HESSE

HESSE

The Wanderer
and His Shadow

Gunnar Decker

Translated by Peter Lewis

Harvard University Press

Cambridge, Massachusetts
London, England
2018

First published in German as *Hermann Hesse: Der Wanderer und sein Schatten,*
© Carl Hanser Verlag München 2012.

The translation of this work was funded by Geisteswissenschaften International—Translation
Funding for Work in the Humanities and Social Sciences from Germany, a joint initiative of
the Fritz Thyssen Foundation, the German Federal Foreign Office, the collecting society
VG WORT and the Börsenverein des Deutschen Buchhandels (German Publishers &
Booksellers Association).

Page 699 photograph of Heiner Hesse (November 6, 2002)
© Gunnar Decker, author's archives.
All other photographs © Hermann Hesse-Editionsarchiv, Volker Michels,
Offenbach am Main.

First printing

Library of Congress Cataloging-in-Publication Data

Names: Decker, Gunnar, 1965– author. | Lewis, Peter, 1958– translator.
Title: Hesse : the wanderer and his shadow / Gunnar Decker ; translated by Peter Lewis.
Other titles: Hermann Hesse. English
Description: Cambridge, Massachusetts : Harvard University Press, 2018. |
"First published as Hermann Hesse: Der Wanderer und sein Schatten,
copyright © 2012 Carl Hanser Verlag Munchen." |
Includes bibliographical references and index.
Identifiers: LCCN 2018012273 | ISBN 9780674737884 (alk. paper)
Subjects: LCSH: Hesse, Hermann, 1877–1962. | Authors, German—
20th century—Biography.
Classification: LCC PT2617.E85 Z678513 2018 | DDC 833/.912 [B]—dc23
LC record available at https://lccn.loc.gov/2018012273

I think that reality is the last thing one need bother oneself about, for it is, tiresomely enough, constantly present, whereas it is the more beautiful and necessary things in life that really demand our attention and care. Reality is something that one ought not under any circumstances to be content with and which one should not on any account worship and revere, for it is accidental, the leftovers of life. And the only way in which we can alter this shabby, consistently disappointing, and barren reality is by repudiating it and thereby demonstrating that we are stronger than it is.

Hermann Hesse, *Life Story Briefly Told* (1921–1924)

CONTENTS

Introduction: Doppelgänger in a Straw Hat   1

1. A Child's Soul: Oppression and Rebellion   15

2. The Self-Proclaimed Writer   88

3. Awakening of Individuality   114

4. At Home Crossing Borders   156

5. Portrait of the Successful Artist as a Young Man Wandering beneath Clouds   204

6. A New Beginning in Switzerland and the First World War   293

7. Escape to Ticino: Making a Fresh Start and Falling to Earth in the South   378

8. The Awakening of Steppenwolf   473

9. Traveling to the East   543

10. On the Nature of *The Glass Bead Game:*
   The Looming Presence of the Third Reich   601

11. The Old Man of the Mountains:
   Hesse's Continuing Journey Inward   665

   Chronology   725

   Notes   729

   Acknowledgments   761

   Index   763

Doppelgänger in a Straw Hat

His look has its own center
somewhere between the contemplative gaze of a mystic
and the sharp eye of an American.

—Walter Benjamin

"His voice had a tanned sound to it. His face was full of deep furrows and folds, the face of a gardener or a mountaineer and at the same time a modern, urban face." That was Peter Suhrkamp's impression on meeting Hesse for the first time in August 1936. This was also the last time Hermann Hesse set foot on German soil, and then only because he wanted to visit an ophthalmologist in Bad Eilsen, whom he hoped—in vain, as it transpired—would be able to cure the unbearable pain he was suffering in his eyes. Thereafter he never left Switzerland again: not when he was awarded the Nobel Prize for Literature in 1946; not to collect his Goethe Prize awarded by the city of Frankfurt am Main or the Peace Prize of the German book trade; not even to attend the funerals of his two sisters.

Indeed, it was only very infrequently that the bird—as he liked to style and often to caricature himself—now left its golden cage, the Casa Rossa in Montagnola. He was intently preoccupied with keeping at bay the external world that was crowding in on him. A note reading "No visitors, please" was affixed to his door, though he did not shirk the daily drudgery of responding to letters. In the final twenty-five years of his life, in fact, he engaged with the world with perhaps even more intensity than he had ever done, albeit in his own particular way—overwhelmingly in the form of writing. For him, devoting attention to others was inextricably bound up with withdrawal—that was the great paradox of his life, and the mainspring of his creativity.

This contradictory nature, even in his outward appearance, was what immediately struck his publisher Peter Suhrkamp at their first face-to-face meeting in Bad Eilsen: the man would fit equally well in either a café full of literati in Paris or a monastery in Tibet. That was Hesse's Janus-like face, turned to the world and away from it at the same time. Suhrkamp's description of Hesse went on:

> He is shorter than me and much thinner, and strikes one as extremely haggard and ascetic. He has a powerful voice, with a heavy Swabian accent. His lips are thin, and the line of his mouth, which turns down sharply on the left-hand side, lends him a skeptical and embittered appearance. His cheeks are sunken and heavily shadowed. At any moment his eyes, behind thick glasses, can take on a softly radiant and very inquisitive look, while at times they seemed focused into a piercing, brooding stare, and on those occasions there is a mad determination about them. His brow is delicate and yet almost completely rounded. His complexion alternates between fresh and pallid, the transition between which is very sudden and violent; at certain moments, the paleness of his face is quite shocking.[1]

Klara, the first wife of Hesse's eldest son, Bruno, also found herself alarmed, not by the sight of her father-in-law but after browsing some of his books: "If I'd known what sort of things your father writes, I would never have agreed to be your wife!" She banned her children, Christine and Simon, from reading anything written by their grandfather. The same sentiment was reported by Sibylle, the daughter of Hesse's youngest son, Martin, who was also forbidden to read these "lewd" books.[2]

Anyone who had such a drastic effect, even on his own family, required an unassuming disguise. Many a person who does not want to appear a murderer becomes a gardener.

So in the old man calmly burning bundles of cuttings and twigs in his garden there lurked a dangerous pyromaniac waiting to pounce. One never knew exactly if he would manage to keep his fascination with fire within legal bounds.

This unmistakable man in a straw hat was in no way a sociable, easy-going person; if one were expecting a carefree rambler, this would not be your man. Here was a notoriously irritable loner, who could tolerate other people—even his own wives—only at a suitable distance. Physical contact was as abhorrent to him as unannounced visits. He hardly ever found an inner harmony, though like Goethe he was constantly invoking this state of mind. His life was always in a state of flux. Phases of creative rapture were followed by periods of the blackest depression. Throughout, he always kept in mind Janus-like nature, above all his own. In the view of this sworn enemy of cities, anyone who denied this nature was in danger of becoming alienated from themselves.

Regarding the sheer multitude of personal testimonies preserved in Hesse's writings, Siegfried Unseld has noted, with an admiration bordering on incomprehension: "Here was a family that wrote a welter of letters and that documented itself in countless notes and diaries. That they kept every last communication, be it in the form of a letter, a postcard, or just a hand-written note, is truly remarkable."[3]

How can one begin to recount a life that ended some fifty years ago, and whose fruits were a twenty-volume *Collected Works,* an oeuvre that encompasses almost 15,000 pages? The task is made still more daunting by the fact that, in the course of his life, which lasted for almost eighty-five years, this man wrote more than 44,000 letters, of which only the most important have been, and continue to be, edited.

Gottfried Benn's observation, which he wrote on the occasion of the fiftieth anniversary of Friedrich Nietzsche's death, applies to Hermann Hesse in a way that it does to few others: "If a life ended fifty years in the past and the person's work was completed some sixty years ago, it is perhaps permissible to switch to the method of regarding that figure as a dream."[4]

Indeed, Pedro Calderón's play *Life Is a Dream* finds a late echo in the work of Hermann Hesse. Without a strong dream dimension there would not only be no Magic Theater and no *Glass Bead Game,* there would also be no author Hermann Hesse, period. In his writing, the constant interplay between the internal and the external brings together autobiographical accounts with reflection and a sense of enchantment through new myth making. A particular tone resonates through his work: namely, that of a "biography of the soul." How could one hope to write a biography of Hermann Hesse without allowing space for this tone to reverberate?

Legends and the fairy-tale form came to play an ever more important role for Hesse than science, whose self-avowedly objective methods he viewed with distrust. To him, the confessor, such methods always seemed to be masking a fundamental indifference and an inner lack of involvement (according to Hesse, this was the cardinal sin in all utterances concerning poetry and art in general).

When faced with the contention that poetry was not a realm that could stand up to serious scrutiny when subjected to the dispassionate parameters of scientific knowledge, Hesse would counter by pointing to the fact that there were other cultures and other ages in which everything that was vital to human existence had been treated in the form of verse.

A biographer should not start from the premise that he or she is conducting a type of police investigation and is expected to produce a series of new pieces of evidence revealing things that the author wished to keep hidden. Anyone writing about the life and work of another person treads a path of convergence with one's subject that is all too readily labeled with the epithet "romantic." Yet in the majority of cases, it is fair to say that the subject of a biography is not some delinquent whom one is seeking to find guilty of misconduct. Errors are legion and certainly form part and parcel of the substance of a person's life and work, but what is guilt in this context, and who decides on it? Biography should be neither an act of willful exposure nor an act of simple homage. Virginia Woolf saw the task of biographers as being the ongoing endeavor "to present that queer amalgamation of dream and reality, that perpetual marriage of granite and rainbow," since they are always writing at one and the same time about a decidedly earthly existence and the mystery of creativity itself. A biographer's integrity thus resides in not neglecting one side of this duality entirely or highlighting it to the detriment of the other.

Early on, Hesse himself attempted to write two biographical monographs: on Saint Francis of Assisi, and one on Boccaccio, both of whom he greatly admired. In both cases he found in retrospect that he had made things unacceptably easy for himself when writing. Nevertheless, today if one reads these texts, both of them relatively short, what was special about these two lives still comes across, and one can feel their charisma across the centuries.

Subsequently, then, Hesse came to take a very skeptical view of the monograph as a literary form; indeed, in his essay "Dealing with Books" ("Der Umgang mit Büchern") he expressly warns people off it: "Extensive consumption of monographs and biographies can easily spoil the magical pleasure a person may take in building up an impression of great writers from their works alone. And in addition to an author's works, one should also not pass up the opportunity to read his letters, diaries, and conversations—Goethe is a case in point here! Where such sources are so close at hand and readily accessible, one should not let oneself be spoon-fed secondhand."[5]

Only direct access to the sources can forestall the danger of relying upon derivative, secondhand material. In the case of Hesse, there are few diaries, and even these few are not very extensive—as compared, say, to those of Thomas Mann. By contrast, his exchange of correspondence is a rich lode revealing his troubles and hopes, a labyrinth of his fears and aspirations, as well as being a chronicle of his humdrum, everyday concerns. In the process, dreams define those themes that form the basis and the hidden depths of his texts. From a reading of these—principally private—communications, Hesse emerges as a man grappling with his inner turmoil. He seemed a neurotic figure to those who had dealings with him, a figure often on the verge of psychopathology. What a robust and rugged artist—one whose stock-in-trade was the shunning of reality—to be able to tap into his own inner contradictions!

No idyll can survive in such circumstances, and things in Hesse show us their light and dark side simultaneously. Nothing here is edifying that does not at the same time immediately destroy every hint of edification. This is also the meaning of the subtitle of this book—*The Wanderer and His Shadow*—an image that derives from Nietzsche's work *Human, All Too Human*. Hesse was a person who constantly carried his doppelgänger within him. In any creative act the spirit of destruction, self-destruction too, must first be overcome. This was a lifelong struggle for Hesse.

Hesse's writings were translated into thirty-four languages during his lifetime. "The Japanese understand me best," he said, "and the Americans the least. But then, theirs is not my world. I shall never go there."[6] He had good reasons for this assumption, for after his works had appeared in several different editions worldwide after the awarding of the Nobel Prize, sales nonetheless proved highly unresponsive in the United States. In the mid-1950s, Siegfried Unseld bought back the American rights to Hesse's works for just $2,000; at dinner later that day, the American publisher even gave Unseld the opportunity to withdraw from this "unfair deal." He did not take it, though he could scarcely have imagined what would happen just a decade later.

For the great Hesse Renaissance of the 1960s came from the United States, of all places. The psychedelic Flower Power movement generated the illusion of a happy antibourgeois rapture. The rebellious sons of the American middle classes read Hesse and felt themselves vindicated in their quest for alternative ways of living. And so Hermann Hesse became an eternal gardener in the last eco-commune, a spiritual guru of Buddhist meditation groups, and the secret leader of the anti–Vietnam War movement. Elsewhere, he had long since been the figurehead of an antiauthoritarian educational ideal.

Indeed, the generation of 1968 in Germany had already discovered Hesse's contrariness for themselves. They celebrated him for the fact that he was patently unsuitable for co-opting as any kind of patriotic cheerleader and for his disaffection for a nation that was characterized by its rigid adherence to diligence, order, self-righteousness, and tidiness. And because many of them had parents who had hailed Hitler's accession to power and who still took that the view that he had done a lot of good things, the rediscovery of Hesse by hippies also took on a political dimension. This, then, represented an expansion of the private garden idyll to a utopia of a future life where people would no longer feel alienated.

The fact that, soon enough, there grew from this movement a new set of ideologues who were destined to make people unfree once more does nothing to change the sense of freedom that people experienced through reading Hesse, or the liberation of Hesse's image brought about by his adoption by this new youthful and antibourgeois readership. The quintessential symbol of this new awakening under the aegis of Hesse was the American rock group Steppenwolf, with their 1969 single "Born to Be Wild": in other words, born to live life without limits. It is a beautiful and necessary dream, at the root of which a dark romanticism shimmers.

In 1968 the German news magazine *Der Spiegel* reported, not without a certain condescending astonishment, that "it was the hippies who dragged Hesse out of the doldrums."

For it is true that, up until that revival, Hesse's reputation had been really very poor in the western part of Germany—with the proviso that it is not readers but critics and competing literary figures who are primarily responsible for a writer's reputation.

Let us begin with the critics. Shortly before his death in 1948, in an interview with Willy Haas, Alfred Kerr was the progenitor of an anecdote that even Hesse could not help but laugh at when it was recounted to him. Haas explained:

> At one point in our talk, he wanted to tell me something about Hermann Hesse, whom he didn't much care for, but couldn't remember his name. He tried prompting me: "You know, that old Swabian who's always claiming he's Swiss!" I couldn't think who he meant. "Yes, you know—that harmless writer! That incredibly harmless writer! That disgustingly harmless writer!" He kept groping around for the name. "That scandalously harmless writer!" he almost yelled at me. "Do you mean Hermann Hesse?" I asked dubiously. "Yes, Hermann Hesse!" he shouted in great relief, his eyes flashing.[7]

And in an essay written for the journal *Merkur* to mark the award of the Nobel Prize for Literature, Ernst Robert Curtius wrote: "Likewise, his use of language is like meticulous painting by numbers, sometimes childish, and on other occasions schoolboyish. His prose never sparkles."[8]

So much for the scintillating opinions of the critics. Those of his fellow authors and rival writers are scarcely less strident. On August 28, 1910, Erich Mühsam noted in his diary on Hermann Hesse: "Even his style I find unbearable. He attempts to pull off some bold strokes. He fawns. He spouts. And I really loathe the way he suddenly breaks into the middle of a story and starts announcing his own personal opinions on the problems that have been raised. How unappealing! How unartistic!—And in general it's true to say that, throughout, his prose has that suspicious whiff of the soil, or rather that earthy stench of the parochial regional writer."[9] Robert Musil expanded on this criticism in the late 1930s: "He tolerates no noise in the house, no irregularity in the strict division of his day into periods for working, reading, walking, mealtimes, and sleep. That's all very understandable; the only funny thing about it is that he displays the foibles of a greater writer than he actually is. Nowadays, it seems, you can be a great writer without evincing any greatness in your writing." And Gottfried Benn provided a postwar perspective: "Hesse. A little man. A German inward-looking nature, which regards it as an earth-shattering event if someone somewhere suffers or commits an act of adultery. He wrote some lovely, lucid poems in his youth. A pal of Thomas Mann. Hence his Nobel Prize, a very appropriate and fitting award in the murky swamp that is Europe right now." Moreover, hadn't Hesse irresponsibly gone off and a found a comfortable bolt-hole in Switzerland (the disparaging term "sybarite" was doing the rounds at the time) while everyone else was having to suffer the privations of the war?

Indeed, Hans Habe, the Hungarian American editor whom U.S. forces appointed to found and run newspapers in their postwar occupation zone, doubted that Hesse even had the right "to speak in Germany ever again."[10]

An opportunist, a curious old bird, a naive nature freak, and a writer of kitsch scarcely any better than the romantic potboiler author Hedwig Courths-Mahler were some of the epithets attached to him. In his obituary of Hesse for the newspaper *Die Zeit* on August 17, 1962, Rudolf Walter Leonhardt concluded, with good cause: "It has to be said, there are no points to be won from liking Hesse nowadays."[11] But that was precisely the root of the great misunderstanding about Hesse: popularity wasn't really what he was all about.

And why was Hesse viewed with the same degree of skepticism by "regional writers" as he was by the urban avant-garde? This is where things begin to get interesting.

For his entire life, Hesse was intent on demonstrating that he was his own person. That made for a lonely existence, but also made him robust. And it is this strength, which made him independent and self-reliant yet also highly neurotic, that many people cannot forgive him for, even to this day. Hesse never managed to keep his own personality out of his writing. He remained a confessing writer, yet one who increasingly hid behind masks—something that not every reader recognized.

There was something about Hesse that antagonized his critics, and still continues to do so. Robert Jungk saw in him a "political visionary who transcended day-to-day politics."[12] *The Glass Bead Game* is precisely not some elitist gentlemanly parlor game, but an attempt—which in the process assimilated Plato's *Republic*—to imagine the future in the light of current catastrophes. In Hesse, any utopia he posits is at any time fully cognizant of the anti-utopia inherent within it. This is what makes him a modern author, because he constantly endeavored to express this inner turmoil and never aligned himself while doing so with any majority or minority.

By contrast, the work of writers from the famous Gruppe 47 postwar literary movement in Germany—Hesse haters, to a man—was engaged, critical, dialectic, linguistically experimental, political, and sociological—all the things that Hesse's writing emphatically was not, nor did it aspire to be.

In the 1960s it was the outsiders who still took Hesse seriously. People like Peter Handke, who attacked West German literature after the war for its "descriptive impotence" and who promoted Hesse's rejection of reality to oppose the cult of social realism and "engaged" literature, positing the inner rather than the external world, and slowness rather than acceleration.

In any case, beyond Germany the picture had long since changed, shaped precisely by Hesse's ambivalent relationship to German tradition. His attitude of attraction and repulsion produces an intensity of language that does not admit of any indifference. As André Gide noted in 1947: "Although Hesse is quintessentially German, he only achieves this by turning his back on Germany. There are very few of his compatriots who have not been influenced by circumstances and who have managed to remain true to themselves. It is to them that Hesse addresses himself, with the message: 'However few of you there are, the future of Germany depends upon you, and you alone.'"

Even before the Beat Generation, admiring voices came first from outside Germany, as Joachim Kaiser recalled. When Henry Miller told him in 1960 that he valued Hesse, Kaiser saw it as a sign of the American's incipient senility and took a grim pleasure in recounting it back in Hamburg—"everyone laughed up their sleeves about old Miller."

The late 1960s saw the publication of a selection of the correspondence between Hesse and Thomas Mann. The initial reaction was irritation. Wasn't this a case of two men talking to one another as if they were equals? This irritation did not last long before being supplanted by prejudices once more. But what West Germany patronizingly mocked, in a cool Anglo-Saxon manner, for being old-fashioned and romantic was exactly what Hesse's readers in East Germany, cut off from the rest of the world and condemned to provinciality, admired about him: his tenacious defense of the spiritual dimension. Hesse was a cosmopolitan figure from the provinces. What a spark of hope this ignited in his readers behind the Iron Curtain! Whereas his books were seen there as an antidote to a world governed by ideologies, a majority in the Federal Republic of Germany, at least a majority of critics, shared Karlheinz Deschner's verdict of 1957—that most of Hesse's works did not even rank as second-rate.[13]

In the light of this, Gottfried Benn's casual dismissal of Hesse, citing by contrast the much-invoked modernity of German literature, should be seen merely as playing around with labels. The clear implication was that "above all a younger German readership was now turning to the prose of writers like Günter Grass, Uwe Johnson, Martin Walser, or Peter Weiss"[14] and had no further interest in Hesse's "epics in search of the meaning of life." Furthermore, there was speculation that the American Hesse renaissance could not last much longer, given that several foreign critics already thought they detected a "faint whiff of metaphysical Lederhosen" about Hesse.

Yet it was precisely not the critics—neither the Germans nor the Americans—who had triggered this Hesse renaissance or even wanted it to happen, but the influential youth culture, which found that Timothy Leary's visions of LSD and beat had something of a flavor of *Steppenwolf* about them, and *Steppenwolf* remained inextricably bound up with the name of Hermann Hesse.

"Destroy what is destroying you!" That was the message that gained currency among readers of Hesse's *Beneath the Wheel* in the late 1960s and early 1970s. A rapturous mood prevailed in leftist, alternative communes and discussion circles of this period. Reading Hesse became a way of stimulating one's own feeling about life, a kind of mystical union of the collectivist, blissful awakening of the new generation, almost a drug.

A late victory for the author of *Steppenwolf*, one might think—yet even that interpretation is ultimately a misunderstanding as well.

On the one hand, if reading leads a person to live life intensely, then that is thoroughly in the spirit of Hesse. On the other hand, Hesse could scarcely have imagined that, among the endlessly debating gatherings of this period, the spiritual dimension would become something that was openly scorned.

Certainly, this headstrong antidogmatist had a highly equivocal relationship with the authorities of Western history. However, his attitude could not simply be summed up as a simple shunning of tradition—otherwise he would never have begun writing *The Glass Bead Game.*

At some stage, the hippies believed that they had pegged this Hermann Hesse as being so fundamentally a fellow traveler of their own attitude of laid-back lethargy that they found it increasingly inconvenient to bother reading him anymore. The most fatal form of fame for authors is when their readership decides it is enough simply to know the titles of their works. Thus began the end of this revival, too.

Then a remarkable phenomenon occurred: in the interim, Hesse's readers, or rather his erstwhile fans, had become for the most part solid bourgeois types, many of them schoolteachers or professors who were nearing or were just post retirement. For them, the folkloric side of their own life story (free love; pacifism; experimentation with mind-expanding substances; an antiauthoritarian, ecological, and communalist lifestyle), which most of them had consigned firmly to the past, was so firmly associated with the name of Hermann Hesse that they came to look upon him as a somewhat embarrassing psychedelic brother to their own, now long-faded, spaced-out former selves.

Many members of this "I-read-Hesse-once-but-don't-anymore" brigade maintained that he was purely an author one read in one's youth, an ideal companion for boys going through puberty. Is that the case? What we were witness to here was, instead, a public display of intellectualizing self-reflection testifying to recurrent identity crises that prompted fresh starts.

No, one does not leave Hesse behind after going through puberty, for his theme remains the new beginning confronted anew on a daily basis. But what had to perish in these beginnings? What had to be destroyed in order that something else might arise?

His invocation of the "child's soul" had nothing sentimental about it and was anything but harmless. Rather, a melancholy of Proustian dimensions runs through Hesse's own very individual "search for lost time."

He was and remains an author of crisis. He was never simply apolitical but instead for the most part found himself compelled to stand above the political fray, and was always keen to demonstrate his willfulness, a trait that could sometimes sound like sarcasm yet that is first and foremost a manifestation of the exuberance that is an essential part of anyone who has made playing with words their lifelong profession.

For example, when asked in an interview with *Die Welt* on June 10, 1962, why he wrote, he gave the succinct answer: "because one can't spend the whole day painting."[15] This exhaustive disclosure was made shortly before his eighty-fifth birthday and less than two months before his death.

What should one read, and most importantly, how should one read? Could there ever be an elite that doesn't read anymore? In that event, what would become of all the dreams of humanity that are contained in libraries? This question becomes even more acute when we consider Hesse's 1929 essay "A Library of World Literature": "The modern world tends somewhat to undervalue books. Nowadays, one encounters many young people who find it risible and undignified to love books rather than real life. They consider that life is too short and far too precious for that, and yet still find the time to spend several hours a week listening to palm-court music and dancing."[16]

He wrote this essay in 1929. Anyone who considers Hesse antiquated must already have ceased to think about the problem of education, at least in the form that seemed so urgent to him: "For education requires something to educate: namely, a character, a personality. If they are absent, and if education without substance occurs, so to speak, in a vacuum, knowledge will result, to be sure, but there will be no love or life about it. Reading without love, knowledge without reverence, education without any heart is one of the worst sins against the human spirit."[17]

Hesse praised idleness and the Romantic ideal of art, yet always remained the son of Pietist parents subjecting himself to an enormous workload each day. Did precisely this paradox conceal a vision relating to the future of our educational institutions?

The first-person tone that Hesse adopted in everything he wrote, in all its many different resonances, comes across as highly cultivated; for this reason it is never strident, but instead manages to retain its fundamental air of openness and listening to the external world.

Hesse was a reader with an instinct for the new—for Franz Kafka, whom he helped popularize, or Peter Weiss, whom he suggested should be awarded the prize that bore his name. In 1927 Kurt Tucholsky wrote: "His book reviews have no peer in Germany at present. One can learn something— indeed, a lot—from every one of Hesse's book reviews."[18]

Only very occasionally did this instinct desert him—for instance, where the urban avant-garde and Expressionism were the subjects in question. In 1960 he said of the diaries of the Berlin Expressionist poet Georg Heym: "He was fortunate in meeting an early death. He was predestined to become a Nazi, his fantasies revolved around officer's uniforms, war, and barricades, and all he can say about Goethe is to call him 'that pig Goethe.'"[19] But even here, in the midst of his incomprehension, his curiosity did not leave him, and he conceded: "Even so, there are some winning aspects to Heym."

Hesse renaissances come and go. But setting aside all fads and fashions, one would hope that any reader cheerfully and aimlessly working his or her way through the twenty volumes of Hesse's *Collected Works* might frequently stray into hitherto unfamiliar territory. For that is when the expedition begins to get perilous, as the author reveals himself to be a visionary author in his precise descriptions of the erosion of an entire era.

His doppelgänger motif, which mirrors his inner conflict, is also a response to the great fault lines in the history of the twentieth century.

"Steps," which he chose to symbolize his life—expressing the metamorphosis that he experienced—always lead both up and down at the same time.

Steps

Just as every blossom fades
and all youth yields to old age,
so every stage of life, each flower of wisdom
and every virtue reaches its prime and cannot last forever.
Whenever life calls, the heart must be ready to leave
and make a fresh start and to enter bravely
into different and new liaisons.
And a magic inhabits every new beginning,
protecting us and helping us to live.

We should joyfully traverse realm after realm,
cleaving to none as to a home,
the world spirit does not seek to fetter us and hem us in

but to raise us up, step by step.
No sooner have we made ourselves at home and comfortable
in some sphere of life than we grow lax.
Only those who are prepared to venture forth
can cast off familiar, paralyzing old habits.

Maybe death's hour too will send us out newborn
toward new realms,
Life's call to us will never end . . .
Come then, my heart, take your leave and fare you well!

1

A CHILD'S SOUL

Oppression and Rebellion

Places of Origin and Yearning

Childhood always had two faces for Hermann Hesse: a precisely identifiable sequence of events from birth to puberty, and the subsequent picture of it in his mind's eye. These reminiscences colored everything he wrote with that familiar background atmosphere, which always comes across as very close at hand and often deeply intimate, and yet at the same time as extremely remote, as if it were part of a legend, almost like an episode from mythology.

Interrupted idylls in Calw and Basel, ominous feelings of security, painful aborting of all-too-emphatic fresh starts, and obstinate forlorn unruliness. That all combined to make him, in his decided outmodedness—he always seemed to have more of the past or of the future about him, but was never wholly in the here and now—a meticulous fabricator of dreams.

Pipe dreams and nightmares interweave in this poetic realm, which can sometimes be very bright and sometimes utterly dark, to form a play of light comprising both the promising and destructive potentials that inhabit individuals and entire cultures alike.

★　★　★

When Hermann Hesse was born, on July 2, 1877, in Calw, his onward path in life already seemed to have been laid out for him. That unconditional trust in God, which had guided all the Hesses and the Gunderts (his mother's side of the family) safely through all of life's unpredictabilities and kept them from the temptation to plow their own furrow, was also expected of him as a matter of course. Hitherto, in this family there had been no dissenters from the rigidly devout world of Swabian Pietism.

Certainly there had been some attempts to break free, but each had been followed by remorse, repentance, and submission: After all, what am I? Nothing but an instrument of the Lord, for it is He who according to his unfathomable will has assigned me my station in life, in which I am bound to humbly serve Him. Everything else is pride, and hence a sin. For the Hesses and the Gunderts, the family was always the smallest unit in a single, great undertaking: the mission to evangelize heathens. And in this, they were successful; they were forced to admit defeat only in the case of one heathen, that new Hermann in the family, whom his maternal grandfather Dr. Hermann Gundert baptized on August 3, 1877.

Family background and tradition—and if those were not enough, God's Commandments—had up until now proved strong enough to ward off any revolt. Up until now. But this latest of the many Hermanns in the family would turn out to be different from its two powerful heads, his grandfathers Dr. Carl Hermann Hesse and Dr. Hermann Gundert. Learned patriarchs both, who left behind vast amounts of correspondence (all diligently archived as if for eternity) and missionary texts. Two guardians of the truth, scholarly men who had even taken doctorates. And then there was the third Hermann, the one who had just been born, and who left school at sixteen. By then, though, he had already gone on an odyssey to Bad Boll to meet Johann Blumhardt, a faith healer and socialist but above all a guru of Pietist revivalism. He had also attempted to take his own life and spent time in the mental asylum at Stetten. His stay there could so easily have become permanent had he not—just in the nick of time— donned the mask of penitence and humility. Breathing a sigh of relief, his family thought they identified glimmers of rationality. A narrow escape once more.

Until he purchased a revolver, that is. His stubborn nature, which did not shy away from self-endangerment, exploited every conceivable loophole in the protection offered by the corpus of metaphysical belief and triumphantly crossed the boundary of what his parents could tolerate.

This Hermann conveyed to his family an outrageous message from Nietzsche: God is dead! And yet, as a legacy of his Pietist background, he too was inhabited by a restless searching for God and an unquestioning certainty in the insufficiency of all worldly fulfillment: "The fact that people see their life as something held in fee from God and seek to live it not through egotistical urges but instead in service and sacrifice to God— this greatest experience from my childhood has had a powerful influence on my life."[1]

The Grandfathers

> When I look at my grandchildren, it increasingly strikes me that God never repeats himself, but constantly serves up something totally without precedent.
>
> —Hermann Gundert (June 8, 1877)

For Hermann Hesse, before the world of fathers, against which he would rebel, there was the world of his grandfathers. This stretched so far back in time that history opened out into legend. And yet even the biographies of his great-grandparents are scrupulously well documented. All the Hesses and the Gunderts lived in the certainty of their Protestant faith, which they interpreted with especial rigor, and felt a vocation to perform their duty as missionaries. Two grandfathers called Hermann, and the grandson too— what did that say about the power of names?

The grandson did not become like either of his grandfathers, and broke with the long Pietist tradition established by the Hesses and the Gunderts— yet he still retained something of this ethos, primarily his awareness of the magical act that is inherent within every naming of a child. He knew when he entrusted his fortunes to a readership and the written word that he was drawing on a broad family hinterland. He would take this knowledge—an empirical knowledge of metamorphoses and of self-realization— over that frontier, beyond which lay the realm of art, governed by different but equally strict rules than that which held sway among the Pietist brotherhoods.

So now once again a new Hermann enters the family, the great-grandson, the grandson, and the son. In later life Hesse would constantly look back

Hermann Hesse's father, Johannes Hesse (1847–1916)

on his forbears, on the one hand with trepidation but on the other with great admiration, as unwavering champions of the divine. His own father, Johannes Hesse, however, whom even his mother, Marie, came to see principally as the assistant of her much-revered father Hermann Gundert, was too much of an obstacle to be given his proper due. So for a long time Hermann found it impossible to accord him the same admiration that he had shown to both his grandfathers. Only in old age would he recognize how like his father he really was.

Hesse's friend and biographer Hugo Ball has highlighted the special role of the grandfather in Pietism: "In Pietist circles, which have a close affinity with the early Christian Church, although the saints in a Catholic sense do not play a role, grandfathers certainly do, and what is more a role that actually surpasses that of the saints."[2] Why was this?

Pietism, a Protestant sect, opposed the established Church. This is also the reason personal role models played such a leading role in the brotherhoods. The wise elder who devoted his whole life to God embodied the highest authority. Because in Pietism the only thing that stands between

God and man is Holy Scripture, and not the institution of the Church, nor any sacraments, dogmas, or other external matters, all that man is required to do is to follow the Bible's commandments. But this places Pietism, which in truth has scant regard for the individual in his or her earthly body, in a paradoxical situation that impacts on the image of man. For a person's ability to live their life according to God's commandments depends entirely on the strength of their faith, asceticism, and forbearance. But above and beyond this, in his or her corporeal existence, a person counts for nothing. In Pietism, individuals were expected to strive to fulfill themselves and through their best efforts and moral purity to try to please God—however, only in order thereby to secure for themselves a promising starting position in the race to paradise. For this reason, on the one hand Pietism was open to the modern spirit (technology!) and even revealed itself to be an ideology of achievement—doing one's duty was paramount!—yet on the other hand, it fundamentally rejected modernity on moral grounds. It regarded as the devil's work everything that did not serve the ultimate purpose of preparing one for the kingdom of God in the hereafter. Freed from the mantle of the Christian faith, Hermann Hesse, the grandson, would attempt time and again to reformulate this contradiction. It is just one of the insoluble questions of modern existence that impelled him to become a writer.

His grandfather Dr. Carl Hermann Hesse did not neglect to leave behind an autobiography in two volumes, an endeavor he spent two years on: his sole aim in this was to give an account of himself before God. Indeed, there were several writers among Hermann Hesse's forebears—but they always wrote with a higher purpose in mind; to do otherwise would have been pure sinful vanity.

Carl Hermann Hesse was born in 1802 in Livonia. His mother also hailed from this region; his father came from Lübeck. Carl Hermann's elder brother studied theology, and he too intended to become a pastor after attending high school. However, low marks in ancient Greek meant that he could not enroll to study theology. His headmaster suggested he study medicine instead, and on the spur of the moment he agreed. And so, just as enthusiastically as always and without dwelling ruefully on his thwarted life plan, he embarked on a course in medicine. This demonstrates the character of the Hesses: they took what happened to them as God's will. They even thanked God for adverse twists of fate, on the grounds that He would surely have His reasons for testing them in this way.

The family's trust in God was complete—and Carl Hermann Hesse was a happy man.

He had ten children with his first wife, Jenny; the first child was Johannes Hesse, the writer's father.

Hermann Hesse's third wife, Ninon, in the epilogue to *Childhood and Youth before 1900,* a volume she edited documenting the writer's early years, attempted a succinct summary of this baroque family history of the Hesses and the Gunderts. Even so, it turned out to be a lengthy essay, because both families had documented in minute detail every step taken by their members and had exchanged hundreds, even thousands, of letters with one another. I will have more to say on this idea of the letter as a form in its own right (somewhere between a compulsion to communicate and an art form). The papers Hermann Hesse left behind after his death were found to contain countless letters that people had written to him, all of which he had kept. We may assume that he also replied to most of them, because a file came to light with commentaries and notes by Hesse on his correspondents, including such remarks as "Don't respond; he's trying to convert me." And in his novella *Klingsor's Last Summer,* we read the following sentence, which sounds like an ironic commentary on the writer's daily exercise of letter-writing: "Are people who write so many letters happy?"

Carl Hermann Hesse's unshakable and firm faith was demonstrated by one of the episodes he noted. His young daughter Agathe was suffering from a bout of severe bronchitis. She began slowly to suffocate and there was no chance of her being cured. Grandfather Hesse reported on this for his readers' edification: "In the evening, while sitting on my lap, and in the presence of her mother and a friend, Agathe said to me: 'Father dear, I know I must die, but if you were to ask God, He could make me well again!' 'Yes, dear child, that is true; but I can't ask this of him, because he told me that he wishes to take you, so you must be obedient and go!'" So died the little girl, whose father had refused to offer up a prayer for her salvation because his own death also was God's will, to which one was duty-bound to joyfully assent. Time and again his grandson Hermann Hesse found himself outraged by this kind of "blind faith." If he were a Pietist rather than a human being, then maybe he would understand, the fifteen-year-old Hermann spit hatefully at his father.

Yet Carl Hermann Hesse also possessed something that in the eyes of the young Hermann was lacking in his father, Johann Hesse: stature. The man appeared unshakable, was a "ladies' man" into the bargain, and had the advantage, where his grandson was concerned, of living—unlike Grandpa Gundert—far away. Hermann never met him in person. Carl Hermann remained a dazzling archetype of his own descent, at the same time attractive and repulsive.

While Carl Hermann Hesse's competence as a doctor has often been called into question—on one occasion, he extracted a healthy tooth instead of a diseased one—his competence as a champion of the faith has never been doubted. Yet he was something extremely rare among Pietists: an Epicurean standing before the Lord. A circle of brothers in the Pietist spirit soon began to form around Doctor Hesse in Weissenstein. Everyone from a baron to a craftsman's apprentice attended his Bible classes. He also founded an orphanage. In fact, the founding of orphanages was something of a specialty of Pietists, with the Francke institutions in Halle acting as a model: children, too, had the capacity to work, which should be exploited for the glory of God. But Grandfather Hesse's favorite activity remained listening to hymns being sung while enjoying a bowl of punch—or conversely singing himself while others imbibed. His unorthodox rhyming motto ran: *Gott lieben macht selig, Weintrinken macht fröhlich, drum liebe Gott und trinke Wein, dann wirst du fröhlich und selig sein* (Loving God makes you blissful, drinking wine makes you happy, so love God and drink wine, then you'll be happy and blissful). Carl Hermann Hesse's passion for wine was one thing at least that his grandson Hermann came to share with him without reserve. When Hermann sent him a long letter from Maulbronn with a poem attached, his grandfather answered enthusiastically—with a poem of his own. And on October 11, 1891, the by-then almost ninety-year-old grandfather responded to Hermann's description of the daily stresses and strains of life in Maulbronn in the following terms: "I can still work and I can still *sleep,* six to eight hours every night, plus an hour's nap in the afternoon, that's a great blessing to me and holds body and soul together and makes me a whole person, so I never need to go to the pharmacy and I am a happy man. Be sure to allow yourself plenty of rest at night, and stay healthy."[3]

In 1921 one of Doctor Hesse's nieces, the singer Monika Hunnius, wrote his biography—this kind of written documentation of a person's life was simply inevitable, among both the Hesses and the Gunderts. Carl Hermann Hesse died at the age of ninety-four in 1896 in the Estonian town of

Weissenstein (now Paide). In 1960, in "A Few Reminiscences about Doctors," Hermann Hesse also included a few observations of his own about his eccentric grandfather:

> This fiery youth, who was enthusiastic and boyish in equal measure, whose lust for life and optimism also embraced a childishly trusting piety, had become the doctor, benefactor, and occasionally also tyrant of a small town in Estonia and a substantial part of the surrounding area with its landed estates. And he remained young, fiery, amusing, pious, and boyish into extreme old age. Aged 83, he still saw fit to clamber up a tree in order to saw off one of its branches, and plummeted to the ground along with the branch but did not sustain any injuries. He was known as "the doctor who gives everything away"—and on several occasions, much to his family's dismay, brought poor patients back home with him and cared for them for weeks or even months on end in his own house. As a doctor, he wasn't in the least bit squeamish, and would "use the wrench" to pull out decayed teeth, or go right ahead and operate without an assistant or using any anesthetics. He had been obliged to work his way up in life from tough beginnings in very primitive circumstances. He had had three wives in all, and buried them all, and in his capacity as a Russian "imperial physician" and state councillor had raised hell about the government's regulations and warnings, if they struck him as being useless or injurious.[4]

By contrast, his other grandfather, Hermann Gundert, head of the Calw Publishing Union, which produced all manner of religious literature for missions to enlighten the heathens, was very much in evidence when the young Hermann was growing up. Even so, they never spoke with one another to any great extent, Hesse noted when his maternal grandfather passed away in 1893, yet he was still shaken by his death.

This grandfather was not one of those missionaries who tried to convince others of the simple truth of religious faith. He was neither ascetic nor sanctimonious, let alone fanatical. He was himself a searcher after truth his whole life and so did not hide his insecurities and doubts, and this gave him even greater stature in the eyes of his grandson. Likewise, something that Hermann Gundert found much more important than any Christian missionary work—about which he had some misgivings anyhow—was his personal passion: his interest in a multitude of foreign languages, especially the dialects of India. Hermann Hesse recalled his grandfather in his 1923

autobiographical essay "The Childhood of the Magician": "This man, my
mother's father, was hidden in a forest of mysteries, just as his face was
hidden in the white forest of his beard; from his eyes there flowed sorrow
for the world and blithe wisdom, depending on the circumstances, and
likewise lonely wisdom and divine roguishness; people from many lands
knew him, visited and revered him, talked to him in English, French, Indian, Italian, Malayalam and vanished into thin air once more after long
conversations. . . . From him, this unfathomable one, I knew, came the secret that surrounded my mother, the secret age-old mystery."[5]

When Hesse later came to write about travelers to the East, he had
Hermann Gundert and his mysterious envoys in mind.

Hermann Gundert was born in Stuttgart in 1814. His father was a busi-
nessman and from 1820 on was secretary of the Württemberg Bible Society; he subsequently became known throughout Swabia as simply "Bible
Gundert." By that time he was already involved in publishing, and for two
decades, beginning in 1823, he was chief editor of the magazine *News from
Heathen Lands*. Hesse's great-grandmother Christine Louise (née Ensslin)
had fallen under the influence of the preacher Jeremias Flatt and become
a religious fanatic. Hermann Gundert was sent to a grammar school at the
tender age of five; it was said that he could then already speak better Latin
than many of his fellow students ever managed to. From the age of thirteen,
he studied at the monastery school in Maulbronn, which served as the preparatory school for the Evangelical-Lutheran College in Tübingen, where
officials of the state of Württemberg were traditionally trained; the highly
educated civil servants produced by this institution could look forward to
lifelong employment.

Yet this Grandfather Hermann also rebelled—like his grandson more
than six decades later—initially against his parents, when he refused point-
blank to become a pastor, announcing instead that he wanted to be a soldier. David Friedrich Strauss, later the author of *The Life of Jesus,* and an
exponent of a form of theology based on the work of Hegel, was at that
time teaching in Maulbronn. Hermann Gundert was deeply impressed by
his teaching; Swabian Pietism was already starting to appear extremely outmoded to him.

Indeed, Hermann Gundert even found himself enthused by political
revolution, with the Paris July Revolution of 1830 stimulating in him

dreams of a new, liberated Germany. He agitated for this cause in political essays.

After passing the entrance examination, Gundert went to Tübingen. Strauss had in the meantime begun teaching there, and his seminars afforded his students insights into the history of philosophy. Gundert was enthralled; by now he found himself between two stools, espousing a new enlightened doctrine of reason while retaining his former religious beliefs. He vacillated, trying to square the one with the other, yet sensed all the while that these were compromise positions that would not be able to withstand a true test of loyalty.

Such a test duly arrived in 1833 when a series of suicides occurred at the Tübingen college and he succeeded in persuading one of his fellow students not to take his own life. He then fell seriously ill himself—with an ailment that, in the spirit of the age, was designated a "nervous fever," and that confined him to bed for weeks. This was the period he later came to describe as his conversion, his return to the old faith. Seen in another light, he could be said to have surrendered to the spirit of his forefathers and to the power of tradition. All these were motifs that Hermann Hesse would include as archetypal and fundamental topoi in his texts, up to and including the great recapitulation of his own life in *The Glass Bead Game.*

After taking his doctorate, Hermann Gundert received an offer to travel to India as part of a missionary expedition to the subcontinent. An Englishman, Anton Norris Groves, a manufacturer of false teeth with an amateur passion for missionary work, asked him to come with him to India as the private tutor to his children. A fellow member of the entourage accompanying the missionary-manufacturer was Julie Dubois, the daughter of Calvinist wine growers from French-speaking Switzerland. To the very end of her life, she barely mastered German.

On their first encounter, Hermann Gundert felt a strong aversion to his woman, whom he took to be a "diligent, bigoted Calvinist." Nevertheless, it was put to him that he might like to marry the young missionary assistant. He vehemently turned the suggestion down. Yet it was not up to him to decide whom he should marry, but rather his coreligionists, a body of people whom Gundert's grandson in Calw would later disparage as an omnipresent "committee." Hermann Gundert swallowed his pride, backed down, and married Julie Dubois. The only thing they had in common was the missionary work they were both engaged in. But there was no question of "only": this was the be-all and end-all of both their lives on the subcontinent.

Gundert wrote to his parents about the bride he had been ordered to marry: "She isn't attractive, and doesn't sing, or play games, or draw, but on the other hand she does have an open, natural spirit, and is a keen judge of character." Later Hermann Hesse would affirm the "passionate sobriety" of his maternal grandmother, and her asceticism, "upright and true, sometimes to the point of utter rigidity."[6] At least the assignment of roles was clear, with the wife from her humble background and with her limited intellectual horizons serving her husband in the same way as she served God: conscientiously.

And the marriage did indeed appear to have functioned perfectly well, even though in later years their son-in-law Johannes Hesse noted that Julie possessed a choleric temperament and was always dissatisfied with herself and in this was the antithesis of her husband, who constantly had a placid and generous demeanor. This was undoubtedly an exaggeration, for at one stage Hermann Gundert had shown himself to be an implacable opponent of all of his daughter Marie's attempts at self-determination. When Marie traveled to India at the age of fifteen to join her parents, she met a young Englishman on the ship. They fell in love and the young man wrote a letter to her father asking for her hand in marriage. In her "Autobiography," Marie Gundert later remarked: "Papa wrote back to him, refusing in the firmest and most serious of terms to ever grant him my hand, since he regarded him as an impulsive fellow and a man of the world." No more disparaging a term could be used of another by a Pietist. And yet who could seriously blame any father—regardless of whether he was a Pietist or not—for forbidding his fifteen-year-old daughter from marrying a chance acquaintance for love? This was surely less a gesture of patriarchal omnipotence than fatherly concern for his daughter.

Marie was unhappy but did not dare to revolt openly. The young man waited for years for her and was then shocked when she married someone else—a missionary, of course—this time with her parents' blessing.

Hermann Gundert himself encountered difficulties in getting his marriage, which had been conducted in India, recognized back in Swabia. For although the union with Julie Dubois had been decided upon by his religious superiors, it had not been authorized by the Württemberg authorities. Fortunately for him, however, his marriage was—supposedly as an "exceptional case"—retrospectively legalized by the authorities in Württemberg, otherwise, in the worst case, his citizenship could have been revoked and he could have been required to pay back the tuition fees for his free education at the college in Tübingen. For it was a legal requirement in Württemberg that all marriages should be officially approved.

Gundert, who during his time in Chirakal, India, had already begun to translate the Bible into Malayalam and to compile a Malayalam–English dictionary—a task that would occupy him for another thirty years—was afflicted for three years in India by an inflammation of the throat and lungs, which at times rendered him completely incapable of speech. This was not exactly a favorable position for a missionary.

Ultimately he and his family quit India. There was a position waiting for him at the Calw Publishing Union, as the deputy to Christian Gottlob Barth, the founder of this citadel of devotional literature. Accordingly, Gundert resided in Calw from 1860 right up to his death in 1893. When his boss Barth died in 1862, Gundert took over control of the Calw Publishing Union.

Hermann Gundert's sons (Marie was the only daughter among his eight offspring) painstakingly collected all of their father's letters, more than 8,000 in all. Most of these letters and chronicles were then published in the proceedings of the Calw Missionary Society, so that their coreligionists might share in the affairs of the family.

Inevitably, one is tempted to say, there is also a biography of Hermann Gundert. His son-in-law—and successor in the post of head of the Calw Publishing Union—Johannes Hesse, Hermann Hesse's father, wrote this work, which was published in 1907 as volume 34 of the Calw Family Library.

Pietism as an Evangelical Revivalist Movement and a Way of Life

It is easy to imagine that the devotional images disseminated by the Calw Publishing Union must have embarrassed Hermann Gundert to the depths of his soul. For this religious propaganda was of an alarming simplicity. One of the posters for missionary work within Germany that was produced by the Union depicted the Pietist dualistic image of the world as consisting of a narrow and a broad path. The world belongs to the devil, and heaven belongs to God. Here below, therefore, people were threatened with punishment, and told that their rewards would be in heaven. The poster showed a signpost with two arms. One pointed to the world, and hence to death and damnation, while the other pointed to God—in other words, to life and blessedness. Broad and comfortable roads lead to the world, whereas the road to God is a narrow and arduous path. The first road tempts a person with the theater, wine, masked balls (a singular attraction in Hesse's *Steppenwolf!*), lotteries, and other questionable entertainments. The second path is the only true one. The stations on its route are the Church, Sunday School, performing humble daily chores, and the deaconess house, and the route leads directly to paradise.

It was as simple as that: Renounce the temptations of the world, and do not let yourself be deflected from the true path! Vital elements in achieving that goal were strict discipline and a multitude of rules. In his rulebook of Pietism, *Pia desideria,* Philipp Jakob Spener promoted the idea that individuals' moral free will should be incapacitated in the name of promoting a higher morality. Thus, every aspect of a person's life was to be regulated, down to the smallest detail, and the individual was to be left no latitude for decision making. The philosopher of religion Ernst Troeltsch counts Pietism, in terms of its fundamental structure, as being a sect, somewhere between an established church and mysticism. And yet precisely this fixation on commandments and literal faith harbors a duality. On the one hand, it is a dogmatism that leaves no room for the individual to maneuver, because everything has already been interpreted, and pleasing God therefore resides solely in adhering to the rules to the letter. On the other hand, however, a faith of this kind increases people's distance from the world, and their view grows more critical as a result. Secure in the knowledge that God is behind you, you can also begin to resist those laws of the world that appear to you to be wrong. Thanks to its moral rigor, Pietism can be an uncomfortable faith, not only for its adherents but also for the outside world. For a Pietist follows through on the Protestant principle that every worldly institution is subject *a priori* to criticism. Pietists must bear witness to the truth, and any dissembling (an integral part of any civilization) is anathema to them. Hence also their boundless reverence for the Word of God. Given that it comes directly from God, it must of necessity always be sacred.

Indeed, every letter that is changed changes the sense of the entire text—that was an attitude that Hermann Hesse did adopt from Pietism for his own writing. Every word is already a world in its own right, and every utterance already a magical act, an invocation of the world that lies hidden within the words.

This, then, was the fundamental tenet of Pietism, manifested at worst in the form of narrow-minded bigotry—but it was also the watchword of the writer, who sees the word as the most fundamental element of his existence, which it was vital to protect. After all, words can be used to construct worlds!

The Son of God-Fearing Parents, Johannes and Marie Hesse

Hermann Hesse inherited his avian appearance from his father. His own son Heiner, when he grew old, would develop the same features—that sharp profile that indicated extreme attentiveness. Hermann also had the "slim, fragilely tender build" (a sympathetic euphemism for a weak constitution) of his father, who was often plagued by severe headaches. A strong spirit in a permanently overworked body. Father and son were alike in requiring rest and in seeking peace and quiet and surroundings that would calm their souls. Hermann Hesse later wrote: "I inherited part of my temperament from my father, namely, my insistence upon unconditionality, along with my tendency to be skeptical, critical, and self-critical. Also, one trait in particular that I get from him is my appreciation of precision in verbal expression."[7]

Johannes Hesse was born in 1847 in Weissenstein (now Paide, in Estonia) on the Baltic Sea. This made him a Russian citizen by birth—a fact that later made the question of his own nationality a virtually insoluble one for Hermann Hesse. In his *Biographical Notes,* we read: "What my nationality was at that time, I do not know—presumably Russian, since my father was a Russian subject and had a Russian passport. My mother was the daughter of a Swabian man and a Swiss-French woman. This mixed heritage prevented me from ever having much respect for nationalities and state frontiers."[8] In actual fact, in his 1919 work *Alemannic Avowal,* he expressly identified that landscape—namely, the corner of the Rhineland that lay between Württemberg and Switzerland—and that culture as his true homeland. National borders, on the other hand, separated people artificially. Here, then, was another root of his vehement rejection of any form of nationalism.

When Johannes reached the age of eleven, his father Carl Hermann Hesse sent him to the Knights and Cathedral School in the city of Reval (modern Tallinn). By the time he turned sixteen, he already knew that he was destined to study theology. Just two years later he applied to join the Basel Mission, because he was eager to serve God in a practical way by converting heathens to the one true faith.

At a time when criticism of religion was powerful and rife (one need only think of Ludwig Feuerbach, and the Young Hegelians!) this was a truly anachronistic idealism. Hermann Hesse later came to regard his father, in his capacity as a belated defender of the faith, as a genuinely unfortunate figure; his tragicomic dignity put him in mind of Cervantes's Don Quixote.

By nature Johannes Hesse was an impractical bookworm, who was never so happy as when he was reading and writing and safely cut off from the outside world. He worked hard purely out of a sense of duty—too hard, in fact, for his fragile constitution. This was not the profile of a born missionary. Then again, what exactly is a missionary? Half a worldly propagandist, and half a divine emissary of a Higher Truth.

Johannes Hesse's nervous disposition may also have been the result of his inability to find a clear answer to this question himself, despite having posed it in several of his own writings. For Johannes was not a fanatic but a reflective person who had committed himself to the Christian faith after much thought. He was well aware, of course, of the Copernican Revolution in Western thought, a paradigm shift that had become irreversible since the writings of Immanuel Kant. When Hermann wrote to him from Maulbronn and touched on the problem of historical authenticity in the Gospel according to St. Luke and in Homer's *Odyssey,* he answered, as a perfect child of the Enlightenment:

> Such things never bothered me unduly, because I always, right from the
> outset, took a critical stance. For instance, when I was still studying to be
> a missionary in Basel, I was convinced that the Judeo-Christian tradition
> was wrong with regard to certain biblical texts, but that this did nothing

to compromise their religious value anyway. Since Kant, we have been living in an age of critical thought, and cannot disengage ourselves from this any more. It may pain us when, in the exercise of this, we shatter this or that fondly held illusion or apparently waste precious time in speculation, but at root it is our *feeling for truth,* that fundamental prerequisite of all scholarly inquiry and all religiosity, which impels us toward critical thought in the first place.

The older Hermann Hesse grew, the more astonished he became to notice his resemblance to his father, who always required a "cordon sanitaire" of peace and quiet and rigorous spirituality around himself. In "The Childhood of the Magician" (1923), we read:

> He stood alone. He belonged neither to the world of idols and my grandfather nor to the mundane world of the city. He stood apart, lonely, a sufferer and a seeker, scholarly and kind, full of knowledge, but far removed from that smile, noble and tender yet also pure and without any hint of mystery. Neither his kindness nor his cleverness ever deserted him, but nor did he disappear in the magic cloud that surrounded my grandfather, or his face ever dissolve into that childlike and godlike demeanor whose interplay could sometimes resemble sadness, sometimes gentle mockery, and sometimes the silent, inward-looking mask of God. My father did not address my mother in Indian dialects, but instead spoke to her in English and a pure, refined, and beautiful German. It was this language which he used to draw me in and win me over and teach me; at times I strove to emulate him, full of admiration and zeal, all too much zeal, and yet I knew that my roots reached just as deeply, deeper even, into my mother's soil, into the dark-eyed and mysterious. My mother was full of music, my father was not, he could not sing.[9]

Johannes Hesse sought to overtrump his father Carl Hermann Hesse in the strength of his religious conviction; he was a romantic knight whose physique had become too weak to bear any sword. At the edges this excessively high-flying staunchness frayed off into pure neurosis. At age eighteen Johannes wrote his father a letter about his own sense of calling: "I long to be accepted into a religious fraternity, in short to become part of some great whole to which I might subordinate myself as a useful member, serving it out of a sense of conviction and duty, so as to play my part, or at least attempt to do so, in achieving a great objective. The Mission Society seems to me to be just such a fraternity." One senses straight away what is missing here: any form of self-evident naturalness; the whole letter comes across as artificial and strained.

Surprisingly, a hint of this same tone—remarkably old-fashioned-sounding for such a young man—can also be found in Hermann Hesse's first books. In *Peter Camenzind,* Hesse sounds as though he is looking back from afar at a long-lost youth—a youth that Hesse (at the age of twenty-six!) was actually still in the midst of.

Like everyone in his family Johannes Hesse lived in order to be able to give an account of his life. In the fullness of time, this would be before God, but here on Earth it was before his spiritual brothers. Hence the sheaves of paper that all the Hesses and the Gunderts continued to cover with biographical accounts, with a zeal that never let up. Hermann Hesse's father not only kept a diary from the age of fifteen on, but also wrote countless letters, initially to his parents and later to his Pietist brothers around the globe. His numerous books, all of which were published by the Calw Publishing Union, had titles like *The Heathens and Us: 220 Stories and Accounts from the Mission to the Heathens* (1901), *Spring Breezes among the Nations: 45 Stories of Missionary Work* (1908), and *A Man of God: Tales from the Life of Henry Martyn* (1913). Yet this adherent of the Christian faith healing practiced by Blumhardt in Bad Boll also wrote two books on truly Christian forms of entertainment: *Guessing Games* and *Games in the Family Circle.* In 1916, shortly before his death among the Korntal Brethren, his final work appeared: *Lao-Tse: A Pre-Christian Witness to the Truth.*

Hermann Hesse, who as a youth had long been at loggerheads with his father, later found himself moved when he thought of the way in which this man had stuck doggedly to his vocation to bring enlightenment to those outside the faith. Now, as his childhood returned to the aging writer and appeared in a different light, he recognized his father's quiet nobility: "He was . . . an alien, a noble and rare butterfly or bird that had strayed to us from other climes, and was marked out and isolated by his tenderness and his suffering and no less by his secret homesickness."[10]

The aging Hermann Hesse returned time and again to the subject of his father, showing him to be, if not a saint, then at least made of the stuff that saints were made of: "And now I saw him before me in his entirety, his knightly face under his long, combed-back hair, his high, noble brow with all its handsome planes, the high dome of his closed lids over his blind eyes, and for the very first time since I had learned of his death, a frosty chill coursed through my innermost being at the realization that all these lovely, fine, precious things were irretrievable."[11]

He and his father were in the same order, "belonging to a secret knightly caste which one could never leave."[12]

His mother, Marie, was, like her own mother, Julie, short in stature and made no secret of her religious disposition. Her passionate dark eyes, set close together in her face, shone out in an almost animalistic way from unfathomable depths. There was something alarming about this demonic look. Hermann Hesse, who as a child and a youth never stopped loving his mother, even in the most difficult phases—in marked contrast to his attitude to his father—and who always asked, even begged, to have that love reciprocated, frequently suffered grievously from the impersonal, far from tender attitude displayed by this woman, who was very artistically inclined but who also had a powerful streak of fanaticism in her. Time and again he imagined that she was completely indifferent as to whether he was her son Hermann or just some other boy. And it was true that she could not and would not treat her children with anything other than the same equable attentiveness and strictness that she displayed toward others.

In a—perhaps not by chance—unfinished sketch from the 1940s entitled "My Mother" and subtitled "A Few Childhood Memories for My Sons and Grandsons," Hesse attempted to create, from the distanced position that the passage of time had afforded him, a personal recollection similar to the one he had managed to write about his father. But he found he could not get close to his subject. As a young man he had revolted against his father and mother in equal measure. He had expected Marie Hesse to at least be more understanding than his father—because she, as a more artistic type of person who wrestled with strong emotions and who was capable of great love and affection, always seemed closer to him than his distant and intellectual father, who suffered for his entire life from a weak constitution. But looking back, he could not establish a closeness to his mother, and despite his best intentions he failed to conjure up a convincing picture: "She was the daughter of substantial and characterful parents who were profoundly distinct from one another in every aspect of their nature . . . and brought together in herself in a remarkable way the inherited traits of both her lines of descent, which in many instances were complete opposites, and made them into something new."[13]

Marie Hesse was the living embodiment of Pietism—and yet still carried India within herself. Her family, who were widely traveled, found the restrictiveness of life in the small town of Calw disagreeable. The milieu of the brahmans seemed to have been closer to them than they cared to admit. And when they arrived, "like gypsies from India," they found not only the small town locals ranged against them but also the church hierarchy. Thus Marie and Johannes Hesse fund themselves equally out of place in Calw—and so, despite his tyrannical side, which compromised their life together, had it not been for the presence of Grandfather Gundert they would have felt utterly isolated.

Although they received numerous visitors from all corners of the world (coreligionists, naturally!), their sense of isolation remained. This was another factor behind the countless letters they wrote. Fundamentally, even in her marriage, Marie Hesse was always first and foremost Hermann Gundert's daughter. She was an unconventional woman, who was rich in investments, although she placed all of these—we may even go so far as to say sacrificed them all—in the service of the mission. Her autobiographical reminiscences began with her birth in India, and were written in an ambitious style: "Over there, in the distant, hot Orient I first saw the light of this world on October 18, 1842, and my earliest memories are an admixture of the dull moaning of the ocean waves on the shoreline, the sound of cocoa palms waving in the wind, and the sweet murmurs and caresses of my brown nurse Rosine, whom I always called Hosianna."[14] Only someone who took great pleasure in expressing themselves in written form could write in this way. And what she wrote most certainly leaped off the page—it wasn't composed of traditional set-pieces and linguistic templates, but instead was deeply personal and so never comes across as officious. The story of her birth had been recounted to her, but when she came to write it down, it sounded as though she had experienced all the events herself. For at precisely the same time as she was born, a wealthy Indian had converted to Christianity and, pursued by his furious relatives, had sought refuge in the Gunderts' missionary house. The angry Indians were massing outside and threatening to set the building on fire, while inside lay the newborn Marie—she came close to becoming, there and then, a martyr in the struggle between the faiths. These missionaries really did have something of the Crusaders about them, though in actual fact they were nothing but colonial officials.

In truth, Marie had no genuine firsthand memories of her earliest days in India, given that her family returned to Swabia when she was just three years old. They went to live with her grandparents in Stuttgart, but she found it hard acclimatizing: "In my grandparents' house, I was once caned because I threw spinach angrily at the wall during dinner, shouting: 'In India, only cows eat green grass!'"[15] After a year her parents decided to return to India—but without Marie. One never ceases to be astonished at how little the prospect of being separated from their children for long periods (or even for ever) seemed to bother people at this time. Hesse's mother remembered how distraught she was when her parents departed, though curiously this did not lead her to behave any differently with regard to her own children. The souls of children did not count for much among Pietists, especially in the late nineteenth century: "My innermost being was appalled; it seemed to me as if the whole world had conspired against me, and my parents had shunned me."[16]

According to the Pietists, a child was a creature that was yet to be formed. No value was assigned to a person's childhood in its own right. An individual had to be brought up, and was expected to learn what was required in order to become a full-fledged adult—where this instruction took place was a secondary consideration. Children were small adults, who simply lacked the faculty of reason as yet.

Initially Marie stayed with her grandparents, but not for long. It was decided that the fourteen-year-old girl should board with a missionary friend in Basel who was already putting up several children whose parents were engaged in missionary work abroad. Marie was fortunate in being housed in the Gundeldingen neighborhood with the family of Dr. Ostertag, who was a well-known Christian author; she was later to call this period "my happiest childhood," although dark forebodings seemed to compromise her disposition to be happy from an early age—even while she was still in India. She was clearly an imaginative child, though this trait was forbidden from the outset by the Pietist: "I wasn't a happy child. Even at a very tender age I was often tormented by a nameless fear, and would wake screaming in the night from terrible dreams, and would lie there shaking silently and listening to the howling of the jackals."[17]

Hermann Hesse wrote of his mother: "I inherited a passionate temperament from my mother, along with my violent, sensation-seeking imagination, and my gift for music."[18]

Marie's foster parents were full of love and care. As she recalled: "I largely forgot about mother and father and often found myself wishing that the Ostertags could be my real parents."[19] A devout harmony reigned in their household, and Marie herself soon learned how to do missionary work. During one excursion to Badenweiler, when they were allowed to ride on mules, the girls had the barefooted mule-drivers recount their life stories, and urged them to pray and do penance and handed out little religious tracts to them. They also promised to pray for the muleteers, and duly delivered on their promise: "A long, long while later, when we were praying together during our devotions, every evening we would call to mind the poor boys who drove the mules and mention them by name: Joggele, Hans, Klaus, Bastian, and Martin."[20] Marie took the business of disseminating the Word of God very seriously.

The idyll at the Ostertags' house proved an illusion, however. A new teacher poisoned the peace of the household through lies and intrigues. Marie remarked of herself how her childlike trust evaporated at this time. For Dr. Ostertag, whom she was accustomed to calling "Papa," chose to believe the teacher rather than the children, who were now regarded as "disobedient" and treated more strictly. Marie recalled how an atmosphere of rebellion began to ferment among the girls at the mission; the Revolution of 1848 was not far in the past: "We suddenly saw ourselves as prisoners, as poor nuns, who only knew freedom and a lust for life as concepts, and we started discussing liberty and servitude and oppression and revolution, and usually ended our conversations with the rallying cry: 'The hour of freedom will yet strike and a new dawn of brighter days will break!'"[21]

Although the teacher left soon thereafter, the idyll had been shattered: "The lovely period of being a child was now gone forever. We never again felt ourselves a family, but rather as inmates of a 'missionary children's home,' a fact for which we were often mocked by the town girls when we walked through the streets of Basel in winter, two by two, in our blue dresses and grey felt hats and heavy clogs, making our way to church through the heavy snow."[22] And because missionaries throughout the world kept bringing more and more children into this sinful world and sending them to Basel, the Committee decided to build their own missionary children's home—where Hermann Hesse was later sent by this same Marie, his mother, when he was fourteen.

The Ostertags' lodging house duly closed. The children were first distributed to other homes, and Marie was sent to Korntal: "I had heard that institute being commended for its strictness." And indeed, she soon came to feel firsthand the restrictive spirit that prevailed there. She suffered from homesickness and the lovelessness of this crammer—the kind of school Hesse was later to expose in *Beneath the Wheel*. Even so, when she wrote about the place, she herself employed the kind of vocabulary used there, such as "naughty," "disobedient," and "stubborn." A curious choice when recalling her own distress as a young girl in such surroundings! There is a good deal of misplaced robustness and very little intuitive sympathy evident in this attitude: from an early age, Marie clearly began to suppress her own sensitivity.

She found only one friend in Korntal, a Russian girl named Olga Bunsen, who was seventeen years old. She comforted Marie, and Marie rewarded her in return with all the love that had been lying dormant within her. How deeply shocked she was, therefore, when Olga was one day upbraided by the institution. In the refectory, the pastor summoned Olga to come forward and ostracized her. She had, it appeared, committed a serious sin and the others girls were forbidden to have any contact with her. It turned out that Olga had fallen in love with a boy and exchanged love letters and poems with him. Someone betrayed her confidence. Marie was outraged and stood by her friend despite the ban, until Olga was finally expelled from the institute. At first sight, this was a noble act on Marie's part. She was even placed in solitary confinement for a spell for attempting to write her friend a letter.

However, in the account she later wrote of her life, Marie Hesse reinterpreted this revolt, which she had staged in the spirit of friendship, as a delusional act. Ultimately, she maintained, those who demand discipline and subordination and who ban all individual emotional impulses are always right. That was her gloomy summing-up of her time at Korntal, during which she had suffered in a way only young people with great expectations and trust can suffer—until even she began to become desensitized.

Her elder brother, who also wrote poems, sent her a volume of Schiller, but the book was confiscated. Yet another transgression! So it was that on March 8, 1855, she was forced to write to her father in India: "You know that I am very interested in Schiller's poetry; however, in Korntal such works may not be read by girls of my age. I asked the pastor if I might read them, but he told me in a very friendly manner that it would be better if I read some Christian verse first, and gave me a volume of Albert Knapp's works. He also said that when I next composed a poem of my own I should show him what I had written, however I know I would find that very difficult."[23]

The fifteen-year-old Marie traveled to India to be reunited with her parents in November 1857. During the crossing on the vessel *Bombay* the love affair occurred that would decide her future fate. She met John Barns, a young Englishman—and it was a case of love at first sight. She didn't know what was happening to her and was emotionally at sixes and sevens—or more precisely, completely hostage to her own emotions. The missionary who was chaperoning her eventually banned all contact with the young man. There ensued various clandestine trysts, chance encounters, swiftly exchanged letters and poems—all in English. On the final evening before their arrival in India, they managed to meet in the ship's chapel: "It was then that I first realized how powerful the bond of love was that joined us, and how impossible it would be for us to part. Afterward we were all alone together for a short while but our emotions rendered us speechless. He wanted a kiss from me, and begged me to give him just one.—I believed I was duty-bound to refuse him. It still pains me now. Oh, if only I had given him that kiss, then our parting would have been easier!"[24] Then, however—not totally unexpectedly—God suddenly emerges once more from his hiding place and interposes himself in Marie's recollections: "God, who deemed it good and necessary to break this bond, He alone knows exactly how things were."[25] God? More like her father, who arrogated a Godlike position for himself. For it was he who turned down John Barns's written request for his daughter's hand as wholly out of the question, but he even hid from Marie the letter that she had been yearning to receive for so long. Only later did she learn of John Barns's communication to her father, asking to marry her, and of a letter addressed to her sent under the same cover, which she never received.

Hesse's mother, Marie Hesse (1842–1902), in a photograph from 1857

Once again, she found herself a sinner. Initially she was angry at her father but then humbly submitted to his will: "Thank God! He has emerged victorious. Mere flesh and blood cannot prevail. If I only have Jesus (and I do have him, just a little), then everything is well."[26] Yet the wound, and her longing, remained, and after a year everything was as it had been on the first day. She could not forget John Barns, and the young Englishman, who was clearly not some frivolous seducer, spent years hoping that her father would relent.

Marie wrote poems full of yearning. These still sound at points like those of the young Hermann Hesse, before they reverted to a purely Pietist tone. For instance, in a poem titled "Alone," we read the following verses:

> Do not ask me, why I am weeping!
> Ah, you cannot understand me.
> Leave me in peace
> Undisturbed and unseen!

The cold presence of other people
Fills my breast with melancholy,
And their consolation only wounds me,
I feel nothing of their passion!

Oh, I am so alone,
I imagine myself far from here,
In spirit, I am sitting in the glow of stars,
Sweet Lord, quietly by Thy side.[27]

Six months later a preacher of repentance, the equally renowned and re-
viled missionary Hebich, who had gained a reputation among the missionaries in India for the coarseness of his conversion methods, would show the
lovesick Marie the sinfulness of her desires. An exorcism, to all intents and
purposes! Marie later spoke of it as a conversion, and dated it exactly to
February 23, 1858. Henceforth, she knew that she only had one purpose in
life: to help her parents in their mission to the heathens. Was this too much
to ask of a young girl? Certainly, a protective carapace of religiosity formed
around her wounded soul. Now she devoted herself only to God and to all
men, never again devoting herself entirely to one individual.

She only married seven years later, at the age of twenty-three. Naturally it was a missionary, Charles Isenberg, whom she wed in 1865, at her
birthplace of Talatscheri.

A year later their first son, Theodor, was born. Their second son to
survive was Karl. In between them there was a son they named Hermann,
who died at the age of five months. The next Hermann to whom she gave
birth was with her second husband, Johannes Hesse. Did Hermann Hesse
perhaps grow up in the knowledge that his mother had already had a son
with his Christian name and that he might therefore in her eyes be a substitute for his dead stepbrother? This is hardly likely. There were so many
Hermanns in the Hesse and Gundert families, several of whom had died,
that the writer surely cannot have been preoccupied with this fact.

After just five years of marriage to Charles Isenberg, Marie was already a widow. Her husband died as the result of a hemorrhage, leaving
the twenty-eight-year-old Marie alone with two children. She and her sons
went to stay with her parents in Calw, where she helped her father in the
publishing house. She also dedicated a biography to her deceased husband:
"Recollections of Charles Isenberg, Recorded for His Children."

Another returnee from India to Calw was Johannes Hesse, in 1873. He had become too ill on the subcontinent to carry out his missionary duties and now likewise came back, to act as a publishing assistant to Hermann Gundert. A year later he and the widow Marie Isenberg were wed. With her second husband, she would go on to have another six children, two of whom died at an early age. Her many domestic chores did not, however, prevent her from writing several books of her own, four in total. The year 1892 saw the publication of *David Livingstone,* a biography of the famous Scottish missionary and African explorer.

The first son Johannes and Marie Hesse brought into their well-ordered world of work—having already produced a daughter, Adele, in 1875—was Hermann Hesse in 1877. And from the very beginning this son showed himself to be a troublemaker.

His brief sketch "My Mother" from the 1940s ends on a melancholic note. His relationship with the mother he had once loved so dearly remained tense, even fifty years after her death. Hermann Hesse could not conceal the fact that he had expected more from this woman, who was forever writing and creating. And it was a source of bitter disappointment to him that she of all people should have failed to acknowledge his literary talent and even attacked his works as sinful. Something had clearly died in him when he reported, in a distanced way and not without an weary under-tone: "It was nice to make one of those little excursions with mother that she loved so much."[28]

The Poet as a Child Who Was Not Allowed to Be One

From my recollection of those days, I often look back, as if from a high tower, on my earliest years, and can see nothing but a sea of mysteries and beginnings, without form but with a sacred scent of remoteness, a veil drawn across miracles and treasures.

—Hermann Hesse, *Hermann Lauscher*

Hermann Hesse was the cause of great pain to his mother even prior to his birth. Marie Hesse, who had already brought three children into the world, was at a loss to explain it herself. She noted in her diary: "I am finding it very hard at the moment. . . . Frequent and severe pains; unless it is twins, I cannot understand it!" The actual birth was problematic as well, but it was not twins that saw the light of the world, but Hermann Hesse, who had already asserted himself while still in his mother's womb. On July 2, 1877, she reported with relief on the arrival of her Hermann, to whom she had successfully given birth "after a difficult day." He was, she recounted, a "very large, handsome child, who was instantly hungry, and who of his own accord turned his light blue eyes to the brightness and his head to the light—a shining example of a healthy, vigorous boy."[29] He was baptized a month later by his grandfather Hermann Gundert: "The little boy cried at first but when the singing began he looked around him, all alert, and kept quiet thereafter." He was bright and alert in every respect and right from the outset. Church rituals seemed to irritate him even at this stage, but music soothed him.

On August 13, 1880, Marie Hesse noted in her diary; "Little Hermann is incredibly lively and intelligent, but he is prone to violent outbursts all the same. Adele is far easier to bring up and gladdens my heart."[30] Adele was greatly loved by her brother (as Hesse was to reiterate in his obituary of his favorite sister). His mother noted the following exchange between the three-year-old Hermann and the five-year-old Adele: "Hermann had stuck an iron nail in his mouth; Adele rushed up to him, pulled it out and scolded him: 'What are you trying to do, kill yourself? Do you think I want to become the baby of the family again, with all the little ones that have died already?' Hermann replied; 'I don't care! If I die and go to my grave, I'll just take a couple of picture-books with me!'"[31] The background to this remark was the premature deaths of their siblings Paul (1879) and Gertrud (1880), which Adele and Hermann had been old enough to register at the time. Hermann's reaction after Gertrud's burial was childlike and unsentimental: "When he got back home, he immediately jumped onto Gertrud's empty cot and started pummeling it and shouting: 'So, Gertrud, have you gone to meet our dear Savior?'"[32] By November 1880 another child had been born, their young sister Marie, whom they called "Marulla."

The prosaic business of giving birth would never be the writer's subject matter. For him, childhood was an imaginary realm, in which he recreated himself over and over in the act of writing.

As a twenty-two-year-old, he made the following precocious observation in his work *Hermann Lauscher:* "It is one of the insufficiencies and privations of human existence that we necessarily become estranged from our childhood and so it sinks into oblivion like some treasure that slips from one's hands and drops over the edge of a deep well."[33]

Childhood in Hesse is spectral and dreamlike. It is a fairy tale, and not just inasmuch as, in childhood, you believe in the fairy tales you are told, but in a much more elemental sense: in and of itself, childhood is an integral part of these fairy tales. As children we have all experienced something that we later so easily forget—namely, that everything has a life of its own and is more than the mere aspect of utility under which we customarily consider it. The animistic-magical worldview of "primitive" peoples, for whom there are no such things as lifeless objects, also inhabits children—and writers are people who nurture their inner child. Likewise, his mother told him stories from the Bible in such a way that that he could still recall these moments some decades later. Her imagination and love of making up stories were first fired by Christian tales—and these also enthused her son, involving him in the joys and sorrows of the protagonists of the stories.

An awareness began to develop in the young Hermann that things have a hidden side, a side that is dark and threatening and even demonic. "My eager mind soon began of its own accord to conjure up mountains with meadows where elves danced in the moonlight, palaces with silken queens, and fabulously deep and terrifying mountain caves unnervingly populated by a succession of spirits, hermits, charcoal burners, and brigands."

The boy's imagination made even the well-ordered parental house into a place where dangers lurked of which the grown-ups were wholly unaware: "A narrow space in the bedroom—the gap between two bedframes—was ideally suited as the constant residence of slit-eyed kobolds, soot-covered miners, the beheaded walking dead, sleepwalking murderers, and green-eyed predators, with the result that for a spell I could only walk past this place in the company of grown-ups, and even for a long time thereafter had to summon up all my boyish pride and courage to go near it."[34]

The Raftsmen of Calw as a Symbol

Even now I have occasional nights of homesickness for Calw.

—Hermann Hesse, 1918

Time and again this small town in the Black Forest, which may be described (albeit not without reservation) as Hermann Hesse's hometown, became the subject of Hesse's writing, primarily his early short stories.

There, it was given the fictional name of Gerbersau. Even the name demonstrates a degree of distance on the author's part, thought this was a notion he constantly played around with in an affectionate way. "Though Wildbad is not far away, our region does not belong to the Black Forest of the Baedeker guide and of international travel; the landscape is very normal and the town itself has no particular attractions."[35] Thus ran the matter-of-fact account in his "Calw Diary" of March 1901, which nevertheless still managed to lend a poetic note to the very featurelessness of his hometown: "The attractive old townhouses may be counted on the fingers of one hand, the town hall is old and pretty but without any truly individual features, and only the old stone bridge over the River Nagold with its Gothic chapel serves as a reminder that this modest, industrious little place is more than just a couple of years old."[36]

He had to get away from here, from the narrowness of this small town, in order to become himself. But once he had successfully escaped, he was able to return later, just on a visit, and allow all the picturesque aspects and the almost militant coziness of the province wash over him once more in all its overblown prettiness. He was no longer a part of it, and yet he could still acknowledge it as something that had had a formative influence on his own psyche. It was rather like an illness that one had successfully survived. Afterward one remembers the long weeks spent laid-up in bed, the dreams, being read to, and one's worried parents. It forms part of the prehistory of one's own life and sometimes it can be remarkably affecting. In Hesse's work "Boyhood" of 1903, we read: "I have always been regarded here half as an outsider, as indeed I am, since neither my mother nor my father were native to this area." That doesn't exactly sound like a declaration of love to Calw. Instead it invokes the "child's soul" that forms the major theme of Hesse's early work, an emphatic affirmation of his own origins in spite of everything: "And so one finds oneself at home wherever one has spent one's boyhood. Not thanks to the school—that was a miserable experience here—but because a boy sees and enjoys and learns and triumphs infinitely better and more beautifully and more certainly than ten adults, and because we never again in life encounter so completely this capacity to claim a piece of land as our own, through and through."[37]

The "remarkable beauty" of Calw to which Hesse draws attention in this work derived not only from the atmosphere of this old manufacturing town (primarily textile mills) but also from the nature of the Black Forest as a kind of fairy-tale forest and the River Nagold, which flowed through the region. One sight in particular that impressed the young Hermann Hesse were the rafts of logs, the traditional method of transporting felled fir trees downstream as far as Mannheim or even all the way to Holland. Each raft, Hesse recalled, consisted of eight to ten logs, bound together with strips of pliable willow bark. The fishermen and even the local farmers felt themselves disrupted by the transport of timber on the Nagold during the summer, especially when one of these rafts got stuck and had to be pushed free. What really fascinated the young Hesse in particular, however, were the raftsmen. These were not petit-bourgeois burghers like the inhabitants of Calw but another caste of men entirely: "The raftsmen clearly belonged to that class of people who were of no fixed abode, untamed, itinerants, nomads—and rafts and raftsmen were not welcomed by the guardians of morality and public order."[38]

Yet for the youth of the small town they were the epitome of freedom. It was surely no coincidence that Hesse later depicted Siddhartha, when on his way to sanctification, as crossing a river, and that he elevated the ferryman Vasudeva into a kind of masked, divine figure. For Hesse, water was always associated with the image of a perilous trial. Could this have been why, when he published his poems in 1896 in the Viennese periodical *Das deutsche Dichterheim,* he added the somewhat boastful explanation that he had been with a lot of Nordic women and that, all things considered, he basically saw himself (because of his father's Baltic origins) "as a son of the Baltic"?[39] In Calw he had to make do with the Nagold as a symbol of the fateful water. It carried goods but could also bring death, in contrast to fire, which could destroy existing things but in doing so also cleanse them and bring forth new life.

As a border, the river separated the worlds of people who belonged together and yet found themselves facing one another on opposite sides of the river. This was the case with Hesse and his parents, and would later be the same between him and his three sons.

The waters of the Nagold were a reality for Hesse that he could experience with all his senses, yet at the same time they were a dream image, a symbol equally for life's dangers and for the means of transportation of his own yearnings, his strivings toward freedom. Was it predetermined that one should drown in them?

Therefore, it was not just a boyish test of courage to travel a stretch as a stowaway on these rafts but also a momentary realization of the dream of breaking free of the all-too-familiar boundaries of the Black Forest into a wider, as yet unknown world. It was no easy matter leaping onto a passing raft, as the rapids carried it forward at great speed—not to mention the fact that the raftsmen reacted violently to the "hoboes" who waited on bridges and weirs to try to catch a ride: "It was strictly forbidden, and it wasn't just the teachers and the police ranged against you. . . . The best time to attempt it was on warm summer days, when you had very few clothes on anyhow, and no shoes or socks. Then it was easy to make it onto the raft, and if you got lucky and could conceal yourself from the raftsmen, it was wonderful to travel downstream for a couple of miles between the quiet green riverbanks, under the bridges and through the sluices."[40] If you managed it, you were soaked through and chilled to the bone, and finally you had to retrace your entire raft journey on foot back up the riverbank—and all you got for your pains was to be sworn at by the raftsmen and berated by your parents.

In his work *Raft Journey* of 1927, Hesse considered what the real value of these adventures during the summers of his childhood in Calw had been. He concluded that it was the formative experience of realizing that one had to pay for every pleasure, and that every genuine and lasting impression of purposeful engagement also brought with it hardships: "You were a raftsmen, a wanderer, a nomad, you drifted calmly past the cities and people, attached to nowhere, and felt in your heart the wide world and a strange burning sensation of homesickness. No—it was certainly not too high a price to pay."[41]

Basel and Missionary Work

The raft journeys, the sheer excitement of putting oneself in jeopardy—all this was the preserve of a late phase of childhood, which began when Hermann Hesse returned at the age of nine with his family—following the death of his grandfather Hermann Gundert's wife, Julie—to Calw.

As it turned out, though, the childhood idyll in Calw, which was peopled with every conceivable hobgoblin and specter, would only last until Hesse was fourteen, when the Committee summoned his father back to Basel. There Johannes not only published the missionary magazine, but also was made responsible for teaching the history of missionary work to others.

Basel as a town—or rather, a great city, in the eyes of a child—was to have a lifelong impact on Hesse. He lived there from 1881 to 1886 and would later return as a young man. From an early stage, Basel became a second home for him. And anyone who, like him, had such early competing recollections of places where he spent his childhood, and who shared his propensity for comparison, never ever binds himself totally to one particular location and is a lost cause where any form of contented sedentary living is concerned. Even many years later, when Hesse stayed loyal to Montagnola for decades, he knew that this came with a caveat: namely, that he was inwardly free to quit his own chosen place of refuge if it should ever in his view cease to be that.

The family lived in a suburb of the city, "on Müllerweg, opposite Spalenringweg; between these two streets, at that time, ran the railroad line to Alsace. The sight of the trains and the frequent spells of standing around and waiting by the level crossing when you wanted to go into town were among my earliest memories of Basel."[42] Finally, this was also the location where his father—up till then a Russian subject—acquired Swiss citizenship.

Marie Hesse was revitalized by the Basel Mission. She was in her element among missionaries, converts, and terminally ill patients. Hugo Ball dubbed her "Abbess" and "Duchess." But her energies focused on the general mass of humanity, and anyone who wanted to be perceived and loved as an individual in his own right, like her son Hermann the troublemaker, was in her eyes nothing but a vain and worldly person.

Hermann was no Pietist—that much was evident—nor, it seemed, would he ever become one. His mother hankered after more than just a family; as she herself noted, what she sought was a "community of saints." And in this her son Hermann, who loved her passionately, was her implacable enemy. Yet even that wasn't quite the case; however ascetic she liked to make herself out to be, that was not her natural disposition, any more than it had been Hermann Gundert's. The complete expunging of all sensuality, the abandonment of any form of corporeality as sinful within the rarefied atmosphere of ascetic rituals—the family was careful to avoid all this.

In 1936, in the story "Herr Claassen," Hermann Hesse recalled how a "heroic hermit" in the spirit of the scriptures suddenly appeared on the scene and how at the time they all—his mother included—regarded the man above all as comical and unappealing. Only later did Hesse begin to appreciate the consistency of this solitary existence and the dignity endowed by the spiritual exercises to which such figures subjected themselves. Back then, however, whenever this strict pilgrim on God's narrow path turned up at their table, he tended to spoil their appetites. For Herr Claassen also denied himself the pleasure of eating well. Anything that people did with relish he considered to be bestial greed. Singing or laughing were sinful in his opinion. But Hermann's mother refused to let this spoil her pleasure. There was a deep chasm between this Pietist coreligionist with his strict observances and Hesse's Pietist parents, particularly his mother:

> For Herr Claassen there was nothing intrinsically sacred about the family and the domestic circle, nor ultimately even about the church and the community; rather, he saw them all as part of the world of base animal instincts and arbitrariness. For him humans existed basically as individuals, and it was incumbent upon them to sacrifice and devote themselves to their Savior by eradicating utterly their private lives. And so it was that he looked down with disapproval, even contempt, upon any show of affection between parents and children, and regarded my father's not infrequent habit of walking arm-in-arm with his daughter as frivolous.[43]

In contrast to this, his parents' and his grandparents' lives seemed positively free-spirited, as Hesse remarked:

> They too lived piously, they too did not indulge in any vices and demanded a great deal of themselves in their daily lives, they had likewise devoted themselves and their lives to the service of God. Yet for all their devotion, they breathed the air like other people, and they lived in an atmosphere of community, friendship, and family, and knew emotions like warmth and affection, and feelings of tenderness, and they even countenanced a certain sensual pleasure in life, baking birthday cakes and cooking Sunday roasts and enjoying music-making, excursions, and walks. . . . Although there was a definite tendency in our household always to relate nature and worldly things to spiritual concerns and to God, this did not entail a radical break

Hermann Hesse at the age of four

with the world and the realm of the senses, and there was no studied rehearsal, technique, or practice of desensualization and spiritualization.

The first letter the four-year-old Hermann Hesse dictated from Basel, in
April 1881 to his grandfather Hermann Gundert in Calw, reveals that
"willfulness and defiance" that his mother had already identified in him at
the age of two, though at that time she still found it "quite wonderful."
Hermann told his grandfather: "I am coughing quite terribly, but I am still
allowed to go out. The doctor wanted to look at my tongue, but I refused
to show it to him, and I didn't drink the bitter tea they gave me either."[44]
     Hermann Hesse was convinced, as he would later explain in his novel
Rosshalde, that human beings throughout their entire lives draw upon
things that they experienced when they were children. This first view of
things conditions all subsequent contemplations. This was a central theme
of his early stories, but not exclusively of these; it remained a constant preoccupation thereafter, too. An incident noted by Hesse's mother shows
how powerfully the five-year-old Hermann had an instinctual awareness
of the connection between wickedness and beauty: "One morning, little
Hermann secretly played truant from kindergarten, so to punish him I shut

him in the guest room. Afterward he told me: 'That wasn't much use as I could see out the window and keep myself amused.' Recently he was singing a song with a tune and words he had made up himself for a long time in bed one evening, and when his father came in he said: 'Is it true that I sing as beautifully as the Sirens and that I'm also as wicked as them?'"

Grandfather Gundert tried from Calw to calm the strained nerves of his daughter and son-in-law in Basel. Nothing less than the fate of his grandson Hermann was at stake. On April 25, 1883, Hermann Gundert, who understood the "complicated and easily exacerbated"[45] character of his grandson better than his parents did, warned them: "I grant that you will need to have a great deal of patience with Hermann. It is God's work too that our children sometimes present us with puzzles that completely baffle us."[46]

Hermann's destiny was also the subject of a letter in which his father, Johannes, ruminated on his son's future:

> Hermann, who as a little boy was regarded almost as a paragon of virtues, has in the meantime become almost uncontrollable. However humiliating it would be for us, I am seriously contemplating sending him away to an institution or to be raised by another family. We are too tense and too weak for him, and the whole household isn't disciplined and ordered enough. He seems to be gifted in all things: he observes the moon and the clouds, he plays long and complicated tunes on the harmonium, he creates truly wonderful drawings with either a pencil or a quill, sings very well when he has a mind to, and is never stuck for a rhyme.[47]

This all sounds just as cruel as Hermann Hesse would himself sound three decades later when he presented his wife, Maria Bernoulli, with the ultimatum that either their youngest son, Martin (whom, in his state of nervous hypersensitivity following a bout of meningitis, he was finding intolerable), be sent away from the house or he would leave.

Nothing less was being decided here than whether Hermann should be exiled from the family for good, as his father wished, or not. The reason for this was that he was a difficult and willful child. Grandpa Gundert in Calw turned out to be the savior of his grandson, when he responded to his daughter and son-in-law: "I feel very sorry about your Hermann, but I must admit that I would be very unhappy if you were to send him far away. It is wrong to say that you have no influence over him. God, who gave you Hermann, has not abandoned you for sure and will not leave you bereft of any means of governing him."[48] By way of intervention, Gundert dispensed the following advice, which Johannes Hesse duly followed: "You couldn't pass him on to anyone who cared more about the boy than you do. That's what I firmly believe and I can only write what I truly feel to be right."[49] This proved no instant salvation for Hermann, however; the arduous business of raising him was only just beginning.

Accordingly, the boy who thus far had been sheltered in the parental home was now brought into the mission house. A self-confident child with a "violent temperament" was placed beneath the wheel. A photograph has survived showing the children of the mission house at this time—a sea of scared, unchildlike faces, looking for all the world like young army recruits. It is instantly apparent what these children are lacking: the ability to play freely and loving care. Instead, they were subjected to tedious drill and were punished for any spontaneous utterance. Hermann was seven years old when his mother wrote in her diary: "Hermann, whose education caused us so much trouble and care, is now getting on much better. He has been away at boarding school from January 21 to June 5 without a break (in other words six months solid), and has only spent the Sundays with us. He behaved well there, but he came home looking pale and thin and cowed." Even so, his parents were delighted; finally their previously so "naughty" boy was now deemed "well-behaved" and "good."

They apparently failed to notice how much their child, who had become pale and quiet, was suffering in this alien and martial environment; or in the event that they did, they saw it as a necessary corrective: a way of finally educating the boy. His mother remarked on the "good and beneficial" effect of this first spell away from home (more were to follow): "He is far easier to deal with now, thank God!"

In "The Childhood of the Magician," Hesse described how society treated children in this period of the burgeoning German Second Empire, when all emphasis was on progress and social advancement: "How pompous they were about their work, about their trades and official posts, how great and venerable they seemed to themselves! If a carriage driver, policeman, or pastor barricaded the street, that was Holy Writ, it was naturally assumed that you should get out of the way, make room, or give assistance. But children going about their work and play weren't the least bit important, they were shoved aside and yelled at."[50]

And so, because he felt himself to be a shoved-aside and yelled-at child his entire life, resistance against these external forces grew in Hesse. One of the fundamental experiences he took from life was how vital it was to protect the inner person from the crude intervention of the outside world.

Childhood: never just an idyll, always concurrently an abyss. This was the phase of Hesse's life when the external world brought him to the edge of total breakdown. This was an ordeal the outcome of which remained for a long time uncertain. A dangerous time, when he was misunderstood and psychologically mistreated not only by his teachers but by his own parents too. Right up to his late old age, that touched a central raw nerve of his existence, prompting him to rebel against a hostile world that was trying to break him and to turn him into something that he was not. But therein already lay the germ of his awakening as an individual. In his *Life Story Briefly Told* (1924), we learn:

> I was the child of pious parents, whom I loved tenderly and would have done even more so had they not made me aware from a very early age of the Fourth Commandment. Unfortunately commandments have always had a catastrophic effect on me, however right and well-intentioned they may be. Although by nature a lamb and as docile as a soap bubble, I always bridled at commandments of all kinds, especially during my youth. I only needed to hear the words "Thou shalt . . ." and my whole inner being changed and I became as stubborn as a mule. As you can well imagine, this characteristic had a major and negative impact on my time at school.[51]

Return to Calw

> I knew my way around the city of my fathers, its chicken runs and woods, its orchards and mechanics' workshops, I knew its trees, birds, and butterflies, I could sing songs and whistle through my teeth and much else besides that is important for living.
>
> —Hermann Hesse *Life Story Briefly Told* (1924)

In 1886 the Hesse family returned to Calw. Johannes Hesse had asked the Committee to grant him this dispensation, as Hermann Gundert had since the death of his wife, Julie, been living in the publishing union house with his cousin Henriette, who acted as his housekeeper.

Marie Hesse in particular was of two minds about this decision, for although her father was the most important person in her life bar none, she preferred living in Basel to a small town. She confided to her diary at this time: "It will be extremely hard for me to leave Basel with its lively, exciting hustle and bustle, the dear circle of our friends at the mission, our sunny, cozy lodgings and our charming neighborhood. On the other hand, I am drawn to Papa. On March 10, the Committee decided we should move to Calw."

Now, with the experience of Basel behind him, the eight-year-old Hermann Hesse saw his birthplace on the River Nagold with very different eyes. Calw was constantly present in the images he conjured up in his mind's eye. Hesse, who as a young writer had all the mannerisms of an old man, increasingly rejuvenated himself through the act of writing. As he grew older, the author always had one place of refuge: his birthplace, which was even more vividly present than ever as an image in his memory:

> The more old age takes hold of me, the more unlikely it becomes that I will ever set eyes on the hometown where I spent my childhood and youth, yet at the same time all the more powerfully do the mental images that I have of Calw and of Swabia in general retain their effect and freshness. When I, as a poet, speak of a forest or river, of a meadow or valley, of the shade of a chestnut tree or the scent of pines, then it is the forest around Calw, the River Nagold in Calw, the pine forests or the chestnuts of Calw that I am thinking of, and also the market square, the bridge and chapel, Bischofstrasse and Ledergasse, Brühl and Hirsauer Weg appear all over the place in my writings, even in those that do not have anything expressly to do with Swabia, for all these images and hundreds of others once came to my aid as a boy as archetypes. As a result, it is precisely to these images and not to some abstract image of the "fatherland" that I have remained faithful and grateful throughout my entire life; they have helped shape me and my view of the world, and they still shine forth to me now no less powerfully and beautifully than they ever did during my youth.

When he wrote these words in his "Calw Diary" of 1901, he had thought that everything to do with Calw was now definitively behind him. With a nonchalant air, he dismissed "this modest, industrious little place . . .

The Hesse family in 1889. From left to right: Hermann, Hesse's father Johannes Hesse, Marulla, Hesse's mother Marie, Adele, and Hans (seated on the rocking horse)

anything warm and praiseworthy that I have to say about our little town is firmly within the realm of my childhood recollections."

Yet soon enough it was precisely those memories that were to become the medium for his own unrest, his restless spirit, and his tendency toward roving. The stories he wrote in 1903, around the time he was composing his first novel, *Peter Camenzind,* took the form of conventional tales of a person's development. But in terms of the subject matter that was bubbling under and searching for expression here, they were pure dynamite. Nevertheless, Hesse would never take pleasure in destruction; he always saw himself first and foremost as a preservationist and as someone who, with unexpected rigor, declared war on anything that threatened the most valuable and time-honored aspects of a civilization: "This was the Germany of the early 'Wilhelmine' period, and a whole host of the concepts and symbols that were current at the time have now disappeared. But this was also the Swabia where an old culture that was as venerable as it was remarkable held sway, a folk existence under whose surface a sacred mythology comprising richly baroque recollections and dream images was still lively and active."

Pretty soon Hesse's parents began to suffer in his grandfather's house. Marie Hesse wrote in her diary: "Of course it is nice being at Papa's. During the first few months here I found everything wonderful, because Papa's presence made up for everything else. But we had a setback in the winter; we got fed up with the bad rooms and the colds we caught, the heating, the toilet, and auntie's patronizing attitude. Plus we were having a bad time with Hermann, and the monotonous uniformity of life here started to get me down." But in the very next sentence, she goes on to admonish herself to show the "discipline and strict morality" that are essential for "inner growth." The fact that her husband was suffering even more than she was in the grandfather's house was no doubt due to the fact that he had been taken on again at the press only in the role of Gundert's assistant, and because Marie remained fixated on her father. This all combined to make the situation a real crisis.

Hermann's father needed a very strong will to get a grip on himself and conceal his growing irritation. They lived like this for three years. On July 26, 1889, however, Marie Hesse noted: "I have spoken with Papa and we have decided to part company. Nobody has any idea what all this has cost me! We should have done this long ago, though, to spare Johnny's nerves."[52] Johannes Hesse was by now in a bad way and could not go on living like this. He sent a letter to Hermann Gundert in which he described his situation as humiliating: "What is more, I increasingly find with every year that passes that I no longer feel that I am living 'among my own people,' but rather in a foreign country to which 'my spirit cannot accommodate itself' despite all the profound concordance that exists." This was a cry for help. Hermann Gundert corresponded about this letter from his son-in-law, who no longer wanted to live under the same roof as him, with one of his own sons, who was also called Hermann: "It was all so considered, so honest and yet so artificially framed that I did not dare to write a reply, given the current excitable state of his nerves."[53]

Hermann Hesse's constitution left much to be desired too. That became the subject of further correspondence among family members: "Hermann was found to be afflicted with deficient limb growth, and he has been prescribed a special treatment. This means an end to things like skating and gymnastics and so forth for him. He will only be allowed gentle, regular exercise with no exertion."[54] Adele, too, was to be subjected to an "orthopedic bed," but she found it easy to fall in with her parents' demands, whereas Hermann was "glowering and agitated." Marie's diary for the year 1889 noted: "Hermann had pain in his arms and legs for half of December, and had to lie down and have an electric current passed through them."[55]

The family rented their own house in Ledergasse. This was not a salubrious residential area of Calw; formerly there had been a tannery there, and the surroundings stank. "But the house was set well back from the street, had a little front garden and behind a really invigorating view of green countryside. With an enclosed corridor, five rooms, a kitchen and a small dining room, everything old-fashioned and simple, and not on a minute scale like most of the dwellings in Calw, either! It's really very snug and cozy."[56] The house was rented by the family from July 28 onward, but then Johannes suffered a complete nervous breakdown. Grandfather Gundert wrote to his sister Emma on August 1, 1889, about what had happened: "Marie traveled to Bern early this morning to go and help poor, distressed Johannes. He is in Dändliker's Hospital in the city and frequently suffers from nervous attacks and fits of uncontrollable crying."[57] Shortly afterward, on August 12, he informed his grandson Hermann: "Almost all these Baltic people have a streak of melancholy in them, and they find my easygoing manner somehow unbearable."

After two weeks Johannes Hesse returned home from the hospital. But he found he could not endure his surroundings, of which his family formed so large a part: "Our mealtimes were too loud for him, so he ate by himself in the adjoining room." And then there was the twelve-year-old Hermann, who was not much inclined to spare his overwrought father's nerves. And so it was that the boy had to be swiftly removed from the house. On

January 1890 his grandfather Hermann Gundert wrote: "Hermann Hesse is now to be sent away to Göppingen to stay with Rector Bauer, who once tutored Carl for his state examination. The boy is pleased to be leaving the family home, and I think the studious atmosphere will do him good. Marie will take him there in about a week's time."[58] That had an ominous ring to it. But Hermann was fortunate: Rector Bauer was different from the general run of dull pedagogues at that time. For all the learning by rote and drill that took place at his Latin school, he kept in mind that it was children he was dealing with, and that they had to be stimulated and given some incentive to cooperate in the learning process.

At Rector Bauer's in Göppingen

> But for Rector Bauer and the spirit that presided over the two classes he ran to prepare pupils for the Swabian state exam, my imagination would have had no occasion to engage with the notion of an ideal school of the sort which, as an old man, I later described in *The Glass Bead Game*.
>
> —Hermann Hesse, letter to pupils of the Hohenstaufen
> High School in Göppingen, June 9, 1953

The young man was thrilled. What a character Rector Bauer was! Unlike Hermann's parents, who always strove to be so restrained, so devout, and so moral and reasonable, Rector Bauer saw things from their entertaining side. Hermann, who thus far had only had commandments imposed upon him, loved him for this. Writing to his parents, he told them: "The rector's wit is inexhaustible." He was an old man who had even more splendid nonsense in his head than the young Hesse, and was not in the least ashamed of it. Looking back on his schooldays in 1953, Hesse would put it somewhat more soberly: "An encounter between a young boy and a superior teacher-genius can be something that continues to have positive repercussions throughout a person's life."

Once released from the stifling atmosphere of Pietism, Hermann, the difficult child, blossomed in Göppingen. He constantly reported back to Calw on the latest idiosyncrasies of his teacher. On February 9 his astonished parents read the following: "Suddenly, the rector will catch sight of something out on the street, like yesterday for instance when he spotted a colossal pig. Whenever that happens the whole school is allowed to go out and look at it." Hermann Gundert also kept his son Hermann abreast about the boy's schooling:[59] "Hermann Hesse sent me a card with the latest joke from Rector Bauer . . . that's the teacher who during school hours can say to one of his pupils: 'You, boy, fill my pipe for me!' And to another: 'Go and fetch me my coffee, but make sure you don't take more than two gulps from it while you're bringing it to me.'"[60]

The school days in Göppingen were long, and the pressure relentless. There were no days off, with teaching even taking place on Sundays. Yet the boys, who willingly subjected themselves to this regime because they found it fun to work hard, soon discovered that they were profiting from it in terms of personal growth.

Subsequently Hermann Hesse would repeatedly make this school, which he referred to as "the crammer," the subject of his writing; its specialty was preparing students, in a short time and under considerable pressure, for the Swabian state examination, that "eye of a needle" through which everyone who aspired to go to one of the free elite schools— Maulbronn, Blaubeuren, and Urach—was required to pass. In turn, those free schools provided the students for the Evangelical-Lutheran College in Tübingen, the alma mater for pastors and teachers throughout Württemberg.

So, what sort of man was this who so impressed Hermann Hesse, the sworn enemy of teachers, at that time? Bauer was already around seventy years old, and was somewhat jaded with the endless drill that parents of the pupils in his charge expected him to provide. The fact that he was judged solely on the numbers of pupils he managed to get through the state exam had not made him meek and complacent in old age, but instead had contrived to engender a special kind of irony in him. Hesse described him in 1926 (in the essay "From My School Days") as "a bent, aged man with wild gray hair, somewhat bulging, bloodshot eyes, dressed in an indescribably old-fashioned garment marked with greenish stains, wearing spectacles low down his nose and holding in his right hand a long pipe with a porcelain bowl reaching almost to the floor, from which he continuously blew huge clouds of smoke into the already smoke-filled room."[61]

Ultimately the Latin scholar Hermann Hesse passed the state examination in June 1891 with the second-highest marks out of seventy-nine candidates. He thus succeeded in becoming one of the forty-five students who were admitted to the academy at Maulbronn. This evangelical theological institution was situated in the building of a former Cistercian monastery. Here candidates were schooled in preparation for entry into the theological seminary of Tübingen University. In order to enroll there, Hermann—whose father had been a Russian national before being granted Swiss citizenship in Basel—first had to become a subject of the Kingdom of Württemberg. "And so, without being subjected to many questions, I was duly naturalized as a citizen of Württemberg in the year 1890 or 1891."

Yet the thing about Rector Bauer that would remain firmly imprinted on Hermann Hesse, what had really fascinated him about this genius of a teacher, as he called him, was his ability to combine learning with play—a highly unusual aptitude for this period! For example, Bauer had his students translate Friedrich Schiller's play *Wallenstein,* of all things, into Latin: "The remarkable and unusual thing about our teacher was his ability not only to sniff out the more intelligent among his pupils and to support and nourish their idealism but also to give proper due to the age of his pupils, to their boyishness and passion for play."[62]

Depths of the Child's Soul: Arsonists and Madmen?

> "In actual fact, a good, proper rocket is almost like an act of worship," said my brother, who sometimes liked to talk in images, "or like singing a beautiful song, right? It's just such a grand event."
>
> —Hermann Hesse, *Youth, Beautiful Youth*

In his 1919 story "A Child's Soul," Hesse wrote openly for the first time—his father had died in 1916—about the dark shadows that had spread over his childhood. What an excess of aggression, what hatred for his father comes to light here! In his autobiographical writings of this period, Hesse is like a barrel of dynamite that often comes perilously close to the fuse. His childlike innocence grapples with a demon that drives him to flout rules and act immorally. Was it ultimately the sheer liberating pleasure of transgressing that motivated him?

All that was missing was just a modicum, a touch more fear and suffering, and things would spill over and move inexorably to a dreadful conclusion. One day, on a day just like today, I would abandon myself entirely to wickedness and, out of a feeling of defiance and rage and an awareness of the senseless and unbearable nature of existence, would do something horrific and decisive, something horrific yet at the same time liberating that would extinguish for good all my anxieties and torments. The only uncertainty was what that thing might be; but a confused welter of fantasies and fleeting, obsessive mental images had already passed through my mind. Visions of crimes through which I might take my revenge on the world and at the same time sacrifice and obliterate myself.[63]

It appears, then, that Hermann Hesse was also one of those permanently overstressed students who harbor fantasies of assassination.

In any event, his pyromaniac tendencies were plain for all to see. This trait reappears in an altered form in his work, in the great mythical opposition between fire and water. Even as an old man, there was nothing that fascinated Hesse more than sitting for hours on end in the garden gazing at the flames of the bonfires that he enjoyed making out of leaves and twigs. And nothing could move him to such expressions of unalloyed joy as fireworks displays, events that had the capacity to both delight and perturb him. In the poem "Hours in the Garden," we read the following lines:

> To me, for instance, fire (among its many other meanings),
> Also denotes a chemical-symbolic act of worship in the service
>   of the divine,
> And the transformation of multiplicity back into a unity,
> And in this act I am both priest and server, I fulfill and am fulfilled,
> I change the wood and weeds to ashes, and administer to the dead.

In a letter of February 18, 1891, Hermann told his family in Calw about a blaze that had occurred in Göppingen:

> Yesterday (Monday), at around 8:30 in the morning, a fire broke out in a weaver's workshop close to our school. Everyone here was in a flat spin; we had to clear away as fast as we could a large pile of maize straw that we had

recently piled up behind the building. Then the fire department came
rushing past the school at full tilt. I found it all very scary. The whole town
was in uproar, with everyone rushing to the scene of the blaze. Nine doves
were burned to death in a locked dovecot. The rector was terribly agitated;
he is a very nervous man at the best of times.[64]

On the one hand, there is evidence here of an elemental delight in fire;
surrounded as he was by repressive benevolence, the young boy had it in
him to turn this delight into a weapon against the pious world of his parents. Is it plausible to see the young Hermann Hesse as an arsonist? Certainly, at the age of thirteen, there was no question that he was aggressive
enough for this. Yet he was caught actually lighting a fire only on one
occasion. Grandfather Gundert lost no time in writing about the incident
to his son Hermann: "On 12-9 a scandal blew up. Hermann Hesse had
gone out walking with George Sturrock. On the way back, they set light
to a clump of dry grass, which immediately flared up. The forest ranger
rushed to the scene, apprehended them, and took them both by the scruff
of the neck to Hirsau."[65] A report was drafted, but it was unclear whether
the matter would be dealt with by the chief bailiff or the district court.
Hermann Hesse's imminent departure for Göppingen, where he was
studying for the state exam under Rector Bauer, was in jeopardy. His parents
were in a frenzy, rushing from one authority to another. Finally, however, Grandfather Gundert was able to report: "No indictment concerning
the fire had yet reached the court, and so Johannes obtained a dispensation
for Hermann to travel to Göppingen this very afternoon, given that
school was going to resume first thing tomorrow morning."[66]
    By the time the forest ranger appeared with the charge sheet "and
dressed in his Sunday-best uniform and carrying his gun," Hermann had
gone. The parents paid a ten-mark fine for their English lodger George,
who returned home a few days later, and three marks for Hermann. His
mother wrote in relief to Hermann's older sister, Adele: "So the whole
sorry business has been resolved, but the English boy will need to send
me the money from home, as he only had barely enough on him to cover
his journey home." The court ruled that the incident wasn't arson but
"wanton recklessness." This was a very fortunate outcome, because for a
moment Hermann Hesse's future hung in the balance here. Yet it appears
that the young Hermann treated the whole matter very lightly. On October 6,

less than a month after the incident in the forest near Calw, he wrote his parents a very carefree and upbeat letter about his activities in Göppingen: "After supper, a few fireworks."[67]

A year before this event, the young Hermann had upset a paraffin lamp in his father's study. His parents had no reason to put it down to anything other than haste and clumsiness. Was it simply that, or was it already that demon which he would later claim had driven him to do this? In any event, the fire was quickly put out.

In 1919, in "A Child's Soul," he traced his hidden aggression and that malign urge within himself to break the law, which—such is the thin line between fantasy and reality—genuinely threatened to take possession of him at one point in his childhood: "Sometimes it seemed to me as if I were setting our house on fire: massive flames would wing their way through the night, houses and alleyways would be engulfed in fire, and the whole town would flare up in one huge blaze against the black sky. At other times, the crimes I committed in my dreams struck me as an act of revenge against my father, a murder, a cruel homicide."[68]

A number of fires broke out in and around Calw at this time. Such incidents were, however, not uncommon in the days of gas and petroleum lamps. On February 28, 1891, an entire factory, belonging to Schill & Wagner, burnt to the ground. Hesse's parents put up the owners, who were made homeless by the blaze, in their house for a few days. Yet the young Hermann Hesse remained fascinated, positively enthralled, by the primeval nature of a blaze and the exceptional situation into which it cast a bourgeois world that otherwise regarded itself as so stable and well ordered.

Just as had happened almost exactly a year previously in Göppingen in the immediate vicinity of the schoolhouse there, so a fire also broke out on the night of January 19–20 in Maulbronn, very close to the Evangelical Seminary. Hermann wrote a detailed account of the incident to his family in Calw:

> We saw nothing and stayed in our beds, but gradually a terrible smell of burning began to penetrate the dormitory and all of a sudden it grew very bright: everything, even the smallest objects, were clearly lit up by an

intense red glow. The colossal benefice house, which stored wood and other combustibles, was ablaze just a few meters away from us . . . the town's public building were in great danger, especially as the wind direction seemed very unfavorable. So, we rushed to the washrooms, grabbed all the washtubs and buckets we could lay our hands on, filled them and carried them to the warden's rooms, which were in terrible danger of going up in flames. But because there was no water supply here, we had to keep fetching water from way down at the bottom of the building. Several students went out into the open, half-dressed, to lend their help there. The fire department was quickly on the spot, but the fire simply swallowed up all the jets of water they directed at it.[69]

The seminarian Hermann Hesse was a keen volunteer fireman on this occasion, as he reported to his parents:

All I had on was a shirt, trousers, socks, a waistcoat and a cap, plus slippers, jacket and a collar—all my other clothes I'd left back in the dormitory, so quickly and unexpectedly did the fire take hold. None of us felt the biting cold, which instantly turned the water running off the roof to ice. I was just wearing slippers on my feet, and I even lost one of them, but kept on working just wearing one until an icy jet of water, which hit my unprotected foot, painfully reminded me that I should go and put on some boots. I snatched the first pair of boots I could find and tugged them on. I couldn't locate my own. The lack of water was so acute that we'd already started using washbasins to carry it. In the meantime, the fire advanced rapidly.[70]

The monastery was in serious danger by now; on the western side it was already surrounded by a sixty-meter ring of fire. "All the while, as we were breathing in thick, hot smoke, water and snow were raining down on us from the roof. We kept on working until past midnight." Then, finally, they managed to bring the blaze under control. But the building was still smoldering the following evening. It was a scene of utter devastation, which Hesse would describe as a winter landscape with smoke: "Today I and some others went to look at the ruins, which we helped damp down. As I walked around, the soles of my shoes were burning under my feet. All around there was nothing to see but a heap of stones, and the instant you lifted one up, flames leapt up from underneath." Hesse soon came to realize that it was a dangerous business standing on the rubble heap left after a major fire. The apocalyptic image of the fire seemed to clutch at him: "No sooner had I stepped back than a huge, heavy section of wall, glowing red-hot, collapsed onto the very spot where I'd been standing." The rubble kept burning for three days. Hesse's sad summing-up, which was not without a sense of the tragedy of what had taken place, ran as follows: "In all, the blaze lasted for some 38–40 hours. The benefice house, with all its storerooms and stalls, has been burnt to the ground . . . its destruction means the loss of a beautiful antiquity; it was an enormous building, several centuries old. When the last ruins were pulled down, I was still marveling at the building's curious construction, especially its alcoves and the like."[71]

In the end, the king donated a thousand marks for the rebuilding of the benefice house.

On April 11, 1892, Hermann tried to set off a firework that he had made himself with a large amount of saltpeter and using instructions from a book entitled *The Knowledgeable Playmate*. In his 1936 work "Herr Claassen"— that important text about the mysterious power of memory, and about hidden history that suddenly comes to light—this event is resurrected with the utmost urgency in the present after almost half a century. All the home-made pyrotechnics had already been let off on a bluff overlooking the town in the darkness of the evening:

> Only a flattish, long cardboard tube, the sight of which had intrigued me, had not gone off; its fuse must have fizzled out or dropped off. I searched around for ages until I finally found it. When I'd located it on the ground with my fingers, I brought it up close and pored over it in the darkness in an attempt to see what had caused it to go out. And just as I was holding the infernal little thing right up to my eyes, it inexplicably ignited after all; for one terrible, beautiful moment, the whole world, beginning with my hand and the small cardboard tube it was holding and extending right up to the heavens, was one single, huge blaze of light, and an immense surge of scorching heat hit me in the face and wrapped itself suffocatingly around me. A profound blackness followed, which refused to lift, and a moment of emptiness and stupefaction, then I awoke in searing pain, and my first thought was that I'd gone blind.[72]

He surely had his glasses to thank for the fact that he actually hadn't been blinded—but the enduring legacy of this incident was a lifelong and extreme sensitivity of the eyes. His face was one large burn injury. He lay for six days with his whole head swathed in bandages, even around his eyes, with only small gaps left around the nostrils and mouth so that he could breathe and drink. Yet his fascination for "terrible, beautiful" fire, even in its destructive form, remained undimmed. It was—he increasingly came to understand—the fairy-tale dimension of his life, where goodness could not exist without evil, nor beauty without ugliness, and where terror exerted its own fascination. Leading a life between these conflicting forces would become for him an ordeal that would last a lifetime.

The Monastery at Maulbronn

> My tribulations began in the seminary. The trials of puberty coincided with my choice of career, since it was already abundantly clear to me that I didn't want to be anything other than a writer, though I knew that this was not a recognized profession and you couldn't earn a crust from it.
>
> —Hermann Hesse, *Autobiographical Notes,* 1922–1923

His future path now seemed mapped out for the fourteen-year-old Hermann Hesse. Pastor Pfisterer, a friend of the family, spelled out what was required of him: "Now, I trust that you will become a proper scholar educated for the kingdom of God and that you will remain steadfast amid the temptations of the seminary."[73] So, even more pressure on the boy, and even less latitude to develop his own personality. At this time, parents and teachers were in accord that the one thing children did not need was time for themselves. Yet after all his cramming for the state examination, Hermann was visibly overstressed and needed a whole summer of rest and recuperation.

On August 19, 1891, his mother wrote in a letter to Adele—and it sounded extremely disparaging—about a long walk that Hermann had gone on with his older stepbrother, Carl: "Afterward, Hermann was so dead-beat and exhausted that Carl doesn't want to go on any more long walks with this big-talking but underachieving boy."[74] Underachieving? Her son had just passed the dreaded state exam as the second best out of seventy-nine candidates. And how could he be expected to stay in shape when all he was required to do each day was to sit at his desk and study? His grandfather, who immediately got to hear of Hermann's "listlessness," noted with concern that it was "unnatural for a fourteen-year-old boy" and added: "I do wish he wasn't so highly strung. . . . Let's hope he finds a good friend who can keep him on an even keel."[75]

Indeed, even before he started at the seminary, things weren't looking good for the future Maulbronn student. He was suffering from unexplained bouts of apnea, though their provenance was no mystery to his grandfather Hermann Gundert: "I sometimes think he's nothing but a bag of nerves, which is scarcely surprising for someone who is the spitting image of his father, since we all know how big a role nerves play in his life."

Regardless of how cocky and confident of victory Hermann may have sounded after passing the state exam, he was in truth very stressed. His parents proceeded to pile more pressure on him, telling him that he ought not to loaf about for the summer but instead prepare himself for Maulbronn. Accordingly, even before Maulbronn came crashing down on him with its huge workload, he found himself back in libraries at the height of summer, with instructions to fill the gaps in his learning. This was exactly the same situation as that facing his protagonist Hans Giebenrath in *Beneath the Wheel*. But the seminarian Hermann did not crack under the pressure, unlike his younger brother Hans, whose fate we shall discuss presently.

(After giving up his job in the Wattenwyl antiquarian bookshop in Basel in 1903 to become a full-time writer, Hermann Hesse returned to Calw to spend some time in his parents' house once more. His mother had died by that stage, and his father was living alone with his sisters. Hermann Hesse's gamble paid off: his first attempt to create a biographical realm from his own childhood, in the form of his debut novel *Peter Camenzind*, was already a hit. This fiction about a wastrel, an express rejection of modernity at the outset of the twentieth century, had been a runaway success. The next task Hesse turned his mind to during his sojourn at Calw was writing the "Gerbersau" stories and fictionalizing his own schooldays in Maulbronn.

Beneath the Wheel became a reckoning with his own past, for sure, but the tone was one of wistful melancholy. All his pain and rage had dissipated and—to borrow a phrase by Heiner Müller about Heinrich Heine—the scar had healed over, albeit somewhat crookedly. The key motifs of his later works—already evident in such books as *Hermann Lauscher* and *Peter Camenzind*—began to emerge, and in later texts were given a wide range of variations but never abandoned. Foremost among these was the motif of the doppelgänger.)

★　　★　　★

On September 15, 1891, Marie Hesse took her son to Maulbronn. There he was assigned to the largest of the dormitories, named "Hellas"; the smallest was called "Germania." Hermann explained what these names were all about in a letter to his "Russian grandfather" Carl Hermann Hesse in Weissenstein: "The seminarian (we're called 'frogs' or 'monks') is a part of a larger, fixed entity, and the individual dormitories all develop according to their own rules. Democracy is, of course, the only proper constitution here. The dormitories are: Hellas, Forum, Germania, Athens, Acropolis, and Sparta. I am a Hellene, and moreover from our standpoint a patriotic Hellene; that is, every good Hellene is my friend, and it is with great regret that I observe that our political constitution tends toward the most rigid form of oligarchy." Clearly evident here is the educational ideal of such institutions, which attempted to combine Greek classicism with Christian values. From this second letter that the seminarian sent to his grandfather in Estonia there developed the humorous correspondence between the young Hesse and his nonagenarian relative that we have already had cause to note. Carl Hermann's grandson sent accounts of his daily routine in Maulbronn in verse form, a bustling kind of doggerel that began thus:

> At crack of dawn while we're still dozing,
> Soundly in our comfy beds,
> A prefect round the dorms comes creeping,
> "Get up," he shouts, "you sleepyheads!"

Grandfather Hesse replied with a parody of this poem and added: "Your ditty made me so happy to realize that I can still see the funny side of things and enjoy joking around myself. So I am sending you a 'second edition' of your nice little poem, and hope that you will be able to come up with a third piece of doggerel soon, just for Christmas. Ha! And why not? We're just finding our rhythm—"

That same day, Hermann Hesse sent a prose version of his daily routine in Maulbronn to his parents in Calw. After reveille at 6:30 A.M., the whole day was scheduled in minute detail, from the morning church service, through lessons, study periods, and quiet personal pursuits until evening prayers. Maulbronn was an expensive place to study; shortly after his arrival there, Hermann had to write home asking for some more money. In this letter—astonishing to modern readers, the fourteen-year-old boy reassures his parents that he only "ordered one bottle of beer (for 11 pfennigs)," and adds by way of explanation, "We're allowed to drink three bottles of beer a week, and most of the boys here do. You can also have milk, but it's too expensive for me."[76] In this way Swabia's future elite was prepared for the old boys' network of convivial socializing through which political deals were struck here, as elsewhere. But although the seminarians were permitted to drink wine and beer in moderation, smoking was banned. And Hermann Hesse hankered after something else in Maulbronn: "The thing I miss, really miss, is coffee."[77]

Grandfather Gundert was not overjoyed at the news he was receiving from Maulbronn: "He gets 42 lessons a week, far too many!" In addition, at Maulbronn there was no Rector Bauer to usher the exhausted children—who were being crammed with ever more dead languages and facts—out into the open air so that they could simply enjoy being children for a while. Here, instead, a great sense of seriousness prevailed, as befitted an elite on whose shoulders the state would rest—even when partaking of beer or wine.

Changes to the routine were sought after, because they were so rare. In the evening the boys would dispute about every conceivable topic. For instance, because there was no consensus on the subject of magnetism and hypnosis, they settled on an experiment. Herman wrote to his parents about this on October 28, 1891:

> Yesterday evening, I agreed to be hypnotized, which duly happened, but I wasn't fully woken from my hypnotized state, with the result that when I went to bed I undressed down to my socks, collar and tie and went to sleep, but with my eyes almost completely open. The other boys summoned Mr. Holzbog. Afterward, I was told that he removed my collar and tie and chided me severely, though I saw and heard none of this myself. Today I have been shivering virtually constantly but I'm glad that I haven't lost my mind (I mean that last statement quite seriously and literally).[78]

Johannes Hesse replied by return post; after telling Hermann about a large fire that had occurred in Calw and reporting the news that, in the Baltic region, Protestant pastors would henceforth only be permitted to preach in Russian, he got round to addressing the subject of hypnosis: "Your tale about being hypnotized really shocked me. I find all such occult things

The fountain in the cloisters at Maulbronn

horrifying. Our bodies should be temples for the Holy Spirit, and our souls tools of His will. Intoxication or anesthesia, whether through the use of alcohol or morphine or hypnosis, is a besmirching and abasement of the being whom God has created to act in His service and has redeemed and sanctified."[79]

The letters written by Hermann Hesse at this time sound like those of a thoroughly ambitious fourteen-year-old who was always keen to be at the forefront of things. On February 8, 1892, he signed off a letter to his parents in lighthearted fashion: "I am and remain for the foreseeable future Hermann Hesse, currently a greenhorn at Maulbronn by the Grace of God."[80]

And on February 14, 1892, his parents were treated to the following euphoric account:

> I am feeling glad, happy, and content! I find the prevailing tone at the seminary most appealing. Above all, it is the close, open relationship between pupils and teachers that pleases me, but also among the pupils themselves. . . . Not to mention the magnificent monastery building! There is a special charm to wandering through one of the majestic cloisters while debating

with a fellow student about language, religion, art, etc. This is no longer
the idle chit-chat of two boys; instead, we address the individual facts of
the matter in depth, generally ask the masters' opinion, and read the relevant books.[81]

Was this a case of Hermann trying to convince himself that Maulbronn
was a great place to be? Or was his enthusiasm genuine—and even as his
euphoria took hold, did an urge concurrently grow within him to destroy
it once more?

His parents found themselves completely taken by surprise by what was to
follow. Marie Hesse noted in her diary on March 7: "The mailman came
at 5 o'clock and called loudly from the door: 'A telegram for you!' I rushed
out, thinking that it must be announcing my 90-year-old father-in-law's
death. But no, it was from Maulbronn . . . 'Hermann has been missing
since two in the morning. Request any information you may have.' What
a terrible shock!" However, his mother's subsequent notes are surprising:
"At first I was worried that Hermann had committed some dreadful sin
and been disgraced, and I was in awful torments imagining that something especially terrible must have preceded his disappearance, so I was
very relieved when I finally got the feeling instead that he was in God's
merciful hands, and had already died and gone to meet his maker. Perhaps
he'd drowned in one of the lakes he was so fascinated by?"[82]

That night the family waited uneasily for further news. The following
morning, around 11:55 A.M., a reassuring message finally arrived from
Maulbronn: "Hermann returned safely." Like all other documents relating
to the family, Hesse carefully preserved these telegrams and they have survived to this day.

But why did Marie Hesse think that Hermann must have done "something especially terrible" before running away and that it would therefore
be better if he'd drowned in one of the lakes? What kinds of evil deeds
did she deem him capable of—and what cause had he already given for
such suspicions?

Inquiries were launched in Maulbronn—and Hermann found himself caught up in the workings of a system that was geared to either clip-
ping the wings of anything that contradicted the prevailing norm or
excluding the disruptive and irritating element. This process now brought

it home to him that it did not take much to become an outsider, or even a heretic.

On March 7, Professor Paulus wrote about how things had stood when Hermann Hesse went missing: "According to the testimony of several of his fellow pupils, Hermann had for a long time—some even said since before Christmas—frequently been in a state of great agitation, in which he was accustomed to composing effusive and sometimes overwrought poems."[83]

The first letter that Hesse—still a seminarian despite his truancy—wrote after being detained by a country policeman and returned to Maulbronn was dated March 9, 1892, in which he gave a down-to-earth summary of his experience: "In the 23 hours I was absent, I roamed far and wide around Württemberg, Baden, and Hesse, and except for the period between the hours of eight o'clock in the evening and half-past four the next morning, which I spent sleeping in the open in temperatures of minus seven degrees centigrade, I was on my feet the whole time."[84] What drove him, during his free period, to fail to return to the monastery from a walk and instead to abscond while dressed only in light clothes and still carrying under his arm the books for his next lesson?

This was by no means a planned attempt to escape; it was a spontaneous decision not to do what was expected of him but instead to simply keep walking without knowing where he was headed.

Precisely this propensity to be led by his instinct and a sudden whim is the hallmark of the wanderer. In his later works, this openness to spontaneous decisions became emblematic for Hesse of the theme of change in a person's life, a topos that he would employ repeatedly. More than once he used it to symbolize the great gulf between the bourgeois individual and the artist. When the young Hermann returned home, Grandfather Gundert was the only one to hit the right note with him about this incident. Hesse expected the same sort of reproaches and warnings he had already received from his father. Instead, his grandfather asked him in Swabian dialect: "So, Hermann, what is this I hear about you going off on a little jaunt recently?"[85]

Otherwise, however, no one in the adult world seemed inclined to take the matter lightly and treat the incident simply as a rather extraordinary whim of a fourteen-year-old boy who felt uncomfortable in his own skin.

Instead, his parents and teachers made a huge fuss about his going "absent without leave" for twenty-three hours.

Nobody offered the opinion that it was good nothing had happened and noted that he must have been terribly cold overnight, or wrote the whole thing down to the inexplicable vagaries of puberty and took it as a *cri de coeur* on Hermann's part to be shown more consideration and love. That would have been out of keeping with the spirit of the age. Instead the incident was seen as having jeopardized discipline and order, which had to be protected at all costs from such flights of fancy. Johannes Hesse reprimanded his son in a long letter: "You must submit without demur to everything that is now about to be visited upon you by way of investigation, punishment, and correction—and not just outwardly but in such a manner that you don't find yourself rebelling inwardly at the strictures placed on you. Instead you ought to be telling yourself: 'even if I didn't deserve it for this transgression, than I certainly did for all my other errors and omissions.'" His father then proceeded to list all the things that were going to be different in the future. Above all, Johannes Hesse maintained, Hermann's "private reading" was distracting him from the real work he should be doing in the seminary: namely, his study of mathematics and Hebrew. The pressure he had always exerted on his son, who was driven by an inner sense of deep unease, now increased. On March 11, 1892, the school's teaching body met to discuss Hermann. Because his lapse was not regarded "as a premeditated and purposeful act of truancy" or as an "expression of willfulness and defiance," the school board was minded to take the "excited and disturbed state of mind in which he acted" into consideration as extenuating circumstances. Accordingly, he was given eight hours' detention. In addition, there was a general consensus that Hermann's continuing attendance at the seminary would not be desirable, as he represented a danger to his fellow students. "He is too full of febrile thoughts and excessive emotions, to which he is all too inclined to surrender himself."[86]

Attached to this communication was a schedule of the expenses that Hermann had incurred:

Telegrams to Stuttgart, to the station, to Bruchsal, to Bretten and one telegram to Calw: respectively, 1 mark 85 pfennigs, 50 pfennigs, 1M 95Pf, 2M 30Pf, and 55 pfennigs, making a total of 7 Marks 15 pfennigs.

    Finders' reward for constables Lieb and Sternenfeld: 2 Marks.

    Ditto for Constable Meier of Maulbronn: 3 Marks.

    Tip for Usher Röhm of Maulbronn: 1 Mark.

    Bill owing to senior prefect Holzbog: 12 Marks 55 pfennigs.

    Grand total: 25 Marks 70 pfennigs.[87]

And so the incident was all properly accounted for. On the morning of March 12, Hermann wrote the first part of his written final examination for the semester, and in the afternoon he entered the detention room. There he was given bread and water—and he was permitted to write and read. It wasn't so terrible, he informed his parents. The only thing bothering him was a nagging headache: "My head is on fire. Goodbye!"

He was delighted to find on the wall of the detention room an inscription by his stepbrother Karl Isenberg, dated May 28, 1885.

He implored his parents to keep loving him. Johannes Hesse wrote back reassuring him, but did not couch his words in the right tone. A sermon was the last thing that his son could endure at that moment in time: "*Our* highest purpose in life is to please God and to serve Him in His kingdom. If that was to become *your* purpose too, we would find true communion and everything would be light, love, and freedom. But so long as this continues not to be the case, there can be no question of complete understanding or hence complete sympathy between us." The letter continues in the same vein: "How happy we would be, and how all the love we have shown you would be rewarded, i.e., reciprocated on your part, if you would only believe and understand that all we have sought in reprimanding and punishing you was to secure your love and your commitment to us. If we meet one another in *this* spirit, then we shall be united for all eternity, since it will be under the auspices of the Everlasting God."

His son was struggling with the business of growing up, and Johannes Hesse chose to play the preacher. But this had nothing to do with God! In the absence of God, did he then count for nothing in the eyes of his parents? To them, nothing counted for anything without God, him included. And this outraged him.

He was also greatly affected by being prohibited from having any contact with the other seminarians. This ban included his closest confidant, Wilhelm Lang, who sorrowfully showed him a letter from his own "pious and conservative" father, "whose content was tantamount to an order to have nothing to do with me."

The authorities in Maulbronn sent Hermann Hesse home even before the start of the Easter holidays; they had still not come to a definitive decision regarding his fate. He was suffering from "a temperature in his head and sleeplessness," his mother noted, and should be treated as carefully as "an egg without a shell." Thereafter he returned once more to Maulbronn—though he already sensed that he was no longer wanted there. David Gundert, Johannes Hesse's brother-in-law, reported from Stuttgart that he had received a letter from his son, delivered by Professor Hartmann. In the letter, he read the following: "Hesse is behaving oddly; yesterday he told me repeatedly that he was going to kill me in the evening, and he really did rush at me in the dormitory (albeit without a weapon) but was wrestled to the ground."[88] Later, he called over from his bed: "He said he had to distract himself by doing such things to stop himself from becoming completely melancholic, and that he had a pain in his head that could only be cured by killing someone."[89] This was not good news for Hesse's parents.

Could this perhaps have been a joke? Was the young Hesse provoking his fellow students, who had turned their backs on him? Professor Hartmann told Hesse's uncle that the boy needed medical treatment: "This will indicate whether it is a nervous condition or whether there's really something physically wrong with him (his brain)." His contemporaries at the seminary had been in no doubt on this point for quite some time already: Hermann was insane! Things were becoming serious.

His parents were now forced to act, and removed their son from Maulbronn. Marie Hesse noted in her diary: "Dr. Zahn talked about doctors and institutions for the insane, but I refused to accept this and took a firm stand against such things, since that would be the very best way of making our son, who suffers from nerves, truly mentally ill. So it was that we lighted upon the idea of sending him to Bad Boll, and made inquiries there."

Christoph Blumhardt, the leading authority in revivalist Christian circles, was prepared to take in Hermann Hesse at Bad Boll for a spell. Hermann's parents were happy, but this marked the start of a dangerous odyssey for their son.

With Blumhardt in Bad Boll

Nowadays Bad Boll is the site of a Protestant training academy. In 1852 the faith healer and "devil exorcist" Johann Christoph Blumhardt established an institution there that combined proclaiming the Gospel with health education. Religious awakening was always regarded there as being a form of healing—and so there developed a kind of Christian sanatorium. For the Christian revivalist movement, Blumhardt in Bad Boll was the principal authority bar none. His son Christoph Blumhardt (1842–1919), who had to overcome the influence of his overbearing father as he made his way through life, succeeded in giving the religious community of brothers a social dimension. He ended up sitting as a Social Democratic Party delegate in the Württemberg regional parliament. Another member of Blumhardt's circle was the poet Gottfried Benn's father, a village pastor who subscribed concurrently to both the conservative *Kreuzzeitung* and the socialist newspaper *Vorwärts*. When his son Gottfried refused to continue studying theology and philosophy, and switched instead to medicine, Blumhardt in Bad Boll was also consulted. He advised Gottfried to become an army doctor, which is what he eventually did.

Hermann Hesse, who was displaying behavioral problems, now made the acquaintance of Christoph Blumhardt. On May 5, 1892, Blumhardt wrote to Johannes Hesse: "If I could only get him interested in practical activities in some measure, that would be a great step forward, since working with your hands give sustenance to the soul."[90] On a brief first visit to Bad Boll, during which his parents introduced him as a problem child, Hermann had taken an instant liking to the place. Like Rector Bauer in Göppingen, Blumhardt was an eccentric original, and Hermann found such people congenial. Furthermore, this place had a totally different atmosphere from the well-tempered aura generated by his parents, who were constantly fixated on godliness and goodness. His first letter from Bad Boll, on May 10, 1892, sounded positively rapturous:

> I find the pastor extraordinarily congenial. Recently he said: "It's so non-sensical for people to tell lies. Like maintaining that Christendom is good, beautiful, noble and so on. It's nothing of the sort; the whole filthy lot of

them have no true conception of what Christ was all about or of morality."
A sermon he delivered not long ago began with a thunderous denunciation: "Sorry to say this—but you're all simpletons!"

He speaks his mind in church as well. For instance, he states quite
openly that, if it was down to him, confirmation and other such things
would soon be abolished.[91]

Hermann was still suffering from persistent headaches, loss of appetite, and
sleeplessness. All possible distractions in Bad Boll were welcome to him,
even those for which his parents had nothing but contempt. The letter he
sent them on June 3 had a thoroughly witty ring to it: "My time is split
between playing billiards, bowling, going for walks, sleeping—or not
sleeping as the case may be—and eating. My headache is still in the same
place it always was: and my eyes are fine." He genuinely enjoyed being at
Bad Boll: "Little by little, I have also worked my way up to becoming the
best skittles player here."[92] However, he spent most of his day listening to
music: "Above all I play Beethoven's sonatas over and over again, there is
a remarkable charm to these works, which are half cheerful and half somber;
they shift between epic gravity and lyrical playfulness and the wildest
passion."

His time at Bad Boll already had something of the sojourn of a sanatorium patient about it. Did his parents approve of how he was spending
his days there? One can sense from Hesse's letters the sheer joy of being
invited by the person his parents regarded as the highest religious authority
to simply enjoy himself to the full. "I devote a lot of time to playing billiards. . . . I find it does me good to have a swig of beer before I go to
bed."[93] Things had been just as relaxed at Bad Boll under the regime of
Johann Christoph Blumhardt the Elder, and his son had simply continued
this therapy through diversion. This approach was highly successful in an era
when the ethos of duty weighed heavy and menacingly, especially on Prot-
estants. The Biedermeier poet Eduard Mörike was a frequent visitor to
Bad Boll in its early years.

Then there happened something that no one expected. On June 20, 1892,
Christoph Blumhardt wrote to the Hesses in Calw: "Today, your son ran

away from here after threatening to take his own life. Prior to this, he secretly borrowed money and bought a revolver. He has now returned. I am treating it as a schoolboy prank, but of such a morbid kind that I need urgently to consult with you."[94] Indeed, that same day Hermann Hesse had told an innkeeper by the name of Brodersen, who had lent him the money: "I borrowed the money from you in order to acquire a revolver; a few days ago, I resolved to shoot myself. You will probably never see me again."[95]

Marie Hesse immediately went to see Blumhardt, and also asked her brother David in Stuttgart to come. They met in Göppingen, where Dr. Landerer, the head of the Christophsbad mental home was already waiting for them. Blumhardt was furious: the suicide of one of his charges would be a fine advertisement for Bad Boll! The boy needed to be sent to a lunatic asylum with all dispatch. Hesse's mother noted in her diary: "Landerer was very firmly against committing such a young boy to a mental institution, and urgently advised them to hold off until there was no other way out. Blumhardt, though, spoke terribly sharply and sternly and, seemingly forgetting that an illness was at issue here, railed so vehemently against evil and devilry that we almost went deaf and blind."[96] Hesse's mother was subjected to a diatribe about how badly she had brought up her son, and what they were now witnessing were the results of that. Blumhardt was after just one thing, namely to be rid of this unpredictable boy as quickly as possible.

It was also his right to decide what was to be done. Hermann was to be sent to the mental institution run by Pastor Schall in Stetten. They were to go there straight away, and give no prior warning they were coming, otherwise the hospital would refuse to take the boy off their hands. The party duly arrived in Stetten that same evening—the sullen, silent Hermann, his uncle David and stepbrother Theo, who had hurried there from Waiblingen to assist. Marie Hesse's diary entry reported on their arrival: "When H. first walked into the courtyard, he exclaimed angrily: 'So, you're planning to lock me up in jail, are you? I'd sooner jump into the fountain there and drown myself!' However, after Pastor Schall had had a few quiet words with him, he pronounced himself willing to remain there of his own volition."[97]

Yet why did nobody think to inquire about the reasons for Hermann's behavior? The fact was, he was in love, for the first time and, of course, unhappily. His half-brother Theodore Isenberg had been living for a spell at the Kolb household in Cannstatt, and here Hermann Hesse got to know the twenty-two-year-old Eugenie Kolb, who naturally was not the right partner for a fifteen-year-old boy. She was in a far better position to recognize this than a hotheaded youth in the first flushes of infatuation. Interestingly, the spark for this impetuous passion was not only the young woman in question, but just as much something that Hermann had just read: Ivan Turgenev's novel *Smoke* (1867). In this work he found a literary template for his infatuation with the young woman. Hesse the gardener and observer of clouds, who had a fine sensitivity for minute changes within nature, needed (and henceforth continued to need) his senses to be prompted by a written catalyst where women were concerned. In these matters he appeared to become detached from any personal experience and give himself over to merely echoing literary antecedents. In other words, with women he only experienced what he had already read about, and when he in turn came to record these experiences, it was to those antecedents that he harked back, thus completing the circle of fictions.

This, then, was why it was such a short step for him (as a living embodiment of the central character of Turgenev's *Smoke*) from his first love for Eugenie Kolb to buying the revolver. This love of his was not designed to be requited—nor would it ever be in his erotic perception. For time and again he would come to realize that he was incapable of experiencing anything in such matters that he had not long since known from his reading. This was a shock—and a pattern that would be henceforth repeated over and over again.

The Insane Asylum at Stetten

For me, Stetten is like Hell.

—Hermann Hesse, September 1, 1892 in a letter to his parents

Hermann's father was astonishingly circumspect in the first letter he sent his son in Stetten. He had a deep understanding of nervous overexcitement. In addition, a medical report prepared by Dr. Zahn after Hermann absconded from the seminary in Maulbronn, which spoke of "Hermann's great aversion to his father," may have given Johannes pause for thought. And so, on June 23, 1892, he wrote to Hermann: "Like you, I too find the business of life very hard and am made constantly and painfully aware of the deep chasm between the ideal and reality. Yet I have always found these comforting words to hold true: 'He who gives free passage for clouds and air and wind, will also find paths which your (my) foot can tread.'"[98]

Hermann's stay with Pastor Schall had to be paid for by his parents, a sum of 1,200 marks. In financial terms, too, their son Hermann was becoming an increasing problem for his parents, who were far from wealthy.

On June 27, 1892, Pastor Schall wrote a positive report on Hermann's period of acclimatization at Stetten: "He works assiduously in the garden the whole day." He would presently begin to participate in schoolwork once more. So what exactly was the condition Hermann Hesse was suffering from? Pastor Schall—whose next professional appointment would be house chaplain at Ludwigsburg Penitentiary—attempted to give a diagnosis: "His handwriting (which is in many cases a mark of character for me) certainly does display signs of absentmindedness and volatility. And an incessant twitch in his temples testifies to his nervous disposition." But apart from this, was there nothing else wrong with him? According to his medical record, the diagnosis was simply "melancholy." Chekhov's short story "Ward No. 6" shows us how dangerous Herman Hesse's succession of stays in institutions could have been for him. Once a person had been pigeonholed as a lunatic and wrenched from the world of "normal" people, they tended to be institutionalized for life. It could so easily have happened that, shut away in Stetten and at first pitied by the outside world and remembered in his family's prayers, Hermann Hesse might over time have been forgotten.

Though Hesse's father was busy with making corrections to the Church Encyclopedia, he followed the fate of his son in Stetten with great interest and concern. The fact that Hermann's nervous debility was hereditary seemed to bring his son closer to him—the condition they shared created a bond between them. Hermann was very compliant in Stetten and dutifully carried out the work he had been assigned to do in the gardens. He knew that his fate lay in Pastor Schall's hands. If he were to deem him insane, then everything was lost. Schall, however, proved to be well disposed toward the young man. He told him that he would get better if he could only learn not to get so emotionally worked up. This meant listening to less music and not getting so passionate about it and reading fewer and more edifying books, but also taking more walks in the woods in order to calm his nerves. There was no mention of the boy's first love for Eugenie Kolb, who was seven years his senior. The only person to broach this subject at the time was his grandfather Hermann Gundert, who wrote to his son Hermann, Hermann Hesse's uncle, about this "young lady" who in his eyes had toyed with the young Hermann and then been shocked when he confessed his love to her: "It really is a pity when a person takes decisions and acts upon them so precipitately."[99] Moderation was the commandment that the family exhorted Hermann to heed, as a way of exorcising all the evil demons that lurked within him. But Hermann, who was in the process of unfettering himself, was farther away than ever from moderating himself.

Likewise, he was only ever able to regard the quiet, imperturbable trust in God, of the kind that his grandfathers and his parents displayed to him, as a reprimand and a provocation. To be sure, in Stetten he suffered from sleeplessness, as did his father. But he had a reason for this (his love for Eugenie), which his parents refused to accept. Accordingly, it did not help when Johannes Hesse wrote to him on July 27, 1892, assuring him of his sympathetic consolation for his predicament: "Sleep is a gift that is granted to us from above, and which no person can take for himself. Likewise the calm, relaxed heart which can bear the vicissitudes of life with tranquility and cheerfulness."[100] Decades later Hermann Hesse would express himself in similar terms, but at this early stage of his development he was filled with outrage at his father's world, which he felt was enslaving him with its strict benevolence. On July 30, 1892, Pastor Schall characterized the young man who was in his care in the following terms: "Hermann strikes me as being like an egg without a shell."[101]

And what of Eugenie Kolb, the actual cause, not only of his purchase of the revolver and his absconding from Bad Boll, but also of his suicide threat and of the emotional confusion that kept him so unsettled? He dedicated his first collection of poetry, "Little Songs," to her. Right from the outset Hermann Hesse laid claim to being a poet. He required a romantic projection of himself that would not have as its ultimate expression a "fictional" persona, but would instead, so to speak, work through and beyond such a construct to achieve a hitherto unknown openness to the world.

Troubled by a guilty conscience, Eugenie Kolb wrote Hermann Hesse a letter, which was not intended to raise his hopes but to make it easier for him to forget her. And she did not address him as a pupil, but as a man—no doubt a friendly gesture on her part, albeit one that did not accord with the facts:

> I implore you, dear Mr. Hesse, please forget the things which are now behind you and look after your own health first and foremost. Please be rational and believe me when I tell you this: "A person's first love is *never* the right one"—and even though it is painful to experience a disappointment in affairs of the heart, it was the best thing that could happen to you, and not to have one's love reciprocated is not nearly so hard a thing to bear as to enter into a relationship that would be torn asunder roughly after several years, nor if you had come to the realization after many years that your young, first love was nothing but self-deception. That is a dreadful thing! You should thank God that you have fortunately been spared such a ghastly thing—but I earnestly ask this of you (should you ever, God forbid, have such a bitter experience again!): please endeavor to display more self-control, indeed I may venture to say more manliness. That is a small matter when set against a readiness to throw your life away in despair! Please, please forgive me my perhaps somewhat indelicate but well-meant words.

Having thus addressed the boy—who, after all, was seven years her junior—in a way that took him seriously (the letter did not offend him; on the contrary, it had a curative effect), as a friendly gesture she went on to issue an invitation that would allow Hermann to maintain their relationship on a different basis: "Come and visit us *as often as you like* and don't forget to bring the poems you have written with you." And in the next sentence, she added: "Dear Mama sends you heartfelt greetings too. Let's presently drink to brotherhood!!!"[102] This was not a letter to a sick person, and when he read it Hermann felt genuinely well—better yet, he finally felt that he was being taken seriously as a poet.

On August 5 Hermann wrote to his mother. By then he had been at Stetten for six weeks and desired nothing so much as to get away from the place as soon as possible: "The doctor does not want me to become a long-term resident here and would like to release me as sound and healthy within a week."[103] It was summer and he could just as easily work in the garden in Calw as in Stetten, and he was sure he wouldn't be a burden on his parents.

Hermann had eaten crow and now begged to be allowed to return home—however, his parents were people of principle and were not to be swayed in their judgment that easily. The authorities in Stetten took the view that an unstable young man who was otherwise perfectly healthy had no place either in a mental institution or as a guest in a private guest house. Pastor Schall also tried to prevail upon Hermann's parents to take him back, sending a succinct note to this effect to Calw: "Under these circumstances it would be best if you were to come here over the course of next week and pick up Hermann."[104] Yet his parents were reluctant to do so, at least not until they had found a new place for Hermann to stay. Hermann, though, deployed all the eloquence he could muster to try and get away from Stetten: "The weather is so beautiful. It's August, holiday time—but there are no bathing facilities here in Stetten, just heat and work with no entertainment, no comings and goings. In the eyes of many people (relatives etc.) we're just insane; I'm not complaining, because I deserved to be sent here and submit voluntarily to my treatment—but believe me, I have been punished sufficiently now . . . I could occupy myself a little back in Calw as well, at least there I would have some human contact, with you."[105] But what was he imagining when he talked in this letter about human contact? A cessation of that urge to normalize, that constant pressure his parents exerted upon him to still try to make a good Pietist out of him despite everything?

Grandfather Hermann Gundert, meanwhile, conveyed further news concerning his deranged grandson to the other Hermanns in his extensive family: "Johannes went to Stetten on the fifth and brought Hermann home with him. He didn't impose any particular rules, but he knows that some kind of discipline must be required of the boy. The pastor in Stetten said that he couldn't have kept Hermann there any longer anyhow, due to the many other patients who needed to be cared for. However, it seems doubtful whether he will be able to continue his studies."

Less than two weeks later, on August 15, 1892, Hermann Hesse found himself back in Calw again. His grandfather takes up the story once more: "Meanwhile, H.H.'s behavior has been erratic; sometimes, he cowers a little while, then suddenly he's full of himself again, saying things like 'anyone who claims I'm mad must be mad themselves.' Under these circumstances, it is hard to decide what to do . . . I feel sorry for Johannes that his son is making his life so difficult. He was doing well at one point, but now his headaches are back."[106] But what was to be done now with Hermann, an abortive student of the Maulbronn monastery school who, whenever he could see no way forward, was in the habit of running away, announcing he was about to commit suicide, and what's more had even bought himself a revolver? Coming straight from a mental hospital was not a good reference to present to any prospective high school. Pastor Schall and his parents tried their best to find a school for Hermann. Inquiries were made at the high school in Reutlingen. But at least Hermann was now back with his parents in Calw. Might this possibly afford him some breathing space, or even mean his salvation?

As early as August 16, Pastor Schall was forced to respond to a complaint from Johannes Hesse that Hermann was becoming extremely difficult at home again. Schall found that strange: "We had no occasion to note a single disobedient word toward his superiors here."[107] But Schall also realized that Hermann now had to be placed at one remove from his parents as quickly as possible, as their intolerance toward one another appeared insuperable.

There then occurred an event that Marie Hesse noted in the meticulously comprehensive family chronicle that she kept for the year 1892: "It was an uncommonly hot summer, and in addition we had any number of visits from German-speaking Russians and others from the neighboring bathing resorts, so that day after day our house was like Grand Central Station. Hermann was dreadfully agitated and irritated and spent the whole time being obstructive and cursing. He refused to come on walks, complained of being bored, and did not do what his father or the doctor ordered." Indeed, it would have been a miracle if the conflicts within the boy and his rebellion against his parents had been resolved so quickly. But then came the great shock: "Finally, Johannes found himself forced to take Hermann back to Stetten on August 22."[108] After just seventeen days of freedom, he had to return to the institution. His mother commented: "The result was that H. became terribly embittered toward us. He did not seem to appreciate all the efforts we had gone to, asking and searching around and writing letters to all and sundry in a vain attempt to try and find a suitable place for Hermann to stay, and that we only put him back into Stetten out of necessity." Could such things be appreciated, though? And what did "out of necessity" actually mean? Whose necessity was in question here? Even the phrase "put him back" betrays a harshness in dealing with a young child that is almost unimaginable to modern sensibilities. This was a wound that would hurt Hermann for his entire life, though it did not deter him from adopting a similar modus operandi when dealing with the mental illness of his first wife, Maria Bernoulli.

So it was that Hermann found himself securely incarcerated within the Stetten mental asylum once more. If one is to believe his parents, there was no other option, as the loutish boy had simply behaved too badly. For the first few days he was struck dumb with rage and fear and did not write a single word to his parents. How could they do such a thing to him? Instead he composed a rhyme:

> Now freedom's just run out on me,
> It always was illusory,
> Sent to the "bin" by Mum and Dad,
> For all they know, I might be mad![109]

But then he had to write to them; he needed them to send certain items. His tone was chilly, ironic, sounding almost like Nietzsche's *Ecce Homo*. All those who have ever tried to find evidence that Hermann Hesse really was insane have found some vindication from this period of his life, in the form of the salvos that the young Hesse, beside himself with fury, loosed off against the world of philistines. Thus, on August 30, 1892, he wrote to his parents: "My dear parents! Although I was minded not to write, I need to ask you for a few things. This would not have been necessary if I'd only been given a little time to pack beforehand. . . . So, I've arrived in Stetten, and things are worse here for me than before, though I haven't complained about anybody but simply confined myself to cursing God and the world in private." The things he wanted from them were his poems, which he had left in the writing desk in his room in Calw. Hermann cautioned his parents against any possible *theft* of these notebooks. His letter ended with the following words: "So, at least you're rid of me, and that was enough. Yours respectfully H. Hesse, nihilist (ha ha!)"

Hermann felt himself betrayed, and the very next day sent his parents a letter in which he screamed his pain into their unhearing ears:

I almost wish I were insane. It must be immeasurably sweet to be able to dream one's life away and forget about absolutely everything—all the joy and the sorrow, life and pain, and love and loathing!

But I've been prattling away for too long. Miserable, no, cold is what I want to be, ice-cold toward everybody bar none! Then again, you are my jailers, so I can't address my complaints to you, can I? . . . I cannot write any more; it would make me start crying, and what I want most of all is to be dead and cold. Adieu![110]

Hermann was fighting against those who, with a clear conscience before God, wanted to break him and divest him of all his self-will. His rage was impotent, though; he knew this and yet still flung this accusation at his parents: "I'm aware that keeping me here must be expensive, maybe even as expensive as Bad Boll, but it's your private indulgence to spend your money in this way; after all there are cheaper prisons than Stetten. Inspector Schall took away my copy of Turgenev's *Smoke*. This miserable existence without any excitement, or education, or entertainment is only fit for an animal. I crave something beyond humdrum everyday life, even if only in my reading matter. Of course, your answer would be to fob me off with Pietism." There then followed a statement of a credo that, despite sounding like Heine, came from deep within himself: "You deliver all your sermons, urging people to 'Turn to God, and to Christ, etcetera, etcetera!' But though you might curse me a hundred times over for saying so, I can see in this God of yours nothing but a delusion, and in this Christ nothing but a man."[111]

His parents looked on helplessly as Hermann tormented himself like this. Why, they asked, did he refuse to comply with the basic rules of harmonious coexistence? Either he was simply obdurate or he was ill. Perhaps the only thing that would work against obduracy was strictness, whereas in the case of an illness all they could do was wait—or do nothing. Hermann's father sent a letter to him in Stetten:

It was a great sorrow to me that you were unable to calm down and recover at home. I tried the best I could and, whenever I noticed you making some effort to take a grip on yourself and to accommodate yourself to living alongside us, I was overjoyed and filled with hope. If only you had found me more congenial, and if I myself had had more patience and wisdom, and particularly if my nerves had not been so bad, things might have turned out well. But that's not how it panned out. And you're not in Stetten as a punishment, but simply because we didn't know of and couldn't find any other place that would be better for you.[112]

Hermann Hesse, now interned in Stetten for a second time, began to become seriously worried about what the future might hold: "The doctor's pronouncements are unfavorable, or he says nothing; for crying out loud, what is to become of me?"[113] What could he do?—he had never been so completely at the mercy of the will of others. How would this all end? He suddenly realized with a shock how quickly one could be catapulted out of the bourgeois world and no longer have any stake in it. A sense of pure desperation now became apparent in his letters to his parents:

If I could have foreseen my present life some months ago, I would have thought it was some bad, impossible dream. This cold, half-educated and half-practical parson with his sermons, these ignorant warders, these inmates with their repulsive faces and manners—I loathe everything here from the bottom of my heart. It is like it has been designed especially to show a young man how wretched life and all its aspects are. . . . But what's the point in me explaining all this to you? You're in Calw and not in Stetten, and I'm in Stetten and not in Calw. You breathe a different atmosphere from me: 'Hermann in Stetten' is a stranger to you, he's not your son.

Now he can no longer hold back the pain he had struggled so hard thus far to keep contained: "I will use my last strength to show that I am not a machine that someone simply needs to wind up. I was put on a train by force and taken out to Stetten, so that's where I am now, not bothering the world any longer, since Stetten isn't part of this world."

In the end, however, he did not suffer a breakdown; instead, a letter of September 11, 1892, contains an unexpected, exultant outburst:

Besides, within these four walls I am my own master, I obey no one and have no intention of doing so. . . . All in all, what I am trying to do here is to describe the conditions as dispassionately and emphatically as I can. So now I ask, purely as a human being (for, in defiance of your wishes and despite my fifteen years, I take the liberty of having an opinion on this matter): Is it right for a young man who, apart from a slight weakness of the nerves, is pretty healthy, to be packed off to a "mental home for the feeble-minded and epileptics," and to forcibly rob him of his belief in love and justice, and hence in God? Are you aware that, when I came back from

The monastery seminary at Maulbronn, steel engraving by L. Hoffmeister

Stetten the first time, I really wanted to live and strive again and that now, though cured after a fashion, I am inwardly sicker than ever? Wouldn't it be better if someone like that were to throw himself into the sea where it is at its deepest with a millstone tied round his neck?[114]

With these words—unheard-of for the period, not to mention for his parents—spoken moreover by someone who was only fifteen, Hermann Hesse for the first time gained some sort of inner independence from his parents. And this general attack on the world of his parents and grandparents culminated in the shocking sentence: "You are Christians, and I—I am just a man."[115]

With this letter, Hermann, the unfortunate son who was incarcerated in a mental asylum, had regained his psychological health. He had put himself out of reach of his parents' monotonous attempts to discipline him; irrespective of how things turned out for him here, he could now genuinely laugh at their endeavors. Unlike on his first visit to Stetten, Hermann no longer had a guilty conscience about his father; he now took his father's words only as the stereotypical speech of someone who had nothing to say to him anymore, as in the letter he received from Calw on September 13: "We are not leveling any dreadful accusations at you over what has happened. But we do believe that you are in a very poorly state, from which you can be cured if you acquiesce willingly and with hope in your heart in whatever is asked of you during your stay in Stetten."[116] No, Hermann would no longer "acquiesce," but he would also come to understand that revolt was not always advisable when faced with a dangerous environment. He would learn what everyone who becomes an outsider quickly learns: namely, to conceal yourself from the world in order to preserve your individuality.

2

THE SELF-PROCLAIMED WRITER

"If Only There Were Some Anarchists Around!"

In his letter of September 13, 1892, Hesse's father wrote to Hermann that he doubted whether his son, who was proving so rebellious behind the walls of Stetten, could stand the "discipline of a school system," given his irrepressible "urge for freedom." As a result, Johannes Hesse continued, he would never be able to study "at all usefully." Hermann Hesse understood the threat—but refused to fall in line. Quite the opposite, in fact. His response on September 14 sounded like one of the rousing calls issued by the character Karl Moor in Friedrich Schiller's "Sturm und Drang" drama *The Robbers*. In later life Hermann was much given—in complete emulation of Goethe—to invoking the principle of moderation in all things. Yet here was an eruption of immoderation, a rebellion of feverish heat against the healthy state of being well tempered: "Dear Sir! Since you show yourself so willing to make sacrifices, may I perhaps ask you to give me 7 Marks, or simply to let me have my revolver? Having driven me to a state of despair, you would surely be willing to allow me to put an end to this and in the process be rid of me for good." There is also something of the Austrian playwright Arnolt Bronnen's "patricide" motif in evidence when he continues: "'Father' is a curious word, I've always thought; I don't appear to comprehend it. It must denote someone whom one can love and who himself loves, from the bottom of his heart. How I would have loved to have such a person!" And then the thing that really divides them—Pietism—comes to the fore in all its clarity: "If I was a Pietist rather than a human being, if I could turn all my inclinations into their opposites, then I could get on harmoniously with you. But I cannot and will not live in such a way, and if I should commit a crime, then you will be guilty alongside me, Mr. Hesse, since it was you who took all the joy in life from me. 'Dear Hermann' has become someone else, someone who despises the world, an orphan whose 'parents' are still alive." And he ends this document of revolt with a call to arms, an explosive outburst that would become the "big bang" moment for his autonomy: "If only there were some anarchists around!" He signed off the letter thus: "H. Hesse, inmate of the prison at Stetten, where he has been sent 'not as a punishment.' I am starting to wonder who the 'feeble-minded' one in this whole business actually is."[1] Yet from these lofty, celestial heights of a Nietzschean immoralist, he plummets in the final sentence back down into the downright childish: "By the way, I'd be obliged if you came and visited now and then."

The hospital inspector Pastor Schall had by now had enough, and had long since reached the end of his tether and his goodwill. In a letter, likewise of September 14, he told Johannes Hesse what in his opinion should now be done with the boy, whom he diagnosed as suffering from a "moral infirmity": "I told him that what he needed was strict discipline." Above all, he went on, this fifteen-year-old should be disabused of the notion that "a person can get through life just by playing the fiddle and writing fiction." This was a challenge to Hermann: the enemy, the bourgeois individual in his worst-case form of the philistine and the bigot, was barring his way. By now he had clearly found his bearings. If he was to become a writer, he had to get away from here, away from these people. And he was certain that was the only thing he desired.

Hermann Hesse would later come to ponder on this momentous decision in a number of ways. It was at the same time a liberation and a burden to him, and forced him to spend his life in an intermediate realm comprising fantasy and a rejection of reality. This was a dangerous existence on shifting ground. But it was the decisive move where Hermann Hesse was concerned: he thereby evaded the grasp of the Pietist world of his parents, the world of authorities, of school, of the state and the Church, while at the same time subjecting himself to a demand that would overtax him (and indeed would overtax anyone)—namely, to make himself the creator of the world that he wanted to inhabit. This world arose within him; the act of externalizing it seemed—as in all artistry—to entail a barely tolerable hubris toward his environment.

His recollections of childhood became a reflection on the place where his writing received its decisive impetus. For Hesse, childhood in its endangered form symbolized the whole purpose of writing. Anyone who was unable to carry his childhood with him across the threshold to adulthood could never be a creative writer. For it was the artist's task to seek after lost beginnings and to recreate them anew in his work over and over again (and in vain). While working on his novel *Demian,* Hesse pondered on these childhood paradises, which could change from one second to the next (it by no means required the *Beneath the Wheel* mechanisms of the crammer for this to happen!) into living hells.

As for the child-soul itself: this was a dream of a succession of summits between which deep abysses opened up. As in fairy tales, good and evil lived cheek-by-jowl there. A comparison of two texts recalling his early life—"The Magician" of 1921, and *Life Story Briefly Told,* which he also began in 1921 but only completed in 1924—demonstrates the alchemistic foundation of his writing. For him, the child-soul was also a testimony of life, in which his worldview and self-image merged. In an added introduction to *Life Story Briefly Told* written in 1944, he dubbed this kind of "conjectural biography"—which had its origins in the nineteenth-century German writer Jean Paul—an *adventure* that also embraced the future.

All this, then, is the world within which Hermann Hesse proclaimed himself a writer—and it was also a world that was already a product of his writing, in part with results that were diametrically opposed to the kind of chronicle of metamorphoses represented by his writings. "The Magician"—a preliminary sketch for *Life Story Briefly Told* and "The Childhood of the Magician"—begins with the sentence: "I was born toward the end of the Middle Ages, on the evening of a warm day in July under the sign of Sagittarius and so I have retained a predilection for warmth, for high summer and for the hours around sunset."[2]

Here we may observe Hesse's need to recollect inexplicable, forgotten, or lost realms—even through such questionable means as astrology—within the rationally explicable world. However, even this is a game to him, a stimulus for his imagination—to conjure up images from signs and to discover in coincidences the possible counterpart to an imperative lurking in the background. "My Horoscope" is the title of a handwritten manuscript composed in the summer of 1919, after Joseph Englert had read what lay in store for Hesse in the stars—this was the one and only horoscope Hesse ever commissioned. Yet it is interesting how intensively Hesse set about interpreting what he was presented with. With a positively violent determination, he began to relate these occult symbols to himself and to incorporate them into his biography. And in them he found a reiteration of all the things that had oppressed him as he made his way south to the Alps that summer: "Many problems with the children, unclear circumstances. . . . Bad . . . !! Bad. Disappointment . . . easily persuaded to indulge in drink . . . disposition toward occult forces, inspiration, knowledge, clairvoyance . . . insincere in affairs of the heart. Sensual . . . tendency to drink."[3] In this way, his commentaries became a truly obscure horoscope of their own, an overconfident hermeneutics at the seat of a profound life crisis. The writer saves himself by playing with words—even if this is only with regard to the hodgepodge of symbols supplied by a horoscope. And more than this, he turns it into an integral aspect of his own inner life.

Factual correctness does not remotely mean that something is true! For how might literature become an important element in life unless it acted as a corrective for Hesse to a reality that he could under no circumstances merely accept as such? It is the mythical dimensions of reality, the truth of the legend, that literature lays bare. Thus it is that we read with astonishment the similar-sounding and yet quite different sentence that opens Hesse's *Life Story Briefly Told:* "I was born toward the end of modern times, shortly before the return of the Middle Ages, with the sign of the Archer in the ascendant and Jupiter in favorable aspect."[4] The end of the Middle Ages in "The Magician" and the end of the modern period here—following poetic logic, the determination of time is perfectly interchangeable for Hesse. What remains is the discovery of an end state—that was the important thing for him. Under such conditions, then, he was indicating that he originated from a continent that had sunk without trace in the interim.

This same fairy-tale logic runs right through Hesse's texts, and owes its origins to archetypal models.

In both textual variations, he invokes his early commitment to wanting to become a writer. This commitment arises in the moment when he ceased to follow the Pietist God of his parents (throughout his life the need for faith and skepticism were constantly in conflict with one another): "However, I only remained devout up to the age of around thirteen. By the time of my confirmation, when I was fourteen, I was already somewhat skeptical, and shortly thereafter my thoughts and my imagination began to become quite secular, and despite feeling great love and respect for my parents, I nevertheless regarded the sort of Pietist devotion in which they lived their lives as something unsatisfying, as something servile and tasteless, and as a consequence I often rebelled violently against it in my early years of adolescence."[5]

By this stage, then, literature, whose unconditionality he perceives like a call within himself, was his vocation. Here, too, we can sense how the text keeps on working in Hesse, how it becomes increasingly radical with every repeated updating. In "The Magician," for instance, he formulates this sense of vocation poetically and at the same time in a nuanced way:

> Shortly before I turned fourteen, I was resolved to become a writer, by which term I understood neither a saint nor a magician, but rather a famous man, whose poems would enchant boys and girls alike and who conceivably might have to starve, and upon whose grave a monument made of marble would one day be erected. I had a very exalted and yet thoroughly bourgeois and conventional conception of the writer, involving books in publication, plays that were performed, and recognition and fame. And yet the sense of being alive that I felt when I was writing was something completely different, detached from the world and untouched and unsullied by reward and renown. It was magic, it was conjuring and playfulness, the most sublime, most childlike, most sacred play with the objects of the world and the emotions within my heart, a form of play in which I was not merely the player, but no less of a plaything myself.[6]

By contrast, in *Life Story Briefly Told* we read a succinct account of what it was all about: "The thing was this: from my thirteenth year on, it was clear to me that I wanted to be either a writer or nothing at all."[7] An all-or-nothing standpoint is concealed within this either/or formulation. His decision was made, but that only prompted the really problematic question: How does one become a writer? One can aspire to learn any bourgeois profession or study an academic discipline—but one cannot aspire to become a writer, such a "professional goal" is simply risible, all one can do is simply be a writer. You don't become a writer, you just are one.

His rebelliousness toward the world resulted from the positively metaphysical certainty of a young man about his vocation. Yet who would believe such a pronouncement of a calling by a pupil who had absconded from Maulbronn and who at present was interned in a mental asylum?

"Primary Insanity"? Why Hesse Did Not Want to Become like His Half-Brothers Karl and Theodor Isenberg

> And so I tried taking up one profession after another, from the age of fourteen to twenty.
>
> —Hermann Hesse, "Autobiographical Notes"

Once again, Hermann Hesse found himself in a hopeless situation. The diagnosis of "primary insanity" was bandied about—however, there was still some doubt on this score; the doctors were not sure, and so his fate was not yet sealed. A duality inhabited Hesse, who had only just turned fifteen: on the one hand, the child who longed to be loved by his parents, and on the other hand, a budding writer who needed to distance himself from this world in which art was at best a pretty ornament on the Sunday-best dress of the bourgeoisie. Yet he knew that as long as he did not reconcile himself with his parents, he would remain in Stetten, and the longer he stayed there, the greater the danger that he would be pigeonholed as insane and vanish into some institution forever. But how could he bring about a rapprochement with his parents without sacrificing his own self-respect, and without abasing himself before the very thing that he loathed?

On September 22, 1892, he wrote to his parents in Calw: "I have no one left to complain to or implore, I am alone. I could make things easy for myself by begging for forgiveness, but I refuse to do so, I have done my penance here in Stetten. But no one gives me any cause for hope." Here the split in his child's psyche is all too apparent; this is the heartfelt cry of a person who has begun to evolve his own personality and who cannot return to the protection of that intact and sheltered world of firm order in which he grew up but in which he can no longer place any credence. No sooner does he set out on his own path, though, than he seems to be riven by inner strife. That is the "obstinacy" of which Hesse speaks, the drama of self-realization: "Only now, when I have lost your love, do I feel that I love you deeply, but I never want to come home, I simply cannot."[8]

Of course, he had a suggestion—if Pastor Pfisterer in Basel (he was not to be rid of the world of pastors quite yet!) was willing to take him in, he could resume his school studies there and Stetten would finally be behind him. But then he received a reply from Johannes Hesse, who had been waiting for a sign of humility from his son: "Dear Hermann! I am now in a position to be able to respond to you. I certainly do not expect you to say sorry. Your last letter is enough for us. In it, you say that it pains you to be inwardly alienated from us. But the very act of uttering those words means that this separation can end. We feel once more that it is your real self, that it is your heart is speaking to us, and not some strange evil spirit to which you have momentarily surrendered yourself."[9] It was not their intention to make further study impossible for him, his father reassured him. But all attempts to find a high school for a person who was being discharged from Stetten had thus far proved fruitless. Even so, Hermann got his father's reassurance that they would write to Pastor Pfisterer without delay: "We will do what we can and will not deceive you."[10] And indeed, in due course Hermann received an invitation from Pfisterer to come to Basel. Not to stay there for good, but to have a break from the institution.

This was a first step toward freedom. The trip was organized, and on October 1 Marie Hesse, who was lying ill in bed at the time, wrote to her similarly ailing father Hermann Gundert to let him know that her Hermann had had a "wonderful day" for his journey to Basel. Except that he never arrived there—thus sending the family into turmoil once more. It turned out that Hermann's stepbrother Theodor Isenberg was at fault, as Grandpa Gundert noted with displeasure: "So then his brother Theodor went and threw a spanner in the works by inviting him to come to Waiblingen and meet some friends from Cannstatt; it appears he had Hermann stay there overnight and so messed up his travel arrangements, with the result that we now have no idea how to proceed."[11]

Theodor, like his brother Karl, was a son of Marie Hesse from her first marriage to the English missionary Charles Isenberg, and had been born in 1866 in what is now Hyderabad in Pakistan. Theodor and Karl were both very talented musicians and sang the solo parts in the church choir. But Theodor wanted more and dreamed of becoming an opera singer. He was always held up to Hermann as an example and a warning at one and the same time. The Romantic ideal of the artist to which Hermann was wedded dictated that the artist must not compromise with the bourgeois world and that it was a case of "all or nothing." And the story of his half-brother appeared to vindicate him in this view. Theodor had given up an apprenticeship as a pharmacist and went off to study music for two years— whereupon he immediately secured an engagement as a singer at the opera in the Dutch city of Groningen. Yet he could never manage to free himself from the pressure of his family—or hence from Pietism. In the end, he gave in. The twenty-year-old Theodor Isenberg, who stood on the threshold of a glittering stage career, returned to Calw, and took up his job as a shop assistant once more. Later he studied pharmacy and opened his own drugstore. The family regarded this as a case of Theodor coming to his senses, the end of an aberration. Marie Hesse—who had once fancied herself a poetess!—also saw Hermann's eccentricities as just such a fleeting interlude. A temptation by sin, which was to be vigorously countered. Hermann, then, was forewarned by this incident: he would have to sever ties completely.

Hermann eventually turned up in Basel five days late and informed his worried parents: "I finally arrived at 6:48 on Wednesday evening after a 13-hour journey via Stuttgart, Mühlacker, Pforzheim, and Karlsruhe. All is well here." In the meantime, Pastor Schall and Johannes Hesse had corresponded with one another about Hermann's future. Schall pointed out, by way of a caveat, that if the diagnosis of "primary insanity" was correct, then Hermann's development would be arrested at the age of puberty. However, exactly what this assumption was based upon remains unclear. Certainly Pastor Schall was not ill-disposed toward Hermann; he was the one who constantly held Hermann's parents in check when they would perhaps have glad to be forever rid of their son, whom they regarded as beyond all control: "Lots of time spent working in the open air will surely do Hermann's nerves a power of good."[12]

Pastor Pfisterer told Hermann's parents that it was his impression that "the boy is too well developed for his age," and that his literary knowledge in particular exceeded what was customary for youths of his age—and that he had even read Bellamy, which was a harmful influence on him—and that, all in all, "there is no longer anything childish about his attitudes."[13]

Bellamy's *Looking Backward: 2000–1887* as a Model for *The Glass Bead Game*

In 1887 the American socialist and writer Edward Bellamy published a novel that was widely read at the time: *Looking Backward: 2000–1887,* a fashionable piece of utopian fiction that for some years was on everybody's lips, though it has since sunk into complete oblivion. The book turned on a bizarre notion that actor-director Woody Allen was later to revisit in his 1973 film *Sleeper,* in which he plays the last human being fighting a losing battle against a world of robots. The utopia of Bellamy's work was steadily transformed by the experiences of the twentieth century into its opposite: a scene of horror played out in a milieu of drawing-room chitchat. The young Hermann Hesse was fascinated by this literary experiment: In Bellamy's story, the protagonist, Julian West, wakes after 113 years of deep sleep to find himself in a socialist America. He is captivated by the new social conditions. In the heated political atmosphere in Germany in Hesse's time, after the passing of Bismarck's antisocialist laws, the battle cry of socialism was "distributive justice," and the Marxist theorist Clara Zetkin wrote the foreword to the first German edition of Bellamy's book, published by the Dietz publishing house. Reading this piece of light, popular literature today is more unsettling than anything else. A dedicated "army of workers" creates prosperity for everyone, and a "nationalist party" holds the reins of power. The utopia imagined here is in the form of a future state—and Bellamy's petit-bourgeois conception of what the world of tomorrow might look like reads like something from the early history of the National Socialist Party, albeit the more "radical" wing of the movement as represented by Gregor Strasser, who took social issues seriously; it also seemed to have an intellectual affinity with Ernst Niekisch's idea of "National Bolshevism."

But it was another aspect of the work that fascinated the young Hermann Hesse: the idea that someone might wake from sleep and find themselves in a "new world." Everything would appear to be different—only you yourself would have retained long-faded images in your mind's eye from the era when you lived, along with yardsticks that would now seem wholly antiquated. We are thus confronted with the picture of an anachronistic person—the inconsistent individual in a constant state of uncertain transition, whose inner life necessarily comes into conflict with the external world. When he began to write, Hesse would make such anachronistic figures his chosen companions. They populate his work: Hermann Lauscher, Peter Camenzind, Knulp, Demian, the Guest at the Spa, the Steppenwolf Harry Haller, Siddhartha, Goldmund, and Josef Knecht!

Bellamy's popular utopia, which had more than a hint of cheap sensationalism about it, conjured up an image for the fourteen-year-old Hesse that suggested to him all the things that might be technologically possible in the future, and how these changes would also fundamentally alter society. Hesse applied the same interpretation to Bellamy and his popular novel about a person who had been asleep for an eternity and wakes to find himself adrift in a future world as he would later apply to the character of Bellarmin in Hölderlin's novel *Hyperion*. In June 1892 he noted:

> Poor Bellamy! Granted, it is easy to dream up happiness or truth, but an unimaginably harder task to imagine others as nothing but unfortunate or to make them pessimists. Even so, it is a splendid, wonderful picture he paints of happy times; the only thing is that he portrays it as good, far too good, and so it is not sufficiently illuminating for a "critical" (!) age like ours! Go ahead, laugh at me if you will, but I am in no doubt that it is sad that we only ever feel compelled to look for beauty, novelty, goodness, and completeness—in a word "happiness"—in the future. Even Bellamy has to first imagine a miracle—namely, someone sleeping away a century and more—before he can identify tolerable and satisfactory conditions.

He then proceeds to express his desire for a metamorphosis that is more than a mere change of scenery: "I too would love to nod off right now and sleep until the advent of a beautiful age in the colors of a fairy tale, where humans and nature once again count for something, and privileges and status, rank and prejudice—indeed, our present system and 'society' as a whole—simply ceased to exist! But who knows, perhaps I would have to sleep millennia, and most likely for all eternity, for such a situation to arise."[14]

Here we already catch a glimpse of the skeptic, who sees the dystopia in every utopia. For although Hesse was curious about what might be effected through change, and although he inquired after the hidden forces motivating both change and conservation—and in the process engaged with the idea of the authorities, and even the secret societies (including "travelers to the East") that were instrumental in these areas—this did not mean that he himself subscribed to those ideas. All too quickly they begin to approximate to conspiracies and never get by without adopting theories of power and that missionary zeal that attaches to all ideologies, which Hesse so despised.

Yet he kept on returning to Bellamy, because he found in this work the blueprint for a possible way in which the whole social and industrial fermentation mass might develop. It was in this spirit that the eighteen-year-old Hesse wrote to his former teacher at Cannstatt, Dr. Kapff, on February 7, 1896: "I don't actually believe that life can be reformed or that social conditions in Germany and Europe can be improved. Instead I take the view that the rotten leaf will have to fall of its own accord to make way for the new. This 'progress' and this nervous feverish energy cannot be repressed, but it will eventually wither and die. . . . One thing I'm certain of is that there will be no Bellamy-state anywhere in the 21st century."[15]

Nevertheless, it was a model of the future whose aroma rubbed off on everyone who came into contact with it. Was it sweet or bitter, fresh or putrid? Bellamy's *Looking Backward: 2000–1887* forms part of the early formative preparation for Hesse's own utopian work—one that was deeply skeptical of all utopias!—namely, the novel *The Glass Bead Game,* which involves a retrospective from the year 2200.

Such travels through time, into the future and the past alike, appear to have fascinated Hesse from an early age. Certainly, the writer who would later invoke the "child's soul" created a positively elderly air in his first books. He wrote like a very old man who could recall his childhood days only with great difficulty. But with increasing age, Hesse's style began to rejuvenate.

Shadows over the "Happy and Jolly Time in Cannstatt": Eros and Death

Once Hesse had—once again on a trial basis—gotten away from Stetten, he found it easier to ask his mother, who was so akin to him in her aptitudes, for forgiveness for all the worries he had caused her. Basel, a place where he had spent some of his childhood, evoked some very particular memories for him. Consequently, Marie Hesse read the following words in a letter of October 20, 1892, from her son Hermann: "My poor, dear mother! Things cannot go on like this, I must finally express my feelings: poor mother, please forgive your fallen son, I implore you to forgive me if you love me and believe that there is a divine spark still within me. It seems as if these streets and meadows where I once played as a child are now accusing me, for I am no longer a child, or a son. I am a wretch who rails against his fate and humanity, a miserable wretch who cannot and will not love himself ever again."[16]

Pastor Pfisterer, a teacher at the Boys' Mission House in Basel, was very taken with Hermann—he believed he should attend the high school in Cannstatt, whose headmaster was an acquaintance of Johannes Hesse. And so he sent an urgent note to Hermann's father: "Quite honestly, I have seen no sign of madness . . . in God's name I would risk it and leave the doctors out of the reckoning."[17]

The reason for Hermann Hesse's burning desire to attend a high school was first and foremost a mundane one: if he passed the one-year voluntary examination, he would only have to serve a one-year rather than three-year term in the military. In November 1892 Hermann was accepted as a boarder at Instructor Geiger's house in Cannstatt. The high school there had agreed to enroll him as a pupil. Finally, Hermann appeared once more to have escaped being institutionalized. Yet this new arrangement entailed new costs for his parents again: "The price for boarding, which amounts to 800 Marks for the school year, is to be paid in advance and in full in quarterly installments of 200 Marks, and regardless of any holidays which might fall within the respective quarter."[18]

Hermann was now a high-school student and reported in his first letter from Cannstatt to Calw: "In sum, I have little hope of ever being able to keep up. I am working hard and for long hours, but I'm finding it difficult and things go so slowly that I get very tired . . . I should say right now: don't take me for someone suffering from a transient illness, but finally please believe that I am seriously debilitated and learn more slowly than I once did, etc. That could only be made worse by having me stay in mental asylums and such places."[19]

For the threat of being returned to an institution still hung over Hesse at this time; it was his parents' main instrument of control. If he did not fall in line, he would have to go back. This threat only served to make him more recalcitrant. In an entry in the family diary for Christmas 1892, his mother recorded: "Hermann was quite remarkably sweet, calm, and agreeable. But before he left he said to me: 'Don't have any illusions about me: I am still as sick and unhappy as I was back in Bad Boll and wish myself dead this instant!'"[20]

And once again his parents' unrelenting attempts to proselytize to him instilled a cold fury in him. No, he told them, he did not regret anything he had done in the past year. Once more he found he was having to defend himself against a kind of soft coercion in the name of the Lord, which weighed down on him as a constant pressure. Especially his dear mother had a fanatical side to her faith that he found intolerable: "And then there's your 'God'! For all I know he may exist, and may even be exactly as you conceive him; but he doesn't interest me. Don't imagine that you can influence me in this way in the slightest." The existing order of the world struck him as unacceptable.: "I could become a D. Phil., a professor, perhaps a teacher or something like that, who has the privilege of being stupid and having a big paunch and wearing a silk waistcoat and a gold watch-chain, and burying himself like a hypochondriac in piles of papers and card-files and books."[21] In the interim he had learned how to agitate his parents, and doing this gratified him time and again. Thus, almost in passing, he informed his parents of something that was bound to alarm them again. He had been reading Eichendorff, he told them, and had been overcome by "all that dismal heartache, and those nagging love pains"—and so, quickly gathering up some of his books, he had gone to Stuttgart and traded them in for a revolver. Another one. "And now I'm back home and the rusty thing is lying there in front of me."[22]

Marie Hesse traveled to Cannstatt straight away to prevent anything worse from happening. Hermann was excitable and aggressive, and swore loudly at her, forcing her to beat a retreat so as not to antagonize him any further. Grandfather Gundert, who was gravely ill and now permanently bed-ridden, noted on January 23, 1893: "Yesterday, Marie returned from a visit to Cannstatt. There, poor Hermann had felt such an urge again to kill himself that he had rushed off to Stuttgart to sell his Livy to an antiques dealer in exchange for a revolver. She could do very little there. He finds the idea of any serious gainful employment repellent and does not know why he should even bother staying alive—in any event, it is not to please God."[23]

In actual fact, Hermann was simply going through a particularly difficult period of puberty. The nineteenth century had little understanding of young people who were no longer children but had not yet reached adulthood. Hesse had had cause to note the problem several times in his life thus far: this harshness of otherwise enlightened parents, teachers, or pastors when dealing with a child's psyche, an entity to which they were incapable of assigning any intrinsic value.

Perplexed, yet in equal measure determined to use any coercion necessary, Hesse's mother wrote: "We are at a loss what to do with him."[24] What this meant was that they were at a loss to decide which mental hospital to pack him off to. In the meantime, Hermann read Turgenev and Heine and felt like every genius always has—misunderstood. Sometimes it seemed to him as if he were already long since dead and that everything he was experiencing now was a "desolate dream of the dead."

As luck would have it, Hermann was examined by a largely incompetent physician by the name of Dr. Landsberger, who diagnosed his condition as a heart defect. This defect—nonexistent, of course—served henceforth to explain Hermann's strange behavior. The blood flow to his head was allegedly disrupted and so—and this was the most important element of Landsberger's incorrect diagnosis—it would be inadvisable to make any external changes to Hermann's routine. So it was, then, that Hermann Hesse was granted something akin to a jester's license; he was ill for sure, but it was his heart, not his mind, that was ailing. Furthermore, he could do nothing to help his condition, and was entitled to peace and consideration.

The prospective writer played his role well. He imagined himself into the twilight worlds between life and death. And his mother wrote to him urging him not to walk so fast, because that was dangerous for people with heart problems.

Hermann, though, was now free to indulge his sensual instincts—not just those associated with indeterminate love, but now also those engendered by the dark and equally indeterminate allure of death: the equipollent primal urges of Eros and Thanatos. On March 7, 1893, the "heart patient" wrote a letter from Cannstatt to Calw, and the scene he portrays conveys to the reader his capacity to generate an atmosphere from an event that is in itself a fiction. Here Hermann Hesse was in his "Tristan" phase: love becomes completely subsumed within death; but as with the singer in the third act of Wagner's *Tristan and Isolde,* this was primarily a matter of good health and an intact voice.

Hesse was likewise training his voice here, in his urge to become the writer of his own life: "Outside there is sunshine and the green of the trees. But spring has gone to my head, there is a constant boom–boom–boom– boom sound in my skull like the drumbeat at a funeral or like the dead, bland tolling of church bells." What follows is already the sketched narrative arc of an as-yet unwritten story: "A girl once lived in the house next door to me. She was pale and irritable and mocking, and at times resembled me. I knew her well and was often her gallant when we were out skating on the ice. I also discussed religion and other things with her—she was Jewish. I hadn't seen her for a few days, and today she died." Here, Hermann Hesse is flirting with a topic that does not correspond to any experience of his—and which precisely for that reason stimulates the writer's fantasy. It sounds like the simulation of a serious reflection on a weighty subject. Despite wearing the mask of a wise old observer, the narrator cannot conceal how helpless he actually is when confronted with the phenomenon of death. And the fact that, despite all his rhetorical effort, he cannot hide this helplessness reveals to us a tentative writer pushing forward the boundaries: "Now she is pallid and dead. When I heard the news my heart felt so strange, so painful and yet so happy. I knew that the girl was neither very pretty nor very witty nor very charming, and I'm sure that no one could ever have fallen in love with her. It's for the best that she's dead." And a few sentences further on, the budding writer reveals himself as Narcissus in the guise of a hypochondriac—for he is now expected to provide the kind of accounts that accord with his "heart defect." By this stage, Hermann Hesse was inhabiting this role with a fervor that no one could doubt: "Yesterday I thought that the end had come for me; in the middle of a lesson I was assailed by a bout of dizziness and the whiff of the grave and I lowered my burning head and felt it grow cooler and thought to myself, this is the end. I sat for a good hour like that, unable to read or hear or speak."[25] Already this passage sounds like Hesse's later protagonist Peter Camenzind. We feel the great pathos of tragedy at his initial appearance, yet in the final clause there is an almost parodistic transition to the actual core of the message: his nervous emotional confusion, which also has something of an apathetic tone here.

"Weak Nerves" or "Moral Insanity"? Apprenticed to a Bookseller in Esslingen for Three Days

Hesse's time in Cannstatt was one of postponed crisis. How could one become a writer when in the eyes of one's peers one was not much more than a schoolboy who had run away and who had severe behavioral problems? By having the seriousness of one's ambitions confirmed step by step by the very people from whom one was trying to escape through writing? This was the vicious circle in which the sixteen-year-old Hesse now found himself caught. No, he needed to make a great leap, a grand entrance through which he could launch himself into the world and present himself in the way he wished one day to be regarded in that world.

His father told him that such aspirations were just "moods"—he used the word "moods," but meant "temptations"—which he himself had once experienced. Yet according to Johannes Hesse (and we may well imagine how every fiber in Hermann Hesse's body must have revolted against this) the most important thing was: "Simply not to make one's self the measure of all things or to let momentary moods govern your life!"[26] That was a fine insight born of the wisdom of age, but it was the antithesis of the approach that Hermann Hesse was currently battling out with himself: namely, a way of giving shape to his awakening sense of self without abandoning what his father called a "momentary mood"—in short, a way of avoiding deadening himself inwardly as required by his parents' Christian faith.

His answer to his father's well-meant instruction was a predictably sharp rebuff: "Do you still take the wrongheaded view that 'all the cares of mankind' have 'taken hold' of me? That's not it at all. I am merely bored and discontent, not least because I do not know of any profession open to me that I might even remotely enjoy."[27]

Easter 1893 was on the horizon. Hesse's parents expected him to come home for the holiday. Hermann complained that he could endure anything except love, especially of the Christian variety, and implored them: "Just leave me in peace at Easter!"[28] More than ever, he was now on a collision course with his parents, who could conceive of only one yardstick for leading a meaningful existence: that of a personal profession of faith.

Hermann Hesse's struggle with his own self had an absolutely insuperable adversary, which never released anybody: Pietism as a sect, with all its moral rigor. The diagnosis of "primary insanity" had by this stage been supplanted by one of "moral insanity"—and if they already regarded him as morally degenerate, then so be it: "I pity you! Such devout, reputable, law-abiding people—and your son a rascal who scorns all morality and everything 'sacred' and 'respectable'! I almost feel sorry for you! I could have made something of myself if only I had been stupider and had allowed myself to be duped by religion and all that stuff right from the very beginning."[29]

In the postscript he appended to this letter he added that he had got to know some "nice, fun people" in Cannstatt. His parents were alarmed. Once again, the family members corresponded with one another about correctional and mental institutions. The uncontrolled willfulness of this stubborn boy had somehow to be broken! In her diary his mother noted the "whole ghastly truth," that Hermann had been taken in by some "seducer and corrupter of youth" in Cannstatt. What did she mean by this? Carousing the night away in taverns, drinking, talking about all manner of godless things and chasing after girls. At least, that was what the family feared was going on. Inspector Geiger, who was supposed to keep an eye on Hermann, was powerless. The boy took no notice of him and sometimes only came home after midnight, apparently the worse for drink. This disturbance of the peace at night was immediately reported to Johannes Hesse. Pastor Schall responded to Hesse's parents' inquiry about a strict institute of correction for their son Hermann by recommending Pastor Blessing in Weiler, near Schorndorf (in his childhood and youth Hermann Hesse was, it seems, surrounded on all sides by pastors!).

The institute run by Pastor Blessing, Schall told the Hesses, was renowned for its successful correction. For instance, a few years ago it had been very effective in the case of a French youth, the *enfant terrible* of his family, who had been "totally transformed." Johannes Hesse spelled out the consequences if Hermann refused to comply with house rules in Cannstatt: "then you will have to be put into an institution, however painful that would be to us."[30] In the meantime, Hermann had become well acquainted with the school's detention cell, and his sister Adele wrote to his half-brother Karl: "I keep hearing the worst reports about Hermann, that many times he doesn't come home at all at night, and that he's been put in detention at the school. Mama thinks he ought to be sent away and that he will go completely to rack and ruin if he is left to his own devices."[31] But the logic that anyone who did not fit in society should be "sent away" was precisely what Hermann was rebelling against. He yearned to feel the love that his parents professed, and which he took to be some abstract platitude, directed at him—most especially when he was making it most difficult for any of them to love him.

Hermann Gundert died on April 25, 1893; Marie Hesse in particular was hard hit by this loss. Johannes Hesse was now chosen by the Basel Missionary Union to be his father-in-law's successor at the Calw Publishing Union. This entailed even more work and a move for the family back to their large, old house. This change of location affected the family's parrot Polly most deeply. Marie Hesse noted that the bird had grown so melancholic that it had "almost suffered seizures." The parrot evidently could count on the family's support and empathy—but what about the "renegade" Hermann?

Hermann's father believed the most important thing now was that he should get through his exams somehow, whereas his mother continued to proselytize. After all, she reasoned, Karl and Theodor Isenberg had already been brought back onto the straight and narrow, so why shouldn't that also happen with Hermann? After Easter came Whitsun, and Marie Hesse decided to try a new, direct approach to the problem—we might well suspect that Hermann, like the parrot Polly, "almost suffered a seizure" in the process. On May 11, 1893, Hermann received from his mother one of those letters that were so unmotherly in their tone that he simply took them to be one big lie—a lie, moreover, that was designed to prevent him from becoming his true self: "Karl and Theodor now look back on all the good advice that they got from their dear grandfather from their early childhood onward, and recognize how wonderful and rich his life was. Wouldn't you now like to open your heart, repent, become a child once more and turn to God your Father and implore him to redeem you?"[32]

It seemed, then, that his parents were not prepared to leave him in peace—while for his part, Hermann was not yet strong enough to let this all merely wash over him. The fact that he was not yet out of the danger zone was indicated by the reference to the two talented musicians Karl and Theodor Isenberg. Theodor—as we have already seen—made it as far as the opera house in Groningen, only to be drawn back to the religious sect by the long arm of the family.

The tragedy for Hermann was that he loved his parents and respected, even admired, them for the strength of their faith, which they lived out in their daily lives—and so it was all the more upsetting for him that they refused to acknowledge his emerging personality. His parents sensed that Hermann was growing apart from them, and in their blindness—there is no other way of putting it—they did everything to accelerate this process. But this time he had no intention of obeying or humbly returning home; he was now on the point of breaking free. Almost daily he was bombarded by letters. Their uniform message was: Change your ways now! His father also wrote to Karl Isenberg at this time, urging him to recognize that "we honestly mean you well, and that God has sent us to give you succor in your need."[33]

The last thing Hermann needed now were missionaries who also happened to be the people who had brought him into the world. By now he was reading books that would strengthen him on his chosen personal path of development (Heine!) and was also busy seeking out ever more friends with whom he could discuss his reading matter—free from the threat of Christian moralizing. In the end Hermann did return home to Calw for Whitsun 1893, but his parents did not achieve their aim of bringing him back into the family fold for good, as evidenced by Hermann Hesse's letter of June 13, 1893, written when he was back in Cannstatt, in which he savored his triumph in gaining his freedom:

> So here we are! I visited you at Whitsun—we went walking, ate, laughed and joked, read the Bible and made music together—but ultimately it all descended into argument and boredom again, with the result that I left a whole day early. And now mother writes to me to tell me that I was there "all too briefly" at Whitsun!! And that I should speak "openly" about "what is preying on my mind"!
>
> Poor parents! You think you're dealing with an eccentric dreamer and his crazy ideals, whose insanity makes him get up to some malicious tricks now and then, but who is otherwise pining away sunk in his own private sorrow and world-weariness. That's how you picture your own son.

You Christians are a curious mixture of optimism and pessimism! . . .
So what's the real state of affairs? What do I wish for? Well if you want to
know in a nutshell, my ideal situation would be: 1.) to have a millionaire
as a father, plus a few rich uncles; 2.) to be more adept at practical things;
and 3.) to be able to live and travel where I liked. . . . Write me again, if
you have the time and the inclination.[34]

That letter had a mocking tone, quite intentionally. In response his mother
sent her "materialistic son" a few tidbits left over from his father's birthday
celebrations, with the waspish observation, "Perhaps this will be more to
your taste than Mama's letters."[35]

The most significant event of this year in Cannstatt, however, was this:
"I have passed the examination, though not with flying colors!"[36]

Apart from this, the legacy of Cannstatt amounted to a commitment
to pantheism—which Hermann Hesse found to be the form of religion
that suited him best—and a not inconsiderable sum in debts, as Marie Hesse
recounted to her daughter Adele: "The bills he ran up are huge, though:
he bought himself the works of Goethe, Lenau, Heine and a pile of other
fiction, without ever asking beforehand." In the next sentence, as a knee-
jerk reaction, she felt compelled to add: "Only a change of heart—genuine
conversion—will bring about a change."[37] At any rate, Hesse was reading
with a thirst for knowledge that was positively unquenchable. Alongside
Heine, it was principally Goethe, whose fictional world exerted a magical
pull on him. At the same time, though, he was constantly tired and suffered
from headaches and pain in his eyes. What was to become of him? For a
start, he would travel to Calw and spend the summer recuperating from
the rigors of the exam. Marie Hesse reported on his condition: "Hermann
is reasonable and biddable, and spends his time fishing, bathing, walking
around the neighborhood, and smoking almost all the time."[38]

By October he was back in Cannstatt and the complaints about his behavior started up again. He was wrapped up in himself and inhabited a
fantasy world of his own, the school told his parents. Indeed, once Hermann
had the one-year voluntary examination under his belt, which exempted
him from three years of military service, all his motivation for schoolwork
evaporated. Ought he to bother studying at all? What subjects, though?

On no account did he want to become a teacher or pastor. His headaches kept troubling him, and he felt exhausted and drained.

Hesse summed up his time in Cannstatt in the remarkable sentences: "I have become a Social Democrat and spend my time in taverns drinking beer and arguing. I am reading Heine now almost exclusively, a writer whom I imitate a great deal."[39]

Perhaps he really should learn a "practical profession"?

Accordingly, an apprenticeship was found for Hermann with the bookseller S. Mayer in Esslingen; his father signed the indenture papers on October 25, 1893. Clearly this was a somewhat overhasty decision. For after just three days of his apprenticeship, Hermann ran away. Once more, for Johannes Hesse, there seemed to be just one alternative—the insane asylum. On November 1 he wrote to Dr. Zeller in Winnenden:

> Dear Medical Counselor, my son Hermann, who is sixteen and a half years old, appears to be suffering from "moral insanity" and last Monday walked out on an apprenticeship at a bookshop in Esslingen, a position he had only just taken up. He had already run away from the Evangelical Seminary in Maulbronn in 1892, and subsequently was unable see his studies through at the high school in Cannstatt.
>
> I hope to be able to bring him with me to Winnethal tomorrow, in the hope that you might to be able to keep him there for observation. Would you please be so kind as to make time to see me when I come and to examine the boy? We simply do not know what we are to do with him.[40]

Mayer the bookseller in Esslingen also did not have a good word to say about Hermann, writing to his parents about his "pronounced lack of any strength of will" and also complaining about his "extremely illegible handwriting." He signed off by telling them: "I will tear up the apprenticeship contract."[41]

So ended the year 1893. No one had been found to take Hermann on, and even Dr. Zeller—to Hesse's good fortune—declined to admit him as a patient at his asylum. And so he found himself back home at Calw. He recalled this period at the family home with a brief note in his diary: "Idle there until May 1894."[42]

Among Clocks: The Exoticism of Machinists' Blue Smocks

There was no longer any immediate aim to find another apprenticeship for Hermann. Instead, he was expected to take time to think things over, rest, and help his father, who was not in the best of health himself, in the publishing house. Marie Hesse had also fallen ill; Hermann Gundert's death hit her hard. For her, her father had always occupied a position far above that of her husband in the family hierarchy. In addition, the battles with her son Hermann had worn her down. Henceforth until her death, she would spend many years struggling with a succession of illnesses. At least now Hermann made every effort not to torment his parents any further—but he found himself unable to fulfill one great wish of theirs: to become like them.

On September 1 Marie Hesse wrote to her son Karl Isenberg: "Hermann is a poor, dear child! He sits at the piano and plays his own compositions, which are all terribly melancholic."[43]

Nonetheless, what his mother recounts here almost in passing was a key breakthrough in Hermann's road to recovery. He had found a way of giving expression to his great internal upheaval: his own songs. In other words, he was on the way to curing himself. This also helped strengthen his own awakening lyrical persona, which would soon be confronted by the world of daily life in all its prosaic dreariness. For the family had come to the view that a practical trade would be better for his nervous constitution than if he were to attempt to continue his academic studies.

In the process, he was to gain some genuinely very interesting insights into the world of mechanics: "In May 1894, I start work as a trainee with the mechanic Heinrich Perrot Jr. in Calw. I am taught how to file, forge and turn metal, but I don't learn how to build or design anything, and don't pick a great deal up. Plus I'm given some very stern talkings-to."[44] The years that followed became a kind of work therapy for the high-strung Hermann. Perrot's workshop was situated on the banks of the River Nagold, whose waters were used to power the machinery.

Here he learned how to forge a flower stand, but Perrot's main specialty was the manufacture of public clocks. The firm's prospectus described these unusual timepieces as "equipped with clock movements and mechanisms for striking the quarter, half and full hours, units for moving the hands and precision movements for the largest church clocks and for cathedrals with bells weighing 7,000–8,000 kilograms and dials over 5 meters in diameter."

The word "trainee" was just gaining currency at that time and did not remotely have the same negative connotations as nowadays, when a trainee is someone who is unpaid, looked down upon and endlessly exploited and who is sustained only by the hope of one day getting a "proper job"—namely, one in which he will actually be paid for the work he does.

Hesse had known another son of bourgeois parents in Calw who had taken up this kind of work—namely, learning on the job in a world of labor hitherto wholly unfamiliar to students on a higher academic study path—and found such an expedition into the world of mechanical work really exciting. The polytechnic educational practice he was exposed to here became a real corrective for the erstwhile dropout from the Maulbronn seminary and the Cannstatt high school.

Furthermore, the workshop he had now entered as a temporary guest worker was a thoroughly humane place of work, almost still a craftsman's studio rather than a sweatshop prefiguring the hellish conditions of heavy industry. For a son of the bourgeoisie and a former Latin scholar, there was a "certain Romanticism" about going around now in a blue machinist's smock, he noted. Despite having neither any talent for technology nor any interest in mechanics, he saw his traineeship at the clockmaker's through to the end. He had, he later summed up his time at Perrot's, "really learned a lot there and lived for the first and only time in my life among working people."[45]

In addition, Hermann Hesse, now seventeen, learned to discipline himself in order to make it through a long working day. He became more physically robust and stronger-willed. He knew now that he could endure other forms of labor—his health would take it and he no longer needed to be cosseted by any special treatment. He had rediscovered a sense of calm and cheerfulness here, he claimed, and was in a much better state psychologically. All in all, he instinctively felt much closer to his colleagues in the workshop than to the petit bourgeoisie—a milieu that he knew only too well. Likewise, he recognized that a new age was reflected in this world of work: an age of industry, which had supplanted the era of the craftsman. Without a doubt, this was a major new departure, in which the possibilities of what was technically feasible were expanding in a hitherto unimaginable way: "Yet if I consider the dark side of this development, the nameless misery, the wretchedness of entire classes of people, then I often find myself assailed by all the woes of humanity."[46]

Everything in this industrialized world was anonymous and soulless, a radical change from the craftworking environment, which was characterized by personal dependencies but also often by a sense of welfare and even domestic coziness. Even at this early stage, then, Hesse was adopting the position of a mistrustful observer of technology, who does not want to miss seeing any of the spectacle but ultimately does not believe that the outcome will be at all positive.

In Calw, however, the clocks went a little slower than elsewhere in the matter of industrialization. Perrot's shop for crafting public clocks was a world of wonder in which time was not merely measured but was also made visible. For Hesse, working here was a formative experience that resonated even in later works like *The Glass Bead Game,* where the mysterious rules and principles of the game mimic the mechanical workings of a public timepiece.

The workshop was a place where the spirit of technology combined with an aura of specialization, which for Hesse always had something magical about it. Only the initiated knew how to construct such clocks for public buildings. This was the genesis of a magical world for the writer.

Hesse, who had of course read Goethe's novel *Wilhelm Meister's Apprenticeship,* was well acquainted with the Society of the Tower, that strange organization of all kinds of eccentrics who could be regarded as a secret elite only through the exercise of all one's powers of imagination. This group was not aloof, but it was exalted and had a far-seeing eye. Yet for all that, it was a self-contained circle of individuals, to which only very few people had access; Hesse would replicate such an atmosphere in the rituals of his travelers to the East.

Perrot's clock workshops did, however, have one invaluable advantage: While it was a real place of everyday labor, the tiring duration of which Hesse was now familiar with, at the same time it became a symbol of the irresolvable mystery, that sense of shutting oneself off from the outside world that is an integral part of any great piece of work—be it a public clock or a novel.

Consequently, the figure of Heinrich Perrot turns up in Hesse's later work, as the inventor of the mechanism in *The Glass Bead Game.* In a letter of May 29, 1895, to Theodor Rümelin, however, there is still no hint of this symbolic aspect of the workshop; the business of the working day, with all its many minor hindrances and frustrations, was still too vividly present for Hermann: "Still, I have learned a bit about mechanics; for instance, I

The Hesse family in 1899

now know how to take apart a sewing machine, how to make a wire cable, turn metal, manufacture screws, and create a saw. I can tell the difference between steel, iron, brass, copper, tin, zinc, antimony and so on, and set up simple ringing mechanisms. I also know how to drink grape juice, eat dry bread, order new trainees about, fall off ladders, tear my trousers and all the other things that are part and parcel of being a mechanic."[47] Along-side this ironic account, though, the main subject of Hesse's letter to Rümelin, his former fellow student at Maulbronn, was what treasures he had unearthed in Grandpa Gundert's library (which now belonged to his father).

His grandfather's library in Calw now became Hesse's real university. Here he eagerly devoured the works of Schiller and the Romantics, Goethe and Heinrich Heine, the last of whom he positively worshiped at this stage in his life: "And in Heinrich Heine, the Romantic School has survived, and laughing, he delivered the coup de grâce to this movement, his old schoolmistress, even though his heart was breaking as he did so."[48] The judgments he was expressing here were the very precise but by no means dispassionate results of the knowledge that he had thus far acquired. His experience of reading always resonates alongside his opinions, and we are here party to his humble declarations of love, which always remained those of someone who was capable of genuine admiration. He would subsequently come to modify his judgment on Romanticism on several occasions. Through the act of reading, therefore, the seventeen-year-old Hermann Hesse, who up until now had been an arrogant and aggressive braggart (and constantly rebelling against his parents' Pietism), finally learned an important lesson just in time: a belief in spiritual matters and a humble respect for the book.

During the daytime in the clock factory and in the evenings in his library at home, he gained his first inkling of the invisible soul that was present within every true work of literature. In October 1895, when the eighteen-year-old Hermann Hesse finally decided to give an apprenticeship to a bookseller another try, this had a lot to do with a new, far more intimate relationship with books than he had had two years before in Esslingen.

3

AWAKENING OF INDIVIDUALITY

Among the Book Stacks in Tübingen

Now I'm in Tübingen, though not as a student or the inmate
of an insane asylum, but working in Heckenhauer's bookshop.

—Hesse, Letter to Ernst Kapff, November 6, 1895

Hesse's dreams took him far away from Calw. Brazil might be the place to make a new start. In any event, he had to find somewhere far from Calw to make his home, as far away as possible, farther than the eye could see from the towers in the town—the towers where Perrot's public clocks measured out the lazy passage of time in this provincial backwater of Swabia.

Brazil was always on his mind, he wrote on October 1, 1895, to Dr. Ernst Kapff. Kapff had been one of his teachers at the high school in Cannstatt. As a sideline, he also wrote novels, though they were not successful. Hesse now began a friendly correspondence with him: "I am now determined to leave Germany and Europe as soon as I can."[1]

His father had other plans, however. Hermann needed a career, and because he did not after all want to become a mechanic and was also incapable of academic study, all that remained was a compromise: making another attempt at being apprenticed to a bookseller.

Just two days after Hesse made his great declaration about going to Brazil, on October 3, 1895, the following advertisement appeared in the midday edition of the local newspaper, *Der Schwäbische Merkur* (The Swabian Mercury): "Young man with a Latin education seeks an apprenticeship in a bookshop. Offers should be sent under 'A.H.' via the paper's Situations

Hermann Hesse in 1895, age 18

Vacant page."[2] Ultimately, the offers that arrived in response to Johannes Hesse's advertisement did not furnish Hermann with much to choose from. But one bookshop had at least replied with an offer to take on the young man—whose citing of a Latin education clearly marked him out as a flunked high-school student—as an apprentice. The establishment in question was Heckenhauer's Antiquarian Bookshop, located, of all places, in the city where the failed Maulbronn student was now fated not to become a seminarian after all: Tübingen. Many of his former fellow-pupils were now studying there. His apprenticeship contract was duly issued, and his parents met the cost of his food and lodging for the next three years. A cheap room was found, a little way outside the old town at Number 28 Herrenbergstrasse, lodging with the widow of Dean Leopold—"an austere, bleak ground-floor room in a bleak, ugly house on a charmless street."[3] He would scarcely have come here to do anything other than sleep, we may imagine, given that he spent twelve hours of every day at the bookshop. And yet it was in this room that Hermann Hesse's real education took place. He consulted books with an almost insatiable hunger for reading. Where would his path in life lead him? Of course, he wanted to become a writer, and nothing else. But for years to come, he was set to be an apprentice, from whom people would expect delivery notes, written in neat calligraphy, rather than poems. Paradoxically, this outward distance from his ideal in life would actually bring him inwardly closer to it. For he suddenly felt, in a hitherto unknown surge of existential seriousness, that he would have to prove to the world that he could do more than deliver books for customers: he was capable of writing some himself! Despite suffering from fatigue and constant headaches, he began studying the history of the world, literature, and art. He wrote his first serious poems and prose pieces at this time, in the evenings after finishing work at eight o'clock or on Sundays (Saturday was a working day at the bookshop).

And so the bird began to break its way out of the eggshell. To put it another way: Hesse started to swim. Water often symbolized destruction in his work. In most cases, the motif is introduced only in order for someone to then drown in it. Here, though, despite the danger: "Swimming in the new and the very latest literature, indeed letting myself be swamped by it, was for me in the first instance a pleasure that verged on the delirious."[4]

Hesse wanted to prove that he was a writer—to the world, but first of all to himself. The welter of intellectual impressions from his reading almost overwhelmed him, but he managed to stay afloat and swim.

In a brief sketch of June 1, 1898, he described the interior of his room on Herrenbergstrasse, and added the note: "Written with a headache and in a state of boredom, and out of my inability to do anything else at present." Here we already encounter someone who was capable of conveying the particular character of a space in just a few precisely turned phrases and who, through his arrangement of his personal effects within that space, made it his own.

All the deities whom he would follow throughout his life were already present: on the writing desk was a "small, yellowish bust of Goethe." There were also some losses to report, even at this early stage: "A few houseplants in pots are no longer there, because my methods of looking after them and keeping them alive were inappropriate or deficient." In any case, of greater importance to him were the pictures on the walls: reproductions of Arnold Böcklin's *Villa by the Sea* and *Isle of the Dead,* portraits of Nietzsche and Chopin (two pictures of the composer, in fact), and also, astonishingly, a picture of the naturalist dramatist Gerhart Hauptmann—despite the fact that Hesse liked to claim of himself he had absolutely no feel for

Heckenhauer's bookshop in Tübingen

the theater. Mozart was an essential presence too, and here he found himself in the company of Beethoven, Schumann, and Weber. There was also a bust of Hermes; this unreliable messenger of the gods was to become for Hesse the archetype of all writers.

Somehow he must then have sensed, however, that it might seem all too self-indulgent to list this selection of guardian spirits in their entirety; accordingly, he ironically summed up the general atmosphere of the room as having an "overall effect that was artistically Baroque." And yet in this description of a room, that special sense of urgency that characterizes all of Hesse's texts is already palpable. His work is always about the totality of things, even when it was a question of describing the way a furnished room was arranged, especially a room that he found bleak. But through his use of language, he was already able here to tease out the life that was hidden within objects. A little world of its own! He addressed these objects and they responded. Therein lay the secret of his apparently simple method of naming things: "The iron stove still grins with desire to be used every so often in June. Today it's not in use, however. But hour by hour, a water glass, an ashtray, cigarette butts and the 'Shorter Meyer's Encyclopedia' keep coalescing into new, surprising groups of a most pleasing effect, supported by a ruler, a piece of billiard chalk, a rubber pot, a pair of scissors, book jackets, bookmarks, cutlery, a clock stand, and various other manifestations of domesticity."[5]

Hesse's father—dyed-in-the-wool Pietist as he was—gave him Ten Commandments to take to Tübingen; in the main, these enjoined him to moderate his expenditure. Pens, writing paper, and clothes would be sent from Calw, he told Hermann, since that would work out cheaper. Most importantly: "On no account should you run up any debts. I refuse to pay any bills for things which have been bought without my prior approval." He also reminded his son that he should not take any book from the bookseller's without asking his employer's permission beforehand. Johannes Hesse's Seventh Commandment read: "Keep your smoking to a minimum, because it reduces your appetite, excites your nerves, and costs money."[6] Playing cards for money was, according to the Eighth Commandment, completely forbidden; his father even provided him with the reason his son was to give in refusing any such invitation to gamble: "I have no money to lose and I don't wish to profit from gambling."

Notwithstanding all the instructions on how to behave, which Hermann continued to receive from his family in abundance during his time in Tübingen, he was finally independent of his parents here—no longer under their supervision in everything he did, and able to put himself at one remove from their well-meaning warnings, whose Pietist militancy he found intolerable. At last, the eighteen-year-old could decide for himself what activities he wanted to pursue, whose company he wished to keep, and whom to avoid.

Yet for all his rebelliousness, the bond with his parents remained close for the time being. His apprenticeship commenced on October 17, 1895, and a day later the Hesses in Calw received their first report from Tübingen. Hermann wrote them that he liked the town: "Narrow streets and nooks and crannies, Romantic in a medieval way, full of sights like little scenes from the works of Jean Paul, but also somewhat misty and dirty."[7]

The tasks assigned to the bookshop apprentices included counting out the previous day's takings every morning, recording all the books that came in, and making sure the stock was complete: "The shop is very large; the main subject areas are Theology, along with Law and Philology, and to a lesser extent also Medicine, etc. Art works and sheet music are less important. The students have their own accounts, including some unpaid bills whose owners have done a bunk."[8] The bookshop also had its own bindery, since many people liked to have the books they had just acquired rebound to their own taste—a nice if expensive way of making a book one's own. During his lifetime, Hesse himself would get several of the books that had found a lasting place in his library rebound.

What kind of people spent their lives holed up in Aladdin's caves of books like Heckenhauer's? Hesse was curious to know. It was easy to turn into an eccentric in such places. He encountered characters like those from the pages of E. T. A. Hoffmann: oddballs who spent their days poring over dusty tomes and who used all manner of magical formulae to practice pedantic bookkeeping. One of these was Hesse's boss, the bookshop proprietor: "Herr Sonnewald works in a heated office dressed in a hat and coat; he usually takes the coat off when he goes out. Instead of speaking normally he whispers. I have boundless respect for him."[9]

The bookshop made great efforts to woo students as customers, and Hesse too embarked on his personal course of study for one or two hours late every evening when he came home from work. Alongside literature, he found himself developing an ever greater interest in art history. He devoted himself to his study more diligently than many a Tübingen student, for he was driven by his inferiority complex and the feeling that he had a lot of catching-up to do where his education was concerned. His stepbrother Karl Isenberg got news of this undertaking from Hermann on December 10, 1895: "I am getting close to comprehending all the innermost ramifications and details and still hope that I might, as far as I am able, reach my goal of really understanding the nature and history of European literature."[10]

Hesse's daily work routine was arduous. He suffered constantly from pain in his eyes and headaches. In the evenings, he did not feel the slightest inclination to indulge in the kind of frivolous entertainments with which the town's students amused themselves. He had become a calmer person, dependent now upon a different yardstick for living. He found this change unsettling: "I don't think about big things much anymore, my brilliant period has passed and I am starting to turn into a philistine; I have even become respectable, inasmuch as I don't frequent taverns anymore and spend the few hours' free time that I have surveying the little garden of my esthetic ideals, which has grown so narrow, and here and there still creating something to get excited about."[11]

For the first time in life he now sensed that he would need a great deal of patience and application if he was to wrest something special, something of his own, from the days that were beginning to pass by devoted entirely to work. On December 8, 1895, his parents received a letter for Advent from Hermann, in which he fought valiantly to suppress his mounting feeling of despair: "Otherwise I only notice that it is December from the mountain of work that has piled up, since the joyous Christmas period is purgatory for the booksellers. . . . I am not in a festive mood at all, because I have a cold and a swelling under my right arm, which is really painful with all the moving around I have to do in the shop and the warehouse." Even so, the news he conveyed to Calw was half-optimistic: "I am being treated decently, though I sometimes have boring work sent my way that no one else wanted to do."[12]

The Autodidact: Writing beyond the Influence of Pietism

My spirit is restless and yearns to be free. It hovers watchfully and keen-eyed over my life like a nocturnal bird.

—Hermann Hesse (1897)

Finding the right circle of friends was difficult for a bookshop apprentice in such a snooty university town as Tübingen. Hesse the autodidact subjected himself to a more rigorous study regime than most of his arrogant customers who were his age. They looked down on him standing behind the bookshop counter as if it was the most natural thing in the world to do. This made him an outsider here, too, since he didn't have much in common with the other bookshop employees either. Where was he to turn? He was by now more distant than ever from his parents in Calw. He wanted to liberate himself from any family obligations, and to be allowed to have his own cares and think his own thoughts. However, this was totally out of the question with his parents, who were completely intolerant toward anything that deviated from their own norms of existence. Hermann Hesse sensed that he would have to make friends with loneliness; he could not afford to succumb to the yearning for security within the family—which of course still went hand-in-hand with indoctrination. And so he wrote his parents on March 29, 1896, that he would not be coming to Calw for Easter, but would perhaps come for Whitsun. He said he would be sorry to miss the crocuses blooming, but told them: "I am very sparing with my time and a terrible egotist, and I positively dread traveling."[13]

He knew that the feeling of loneliness, which he now had often, did not make him appear exactly attractive. Even among the most worthy of his old school friends who were now studying in Tübingen, he was regarded as a small-minded pedant in the making.

He cannot have excited any particular interest from anyone at this stage; it was a vicious circle: "Admittedly my isolation, which was partly of my own making, has made me brittle and temperamental in many respects, though I constantly fight against it."[14]

Yet this humiliation spurred on his ambition. Now he studied with an intensity never seen before in his life. And all that after long, grinding twelve-hour shifts at the bookshop, when he was so tired he could hardly stay on his feet. His eyes hurt, he had thumping headaches, and on top of all that the lump under his arm refused to go away. Not that any of that really mattered to him, though. What was important was that he should be something more than just a trainee in a Tübingen bookshop. That was his sole concern, and to that end he devoured book after book. His favorite pastime was immersing himself in Goethe's *Wilhelm Meister's Apprenticeship.* With its central character's peregrinations and its magical transformations, this work was to become the model for his later writings.

He knew that, in order to make friends with students, he must be more than a simple apprentice who hadn't managed to get into university. He had to be a writer! But equally, the students had to be more to him than just students, for he was also quite particular about the company he kept. And, as he was later to recall in a letter to Alfons Paquet on March 20, 1903, even as a bookshop apprentice he had a deep aversion to the conceit of university students; he broached this subject after self-confidently stating his position on the topic of how a person becomes the way they are: "I found the whole university setup ridiculous and think it's a shame that so many of the young generation regard study as the only decent and correct career choice open to them. . . . The company of students, professors, musicians, actors, and literati has always been anathema to me, whereas I am fond of visual artists, especially painters, and so tend to socialize almost exclusively with such people." The same letter also reveals much about Hesse's personality traits, which throughout his life would make him an outsider who was afraid of other people. In the estimation of others, he was, he said: "very incompetent, I must confess, for while I regard myself as pretty free of any kind of prejudice in intellectual matters, in my practical dealings with people I am the oddest of oddballs and I go out of my way to give a wide berth to any kind of social intercourse that I do not absolutely have to engage in. I have a complete dread of anything that looks like it might have the capacity to commit or constrain me—be it societies, associations, family visits, or friendships."[15]

Alongside Chopin, Goethe, and Nietzsche, there were three other role models who impressed him at this time: Jens Peter Jacobsen, Gabriele D'Annunzio, and Maurice Maeterlinck. He wrote about these figures in the collection *Plauderabende* (Evenings of conversation), which he wrote to mark his mother's fifty-fifth birthday in 1897. Once again, the first thing he does here is to evoke the kind of atmosphere appropriate to the treatment of intellectual matters. He describes the sensory counterpart to each idea, in order that those ideas might not dissipate into theory but instead give rise to an esthetic form in which the intellect can appear as far more directly relevant to real life. At this stage he still could not shrug off thoughts of Calw and the family. He knew that he had to free himself from the idea that the family was the primary yardstick for his life, but this was a difficult task for him, and one that he never fully achieved. Hence his constant propensity for immersing himself in childlike worlds in his writing. Having never experienced much love or tender devotion from his parents, but for all that a great willingness to make sacrifices and strict attentiveness, he found that his feelings were extremely conflicted. His parents and his siblings were thus closest to him when the spatial distance between them was at its greatest. Because he had chosen the pantheist Goethe as his god, his relatives in Calw were treated to the following missive, which sounds both presumptuous and helpless at one and the same time: "Goethe says of Lavater that he wrote about the journey they took together incessantly and almost on a daily basis to his loved ones, just in order to tell them every day that he still loved them. If you want to try and divine this from my lectures on Goethe and Homer, it isn't there—it's between the lines, and it's the most important thing between the lines, too."[16]

Though he was so "sparing with his time" and thought he had so many things to catch up on, on which his contemporaries already had a head start, apparent inconsequentialities began to take on greater importance—lighting questions, spatial geometry, and the kinds of surfaces in his room: "My lamp has a red, tired glow about it. Here and there on the walls a harshly lit profile stands out from the picture frames, or a single, strident color. In the corners and right up to my feet kneel saturated, black, fatigued shadows."[17]

Here then, so to speak, Hesse was preparing the canvas for the color he was about to add. During his time in Tübingen, there are also already signs of Hesse the neurotic, who reacts to every disturbance and every noise with nothing less than sheer panic. For a while the room above him was occupied by a noisy lodger who tramped across the floor in his boots while declaiming loudly in Arabic. This too prefigures a scene in his later work—namely, the episode with the Dutchman in his autobiographical novel *A Guest at the Spa* (1925).

All things considered, his relationship with Tübingen remained ambivalent. On the one hand, with its famous Lutheran seminary and its association with Hölderlin and the Romantics, the town exerted a strong intellectual allure—but on the other hand, it was rather conservative and monotonous there. Hesse complained in a letter of February 1897: "I sometimes find Tübingen too cramped and my whole life here squeezes me like a coat that's become too tight for me but that I keep wearing out of thrift. I yearn for people, life and abundance, and for a country and a society where I could really let loose and give my all."[18] But that was exactly what he didn't find in Tübingen. Hesse remained isolated, and where friendly conversation was concerned had only his books, which he now fell upon with enormous intensity. He expected them to first heighten his longing for another life and then to assuage it. Was this asking too much, though?

Above all, Jacobsen's *Niels Lyhne* was a book that, by Hesse's own account, he knew almost by heart. Jacobsen's name was on everyone's lips at this time. Rilke had been a great fan of his work, and now Hesse followed suit. He called it a "miracle of a book" that seemed to have been written by someone who had just awakened from a dream. "I do not know if there is another book where the magical power of the unspoken and of the mood is so vividly alive and where so few words convey so much beauty, perfume, and sun."[19] Does that sound like a note written by someone who had only just turned twenty? During this period in Tübingen, Hesse undoubtedly matured into a reader with a real sense of humility and admiration for the written word, and also began to express his own thoughts differently.

It no doubt still pained him greatly that his mother steadfastly refused to accord him any recognition. His father was a far less passionate individual, who led the quiet life of a scholar specializing in the history of missionary work. But his mother, who harbored urgent aspirations of her own and wrote poetry and who came across as far more impetuous than his father—surely she should be able to understand him! But no, she refused to give him any encouragement, and shunned his writing (which he had hoped would win her love) as sinful.

Consequently, an unbridgeable rift opened up between them; nevertheless, his sense of vocation remained strong. With a great deal of pain, but nonetheless without the slightest hesitation, he would subsequently sacrifice his mother to his mission in life.

Much later, on July 4, 1920, Hesse wrote to his sister Marulla about this scar that never healed: "What a truly magnificent person she was! It is a shame what happened between us—for me, one of the most depressing and hurtful experiences of my youth was to receive a letter from her in which she responded to my very first attempts at poetry with prudishness and by giving me a sermon. She ought to have read my 'Klein and Wagner' and realized that her moralizing tone back then was one of the things that impelled me on my way as a writer!"[20]

For his parents, the sole definition of love was something that pointed the way to God, while sin was synonymous with taking pleasure in the world. This attitude was enough to make Hesse despair; for him, nothing could have been more important than being acknowledged by his mother as a writer.

But there were verses in the *Plauderabende* that were guaranteed to displease his mother in her restrictive Pietist corset of faith. One of the poems, entitled "What I Love," began:

I love silent women
With narrow, regal hands
Which, caressing my hot temples,
Ward off all my dream specters.

Whereas, at the beginning of his time in Tübingen, his letters to Calw were still packed with everyday descriptions, and the literary vignettes of a young man who aspired to write more than just letters and who was proud of every step he took toward independence, the relationship began to cool insofar as he received either no responses or downright negative ones to his embryonic sallies into authorship. In addition, he felt increasingly bothered by the family's habit of always putting up coreligionists and even going to visit them in their homes. This was an integral part of the communitarian way in which Pietists lived—but even in Calw Hermann had hated the constant comings and goings of visitors from all parts of the globe. He was also adamant that the family should now finally refrain from sending emissaries to Tübingen to check up on him and to proselytize to him. It was in this vein that he wrote a very determined-sounding letter to Calw on November 10, 1897: "I would be grateful if you would desist, because I have a fear of making new acquaintances, especially with aspiring pastors or entire families. Our family's way of socializing is a torment for me, plus to my great regret I have already been marked down here as too much of an oaf."[21]

Original Location for *A Guest at the Spa:* The Palmenwald

On May 29, 1896, Hermann Hesse wrote his parents from Tübingen: "On Sunday I was in Freudenstadt; I liked it there and feel something resembling homesickness for sun and freedom. The 'Palmenwald' seemed such a friendly place to me, and I'm still trying hard to erase this pleasant impression from my thoughts, since one is required to be down-to-earth and industrious here."[22]

The Palmenwald spa hotel had just opened the year before—and before long Hesse's parents would become regular guests there. What, though, were Pietists doing in a spa hotel? In Bad Boll, Blumhardt had been the proprietor of an institution that was a cross between a sanatorium and a Moravian Christian revivalist meeting place. In Freudenstadt, the Palmenwald was run in cooperation with the Basel Mission. Accordingly, the

Palmenwald also played host to "missionary courses," which Johannes Hesse attended. Because they were "among brothers and sisters," even Hesse's devout parents (who abhorred mere idleness) found themselves able to stay here. A rest cure at a spa as an act of worship!

The nineteen-year-old Hermann Hesse broached this motif in a letter that took him several days to compose—from September 13 to September 19, 1896—which prompted Marie Hesse to pass it on to Hesse's sister Marulla with the remark: "Here's an extraordinary letter from Hermann."[23] Extraordinary? It was certainly a great sense of liberation for him to feel that he, who had worn himself out inwardly resisting the god of the Pietists, was not intrinsically a godless person. Anyone who writes poems and loves nature cannot be godless, and was also a religious person!

In the Palmenwald—even in discussions with the many theologians who stayed here, which of necessity were more broad-minded than talks with his parents—he discovered that pantheism was the form of religiosity that best suited him. So it was that his astonished parents—albeit without much understanding, as the reaction of his mother demonstrated—came to read such statements as "My recollections of Freudenstadt keep coming back to me; I became a 'seeker after God' there." A seeker after God is the antithesis of a person who believes he already has his God and who knows from the outset where any search will lead him and where it will not, as became apparent from the next sentence of Hermann's letter:

> Time and again I encounter the Sunday God of churchgoing Christians and notice that he doesn't offer much help on weekdays. There are undoubtedly many Christians like that among our own acquaintances. I must confess that my own ideals in life, my poetry, even my little Goethe cult are better and more faithful deities than that Sunday God. They stand by me, even when things look dismal and hopeless, but there's the rub— they suffer and complain alongside me, but they are too much my own creations to have the strength they would require to pull me up and rescue me.

Hesse's gods are thus weak gods, almost as weak as him. Salvation was not to be expected from them—so what was he to do? "I am searching the heavens again for the stars that represent my previous ideals, and will endeavor once more through poetic pantheism to discover the secret to peace and health."[24]

At this stage he was already the wanderer, a figure who would always for Hesse have a close affinity with the "cherubinic wanderer" of the German Baroque mystic poet Angelus Silesius. Hesse expressed his feeling of likewise being a seeker after truth in the following terms:

> I haven't found a God yet, but I am grateful that I have at least found some revelation. You may well regard my intellectual world as nothing but a little kindergarten, but as I haven't found anything better, I intend to remain faithful to this world of beauty whose ultimate limits are hidden from our gaze. I realize that everything, even the highest achievements of our poets, are mere patchwork, and there are times when our whole canon of literature strikes me as truly puny and impoverished; by contrast, the term "the world of poetry" that I use is meant to denote something far greater—a world for which all existing works of literature, including even the *Iliad, Hamlet,* and *Faust,* are nothing but a poorly furnished anteroom.[25]

Hesse's poetic religiosity is a form of mysticism. This is similar to Pietism in certain respects, especially in the magical properties it ascribes to the Word, but in its basic pantheistic nature it has none of the asceticism associated with Pietism. It has no desire to renounce the world, and so does not condemn sensual things as sinful but instead affirms them every bit as wholeheartedly as it does the spirit. God, Hermann Hesse now knew, was to be found only in the world and not in any renunciation of it. Accordingly, he saw himself as a seeker after God who appears in the guise of a wayfarer.

Hesse did not require any theological legitimation for idleness; he was happy to come to Freudenstadt in order to rest and recuperate from the twelve-hour days at Heckenhauer's in Tübingen, especially since his parents were footing the bill. He had also enjoyed his time with Blumhardt in Bad Boll—Hesse was born to be a spa patient, though during later stays in sanatoria he would forego such dramatic escalations as the purchase of a pistol and the threat to shoot himself with it.

Thus, even as a young sanatorium patient, he became an observer of the bizarre aspects of a place where people came for psychological rest cures—or a *Psychologia Balnearia,* as he would entitle his reminiscences of this period (subtitle: "Glosses of a Spa Guest in Baden"), which appeared

in 1924. Sanatoria were very much part of the Zeitgeist then, as epitomized by Thomas Mann's novel *The Magic Mountain (Der Zauberberg)*—
as people became unsure to what extent they ought to keep their distance from a world that was growing ever louder and more hectic yet still
make efforts to maintain their status within that world. This atmosphere
gave rise to the hysterias that manifested themselves during rest cures, and
that are described in the works of Thomas Mann and Hermann Hesse—
and these hysterias were never personal in nature but instead inherent
within an entire era.

The Palmenwald spa hotel also regarded itself as a hideaway, a place
where people could take refuge from the increasing "nervousness" of the
world. The first manager of the sanatorium here was a man named David
Huppenbacher, who had previously been a missionary in Africa. He was
a strict warden of the hotel and ran this large establishment in the manner
of a mission house; this pleased the first generation of spa guests (which
included Marie and Johannes Hesse), but after the First World War it began
to seem like a relic from a bygone age. As a business model in the new
American leisure culture that was then developing, it now fell woefully
short.

In the 1890s, though, it was still quite normal for the manager, who at
the same time was the spiritual head of the establishment, to come into the
hotel parlor at ten o'clock in the evening and announce: "Time to go to
bed now, ladies and gentlemen—I wish you all a good night." And the
guests would indeed dutifully slink off to their rooms, while Huppenbacher
turned the lights off behind them.

A quarter of a century later, guests at the Palmenwald inhabited a completely different world. Right from the start, the building looked like one
of those grand hotels that existed everywhere during this period. It was
technologically advanced and lit by electricity; the only economy made
was in the number of bathrooms, with only one apiece on the first and the
second floors. That accorded with the spirit of the age, which did not put
much of a premium on wellness and which, as an entry in the *Architects'
Handbook* of 1885 indicates, deemed one bathroom perfectly adequate to
serve 40 to 50 beds. Thus, the Palmenwald, with its two bathrooms to
120 beds, was well within the bounds of what was customary.

The founder and managing director of the Palmenwald, Paul Lechler,
was a typical representative of Pietism. He was a conservative patriarch
and a social reformer rolled into one. In this he was similar to Count Finck-

enstein from Trossin in Saxony and his circle, of which Gottfried Benn's father, Gustav, was also a member.

In such circles, the question of health took on a spiritual dimension, on both a personal and a universal level. At the end of the 1870s the Pietists identified the emergent German Empire and the dawning Wilhelmine period as being in a state of crisis. According to them the system was sick and it was making people sick. Or, as Lechler trenchantly formulated it: "The upper echelons of society are proving to be too shortsighted, while the property-owning classes are too selfish."[26]

How, then, was social—and with it spiritual—peace to be restored in the country? What was to become of the labor unions and the Social Democrats? In any event, the Pietists regarded Bismarck's draconian antisocialist laws as the wrong response to the pressing question of an equitable distribution of wealth. Could capitalism be regulated at all? These were the burning topics of the age, and they were also discussed in Pietist circles—particularly with an eye to the mission areas of Africa and Asia, which were also the scene of clashes between competing colonial interests. Ultimately the question of morality kept rearing its head in all these realms. Could there be a "happy medium" between self-interest and the common good?

"Rest cures" at the Palmenwald consisted primarily of peace and quiet, fresh air, prayer, intellectual discussion, shared mealtimes, and communal recreational activities. At this time, this was the general tenor of spa hotels, which acted like hybrids between sanatoria and grand hotels. Medical treatments did not play a central role, but were generally only peripheral to people's stays at health spas, which could last for months. The typical spa guest was an idler with the alibi of a weakened constitution; the actual clinical diagnosis largely remained extremely nebulous ("nervous debility"). It could be deemed an attempt to ward off modern life—albeit through employing a number of its methods, such as the railroad to ensure a comfortable trip to and from the sanatorium.

Lechler, the founder of the Palmenwald, was an entrepreneur through and through, and was loath to give any money away. He built the hotel as a commercial undertaking. To finance the venture, he established a limited company and promised a 4 percent return on investments. With considerable diplomacy, he managed to assemble enough shareholders to make it viable.

His concern was to run the institution as a solid business venture and not merely with an eye to the dividends. Entrepreneurs at this time were people who genuinely desired to create something new—the antithesis of the kind of stock-market speculator who has largely supplanted the true entrepreneur nowadays.

The ideal behind the Palmenwald was strongly reminiscent of the thoughts of Jean-Jacques Rousseau: simple living, albeit here in comfortable surroundings, but without any form of superficial luxury. Being close to nature meant being close to God—something Hermann Hesse found very congenial during his stay here. Hesse's love of nature had a strong element of piety about it, which revered the divine aspect of the natural world. He learned the magic of words from rocks, plants, clouds, and butterflies and saw as something truly magical the force that held nature in a constant cycle of growth, decay, and new efflorescence. This also conditioned his conception of reading and writing. There is always concealed in these activities, Hesse believed, something that repays attentive listening, something that binds God and man together in a new unity in which they become—in brief moments of transformation—two names for the same entity. This formed the basis of Hermann Hesse's deep-seated mysticism; although this had its origins in Pietism, it nevertheless surpasses it in several key aspects (notably its conception of nature!). As a result, the symbols of his life, which at the same time are also those of his work (the wanderer, the Steppenwolf, the glass-bead player) achieve a new synthesis of sickness and health, life and death, origin and decay. "Crisis" thus becomes a key word for all these metamorphoses—and the first signs of this can be found here in the Palmenwald. By contrast, the poem that he writes in the hotel's guestbook in May 1896 appears remarkably artless and innocent—simple goodwill in rhyming form. It begins:

> I love these somber fir trees,
> When the young summer spins it web in them.

Into this conventional rhyme there then steps a herd of startled roe deer racing past, wide-eyed like shy children, and the poetic persona's breast swells and his gaze broadens and his heart beats wildly and so on. Only at the end does the lyrical voice, conversant with Hesse's struggle with his family over God, pause for reflection:

> As on life's twisting paths we stray,
> O God of love, stretch out thy hand,

And lead us firmly, this we pray,
Homeward to a peaceful land!

The eighteen-year-old Hermann Hesse can only still speak of God with
the epithet "God of love." The God of his parents was a different deity, a
stern presence judging what was Good and Evil.

In order to survive the changing times, over the coming decades the Palmenwald spa hotel repeatedly sloughed its skin and emerged in a fresh
guise. Many things were abandoned in the process—first to go was the
tradition of long refectory tables for communal meals, then the courses in
cookery and sewing, and the group prayers in the hotel's own specially
built chapel. During the two world wars, it became respectively a hospital
and a home for refugees. After housing various military administrative divisions, it reverted to being a hotel. At the start of the twenty-first century
one could sit in the same dining room and eat with antique silver cutlery
and take a strangely moving tour through the many beautiful wood-paneled
lounges, which in the interim had become storerooms, now that there are
no longer any communal evening entertainments like in the hotel's early
days. In the 1920s, baths were finally installed in almost all of the rooms,
followed later by a swimming pool and sauna in the basement. The hotel
finally closed a few years ago. Thus ended a tradition that had been stoutly
defended for over 110 years.

Hesse's First Female Admirer, Helene Voigt, and a Consistent Non-Admirer, Marie Hesse

Wandering, and giving, on the trail of happiness
And constantly ailing from as-yet unborn songs

—Hermann Hesse, "On Being a Poet" (1896)

For Christmas 1896, Hermann Hesse sent his mother a collection of poems
under the title *Lieder vom Leben* (Songs of life). Its dedication ran as follows:

Und dennoch will es mich betrüben,
Dir stumm und fremd vorbeizugehn;
Ich will dir nah sein, will dich lieben,
Und will, du sollst mich ganz verstehn.

[Yet it would grieve me
To pass you by silent and unheeding;
I want to be near you, want to love you,
And want you to understand me completely.]

A very frank avowal, in which the son asks—no, rather begs—for his mother's love. He yearns for her to take him as he is and not how, in her eyes, he should first become in order to be worthy of her love. In the Hesse household, the love of one's nearest and dearest always took a detour through God. To them, it was imperative to lead a godly life. This was the love of missionaries—a means to an end.

Among the poems in the collection there is one entitled "Ein Dichter Sein" ("On Being a Poet"). Without a doubt this was a personal credo, but equally it was a deliberate provocation to the closed worldview of his parents:

Ein Dichter sein, das heißt mit kranker Brust
In jedem Glück, in jeder kleinsten Lust
Den eig'nen Idealen zu entsagen,
Die Schönheit lieben und sie leiden seh'n,
Und schwer am Zwiespalt seines Lebens tragen

[Being a poet, that means with a sick heart
Renouncing one's own ideals
In every happiness and every delight, however small,
And loving beauty and watching it suffer
And wearing the dichotomy of one's own life heavily.]

The Vienna-based journal *Deutsches Dichterheim*, to which Hesse offered his work, told him it planned to publish a poem of his on Chopin. He had every reason to be proud of himself. Thinking that this might also please his parents, he wrote a letter to Calw on September 10, 1897, telling them about his success. His parents replied on September 21. Their letter began with news of all the foreign visitors who had been staying with them lately, "mostly missionaries." There then followed a brief postscript from his father, which began by expanding on his mother's domestic news before concluding: "I too send you warmest thanks for your letter, and for the copy of *Deutsches Dichterheim* that you sent under separate cover, though I must say it contained nothing I am capable of appreciating."[27]

This callous snub epitomized everything that was wrong with the Hesse parents' relationship with their son. Masquerading as strict adherence to his religious convictions, the emotional coldness of his father's reply revealed a complete lack of sensitivity. His parents found it impossible to see their son Hermann's urge to express his feelings as anything more than evidence that he was ensnared in sinfulness and defiant rebellion against God's commandments. The rebuff was a shock to the literary debutant Hermann, who was eagerly anticipating his parents' response; although he had already had to contend with other instances of their emotional crudeness, he was still loath to sever entirely the ties that bound him to them.

It is unsurprising to learn that Hesse now commenced a series of violent rearguard actions—he was no longer his parents' offspring, he was the writer Hermann Hesse. He now knew that if he was to plow his own furrow, his parents could no longer be allowed to be a yardstick for him. His letters became rarer and briefer, his visits less frequent, and he stayed away entirely from larger family gatherings. He no longer had any desire to subjugate himself to the narrow little world of Calw, with its humdrum everyday dramas that did not concern him. He found this disengagement difficult, however, and over the following years he would try time and again to please his parents, albeit only in his new role as a writer.

Hesse's parents were not conscious of any guilt in reacting according to the precepts of their faith to what they saw as the wrong course taken by their son. As for Hesse himself, he was still torn this way and that between revolt and attempts to persuade them. Accordingly, he wrote to Calw to tell them that he had drafted "a few little essays" to mark his mother's birthday—as a substitute for his recent lack of correspondence, so to speak—but that he was now unsure whether these would be well received as a gift.

The answer he received was another cool one. On October 3, 1897, his mother replied to reassure him that his father had been referring in his postscript "more in general terms to that edition of the *Dichterheim* rather than to your poems in particular." That didn't sound much better, in truth. She went on to say that he should go ahead and send what he'd written for her. Fair enough—but then came the thoroughly nasty addendum: "Yet one doesn't need to have so much material *put into print,* I admit. Then

Hesse as a bookseller's apprentice in Tübingen, 1898

again, in an age when so much wicked rubbish makes it into print, ultimately something mediocre cannot do any harm."[28]

This already hints at a major rift between Hesse and his parents. What appeared to Marie and Johannes as an irrelevant aberration that should be corrected as energetically as possible was for Hermann the very core of his life as a writer. His recently awakened poetic self-awareness was duty-bound to protect him against such authoritarian presumption if it was not to be immediately snuffed out once more. And Hermann Hesse had become sufficiently aggressive and self-confident to take up the fight, as his mother noted with displeasure: "You judge devout verse very harshly." And it was certainly true that the much-dishonored son had flung down a savage challenge to her:

May God help art if even the Swiss have started to discover popular lady poets! This sector is really thriving at the moment. And religious verse, what's more! That's the most awkward and generally dreariest type of poetry I know. The more poetic a piece, the less devout it is—and vice versa! But the Moravians have already milked this genre for all it was worth.

I'm sorry, but from the word go, religious, and especially non-church-based, Protestant, Pietist verse is something truly tragicomic—and this insight need not in the slightest stand in contradiction to the gems written by Gerhardt and Claudius.[29]

In this letter Hesse already shows clear signs of having a considerable talent for polemics. Yet the missionary parents, whose faith was as solid as a rock, were unperturbed by his attack. With friendly smiles, but doggedly sticking to promoting their own message to the exclusion of all else, they continued to importune him. The next disappointments for Hermann Hesse's sense of a literary calling were therefore already preprogrammed. But with each successive snub, he grew colder and colder. The family in Calw, he became convinced, was not the public for whom he was writing!

Instead, he received his first letter from a reader—almost a love letter. The sender was one Helene Voigt, and young woman from the north of Germany who had grown up as the daughter of a country estate owner. She wrote too, predominantly about life in the countryside. When horses whinnied outside—as they do in "Grand Valse," Hesse's poem on Chopin—she appeared not at all surprised; after all, that was part of her everyday life. Helene Voigt inquired at the magazine *Deutsches Dichterheim* in Vienna after the poet's address and subsequently wrote to him on November 22, 1897: "What is it I wanted to say to you, you may ask. Ah, what can one say when someone, with just a few words, has struck a chord in us that keeps resonating for a long, long time after? Thereafter, one cannot help but turn one's head and harken to the deep, mysterious sound. This voice is too fine for anyone to grasp it with their hands and inquire after its nature and where it comes from." Hesse was enchanted; this was exactly the kind of encouragement his downtrodden bookshop apprentice's spirit so urgently needed. And the passage about "harkening to the deep mysterious sound" especially pleased him, so much so that he named his "Hermann Lauscher" after it.[30] He sent a reply to his young admirer on November 27, making great play of his persona as a writer in the process. As a precaution, he suppressed the fact that he was an apprentice in a bookshop, preferring to talk in vague terms about his "exhausting profession," which left him little time to turn his mind to greater things. The letter that Hesse sent to Helene Voigt—who was two years older than him and who clearly had no inkling of what a young stripling it was who was making his horse whinny outside her door—began thus:

> My dear young lady, please accept my heartfelt thanks for your letter! I was sitting with friends, tired from work and weighed down with troubles and

Helene Voigt (1875–1961), seen here in the photograph she sent to Hermann Hesse in 1898

cares. My friend, a dear artist who shall remain nameless, was playing an old, simple gavotte on his fiddle for me. And I was thinking of the few people whom I should really like to count among my listeners and friends, and of better times and songs that have yet to be sung . . . and then your letter was brought to me, and it made me feel instantly at home and did me a power of good.

Here, we observe how Hesse straight away adopts the Romantic pose of the *fin de siècle* artist, with his weary, melancholic demeanor, a role that we never quite believe is anything more than mere posturing. Art here always smacks of craft, and the loneliness on display seems like a trademark: "I am so unused to friendship and friendliness!"[31]

At this stage Hesse still had no idea how important this "dear young lady" would be to his identity as a writer. Was this as his muse, even his "fever-muse"?[32]

Perhaps she was that too, but only at the outset. But later she began to exert a far more practical influence. Initially Hesse was entranced by a woman devoting so much attention to him. It led to his work taking on an erotic dimension, which was more in keeping with his beloved Chopin than the image of a whinnying horse outside the door. Henceforth, Hesse and Helene Voigt would exchange ever more intimate letters.

Hesse's First Book: *Romantic Songs*

> On the far bank of my sick soul
> Lies the land of my homesickness
>
> —Hermann Hesse, "To Beauty," in *Romantische Lieder*

Hesse's three-year period of apprenticeship came to an end on September 30, 1898, whereupon he immediately gained a position as a sales assistant at Heckenhauer's, with a steady income. He sunk his very first paycheck into publishing his *Romantische Lieder (Romantic Songs)*.

On November 28, Hermann Hesse received a postcard from his sister Adele, thanking him—on his mother's behalf—for the copy of his book that he had sent to Calw. He had not given up seeking his parents' acknowledgment. Yet once again he was destined to be disillusioned: "Mama wanted to thank you straight away for your poems, but yesterday we had the Aidlingers and the Marulls over to visit, and everyone left at 4 o'clock, and then there was a church concert. And today we held a sale to raise funds for the mission—we've already made 200 marks—but Mama was exhausted after that and had neither the time nor the energy to write. So, in the meantime, please accept my thanks; I was astonished, though I had expected something of the sort from you."[33]

What Adele meant by "something of the sort" later became clear in the follow-up letter that Hesse's mother naturally could not resist sending her son three days later. The poems, which had been published by the house of E. Pierson in Dresden and Leipzig—a vanity publisher with a moderate reputation—in the fall of 1898, had been reviewed enthusiastically only by Ludwig Finckh and had otherwise been ignored. Even nowadays, it is hard to see them as anything other than very lightweight. The only genuine-sounding thing in this labored doggerel, which deals in clichéd, manufactured images, is Hesse's attitude. And this is avowedly Romantic, an apologia for the island as a place of refuge for the artist. In his very next book, *Eine Stunde hinter Mitternacht (An Hour Behind Midnight)*, Hesse would revisit the theme of the island (for which read "art" in a bourgeois world) in a much more thought-through and disciplined way. There, his dreamlike prose has a surreal dimension of the kind that the Austrian illustrator Alfred Kubin would perfect in the twilight atmosphere of his fantasy novel of 1908 *Die andere Seite (The Other Side)*. Both Hesse's and Kubin's works were very much in the same vein as Francisco Goya's aquatint cycle entitled *The Sleep of Reason Produces Monsters*.

In her letter Marie Hesse reassured her son that she had found "some things to admire" in his slim volume. "You have mastered poetic forms and language very well—though I would have liked to see you treat some more exalted themes in verse." Yet some of the poems really pained her, "because they arouse the suspicion that love is not always chaste and pure." This Pietist neurosis about chastity continued to annoy Hermann Hesse. Even so, all the poems in *Romantic Songs* feel so disembodied and anemic; take, for example, the poem "Königskind" ("Royal Child"):

> And my soul strains mightily
> In ardor and longing, strong and pale,
> And under cover of midnight silently creates for itself
> A moonlit realm of homesickness.

The poems in the collection all basically evoke the poet's own sense of loneliness; contrary to the view of Hesse's mother, there is nothing about them that suggests anything "unchaste." In his constant state of feeling misunderstood, Hesse clearly had the Romantic writer Novalis's "stranger" figure in mind, whom he regarded as a kindred spirit. An outcast like him! Here is someone trying to find his own poetic voice, yet in this instance the attempt fails.

It is not for that reason, though, that his stern mother criticizes him, but instead for even making the attempt in the first place! "God gave you talent, and once you have found him and dedicated this beautiful gift to his service, only then will your old mother be happy for you. In the meantime, I will continue to intercede for my 'royal child,' praying that you acquire a truly kingly profession and gain your rich royal inheritance."[34]

A twenty-one-year-old literary debutant who had just sent his first book to his family—a family where reading and writing were among the main activities—would seldom have been so rudely rebuffed as Hesse was here by his mother.

Nevertheless, on December 2, 1898, Hesse wrote his mother a letter from Tübingen that was remarkably humble in the light of the total lack of respect he had been shown:

> Believe me, mother, your judgment was far more important to me than any professional criticism, and I set great store by your opinion and sensitivity. My heart is not so alien to you that I am incapable of understanding and respecting your motherly reprimands and concerns. You cannot know how much of what you say rings true with me, although I have up to now been unable to embrace it despite my best intentions to do so. When I think back to my bad years—how could there still be any part of me that is not grateful to you and does not submit to your better judgment?[35]

How close was Hesse here to capitulating? Did he merely want to make peace with his parents, who had had so much trouble and strife with him, or did this permanent disrespect on their part unsettle him more than he was prepared to admit? What a piece of good fortune for him, then, that he now had Helene Voigt as a corrective female voice to all this! He could explain his feelings to her, and what's more from the position of a revered writer. The only pity was that in March 1898, Helene had suddenly got engaged to the publisher Eugen Diederichs; they were married in June. At least Hesse had not offered Diederichs his *Romantic Songs*. But Helene Voigt, who had been so instrumental in strengthening his self-confidence, had ended her debate through correspondence with Hesse about art, love, and life in order to devote herself to a man who wanted to possess her. This gave Hesse pause for thought. For in actual fact, the problem with Hermann Hesse was exactly the opposite of what his mother had been criticizing him for. He, like Helene Voigt before she met Eugen Diederichs, was all too firmly ensconced within the carapace of his virginity and of a fear and loathing of carnality that had been inculcated in him from an early age. He could still not find the strength within himself to leave this all behind him. He now referred to Helene Voigt-Diederichs as his "alien-familiar friend."[36]

Hesse would never be entirely free and easy in affairs of the heart. The barb of Pietism was too firmly embedded in his flesh for that. Even later in life he was given to talking about a state of "desire-less love," and throughout his life he remained a contact-phobic who could not bear others to get too close—indeed, for whom it was a matter of life and death that people kept their distance. What remained was a dreamworld, which could furnish expressive material to the writer in him.

The Petit Cénacle: Bohemian and Bourgeois

> I am a gypsy, with my hands in my trouser pockets and only writing my poetry on those rare days when I am neither working to earn a living nor am drunk. Alongside books, wine, and women, I know of only one other pleasure: walking.

—Letter to Richard v. Schaukal, November 10, 1901, *Romantische Lieder*

People of a similar disposition now began to emerge. Not stupid students from dueling societies who made it a point of honor to drink more than anyone else on any given occasion, but friends who like him expected something special from life. With them, he was able to debate about Nietzsche and discuss what he was working on.

This circle of contemporaries named themselves the *petit cénacle* and aspired to be a kind of bestiary in miniature. Hesse wrote to his mother on January 24, 1898, about his working life in the bookshop, telling her that "the rather monotonous work can turn you into a bit of a knucklehead." But that was just the preamble to his letter, the justification for what he had to report about his burgeoning social life outside the confines of work: "Many of my evenings are almost completely taken up by socializing with my friends (Rupp, Finckh, Hammelehle)."

A circle of bohemian acquaintances for the weekend and at the end of the working day—that surely must have displeased the family back in Calw, despite the fact that Hesse was at pains to make it all sound as harmless as possible: "We get together most Sundays and go for a walk, or read together and eat our supper together, and sometimes we even treat ourselves to a few hours' worth of worldly fun in a tavern."[37]

One of their number was Ludwig Finckh, who studied law (later switching to medicine) and wrote poems. Subsequently he was to become what some people wrongly accused Hermann Hesse of being: a popular folk poet of a rather sentimental kind. Their group was a utopian band of young enthusiasts, who followed the French Romantic model of styling themselves as a *cénacle* (literary coterie), albeit with the addition of the ironic qualification *petit*.

He first introduced his three friends to his parents in a letter of November 10, 1897. Finckh, he informed them, was "a friendly, naive person, and somewhat superficial." The other two were more serious individuals, though in radically different ways: "Hammelehle is very passionate, brimming with questions that have no answers; he is a lawyer and a philosopher—Rupp is a calm, extremely diligent, and worldly-wise person; he listens more than he talks, but we really miss him if he is absent."[38] Here, Hesse was not only beginning to observe his surroundings precisely, but also to place it into a fairy-tale-like context. He was only ever half immersed in his new community of friends, while the other half of him remained outside as an observer. It was therefore from this dual perspective that he also described the *petit cénacle* in his work *Hermann Lauscher*—and occasionally the insider and outsider switched roles. Hesse thus played not only with different distances to his subject but also with a dreamlike state and actuality as parallel planes of reality, which—already prefiguring the magical theater of his later work—start to become indistinguishably similar to one another. Hesse's magical style already manifested itself in his earliest prose works, while his poetry remained by contrast oddly one-dimensional.

For the first time in his life, in the company of his brothers in the *cénacle* Hesse felt himself to be in a circle of like-minded individuals. Here, his *Romantic Songs* were admired, and he was even rather effusively accorded the rank of the "greatest German poet alive today." At least, as Ludwig Finckh recalled in his autobiography *Himmel und Erde* (Heaven and earth), those were the words he used when giving his mother Hesse's book. Her reaction is not recorded, though we may fairly assume that it was more positive than that of Marie Hesse. By now, though, things had changed. Hermann was financially independent of his parents in Calw. This further boosted his self-confidence, although his unpredictable mood swings still remained. Sometimes he was positively manic in his euphoria, while at other times he was apathetic and depressive. This would be the case for the whole of his life, and was one of the shortcomings of his constitution against which he struggled with all his might. As a consequence, for him the act of writing would always be partly an attempt to save himself.

The circle of young geniuses would meet in the evenings in a wine tavern or play billiards. Hesse attained an astonishing degree of proficiency in the game. The real life and soul of the party in this group was undoubtedly Ludwig Finckh. Hermann Hesse was much too withdrawn and introverted to be able to hold together a circle of friends like the *petit cénacle,* made up of young poets with a sense of mission. They met up once a week for readings, invariably from half-past eight to almost eleven in the evening, at which they recited both their own and others' poetry, and felt a real sense of comradeship in the company of congenial friends.

In the "Lulu" chapter in *Hermann Lauscher,* which was only added in the second edition and which Hesse dedicated to E. T. A. Hoffmann, the author portrayed this literary circle. He could not help but poke friendly fun at their well-practiced poses, which unmistakably contrasted with the clear limitations of this assemblage of beginners of very variable talent. Ludwig Finckh appeared here in the guise of "Ludwig Ugel," Oskar Rupp as "Government lawyer Oskar Ripplein," Otto Erich Faber as "Herr Erich Tänzer," and Carlo Hammelehle as "Karl Hamelt." Hesse depicted himself as the "perambulatory esthete Hermann Lauscher," whose (posthumous, naturally!) sketches supposedly composed the substance of the book. Another character in this work was "Princess Lilia"—in reality Julie Hellmann, the niece of the landlord of the Crown, a tavern in Kirchheim, to which the *petit cénacle* made their last communal excursion in August 1899.

Hesse, the least disposed of all of them to conviviality, was surprisingly the one among this group of youthful Knights of the Round Table who was hardest hit by the inevitable breakup of the circle of friends. The first of them to depart was Ludwig Finckh, who returned to his parents in Reutlingen in the fall of 1898. The other hitherto self-styled young poetic geniuses quite naturally found themselves presently having to pursue the bourgeois careers that had been marked out for them. Apart from Hesse, Ludwig Finckh would be the only one not to leave poetry behind him as a mere youthful episode. In *Hermann Lauscher* Hesse would subsequently portray all his erstwhile friends from the *cénacle* in all their later bourgeois

The *petit cénacle*. From left to right: Otto Erich Faber, Oskar Rupp, Ludwig Finckh, Carlo Hammelehle, and Hermann Hesse

respectability and comfort—which at the time appears so grand but through that very portrayal suddenly takes on the aspect of something perilously on the cusp of decline. It is as though the Steppenwolf and Goethe enthusiast were already standing in front of the bourgeois professor and owner of a marble bust of Goethe the Weimar privy councillor.

So, Hesse's portrayal of the hopeful student of jurisprudence shows us what he would later become—an established lawyer with his own practice, small but successful enough to provide him with a living: "A premature tendency to corpulence lent his not displeasing figure the hint of a rather comically sedate appearance, while on his shrewd, determined face his strong nose was at variance with his remarkably plump lips and puffy cheeks. Beneath his broad chin, ample folds of skin pile up on his tight stand-up collar, and his close-cropped hair, sweaty and without a parting, poked out impertinently between his forehead and his hat."[39]

This depiction shows that Hesse was adept at turning a wickedly scathing eye on a subject for literary effect.

Hesse would later finally take his leave of the *petit cénacle* circle in a more lightly humorous way in verse:

Wir galten für dekadent und modern
Und glaubten es mit Behagen.
In Wirklichkeit waren wir junge Herren
Von höchst dezentem Betragen.

[We were thought so decadent and modern
And were content to believe it ourselves
But in truth we were young gents
Of extremely modest demeanor.]

Livingstone

While Hermann Hesse, as a young rebel in a circle of like-minded friends, felt accepted like never before in his life, the threat from his family still remained. For both his mother and his father were already experienced—and thoroughly successful!—authors. It would take a Herculean effort, one that almost proved too much for him, to disengage himself from their judgment.

As the author of Pietist texts on missionary activity, Marie Hesse was not without her own depths. Missionary work in the nineteenth century was synonymous with expeditions, the discovery of unknown lands and peoples, and ethnographic research. It was oftentimes the case that scientific research expeditions had a missionary background and a missionary organization as their financial sponsor. Marie Hesse's interest in advancing the Christianization of Africa was also combined with an interest in the exotic. Accordingly, David Livingstone provided her with the ideal subject matter for an exciting biography that would not be lacking in dangerous episodes—and yet that could also quite legitimately claim to be a book driven by religious conviction.

At that time Livingstone's name was on everyone's lips. He was a legend; after being thought lost without trace for many years, he was tracked down by the reporter and adventurer Henry Morton Stanley (his diary of the expedition, *How I Found Livingstone,* became a best-seller) and became a media star before returning to the jungle once more, where he succumbed to disease. Marie Hesse set about writing the story of Livingstone's perilous life, full of often-shocking details of an alien civilization. The subject matter of her biography, which was published in 1900 and met with instant acclaim and success, could almost be called racy. Her Pietist outlook in the work displayed a strikingly modern trait: namely, the idea that one can justify oneself before God through strenuous and success-oriented activity.

Nor did Marie and Johannes Hesse lived reclusive lives secluded from the economic and political realities of the age. On the contrary, they were extremely assertive in trying to spread their spiritual message to the farthest corners of the world with all the modern technological means at their disposal.

It was in this spirit that Marie Hesse also presented David Livingstone, who was born in 1813 into a family of tea importers. The Livingstone family thus lived four-square within the world of profitable commerce while at the same time being members of a temperance society and taking an active interest in missionary activity, which primarily took the form of distributing religious pamphlets. As Marie Hesse put it, this was a family characterized by "a contented cheerfulness." This was a reflection of her own ideal model for life, which she militantly sought to implement within her own family: "Frugal contentment teamed with steely hard work, unflinching self-denial and true godliness, that was so to speak the atmosphere within which the children grew up."[40]

And David Livingstone grew up in a way that she would dearly love to have seen her own son Hermann grow up. Namely, in the kind of firmly disciplined way with which the Hesses themselves were familiar. Thus, every evening in the Livingstone household, as dusk began to fall, the front door was locked. One time when the son of the house, who had become too engrossed in playing outside, came home too late, he did not dare to call or knock and so lay down dutifully and quietly to sleep on the doorstep.

While staying overnight in his parents' house on one occasion, the young writer Hermann Hesse also reported on the front door being locked early, confining him to the house on a summer's evening. The Hesses retired early to bed so that they could wake up at the crack of dawn and begin their daily task of acting in accordance with God's wishes. In Marie Hesse's book on the young David Livingstone, one could read the following account: "Often his good mother would jump out of bed herself in order to put out his bedside lamp and force the assiduous boy to go to sleep, as he had to be at work at the spinning mill at six o'clock the next morning."[41]

Marie Hesse shared David Livingstone's strongest conviction—that science and religion were by no means inimical to one another. Marie Hesse could thus invest all her restrictive morality in the service of progress. David Livingstone served as her model in this, because he was "extremely aloof and cold toward the female sex" and lived in Protestant celibacy, as it were. He was entirely in thrall to his godly duty, which occupied the whole of every day. Marie Hesse described in punctilious detail the journeys that the missionary, whom she called a "collaborator with God," now embarked upon. Depending upon one's perspective, Livingstone's expeditions were undertaken either primarily or coincidentally in the service of the Geological Society, in search of the mouths of African rivers.

Here the fundamental ambivalence of such missionary activity becomes apparent. On the one hand, it was part of the whole colonial enterprise, the exploitation of Africa and the subjugation or even extermination of indigenous peoples. On the other, parameters of civilized behavior were being set here for all people. Admittedly, the ideal citizen of the world aspired to in such a process looked very much like a Pietist from the provinces, who live solely for his work, his family, and the Bible. Livingstone protested vehemently against slavery, and Marie Hesse's book portrays massacres conducted by the slave traders and clashes between enemy tribes, whose chiefs not infrequently made common cause with the human traffickers.

Slavery was the work of the devil, according to Marie Hesse, who greatly admired Harriet Beecher Stowe's *Uncle Tom's Cabin*. The rivalry between the great colonial powers, and especially the role played by the British, was followed keenly in the Hesse household.

Yet Livingstone—who, as Marie Hesse noted, had "died while at prayer"—also provided ample material for a writer's imaginative powers to conjure up lurid pictures of the terrors of violence, disease, and death—and it is indeed astonishing to see quite how eagerly Marie Hesse (in contrast to other biographers of Livingstone) devoted herself to doing this.

In great detail she described the embalming of Livingstone's body and the journey of many weeks that it took to carry him from Ilala near Lake Bangweulu in East Africa—culminating in his solemn interment as a national hero in Westminster Abbey. The chapter in which she recounts this has as its epigraph: "The Power of the Prince of Darkness Is Dreadful." She tells the story of the bizarre transportation of Livingstone's corpse through the domains of various tribal chiefs almost as a piece of hagiography. For nothing was as inexplicable to "primitive" peoples as a funeral cortège of this kind. Thus, the hastily embalmed body of the missionary had to be concealed from the gaze of native peoples as it was spirited through their territories:

> The corpse, which could only be treated with salt and a bottle of surgical spirit, was dried out by exposing it to the air for fourteen days, before being wrapped in tree bark and sewn into a shroud made of stout sailcloth; the whole thing was then dipped in tar to prevent moisture from getting to it. And so, in somber mood, the funeral procession set off on its long, long march, the like of which had never been seen before in the whole of history. The pallbearers had to carry their precious burden on their shoulders on unpaved footpaths for some 1800 kilometers in a tropical climate![42]

It was therefore far from being the case that Hesse's mother would have been easily shocked by the more macabre aspects of life. Every horror story was welcome so long as it had the payoff of being recounted to the greater glory of God!

Africa was here being used as a metaphor for the unknown, for nature as wilderness, which promised adventure to those who sought to explore it and open it up. This yearning, which is like a variant of Novalis's famous "blue flower," was not confined to writers such as Rimbaud. What is remarkable, though, is that this longing for an unknown continent, for another life, also resonates unmistakably in Marie Hesse's work, though it is well concealed there by the book's ostensible missionary purpose. We are already on the dark side of reason here, and well on the way to Joseph Conrad's *Heart of Darkness*. Whereas for Marie and Johannes Hesse, exploring this psychological realm of darkness was a taboo that could never be broken, it became a key motif in the writings of Hermann Hesse.

The End of a Romance in Letters: Eugen Diederichs's Wife as a Useful Friend

Hesse's connection with Helene Voigt continued to be what it had always been: a conversation in letters that took pleasure in indulging in romantic projection. Essentially, what Hesse was doing in these letters was conducting exercises in style for stories that he was yet to write. Somehow the young woman must have intuited that she was not actually the focus of any amorous intent in these poetic missives, since Hermann Hesse never made any serious attempt to meet her. Instead, she was treated to confessions such as this from February 12, 1898: "Where friendship is concerned I have always been an unlucky person, and eagerly attach all of my mute devotion to every little piece of my homeland."[43]

It may perhaps have dawned on him that he had missed an opportunity for more when he received an uncertain and hesitant letter from Helene, dated March 1, 1898: "My dear friend, for I trust that I may still call you that? It is strangely difficult for me to write to you today, although what I have to tell you may perhaps not affect you in the slightest. Your last letter to me was dated February 12, the very day on which I renounced my youthful freedom. I am a bride, laughing and crying at the same time."[44]

A laughing and crying bride? It must have shocked Hesse to learn that he was the drop of bitterness in her newfound love, especially because she added the following note (which must have sounded awful to him): "From Strasbourg I traveled (not without having first looked at the map one more time to see where Tübingen was) to Leipzig. There, at my publisher's office, I made the acquaintance of the publishing bookseller Eugen Diederichs. Within a few days, we were an item."[45]

This was a stroke of bad luck—but for Hesse it would soon prove to be an advantage that his female pen-friend was now the wife of a (renowned) publisher. Even so, it was an object lesson for him that he would never forget: when push came to shove, it was not enough simply to write women rapturous letters! To make matters worse, this was presently confirmed in as many words by Helene Voigt: "One is alone with one's dreams for so long, and so proud of these lonely dreams—and then along comes someone." It was scant comfort to Hesse to now be offered friendship rather than love. It must have sounded like pure mockery to him: "But if you'd like to, why don't you move to Leipzig at the same time as me? It's important to me that you shouldn't think you have been jinxed where our friendship is concerned."[46]

Hesse sent a polite reply on March 8, but his tone makes it clear that he has taken the news badly: "Many thanks for your noble and honest letter! It tells me more about you than even your previous ones. The truth is that it caught me at a bad moment. Just as I had finished reading it, the sound of a funeral march drifted up from the street, accompanying the procession to the cemetery for an acquaintance of mine who had taken his own life. . . . Forget me and everything that is happening right now; but later let me accompany you into your new life!" The letter ends with a curious misfire of a complimentary sign-off: "I wish you and everyone a sunny spring."[47] Everyone? That was tantamount to lumping her husband, Eugen Diederichs, in with all and sundry—however, Hesse would soon change his stance and begin to take a greater interest in the publisher than his wife.

So ended a brief romance through letters, though Hesse would by no means break off the contact entirely—throughout his life he was careful to nurture all the contacts he made, even if only at a distance and irregularly. He would continue to exchange greetings with Helene Voigt-Diederichs into old age. Hesse did not attend their wedding, however. Nor was he invited, but he maintained such a stony silence on the whole affair that he was reprimanded by Helene Voigt-Diederichs on June 20, 1898: "You know what would have made me really happy? If you had at least said something to me about July 4. You wouldn't have had to send me your congratulations, I've had plenty of those already. But just a word in acknowledgment would have been nice and friendly of you."[48] But Hesse now had even less inclination than usual to be "nice and friendly."

Instead, he threw himself with even greater vigor into the meetings of the *petit cénacle*. "Sundays are reserved for my friends,"[49] he told his parents when they asked why he had not visited them for so long.

The high point of communal activities with his friends was ultimately also their swan song, as the members of the *cénacle* all had other obligations. Accordingly, an excursion to the village of Kirchheim an der Teck became a formal occasion at which the *cénacle* brothers took their final leave of one another.

Lulu from Kirchheim: The Landlord's Niece as Princess Lilia

In the summer of 1899 Hermann Hesse handed in his notice at Heckenhauer's bookshop. He had the prospect of a post at Reich's bookshop in Basel, where he hoped he would be able to switch to the antiquarian book department. He had completed his apprenticeship a year before, and the period he had spent thereafter as a sales assistant left him all too little free time for writing. Writing, though, had become increasingly important to him. He spent the summer of 1899 in Calw. He arranged to meet Ludwig Finckh and the other members of the *petit cénacle* for their summer excursion to Kirchheim, a gathering that would later go down in legend. The group of friends walked, debated, and drank together—and Hesse found himself inflamed once again, albeit in a very indeterminate way, by his erotic fantasies, though on this occasion he was in rivalry with Ludwig Finckh. The object of their adoration and desire in equal measure was Julie Hellmann, the niece of the landlord of the Crown (the tavern in Kirchheim). Hesse was enchanted by the pretty girl. Only after ten days in the village—he had originally meant to stay for two—did he finally leave. The mistake he then made, which at the same time proved him to be a writer, was to follow the dictum that one can express one's love far more poetically from a distance. And so, on August 26, after arriving back in Calw, he wrote to the "Lulu girl," confessing what a state of confusion he was in: "When we said goodbye, didn't you notice how I couldn't stop my hand and my voice from trembling?"

The way in which Hesse retrospectively worked himself up into an erotic rapture in a letter must have appeared very strange to the simple country girl. Was this a declaration of love to the girl, or was he already writing the draft of a love story for which Julie Hellmann had merely provided the impetus? Wasn't "Lulu"—the name she appears under in *Hermann Lauscher*—in fact entirely Hesse's creation, a product of his poetic inventiveness? The innkeeper's niece must have had some inkling of this, as she kept Hesse very much at arm's length. Hesse meanwhile waxed ever more lyrical in his love frenzy, which quickly revealed itself to be, instead, a writing frenzy: "But I am also grateful to you. What for?—For being so beautiful, and for the fact that I was allowed to gaze upon you and that your image pursued me and enthralled me. From the moment I departed Kirchheim I regretted leaving, and since then every hour that I have missed being with you cuts me to the quick." Hesse goes through the motions of how a lovesick person feels, but he is playing by rules that he set himself.

And what of the girl? She was nothing but a projection, a beautiful image: "I hope you will believe me when I tell you that I do not want to force myself on you, all I want is that you should know about my devotion and tolerate me as your love slave. No matter whether you laugh at me or have pity on me—please be my fairy-tale princess and let me know soon if you will deign to look upon me as your captive. I am completely at your disposal to be treated as a hero or as a buffoon, as you see fit."[50]

An Hour Behind Midnight: A Report from the Verge of Art

A shipwrecked dreamer left the rowing bench and stretched
out his arms to the mute land ahead.

—Hermann Hesse, *An Hour Behind Midnight*

Once he had got over the painful moment of disappointment, the fact that
Helene Voigt married the publisher Eugen Diederichs was a fortunate side
effect of this romance through letters for Hesse. Helene Voigt-Diederichs
continued to greatly admire his poems and in addition probably felt that
she needed to mend fences with him. Nor could the experienced publisher
Diederichs prevent his new wife from following her impulse in this matter.

Hesse sent Eugen Diederichs the manuscript of *An Hour Behind Midnight.* The publisher now had a problem. He knew how inappropriate a
gesture it would be to his wife to turn down this author out of hand. Consequently, he did not send Hesse any reply for a while, finally explaining
his delay to the author on April 4, 1899: "You see, I was unsure for some
time whether to accept your draft, more from the personal sense that it
was my duty to act solely in my best commercial interests." In saying this
he clearly implied that publishing Hesse's work would not be a sound business decision. He then continued: "So, when I declare myself willing
today to publish your book and to get on with printing it without delay so
that it will be ready for your mother's birthday, I should say that I am not
doing this because of your friendship with my wife, but rather because of
the high regard in which I hold your literary work." This is exactly the
kind of argument advanced by husbands who are acting under their wives'
instructions. What's more, Diederichs was happy that Hesse had missed
the opportunity to get together with Helene, who had quite obviously been
head over heels in love with him, though this had only ever expressed itself in writing.

The publisher took a magnanimous attitude; he had, after all, emerged
victorious. He already suspected that he would lose money from publishing
An Hour Behind Midnight. He had, he wrote Hesse "quite frankly little faith
in the book's commercial success." And there was even something lacking in
the texts, he pointed out: "For all the individual elements of your work
that I admire, I find that there is still something missing from your authorial voice as a whole, something I might call a conscious sense of being at

ease with yourself. I must say in general that I don't get a great feeling of release from your work."[51]

In saying this, Diederichs had touched on a sore point, for the ties had not yet been severed and the bird of Hesse's creativity was still caged. In an introduction to a new edition of the work in 1941, Hesse quite dispassionately diagnosed the problem: "In the prose pieces of *An Hour Behind Midnight,* I had created an artistic realm of dreams, an island of beauty, and its self-consciously poetic nature was a retreat from the storms and the low points of everyday life into the night and the world of dream and beautiful solitude, and as a result the book had many estheticizing features."[52]

Diederichs had 600 copies printed; he could scarcely have ordered a smaller print run. But it was not for his mother's birthday, as Diederichs had mistakenly assumed, that Hermann Hesse eagerly wanted to get his hands on copies of the book, but for his father's. It was touching—or perhaps more disconcerting?—to see how much Hermann Hesse was still concerned to be taken seriously as a writer by his parents. When the book duly appeared, he immediately sent a copy to Calw.

In the meantime, his father had fallen ill again and his mother replied on July 15, 1899, in her customary manner: "Papa was therefore unable to look at your book. I skimmed through it, but then found I couldn't get to sleep that night. Shun your 'fever-muse' like you would a snake; it was she who slithered into paradise and who nowadays still wishes to poison thoroughly any paradise of love and poetry." But the fire-and-brimstone preaching tone she adopted here was still capable of being cranked up a notch, it seemed: "O my child, flee from her, hate her, she is unclean and has no claim on you, for you belong to God; you were pledged to him at your baptism and even long before that given over to His loving heart by your parents. . . . However beautiful her external form may be, she is totally lacking in any nobility. Remain chaste! Everything that comes from man, from his mouth and even more so from his pen, sullies him—have you considered that? . . . My heart rises up against such poison."[53]

Even Hesse, who was to some extent accustomed to his mother's sanctimonious reactions, was taken aback by this outburst. So, what he had written was "poison," was it? And everything produced by a man defiled him and was sinful? He could no longer expose his poems to such militant religious ideology! However, his mother the missionary was so incensed by her son's sinful outpourings that she sent another letter to him later on that same day, in which she wrote: "Some sentences are so indecent that no young lady should ever read them; you talk about animals in such a way, not people."[54] What passages did she mean? Perhaps those in the section of the book entitled "The Fever-Muse"; the title alone must have been a provocation to one whose business was promoting virtue. A muse who inflames, arouses desires, and stimulates a creativity that emanates from the loins—his mother could only be filled with disgust and condemn such a thing as the work of the devil. Was it his words, which gave voice to his need to express himself, that so upset her—or was it simply that the only words that had any value in her eyes were those uttered in praise of God and in renunciation of the self? So, was nature—including man's nature—the work of the devil? At this stage Hesse already knew that man and God cannot be torn asunder, or treated as mutually hostile worlds, in the way that his parents did. If the love of God was the greatest imperative for a Christian, why shouldn't sensual love also be paramount between two people? In any event, the "fever-muse" heightened his poetic potency, and he would henceforth never let anyone sway him from this certainty; "This muse taps into the tremblings of my blood and goads my thirsting eye from one longing to the next, and smiles as she does so, until my gaze and my heartbeat break . . . she has led me through ghost-pale nights and has fixed her beautiful, all-powerful eye full of deceit and love on me, eager to revive the dreadful sensuality of our former dreams."[55]

The nine prose pieces in *An Hour Behind Midnight* are nocturnal dreams of islands. Dream landscapes penetrated by nightmare like a thorn in the hand of a person reaching out all too dreamily to pluck a rose. Here the writer stylizes his solitary nature into a lyricism of loneliness. Terror waits at the end of each insular dream, whose true fulfillment can only consist of disappearing in the moment of waking—like fog lifting when the rising sun shines on it.

There is a pronounced tendency toward estheticism in these texts, and doubtless also a hint of something mannered, and Eugen Diederichs was right when he remarked that there is no sense of anything or anyone actually being alive here. This kind of somnambulistic prose was familiar from the work of Maurice Maeterlinck and Gabriele d'Annunzio. The latter's 1928 novel *The Comrade without Eyelashes,* contains the observation: "What is imagination, then, if not the dream of dreaming?"[56] Here, the night is revered and the day shunned—another possibility that has its roots in Romanticism.

Hesse would later contend that the "artistic realm of dreams," and the "island of beauty" envisioned here, were things that could find no further place in his works and therefore "disappeared from my list of books."[57] We should, however, add the caveat here that it was only in this particular form that the theme of the "artistic realm of dreams" was not revisited in Hesse's work—in actual fact, after undergoing several metamorphoses it was to reappear regularly as one of his central motifs.

The book was indeed not a commercial success, with the publisher selling a grand total of fifty-four copies in its first year of publication. Hermann Hesse received royalties of 35 marks, 10 pfennigs. Even so, it did receive some positive reviews, which identified something extraordinary in the young author.

In his review, Wilhelm von Scholz pointed to the similarity of tone in *An Hour Behind Midnight* with that found in the writings of Maurice Maeterlinck and Stefan George. Hesse would subsequently concede that Maeterlinck's work, which had a "certain artificial twilight feel" to it, along with "a rather sickly form of introversion that was enamored of itself,"[58] really had made a strong impression on him at this time, though he vehemently rejected the suggestion that he had been influenced by George: "When my book came out, I still had not read a single line by George." Shortly thereafter, he claimed, he had identified in the cult that began to grow up around Stefan George a form of estheticism whose "cultivation of a secret-society-like pathos and a pretentious cliquey esotericism"[59] he instinctively rejected.

The young Rainer Maria Rilke also discovered *An Hour Behind Midnight*. He recognized the authorial voice as one akin to his, and soon after its publication, discussed the slim volume in the journal *Der Bote für deutsche Literatur* (The German literature courier). Only two years older than Hesse, Rilke found that Hesse's prose resonated with him. His review began by stating that it was decidedly "worthwhile" discussing a book "that is fearful and pious and arises from a dark voice at prayer." He then proceeded to give a disquisition on what constitutes a writer. Rilke's words here were not yet those famous lines from his novel *Malte Laurids Brigge,* in which he corrects his own tentative beginnings as a writer—the point of writing, he maintained there, was not to express feeling about things, but to address things in such a way that they can be felt!—but instead made godliness the yardstick of writing. In the process, Rilke raised *An Hour Behind Midnight,* which for Hesse's parents had been a book of the most disgusting sinfulness and pure poison, to a work of pious reverence: "The starting point for all art is piety: piety toward oneself, toward each experience, toward all things, and toward a great paradigm and one's own untried strength." Hesse would later express very similar thoughts of his own, though he replaced the word "piety," which he found deeply suspect, with another: self-will. Yet piety is a fitting term to apply to the kind of Romantic religion of art that both Rilke and Hesse advocated at this time, a religion that celebrated the redemptive power of art in place of a church-based faith.

Rilke called the aim of art that proceeds from piety understood in such a way "the new life, the *vita nuova.*" And it was this profoundly secret wish to have the capacity to change one's own life through the act of writing that Rilke identified in Hesse as well. He expressed this idea in an image that was very pathos-laden but highly apposite in all its resonant ambiguity: "His words kneel." Similarly he also maintained: "It is as if his words were made of metal and read very slowly and heavily." Yet Rilke also remarked on the shortcomings of Hesse's prose. A great deal of abstraction had found its way into the book, he claimed, and these elegant formulations had not blended well with the rest of the material. Here Rilke was addressing the fact that Hesse's style in *An Hour Behind Midnight* comes across as extremely aloof—sometimes bordering on the kind of "arts and craft" esthetic he despised. Rilke identified in this "a certain Sunday-best language . . . yet the author seems to have actually felt too few Sundays; many words appear just too new and unused for that." Nevertheless, the work was very unliterary, by which Rilke meant: "In its best passages it is vital and idiosyncratic. His reverence is sincere and profound. His love is great and all emotions in the book are pious: it is on the verge of art."[60]

This was a truly prophetic designation of the position from which Hesse wrote and which he would henceforth defend throughout his whole life: on the verge of art.

4

AT HOME CROSSING BORDERS

Alemannic Avowal

Hesse repeated it time and again: he had no idea what nationality he was when he was born. His father, as a Russian citizen, he maintained, had a Russian passport. His mother, meanwhile, who had lived for a spell in India while she was growing up, was the daughter of a Swabian father and a Swiss-French mother. He himself had spent half of his childhood in Basel and half in Calw. "This mixed heritage prevented me from ever having much respect for nationalism and national borders."[1]

Did this attitude preclude him from ever declaring his nationality, and was he even interested in addressing the topic of a homeland as such? Indeed he was, though in a far more detached way than most other writers. For him, a homeland was not something that one possesses from the outset, but instead something that one must go in search of—this was an article of faith for Hesse, who would elevate the transgressing of boundaries to a joyous art form. Accordingly, the wayfarer became the symbol par excellence of Hesse's life as a writer.

To give his existence some spatial coordinates, though, Hesse was keen on referring to the Alemannic region, that corner of the Rhine divided by the border between Württemberg and Switzerland. Hesse always identified this area as being somewhere apart, a thoroughly secondary phenom-

enon that one did not have to take so seriously. It is not that he would
have been a separatist who could have revolted against national claims to
power in the name of a minority—for him, the politics of nationalism were
a largely uninteresting affair, and a question he thought it fruitless to try
to answer. Only the pressure of external circumstances would eventually
change his stance. Reluctantly, Hesse was forced to concede that nationalism would not tolerate being provoked by his refusal to acknowledge its
existence. Especially in times of war, this was a surefire way to make oneself the target of an inexplicable hatred. This kind of nationalism, which
was constantly prepared to make the leap to fanaticism, was always deeply
abhorrent to Hesse, who otherwise was always eager to invoke the underlying mainspring of things. For him, it always had more than a whiff of
ideology, party-politics conflict, journalism, and a latent threat of pogroms
against outsiders. And yet it was precisely for this reason that Hesse found
himself drawn over and over again into debates about nationality and the
nature of German-ness. Right up to his *Rigi Diary* after the Second World
War, his statements on this subject had the capacity to provoke his readers
to what could sometimes be violent reactions: on questions of German nationality they always expected more emotion from him than he was prepared to expend. Hesse the German national poet, who spent most of his
life living in Switzerland, always regarded it as unreasonable that people
should require him, of all people, to pledge his allegiance to the German
nation. He was unqualifiedly in support of German culture, literature,
art—but the German nation? Hesse was at a loss where this was concerned;
the concept did not resonate with him at all.

Writing in 1937, Thomas Mann saw Hesse as the antithesis to a Greater
Germany—as a great poet of Little Germany, as it were, of its niches and
provincial peculiarities, which were not all designed to lay the ground-
work for disastrous resurgences of nationalism. Mann noted: "There is
nothing more German than this writer and his life's work—nothing that
could conceivably be more German in the old, joyous, free, and spiritual
sense of the word, the one that has given the German name its best reputation
and earned it the gratitude of humankind."

After the First World War, Hesse wrote his "Alemannic Avowal." By that
stage he had been living in Berne for seven years. Altogether, he spent sixty
years of his life in Switzerland: initially in Basel, thereafter in Berne, and
finally, the longest spell, in Montagnola on the southern slopes of the Alps.

There, political conditions in Germany receded into a distance from which he was bound to judge Teutonic ideology and the battle between partisan groups in a different—primarily freer—light. All the while, however, he remained dedicated to the spirit of Goethe, Mozart, Nietzsche, or Novalis. These artists had become part of the very fabric of his existence and embodied for him the other Germany, distinct from the political realm of the Wilhelmine Empire. He did not even have much connection to the Weimar Republic, and he completely rejected Hitler's Germany.

The "Alemannic Avowal" was an attempt to bridge the gap between himself and Germany. Writing from his home in Switzerland, he proclaimed the things that mattered to him about Germany. Of course, as always happens in times of strident political sloganeering, this attempt at a biographical self-analysis was largely ignored, and where it was taken notice of, it was predominantly misinterpreted as a betrayal of German-ness (which Hesse had never claimed for himself anyhow):

> If two villages are closely related to one another and as alike as twins and war comes and the one village sends its men and boys off, and bleeds to death and descends into poverty as a result, while the other village continues to espouse peace and goes on thriving, this situation strikes me as in no way right and proper, but unnatural and hair-raising. And if a person is forced to repudiate his homeland and sacrifice his love for it in order to serve a political fatherland more effectively, that seems to me tantamount to a soldier shooting his mother because he deems obedience to her to be a greater imperative than his love for her.[2]

The foundations of this attitude were already laid by his background and in particular his uninhibited switching between his twin hometowns of Calw and Basel, as well as in the polyglot lifestyle of his missionary parents and grandparents. As a result, in both locations Hesse developed one and the same awareness: anything that ties you to a particular homeland—no matter in what country—is also something constricting, which you must shake off and only possibly rediscover in later life.

Hesse in Basel: Reich's Bookshop

By the time he moved to Basel, Hesse was twenty-three years old, had already published several works, and knew that hard work was required in order to fulfill the dream of becoming a writer. He needed more time to do his own work; the twelve hours a day he had spent working as a sales assistant in Heckenhauer's bookshop in Tübingen had made too many demands on him. In Basel, he hoped to switch over to working in an antiquarian bookshop, which would give him more leisure time in which to write. Toward the end of his time in Tübingen, he had been suffering constantly from severe headaches and had been forced to interrupt work on his novel *Schweinigel* (The hedgehog)—the manuscript of this is now thought to have been lost. It was also now high time that he distance himself still further from his parents.

On September 17, 1899, he sent his first letter from Basel to Calw. In it he reported that he was doing lots of work at Reich's bookshop in the city (albeit in the regular retail bookshop once more, not the antiquarian division), but that at least this establishment was "new and wonderfully well appointed" and that he found Herr Reich to be "clearly a very pleasant boss."

At first, recollections of Basel from his childhood clashed with the intellectual atmosphere of the city, which impressed him and opened up a new dimension in his thinking. His parents were once again taking a rest cure at the Hotel Palmenwald in Freudenstadt when they received some very conflicting reports from Hermann about how he was getting on in Basel. His need—oftentimes disappointed—for closeness with his family was clearly still in conflict with his awareness that he had to get some distance from them. He knew full well that he would be able to start living his own life only after he stopped using his parents as a yardstick for his behavior. But he was also aware that he did not have sufficient rigor to achieve that. It was precisely in this contradiction, which he found quite insoluble, that he began to grow as an author, who senses that he is not entirely free after all and can never completely leave his origins behind.

Yet how was one to live with a strong sense of tradition, of one's origins, and of family without being completely controlled by such factors? How could one gain the necessary freedom to affirm a strong connection to one's own background while at the same time knowing that one had to overcome that background in order to become oneself? Hesse would never be able to resolve this question and raised it with himself repeatedly. As a result, his writing henceforth was characterized by an urge to forever justify the way in which he lived. Basel was now the place where he came to experience firsthand the irresolvable contradiction between the past and the present. On October 1 his parents read: "This afternoon, I called you and the old times to mind especially vividly. I had been walking along the Spalenringweg, the Steinenringweg, Birsigwäldchen and also St. Margarethen. The park behind St. Margarethen, which had always been shut in the past, is now open and has been laid out with lovely paths and shrubs, with lots of squirrels running around."[3]

Hesse did not go back to Calw in November to attend his parents' silver wedding anniversary. Instead he wrote them a letter: "I am all too painfully aware how many of the difficult times you have endured over the past 25 years were down to me, and I thank you and God from the bottom of my heart for your forbearance."[4] He immediately followed this up by announcing that he would not be coming home for Christmas either. He no longer wished to be drawn into the family's everyday concerns in Calw. He continued to write to them frequently, and replied politely and even cordially to their letters, regardless of whether they informed him that his stepbrother Theodor had just had a nervous breakdown or told him the latest news about the worrying state of health of his mother, who was suffering from a painful softening of the bones [osteomalacia]. His younger brother Hans, who had secured a position with the mission in Basel, gave up his post in order to be with her in Calw. Not once did Hermann Hesse ever entertain the thought of doing such a thing. He wanted to live his own life. Accordingly, he increasingly came to regard himself as the guest of his own family: in other words, as an outsider there too. For he wanted nothing to do with an unconditional faith in Pietism, the glue that kept the family together. The draft-board medical exam for his one year of voluntary military service in 1900, which he was very apprehensive about, had a happy outcome: his severe nearsightedness rendered him unfit for active duty, and he was assigned to the reserves.

Hesse really liked Basel; he rented a handsome room with parquet flooring and a large old tiled oven in an old Basel townhouse that promised to be a quiet location. He spent most of his free time visiting the city's museums. In the process, he developed a "serious and lively relationship with the visual arts" and with it a desire for the first time to live comfortably.[5] However, the "room with history" was not conducive to this; "the room was wonderful, but it was never warm, despite the fact that the huge oven consumed unfeasible amounts of wood; meanwhile, right under the room's window from three o'clock in the morning, milk and market wagons rumbled over the cobblestones of the apparently quiet alleyway on their way from St. Alban's Gate, making a hell of a racket and rousing me from my sleep. After a short while, I gave up the struggle and moved from the lovely room to a modern suburb."

Ebulliently he wrote to his parents telling them they should spend a bit longer recuperating at the Palmenwald. He knew how much it provoked his parents when he wrote sentences such as the following, but he couldn't help himself: "My dear parents! It's a bright Sunday morning and I'm sitting here in my room smoking a bad but wonderfully cheap Basel cigar and feeling too lazy to work."[6]

Even so, all the new things that he had encountered in this city were fermenting inside him. Basel was the birthplace of the symbolist painter Arnold Böcklin and the historian Jacob Burckhardt—Burckhardt died just prior to Hesse's arrival there.[7] The intellectual atmosphere of the city was still very much colored by the work of these two figures. Hesse had brought with him a reproduction of the painter's *Isle of the Dead;* paradoxically, it had become for him a symbol of his new start in life. Romanticism, which he had dismissed not long before in less than flattering terms, was now before his very eyes in all its intensity. He found himself at a crossroads (a Pietist image for a decisive juncture in a person's life!) and had to choose how he wanted to grow up—and what should happen to his childhood in the process. He sensed that there was only one way he could become himself without having to kill the child within him, and that was the way of the artist. Looking back at this phase of his life, he noted: "I was not a child any longer and thought I had nothing whatsoever to do any more with the Basel of my childhood and the Mission house and its atmosphere; I had already published a small volume of poetry, read Schopenhauer, and was enthralled by Nietzsche. Basel for me was now first and foremost the city of Nietzsche, Jacob Burckhardt, and Böcklin."[8]

Burckhardt especially, with his works *Reflections on History* and *The Civilization of the Renaissance in Italy,* which he had read while he was still in Tübingen, shaped Hesse's view of history. He now knew that the attitude with which he approached the subject was decisive. And he was aware that history was not just a question of amassing facts, nor was the subject an objective academic discipline from which one could remain aloof in one's own life, but instead an art form that was difficult to master, in which intuition and diligence were inextricably linked.

In Basel he also came into contact with Hans Trog, an editor at the *Allgemeine Schweizer Zeitung*. Trog was the author of a biography of Burckhardt, which Hesse had also read in Tübingen. Their mutual veneration of the historian led to an invitation to Hesse to come and work on the newspaper. His first book reviews appeared in 1900.

Working as a Reviewer at the *Allgemeine Schweizer Zeitung*

The eight reviews Hesse wrote for the *Allgemeine Schweizer Zeitung* in 1900 all had to do with Romantic works; in addition, four of the books in question had been published by Eugen Diederichs. One of his reviews related to his own book, which he presented as the work of a highly promising but unfortunately now deceased unknown: Hermann Lauscher.

By discussing the books from Diederichs's publishing house, Hesse presumably was attempting to make amends for the losses he had saddled the publisher with from his slow-selling *An Hour Behind Midnight*. The first of these reviews appeared on January 21, 1900, and was devoted to the collected works of Novalis, which had been published in 1898. The review began with great intensity: "There are certain quiet children with large, soulful eyes whose gaze is hard to bear. Customarily, they are not given long to live and are looked upon, like distinguished strangers, with reverence and pity in equal measure. Novalis was just such a child." This was a powerful way of broaching the theme of Romanticism, in which Hesse had taken a sudden interest after his arrival in Basel, not least as a result of Diederichs's publishing program. But then the quality of the review quickly declines, betraying the tyro journalist, who now begins to struggle ineptly with his words: "The purpose of the lines I am writing here is to make readers aware of this edition. It is to be recommended—leaving aside the fact that it is the only one available—due to its thorough and largely successful way in which it amasses its material; furthermore, it is well printed and inexpensive." He then takes an even more direct and explicit approach, which reads like a piece of advertising copy: "This sensitive and infinitely helpful publisher has once again done us a great service in having prepared this edition and thereby filled a positively embarrassing gap for the literary historian."[9]

Hesse's other reviews are devoted to Jens-Peter Jacobsen, the anthology *The Blue Flower*, Rudolf Kassner's *Mysticism, Artists, and Life*, Dante Gabriel Rossetti's *The House of Life*, Maurice Maeterlinck, the collected works of E. T. A. Hoffmann, and Hermann Lauscher's posthumous writings and diaries, which appeared under the imprint of the R. Reich publishing house (with Hesse as editor). These newspaper pieces help Hesse make a modest name for himself in Basel as a young reviewer and writer.

One encounter in Basel proved especially important for him. His father's recommendation opened the door of the historian and state archivist Rudolf Wackernagel to him. His house was a place where the intellectual elite of Basel frequently gathered. Wackernagel himself had written a *History of the City of Basel*. At this house Hermann Hesse would learn to present himself as a promising young author, a role that did not necessarily sit easily with him, but one that he nevertheless took on. For there was one thing he wanted badly—success as a writer. Marulla wrote to him on December 9, 1899, evidently somewhat piqued at her brother's new "lifestyle": "Evidently you are enjoying a fine life of social engagements, at least in the evenings. You're becoming quite the man of the world, so much so that you will end up putting us country bumpkins to shame."[10]

Romanticism and New Romanticism: Early Steps toward *The Glass Bead Game*

> He can do what very few others can. He can not only describe a summer's evening and a refreshing swimming pool and the delicious feeling of tiredness after physical exertion—in itself that wouldn't be difficult. But he also has the ability to make our hearts feel hot and cool and tired.
>
> —Kurt Tucholsky on Hesse (1927)

As early as 1899, Hermann Hesse wrote a small piece on "New Romanticism" for Eugen Diederichs: "It is the Romanticism of Friedrich Schlegel and of the young [Ludwig] Tieck, but especially that of Novalis, which is now experiencing a curious and significant revival. Above all the New Romantics value and love the sweet, apprehensive scent that lies wistfully and wonderfully pleasantly over the unfinished oeuvre of Novalis—the scent of the Blue Flower."[11]

Remarkably, we already find here a motif that would continue to resonate throughout Hesse's work—that of fire. Here, however—unlike its later use in, say, *Demian*—it is still fraught with negative implications. As the young Hesse said, it was the fate of the young circle of philosopher-poets around Novalis to all be ultimately "consumed by their own fire."

Hesse then goes on to address the estheticism of the turn of the century—the prevailing *fin de siècle* atmosphere, the vogue of "art for art's sake" within which he identified a renaissance of Romanticism, a development that was completely in keeping with his own conception of himself as a writer in *An Hour Behind Midnight:*

> New Romanticism also has the Blue Flower as its symbol. But it has understood the meaning of this symbol better than Novalis's contemporary age. The Blue Flower, the goal of all poetic yearning, is invisible and thrives on the soil of very serious and longing soul, and it is itself at one and the same time both yearning and fulfillment. The essence of Romantic poetry is to capture and convey its scent. As a result, this form of art is always non-classical, characterized by tender forms and its search for quiet paths, because the route from the first vision to the writing of poetry is long and perilous. Reverence for the voice of eternity, harkening to the rhythm of the inner life, and being at home with the secret wellsprings of the soul—these are the foundations of the Romantic creed.[12]

The most momentous, and surely therefore the most important, text from Hesse's early years was his essay "Romanticism and New Romanticism" (1902). Here it becomes apparent how intensively the autodidact Hesse had steeped himself in the literature of the nineteenth century. In the process, Hesse always wrote from the position of one who regards himself as a writer. But suddenly this was now supplemented by something not seen before in his work: a deeply existential frame of reference, a radical realization of poetry. This experience opened up new worlds for him. All of a sudden Hesse shows his special talent—his capacity to express something fundamental about existence beyond all the abstract concepts of academic discourse, and in his own unique voice. Things began to oscillate at this point, as the multiple layers of Hesse's thought strained toward a unified vision that had nothing dogmatic about it.

What is Romanticism? The twenty-five-year-old Hesse immediately recast this question to inquire instead after all the works of art that could be construed as Romantic. His way of seeing was inclusive rather than exclusive. Even at this stage, Hesse owed it to himself to be a sophisticated composer of his mental images. The opening sentence of his essay "Romanticism and New Romanticism"—"No one knows precisely what the term 'Romantic' actually means"[13]—reveals a sure instinct for the dramatic.

In his youth Hesse had found his way to Romanticism via the works of Heinrich Heine. Heine was the first author he read who seduced him into the notion of freedom, which in Heine's case was unthinkable without an attendant measure of facetiousness. It was through Heine's eyes that Hesse first viewed Romanticism, and he sensed immediately its proximity to the "Romantic School" that he had so roundly ridiculed. The seventeen-year-old Hesse had written to Theodor Rümelin on February 7, 1895:

> Heine undoubtedly delivered the *coup de grâce* to Romanticism, yet he also sang the last, most mature songs of Romanticism, tones that captivate the heart with their naive simplicity. . . . I feel sorry from the bottom of my heart for poor Heine, who at root was the knight of Romanticism, an enthusiast and dreamer who knew how to sing so ardently of the flickering moonshine and faded knightly splendor and the olden days of the troubadours; and once he had been forced to adopt a mocking attitude, he started to pour his Aristophanes-like, sparkling, witty scorn over everything, but most of all over his own corrupted and deeply miserable heart. And so he ultimately became the "German mockingbird" and the poet laureate of world-weariness.[14]

Hugo Ball picked up on this "knight of Romanticism" label in his monograph on Hesse when he described him as "the last knight from the magnificent cavalcade of Romanticism," only to then place this talk of the "last knight" in the context of the oppressive present: "He is defending the rearguard. Will he suddenly turn around, this knight, and establish a new front?"[15]

By the age of seventeen, Hesse was more familiar with Heine than he was with the Romantics. Certainly, he loved Eichendorff's *Aus dem Leben eines Taugenichts (The Life of a Good-for-Nothing)*, but he couldn't get on with Ludwig Tieck at all. And so, lacking any firsthand experience, he sounded quite schoolmasterly when he noted on May 29, 1895: "Romanticism is a standpoint that is already played out."[16]

Romanticism only became interesting for him again when he read Novalis, in the edition published by Diederichs. He realized that Novalis did not represent a "played-out standpoint." Quite the contrary, in fact—his work, Hesse felt, had a spiritual topicality about it that set a course for the future: "I really love him now."[17]

The land of the blue flower was an internal realm. Hesse wrote to He-lene Voigt-Diederichs in 1898: "This Romanticism! Everything secret and youthful about the German heart is contained within it, all its excessive vigor alongside its sickness, and above all a longing for spiritual elevation, a brilliant youthful sense of adventure that is totally lacking in our own time. The religion of art—for me that is the essential thing, that is the aim of Romanticism in both its most naive and its most sophisticated products."[18]

In the essay "Romantic: A Conversation" (1900), he goes on to enun-ciate clearly what Romanticism is: a modern sensibility. A divine order no longer exists. The only things that existed now were the individual and the crisis of the age—and any attempt at an answer could only be tentative. The way forward seemed self-evident for Hesse: "greater pro-fundity through internalization." Accordingly, Novalis's novel *Heinrich von Ofterdingen* became for Hesse a "dreamlike reflection of the human soul up on itself, a wing-beat lifting it out of distress and darkness."[19] Moreover there were successors to Novalis: even in his most trenchant mood of negation, Nietzsche remains a Romantic. *Thus Spoke Zarathustra* is the source of the infamous statement "God is dead"; yet the same work also contains the Romantic music of the "Wanderer's Night Song": "It is night: now all gushing fountains speak louder. And my soul is also a gushing fountain. It is night: only now do all the songs of lovers awake. And my soul too is the song of a lover."[20] For Hesse, the successor to Nietzsche was Jacobsen with his *Niels Lyhne,* which represents the dis-covery of the "child-soul."

All this became the background to Hesse's work from *Peter Camenzind* to *Rosshalde.* After the First World War his field of vision broadened, first in *Demian,* with its aspect of dream interpretation, and then in the Buddhism of *Siddhartha,* and it finally reached its apogee in the—likewise deeply Romantic—figure of Harry Haller, the "Steppenwolf" trapped in the Magic Theater. Hesse was to write one further essay on this subject, en-titled "The Spirit of Romanticism," this time from the perspective of 1926, which will be discussed presently. But he never abandoned the theme of Romanticism as an attitude to life that savored the paradox of modernity to its happy / bitter utmost, as he clearly intimates in this later essay: "Somehow the feeling exists that the German path to self-discovery must once more lead past the Magic Mountain of Romanticism."[21] This path culminated in *The Glass Bead Game,* with its synthesis of tradition and utopia, life and art, skepticism and love, and freedom and monastic seclusion from the world.

Elisabeth, the Distant Muse: Esthetic of the Clouds

> If all women were like you, so pure, so honest, so implacable and so thoughtful, then the world would perish. But there are few women who are like that—maybe as many as ten, maybe as few as none, and that's why I love you.
>
> —Hermann Hesse, "The Poet" (1900 / 1901)

"Lulu"—Julie Hellmann, the pretty waitress from Kirchheim—had not found it hard to resist the young poet's hyper-artificial attempts to woo her by sending her poems rich in literary allusion and letters shot through with fairy-tale and didactic elements. With her, he had nothing to gain from such an approach. And so, standing behind the bar in Kirchheim, Lulu would eventually read the lines: 'To my great alarm, I am noticing more and more that the beautiful princess is in actual fact sadly a witch. My God, I can write such beautiful letters, but when I address them to you, they might just as well be rubbish."[22]

So it was almost with a sense of relief that in December 1899 Hesse informed Ludwig Finckh—until recently a rival for Lulu's affections but who had now also turned his attentions elsewhere: "There's no romance between Lulu and me any more, and she now just shines like a sacred star in heaven."[23]

There were good reasons for this, which had much to do with his new fascination for Basel. In this case it was not his general enchantment with the city but a quite specific focus of interest. At Wackernagel's house he had met Elisabeth La Roche. However, because he lacked the gumption to approach her, this pastor's daughter, who indifferently failed to notice his presence at all, became for him like a cloud—an ideal subject for his poetic raptures because she remained a remote entity, sailing past him and marveled at by him but forever beyond his reach.

Before long his old malaise had set in, and he was plagued by headaches and sleeplessness. Hesse still felt himself very much an outsider. At the same time, though, there is much talk in his diaries of evenings spent in wine taverns, and of people visiting him and he in turn going to see them— never before had he been so much a part of society as he was in Basel now. And yet his inner discontent had only increased as a result of this conviviality, which was alien to his nature. He felt himself to be an outsider, and the soirées in the company of others were nothing but superficial stage props.

He watched Elisabeth playing music, but this did not provide any opening to him, and no confidential conversation resulted from it: "The evening at Wackernagel's (which lasted until 1 A.M.) was enormously grand and showy, and the highlight was the marvelous supper. A throng of professors in black frock-coats and professors' wives in evening gowns made their stately and graceful way around the roomy and attractive house as best they could. As for me, the young whippersnapper—I was by far the youngest person there—I sat between them, looking somewhat irritated."[24]

Elisabeth, the object of his adoration, was blind to his desire and failed to notice his love pangs. At the age of 87, shortly before her death in 1965, she recalled these gatherings at the Wackernagel house—and in her testimony, the indifference she felt toward Hermann Hesse was still clearly evident: "The young writer seemed very much at home in this setting, and the entire Wackernagel family was fond of him. But all my attention and thoughts at that time were still focused on Lake Garda, so I didn't take a very lively interest at all in my Basel acquaintances."[25] Could it perhaps have been this very lack of interest, this melancholic and ostentatious indifference of hers, that drew Hesse to Elisabeth in the first place?

Where women were concerned, Hesse made one mistake after the other—and this trend would continue. Even so, the poetic capital gleaned from this particular encounter was not inconsiderable. In the novels *Hermann Lauscher* and *Peter Camenzind,* a series of melancholic poems, (unsent) letters, as well as the (unpublished) story "The Storyteller," Hesse increasingly came to eulogize Elisabeth in the metaphor of the cloud.

Elisabeth

Like a white cloud
High in the sky
You are bright and beautiful
And so far away, Elisabeth.

No sooner have you noticed it
Than the cloud moves and drifts away
And yet in the dark night
It still drifts through your dreams.

It drifts and shines so silver
That henceforth you feel
Forever a sweet homesickness
For the white cloud.

In a diary entry of February 5, 1901, Hesse spoke of his "half-sad, half ironically skeptical sense of isolation, also from women."[26] By this stage his love affair in letters with Julie Hellmann (Lulu) had taken on almost comic traits; Helene Voigt-Diederichs was married (thanks to his prevarication) and furthermore to the publisher of his first book; and he had not had a favorable experience with Elisabeth La Roche either—Hesse called it a "half-love."[27]

His futile attempts at romance were mounting; he had, it seemed, no talent for dealing with women. He summed up the year 1900, a year in which he nonetheless scored a modest success with his publication of *Hermann Lauscher,* in a mood of gloomy resignation: "In general, my character took on a more masculine, cooler demeanor during this year. My expectations of gaining pleasure from life (intellectual pleasure, that is) increased suddenly, and presently grew insatiable. Yet all my hopes that the future might bring great fulfillment have ceased and I see myself instead resignedly settling for merely enjoying the moment." All in all, then "this year has seen the temperature of my being drop quite considerably."[28]

Over the following years, up to the publication of *Gertrud,* Elisabeth became the symbol of an eroticism that, because it went unfulfilled in real life, looked for expression on a more exalted artistic plane. Only with the appearance of *Peter Camenzind* and the shift to a more practical, workaday sensuality that did not make every day a celebration did this overwrought mechanism of self-frustration begin to dissipate. By then Hesse had already taken two trips to Italy, the second time with Maria Bernoulli, a photographer from Basel who was nine years his senior. But during his time in Basel, Hesse had not yet attained that Rousseauesque simplicity of existence that, following his marriage to Maria

Bernoulli, he tried to act out in Gaienhofen. Everything was still complicated and unclear. The Bermuda Triangle of Eros, Nature, and Art generated its own undertow, which held an almost morbid fascination for him.

In the fall of 1901 Hesse wrote six letters to Elisabeth that he never
ultimately sent, and that were only discovered among his papers after his
death. They are not traditional letters that address themselves to a correspondent or that try to effect some outcome or another; instead they are
monomaniacal exercises in style written by a poet who is intoxicated with
his own misfortune.

In them, the author speaks to everyone—that is, to the anonymous
reader rather than to a particular individual. Yet these letters are extremely
revealing. They bear witness to that dreamlike estheticism that decisively
shuns any form of sensuality and in so doing heightens the dream image
to such a degree that the woman who is the object of desire ends up resembling a cloud rather than a human being. Something similar is found
in the work of the young Rilke, though there it has more of the pathos of
humility about it. Hesse, on the other hand, would dearly love to be a significant poet who radiates a profound knowledge about the mysteries of
life, an aspiration that, given his youthful inexperience, required that he
keep the actual exigencies of real life at bay. The first letter begins: "When
I send someone roses that have grown in a fairy tale I created myself, then
that someone must have a degree of callousness about them to place them
in the shallow water-dish of pallid prose. If only they had at least torn the
roses to pieces! And, laughing their peculiar laugh, strewn the petals into
the night!" Here one can sense a powerful impulse to preserve a dream of
love against any harm and any diminution by life itself. Fulfillment thus
remains only in the world of dreams.

This follows a fairy-tale logic that can also been seen in Hesse's later
works, though there it has been ruptured in many ways and become, as it
were, permeable to experience. This fairy-tale logic constitutes Hesse's esthetic defense against the world:

> I am a person who has a talent for having frequent and vivid dreams. I live
> out everything that I dream: as a child, as the sea, as a storm, as a hero, as
> a penitent—however, I am in a mysterious way always the same person,
> entirely the same person. In between whiles, I "wake" for short spells, and
> then I see things "as they are"—cool, hard, raw, and strange—and hear the
> turgid, murky river of real life rushing by. Every time that happens I find
> myself seized by the desperate question: "Is that really what life is? Is it truly

that grey, that sluggish, that sordid?" But before I can think the question through to the end, the whole miserable apparition of this life suddenly collapses into the abyss and I am gripped once more by the world of dreams.[29]

We may read this as Hesse's esthetic manifesto for the period prior to the writing of *Peter Camenzind*—while a measure of it also continues to leaven his writing thereafter, through *Demian, Narcissus and Goldmund,* and the *Fairy Tales,* right up to *The Glass Bead Game.*

Elisabeth also made an appearance in his lengthy though unpublished story "The Poet" of 1900–1901, which has the subtitle "A Book of Longing"—here in an energetic attempt by the author to drag the dream image into real life and to capture the woman behind her dream persona. The result was a fiasco! The Elisabeth of the story, a pianist, is so plagued by the love of the poet and his furious urge to confess it that she takes flight from the humdrum reality of their actual life together. It sounds as though Hesse wrote this story as a warning to himself. This was a cul-de-sac, in which only cheap sensationalist writing thrived, and in which nothing was genuine or natural! Yet the artificial and unnatural was far from being art— Hesse would learn that though the act of writing.

Somewhat mischievously, one might claim that Thomas Mann, who wrote his own story of youthful angst about the purpose of life in *Tonio Kröger,* had in mind Hesse's poet figure Martin (an alter ego of the author) when he embarked on his story *Tristan* (1903), which features a highly mannered writer who is referred to simply as the "putrid infant." Certainly, Hesse's story is completely without any irony. Instead, he employed that old-fashioned condescension which is designed to conceal how bloodless and devoid of passion the beginning of the story is: "Alongside his mourning for the lost sensory freshness of his early youth, the poet was also overcome by a terrible bitterness toward everything that had occupied his life for many years. The few vestiges of verve and youth that still clung to him following a brief period of reveling indiscriminately in all manner of debauchery he henceforth placed, in an act of dogged self-education, at the sole service of his burning artistic ambition."[30] The twenty-three-year-old (!) Hesse meant this quite seriously—and yet he did not then simply cast aside this mannered piece of artistic posturing like his character Peter Camenzind, who after a long search ultimately deemed it a more meaningful role in life to work in a tavern in his home village dispensing wine and spirit to drinkers

Hesse as a naked rock-climber (at Amden in 1910)

than to belong to an artistic clique in a city like Paris or Berlin, even if it did happen to be the predominant clique at the time. No, poet Martin carefully assembles everything that he has written in his life (which doesn't amount to a great deal) and voyages by boat in the company of these unique pieces of work to the middle of the ocean, where he drops everything overboard. Was what he wrote meaningless, or was the world too meaningless for his work? Hesse forbears to give a response to this question.

So, now that Martin was freed of the burden of his past work, couldn't he begin to lead a different life? Not for Hesse in 1900. Thus, although in fact "The Poet" ends dramatically, the way in which the end is expressed is refreshingly succinct: "Martin traveled to Grindelwald, where he disappeared without a trace in the high mountains."[31]

Whichever way one turned the image of Elisabeth—and Hesse did just that incessantly during this period—she remained a wretched muse, a woman who was as cold as marble.

Love seemed to Hesse a topic that was as remote as it was mysterious. He could never quite make it his own, nor could he completely leave it behind. That was Hesse's dilemma at the end of his time in Basel, as he envisioned his Hermann Lauscher, this eccentric character on the border-line between outsider and heretic, being haunted by the "muse of sleep-lessness," to borrow a phrase from Nietzsche's *Zarathustra*. Lauscher is perplexed; his only knowledge of women relates to the dream image in his head: "Was this love? I have no idea. Love is just a name, and for me love is precisely that softly dissolving lyricism that affects me as a special form of sentimentality and is as sweet as it is debilitating."

Fewer and fewer things were now keeping him in Basel. As early as December 3, 1899, shortly after his arrival there, he wrote the following to his parents: "The true denizens of Basel are very stiff and mistrustful toward foreigners, especially young unknowns."[32] With the exception of Rudolf Wackernagel and his family, that would remain the case for the next four years. Plus Hesse was no longer as enthused about his boss, Herr Reich, as he had been at the outset. For sure, he was genial enough, Hesse noted on February 5, 1901: "However, the range of books doesn't meet my expectations and in fact irritates me so much that I am currently, as I write this, contemplating transferring to an antiquarian bookshop." There then follows a sentence that the reader must find remarkable: "I haven't found a single friend in Basel."[33]

Inwardly, Hesse had already taken his leave of this city, to which he felt bound by so many things since his childhood that he once maintained he had actually always felt himself to be Swiss. Although he did indeed now accept a post at the Wattenwyl antiquarian bookshop, where he would earn only 100 francs (only as much as he had been making back in Tübingen, but now with more free time at his disposal) and was reliant for additional income on the royalties from reprints of his works—in other words, he was already trying out the "semi-free" existence of a professional writer—he still yearned for another kind of life entirely. His dream was to be able one day to live entirely from his writing.

Chopin and the Pure Essence of Music

> You are an educator and hence to all practical intents and pur-
> poses an enemy of art.
>
> —Hermann Hesse, letter to Karl Isenberg June 12, 1897

On October 4, 1897, Hesse had written to his parents from Tübingen to tell them that three-quarters of the poetry written by the Moravian

Brethren was, if one disregarded its morally uplifting purpose, "nothing short of criminal." Or perhaps that was precisely because of its "morally uplifting purpose"? Hesse does not goes so far as to say that here, but what he does write about the connection between morality and esthetics (in the mold of Nietzsche) almost prefigures the basic principles of Theodor Adorno's *Esthetic Theory:* "For the simple fact is I have for a long time now been of the firm belief that morality in the artist is replaced by esthetics (though this need not necessarily be so) and that art, and the art of poetry first and foremost, is not there to do good in any moral sense."[34] This was a powerful thesis that the twenty-year-old Hesse was positing here against the one thing that had up till then given art any rationale for existing in the eyes of his family. This act of disengaging art from any moral purpose had a number of causes—one of which was the overpowering effect that Chopin's music had had on Hesse.

"Grande Valse," one of several poems by Hesse on the subject of Chopin, was written in the spirit of emotional self-exploration. It therefore comes across more powerfully as the poet's declaration of belief in the composer he so admired than as a real expression of the nature of his music. All the more reason, then, why it should have merited his parents' paying some real heed to it rather than passing over it with scarcely a mention as if it was some embarrassing faux pas:

> A candle-bright hall
> And the sounds of spurs and gold braid.
> The blood sings in my veins.
> Pass me my goblet, my girl!
> And now let's dance! The waltz romps on;
> Warmed by wine my sparkling spirit
> Yearns for all the pleasures I have not yet tasted—
>
> And outside the window my horse is whinnying.

Certainly this poem has that same tantalizing triviality that is often encountered in Hesse's later poetry. Curiously, he declared the lyricism of the nineteenth century and its propagation of emotion to be the ideal of poetry. The Chopin poem would go through three further versions, and in all of these the line "And outside the window my horse is whinnying" reappeared, twice in each case, as a leitmotif. Is it perhaps not understandable that Hesse's parents, who were not only familiar with Pietist morally improving verse but also knew their Schiller, should find this kind of poetry both ungodly and devoid of any spirituality?

Hermann Hesse was deeply wounded by their attitude. Even so, he attempted to explain why Chopin was so important to him: "I can appreciate how my Chopin poem did not appeal to you. There's nothing that great about it. But you should understand that what Wagner was for Nietzsche, Chopin is for me—or even more so. All the essential features of my spiritual life are connected with those warm, lively melodies and those piquant, wanton, and nervous harmonies, indeed with the whole of Chopin's musical oeuvre, which is so uncommonly intimate."[35] This explanation touched on the sore point: the intoxicating aspect of art, particularly in music. For his parents, and their whole religious worldview, this crossed a line into the realm of evil.

Throughout his lifetime, Hesse, whose fiddle had been a strong emotional prop in times of growing pressure in the midst of his own neurosis during puberty, but who never played it in public (something he confided to Helene Voigt-Diederichs), found his greatest inner stability in music. This role, which was initially filled by Chopin, was later taken by Mozart. But the first music that really shook him emotionally was Chopin's. Listening to his work, Hesse experienced the Romantic aspect of music as a moment not only of rapture but also of intensity and enchantment and ultimately of transformation. During his time in Tübingen, the only person he could talk to unguardedly about this was Helene Voigt-Diederichs: "You understand that I feel creatively stimulated through music like I do through nothing else. The poems of my own that I like the most can in almost all cases be traced back to Chopin or Beethoven."[36]

Later, too, he would always hark back to this first encounter with Chopin, which for him was like a rite of passage. In his 1956 work *Funeral March: Memorial Sheet for a Young Comrade* he spoke once more about an event that in his memory was inextricably associated with the Funeral March movement from Chopin's B-flat minor sonata. A student had shot himself. Hesse knew him from his time at Maulbronn and had also run into him a few times in Tübingen. The funeral of a student was a big event for a small place like Tübingen, and Hermann Hesse also took a break from his monotonous work there and went outside onto the street with the other sales assistants from Heckenhauer's bookshop so as not to miss the macabre spectacle.

> There we stood watching the cortege coming slowly toward us, at its head the black hearse carrying the wreath-bedecked coffin, and behind it, in a solemn and ceremonial procession, the officials of the fraternity the student belonged to, all spick-and-span and wearing caps, sashes, top boots, with lowered dueling rapiers, alongside other fraternities and sundry student organizations. The town band marched along in their midst. It was a long, splendidly colorful funeral procession and drifting and surging over it all like a flag of mourning came the ponderous, mournful, magnificently solemn music of Chopin, in its pathos-laden marching rhythm, a piece I would hear many times again in my life, and that would unfailingly be accompanied by a painful recollection of this sad occasion.[37]

The paradox remained, however, that on this occasion a deeply serious event—notwithstanding the solemn dignity that was lent to it by Chopin's Funeral March—ultimately degenerated into a spectacle with a positively obscene carnival aspect to it. For among the throng of rubberneckers who gathered to watch the procession, who was actually mourning the poor person being laid to rest there? As the funeral cortege made its way through the streets, Hesse detached himself from the frivolous crowd and, with a feeling of disgust and loneliness, returned to his post in the shop. Yet in spite of himself, he too found his senses stimulated by the showpiece that he had just witnessed with a dead person as the leading character.

Hermann Lauscher: Art and Life Meet

The world becomes dream, and dream becomes the world.

—Novalis

Hesse noted that he intended to imitate *Niels Lyhne,* not without adding his own personal flavor, and to overtrump the most sublime of Viennese artists in their ecstasies. Tübingen now lay behind him in actuality but ahead of him as the subject of artistic description. Basel had awakened the music within him. There, he began to see images in a different way; henceforth they took on the most intense spiritual actuality for him. And in Basel he discovered the inner freedom to tell stories dealing with errors and ignorance, wayward love, and betrayed faith.

In the process of writing he now had the reader more clearly in mind than he had during his hermit-like creation of *An Hour Behind Midnight*. He banked on the effect of certain phrases, created deliberate points of emphasis, and ironically generated the kind of playful atmosphere for himself—and the reader—that is the key element in making the act of reading (and of writing) an intimate experience. In his biography Hugo Ball described Hesse as belonging to a generation that looked back in lamentation to the very beginnings of the human soul: "There they are, Apollo and Dionysus; only they now relate not so much to culture and history as to the individual, personal realm."[38]

The *fin de siècle* covered everything it touched with the mildew of melancholy. That is also true of Hesse, albeit only halfway true. He was far too impetuous to exhaust himself making nothing but valedictory gestures. Undoubtedly Hugo Ball was right to remark that *Hermann Lauscher* contained the same kind of vocabulary that could be found in the works of Friedrich Nietzsche, Hugo von Hofmannsthal, Stefan George, Maurice Maeterlinck, and Georg Trakl—yet there was something different about it all the same. Amid the great round-dance of characters, which does not comes across as especially original because it follows the Romantic model somewhat too mechanically, other elements—things that constitute the essentially modern characteristic of this prose—shine through: Hesse's playful manipulation of his own doppelgänger figure, and his audacity in using a fragmentary and open form of narrative. In order to be able to recount the story in the first place, he creates his own double, Hermann Lauscher, whose suicide is in turn presupposed. Then, however, the prose piece "The November Night," which has Lauscher as its central character, tells the story of another suicide. It is a ghost story in the style of E. T. A. Hoffmann.

At the same time Hesse himself also made an appearance as an author—for instance, in his *Diary 1900,* which reads as aphoristically as if it were the working journal of a writer, the collection of reflections of a person who seems determined to exploit the literature of the nineteenth century in a highly individual way. The perspective of the author Hermann

Hesse is, so to speak, split simultaneously into an inner and an outer persona. Hesse appears by name in the book, but only in the form of a note by Lauscher mentioning him as someone he met in Basel: "There I had a long conversation with Hesse, who of course complained and nitpicked so much again that I eventually lost my temper." And at another point: "Hesse is trying to get me to write a piece on Tieck, whose work he ought to know far better than I do."

Here, then, the young author Hesse proves himself a sophisticated narrator—time and again, what claims to be reality reveals itself to be a new story. Does one ever get to the bottom of things here, or is it rather the case that when one curtain opens here, another one always closes, shutting off what had only just been glimpsed from view once more? In the prose piece "The November Night" we enter a kind of cabinet of mirrors. There, in what is heralded as a retrospective account, we find Hermann Lauscher—long since dead, by his own hand—sitting in a wine tavern, seemingly very real and present, oppressed by the pain of existence, and beset by a pathos at the meaninglessness of life:

> Poetry be damned! My humor consists of sitting here, drinking your wine and contemplating your desperate faces when I have gold, silver, fairy tales, and treasures inside me. What is it that you're squandering here? An exam, a bit of family capital, a post in which you've worked your fingers to the bone and become bored to tears. And why are you doing it? Because it's dawned on you that it's not worth living for all that stuff. Now I, on the other hand, drink down a little bit of poet's blue sky with every sip of wine I take, a province of my imagination, a color from my artist's palette, a string from my harp, a bit of art, a bit of fame, and a bit of eternity. And why do I do that? Because it's not worth living for all that either. Because life isn't worth living whichever way you slice it; a life without a purpose is bleak, and a life with a purpose is sheer torment.[39]

In this way, Hesse's alter ego Hermann Lauscher launches into his voluble diatribe by emphatically stating his nihilistic outlook on life. And what does his interlocutor do, who is sitting opposite him and is the target of this rant? He laughs in Lauscher's face, and brushes aside his lofty graveyard pathos: "Drink up, Lauscher, and stop talking nonsense!" And shortly thereafter the wheel of life and death rolls on once more—and at the end of a long and boozy night the second suicide is found lying dead on a bridge: the scoffing drinking companion known as Elenderle ("Miserable"), a washout whose keen sense of irony was of no use when he found himself caught in a moment of terrible loneliness. Lauscher is shocked; perhaps this death before his very eyes might have cured him of his own death wish if he hadn't been long dead already.

Hermann Hesse drives the role-play forward in *Hermann Lauscher,* appearing in a succession of different transformational forms. Motifs are broached here that are generally only associated with Hesse's later texts. Thus, the dramatic departure of the philosopher Drehdichum ("Turn-around") in the prose piece "Lulu" anticipates the surreal closing image of *Life Story Briefly Told* (1921–1924), where the author, who has been imprisoned for the "seduction of a young girl," makes himself small, steps into a picture and, stepping into a train that the artist has just painted, makes good his escape: "The prison wardens were left behind in a state of great embarrassment."[40] Here, in the thinly disguised setting of the tavern in Kirchheim, the domain of Lulu (Julie Hellmann), the philosopher departs an inhospitable situation just as dramatically: "Lulu was crying again, the landlady was protesting and cursing; and so neither of them noticed how the philosopher blew a large smoke ring from his stubby pipe, sat himself down in it and quietly drifted out of the open window on a light draft."

The slim volume first appeared in 1901 under the title *Writings and Poems from the Estate of Hermann Lauscher,* purportedly edited and published by Hermann Hesse. This was a trick that he would later repeat under the pseudonym Emil Sinclair. This was an outward manifestation of the fact that a new departure seemed to call for a new name for the author.

And so, on December 2, 1900, the following lines written by the reviewer Hermann Hesse appeared in the local paper in Basel, discussing Hermann Lauscher's posthumous writings: "I felt his (Lauscher's) sudden departure to be a blessed release for his soul, which swung distressingly between extremes. I can think of no more fitting monument for his ardent, unstable but at root noble and in any event always upright nature than publication of the works he left behind."

Hesse did not omit to note discreetly that Lauscher's writings might be of particular interest to a Basel public, because the deceased writer had lived there. The book was indeed a success, albeit one that was confined to Basel. Before long it came to light that Lauscher and Hesse were one and the same person. And in truth the symbol of the "listener"—a person both harkening to the outside world and listening to what was going on inside himself—was a new element to this prose. Helene Voigt-Diederichs noticed this change in attitude early on. Hermann Hesse experienced the world—and Basel in this regard offered more than Tübingen had—with a new sensual openness. He had acquired a new sensitivity—to what was going on around him as well as for what came from within him, or recollections of his childhood. Anxiety and longing now combined with descriptions of nature and studies of milieu, and with those dream landscapes of the "blue flower," which Hesse (following Novalis) was in search of.

Yet Hesse's departure from a reduced nature—namely, a form of art deriving from stylized artificiality—is also already half-complete in *Hermann Lauscher*. In the story "Lulu," the title figure looks at the seminarians, who are attempting to pass themselves off as men of the world, with the sobriety and wit of a real, lived life that will not allow itself to be deceived about the hardships of everyday existence: "These young men seemed to her like poor moths that had been misled into fluttering around little lights. All the same, they held forth at great length, and it struck her as sad and laughable how they kept going on about beauty and youth and roses, constructing colorful stage scenery of words around themselves while the whole harsh business of real life passed them by unnoticed. That reality was inscribed simply and deeply upon her uncomplicated little girl's soul, instructing her that the art of life consisted of learning how to suffer and still smile."[41]

First Encounters with Goethe and Nietzsche

When Hermann Hesse began to take responsibility for his own education in Tübingen, he focused above all on German literature between 1790 and 1890. There, the eighteen-year-old made a remarkable discovery, which he recounted to his parents in a letter that took him three days to write, from January 11 to January 13, 1896. He could sense momentous changes taking place within him:

> Learning and forming judgments has become remarkably easier for me, since I applied myself to reading Goethe, where I discovered a definite standpoint from which I could judge. It is curious how, starting from Goethe, even the newest developments can be understood. My real literary

Gospel, though, has not been *Faust* but instead *Wilhelm Meister's Apprentice-ship* and *Truth and Poetry.* I am very fond of *Reineke Fuchs,* whose carefully constructed reliefs I studied with both a sense of happy application and pure pleasure such as I have not yet encountered in life. Reading something like this you become a child once more, yet you can also bring to it the customary baggage of your previous education without ever feeling disappointed.[42]

To Hesse, Goethe seemed to be worldly-wise and party to all the mysteries of the world. In Goethe's work he discovered an attitude toward religion that was liberated but not blind and deaf to transcendental experi-ence. This was expressed, not in the form of dogmas or ready-made answers, but as an appreciation of openness, inconclusiveness, and the mysterious power inherent in all material things, be they organic or inorganic. In his own period of "crisis," when he arrived in Frankfurt in 1768, Goethe en-countered Pietism in the shape of one Madame Klettenberg, who recom-mended he read Gottfried Arnold's *Impartial History of the Church and of Heresy* (1699 / 1700). For Goethe this meeting was a liberation. However, among Pietists, Gottfried Arnold was an exception rather than the rule and as a mystic was an outsider, almost a heretic himself.

This chronicler of heresy energetically lambasted the institution of the religious sect, which formed the center of Johannes and Marie Hesse's life. In book 8 of *Poetry and Truth* Goethe would later recall: "The spirit of con-tradiction and enjoyment of the paradoxical is inherent in all of us. I ea-gerly studied the most diverse opinions. And because I had often heard people say that everyone ultimately has their personal religion, nothing seemed more natural to me than that I should create my own, so that is what I did, much to my satisfaction."

How Hermann Hesse must have inwardly rejoiced when he read this! In Goethe he found that pantheism that recognizes a divine spark in all things. There is nothing that is simply holy, or simply profane—such a clear division was only brought about by his parents' demonic view of the world, which Hesse firmly rejected. In Goethe, by contrast, magic and alchemy combined in enlightened autonomy and in the *Sturm und Drang* spirit of his poem on Prometheus. Goethe had a sense of the fateful vulnerability of the individual adrift in an ocean of time.

As it was for Gottfried Benn, Goethe's concept of nature was fasci-nating for Hesse in its opposition to a simple codification of the world, such as that practiced by the modern natural sciences. Isaac Newton, whose theory of optics propounded technically verifiable spectra of light, was a source of irritation for Goethe and only served to strengthen his magical conception of nature. To Goethe, nature was a living entity. What, he asked himself, was this power, this transformative spark in nature that lent it its peculiar qualities? For Goethe, the enlightened statesman and Weimar classicist, nature was quite unashamedly a treasure trove of various magical arts of transformation—and that in turn also fascinated Hesse. Goethe managed to powerfully unite—and was the only person of his era to do so—the contradicting realms of modern natural sciences and traditional interpretations of the natural world. Here was a model for Hesse of someone who was a writer and yet also concurrently a philosopher!

Unlike his attitude to Schiller, Hesse did not consider Goethe a genuine dramatist. Yet even though he was not a dyed-in-the-wool man of the stage, he had still successfully headed a theater. Hesse, who had no time for bourgeois theater (but who, despite this, or precisely because of this, created the Magic Theater) and who condemned it every bit as vehemently as his Pietist parents as a place of superficial effects, would have dearly loved to elevate Goethe out of the milieu of the theater, believing him to have very little in common with that world: "I am positively happy that Goethe was not a great dramatist; despite being a heretic, I don't pay homage to the theater and consequently always find myself somewhat distant from Schiller, that one-sided writer for the stage." And here his rather conceited objection to the theater becomes apparent, though the particular line of argument he advances makes it audacious of him to adduce Goethe, of all people, as a witness for the defense: "The stage is the most fashionable and conventional of all art forms; alongside journalism, it generates the most toadies."[43]

Nevertheless, Hesse had a farsighted understanding of Goethe's positively cosmic humor. In Goethe, irony, parody, satire, caricature, and wit are always organically linked with their opposite—namely, tragedy and pathos. They remain related to one another and do not disintegrate, as they do in later writers. Goethe differs from Schiller in having a sense of the scurrilous, the absurd, and the risible in human relations. The autodidact from Tübingen is able at this juncture to pinpoint this distinction, too: "Schiller could also have portrayed a Faust, but not a Wagner [Faust's assistant] or a Mephisto, and a proud monologue would suddenly have carried a Schillerian Faust off into the blue yonder, into heaven, and then there would have been no earthly ties to bind him any longer."[44]

If he were to emigrate to Brazil, the young Hesse informed his parents, he would find no difficulty in restricting his library to the works of Goethe. As we know, such a journey never came about, and instead of going to Brazil he found himself back in Basel. There his preferred reading material expanded to include, alongside Goethe, the Romantics, Nietzsche, and Jacob Burckhardt.

In a letter of November 6, 1895, to Dr. Kapff, Hesse complained that he only knew of Nietzsche's work "from a thousand reviews" and that he surely wouldn't get around to reading the philosopher firsthand anytime soon. It was only when he was back in Tübingen that he began reading Nietzsche—and in July 1896 his father in Calw received a letter explaining: "You mentioned Nietzsche briefly when you wrote to me recently, father. I am familiar with some of his writings and in general I find his high-minded, esthetic approach by no means unsympathetic; now and then his work gives you a breath or two of refreshing mountain air. Most of all, I admire his powerful linguistic and poetic genius. To cite just a couple of isolated poetic turns of phrase from his work: 'Virtue is the will to destruction and an arrow of longing' and the sentence 'Do not be ashamed to stammer about your virtue.'" Hesse then follows this up with something that was calculated preemptively to mollify his father, who despised the kind of decadence evident in the passages from Nietzsche: "The shame about him is that he ought to have written an 'esthetics of the master class,' which would have been more worthwhile than his 'morality of the master class.' It seems to me that, in contrast to other forceful geniuses, he is especially dangerous precisely for well-educated people."[45] It seems fair to regard this as a semi-Pietist reading of Nietzsche. Presently, however, it dawns on Hesse that Nietzsche's problem is another one entirely: Don't follow me, follow yourself! Henceforth, Hesse would frequently identify the often failed task of the intellectual as having the courage to take his fate in his own hands and to live the autonomous life he had always hankered after even in circumstances where it was accompanied by bitter mistakes and failure.

Embarking on His First Journey to Italy:
A Feast and a Torment for the Eyes

This was a journey through a Europe in the absence of war,
through a Canton of Graubünden without dust, though an
Italy without automobiles; back then it was still a pure delight
to walk for whole days at a stretch along highways. I did not
know at the time that most of the little joys I experienced in
traveling belonged to a world that was about to vanish and
would soon no longer be found anywhere.

—Hermann Hesse, "Recollection of a Journey"

Unlike Thomas Mann, who has his character Tonio Kröger say that
people should stop going on to him about Italy and all its *bellezza,* and
that he would rather go to Denmark for a spell, Herman Hesse followed
Goethe and the Romantics in pursuing the dream of the "land where the
lemon trees blossom," that place where darkness and chilly senses are dis-
pelled by the pleasures of the here and now. Here, many an out-and-out
good-for-nothing who had no intention of obeying the Protestant work
ethic, like the title character of Eichendorff's famous story, had found
happiness and peace and repose, at least for a certain amount of time.

Hermann Hesse, though, lacked the money to go on a journey, especially since he had quit his job at Reich's bookshop.

Yet even at this early stage there came to the fore a characteristic of
Hesse's that would subsequently help him through several lean financial
periods: his inventiveness and his joy in producing handwritten manuscripts; this was a task in which he displayed genuine handicraft skill—in
later years he would often painstakingly illuminate them. He made twenty
copies, for instance, of his small poetry selection *Notturni,* which he offered for sale to friends and acquaintances. In this way, he succeeded in
raising no less than 400 francs for his travel fund.

Hesse wrote to his parents on May 2, 1896, explaining the effect that
Italy had had on his idol Goethe: "When he travels to Italy, that's the
point at which Goethe's work starts to become ambiguous. The experience changes him, he becomes more complete and self-aware, but after
Italy he is also the quiet, enigmatic creator who becomes estranged from
the people and sees his own past in an ambiguous light . . . that dual truth
sets in, and that divergent double path starts, which one cannot follow

without putting one's feet too far apart; there's rarely a happy medium there."[46]

Hermann Hesse knew that his yearning for Italy was already antiquated at the beginning of the twentieth century. New things were happening not in southern landscapes but in the metropolises of the North. Rilke was just experiencing that in Paris at the time. His work *Malte Laurids Brigge* became a seismogram of a fragmented modern reality, in which deep fissures were becoming apparent through the simultaneity of the rapid acceleration of life and stasis. What emerged from this was a damaged new kind of human being who was experiencing pain as a result of being cut adrift from all the old natural opportunities open to him even as he strove to free himself from them by exploiting the rapid expansion of technological opportunities. If this liberation did not come about, then at least he could achieve a kind of numbness.

In his "Letters to Elisabeth" Hesse placed himself firmly on the side of the *Southerners,* and declared his allegiance to that "world of yesterday" that Stefan Zweig regarded as being in terminal decline. Even at this stage, then, traveling to the South was tantamount for him to traveling into the past. As regards the new metropolises, those places where the hysteria associated with the acceleration of life and the neuroses of the emergent mass society held sway, these letters convey a very clear feeling of "Count me out!": "Berlin is right: the art of the future comes from up there, from Prussia, Scandinavia, and Russia—in other words from those countries that we Southerners can only regard with horror and pity when we look at them on a map." Hesse sensed what the dawning twentieth century had brought with it: a new mentality, an era in which economics governed everything, even time. "With this, the death sentence has been pronounced against us fantasists of the old school. For our art and our taste—mine, yours, and that of all of us—is at home in Florence, Venice, and Rome, in empires that have long since declined and fallen. The modern-day Rome is called Berlin."[47]

Hesse entered the twentieth century with the distinct sense of being a residual figure. In no other author of his generation—we should remind ourselves that he was only twenty-three at the time—was the conviction so strong that an era of banality, of the devaluation of all values, and of irrevocable losses was now dawning. However, it would be wrong to see this as simply backward-looking and Romantic—for Hesse had already studied Romanticism so intensively during this period that he knew how this movement promoted the realization of art more assertively than any other intellectual trend. After having been let down by the state, by the Church, and by rationality, the individual stands there with Novalis's "blue flower" in his hand—and does not cease to search for the garden where it grows. This is what explains Hesse's yearning for Italy.

He consigned Nietzsche to the things he needed to leave behind: "I am convinced, though, that it is precisely the readers and writers on Nietzsche who have no future; for when all is said and done, Nietzsche too is of the old school. Secretly he had more homesickness for the land of the Greeks than for the country of Zarathustra's childhood. . . . If I voyage on the ship of modernity, then I am one of those who look past the busy industriousness and the revelries of my fellow passengers and gaze back at the sinking, temple-strewn shores of the land we have left behind." But the way in which he concludes this passage does not sound at all melancholic, revealing instead an impetuous urge to plow his own furrow: "Indeed, what is Nietzsche to us? Or philosophy in general? An exercise, mental gymnastics, something pleasant and useful! But what's the point of that?"

This would prove to be the case as he made his way south. Hesse's journey to Italy was his way of putting to the test a dream that he knew full well most people regarded as a museum piece. Not in his eyes, however: for him the South lived with an intensity he envied with every fiber of his body, which had been so abused by the demands of asceticism. For someone who was leaving his homeland not just in order to reject Pietism but also to counter it with a totally different attitude to life, Italy still represented a highly relevant and vivid challenge to the senses.

On March 25, 1901, Hesse finally began his long-planned journey to Italy, starting from Calw. He wanted to continue dreaming the dream that Goethe had dreamed before him. It was not Rome that attracted him— no large city ever cast a spell over Hesse—but a dream of the southern landscape, where nature and culture in German eyes combined in spectacular natural ease. By the time he came to write a foreword to his work "Mood Pictures from Northern Italy," which was published in book form in 1904 in the style of travel reports, he had already made two trips to Italy: "For when I finally set foot on Italian soil, something I had been longing to do and dreaming of for many years, it gave me an intensely heightened feeling of happiness such as I had scarcely known before and would in all likelihood never feel again."[48]

In Stuttgart he spent a night at the house of a great aunt on the Gundert side of the family. The following evening he arrived in Milan, his first port of call south of the Alps. He was keen to see the cathedral at the very least: "Enormously impressive in terms of its ornamentation, the interior colossal (principally due to its height), and the light cast by the stained-glass windows and broken up by the marble columns quite beautiful."[49] There is no real enthusiasm in this description, however; Hesse was disappointed by Milan. It was a bustling, very northern, very business-oriented city that did not at all fit his image of the South. Two years later he would discourage Stefan Zweig, who was planning an Italian journey of his own, from going there, "since, as a city, is it disappointing." Modern Milan simply did not accord with his image of a place of refuge for the overstimulated senses. For if Hesse was searching for anything in Italy, it was salvation from his Protestant compulsion to work and the pressure he felt to account for every minute of the day. Was wasting time a sin? No, it was the starting point of all art, of that art of seeing, hearing, smelling, touching, and tasting that precedes the hard work without which no work of art would ever see the light of day. As a result, he told Stefan Zweig: "I strongly recommend that you don't go dashing around Italy but instead take your time to stroll about at leisure, even if that means you only get to know one city."[50]

He hardly needed to convince his correspondent not to spend the whole day dashing from one major attraction to the next with a Baedeker guide clutched in his hand—for of all the authors of his generation, Zweig, together with Hesse, was undoubtedly the one who thought most deeply about the art of traveling.

These two writers had in common a strong aversion to "the new bureaucratic, mechanistic form of mass wayfaring: namely, the tourism industry." Austrian writer Joseph Roth had already voiced the sense of disenchantment that afflicts everyone who crosses a state frontier with an image of flourishing landscapes in their head—only to immediately find themselves in the next state: "Foreign countries only come into bloom behind borders that are guarded by customs officers and hemmed in by passport laws, and the distant place that was the object of your yearning, is itself just another state with a head of state and constabulary, its population growth and its tax declarations."[51]

Stefan Zweig's short essay "Traveling or Being Traveled" of 1926 is a kind of manifesto of the individual in an age that thought only in terms of masses, yet that, perversely enough, had chosen to fly the banner of individualism, behind which the people manipulated in this way willingly marched, following every fashion that led to a new uniformity and misconstruing it as the very epitome of freedom. Against this ideology of freedom, Zweig and Hesse felt it was incumbent upon them to defend the kind of freedom that people lived every day. For Zweig too, it was the figure of the wayfarer who was the guardian of the magic of the unknown against the standardization imposed by the newly emergent tourist industry. Yet the state of "being traveled" was the "shape of things to come," because it was practical and comfortable.

> And yet, doesn't precisely the mystery of travel get lost amid such random communality? Ever since ancient times, the word "journey" has been tinged with a faint whiff of adventure and danger, a breath of capricious chance and engrossing precariousness. When we travel, we don't do so just because of the lure of far-off places, but also in order to get away from our own world, from the daily well-ordered and tabulated domestic sphere, just for the sheer joy of not being at home and therefore not being ourselves—We want to interrupt the business of simply living from day to day by experiencing things. However, those people who are content to "be traveled" merely journey past many new things and not into the new, with the result that everything that is special and individual about a country must of necessity elude them, as long as they are led rather than letting the true God of the wayfarer, chance, guide their steps.[52]

In his 1904 text "On Traveling," Hermann Hesse also saw the poetry of being under way as an exile on the part of the individual who wishes to escape being absorbed into the mass by technology and bureaucracy. Yet everywhere this quintessential embodiment of the traveler, the wayfarer, now comes up against "the blight of city dwellers who when they are in the Alps want to live like they are at home. . . . However, one time on a train between Verona and Padua, when I could not help but share my views on this subject with a German family, the frosty politeness I encountered reduced me to silence; and on another occasion when I boxed the ears of a vile waiter in Lucerne, I was not requested to leave but positively forced to quit the establishment in unseemly haste. Since then I have learned to control myself."[53]

According to Hesse, one ought only to travel to places with which one has a spiritual connection. One must surely have dreamed one time during the night of what one would dearly love to see by day with one's own eyes. But where does it lie hidden, this "poetry of travel" that Hesse invokes so fervently? It does not, he maintains, reside in merely taking a rest from the monotony of everyday life at home, nor is it to be found in the simple gratification of curiosity: "It is to be found in experience, that is to say in enrichment, in the organic assimilation of things newly acquired, in the growth in our appreciation of unity in diversity and of the great fabric of the Earth and humanity, and in the rediscovery of old truths and laws in completely new circumstances."[54]

This, then, was why he was now in Italy. For the very first time. He knew Goethe's *Italian Journey,* Heine's *Baths of Lucca,* and Count Platen's poems about Venice. But all of that was subservient to looking at himself. Milan was a letdown; this big city had already become as soulless as Hesse imagined every city in the world to be—and this was a question of nerves, since everyone navigates in life by their physical and psychological presuppositions.

Hesse, this intensely visual person, for whom seeing was the greatest of pleasures, also tormented himself through the act of seeing. Vision for him was not just a self-evident fact, but was always associated with pain. There were times when he had to forbid himself from looking—no idle sauntering round towns, no art galleries, and no reading—just constant headaches and sleepless nights as a result of his eye condition (muscles spasms in both his right and left temples). He could only ever sit and in quiet enjoyment or in edifying contemplation of a scene for a short time, and even that came at a high price. He captured what was so fundamental for him about the act of seeing in a 1902 sketch entitled "At the Eye Clinic": "I recall the only great passion in my life, namely, my quiet friendship with mountains, fields, trees, and water, and found to my astonishment that, almost without exception, all the pure, genuine, exquisite joys that I have ever experienced came to me through my eyes. This feeling was so vivid that I felt an overwhelming urge to run away and find a spot somewhere in the city where I could lie down in the tall, sparse grass."[55]

He stayed in Milan for only two days before traveling on to Genoa. Here, too, he found himself confronted by conflicting impressions: "The Novi railway station, as dirty as the one at Basel Bad." That was a very German perspective, to be put out at finding that the nonchalance one was seeking in the South was actually just messiness. But a sigh of relief is also clearly audible: "Genoa furnished me with my first genuinely Italian scene: sun, shining white houses, a sparkling blue-green sea, colorfully dressed people, and beggars and dawdlers on the steps of the houses and churches."[56] Around the turn of the twentieth century, Italy was not just a country of art treasures and beautiful landscapes; it was also a very poor country where child beggars were part of everyday life. And if that were not enough, it also started snowing when Hesse was in Genoa. Accordingly he resolved to head farther south. He had no desire to remain in Pisa; the weather there was appalling. Even in the very first few days, the South was showing him what potential it held for disenchantment. Then he moved on to Florence; even here, things were not as he had dreamed they would be: "The Piazza was very noisy until the small hours of the morning." Despite this, though, "the weather is mild in Florence, almost warm. The room, bed, and furnishings are good." He found the cathedral and its tower staggering, and the wine "first-rate and cheap for the most part, not light but very palatable all the same." He ambled through the streets clutching Jacob Burckhardt's *The Cicerone* and wearing the expression of a *flâneur*. The disappointing reality that all foreign visitors encounter stood cheek-by-jowl with art and architectural history: "Bad cup of chocolate in a café. Then on to the Uffizi."[57]

Hesse remained in Florence for the whole of April. In the diary he kept of his journey, he confessed that he enjoyed looking at beautiful women even more than he did at paintings. "Here you can see artists, German moneybags, and slim, fantastic, Pre-Raphaelite Englishwomen." Hesse drank in all of this eagerly, the exotic and the familiar alike, colorful and dreary things, and the sun and the rain. He was living a more intense existence, even when he was doing nothing more than strolling around the city. Italy awakened his senses. And he admired the Italians for the fact that they had—still!—managed to preserve their naturalness in the face of the trend toward the mechanization and uniformity of modern life: "Unless they're actively engaged in business, these people have a naivety and generosity of manner, and have such a natural and flexible mode of existence that makes us Northerners seem like marionettes in comparison."[58]

For Hesse, as for many Germans who loved Italy not just for its art treasures but also for its way of life, it seemed as though he could suddenly spend his days walking about without having a guilty conscience and could finally shrug off that rigid corset of order and dutifulness that constrained him. This was the same kind of freedom to simply live life one day at a time that Eichendorff had already glorified in his work *From the Life of a Good-for-Nothing*. The word that Hesse uses most frequently in the diary of his first Italian journey is "splendid" *(famos);* he even uses it to describe things that might on the face of it appear instead to be irritating—but in Italy even such things often had a comical aspect to them: "Today, when I was out on the street and had a half-smoked cigar in my mouth, a man came up to me and asked me to give it to him. I thought he wanted to light his own from it, so I handed him it, but he cheerfully stuck my cigar in his mouth and walked off."[59]

At the end of April he traveled to Venice via Bologna, Ravenna, and Padua. Ravenna did not make a very overwhelming impression on him to begin with when he arrived there on April 30, 1901: "It is raining, the city is showing me the most unfriendly face it possibly can, and on top of all that I've got a cold with a miserable runny nose." He bought himself some Antipyrin in a pharmacy, "which didn't look at all like Antipyrin, and seemed dirty when it was handed to me."[60] It would have been hard for someone to feel more dejected in a foreign city than he did—and yet Ravenna ended up impressing him for that very reason. The visit resulted in one of his most beautiful poems. It sounds cooler and more "down to earth" than those he mostly wrote during this period—and, for that matter, later too—which often have an unpleasant whiff of sentimental doggerel about them, which quickly engenders a queasy sensation in readers who are schooled in the conventions of modern poetry. "Ravenna," on the other hand, belongs to that body of magnificent poems that also emerged from Hesse's pen:

Ich bin auch in Ravenna gewesen,
Ist eine kleine, tote Stadt,
Die Kirchen und viel Ruinen hat,
Man kann davon in den Büchern lesen.

Du gehst hindurch und schaust dich um,
Die Straßen sind so trüb und naß
Und sind so tausendjährig stumm,
Und überall wächst Moos und Gras!

Das ist wie alte Lieder sind,
Man hört sie an und keiner lacht,
Ein jeder lauscht und jeder sinnt
Hernach daran bis in die Nacht.

[I have also been in Ravenna;
it is a small, dead town,
which has churches and many ruins
that one can read about in books.

You walk around and gaze about:
the streets are so dismal and wet,
and so mute with the weight of a thousand years,
and everywhere moss and grass is growing!

It is like old songs:
people hear them but no one laughs,
and everyone listens and ponders
on them until deep in the night.]

This is a poem that shatters all the clichés about the South. Scarcely can the sun-craving travelers who came to Italy in the eighteenth and nineteenth centuries have felt so cold as they did when spending Italian winters in barely heated rooms! But that did nothing to dispel the myth of the warm South. To this day, anyone who finds themselves cooped up in Italy while it thunders, rains, or snows outside regards this as their very own personal occupational accident. The fact is that the weather south of the Alps is and remains unpredictable—yet this experience, suffered anew by groups of travelers every year, seems incapable of denting the myth of the sunny South. Likewise, a note written by Hesse in Padua attests to his imperturbable inner feeling of exultation: "It is marvelous that the charm of life in Italy can even overcome a truly foul case of catarrh. Despite feeling physically thoroughly miserable I am in the best of spirits."[61]

Yet despite the month he spent in Florence, the real shock for Hesse came when he first set eyes on Venice. Defiantly exotic in the way it seemed to have fallen out of time, the lagoon city fascinated him with its fluid sea borders, its hazy play of light, and a cityscape that was virtually unchanged for centuries. Venice stimulated the painterly eye of the young writer. Here his travel reports suddenly began to breathe a different atmosphere, as his sense of nuances of color and refractions of light, and for unexpected points of transition between the past and the present, came to life. He arrived there on May 1, 1901: "Nothing is as thrilling as the railway journey to Venice, as the train gradually makes its way across the lagoon and then the city rises up out of the water." Yet even here the writer's elation had to overcome a poor state of physical health:

> The circumstances were as bad as they could be for Venice. I arrived there freezing in really gloomy weather: even so, the city exerts a quite ineffable magic. The best experience of all was a gondola ride one evening down a completely dead, dark, narrow canal hemmed in by tall houses; everything there was as quiet as the grave, with no noise of footsteps or wind, and no sound at all except the gentle splashing of the gondolier's oars. When you first arrive here, finding your way around Venice on foot is almost impossible. I am writing this in a tavern, and still have no idea how I will get back to my house, and even when I do, I will have ample opportunity to lose my way around it too.[62]

His "pad," as he put it in student slang, was directly opposite the La Fenice theater on a small canal. How quiet it was in Venice at night! Anyone who has ever lived in one of the quarters of the city not yet overrun and ruined by mass tourism—around the Arsenale or the Ospedale, for instance—is perplexed by the almost unsettling silence that falls over the city by late evening. Hesse, too, who had roomed next to a noisy piazza in Florence, was amazed at how quiet it was on the "silent canal."

Venice remained a living paradox. Genteel and squalid at the same time, high-minded yet concurrently displaying such baseness that, even as you genuflected, you felt a sense of outrage at the disproportionality of things here. In *A Tramp Abroad* (1880) Mark Twain noted: "I have not known any happier hours than those I daily spent in front of Florian's [a famous café on the Piazza San Marco] looking across the Great Square at the cathedral. Propped on its long row of low thick-legged columns, its back knobbed with domes, it seemed like a vast warty bug taking a meditative walk."[63]

In Venice, Hesse cast a detached eye on philistine impulses, a tendency he was all too aware of in himself. He viewed things differently now, his gaze had grown more malicious, like that of Heine, Nietzsche, or Twain: in contrast to his former attitude, in Saint Mark's Cathedral he found himself annoyed by the "German beer bellies." More and more often now, he tended to take an outsider's view of things German, which for his whole life henceforth he would try to leave behind him—albeit with only partial success: "How ugly a fat German commercial counselor can appear when put next to an Italian beggar boy!"[64]

The whole of the strung-out city seemed to Hesse to be like one great long, slim gondola. He enjoyed his indolence, and liked to wander through the Academy, where he was particularly impressed by Bellini and the Venetian School of painters; he also went to bathe every day at the Lido. In his "Mood Pictures from Northern Italy," which first saw the light of day in the fall of 1901 as a series of newspaper articles, Venice took center stage. From "cheap Tuscany" to "expensive Venice"—that was a stretch even for his travel fund, although gondolas at this time were still a common mode of transport and not a pointless and extortionate tourist attraction. So why did Venice hold a more powerful spell over him than any other Italian city? No doubt this had to do with its dual nature: as a real place and as a tourist trap even back then, but also in its role as an indestructible dream image. The canals were imbued with an aura of music, and love and death merged there in an uncanny way. Even nowadays, Venice remains a spectacle of rise and fall that one can experience with all one's senses. Time and again, one finds oneself at the center of humanity's destiny here and cannot grasp it:

> As the result of all its centuries of history, modern Venice and its people now stand as unconscious, or perhaps semi-conscious, bearers of boundless memories, devoted to the moment, genial, and superficially musical—and

yet within this powerless and far from haughty people, a hidden flash of superiority and majesty, the occasional enchantment of an incomparable local tradition. . . . One admires and pities this peculiarity of Venice, which is in a permanent state of decline, twice over, since one clearly senses how the core of its power and beauty resided in its isolation, in its autonomous separation from the mainland and how with the decline of autocratic rule the potential for new developments also withered and died.

Venice, then, was imbued with the music of doom. Another factor that came in to play was the fact that Venice was only half Italian, and that the other half concealed that uniqueness which we nowadays do not have the right mindset to comprehend. Venice was a gateway to Greece and Byzantium. Hesse came to see this city, which eludes any quick appropriation, less and less from the perspective of a foreigner; he grew accustomed precisely to its strangeness. His eye for nuances became ever keener. So it was that he noticed with astonishment how "the lagoon cast only faint reflections." Venice had something impressionistic about it, arising from indefinite depths, a veil-like haze that did not settle on things from the outside but instead appeared to be an integral part of them: "In reflections, color is remarkably faded and takes on an exquisitely delicate nuance. It seems to me as if the water resists the colorful object that is forcing itself upon it and that it is relatively most receptive to very pale colors, namely whites."[65]

With his writer's eye thus strengthened, Hesse assimilated himself to Venice in the two weeks and more that he spent there. This did not prevent him from writing some semi-adolescent poems that were in noticeable contrast to his grown-up discernment. So, the very lengthy poem "Wave," with the addendum "A Lyrical Diary," ends like this: "My boat crunches ashore. Welcome, girls!" Hesse never ignored pretty girls or beautiful women. Even so, he noted with disapproval, the women in Venice always had remarkably dirty hands.

On May 16, 1901, his call-up for the army reserve came through. He had no choice but to leave Venice the very next day. In September he wrote to Carl Busse to tell him he was 'stuck fast' in Basel and was really unhappy. And on November 3 he sent his parents a letter thanking them for helping him out with money and complaining about the poor payment practice of the *Basler Anzeiger* newspaper, which had published his "Mood

Pictures from Northern Italy" in six installments. The prose of the daily life of being a writer had him in its grip once more: "After I had twice sent them overdue payment notices without success, I visited their editorial offices in person and demanded payment for my articles. The editor was caught unawares and was forced to give in, and counted me out the money owing to me, in dribs and drabs, first in ten-franc notes, then in five-franc coins, pausing between every one to see if I would withdraw my outstretched hand. 'Isn't that enough?' he kept asking."

But new clients also began to show an interest—and Hesse as a budding career writer was determined to produce work for all of them. So it was that his parents in Calw learned from him that a Berlin magazine had asked him to write a poem on the theme of winter for its Christmas edition. Not a good topic for a melancholic traveler to Italy: "I looked at my manuscript and discovered that the words 'snow' and 'winter' hadn't made a single appearance in any of my poems for the past four years."[66]

Distancing Rituals: The Death of His Mother and a First Volume of Poetry

Even during his time in Basel, his family kept on pestering him to come to his senses. But his standard ploy now was to keep them at arm's length with a studied coolness. He replied to his mother on March 10, 1900, responding to her incessant reproaches with growing aplomb: "Everyone has faults and weaknesses that bother them and keep them awake at night, and that is the case with people who are not devout just as frequently as for those who are, in fact it is even more bitter and painful for them. Besides, I can't be moved by the sound of church bells; you soon become pretty indifferent to such things in Basel."[67]

Hermann Hesse's siblings were not so capable as he was of making a clean break from the moral dictatorship of their mother. His half-brother Karl Isenberg had suffered a nervous breakdown in January 1900 and was admitted to hospital. Hermann wrote to him, telling him that he himself had often wished, during times of great nervous stress, just to be left in peace and "to worry only about myself and getting better."[68] Ultimately to only have to think about himself—that seemed to him to be the best way to good psychological health, and one that he was determined to pursue here in Basel. He asked his parents, who were greatly agitated by Karl's condition: "I implore you to keep sending me news of Karl, and I mean to write to him myself soon." Then, with a cry of "But enough of such things!" he returned to talking about his own affairs. It was fair to say that he was by now taking himself and his writing much more seriously than anything that counted as an important topic among the family. He was in the process of forming his own intellectual sphere of life, finishing his third book, *Hermann Lauscher,* and living his own life as an author. His mother, however, had declared that she was having none of this. Accordingly she found herself increasingly excluded from his new life. Hermann had also moved to a new flat, as his parents learned quite coincidentally. He informed them that he was now living in a commune comprising three rooms with an architect named Jennen: "Admittedly, we don't chat much about art, as he is a sworn enemy of all talking and writing, almost never reads a book, and looks at the world through the eyes of a child, such sparkling and kind eyes as I have never before seen in my life."[69]

More and more, he received the news his mother sent about family matters without responding to it. It mattered little to him now, for instance, that Marie Hesse's uncle Hermann was planning to forward to Basel his account of the silver wedding celebrations of his brother-in-law in Tallinn, or that Uncle Hermann's fifteen-year-old son Georg had become "moonstruck" and ridden his bicycle through the house while sleepwalking. This was no longer his world, it did not reflect his hopes and fears, and he simply had no time for it.

Despite suffering various ailments, his parents kept on working. Alongside the regular missionary reports, there was a constant stream of new books. But even that wasn't something that really concerned the author of *Hermann Lauscher.* At Christmas 1900, Marie Hesse told her son the title of his father's new book: *The Heathens and Us.* Was Hermann Hesse one such heathen now? In her eyes, he undoubtedly was. Yet terms like this, which were born of Christian missionary zealotry, meant nothing to him any more, they were too narrow-minded and ideological for his way of thinking. He had long ago ceased discussing theological matters with his parents.

Marie Hesse was afflicted by an incurable softening of the bones, and by chronic kidney failure. Yet Hermann refused to let this be a reason for him be drawn back into the family circle. However much he loved his mother, he could not abide her religious fanaticism. All his misery and happiness were now focused on his "fever-muse," Elisabeth; he exchanged letters with Eugen Diederichs, whom, despite the failure of *An Hour Behind Midnight,* he was keen to interest in a new publishing venture—Diederichs, though, refused to be won over. Instead, Hesse received an unexpected offer from Carl Busse, the editor of the New German Poets series at the Grote publishing house. Busse had read Hesse's *Romantic Songs* and invited him to contribute a volume of verse to this series. Somewhat taken aback by this invitation, Hesse replied to Grote on September 26, 1901: "But as a hypochondriac and grumbler I have fallen midway between the two extremes of hero and silent sufferer, and both inwardly and outwardly I am somewhat spoiled by indolence. My "Songs" contain a lot of bad stuff, but nothing fake—that's all I can really say about them."[70] Unsure about the terms and conditions of publication Grote was offering, he added that he was eager to see his poetry in print, but had neither an agent, nor a publisher, nor any money.

In a piece he wrote for the *Neue Zürcher Zeitung* on December 3, 1928, ten years after Busse's death, Hesse recalled:

> He was one of the few people who placed any faith in me in my younger years and boosted my morale so that I was able to survive the years when I was starting out, and was either ignored or laughed at. . . . Admittedly, this volume of poetry did not have the slightest success either. But the very fact that I, without any intervention on my part, was invited by a famous writer to publish my work, and that my volume of verse could appear under the imprint of a distinguished publisher, kept my faith alive for the following two years.[71]

Following his first trip to Italy, Hesse took up his post at the Wattenwyl antiquarian bookshop in Basel in August 1901. This establishment was also owned by his boss Reich, but here the pay was far worse than in a commercial bookshop. Hesse's younger brother Hans, who worked for the Lutheran Mission in Basel—Hermann kept his distance from him as well—had by this time returned to Calw to be with their mother. Hesse shared in her sufferings, but remained in Basel.

Marie Hesse died on April 24, 1902. The next day Hermann Hesse sent a postcard to Calw: "My dear family: I was already in my traveling clothes when both of Papa's cards arrived. After much soul-searching, I decided to stay here."[72] Hesse shared Goethe's aversion to sickness and death. It was something he couldn't deal with, and preferred simply to blank out. Moreover, his feelings toward his mother had been too conflicted to go and play the grief-stricken mourner now at her graveside. He harbored too much pent-up anger at the lack of understanding shown him by the family member who had been spiritually closer to him than any of the others. On April 30 he excused himself for his absence: "While I am deeply sorry not to have come to my dear Mama's funeral, this was perhaps a better outcome for me and for you than if I had come. I was and still am very saddened, yet in the days after the 24th I have suffered less than in the preceding weeks."[73]

Was this an allusion to her suffering prior to her death, which he found unbearable, or the upsetting knowledge of his mother's rejection, who refused to see in him any kind of poet who would be pleasing to God? On May 11 he wrote to the family in Calw: "I was not spared the most difficult aspect of mourning, however, namely my regret over all the unkindnesses by which I hurt Mama, and for which she went out of her way to forgive me." Had he also forgiven her? On July 8 Carl Busse received a letter from Hesse, who seemed to be at the lowest emotional ebb. His eyes had given up under the strain, he could neither read nor write, and muscles spasms and pain in both his left and right temples condemned him to inactivity: "I am furious and spend all my free time in taverns, sleep away my Sundays lying in the grass by the Rhine, and am really only one-quarter alive."[74]

One of the remarkable things about the life of the writer Hermann Hesse was that he seemed able to overcome his repulsion at life only through the act of writing. He played out in his writings events that had failed to materialize in his actual life. Thus, in *Peter Camenzind* we find a portrayal of his mother's death, an ordeal that he had not put himself through in real life, true to his motto that reality was something that one ought under no circumstances to settle for. So, it was only in writing (be it retrospective or anticipatory), the activity that constituted his actual life, that death came to prominence—though there its sting was drawn through having the spell of poetry cast over it.

The reversal of roles in *Peter Camenzind* is peculiar. Here the father figure, who in reality watched his mother die, is asleep, while his alter ego, the title figure, receives a life lesson at the sight of his dying mother.

Camenzind's father, though, is an evil drinker, whereas Johannes Hesse was a teetotaler plagued by headaches. It's not an act of patricide here right away, but perhaps more of a revenge tackle in the decider game between father and son:

> Early one hot summer morning, while I was still lying in bed, I felt thirsty, so I got up to go to the kitchen, where a pitcher of cool water was always kept. To get there, I had to pass through my parents' bedroom, where I was struck by the odd groaning sound my mother was making. I approached her bedside; she didn't notice me or respond to me, but just kept emitting the same dry, frightened moans. Her eyelids were twitching and her face had a bluish pallor. I wasn't especially alarmed by this, though I was slightly anxious. But then I caught sight of her hands lying on the sheet as motionless as sleeping twins. I could see from these hands that my mother was dying, because they looked curiously drained and listless in a way that no living person's hands look. I forgot my thirst, knelt down beside her bed, laid my hand on my sick mother's forehead and looked into her eyes. When her gaze met mine, it was benign and untroubled, but close to flickering out altogether. It didn't occur to me to wake my father, who was sleeping nearby, breathing heavily. I knelt there for almost two hours and watched my mother die. She was calm, grave, and courageous in the face of death, as befitted her kind. She set me a fine example.[75]

Something in Hesse would surely have dearly loved to act like Peter Camenzind, an alternative ego that he carried within him, but he could opt for decisive action only in his imagination.

Hesse now set about planning another stay in Italy. It would, however, take until the following April before he finally managed to get away. In 1902 he was offered a post as an assistant in the Leipzig Museum of the Book Trade—but he turned it down. Leipzig was too far north for him, almost as far as Berlin. Those were places where no vines grew, big cities he didn't know and that he had no wish to get to know either. His aspirations were focused elsewhere, as he emphasized in a letter of January 29, 1903, to Paul Ilg. We can hear the voice of Peter Camenzind speaking through his creator: "I have an eternal and unfulfilled desire to live independently as a private individual, be it ever so modestly—I would inhabit far-flung Italian jerkwater towns, go on long walks, and feel myself completely and grati-fyingly cut off from all the hustle and bustle of modern life."[76]

Sleepless Nights

> The idea of "endless recurrence" is a dreadful one. I only know it firsthand from a single situation: sleepless nights. You see a pale window, hear the ticking of the clock, and keep opening and closing your eyes. You feel an exhausted sense of hope-lessness, and sense you've experienced this all before, many times over. It's the route to insanity.
>
> —Hermann Hesse, notebook entry (1907–1914)

Even as a child, Hermann Hesse was frequently, to employ a word much used at the time, "indisposed." And this continued into adulthood: one of his diary entries written at the age of twenty-two, dated September 20, 1899—when he had just begun work on the manuscript, since lost, of the novel *Schweinigel*—broached a theme that would recur in variations throughout his lifetime: "Headaches and a total lack of sleep."[77]

Dreams and sleep were precious gifts to Hesse, in much the same way as he managed to wrest visual pleasures from life despite his constant eye pain. On February 8, 1900, the *Allgemeine Schweizer Zeitung* published his article "Sleepless Nights," which demonstrated his great powers of creativity and interpretation when dealing with an apparently trivial ob-ject. This was more than just an imaginative piece of whimsy; it was a profoundly existential text that refrained entirely from proclaiming an authorial viewpoint, preferring instead to conceal it almost humbly within an account of a personal experience. Many of his notes and reports are observations of this kind, which select inconsequential incidents as a springboard for addressing fundamental questions. In his writing Hesse developed a mastery—often underrated—at linking the spirit of his age with one that transcended all space and time in such a way as to lay bare the prevailing Zeitgeist.

Hesse was aware that sleep was only an apparent pause, a diving be-neath the surface of the consciousness that governed our waking hours. Sleep was life at night, which was controlled by subconscious powers dif-ferent from those of the daytime. The feeling grew within Hesse that it was not just the powers of the individual that were endowed or withheld by sleep (or the lack thereof). The night demonstrated how disastrously arrogant it was for the logic of the daytime world to believe that all aspects of life were within the firm grasp of reason. The arc of life from birth to death only revealed itself to the nocturnal eye, which saw different things in the dark than it did during the day. With an imperious gesture of contempt, the day destroyed the very foundations on which it was based: the night. And in so doing it once more formed a hindrance to the ability to sink down into the very same world of myth from which it had arisen. If the day conquers the night entirely and insists that it be adjusted to fit in with its own logic, then people die a dreamless death.

Anyone who lies awake at night, yet is accustomed to performing his daily tasks quickly and effectively, is humiliated by his sleeplessness. For something there is defying his strong will, something that is not owned or controlled by him and that surrenders itself to him only as it sees fit—an inscrutable process. Reason cannot fathom why it has no purchase on sleep. And the more reason mulls over this question, the more sleep fights shy of it. For sleep—as Hesse knew very well—is nothing but the mirror image of our waking state. A person who is restless during the day will likewise find no peace at night. And anyone who has not mastered the art of indolence also finds he is shunned by those muses that only emerge from the depths of sleep. Yet that is only half the truth. For just as one can never possess God except in the most naive of ways, and just as one must first seek out the eternally absent God in order to have the potential to divine the presence of God in all things, the same is true of sleep, which is the guardian of both dreams and rationality.

Consequently, half-sleep becomes a place of constant transition, such as the stream that at the same time both separates and joins life and death in *Siddhartha*. The night sits in judgment over the day. The day, and with it everything that makes it significant, sinks in the darkness of the night, where no aspect of the day counts for anything anymore and suddenly quite different phenomena loom up threateningly before us:

> Who in their youth has not made life difficult for their nearest and dearest, rejecting love and scorning sympathy, who has not, through their contrariness and cockiness, missed a piece of good fortune that was theirs for the taking, and who has not at one time or another violated the respect of others or their own self-respect or offended friends by saying something foolish, by breaking a promise, or by making an unpleasant or wounding gesture?

And now they are all standing in front of you silently and staring at you with an oddly calm look, and you feel ashamed of yourself now you are faced with them. . . . You just got on with the business of life, and read and talked and laughed a great deal during your lifetime, but now it is all as if it never happened, it all seems alien to you and slips away from you, while the blue skies of your childhood, the long-forgotten images of your homeland and the voices of long-dead people seem uncannily close and present to you.[78]

Spending the night wide awake makes one feel forlorn. In the worst case a feeling of aggression, and in the best case a restorative helplessness, sets in after all the certainties of the waking hours. The time that remains to us before our deaths is not in our hands. That alone is a good reason to adopt an attitude of humility and to seek out and cultivate tranquility. Perhaps then, when one has become intimate with the secrets of the night even in the daytime, one will be visited more often by sleep during the night. According to Hesse, "being made to wait," just like being ill, was "a mentor whom it was impossible to misunderstand." This was a "schooling in respect" for that "veiled final secret of life." Mastering the art of waiting, Hesse maintained, made it easier for a person to discover the correct measure of their own desires: neither too insipid nor too strong, while all the time remaining in expectation of something special—namely, the capacity to enter into that inner space that is our homeland and that manifests itself solely in dreamscapes as those possibilities we run through for the life that we did not live, yet that we still carry within us.

Young though he still was when he wrote "Sleepless Nights," Hesse already knew a great deal about this subject: "Sleep is one of the most precious gifts of nature, a friend and a place of refuge, a magician and a quiet consoler, and anyone who knows the torment of enduring sleeplessness, and who has learned to make do with snatched half-hours of feverish dozing, has my deepest sympathy. But I would find it impossible to love a person whom I knew had never suffered a sleepless night in his life, unless he were a child of nature with the most innocent of souls."[79]

5

PORTRAIT OF THE SUCCESSFUL ARTIST

AS A YOUNG MAN WANDERING

BENEATH CLOUDS

Peter Camenzind, or the Art of Self-Discovery: Brother Eros's Rebirth in Wine

I can endure everything except love.

—Hermann Hesse, letter to his parents, March 24, 1893

Hermann Lauscher, which was only a slim volume of prose, went virtually unnoticed outside of Basel. Although Eugen Diederichs had previously, politely but firmly, declined to publish it, this work was nevertheless key to Hesse's further development. For the writer Paul Ilg, who edited the literary magazine *Die Woche,* recommended the book to the official reader of the Fischer publishing house, Moritz Heimann, and suggested to him that he might like to review *Lauscher* in the in-house Fischer journal, the *Neue Deutsche Rundschau.* Heimann subsequently contacted Hesse directly: "We would be pleased to receive notification of any new works of yours." This communication reached Hesse on a sheet of paper with the firm's letterhead on it but with no signature. For him, this opened the door to one of the most prestigious publishers in Germany. This invitation marked the beginning of an era that was to last for more than thirty years. In his memoir "In Memory of S. Fischer" ("Erinnerung an S. Fischer"), Hesse wrote: "And I recognized that Fischer had a very particular conception of his publishing house, both as it existed at that time and of its future shape, an idea that he pursued with a sense of high-minded duty but also with a very keen instinct. . . . You couldn't catch him at an auspicious moment and seduce him into flights of fancy over a glass of wine like you could, say, Albert Langen or Georg Müller."[1] But at this juncture, at the start of 1903, things were not yet at a stage where Hesse could have discussed future plans over a glass of wine with Samuel Fischer anyway. For the head of the firm still had no knowledge of the young author whom his reader had invited to collaborate with the company.

Hesse was already working on a novel in the style of nineteenth-century Swiss writer Gottfried Keller's work *Der grüne Heinrich (Green Henry)*—it is for this reason that many people came to refer to the resulting work, *Peter Camenzind,* as *Grüner Peter.* Hesse loved Keller's work, as he also did the work of Keller's contemporaries Wilhelm Raabe and Adalbert Stifter, and in particular he admired their ability to tell stories in a very unobtrusive manner—stories in which nothing momentous occurred yet where the dramas and comedies of provincial life took on a compelling, quiet intensity of their own. By this stage Hesse too had traveled to Italy—and these excursions to the South had suddenly raised the temperature of his writing. A Dionysian element took hold of his style, and the serious, beer-fueled artistic intent that had informed the writer's work hitherto was supplanted by a lighter mood lubricated instead by the fruit of the vine.

Whereas in *Hermann Lauscher* Hesse had recounted the outsider's journey into his inner psyche, the direction of travel in *Peter Camenzind* is to the outside world. And what a liberating effect this had on his writing! So what is *Peter Camenzind* exactly? Primarily it is a book about the many distortions of the modern outlook on life. It is played out between two poles—on the one hand, Nimikon, for centuries the home of the Camenzind family, and on the other hand, Paris, a place where one avant-garde movement follows hard on the heels of another. How is it possible to become a writer in such a disjointed world? It was common knowledge that no one had much time for eccentrics who spoke a language that others first had to learn in order to make any sense of it. The eponymous hero of Hesse's novel was just such an outsider, whose otherness was bound to act as a provocation to the guardians of utilitarianism and the kind of system that since time immemorial has guaranteed commissions and success. For Peter Camenzind does not emerge either as a person who suffers in silence or as a revolutionary who is ready to sacrifice himself in the service of the new, but instead as an odd fish, a drinker and a braggart, a rogue who is equally prone to displays of impetuous love and abrupt cooling of ardor, a feckless drifter upon whom no one should rely.

And yet precisely for that reason, this "Outlaw Prince" turns out to be the only person who remains true to himself and who refuses to engage in any compromises or false appeasement.

No doubt Hesse felt spurred on by the fact that he was now writing for the Fischer publishing house, and also because he no longer had to fear the strict moral injunctions of his mother. *Peter Camenzind* is dedicated to his friend Ludwig Finckh from the *petit cénacle* in Tübingen. Hugo Ball was undoubtedly right in his uncompromising judgment on Finckh. It is surely incorrect to suggest any similarities between these two authors, who lived close to one another in the Lake Constance period and who constantly assured one another of their abiding friendship. For whereas Finckh wrote novels with a bucolic flavor, in his own writings Hesse treated this genre of regional fiction with irony and parody.

Even so, his Rousseauesque revolt against a life lived far from nature was in deadly earnest, as was his plea (echoing the works of the Romantic writer Joseph von Eichendorff) for a new art of idleness. This is how Peter Camenzind sees himself: "Incomprehensible and wanton nature had seen fit to combine within me two opposing gifts: an uncommon physical strength and an unfortunately not inconsiderable aversion to work."[2]

The character's favorite occupation is to take long walks regardless of the weather conditions and to go mountain climbing. Or simply to lie on his back in the grass and gaze at the clouds. Indeed, Elisabeth La Roche and the metaphor of the cloud associated with her continues to play a part here—Hesse proved himself to be faithful in the choice of his imagery. And yet what these images revealed began now to change imperceptibly.

All at once, Peter Camenzind's biography seems to become an aspect of the study of clouds:

> Show me a man anywhere in the whole wide world who has a greater knowledge and love of clouds than I do! Or show me anything in the world that is more beautiful. They are a plaything and a comfort to the eye, a blessing and a gift from God; yet they are wrathful too and have the power of death. They are as delicate, soft, and gentle as the souls of newborn babies, as beautiful, rich, and prodigal as good angels, but also lowering, inescapable, and merciless as the emissaries of death. . . . O lovely, floating,

restless clouds! I was an ignorant child and loved them, and observed them, little knowing that I too would drift through life like a cloud—wandering aimlessly, everywhere a stranger, and suspended between time and eternity.[3]

A wealth of experience with the symbol of the cloud is evident here—the preliminary stages in other texts all pointed here, to this tempestuous symbiosis of the self and clouds, a metaphor that comes across as being handled with a light touch and not at all forced.

In 1904, the year that *Peter Camenzind* was published, Hesse also wrote a small text with the title "Wolken" ("Clouds"). Here the author's method of working with motifs becomes apparent—he treats them not merely as portrayals of reality but always as symbols as well. Indeed, this is how he proceeded with the character of Peter Camenzind himself, in whom we can already identify traits of Klingsor, the Spa Guest, and also Steppenwolf—albeit still under other auspices, and paying greater attention precisely to clouds, whose different aspects he once more thought about afresh. That meant not just giving them a cursory look or even observing them once or a few times; rather, quintessential observation of a subject came about only through frequently repeated and long-term contemplation. And so, in "Wolken" he reached the following judgment: "Yet the more time and effort you subsequently expend in looking at them, the more clearly and sadly you realize that 'nice' poems and 'nice' clouds are a cheap commodity and very rarely withstand unflinching scrutiny."[4]

It now seemed especially important to him that clouds should move and "create distances and spatial intervals in the sky, which to our perception is otherwise nothing but dead space." In this way, Hesse fashioned a bridge to the next image, one that reappears throughout his work . . . the bird! "What the bird does in microcosm, the clouds do on a larger scale."[5] And yet, Hesse maintained, the cloud as an allegory of transience also had an intimate connection with art, becoming the mediating entity between heaven and earth, between the eternal and the transitory: "Clouds are the equivalent in nature to winged beings, genies, and angels in art, whose human–earthly bodies have wings and defy gravity."[6]

★   ★   ★

Peter Camenzind, the well-read farmer's son from the village of Nimikon, makes the mistake of thinking that he has been put on earth to become a professional writer. He has studied literature—and by some fortunate chance, which actually turns out to be unfortunate, he gets the opportunity to write for a newspaper. He breaks off his studies and is caught in the trap. A journalist must write in such a way that his or her piece can be printed without too much difficulty. And so Peter Camenzind finds himself caught up in the literary business where the sole concern is to increase his own market value—in other words, to keep shamelessly promoting himself. Hesse, one feels, wrote this book in order to exorcise the fear of an inevitable fall from grace that his Pietist parents had kept on predicting for him. Indeed, in his telling of the story, Peter Camenzind seems similar to him in many ways—though it is by no means a foregone conclusion that he, Hesse, would come to the same end. But what if this were to happen? There are worse things than going back to where one started from and occupying a minor station in life—he had already read of such an outcome in the works of Gottfried Keller. No one is condemned to produce literature for their entire life. Hesse sharpened the perspective by having Peter Camenzind end up as the landlord of a tavern, which from a petit-bourgeois standpoint was the fate of all those who once left their hometowns to try and pursue a life in art.

However, within the story Hermann Hesse also recounts another story: namely, one of a change of direction in a life, and of growing doubt over what can become of the creative will of the individual in a mass culture that subscribes solely to cheap sensation. In the figure of Peter Camenzind he mirrors his own distance from popular expectations of him as a writer. Moreover, he is sufficiently carefree and confident enough of his own calling as an author that he can now address all those objections to the insecure existence of a writer that he had heard so often and act them out through one of his characters. His conclusion is that not everybody is cut out for such a life, and that the people who fail at it are primarily those who lack the strength to isolate themselves from the external world and who cannot assert their position of being alone and misunderstood against both the temptations of a feckless bohemian existence or those of rapid success. If one knocks off and smooths over all one's own rough edges, then one can fit in anywhere—precisely because one doesn't have anything original to say anymore.

★   ★   ★

All the elements of criticism of the "age of the feuilleton" familiar from *The Glass Bead Game* are already evident in *Peter Camenzind*. And yet for all that, Hesse himself wrote for newspapers throughout his life (unlike Rilke, who feared such activity might compromise his integrity as a writer); during this time he turned out not only hundreds of reviews but also travel sketches and atmospheric vignettes from his journeys. Nor did he shy away from occasionally adding polemical pieces to the seething cauldron of contemporary controversies, which was kept constantly on the boil despite—or perhaps precisely because of—the loose spectrum of viewpoints it accommodated.

Yet he was certain that this was not what his life was really all about. In this, he was of the same mind as Otto Julius Bierbaum, who wrote in his 1897 novel *Stilpe* that if one went to seed by staying up late and drinking, one could always become a journalist. And even at this early stage Hesse had cause to note the damaging effect of constantly trying to intensify superficial sensationalism, as well as the neuroticism of an age, which, swamped as it was by a welter of information, had forgotten how to concentrate on the essential.

Hesse sent Peter Camenzind off on a journey through highs and lows, through the cultural landscapes of Tuscany and Umbria, which he experiences wholly in the spirit of Saint Francis of Assisi, but also through metropolises, of which Paris proves to be the most repellent Moloch to him. Yet it is here that his lack of a cosmopolitan outlook truly reveals itself. Having never before visited Paris, he portrays it in much the same way that Karl May depicts the wilds of Kurdistan: "Nothing but art, politics, literature, and sluttishness, nothing but artists, literati, politicians, and low women. The artists were as vain and importunate as the politicians, the literary types were even more vain and pushy, yet the vainest and pushiest of all were the women. One evening I sat alone in the Bois de Boulogne wondering whether to have done straight away with Paris or preferably with life itself."[7] The city glittered with many allures that were nothing but cheap trash. Hesse knew about clouds and about Italy, at least to some extent, but he was as ignorant of Paris as he was of Berlin, which he avoided visiting throughout his life for that very reason, because he was afraid that it might be as he had pictured it in his provincial backwater. The only time he went there was to consult an ophthalmologist—but on that occasion did so in modern and rapid style by flying there on Lufthansa.

His ignorance of metropolises, for which he has no feel whatsoever, comes across as a serious and quite obvious weakness if one compares the novel with, say, the depiction of Paris from a position of intimate knowledge in Rilke's work *Malte Laurids Brigge,* written a few years later. And yet there are certain advantages to consciously adopting a defensive attitude toward the modern world, a topic we shall return to presently.

However, the prime mover behind Peter Camenzind's long, restless journey is quite genuine, and is an impulse that Hesse knew well—namely, his chronic insecurity. His own sense of vocation appears to consist of an explosive mixture of euphoria and anxiety, of initial triumph followed by a lassitude that grows progressively stronger: "I thought I was at the beginning of an upward trajectory. I had no idea that everything I had experienced thus far was mere chance and that my being and my life still lacked a deep individual keynote of its own. As yet, I was unaware that I was suffering from a yearning that neither love nor fame could satisfy."[8]

Art is not an end in itself, but instead life is—this is the lesson that the absconding son of Pietists has his fugitive farmer's son learn. And all the vain, self-satisfied literati whom he encounters in the big cities appear to have very little appreciation of this fact. Hesse lets us know through Peter Camenzind that he wants nothing whatsoever to do with them: "I can only look back now with horror and pity on this half-formed bunch of eccentrically dressed and coiffed poets and esthetes, for it was only retrospectively that I realized the danger of keeping such company. Fortunately, my Bernese Oberland peasant background saved me from falling prey to this circus."[9]

Hugo Ball saw *Peter Camenzind* as Hesse's strenuous attempt to create a homeland of his own—to fabricate it in words according to his own ideas, because his predilection for inventing stories had been suppressed for so long:

> When one reads it nowadays, the book sometimes appears to be a parody of the serious Swiss; the writer's fresh approach really does extend this far. In all seriousness, the sound of nearby yodeling is counterpointed to the refinement of Richard Wagner at his villa at Tribschen on Lake Lucerne as the antithesis to his opera "Tristan and Isolde." That is the humor of this book; that is the ironic streak already evident in Hesse when he wrote it.

The novel was conceived and executed in the very best of spirits; there is
no more depression on display here, and no sign of any stress. The Alps serve
to suppress any inner nightmares.[10]

Very true; this is not a manifesto but a high-spirited playing with progressive attitudes, with artistic obfuscation and the mania for success; it is
a deep gouge in the smooth veneer of the prevailing spirit of the age. Hesse's
novel is an early apologia for the self-will of the individual, and not remotely an advertisement for communes of dropouts or the contemporary
back-to-nature-oriented *Wandervogel* (Ramblers) movement. What it most
decidedly is, however, is a revolt against a modern world characterized by
the division of labor, against civilization as a form of alienation, and against
a system lacking the vital element of anarchy. A book entirely in the spirit
of Rousseau, but enriched with a dimension of irony.

Even the young Bertolt Brecht, during the phase when he wrote his
play *Baal*, recalled *Peter Camenzind* as "something cool and refreshing, a
tract filled with autumnal color and acerbity. All we're left with at the end
is someone who resolves from then on to do nothing but drink red wine
and go to the dogs and watch the passing decades and the moon rising—and
that's his sole occupation."[11]

Another allusion to the oft-invoked "Art of Idleness"! Following Goethe's
example, Hesse learned this in Italy. Only partially, however. The deep
depression into which he plunged after the death of his mother and which
he tried to sit out by drinking too much wine in taverns, and the idleness
that he put down to his constantly painful eyes—these were other symptoms of a crisis, a severe paralysis that rendered any activity impossible.
This was the miserable situation in which he found himself in 1902 and
which he now, in the writing of *Peter Camenzind,* took as the basic material from which to fashion a great celebration of life. All he had to do was
affirm it—this attitude had something of Nietzsche's *amor fati* about it—
namely, learning to love one's allotted fate—but something else too. Carl
Busse's publication of his poems and Samuel Fischer's offer to bring out
his next book stirred Hesse from his state of apathy and enthused him to
a degree he had not known before. He wrote like he was intoxicated—and
all the motifs he had used before that reappear in this novel, come across
with greater energy and humor and a deeper meaning.

★   ★   ★

The style he employed here had something of a controlled drunkenness and dispassionate ecstasy about it. It is no coincidence that *Peter Camenzind* also became a hymn to wine. Hesse drank a great deal of wine, for sure, though he could not be classed as an alcoholic: the measure of his drinking was (almost) always synonymous with that of his enjoyment. He was not some self-destructive drunkard, nor did he drink to forget, but instead in order to remember better. This was a crucial distinction. Yet in the period following his mother's death and prior to the success of *Peter Camenzind,* wine became for Hesse both his stimulant of choice and a form of sedative. The year 1902 was one of the many crisis years of his life. And this time he genuinely ran the risk of sinking into depression and alcoholic overindulgence. The only thing that saved him was the act of writing.

He quite openly told everyone he knew: if *Peter Camenzind* was not a success, then he would have to seek permanent employment—and nothing made him more afraid than that. The pressure on him was great: the new book was meant to finally make the breakthrough he had been hoping for—and Hesse was smart enough to realize that things are least likely to succeed when it is absolutely crucial that they do so. Fischer's advance commitment to publish gave him some kind of security, certainly. But above all it was the two journeys to Italy and the wine that allowed him to adopt in the book that high-spirited tone that was so difficult to achieve. This tone also made *Camenzind* a picaresque novel. A *Simplicius Simplicissimus* for the industrial age, a *Candide* that attacked the foundations of a belief in progress, and a piece of brash impudence cloaked in geniality.

Henceforth, wine would come to play an increasingly important part in Hesse's life. Wine would always remain more important to him than women or friendship; to him, wine was that friend who contributed something to his desired state of solitude that people could not provide: namely, a hint of the transcendental, a taste of the silence that whispered deep inside him of hidden secrets. That enabled him to get up and continue writing again every morning, despite the fact that there was already so much written material in the world. Wine is revealed to us as a great catalyst, a "hero and magician," a "brother of Eros." In the fourth chapter of *Peter Camenzind,* Hesse presents wine as a tempter who is well versed in hovering over the abyss: "He [the god of wine] can do the impossible; he imbues impoverished human hearts with beautiful and wondrous poetry. He has transformed me, a peasant and a recluse, into a king, a poet, and a sage. He fills the emptied vessels of life with new destinies and impels those who are stranded back into the swift current of active life." So much for the promise held by wine; its threatening side, though, sounds like this: "He demands to be loved, sought after, and comprehended and wooed with great effort. Few are equal to this feat, and so he kills thousands and thousands in the process. He ages them, destroys them, or snuffs out the spirit's flame within them." But then Hesse describes the god of wine as building a bridge over to a shore inhabited by a seemingly quite different spirit: the Franciscan world of joyous creation: "He transforms the confusions of life into great myths and plays the hymn of creation on a mighty harp."[12]

Hesse gives Peter Camenzind a drunk as a father—and the apathy that accompanies that condition repels the young idealist. Drinking is another art that has to be learned! Is this now part and parcel of world wisdom or does it instead belong in the category of self-deception? Only the fact that Hesse constantly remained an ascetic, who each time he indulged in excess had to come to a conscious decision to do so, and that such self-indulgence, like the idleness that he praised so highly, was basically quite alien to his nature, allowed him to write his extensive oeuvre. Without his unrelenting diligence and his strict self-discipline, we would not have Hesse's twenty-volume *Collected Works* or the dozen or more volumes of letters, plus hundreds of drawings and watercolors.

On the other hand, nothing original ever comes simply from industry and discipline. Hesse remained trapped in this paradoxical condition for the whole of his life. He was well aware that he could not escape it. But perhaps he could keep it flexible by remaining constantly versatile himself?

Notwithstanding his serious crises in puberty, Hesse did not have to first work at acquiring self-discipline. Quite the contrary, in fact: he repeatedly had to moderate this trait to keep in within sensible bounds. Not only wine but also the Franciscan ideal helped him to do this. Paul Sabatier's book about Saint Francis of Assisi is not a hagiography in the traditional sense but instead a novel of personal development about a person who combined a love for all of God's creations—be they plants, animals, or people—with a social conscience.

This presentation of Saint Francis as a critic of capitalism made Sabatier's book explosive at the end of the nineteenth century. Accordingly this treatise, which did not remotely provide an overview of all aspects of the figure of Saint Francis, preferring instead to concentrate on the most pressing facet at this period, is closer to the work of Émile Zola than the Catholic Church.

Likewise *Peter Camenzind* is avowedly a book extolling the virtues of brotherly love amid increasing division of labor and the mechanization of life. Love, then, becomes the binding factor among those elements that want no part of such a society. Peter Camenzind and his creator Hesse alike experienced Italy through the Franciscan "Canticle of Brother Sun and Sister Moon," but alongside Brother Sun there was also for Hesse Brother Wine and Brother Death. The circle of life closes and at the end we come face-to-face once more with the point where it all began: "in the beginning was the myth." What might at first sound somewhat bewildering to an impartial reader quickly becomes clear. For the great story of the creation of the world occurs afresh in every newborn child, and the myth that is to be recounted here resides within the "child-soul." This child-soul can endure even into old age—only there it wears the mourning clothes of melancholy. The poet figure in *Peter Camenzind* is the person who lives with both the yearning and the melancholy of lost beginnings, of missed or even thwarted connections. And so, at the age of just twenty-six, in *Peter Camenzind* Hesse was already embarking on his own quest "in search of lost time."

There is a significant gap left by Brother Sun, Brother Wine, and Brother Death—the love of women. This was a problem that Hesse posed for his character Peter Camenzind on his odyssey through life. Unlike Thomas Mann, who was working around this same time on his novella *Tonio Kröger,* Hesse in no way had a dominating homophile tendency. With him, the matter is far more complicated and has a great deal to do with his Pietist background, which, like Rilke with his Prague Catholicism, he would never completely leave behind. It is a kind of virginity complex, a neurosis about chastity, which all his transfiguration of nature and the natural physicality that he tried so strenuously to cultivate could not dispel. Even posing for the camera as a determined naked rock climber did not help. This appeared just as strained as the photo Rilke shot of himself wearing a suit but barefoot in one of the grand hotels he liked to frequent.

In *Peter Camenzind* the concept of "lustless love" is mentioned for the first time, a coinage after Hesse's mother's own heart. This formulation was meant to invoke his own harmlessness, something he himself could not believe in. Certainly, one could "lustlessly" love creation in general, along with nature, plants, animals, and one's parents and siblings and children. But women? Of course, one was capable of loving most of them free of any sexual desire; otherwise the civilized world would turn into a bestiary. It counts among both Hesse's virtues and the great depressions of his life that he could never quite believe in the civilized forms of human nature. All or nothing, ice cold or overheated—Hesse was all too aware that he had not been endowed with a natural, easy, and playful manner when it came to erotic encounters. He could always sense within himself some lurking urge to commit sexual violence, and so preferred to seal himself off from any temptation—this is already the stuff of *Steppenwolf.*

In *Peter Camenzind,* Hesse therefore steered clear of any intense display of emotion, preferring instead to oscillate between love and friendship. In the process, he discovered within himself Jakob Böhme's "androgynous Adam" and the "other gender," and shied away from the directly sexual sphere. His guiding principle in this was the code of conduct of religious orders, and he followed the Franciscan ideal, which so to speak relieved him of any sexual consummation. In this matter too, therefore, Hesse remained a man of potentiality who avoided overly explicit facts.

According to Hesse, it was essential to remain alive to the hidden forces within things. Thus, in the second chapter of *Peter Camenzind* we read: "As for love, I must confess to having retained a juvenile attitude to it throughout my life." There then follows a formulation, telling in its enigmatic nature, that points to the neurotic root of this condition: "Due to my mother's influence and my own indistinct feelings, I venerate womankind as an alien, beautiful and mysterious race, superior to men by dint of innate beauty and constancy of nature, a race that we must hold sacred. For, like stars . . . they are remote from us men and appear to be closer to God." So his mother inculcated him with this image! Hence his talk about maintaining the sanctity of the remote female figure. Of course, Hesse knew full well that such attitudes would lead him into a blind alley from which he could not escape just by applying pure reason: "Since, in this matter, life has oftentimes put its rough oar in, the love of women has always brought me bitterness and sweetness in equal measure. Although I still put women on a pedestal, my chosen role of solemn priest has sometimes changed all too readily into the painfully comic one of a fool."[13] This sounds like a leave-taking from Elisabeth, that cloud drifting by in the sky as an object of simple transfiguration—and indeed that is precisely what it was.

So, friendship rather than love—that was not an easier option, in fact presumably an even harder one, and not without an erotic motive, though free of sexual pressures. Peter Camenzind travels through Italy with his friend Richard, and this both heightens his urge to express himself and gives him the certainty of brotherly support—but then Hesse does something that he often did with characters of his own creation as soon as readers began to invest hopes in them: he killed him off. Richard drowns, a common death in Hesse's works. Water for him was a medium of death, whereas fire was one of life.

It is these little twists and turns in what is only seemingly a conventional narrative flow, and these ironic reservations and skeptical incisions into the flesh of broad acquiescence with the course of life, that save the book from teetering over into cheap sensationalism—something it is always threatening to do. The reader is enthralled by Hesse's emerging delight in storytelling, which he takes to the limits of the absurd. The work is imbued with an audacious courage to fail—something that has retained its appeal—and hence full of ironic distancing from his own earlier flights of fancy, which are now over and done with for the present. This makes the character of Peter Camenzind the prototype of all those oddballs who will come to populate Hesse's subsequent writings: figures who are part saint and part conman and always outsiders. They are the guardians of obstinacy, defenders of the self against a world that always directs its promises to the generality of humankind, never to the individual. A more resounding affirmation of life in all its imperfection is scarcely imaginable: "So what has been the outcome of so many wanderings and wasted years? The woman whom I loved and still love is raising her two beautiful children in Basel. The other woman, who loved me, has got over me and continues to trade in fruit, vegetables, and seeds. My father, for whose sake I returned to the nest, has neither died nor got better, but sits opposite me on his daybed, staring at me and envying me my possession of the cellar key."[14]

★   ★   ★

Within just a few weeks Hesse had completed the manuscript of *Peter Ca-menzind,* which he had expected to spend years working on. On May 9, 1903, he sent it off to Berlin. Samuel Fischer replied to Hesse on May 18, congratulating him on the book, which he said he was delighted to be publishing under his imprint: "Not only the story you recount, but the way in which the experiences of the central character, which are not significant in and of themselves, are conveyed through the sensibility of a writer, lend the work richness and brilliance."[15]

Hesse was given a publishing contract (with terms that were double what is customary nowadays: 20 percent of net receipts) and an advance against half of the first 500 copies sold. He immediately quit his job in the antiquarian bookshop and announced that he was becoming a free-lance writer.

On June 24, Hermann wrote to his father; the nagging unease at the decision he had made is palpable: "A well-known major publisher has purchased my last manuscript, a short novel. . . . If success still eludes me after, say, a year I will apply for a regular position in a bookshop."[16]

Shortly after handing over the manuscript of *Peter Camenzind,* Hesse was once more assailed by doubts. Given his experiences thus far, he found himself unable to believe in the possibility of a major success. He formulated his concerns in a letter to Stefan Zweig on November 2 in the following terms: "Even good old Camenzind is beginning in retrospect to mockingly reveal his evil defects to me. Whenever you're writing you always feel like a little deity, but afterward it all seems like the scribblings of a schoolboy, and this book is no different."[17]

Yet certain things were most definitely different now—for example, the very fact that the addressee of this letter was Stefan Zweig. Hesse had first written to him in January 1903, sending him his volume *Poems,* which had been published by Grote, and drawing his attention to a translation in them of a piece by Verlaine. He inquired whether the "most esteemed Sir," whose work *Silberne Saiten* (Silver strings) he already had, might be so kind as to send him a copy of the anthology of Verlaine's work that he had edited? This was Hesse's first attempt at contacting a young author in whom he had identified a kindred spirit.

Zweig immediately understood this attempt to establish a friendship—and indeed, each found in the other a counterpart to whom he could confide, with unaccustomed frankness, the joys and sorrows of embarking on a career as a writer. A new tone emerges in Hesse's letters, on the one hand more open and profound, but on the other hand also already consciously presenting himself in his role as a writer. Zweig found himself in a similarly uncertain situation to Hesse. When would success finally arrive? They both shared the same anxiety, and the fear of "perhaps never" formed a bond between them. But of all the disappointments encountered by the young authors—who are at first intoxicated with one another and thereafter all too sober—one is the most severe: the readers. The writers found it impossible to gauge how highly they were thought of by their readership thus far.

Ultimately both Hesse and Zweig were able to express the demystification inherent in the start of every new piece of work. Even so, it may well be that Hesse was rather playing up his sense of disenchantment when he wrote to Zweig on February 5, 1903:

> I acquired some more tangible, solid knowledge in a few of my favorite subjects: the history of German Romanticism and Tuscan easel paintings of the fifteenth century, among others. In addition to this an acquaintance based on serious experience with the table wines of Baden, Alsace, and Switzerland. I studied philosophy for some years without discovering any pearls and finally put it aside. Up to now, I have been completely spared any literary successes. My little books lie tied up in bundles at the publishers. From time to time I have been angered by that, but never disheartened, for I know only too well that as a misfit I have nothing to say to the world at large. I am in part too unskillful, too proud, and too lazy to become a feature writer. The act of creation is always a pleasure for me, never work. Even so, thanks to the tiresome business of having to buy things, I find myself obliged now and then to engage in such activity.[18]

Somehow he seemed to have now made the Camenzind role his own, and his character's fantasizing tone of braggadocio also crept into his letters—for instance, when he confessed to Zweig: "In truth, I am not an unsociable person. I really enjoy the company of children, peasants, seamen etcetera, and can always be persuaded to go drinking in sailors' bars and other such places."[19] This comes as something of a surprise; one is tempted to ask what sailors' bars Hesse could possibly have frequented in places such as Calw, Tübingen, or Basel. But here an element is being introduced into an autobiography that—especially in the case of Hesse—we would be ill-advised to disregard. Self-disclosures are always at the same time tests of the imagination, and demonstrations by the self of its own potential. Anyone who writes, particularly about himself, creates a doppelgänger—even if only for the purpose of making him a denizen of sailors' bars.

Zweig, who was studying in Berlin and who in 1904 was awarded his doctorate for his dissertation "The Philosophy of Hippolyte Taine," was envious that his correspondent had been offered publication by Fischer. In that regard, Hesse was a decisive step ahead of him. This is one of the reasons Zweig paid so much attention to Hesse. Subsequently, in his 1923 essay "Hermann Hesse's Journey," he would come to praise *Demian* and *Klingsor's Last Summer* as milestones of German contemporary literature, while dismissing out of hand all the works that had led up to them, such as *Hermann Lauscher, Peter Camenzind,* and *Knulp,* as "scenes like those from the paintings of Carl Spitzweg" and "endless snapshots of Little Germany" (and in this his attitude was very akin to Hesse's own abjectly unjust critique of his early efforts). Yet when he referred to *Beneath the Wheel* and *Rosshalde* as "classic examples of the bourgeois German art of narration," this failed to recognize the antibourgeois explosive power of this kind of description of conditions. However, even the logic that Zweig was applying here—"the more grim life is, the sweeter music and dreams are"[20]—seems to fall badly short of the mark, and is unjust to both Hesse and to his and Zweig's shared beginnings. In his first letter to Hesse, Zweig displays none of his later misgivings in invoking the "secret society of melancholy" to which they both belonged.

In the fall of 1903 *Peter Camenzind* began to appear as a preprint, in several installments, in the journal *Neue Deutsche Rundschau.* In February 1904 it was published in book form, and five editions were printed in swift succession. In his first year as a freelance writer, Hesse earned more than 9,000 marks, which was many times more than his annual salary at the Wattenwyl antiquarian bookshop.

Why was this book so successful, though—much more successful than Thomas Mann's *Tonio Kröger?* Primarily, it touched the nerve of the age. Even more than its Rousseauesque revolt of nature against alienated civilization and of the provincial world against the metropolis, it was its clear declaration of sympathy for the losers from the process of modernization that spoke to its readership.

Overnight Hesse became a figurehead of a counterculture—one of the first of the twentieth century. Before long the Wandervogel and reformist movements of all kinds would heed and take as their own the call that he issued in *Peter Camenzind*—just as, sixty years later, a global counterculture youth movement would adopt *Steppenwolf.* Hesse himself regarded this as a misunderstanding of his message. But who can control the way in which their works are received?

Of course, Hesse—who was well aware that such models of his as Romanticism, Nietzsche, Goethe, and Burckhardt also shunned such things—was a sworn enemy of anything that smacked of organized communality. His concern was always with the individual who was destined to be an outsider. Indeed, what else could one be when one was defending such a lost cause?

This question cropped up time and again throughout his life. When, in advanced old age, he was asked about the rise of the American hippie counterculture under the aegis of *Steppenwolf,* Hesse recalled an early manifestation of this same kind of effect, arising from *Peter Camenzind.* It had been far from his intention, he claimed, to promote campfire Romanticism and a guitar-strumming dropout lifestyle, or the reform of a communitarian ideal. After all, he had expended a great deal of time and effort precisely trying to break free of the latter, in the form of the Pietist circles around his parents. Retrospectively, he summed up the principle of what he had been aiming at in *Camenzind* in the following terms: "He [Camenzind] does not want to follow the path trodden by many, but to resolutely plow his own furrow; he does not wish to run with the pack and fit in with others, but to reflect nature and the world in his own psyche and to constantly experience it in fresh images. He is not made for the collective life; instead he is a solitary king in a realm of dreams that he himself has created."[21]

Hesse's success was also reflected in the fact that certain people around him began to envy him his newfound fame. Robert Musil, for instance, waited in vain for a follow-up commercial success after the acclaim given to his debut work *Die Verwirrungen des Zöglings Törleß* (The confusions of young Törless) in 1906, and noted bitterly in 1910 in a sketch (which remained unpublished):

Hesse: the product of a union between Gottfried Keller and Marlitt, and taking more after his mother.[22] Camenzind begins well and sounds good. But does no one notice the chasm between the tone of the ending and the rest of the novel? Or that simply saying that nature is beautiful does not make a work of creative fiction? Does no one feel that even a better description of nature wouldn't amount to much? Is one entitled to simply rerun Jacobsen? Does nobody else feel the strange absence of eroticism in this book? The sentimentality of the main character's friendships. The matter-of-factness of men kissing one another, living together, and doting on one another—as if that were all perfectly self-evident! Unremarkable! Humdrum! In sum, the homosexual tenor of this book? Does no one feel the bogusness of the encounter with the good woman in Italy, who like other such good women surely goes swimming only very rarely? That is not to say that such woman do not have a certain allure, but it's problematic and should have been dealt with differently . . . and does nobody else notice the poor and common German in which this book is written? This barrack-room style? Does no one feel the clumsy pacing, the dilettantism, and the unwieldy construction of this novel?[23]

In this critique, Musil's own polemical zeal then causes him to forget himself and start expressing himself in "poor and common German." It is clear from this how strongly some people felt about the overnight arrival and instant success of Hermann Hesse. This is in glaring contrast to how Hesse spoke about other writers and their books—a fact that becomes quite evident from looking at volumes 16 to 20 of his *Collected Works*. If one reads these, one comes to understand Ernst Jünger's assertion that every piece of polemic that a person can refrain from uttering redounds to their benefit. Incidentally, Musil, who often made caustic remarks about other writers, wrote to Hesse in 1931 to tell him: "I am a great admirer of your art."[24]

Italy Once More, This Time in Company

Hesse's favorite word of 1903 was *fidel* (cheerful). Two years before it had been *famos* (splendid). On March 20, 1903, he wrote to Alfons Paquet to inform him that it was his life's ambition to one day have enough money to disappear from the literary and social world and make his way "through beautiful foreign lands on my own and carefree, as a wayfarer and connoisseur." Just a few days later he had the opportunity to do exactly that.

On the evening before the Basel photographer Maria Bernoulli was due to travel to Italy, Hesse decided on the spur of moment to go with her. He would note in his journal of this trip that he had been "persuaded" to accompany her. The word *fidel* appears a dozen times across the barely twenty pages of this journal, creeping into all kinds of sentences. In general, any reader of Hesse is surprised time and again at how artlessly the writer uses certain words, from *lecker* (tasty) to *nachhaltig* (lasting) that weren't even really permissible in the slang of the period.

So, can we deduce from this that everything was jolly and carefree during this spontaneous adventure? Far from it—reservations and doubts run through Hesse's notes right from the very first section. This first section closes—after a reference to a "very tiring" overnight journey to Milan traveling in third class—with the phrase "gallows humor."

What gallows was Hesse being led to here? Italy was, after all, the country he always longed to visit, and he would have been absolutely delighted at the prospect of making a second trip there. But right from the outset there is something not quite right with the atmosphere, as evinced by the clearly forced jollity of many of his descriptions. Perhaps Hesse did not even want to admit it to himself, because another woman, a friend of Maria Bernoulli, was also traveling with them, the painter Maria Gundrum, with whom Hesse quite clearly did not get on. Yet what Hesse wrote about Maria Bernoulli sounds remarkably "Biedermeier"-like in its tone: "The smart young lady chatted intelligently and cheerfully with me, we told each other about our amorous encounters, made various observations and reflections and laughed a lot. In sum, we 'hit it off' with one another." Yet how differently he viewed the dark young Italian women, what very different associations they awakened in him! There is no sign here that Maria Bernoulli held any erotic fascination for him. In all respects she resembled his mother; she too was adept at chatting "intelligently and cheerfully." He was discontented. The weather was as bad as April weather elsewhere—and even familiar Florence did not appeal to him this time. As early as April 4 he notes in his diary that he often had occasion to get annoyed, "partly just because I wasn't able to soak up the atmosphere in peace and quiet and partly because of Gundrum and her incessant art history."[25]

The upshot of this simmering discontent was: "I drank too much Chianti and was rather too carefree and boisterous one evening." In the meantime, Maria Bernoulli had caught a cold and was suffering from earache. Hesse found himself experiencing even greater an aversion to her friend Maria Gundrum and her opinions on art history. And so the phrase "gallows humor" appears again repeatedly. Here, Hesse comes across in exactly the same way as he would later sound as a husband and *paterfamilias* in Gaienhofen—ready at any moment to escape and talking in a tone of barely suppressed displeasure. On April 8 the Hesse family in Calw received news that he was in Florence; the letter sounded allusive and yet downbeat at the same time: "A painter friend of mine, Fräulein Gundrum, recently left Basel in order to move permanently to Italy, and invited various acquaintances and friends to join her in Florence over Easter. I was disinclined to go until, at the last minute, another artist got enthused by the idea and persuaded me to accompany her. I just had time to change my clothes and pack a few things before setting off."[26]

Hesse repeatedly disengaged himself from his two female companions, as when he went to visit certain favorite old haunts, and noted on such occasions: "It suited me just fine to enjoy seeing Fiesole again without anyone else in tow. I was fortunate: that day, it was unexpectedly hot and sunny around noon and I was able to stroll happily along familiar old paths." Even by this stage, Hesse was a notorious loner.

On April 13 they left Florence. Their next stop was Genoa, which made a "terrible impression" on Hesse. Maria Bernoulli was just as annoyed as him (the painter was no longer with them) and this led to some "friction"—the coffee was "execrable," and Hesse noted that "we argued about what to do with the day." Though they were on holiday, that sounded too much like the frustrating humdrum of everyday life. In the end it was Maria Bernoulli who revealed an affectionate streak and began to look after Hesse, who was nine years her junior; his reaction to this attention was to be half embarrassed and half flattered. And so it was, on her final day in Italy, that she was up at 6:30 A.M. waiting him to come down for breakfast and accompanied him to the onward train that he was to take, on his own, to Venice. Had this woman actually made a deeper impression on him than he was revealing?

Hesse appears to have arrived in Venice in a state of some confusion. In any event, he noted the shocking absence of the campanile on Saint Mark's Square, which had collapsed the previous year (and which was only rebuilt in the form in which we see it today in 1905) and reacted with irritation to the crowds of tourists in the city. He didn't like the food in the Cavaletto Hotel, and he found the waiter "impertinent." He resolved not to return to this place, which had been a favorite haunt of his during his first stay in Venice. At this early stage Hesse was also displaying his irascible nature. At any rate, the time he had spent with Maria Bernoulli had done nothing to put him in a more even-tempered frame of mind, as evidenced by a remarkably terse diary entry on April 15: "Stupid escapade with a fat Viennese woman."[27]

Conflict and discontent now seemed to dog his every step, and the magic of his first sojourn in Italy never materialized. At the post office in Venice he endured hours of inconvenience trying to arrange a money transfer; here, he only notes his greatest handicap in passing: "My eyesight was very poor."

Then again, it was not so poor that he was unable to capture the cityscape, through which he now wandered aimlessly for the most part, in all its essential features: "A light rain sets in, so I sit out most of the afternoon in the vestibule of the Doges' Palace, amusing myself at the sight of the drenched crowds passing by outside and observing the exquisitely delicate grey-silver color the lagoon always takes on when it rains. A tour party arrived, and was herded past the 'tourist attractions' like a flock of sheep."[28]

All in all, as he would conclude when he took his leave of Venice on April 24, this was a trip that was flawed from the outset by being "totally improvised and devoid of any plan."

But perhaps it had even greater flaws. First and foremost the fact that it hadn't been his idea and also that it had failed to make the same strong impressions on him as his first journey to Italy, when he had traveled alone through this foreign yet familiar country. For him, this journey was to have only one enduring consequence: his relationship with Maria Bernoulli.

Boccaccio and Francis of Assisi: Intermezzo as a Monograph Writer Who Fabricates Myths

The success of *Peter Camenzind,* which was evident even from the advance publication in the *Neue Deutsche Rundschau,* resulted in an invitation to Hesse from the Schuster und Loeffler publishing house of Berlin and Leipzig to write a volume on Giovanni Boccaccio for their forthcoming series of monographs on poets. Hesse was happy to accept this commission, as he had already spent two extended stays in Florence, the home town of this fourteenth-century Italian writer, and was equally in awe of this unique Renaissance city and its famous author son.

He finished this manuscript within a few weeks—even in the most generously spaced typesetting, it only came out at around sixty printed pages, an uncommonly slim monograph. But Hesse had absolutely no intention of assembling all the available facts about Boccaccio's life, let alone of searching out any new ones, nor was he trying to present a detailed account of his work.

Instead, he was aiming at something else entirely—namely, to identify the one point that crystallized the essential truth of his subject's life. This short text, which is far more than simply an abridged biography of Boccaccio, makes for some quite astonishing reading. Hesse retrospectively—and excessively harshly—claimed that he had written this work in a flush of youthful enthusiasm and what he self-critically termed a spirit of "ignorance and impertinence" that he no longer wished to recall. Accordingly, from even as early as 1905 Hesse was adamant that he did not want to see his essay on Boccaccio—or the subsequent one on Francis of Assisi—reprinted ever again, with the result that a new edition of these works had to wait until the 1980s to see the light of day.

Yet both texts are biographical essays in the best sense of the term. For the life of a person who is long dead has to be reinvented by us in order to really come alive. The amassing of facts alone, which as the fruit of scholarly research can always be added to at any time, does not in and of itself create a picture capable of truly enthralling us. This requires the kind of atmosphere that can only be generated by poetically heightened expression. And this in turn presumes that the writer himself is captivated or at least enthused to some degree by the subject he is intending to write about—a cardinal sin in the eyes of the prevailing academic world, whose aim it was to expunge the subjective element from any form of biographical account, and consequently also to rigorously prohibit any fruitful access to legend and myth in the highly vulnerable accord between a writer's life and work.

Hesse himself pointed to another approach, which to modern sensibilities seems far more productive. The motifs of both biographies sound similar. For both are inextricably bound up with the landscape of Italy, in the case of Boccaccio that of Tuscany, whereas for Saint Francis it is

Umbria. For Hesse, describing someone's life entailed an intensive process of getting under their skin and discovering that person's true character, which required a poetic mode of expression to bring out its particular individual stamp.

Boccaccio and Francis of Assisi were both wayfarers, fellow pilgrims on a route that they first had to reconnoiter for themselves. Hesse wrote that the "gate to the garden" opened for them. At this point at the latest, it should become clear to us how inseparable Hesse's portrayal of Boccaccio is from his attempt to chart his own self-image:

> Have you never walked past an unfamiliar garden on a fine, warm day in early summer? You were alone and unhappy, and a wind blowing from the garden wafted the scent of roses and orange blossom over to you, along with the tinkling, silvery sound of a splashing fountain, the strumming of a guitar, and the noise of happy young people's conversation, interrupted occasionally by laughter. And you were seized by a sudden wave of melancholy and a powerful longing to enter the garden, to exchange the dusty country road for green lawns and flower beds, to listen to the singers' songs and the pleasant chat of the happy people and sate your yearning to your heart's content on all the jollity and joy there.[29]

A refuge akin to that of the *Decameron* itself, that collection of ludicrous and erotic tales, which become a mirror held up to the eternally identical human comedy. Yet the material from which these immortal stories are woven often seems impure and mired in the banal humdrum of everyday life. It is those facets of our nature that are animalistic and that, without a saving spark of intellect, often body forth in the most depraved and demonic form. And it was precisely those dangers of an itinerant existence that interested Hesse.

Boccaccio wrote the *Decameron* at around the age of forty—when his time as a young man impelled by a sense of unrest was past, yet before he was stamped with the staid dignity of old age, took up diplomacy, and repudiated his own masterpiece. Boccaccio's work was the source from which Lessing borrowed the parable of the ring in his play *Nathan der Weise (Nathan the Wise)*. Yet much of the *Decameron,* perhaps the bulk of it, was not actually Boccaccio's own invention. These were tales that people had told one another since time immemorial in Naples, where he studied, and in Florence. The spirit of the Renaissance—the exaltation of all things natural—is expressed in its poetically most vigorous form in these liberal-minded stories. Priests, abbots, nuns, bishops, and dignitaries of all kinds—at root these are all the same type of human being, who can all be surprised in similar, and all-too-human, situations. Even better, having been caught out in such compromising situations, they are free enough to laugh about it! This dismantling of dogma and acknowledgment of nature, human nature included, became in the Renaissance the prerequisite for an unprecedented blossoming of the arts. All forms of hypocrisy and sanctimony are exposed with wit and humor, and parodied. And the *Decameron* was right at the forefront of the barricades in this literary revolution. So it is that we read in Boccaccio's stories (and Hesse quoted this very passage): "In my time, I have witnessed thousands of those who covet, seduce, and haunt not only laywomen but also those in convents—and they were precisely the people who raised the loudest outcry from the pulpit."

But the catastrophic flipside of the new freedom—the horror of the Black Death, which carried off almost a hundred thousand people in Florence—also came to the fore. Hesse expressed this elementary logic of creativity when he wrote: "Without a doubt, seldom can such a terrible disaster have borne such exquisite fruit as the great plague of Florence, in remembrance of which the *Decameron* was written."[30]

Hesse's monograph on Boccaccio was a success. That was one reason he went on to quickly write another short profile for the monograph series—this time on Francis of Assisi. This was an extraordinary choice insofar as he was a principal saint of the Catholic Church. Yet at the same time he was someone who had only escaped by the skin of his teeth the fate of Peter Waldo, who was stigmatized as a heretic and persecuted. Also, Hermann Hesse's Pietist parents would have been in sympathy with Francis's ideal of a poor church. They were unequivocally skeptical toward the institution and dogma of Catholicism.

But with Francis of Assisi it was a quite different matter, at least in the light in which he appeared to Hesse. Hesse loved him for the fact that he revered the presence of God first and foremost in nature, in streams, meadows, clouds, or birds. And also within human beings themselves, especially the poor and the sick and those who were shunned by the community of "normal" people. Yet this biography of Francis of Assisi is astonishing because here Hesse explicitly addresses the question of religious faith—a subject toward which he had hitherto adopted a demonstratively hostile stance. His parents had tormented him for years with their insistence on true faith in God and genuine piety, and yet here he was choosing to address this question of his own volition.

This is why this short essay is so important: it is, effectively, Hesse's religious credo, a clear statement of what he believed in after he had stated often enough what he did not believe in. Nature and love, sincerity, greatness in the smallest and most miserable of things—Hesse saw in Francis a figure plowing his own furrow, quite alone at first, misunderstood and mocked. It was G. K. Chesterton who had identified what distinguished Saint Francis from all other preachers of the religious revival. It was not his social conscience; this was not the source from which he drew his strength on his pilgrimage, which was a lonely enterprise at the outset. It was not his mission to "help" others. He was going in search of the true faith—and the path he took to it made him an outsider. Without his stubbornness, as Hesse would formulate it (Chesterton put it even more provocatively, calling it "insanity"!), he would never have embarked on this quest. How otherwise would he have begun listening to birds, in order to divine in their song the voice of God? Saint Francis's work was his life—and yet, according to Hesse, he was also a poet: the poet of his own life, which was one long pilgrimage toward God. He adapted himself to things and, rather than seeking to gain mastery over them, sought to become their brother. Brother Sun, Brother Water, Brother Fire, Brother Death—but Mother Earth.

Francis was not driven by ambition or by a sudden religious zeal to completely change his life. It was a pure moral dilemma, a voice inside him that he could no longer ignore. He was no knight of the faith in gleaming armor, no missionary who went out into the world to convert nonbelievers or, if they refused to be converted, to kill them—but instead someone who in the midst of the deepest personal crisis, his most abject misery, began to praise God, because it was He who made seeds germinate, flowers bloom, and fruit ripen and grow. And because He caused new life to emerge from every act of dying. Just in the same way as Vincent van Gogh painted Him, God for Saint Francis was both the sower and the reaper.

Francis became a person on whom others pinned their hopes, not because he showed them the way, but because he shared with them his uncertainty about the correct path to take. Because rather than offer proclamations, he asked questions and listened to nature. His God is immanent in actual things, in their growth and decay.

Hesse learned from Saint Francis the true meaning of "lustless love" in its deepest sense (as something more than and different from a simple vow of chastity!). He also learned about the truth that resides within myth. It is the spirit of brotherhood that fascinated Hesse: "His speech was not that of a dreamer and wordsmith, instead he spoke like a peasant with peasants, like a townsman with townspeople, and like a knight with knights. He spoke to everyone about what moved his heart and above all he talked as a brother to his brothers, as someone who had known suffering to those who had suffered and as one who had recovered to those who were sick."[31]

As already noted, when Hesse wrote this biographical sketch in 1904, he was influenced by two books that excited much controversy and discussion during this period and that disengaged Saint Francis from the narrow horizon of being seen just as a Catholic saint, depicting him instead as the creator of a new—natural—image of man. Paul Sabatier's *Life of Saint Francis of Assisi,* which was published in German translation in 1895, was frowned upon by the Catholic Church because it dared to cast a socially critical eye on the founder of the Minorite Order and to view him entirely as a human being who operated within a concrete historical context. When Hesse spent some time in September and October of 1902 recuperating in Calw from severe eye pain, during which time he was told not to overstrain himself, his sister Marulla read Sabatier's book to him. Another groundbreaking book that appeared at around the same time was the German art historian Henry Thode's *Franz von Assisi und die Anfänge der Kunst der Renaissance in Italien* (Francis of Assisi and the beginnings of Renaissance art in Italy). Thode's book—which is still fascinating today for the richness of its inspiration—reveals the connection between the new Franciscan piety and the revolution in the image of man and nature as reflected in the painting of Giotto. Hesse formulated this idea in the following way: "He constantly practiced, as an incomparable master, the marvelous and splendid art of rejuvenating himself daily by experiencing the life of nature and as it were of imbibing the powers of the Earth, a skill that one encounters only in poets and truly blessed people. He conversed like a child and like a sage with flowers, grasses, waves, and all manner of beasts, singing hymns of praise to them, loving and consoling them, exulting with them, and sharing in their blameless lives."[32]

This vision of Francis of Assisi as a wayfarer on a pilgrimage to God and to himself on one and the same path stayed with Hesse throughout his life, and was especially prevalent at moments of crisis. It was the dual nature of Saint Francis, whom Hesse called the "favorite of all artists," that fascinated him above all. At the same time, he was constantly both saint and heretic, ambassador and outsider, mystic and enlightener, ecstatic and rational. The internal and the external merge in his image. For he never stood outside nature, even his own.

Intermezzo in Calw: Waiting for the Novel

By the summer of 1903 Hesse had quit his job at the Wattenwyl antiquarian bookshop and turned his back on Basel. He would return to live for the next six months at his parents' house in Calw. There he wrote his first Gerbersau stories and started work on *Beneath the Wheel*—his way of set-tling his account with the authoritarian school system of his age. Above and beyond this, though, this novel was also a double portrait of a mal-treated "child soul." Hesse spent the months leading up to the appearance of *Peter Camenzind* in the greatest imaginable emotional turmoil. He wrote to Stefan Zweig on October 11, 1903: "Literature continues to bring me little joy. I recently read a nice review of my poems, but not a soul is buying them, and if the latest novel flops as well, I'll give up the whole stupid business and try my hand at something else instead."[33]

From Whitsun onward he was engaged to Maria Bernoulli—much against the wishes of both his and her parents. He was intending to marry her the following year—but if he failed to finally score a commercial suc-cess with his books, what were they to live on? For the time being, though, the impecunious young author, who had only earned 400 marks for the preprint of *Peter Camenzind* and a 300 marks advance on the book edition, was content just to be able to sit in his old room once more: "I found what I was looking for here—namely, complete peace and quiet and solitude. There is no one here who reads books or writes poetry or drinks tea and smokes cigarettes and is a know-it-all; no one who has just been in Italy and Paris and speaks several languages, and that's just fine by me."[34] Hesse meant to spend the winter here and, transported back once more into the atmosphere of his family, to write *Beneath the Wheel*. His mother was no longer there, against whose dominance he rebelled and whose great strength he was nevertheless in awe of. Marie Hesse's photograph hung on the wall of his room, alongside one of Maria Bernoulli, a fishing rod, and a map of Italy. At least when viewed from a distance, the portraits of the two women looked strikingly similar. Booth of their faces were strong and coarse-featured—they were certainly no beauties but rather what one might term "countrywomen"; yet both possessed a considerable gift for music (Maria Bernoulli was a great music lover too, and played the piano very well). Equally, both women had a deep mistrust of art when it shifted from being a pleasant adjunct to everyday life and took center stage. In other words, Hesse should have been warned. The last person Maria wanted as a husband—indeed, she had nothing but contempt for such a figure—was a professional writer who had to constantly struggle for success and recognition and who had to somehow square his neuroses with the commercial demands of the book market.

Hesse, who had rushed into his engagement to the Basel lady photographer shortly after his return from Italy, was determined not to rescind his offer of marriage. Why, though, did he insist on honoring the kind of liaison that an inner voice had been warning him against for a long time?

In late 1903 Hesse was concerned to suppress any speculations on what his future as a married man with a family might look like. In any case, if *Peter Camenzind* sold as badly as his other books had, the question of marriage would be taken care of. So he devoted his time to "collecting two small sacks full of pine cones every day," which he meant to use to heat his room in his parents' house in Calw over the coming weeks. Though he made much of the art of idleness, Hesse nonetheless took a highly disciplined attitude to his work and could be prized away from his desk only by illness, chiefly his overstrained eyes and his bouts of deep depression. But he knew that this sacrifice of time he could have spent on the real business of life to describing it on paper had to be a voluntary one, for no one could release him from living with the results of his artistic endeavor. Whether such an enterprise was sensible did not depend upon outward success—however important that may have been both for his bourgeois status and for his ability to furnish himself with the simple physical necessities of heating, coffee, and wine; rather, the decisive factor in determining whether his chosen path as a writer was the right one for him was his inner voice, and nothing else. And it was vital that he protect this from all persuasion and from all calculation about the practical pros and cons.

The freelance author may be amenable to all kinds of things attracting a fee, but one thing cannot be bought: the inner voice, the writer's own yardstick for judging success and failure. In a text that Hesse wrote in 1904, "Die Kunst des Müßiggangs: Ein Kapitel künstlerischer Hygiene" (The art of idleness: A chapter in artistic hygiene)—a very short work, yet remarkably profound in its observations for such a young writer—Hesse already set a "cordon sanitaire" around those so very vulnerable wellsprings of creative endeavor that anyone who aims to write from the heart about what he sees as the truth must keep from becoming sullied. Hesse's text is astonishing in its vigorous rejection of the increasing functionalization of the spirit by the state and the education system, as well as by science and fashion. This was an unequivocal declaration of belief. The kind of critique that Stefan Zweig would express with the same degree of vehemence in his famous 1939 lecture "The Monotonization of the World" is here anticipated by Hesse:

> The more intellectual endeavor fell into line with tasteless, oppressive industrial enterprise, which is devoid of all tradition, and the more zealous the scientific community and schools became in divesting us of our liberty and personality and in drumming into us from earliest childhood the notion that a pressured, breathless state of exertion was the ideal to aspire to, the more the art of idleness fell into disrepair and discredit through lack of practice, alongside a host of other outdated skills. It is not as if we had ever become past masters at it anyhow! In the West, indolence honed to an art form has only ever been practiced down the ages by harmless dilettantes.[35]

These words come from the pen of an author, of all people, who like scarcely any other of the twentieth century—excepting Gottfried Benn—pushed radical Protestantism to the point where a Pietist obsession with words is transformed into linguistic poetic magic!

Life after the Bestseller: Hesse as a Family Man in Gaienhofen

My exterior life now ran smoothly and pleasantly for a while.
I had a wife, children, a house, and a garden. I wrote my books,
was regarded as a genial poet, and was at peace with the world.

—Hermann Hesse *Life Story Briefly Told* (1924)

The book edition of *Peter Camenzind* was published on February 15, 1904. The first print run was sold out after just fourteen days—edition

Hesse pictured with a glass of red wine in October 1910

after edition would swiftly follow. This success surprised the author and publisher alike. Hermann Hesse said of his life after the publication of *Peter Camenzind:* "I had arrived." But as he would soon learn, this was a double-edged sword. What a complete reversal of roles! All of a sudden he did not have to struggle to get his work published anywhere, as the world flocked to his door to woo him. A lot of wheeling and dealing ensued, vanities were incited and wounded, and jealousies arose, both Hesse's own and those of others. Life began to grow complex. Even Hesse, a textbook example of an unclubbable individual, was forced to recognize this when, at a Fischer publishing house reception in Munich in the year *Camenzind* scored such a hit, he met Thomas Mann and— naive provincial that he was—asked him if he was related to the author of the work *The Goddesses: The Three Novels of the Duchess of Assy.* This was the work of Thomas Mann's brother Heinrich, whose books were widely read during this period.

Hesse's *Life Story Briefly Told* recounts the period following the success of *Camenzind:* "I had triumphed, and now, when I did the stupidest and most worthless thing, people found it delightful, in just the same way as I was delighted with myself. Only now did I realize in what a state of horrible loneliness, asceticism, and danger I had lived year after year; the balmy atmosphere of recognition did me good and I began to become a contented person."[36]

This new role as an established writer irritated Hesse, however. To be sure, he was flattered by success and relieved by his steady income, which exceeded all expectations. But he also sensed that if his yearning was walled in with false security, this might well strike a death blow at the root of his creative restlessness. So it was that, in 1906, he quite openly confessed: "Leaving aside a brief trip to the mountains, my life over the past few months has not been enjoyable. I would give my last cent to have published 'Camenzind' anonymously. This newfound fame is a miserable, sad, and at root deeply ridiculous business."[37]

Hesse and Maria Bernoulli were married in August 1904, in defiance of the wishes of her father, a lawyer from Basel who was almost eighty years old and who had no confidence in the writer as a suitable husband for his daughter. On September 11, Stefan Zweig learned from Hesse: "My wedding went off at a gallop! Because my father-in-law was not in agreement with the marriage and wanted nothing to do with me, I traveled to Basel when he was absent from the city and we headed off to the registry office without delay. Now, from a distance, the old man is moaning about it but does gradually seem to be taking a calmer view of things."[38]

Was getting married a liberating act for Hesse? Certainly, but not only that. To an even greater extent it was the beginning of a new period of captivity by the things that Hesse found most unbearable: a family and children.

Hugo Ball took the view that Maria Bernoulli became a "placeholder" for Hesse's dead mother, and Hesse never contradicted this assertion by his friend and first biographer.

The tone in which Hesse speaks about his wife is irritating. It is not that of a person who adores their "other half" or even considers her as an equal and takes her seriously. He states that marriage means his life as a roving gypsy is over, at least for the time being—and he almost sounds resigned when he concedes: "But the little woman is sweet and sensible."[39]

Even so, a definite bond existed between himself and Maria Bernoulli: their shared ideal of a life on the land, based half on Rousseau and half on Tolstoy. While Hesse was still living with his father and sisters in Calw, Maria was already on the search for a house that would meet her expectations, as a patrician's daughter with a penchant for an alternative lifestyle. Hesse recalled that the kind of property she was looking for was a "half-rustic, half-manorial country house, with a moss-covered roof, spacious, beneath ancient trees, and if possible with a rushing stream outside the door." She found just such a property at Gaienhofen on Lake Constance.

As early as 1903 Hesse had written a "biographical piece" for Franz Brümmer's *Encyclopedia of German Poets and Prose Writers,* published by Reclam in Leipzig. In this contribution, we read the following: "I like to travel and live on my own. My passions are: looking at paintings, walking, and books. I am poor and have trouble making ends meet."[40] His circumstances altered rapidly after he wrote that—but did his own conception of himself also change at the same time?

Now he had to attend to matters other than writing. When the couple were about to move into a simple farmhouse in August 1904, the first unexpected problems already started to become apparent: "Our furniture has not arrived yet, and for several days we've been living without a table or chairs in our empty little farm cottage."[41]

The newlyweds had rented this accommodation, which one could only call primitive, at a cost of 150 marks a year. Ludwig Finckh, Hesse's friend from the *petit cénacle* in Tübingen, now a doctor and writer, and who was also planning to move to Gaienhofen in 1905, spoke in terms of a "lonely eyrie" for Hesse here on the Untersee [the smaller of the two lakes that make up Lake Constance]. The house had no electricity, running water, bath, or toilet. Moreover, Hesse and Maria Bernoulli only had half the house at their disposal; the other was used by a local farmer as a byre and barn. Even so, Hesse tried to infuse this ramshackle place with a large dose of poetic idealism. If the Gaienhofen house was an idyll, it was one that laid claims to all his artistic powers. He told Stefan Zweig:

> Gaienhofen is a tiny, pretty hamlet, with no railway station, no shops, and no industry. It doesn't even have its own parish priest, so that early this morning, when I had to attend a neighbor's funeral, I had to wade across the open fields for half an hour in the most appalling downpour of rain. Also, there is no mains water supply, which means I have to collect all the water we need from the well, and no handymen hereabouts, so that I have to do all the necessary repairs in the house, and no butcher, forcing me to row across the lake every time we need meat and sausage and so on and fetch it myself.[42]

Switzerland began on the far side of the lake, where there was a railroad connection and various shops. Although Hesse rowed there in order to shop, there was of course a customs post right on the jetty: "I can already recite off by heart the entire customs tariff for all kitchen requisites, etc., but where practicable I prefer to smuggle goods."[43] So, Hesse's idyll lay at the back of beyond. Almost beyond the edge of the world. What was he supposed to write about there? Like subsidized dropouts, the Hesses lived off the money earned from *Peter Camenzind,* and the new lord of the manor, who at the same time was also the manservant, found himself with no time anymore in which to write. Even at this point *Camenzind* had already netted some 2,500 marks, and Hesse estimated that they could live on this for two years if they weren't too spendthrift. The question still remained, however, whether that was what he wanted to do.

Maria Bernoulli, whom Hesse called Mia, reveled in this kind of life. Reclusive, with no ambitions, in the midst of nature, and far from the world and all visitors. Yet by September 2, 1904, exactly a month after the wedding, Hermann Hesse, who by now was well on the way to becoming a very successful writer, was at his wits' end: "I have finally sweated out and forgotten everything literary, but need to pick it up again soon."[44]

The house was very modestly furnished. On the ground floor was the kitchen and Mia's room, which also housed the piano. The first floor comprised Hesse's study and two small bedrooms. There was a tiled stove, however, and an oven in the kitchen. Hesse would later claim that this house left a lot to be desired, primarily a garden, which they had both greatly hankered after, though it did have one big advantage: it was their first abode! But he also noted that this kind of sedentary lifestyle was at the same time a form of captivity, a "state of being shackled to limits and systems."

It was a good feeling to break free into a new life. Initially the thrill of the new distracted him from what he was actually doing here yet was not admitting to himself: namely, putting down bourgeois roots, albeit with an alternative flavor. Wasn't he meant to be doing something else with his life? At first, he suppressed this question in favor of trying out a life as a handyman with an idealistic streak:

Hesse on the verandah of Am Erlenloh, his house at Gaienhofen on Lake Constance, silhouette from a shadow theater by Otto Blümel

All the nails in this room I have hammered in myself, and they weren't nails bought in a hardware store either, but the nails from the crate we brought our belongings in, which I hammered out straight on the stone front step. I have plugged the gaping holes in the floorboards of the upper story with oakum and paper, and painted them red, and I have struggled against drought and shade to keep alive the few flowers I planted alongside the wall. When I fitted out this house, I did so with the charming pathos of youth, with a feeling of genuine responsibility for all we were trying to achieve, and with a sense that it was going to last a lifetime.

However, the young married couple did not have a lot of time to practice their life together in the old/new house, for Mia fell ill in October and had to move to Basel for the next two months for a rest cure. During this time Hesse was left alone in the remote house—yet he found this solitary existence more to his taste than living as a couple. His sense of unease grew. Had he made a big mistake? In 1960, in his "Lake Constance Memoir," he recalled: "Something was not quite right about our leap into our new life, something I had rather childishly imagined half as being an idyll, and half as some kind of Robinson Crusoe-like existence; some gremlin seemed to haunt our time there."

In 1905 Hesse's eldest son, Bruno, was born—and from this point on, life became really difficult. Every pail of water had to be drawn from the well and heated on the stove. Fetching water from a well, lighting stoves and ovens, and rowing over to Switzerland to buy provisions, either going through customs or sneaking about on smugglers' paths, might be all very fine and exciting for the duration of a summer, but over the long term it became more and more uncomfortable and inconvenient for a writer with a wife and child. And yet, during the lonely evenings in the fall of 1904 while his wife was away on her rest cure, Hesse's life actually struck him as much too comfortable. For the first time in his life he had more money than he needed for his immediate survival. And that got under his skin somehow. He felt himself already on the way to the "land of the Philistines" when he portrayed the dilemma of his new existence in the 1904 essay "Autumn Nights" ("Herbstnächte") in all its raw intensity:

> There are my books, over a thousand of them, all painstakingly collected during my bitter years of hunger, a wonderful treasure trove containing many gems. They are on good, solid boards and are not lying around on the floor or on the bed or the sofa like before. There are a couple of good pictures hanging on the wall and I can keep the large stove alight for as long as I like. I don't need to count the logs and ration them anymore. There's even a little barrel of wine in the cellar, with a friendly little tap in the bung-hole, and there's always plenty of tobacco in the old tin box. In other words, I'm doing well; even the cat is growing fat; it's getting as much milk as it wants.

Hesse found all this a sobering discovery.

So, the euphoria he felt on making this fresh start cannot have been so great after all. There was something not quite right about his new life. A deep fissure ran through the image of the writer with a house and wife.

A doctor can settle down with a practice, but could a writer? And not just any writer—but Hesse, who had only just got free of the clutches of his Pietist family and who had an allergic reaction to any form of forced community? What would become of Hesse the solitary wayfarer, the restless free bird? After just a few weeks, Hesse was already greatly afflicted by his new life, which he knew to be a lie:

> When I walk down to the shore at dusk, the poplars by the jetty rustle loudly but tenderly in the wind, and the moist breeze quickly embraces me before leaping on to the lake and sweeping with a moan across its choppy waters. It is then that I begin to grieve from the depths of my soul that I am no longer a loner and a drifter, and I would cheerfully trade in my little house and my modest success for a battered old hat and a satchel, so I could go out and greet the world once more and carry my homesickness over land and sea.[45]

Homesickness for faraway places, and a yearning for the unfamiliar—these would become the principal themes of Hesse's work in the ensuing years, as he lived all too remotely from the world in an idyll that was in fact no such thing. False beginnings—anyone searching for this theme will find it over and over again, in a host of new variations, in the works that Hesse wrote during his Lake Constance years.

Several visitors came to see him in his house. And so many a person got to experience firsthand the fact that Hesse's lodgings at Gaienhofen, with its cramped rooms, was far from being some spacious bourgeois mansion: "On entering the house, you had to watch out for the high step up; if you didn't, you cracked your head against the low-set doorframe—several visitors fell foul of this. On his first visit, the young Stefan Zweig had to lie down for a quarter of an hour and recuperate before he could speak; he had come in too quickly and enthusiastically before I had a chance to warn him about the high doorstep."[46]

Yet a serious question lies behind this false start—namely, that concerning a refuge. Gaienhofen was always the place where, hidden away from the importunate outside world, that omnipresent vampire, he could be himself. Even in facets that had to remain incomprehensible to others, yet without which he would have been another person. In everything that he wrote, Hesse was at the same time both in search of and on the run from any form of refuge that promised protection: "The purpose and main point were always one and the same. Whether it was a country house or a ship's cabin, or an Alpine hut or a garden in Tuscany, or a clifftop in Ticino or a hole in the ground in a cemetery—the purpose was always to find refuge!" And time and again he met with disappointment and disenchantment, though this never meant that he felt he ought to stop himself from yearning for something that could never be fulfilled: "But also my sorrows became more forceful and more enduring and were directed against my dream: the time came when I realized it was all to no avail. The 'refuge' would not cure me, my sorrows would not vanish in the woods or in an isolated hut, I wouldn't become one with the world or put things right with myself there."[47]

For three years things went on in this same vein in the rented house. Years in which the success of Hesse's book sales continued unabated. Instead of running away, he resolved to do the opposite and increase his level of comfort. He duly became a house owner! The modern house he had built—almost a villa—was the first and only dwelling in Hesse's life that truly belonged to him and in which he was more than just a guest or a tenant. It was designed according to his plans and erected on a site above the lake shore, with a large garden surrounding it.

> We chose a location outside the village, with a clear view over the Untersee. From there you could see the Swiss shore, Reichenau Island, the tower of the minster in Konstanz and the distant mountains behind it. The house was more comfortable and larger than the one we moved out of, with plenty of room in it for children, a maid, and guests. Cupboards and chests were built in as fitted units, and we didn't need to fetch water from the well anymore as the new house had running mains water, while below ground there was a cellar for storing wine and fruit and a darkroom for my wife to develop her photographs, along with many other pleasant amenities.

This was how successful writers lived, and Hermann Hesse now counted among their number. And yet it wasn't him who paid for the new house, as he would report—in a very brisk tone—to his family in a letter of January 17, 1907:

> Besides, Father Bernoulli will be advancing us a large part of the building cost, interest-free, so that we might regard the house as our inheritance from him ahead of time, so to speak. Although I will have to contribute several

thousand myself, the total cost of the build will be 20,000 marks at most. It's estimated the actual construction will account for around 16,000 of this, then on top of that we'll need money to buy furniture, erect a fence and put the garden in order. The location is very pretty, with water from a spring nearby, and the whole place just three minutes' walk from the village, with extensive views over the lake from two sides of the house.[48]

But before the house was finally ready to occupy in October 1907, Hesse was plunged into a deep health crisis. In April he traveled to Monte Verità for a special course of treatment.

For Hesse, the question of the sort of house one should inhabit was directly linked to his abiding preoccupation with how to lead a proper life. In 1930—by which time he had already been resident for some time in Ticino in Switzerland—he confessed: "I have unfortunately never understood how to make life easy and comfortable for myself. However, I have always had at my command one single skill, namely the art of fine living."[49]

By this he meant first and foremost having in front of his windows "a characteristic extensive and broad landscape." In a retrospective account of the locations where he had lived and worked, entitled "On Moving into a New House," which Hesse wrote in 1931, we read about the mistake of wanting to live like a character from Tolstoy while at the same time achieving success as a bourgeois writer—during the years spent at Gaienhofen he came within an ace of finding himself saddled with the label "popular author," just like his "rose doctor," his neighbor Ludwig Finckh. Finckh undoubtedly deserved this label—but Hermann Hesse sensed that he was in danger of heading down the wrong track here and that an image of him as an idyllist was beginning to do the rounds. Nothing could have been farther from the truth. He increasingly began to doubt if he had arranged his life here in Gaienhofen properly, in either his first temporary rental or in his second, more comfortable house.

His second son, Heiner, was born in 1909, followed by his third, Martin, in 1911. It now almost seemed to Hesse that he was a rustic writer rooted in his own little patch of land. Did he really want everything to stay just as it was?

Hesse's sons Heiner (1909–2003) and Bruno (1905–1999)

And so we thought, and said as much, that it would be nicer and more fitting if our children were to grow up here in the countryside, and do so on their own plot of land, in their own house, and in the shadow of their own trees. I can no longer remember how we justified this opinion to ourselves, all I can recall is that we were really serious about it. Maybe there was nothing more to it than being middle-class and house-proud, though that was never a very prevalent attitude for us—but ultimately there's no denying that we were corrupted by the good years following that first flush of success. Or maybe we were also haunted by a pastoral idyll?

During his time at Gaienhofen, Hesse came to realize that he was anything but cut out for the farming life: "Today, at least, I fancy I know nothing with greater certainty than that I am the exact opposite of a farmer, namely (according to my innate character) a nomad, a hunter, a person of no fixed abode and a loner." Later he would ask himself whether he had ever truly desired to live in the manner that he attempted during these years he spent on Lake Constance. His answer seems quite unequivocal: "I cannot say to what extent I allowed myself to be dominated by the ideas and wishes of my wife Mia; however, it is only looking back now that I realize her influence in those early years was far stronger than I had admitted."[50]

Meanwhile, Bruno had reached his second birthday and Hesse started a "Bruno Book," a kind of diary charting his son's development—but he lost interest after little more than a page and left it to his wife to complete it. Yet Hesse himself did record for posterity the first words his son spoke: "His first words were *Duta* (=sow, pig), *No* (=dog, from our dog's name 'Fino'). *Mäm* (=bottle), *Gaga* (=chickens)."[51] Bruno Hesse was surely one of very few under-twos who could say the word "bottle." Yet something else, this time noted by Mia Hesse, also characterized Bruno: "Father often lights a bonfire in the garden in order to get rid of all kinds of rubbish. One time, he couldn't find his matches, or for some other reason the fire refused to catch light. Immediately, Bruno dashed off and came back with a nasturtium flower. 'Look, Daddy, here's some fire!' he announced."[52] "Brother Fire" always appeared, it seemed, wherever Hesse was, and not just in his garden at home.

Hesse began to feel more and more out of place at Gaienhofen. Local people there were suspicious of his eccentric life as a writer. And because Hesse had never possessed either the talent or the slightest inclination to integrate himself into a community, he tended to be rather brusque in his dealings with people. The distance between them remained considerable. He never made any effort to ingratiate himself with locals at places where he lived—even though here he didn't go so far as to put up a sign on his gate, like he did later in Montagnola, reading "No Visitors Please!" One of his friends from the *cénacle,* Ludwig Finckh, who arrived in Gaienhofen a year after Hesse, ended up staying there for the rest of his life. Yet shortly after Finckh's honeymoon, his fully furnished house burned to the ground and had to be rebuilt from scratch. Hesse collected books to replace his friend's library.

On March 11, 1908, the two went together to a local municipal meeting, of which Hesse recounted in a letter of the same day that it had lasted for two hours and "made you stupider by the minute, and didn't exactly instill you with love for the local farmers."[53]

"Schoolmate Martin" or the Ambivalence of Memory

In 1949, in a text of ten pages or more entitled "Schulkamerad Martin" ("Schoolmate Martin") Hermann Hesse addressed the topic of the curious paths taken by a person's memory. What, and how, does one remember, and what does one forget, and why?

For any writer the unconscious selection of experienced events as subject matter is a provocative theme. Recollection is unjust, but not intentionally so; rather, it follows a logic that is never wholly accessible to logic. Which aspects of occurrences make an impression, and which get lost without a trace? How does it come about that one sometimes remembers an event quite differently from another person who was also there? Furthermore, could it be that, with the passage of time, one's own recollections of things that are irrevocably past begin to take on a life of their own in one's head, which dispenses with any corrective from "outside"?

These are momentous questions not only for our image of our own life history but also for historiography in general.

In "Schoolmate Martin," Hesse presents a subtle psychological sketch of a fellow school student from Calw and then Maulbronn. In later years he had run across this young man once more, whom he had never been especially close to, in Tübingen, where he was studying theology at the same time as Hesse was doing his apprenticeship in Heckenhauer's bookshop. Again, they did not strike up a really close friendship; whenever they met, they simply acknowledged one another and gave each other a friendly but brief nod.

And now, in the fall of 1904, Hesse the married writer had just made his new house in Gaienhofen habitable and taken his wife, who had suddenly fallen ill, to her parents' house in Basel. On his return journey, at Basel station, he again unexpectedly ran into his former schoolmate Martin. And this time, curiously enough, they did not just pass one another with a nod. They had by now grown old enough to have developed a closer interest once more in their childhood: "So we ran into one another and were both delighted at this chance encounter, for we were both at a stage in our lives where getting together with a classmate and talking about our boyhood was no longer an everyday occurrence, but something special and rare—a stroke of luck and cause for a small celebration." Hesse, the person who shunned others and was afraid of human contact, approached other people only sporadically and even then only when he expected something from the meeting. And so it was on this occasion too: "At any rate, we greeted one another more excitedly and warmly than we would have done, say, a year or two ago, and each of us found the other to be a voice from a time when we were young that reinforced our own impressions; and as we talked, that time seemed quietly to be transfigured and we both felt the need to prolong the time we were spending together."[54]

And so Hermann Hesse, who seemed ill at ease at the prospect of returning alone to his farmhouse in Gaienhofen, invited his former schoolmate Martin, who was in truth just a fleeting acquaintance, to come back with him and spend a couple of days at his house. Was this a sentimental impulse or, as in the later story "Kinderseele" ("A Child's Soul"), a conscious attempt to reimagine a period sunk in the past? Both, surely—a sudden emotional response, but above and beyond this also Hesse's burgeoning interest in a period they had both lived through, albeit one that was long past. Of course, he knew that they had never actually experienced that time together, but that each of them was confined within his own bubble of memory.

Perhaps Hesse was succumbing here to the temptation to present himself in a rather intriguing and spectacular light. Hesse, who for a long time had only been known to those around him as a school dropout and as something of a dreamer and an outsider, could sense his well-educated school friend's inquisitive admiration, something for which Hesse had the success of *Peter Camenzind* to thank.

Their encounter took a course that is common on such occasions. The two men wallowed in reminiscences, drank a lot of wine, and enjoyed one another's company—and in the process increasingly shifted the time they were recalling into the realm of myth. Was that really so reprehensible?

This phenomenon captivated Hesse's interest more than ever with the passing of the years. After all, he wrote this story almost half a century after the meeting and many years after the death of his former classmate. And yet it contains certain key elements of the present that tenaciously defy any attempt at objectification.

Then something happened that imprinted itself for ever in Hesse's memory and determined his portrayal of his schoolmate Martin: "That night, long before it was time to get up, some alarming noises roused me from my all-too-brief sleep. I opened the door and found my guest standing on the landing in the gray light of dawn, leaning against the wall in his nightshirt and clutching a candle that had gone out. He was moaning, and was as pale as the whitewashed wall—something that particularly disfigured him, since from childhood I had always known him as a rosy-cheeked fellow with a healthy complexion." His school friend Martin had suddenly fallen ill, "a form of dysentery," which forced him to break off his visit and head home with all speed the following morning despite the wretched state he was in. Hesse took him to the station, and the image of his pallid face peering solemnly and miserably out of the window as the train pulled out remained imprinted on Hesse's mind long after. His conclusion about this encounter may sound eccentric, but it is completely understandable: "I never saw Martin again. After that visit—which ended for him in a sudden overnight illness and a hasty departure the next morning, and for me in an almost angry disillusionment and a bitter return to my empty house, where first my wife and then my guest had fallen sick—I didn't hear anything more from him in over twenty years."[55] On his fiftieth birthday, however, he got a long letter from Martin, and then some years later another. Thereafter, all he received was a printed notification that Martin had passed away. In the first of these letters (the second one appears to have gone missing) Martin recalled his visit. Yet how astonished Hesse was when he read Martin's account, which recalled a totally different evening! Their memories clearly clashed. Hesse had no reason whatsoever to doubt the integrity of his former classmate, who had painstakingly reconstructed what he had retained in his memory. "But the majority of experiences he recalled in that letter were absent from my own recollection of events. . . . What's more, he had absolutely no memory of the incident that for me had been the main event and the most unforgettable aspect of the time we spent together, namely his serious illness!"

What remained for Hesse from this episode was a mistrust of memory. It prompted him to question how we compose our image of the life we have experienced and of history in general. Should we continue to trust our memories if we know that others recall the selfsame event very differently? Yes, we have to go along with our own memory; after all, we have no other. But we should always be mindful of the fact that this memory does not end where our consciousness ends.

Any image of a period in the past is therefore just as a much a new creation as it is a reconstruction. That seems inevitable. Yet the person giving the account, aside from recognizing the ever-widening gap in time, should also always acknowledge that he is not just retrieving something from memory but also putting something new in. Anyone wishing to return to the beginnings of their own life must always make a very contemporary start. And every time that is a decision to be made in the here and now.

Beneath the Wheel: A Journey into the Child Soul, "in Remembrance of Hans"

> For all their attempts to paint themselves as righteous, strict,
> indeed even military, authorities such as the state, money, and
> vested interests never have much time for a selfless and un-
> wavering will.
>
> —Hugo Ball

Before success, money, and marriage overwhelmed him, before he moved to Gaienhofen with Maria Bernoulli, Hesse had spent time living back in Calw. He had long since quit Basel, and his recollections of childhood after his mother died took on a dual aspect: rage and tenderness, bitterness and its resolution in the act of writing. Adaptation to the milieu he came from and that might almost have destroyed him. But he left behind only a part of himself, the petit-bourgeois part that sought to give fixity to his existence, and made off with the other part in order to embark on his new life. The life of a drifter and storyteller. This was how he saw his future when, with the success of *Peter Camenzind* already behind him, he began writing his Gerbersau stories and making a start on his most serious book to date, *Unterm Rad (Beneath the Wheel)*.

Without a doubt, the book became a reckoning with the school system of his time and the view of the child as a pupil, but it is a melancholic reckoning all the same. All pain and fury had by now dissipated and—to borrow a phrase from Heiner Müller in reference to Heine—"the wound had scarred over," albeit somewhat unevenly. Motifs from his later books emerge here, and are subsequently treated to all manner of variation. For Hesse never abandoned any element that he had once used to symbolize his wanderings through life. Thus, the principle of the doppelgänger, which he formulated openly here for the first time, continues to resonate throughout his later work. Henceforth these mismatched pairs, which are presented like the light and dark sides of his own self, crop up in all his major stories.

Nowadays *Beneath the Wheel* is often mentioned with something of a disparaging undertone. Has not the problem of an authoritarian school system, which was geared to breaking an individual's character, now completely metamorphosed into its antiauthoritarian counterpart? Today teachers fear for the last vestiges of their authority, and scarcely any pupils now dread attending school, which has long since ceased to have any hint of a military drill-hall about it. Learning by rote seems obsolete, and the very notion of a teacher standing up in front of a class is now lampooned as an outmoded "chalk and talk" mode of education. Students are now meant to feel comfortable and positive at school, and if they encounter problems that they find hard to talk about, a battery of psychologists is at hand to assist them. So, it would appear that there is no longer any sign of the "Wheel" that crushes the individual.

It is a widespread assumption in liberal social democracies that one need only implement an ongoing program of improved conditions in order to automatically make the demons vanish from people's heads as circumstances get better. But is it the conditions alone that cause such demons to arise there in the first place?

To see Hesse's *Beneath the Wheel* solely as an indictment of the school system of its period is to misunderstand it. For sure, such criticism is definitely present in the book—indeed, in later life Hesse was to rue his having made this theme so blatantly obvious, not because he wanted to recant his position but because he felt he had overstated it as the main focus of the work. Yet surely only the external manifestation of forms of oppression has changed rather than their fundamental nature? Has the pressure to achieve disappeared from society? Aren't people who cannot endure the daily struggle to compete and get ahead still pushed aside? Having said that, over the last 120 years the individual's prospects of regeneration have increased. When Hesse wrote his book, paid leave for rest and recuperation was not universally available; such an idea fitted neither into the rural worldview nor into that of laissez-faire free-market capitalism. Protestantism revealed itself to be a religion of achievement and effort; coupled with the Enlightenment, the Protestant work ethic completely asserted itself as the spirit of the age. Romantic protest against this state of affairs remained the preserve of an intellectual, artistic, and religious minority, who couched their opposition in terms such as "idleness," "meditation," and "monastic solitude."

Nowadays, "executive burnout" is a fashionable complaint, which says something not only about the power of fashion but also about the partic-

Maria (known as Mia) Hesse, *née* Bernoulli, Hesse's first wife (1868–1963)

ular forms of depression that characterize different historical periods. In the nineteenth century, such forms of depression had other names—nervous fever, anemia, consumption, or even moral insanity—and in much the same way as today were circumlocutions for a concurrence of real symptoms of illness with a widespread psychic constitution characterized by excessive stress. In this respect, *Beneath the Wheel* portrays one of the archetypal scenes of our modern—that is, urban and hence also neurotic or hysterical—existence. The lessons one has learned in school have no application in life, or if they do, they turn out to be quite different than expected. Anyone who wants to pursue a path other than that leading from school pupil to well-educated subordinate (the path prescribed in Hesse's youth) or, nowadays, to a trusted employee and committee member, cannot avoid taking the decision to kill off the inner schoolchild.

But there is more to *Beneath the Wheel;* it is also the story of an act of individuation by a young person with Rousseau and Gottfried Keller in his schoolbag. The inner story behind the external one distinguishes *Beneath the Wheel* from comparable boarding-school stories like Musil's *Die Verwirrungen des Zöglings Törleß* or Rilke's *Turnstunde.* In his novel *Buddenbrooks,* Thomas Mann employs a similar perspective to examine his character Hanno, the oversensitive scion of the eponymous family of merchants. But this is in a very different context—the story of a dynasty in decline. Hanno drowns, he is too weak, which, incidentally, is the view that both Hesse and Mann took of the art of the *fin de siècle*. The tale most similar to *Beneath the Wheel* is Mann's *Tonio Kröger,* although the stories appear to treat different subjects. Certainly, the background to each is different: for Hesse, the benchmark of nature for culture is paramount, and a properly lived life is one that must even be prepared to forego art if need be—whereas in Mann's work, the view of nature is ironic through and through. Art that seeks to serve the purpose of a healthy life strikes Mann as being little more than Rousseauesque naivety. And yet both authors consciously share the atmosphere of a fresh beginning on the threshold of a new century mixed with a melancholy at the demise of the passing century.

In Hesse's novel, something (Hans Giebenrath) declines in order that something else might rise (Hermann Heilner, making his way in the world). Anyone who recognizes in this the immanent process of consciousness quickly arrives at the figure of Hermann Hesse in Calw, where he ruminated about how to make his way as an artist in a bourgeois world. *Beneath the Wheel* was Hesse's first substantial contribution to the theme of the existence of the intellectual in an increasingly mechanized environment. At this early stage Hesse already broached the problem of how to be a "spiritual guide," along with the question of how the spirit might even begin to have an effect in such a world—both internally and externally.

Beneath the Wheel opens with a rage-fueled characterization of the "philistine." For Hesse this denoted a state of "inner existence" rather than the way a person publicly conducted his or her life—namely, the kind of passionless, moderate temperament that was wholly at variance with the romantic ideal of the artist. The most that the philistine type can ever achieve is a kind of scholarly stupidity, because he lacks the essential qualities of empathy and inspiration.

Hans Giebenrath's father, a central character in the novel, is by nature just such a petit-bourgeois figure. Hesse knew such people to be close at hand—in fact, just around the corner in Calw, near to number 4 Bischofstrasse, where first his grandfather and subsequently his parents and siblings lived in the house owned by the Calw Publishing Union. This was the location of the "Heinrich Giebenrath Saloon and Bakery," which coincidentally supplied the name the author gave to Hans Giebenrath's father, the person whom Hesse made primarily responsible for the spiritual under-development of his son. Instead of love, all Hans experiences is ruthless education by rote; and reaching the top of the class by such means is the only way of gaining recognition. A vehement reproach by Hesse against his own father resonates here, which later in life he kept relativizing and even-tually, in old age, completely retracted. Hans Giebenrath's weakness in life therefore cannot simply be explained from the outside as a failure to offer any resistance to his environment; it is also an expression of a weakness inherent in himself, with internal causes. Why, for instance, did Hermann Hesse rebel against his parents, whereas his younger brother Hans did not?

Hesse's choice of first names—Hans Giebenrath and Hermann Heilner—was not accidental. Hans Hesse, the ambitious and yet at the same time cowed brother of Hermann Hesse, tried to do right by everyone and really was crushed by the "wheel" of school; he emerged from his time in education a broken individual and later, as an adult, took his own life. "Hermann," of course, was a reference to himself, anarchic, untamable, and dam-aged—but not broken. Astonishingly, Hermann Hesse, who on several occasions during his lifetime made strenuous efforts to sever all family ties, repeatedly made his family the subject of his writing in a way that few other authors have ever done. His father, his mother, and his sisters Adele and Marulla—about all of them, he wrote some very beautiful and empa-thetic texts. He also composed a positively alarmingly long piece of more than forty pages about his brother Hans after his suicide in 1936. It reads like a reckoning with himself over his unkind attitude toward his younger brother, in whom he showed no interest—indeed, whom he despised and even as a child treated very badly. Two images of Hans from their child-hood had imprinted themselves on his memory: the blissful look on his face as he stared happily at a present he had been given one Christmas Eve, and his expression of docile self-sacrifice when Hermann once hit his younger brother in a violent fit of temper. Hans was the boy who did not rebel, and who cracked under the pressure. All the piety that he had imbibed from his parents could not help him cope with life, any more than could the music he loved or his ability to become completely ab-sorbed in games.

"In Remembrance of Hans" is one of the most important—yet also one of the least known—of Hermann Hesse's confessional texts. Here we find a summation of the wrong-headedness of the upbringing provided by Hesse's parents. How could musically gifted people like them be so hardhearted and cruel to their children? According to Hesse, this was down to the principle they followed, and their view of education, which proceeded from the assumption that the first thing that needed to be done was to break a child's will: "We lived under a rigid principle that took a very distrustful view of the young person, his natural inclinations, dispositions, needs and developments and that was not prepared to promote or even compliment our innate gifts, talents and peculiarities."[56] Only a handful of years separated this kind of attitude from the publication of Ellen Key's book on education, *The Century of the Child,* but in spirit they were worlds apart.

Hermann Hesse's younger brother Hans was a magnet for all manner of sadistic violence, especially for that perpetrated by teachers:

> Hans was utterly obliging, obedient and ready to recognize authority, but he was not a good learner. He found many subjects very difficult, and because he neither possessed the naive stolidity to simply shrug off all the drudgery and punishments to which he was subjected, nor the native cunning to con his way through difficulties, he became one of those pupils whom the teachers, that is to say the bad teachers, kept on at and couldn't leave in peace. Instead, they hassled and mocked and punished him over and over again. There were several really bad teachers at our school, and one of them, a real little devil, made a point of tormenting him to distraction. Among various other evil habits, this fellow liked to stand threateningly close to a student while asking him a question, bellowing at him with a terrible judge's countenance and then, when the terrified pupil naturally faltered and started to stutter, began repeating his question over and over, in a rhythmical singsong voice, and beating time to it on the pupil's head with his heavy iron door key. I know from my brother's later accounts that this nasty little tyrant with his key not only tormented poor little Hans like this day after day for two years but also found his way into Hans's nightmares, where he continued his assaults. Hans often came back from school abjectly doubled-up with a combination of a splitting headache and sheer dread.[57]

Hans Hesse would remain a broken person until his suicide, pursuing an occupation that was totally wrong for him and that brought him nothing but pure torment. He meekly accepted his life like a form of punishment—without ever finding the presence of mind to rebel against his treatment or even to run away. He was a deeply unhappy individual who, on the one and only occasion he ever kicked against the goad, only succeeded in fatally wounding himself.

And so when Hermann Hesse characterized the world of the philistine, it quickly became apparent that he too had only half left it behind. And perhaps only ever wanted to half leave it behind? For, just like Gottfried Benn or Thomas Mann, he felt that any form of affectation as a bohemian was abhorrent, and he needed the almost bourgeois grounding for his artistry. All his adventures are played out in his head, and for him the definition of a writer is a person who can stay detached enough not to get swept along by his own fantasies in "real" life. Anyone who writes also in the process exorcizes whatever dangerous fancies might be lurking inside ready to pounce—be this the temptation to establish themselves in the literary world, to lust after fame and fortune, to engage in erotic adventures, or by contrast to set themselves up in great comfort as a mouthpiece of the middle classes.

A few months later, in the summer of 1904, Hesse was already playing at being happily married and settled in Gaienhofen, and soon thereafter felt himself firmly ensconced with the land of philistinism. What was the truth here—the life he was leading in Gaienhofen or what he had written about the philistine shortly before in *Beneath the Wheel*? The relevant passage there runs as follows:

> The sensitive side of his personality had long since fallen into abeyance and now consisted of little more than a traditional, rough-and-ready "sense of family," pride in his only son, and now and then a charitable impulse toward the poor. His intellectual talents did not extend beyond an innate shrewdness and an aptitude for figures. His reading was confined to the newspapers, and his need for artistic diversion was sated by the annual amateur dramatic performance of the Chamber of Commerce and an occasional visit to the circus.[58]

At this point Hesse broadens his terms of reference. We see emerging before our eyes the modern type of the "man without qualities." The traditional subservient subject combines with the representative of mass culture. Interchangeable identities whose roots were severed even in an earlier age, not that this curtailment had had the slightest effect on their current patterns of feeling and thought: "He could have exchanged his name and address with any of his neighbors without a single thing changing. From the depths of his soul, and in common with every bourgeois *paterfamilias* in the city, he also harbored a deep-seated distrust of any power or person superior to himself and an instinctive hostility, born of envy, toward anyone out of the ordinary and more liberated, refined and intelligent than him."

Hesse's view of this type of opinionated philistine exposes its subject to ridicule every bit as uncompromisingly as that of Heinrich Heine, except that Hesse, like his model Gottfried Keller, also attempts to love the "People of Seldwyla" (that is, the "common" people), albeit not without ironic allusions to the spirit of conservatism he encounters there: "It would take a profound satirist to convey the shallowness and unconscious tragedy of this man's life."

At the beginning of the novel, Hans Giebenrath seems to be well on the way to becoming just such a philistine. He is already a striver, and has accepted external achievement as his only criterion of success: "It was his ambition to get on in life, to pass exams with flying colors, and to find his role in life, albeit one that wasn't romantic or dangerous."

And here we can see what it is that makes this book so truly explosive—namely, the successful "corruption" of Hans Giebenrath, who has already embraced philistinism almost completely. This aspect also has an autobiographical basis, in Hesse's fear of coming down in the world and becoming a loser in the eyes of his peers. After all, it was deeply humiliating for Hesse not to have the opportunity to pass his final school examinations, but instead to find himself committed to a mental institution—and thereafter to fail even as an apprentice, and to have to be taken in once more by his parents—and all the while to entertain such grandiose literary dreams of his own glittering future. And then to have to don his mechanic's overalls or to present himself to former schoolmates in the guise of a subservient apprentice working behind the counter of a bookshop—for Hesse this was all a bitter schooling in being an undervalued member of society. And even during his time in Tübingen, he already got an inkling that life as a writer might just as easily turn out to be a marginal existence, but this he accepted.

This ran counter to the attitude of his alter ego Hans Giebenrath: "Hans . . . tried to imagine what life would be like if he failed to get into the seminary or the high school and thereafter university. They would make him an apprentice in some cheese shop or office, and for the whole of his life he would be one of those common, wretched people whom he so despised and was determined to rise above."[59]

His encounter with Hermann Heilner awakens the other side of Hans Giebenrath: the creative euphoria, the whiff of genius. It was that same side that the thirteen-year-old Hermann Hesse had once discovered within himself and that he henceforth asserted in his resolve to become a writer, in the face of all external pressure and opposition.

From an external perspective, Heilner is an independent protagonist of this story, but from an internal perspective, he is every bit as much Hesse's alter ego as Hans Giebenrath. Can there be a friendship between Hans Giebenrath and Hermann Heilner, and hence a surmounting of the dichotomy between the bourgeois and the artist? For a while it seems so. Giebenrath is fascinated by the anarchically brilliant Hermann Heilner, who couldn't care less what the world around him believes is good and right.

Heilner, whom Hesse called "lyrical" and a "dreamer," carries his own yardstick of behavior within himself. This makes him a spiritual kinsman of the cobbler Flaig, the town's religious outsider, who regards the priest as a heathen. There are echoes here of the historical mystical figure (and also a cobbler!) Jakob Böhme (1575–1624), as well as Blumhardt in Bad Boll, who exerted a strong influence on Hesse. Paradoxically, Hesse was here bridging the gap between Pietism (the world in which he grew up, in other words) and the art of the brilliant dreamer Hermann Heilner, that endangered and—as Hesse knew only too well—also dangerous ideal that he pursued in Gaienhofen.

Hans Giebenrath and Hermann Heilner symbolize different progressive forms of that "sickness of youth" that was the subject of a play (1926) by the Austrian writer Ferdinand Bruckner. This alluded to that generation of readers of Nietzsche who saw the worldview of their parents dissolving in front of their eyes before they had a chance to formulate their own. There is in this already a glimmer of motif of murdering one's father, which was so beloved by German Expressionist writers like Arnolt Bronnen, though Hesse shies away from giving the action of his novel such a melodramatic turn.

For Hans Giebenrath, the encounter with Hermann Heilner becomes a deadly threat to his existence. The intensity of their ensuing friendship wrenches Hans Giebenrath away from the regular sense of order that has governed his life up until then. Now emotional anarchy holds sway, a torrential rush of feeling such as can only be engendered by youth. Friendship between two dissimilar boys is an important motif in Hesse's work. Is there perhaps a homoerotic angle at work here? Possibly, but if so, no more than in any individuals who feel within themselves something of both their own and the opposite sex. It would be more fitting to adduce that motif from Protestant mysticism, which invokes the "androgynous Adam." This is not homoeroticism in the modern sense, where one—at least in western Europe—is equally free to profess either homosexuality or heterosexuality. Such a course was in any case forbidden to boarding-school boys of Hesse's time; it lay beyond the realm of things that could be openly expressed.

As a result, friendship, especially during puberty, was far more erotically charged than it is nowadays. Yet for Hesse it always remained something natural, which had the ability to provide a safe haven from the oppressive features of urban life, a mode of existence that in Hesse's eyes was synonymous with anonymity and soullessness. On the basis of his earlier work *Peter Camenzind,* Hesse had already been accused by Robert Musil of writing about homosexuality—but this was a wholly inaccurate description of the problems that Hesse was attempting to highlight. We may easily divine this from the simple fact that there is no hint of psychological stress in Hesse's novel, and that no proscription is under discussion here. For Thomas Mann, for example, the unequivocal rejection of homosexuality demanded by bourgeois society acted as a provocation to his own erotic self-image, which, along with other, earlier instances, found its artistic expression most famously in the scandalous portrayal of pederasty in the novella *Death in Venice.* This theme did not act as a spur to Hesse's writing. Instead, he took the liberty of playing impartially with both homoerotic and heteroerotic facets. When Hans Giebenrath and Hermann Heilner—after vehement attempts to fend it off—ultimately do join together in intimate friendship, it instantly conveys the point that is always evident in relationships between couples in Hesse: namely, that these are two sides of himself, two poles of one and the same person. They serve to illuminate the self psychologically and mythologically from various angles and to reveal the contradictory aspects of character that reside therein.

If, against this background, we consider the encounter between Hans Giebenrath and Hermann Heilner—which it would be accurate to call thoroughly erotic—we can see that Hesse not only gives his portrayal of it an autoerotic frame of reference but also sends it in a surreal direction:

> Hermann Heilner slowly extended his arm, took Hans by the shoulder and drew him toward him until their faces were almost touching. Then, all of a sudden, Hans was startled to feel the other's lips brush his mouth.
>
> His heart was gripped by an unaccustomed anxiety. Their being together in a dark dormitory and this sudden kiss was something risky, something new, maybe even something dangerous; it struck him how dreadful it would be to be caught in the act, for he was in no doubt how much more laughable and scandalous this kissing would seem to the others than his earlier tears.[60]

On October 17, 1905, Stefan Zweig wrote to Hesse about *Beneath the Wheel:*

> There are things in it that I experienced myself when I was a boy and then lost once more; and reading the book put me in mind of those bittersweet hours in the past that we never realized were the best times of our lives. You have described all this so enchantingly that I want to grasp your hands in gratitude across the distance that separates us. And then there are the two love scenes: these now seem to me like events from my own life.
>
> Isn't that ineffable? Can a writer do more? Hardly. All know is that I have a few reservations about details of the composition (we have all been schooled in too literary a fashion not to notice such things), but that all such minor quibbles vanish when set against the overpowering impression that the *soul* of your book has made upon me.[61]

The soul of the book? In the Magic Theater in *Steppenwolf,* Harry Haller experiences a spilt personality. There we find ourselves confronted not just by the pair of doppelgängers Hermann and Hermine but by Pablo as well, that fallen Mozart angel with his saxophone, who is also a spin-off of the Haller / Hesse personality. Art as a substitute for metaphysics remains for all those involved a game of deceptions in the center of a cabinet of mirrors. Yet it is a pleasurable and inventive game, for all that, so long as one realizes it is a game and does not start attacking one's own mirror image with misplaced seriousness.

In *Beneath the Wheel* we find ourselves in the very early stages of a great process of acquiring self-knowledge, which will one day pass through Goethe and Mozart and in the historical laboratory that is the "Magic Theater" will come to both celebrate and curse the here and now. In *Beneath the Wheel* this process occurs, still at this stage quite straightforwardly, between Hermann Heilner and Hans Giebenrath, who must be overcome if the former is to stand any chance on his escape from the bourgeois world.

So, is Heilner a vampire who sucks the last drop of lifeblood from Giebenrath? He certainly could be seen in this light: Heilner uses up Giebenrath, he kills him—not directly, but certainly indirectly—in order that he might become himself. This is why Hans Giebenrath also feels so exhausted and increasingly unwell when he is in close proximity to Heilner.

There were many ways to drop out of the seminary at Maulbronn, prematurely, without graduating as a perfect servant of the Church or state. Hesse provided a succinct list of them: "Now and then one of them will die and be buried to the accompaniment of hymns or carried back home by a cortege of his friends. At other times, a boy will simply abscond or be expelled because of some outrageous transgression. Occasionally, though rarely and then only in the senior classes, it can happen that some desperate boy will find a short, dark route out of his adolescent misery by shooting or drowning himself."[62]

Contemporary critics were incapable of seeing *Beneath the Wheel* as anything much more than an indictment of the authoritarian education system of the late nineteenth century; moreover, many of them found this denunciation far too sensationalist. The aversion to the form of the story, which was initially designated as a novel, has persisted until the present day. But is Hesse's mode of narration really as conventional as his critics claim? As early as May 13, 1907, in a letter to his stepbrother Karl Isenberg, the author himself voiced his own discontent:

Although, when I first conceived *Beneath the Wheel,* it arose purely from my need to present an important period of my own youth in concentrated form, it's fair to say that a tendentious element crept into the work only when I actually started writing it; this was quite unintentional and was prompted by my bitter recollections. But it was also unnecessary. In the future, although I still intend to get up on my soapbox every so often, I won't preach in such a negative, critical way but instead will set forth my own experiences and my own ideals, in other words by presenting something positive.[63]

But is Hesse guilty here of making too strong and self-critical a case against *Beneath the Wheel*—as he tended to do with all his early works? Certainly, by the time he wrote *Demian* in 1919, he had developed a quite different concept of narration. But could the foundations of this have been actually laid, perhaps more firmly than even he was aware of, in the works he completed before the First World War? Theodor Heuss showed himself to be one of the few perspicacious readers of *Beneath the Wheel* when he wrote in 1905: "Is it a polemic? Undoubtedly so in those passages where it makes an impassioned plea for the rights of young people to enjoy their youth. But what raises the book above the great mass of other, run-of-the-mill works is not the story as such, but its development and dénouement."[64] The truly novel thing about the work, and what in formal terms makes it a qualitative leap forward in the art of narration, is the dual perspective it offers on a breaking soul in its simultaneous presentation of internal and external worlds.

In the course of his "sickness of youth," which all of us experience in some measure according to our temperament, Hans Giebenrath is swamped by the maelstrom of his former benchmarks and values. He drowns in the river; whether this is the result of suicide or an accident is left open, though the fact that he dies is unequivocal. Hermann Heilner has long since moved on. With him, the figure of the wayfarer in Hesse's work is born.

When Hesse wrote *Beneath the Wheel,* he could not know that its deadly finale would also claim his own brother Hans more than thirty years later. The wheel keeps on turning, not just that great wheel of world events with which our own life cycle is inextricably linked, but also the wheel as a cruel instrument of torture on which all those who are not strong enough to wrest control of their own environment and yet who remain clearly identifiable as outsiders are flayed alive. And this is invariably at the hands of an indifferent majority and their anonymous institutions.

Studies in Wine

> I get the impression that your life is now ticking along at a very calm pace.
>
> —Stefan Zweig in a letter to Hermann Hesse dated September 8, 1904

In 1904, in *Peter Camenzind,* Hesse wrote a declaration of love to the god of wine:

Who is as mighty as He? Or as beautiful, as fantastic, as lyrical, and as joyous and melancholic? He is a hero and a magician, the tempter and the brother of Eros. He can do the impossible, filling poor human hearts with lovely and wondrous poetry. He has raised me from being a hermit and a peasant to a king, a poet, and a sage. He fills the emptied vessels of life with new destinies and drives the stranded back into the swift current of life. Such is the nature of wine. Yet as with all precious gifts and arts, it must be cherished, wooed, understood and acquired at some considerable cost and effort.

Hesse was twenty-six when he wrote these words. His constant pitting of reason against passion was almost a form of love, albeit a dangerous one. Wine, on the other hand, did not pose the Either / Or question, it had no urge to dominate, but instead tolerated—indeed, promoted—dalliances, for instance with poetry. Nevertheless it still led to intoxication, though this came on slowly, and a true love for wine manifested itself in avoiding getting drunk. A genuine lover of wine tasted the aromas of sun, wind, and soil in the grapes, each variety of which had its own story to tell and exuded its own unique atmosphere.

Wine was another reason Hesse would later feel that he had immediately arrived in a new homeland when he move to Ticino. In 1921, in a sketch entitled "Summer Evening in Ticino" ("Tessiner Sommerabend"), he enthused:

In the forest, on the shadowy side of the mountain, lie the *grotti,* the village's wine cellars, a small, Lilliputian, fantastic fairy-tale settlement in the woods comprised of just the façades of little stone gabled houses with nothing behind then, since the roof and the rest of the house are embedded in the ground, and the rock cellars have been bored deep into the hillside. The wine is stored there in gray barrels. Wine from the previous autumn and also wine from the autumn before last; there's nothing older than that, however. The local wine is very gentle, light, and grapey, red in color, and has a tart and cool taste reminiscent of fruit juice and big bowls of grapes for eating.[65]

Perhaps wine is the only form in which metaphysics becomes truly liquid and capable of building bridges between the individual and the Universe. Wine renders borders transparent, especially those between the internal and external worlds. Instead of drunkenness it engenders a sort of stream of warmth of the kind that Ernst Bloch saw coursing through history—a heightened sense of creativity, not in the sense associated with taking drugs but instead a feeling of being gently disengaged from all the disruptive concerns of everyday life. Good wine has the capacity to generate a solemn moment, in which the fleeting instant reveals itself to be precious.

Hesse had occasion to experience firsthand the fact that this remained an ideal image of the beautiful art of true wine connoisseurship, or even an expression of inner harmony. As early as 1905, in his wonderful sketch "Wine Studies" ("Weinstudien"), he described a situation where wine was a false comforter, a dubious means of lightening one's mood, that took more from a person than it gave. This coincided with a time of crisis in his own life, where he no doubt drank too much and was aware that this situation could be changed only through a strenuous effort to alter his lifestyle. Outwardly, though, he remained on a path to conventional bourgeois success. Where, then, was the crisis? In "Wine Studies" he runs through the demise that he—perhaps as the only one—had noticed in itself, and he brings all his intellect and wit to bear on this very short text. It is also a wonderful parody of the great and specious gravity with which the world distributes fame and recognition, as well as of the eternal inadequacy of the means we have at our disposal for comprehending the mystery of wine—a mystery that is not so very far removed from that of writing, or of art in general.

The purpose of the sketch, we read in the very first paragraph of "Wine Studies," was to divine the personality of wine. The scenario is that a chemist by the name of Konrad Pfeuffer wishes to establish objective criteria for the enjoyment of wine, a sort of "Baedeker Guide to the Wine-Growing Regions of Switzerland"! Yet he finds that he cannot make much headway: "For, despite being a chemist, he was a harmless and childishly honest person."[66]

At this point a first-person narrator comes into play, who does not appear to be so very dissimilar to Hesse: a writer who is told by a publisher-bookseller of his acquaintance that he, the publisher, is keen to commission a wine guide for his book program. Once the contract has been signed, the narrator and Pfeuffer begin ordering samples from various estates in order to assess their wines for inclusion in the forthcoming work: "Their efforts were soon crowned with success. Some of the estates they invited to contribute did not reply, while others sent laughably tiny little sample bottles, but on the other hand many did respond in the proper spirit to the discreet suggestion and sent us small cases of full-sized bottles, and some even sent little barrels."[67]

This response, the narrator tells us, ensures that they can pursue their studies right away. But problems begin to arise: What criteria should they use for judging the wines? For the wine researchers approach the wine in quite different ways, and the question prompts very divergent responses in them:

> Konrad Pfeuffer saw colors when he drank. There were wines that evoked in him impressions of red, pink, ultramarine, opal-blue, green, and yellow, as well as every imaginable hue of lilac, brown, and violet. For certain favorite wines, whose color impression he found quite unmistakable, he possessed such a reliable "tuning fork" of taste that he could have unerringly characterized every wine list in terms of colors. But who else could possibly have understood this? His approach was no worse and no better than a spectrometer analysis. For me, though, the wines did not stimulate color impression, but instead stirred memories.[68]

In comparing colors and memories, they hit upon an "undeniable parallelism" that leaves them at a loss how to proceed. "What we needed to do was to identify a generally comprehensible spectrum between his coloristic and my mnemonic scales." But they fail in this task, and in their despair their drinking goes beyond all reasonable bounds. And so wine eludes their attempts at diligent and scholarly categorization and begins to slip back into being a mystery. The supplies that they obtained for free run out, and the wine guide is never written. The researchers start frequenting taverns again, but now without any real pleasure; their mood is black. And because they had become accustomed to ordering wines that ranged from good to the very best, they now begin to drink away all their money.

The writer ultimately cashes in his bibliophile's collection of valuable first editions to buy wine, while the dipsomaniac chemist starts to become unreliable at his job, and is duly sacked. Both face imminent ruin. This was the point Hesse himself had arrived at in 1905. Is there a way out? "So, I packed the remainder of my wardrobe into an old suitcase and put the remnants of my library in a crate and went on my way."[69]

Fantasies of Dropping Out: "Tales about Quorm" Remains a Draft; Knulp—Half Hobo, Half Tramp—Becomes Hesse's Idol

It was not just Hesse who experienced a sense of unease at the new century. The growth of industrialization offered undreamed-of possibilities, but fears were also on the increase. Were not the great metropolises simply molochs that devoured their own children? When viewed from Basel and Gaienhofen, at least, they certainly appeared to be so, especially to those who had never traveled to Paris or London. But Berlin was bad enough, where the traffic created a constant roar, where there was no air to breathe amid all the smoking factory chimneys, and where the noise on the street was infernal. Electricity not only turned the night into day, it also provided the motive force for the accumulation of all manner of machines— even within people's own houses.

How peaceful and tranquil life in the countryside still was! Here, the nineteenth century seemed to have stood still. The Romantic writer Eichendorff's figure Good-for-Nothing (Taugenichts), who travels as far as Italy on foot and by mail coach, and who is the epitome of an aimless wayfarer content to savor the journey through woods and fields for its own sake, increasingly now became an anxiously protected dream image of a bygone era.

People began to sense that the world was in the process of decline. And precisely for that reason, they started to dream the dream of a still-

intact world of small towns and villages, in which life went on just as it
always had done. This dream was nurtured with almost desperate intensity.
And Hesse, first in Basel and then in Gaienhofen, infused such dreams into a
landscape that was an inviting place in which to live. His readers clutched
at it like a straw. Peter Camenzind was a reassuring figure, whereas by contrast Hans Giebenrath and Hermann Heilner in *Beneath the Wheel* were
rather unsettling. And so his readers bestowed their love instead, in a positive avalanche of adulation, on the sympathetic enemy of modernization
Knulp, the eternal pedestrian, who continues to set the appropriate speed
for all motion relating to humans as being no faster than his own walking
pace. Knulp became a secret byword for that "Little Germany" that wanted
nothing to do even with Bismarck and the Wilhelmine era, let alone
heavy industry and imperialist colonial policy. Knulp was a charming
refusenik figure who opposed striving and achievement and who was completely immune to all blandishments of career advancement or material
consumption. A dropout for sure, but with elements of the dandy about
him, who despite dressing in rags still managed to exact a modicum of
grudging respect from assiduous citizens. A southern German, an anti-
Prussian by nature. There is something of a cosmopolitan aura about this
attitude, but also something that Hesse invented and explored and dreamed
up himself while lying on his back in the grass, and that was not conditioned by anyone else's educational criteria. This state of mind was mirrored in a number of stories Hesse wrote during this period. The first of
these—"In der alten Sonne" ("In the Old Sun")—was written in 1903, as
if in anticipation, and at the same time as a defense against, false dawns.

The main protagonists of this story, the "sun brothers"—poor urban
dwellers who take refuge with a hostel warden (a sanctuary they disdain,
but which at least is safe)—are at the same time vagrants, "hobos," but also
hedonists who find themselves in revolt against the prevailing norms of
society: "They only value security for a brief spell before the dream of a
free life on the open road becomes all-consuming once more. For Hesse,
this was a deeply poetic configuration of ideas. Pure dreams of escape from
an excessively restrictive everyday existence." "The sun brothers also had
this in common with other people: they lived out the great majority of
their fortunes, their gratifications, their joys and their sorrows in their
imagination rather than in reality." So, were these "discarded" and "left
by the wayside" individuals no different from all the other worthy citizens of the small town on whom they were currently a burden? No, in

truth they were no different; all that appeared to have happened was that they had experienced too much ill fortune in their lives, though at the root of this there also lay a stroke of good luck: namely the childlike nature retained by those who in the eyes of their fellow citizens would "never properly grow up." Hesse not only had great sympathy for such people, he also felt himself to be one of them.

Knulp reflected Hesse's yearning, increasingly frantic during his final years at Gaienhofen, which impelled him to both move on and regress at the same time. His marriage was unhappy; he was working on the short novel *Rosshalde* and asking himself why he did not simply get up from his desk in his comfortable library, pack up a few essentials, and head off somewhere, anywhere, where he could be himself again.

Knulp had a precursor, a figure in the "Tales about Quorm" ("Geschichten um Quorm") that he had jotted down during his time in Basel and Calw, though they had remained just rough drafts. The prelude to this was "Portrait" ("Porträt"), written in 1902. This was a time when Hesse staked everything on achieving success as a writer and on trying to earn a bourgeois livelihood from his writing—yet at the same time he presented here the anti-philistine parameters for such a course of action in a strikingly uncompromising way. This is a wonderfully accurate sketch, with a complete lack of self-irony, about the frankly unviable twilight existence of a person who in the eyes of the world is utterly insignificant. In such circumstances, what use was there in not giving into despair and in continuing to live according to one's own standards?

This was the seedbed for that obstinacy of Hesse's, which first came to light in his childhood and for which he later became infamous, albeit in a misleading way. For this obstinacy—which will be the subject of further discussion presently—was two things above all else: a form of self-defense against the impositions of the outside world, and a strengthening of his internal being. And this inner being truly had need of reinforcement. Had he perhaps shown too much disregard for the world and its standards? The threat of sinking into poverty loomed—or worse, of going to rack and ruin and ultimately leading the life of a beggar or tramp. What could be done to prevent that? He found the only answer in Nietzsche: an enthusiastic affirmation of the danger. And so we are presented with this quasi-self-portrait of an individual who is well on the way to failing and vanishing without trace in the Hades of the bourgeois world. A man who, as Gottfried Benn would have put it, is only now sending out very faint, intermittent signals:

> You might have taken him to be a very young man. His speech, his gait, his waistcoats and other clothing all had something ill-assorted and unsuccessful about them, like those of young people who do not know how to present themselves. But this awkward gait was often very tired, heavy, and sullen. And his voice was often reticent and had an unassuming ironic tone unknown to youth, whereas his mouth was frequently twisted and bitter and the traces of intensive mental effort, headaches, and sleepless nights were etched on his forehead. When he was in company, he often had a quite unabashed way of clamming up and yet paying an exaggerated, sneering attention to the conversations other people were having.[70]

This person attracted attention, he was undoubtedly something special—but what had he achieved? Had he then already enjoyed some success, or did he at least have some position or private wealth? At worst, this stranger could not even lay claim to genuinely coming from abroad. He was an alien presence all the same, even though he came from their midst: "Among Philistines he looked provocative and almost like a child prodigy, while among important people he looked almost foolish. Among young people he appeared sober and old, and among old people unformed and embarrassed." Evidently a dilettante who had been unable to decide in a timely manner to become a specialist in any walk of life. And in addition to all the skills that he has, at best, only ever half-mastered (and he has never claimed otherwise), there is one about which he understands absolutely nothing: the art of living. That could assume a tragic dimension, though it scarcely comes across to the reader in this way. For Knulp appears too much in accord with his fate, so that the poetry of ruin shines out to us beyond the bitterness that is inherent within this situation. Rilke once wrote that poverty was a great radiance from within—and in Knulp that poeticized poverty appears to have found its most beautiful embodiment, for the very reason that it is also its most obstinate. Here, in the "Portrait" that Hesse did not dare to call a self-portrait, it sounds far more sorrowful, almost gloomy: "Of all the arts through which blissful, naive people know how to while away the time, he was conversant with just two: improvising on the violin and spending long afternoons lying on his back in the grass and casting a studious eye on the passing clouds. And yet he practiced both only infrequently." This lack of practice had consequences, with which Hesse seemed to threaten himself.

When he wrote this passage in 1902, he was a paragon of diligence and ambition. As a result, the vision of destruction ultimately leans gently into the corner: "Everything in his soul that was good and undamaged now consumed itself in a conflagration of hopeless love for a beautiful woman, which he would not even admit to himself, and in verses that he dashed down on paper night after night. From time to time, he also observed himself, with astonishment and mistrust. It was at such a time that he wrote these lines."[71]

The "Tales about Quorm," which Hesse wrote later in 1902, never got beyond an eight-page draft. Hesse here already makes playful use of his initials H. H. in a preamble where he uses the same device he had employed in *Hermann Lauscher* of appearing in the guise of the editor of the manuscript. For him, presenting himself as an anti-philistine also meant laying out his credentials as an autodidact, and moreover doing this in a playful manner. A special dignity attached to someone who was unattached to any position and had no academic degree; this was the pride of a person liberated from all external forms of acceptance and accreditation. Here this impulse was so intense it expressed itself as an inverted snobbery: "I am not a doctor, and can present proof positive that I have never been a student."[72] This is powerful stuff, and brazen in a winning and enchanting way! The sense of unease that competed with Hesse's urge to finally establish himself in the bourgeois world manifests itself as an ironic retrospective on his own time as an apprentice in the clock workshop in Calw. What becomes of a person's dreams when they have got a career, a wife, children, and a house and garden? And does that represent the fulfillment of a person's desires or only ever a hindrance to it?

The realization began to dawn on Hesse that it surely had to be both at the same time, and that the only way to retain a small vestige of freedom was to employ an ironic switching technique; even so, it was essential that one did not then broadcast this sense of liberty with the pathos of certainty. Here the wayfarer figure announces himself, someone who is constantly in the search of something and in the process is on the run from something also. A person held by little but drawn by much, who tries repeatedly to carry the security of his childhood on into the future, while actually entering into a completely unknown realm while he is under way: "It's great that you are planning to go off on your travels again in April; I really thought you were going to stay put now. At some stage, when you get older, this endless wandering will have to come to an end. I myself have become far more tame and intend to get married soon. If had remained a clockmaker, I would surely have a wife and child by now; but writing books is a slow business and often costs more than it brings in."[73] Likewise, the "Tales about Quorm" earned nothing for Hesse, since he laid them aside after writing just a few pages. But the motif of the wayfarer had been established, the vagrant with rich potential within him—to become both an antibourgeois artist and a beggar or even a criminal.

The three stories concerning Knulp appear to us today like a curtain drawn aside to reveal the stage of prewar Europe. One can imagine the vagrant Knulp, a rather introspective provincial individual from the nineteenth century, transposed into Charlie Chaplin's movie *Modern Times*. They are the same romantic types: in Hesse's work living and dying in harmony with nature, and in Chaplin's movie exposed as an incurably deficient being when caught up in the rhythm of the machine. The former perishes covered with snow by the side of a road that he has kept walking until the very last—making for his hometown Gerbersau (appearing once again, but here for the final time in Hesse's work), whereas it is clear that the latter will inevitably be struck down by either a nervous breakdown or a heart attack. This is an unavoidable consequence of modern times and the dominance of the time-punch clock.

"In Remembrance of Knulp" ("Erinnerung an Knulp") was written in 1907 in Gaienhofen and was preprinted in the *Neue Deutsche Rundschau* the following year. Thereafter, the Knulp theme took a back seat as *Rosshalde* and the problem of marriage for the artist took priority. In 1913, on the eve of the First World War, when Hesse was already living in Berne, Knulp suddenly reappeared in the story "Early Spring" ("Vorfrühling"). War had already broken out by the time he wrote the third story involving Knulp, "The End" ("Das Ende").

All three stories were subsequently to appear in book form in 1915, in the Fischer Library series. Knulp in the midst of hails of bullets and shells and trench warfare? One can hardly think of anything more anachronistic— and yet precisely the antiquated form of the Knulp figure had the effect of a vision of an undamaged world amid all the death and destruction. The scent of woods and meadows, and clouds drifting by that were not composed of poison gas—all this served to make Knulp a dream image of a peaceful little provincial world that knew nothing of geopolitics.

But if we read the text more closely, this Knulp does not stand before us as quite such a harmless and charming figure. We see, rather, someone who is stuck in an unsuccessful life that he neither can nor wants to relinquish. For all that, though, it remains a façade. Once again, Hesse was here alluding to himself and his failed marriage, and his dream of being liberated from all the obligations that were hemming him in. Yet involuntarily the scenery broadened out and the old-fashioned Knulp, who preferred to die in his own way rather than have his life lived by others in a different manner, takes on a truly anachronistic symbolism. Is Knulp, then, a good subordinate whom one can picture yelling slogans of hatred as he charges at the enemy with a fixed bayonet? This vagrant, the illegitimate descendant of Eichendorff's Good-for-Nothing, embodies the question, suppressed during times of patriotic fervor, as to what the purpose of all this is. Why not instead just lie back in the grass, with a bottle of wine by your side and the sun up above? Knulp is a poor subordinate, and as a soldier he would at best have become a figure like Jaroslav Hašek's "The Good Soldier Švejk."

In a letter of October 1915 to Romain Rolland, Stefan Zweig said of Knulp that he embodied an aspect of Germany that no one knew about, not even the Germans themselves.

When the aging Knulp appears before us, he is already old and his days of roaming have come to an end. Only death lies ahead of him now. And yet—in contrast to the soldiers at the front—Knulp's end is a peaceful, gentle one. Ultimately he finds himself reconciled with his squandered life, which turned out not to have been in vain.

Critics have accused Hesse of slipping into sentimentality with the figure of Knulp. That is inaccurate, however, insofar as Knulp the great survival artist has to learn, of all things, the difficult art of dying. This rogue does so with a great deal of irony, occasionally casting a glance of bitter mockery at his former schoolmates, who are firmly entrenched in their little worlds and who have long since been practicing a useful trade or occupying important positions. Yet mingling in with this pitying condescension toward the philistines there is a hint of melancholy that he can never fully be one of their number. In much the same way, the "Steppenwolf" Harry Haller is later described as sitting on the landing of his landlady's house close to the monkey-puzzle tree in order to breathe in the aroma of floor polish and cleanliness that reminds him of his childhood. That is now past, and he has fortunately escaped the restrictiveness of his background—and yet a hint of sorrow mingles with his thoughts. An ambivalent feeling regarding his own origins: wistfulness over the lost sense of security along with satisfaction at his successful escape—both remain a constant in Hesse's works.

Knulp has mastered the skill of being able to go on his way unmolested. Despite being a suspicious character *per se,* he is allowed to pass everywhere unimpeded, for in fact he always comes across as sympathetic—almost like one of the upright citizens in the small towns where he is a familiar face. But this does not happen without the requisite amount of deception:

> One of Knulp's hobbies was to keep his little journal of perambulations up to date. In its faultlessness it represented a charming myth or fiction, and its officially accredited entries described nothing but glorious stations in a respectable and hardworking life, in which the only striking thing was his wanderlust, evidenced in the form his extremely frequent change of location. Knulp had entirely fabricated for himself the life that was attested to in this official passport, and he employed a hundred different arts to sustain this spurious existence on a sometimes dangerously thin thread, whereas in reality, although he did little that was actually forbidden, he did nevertheless lead an unlawful and scorned life as an unemployed vagrant.[74]

Knulp resembled Baroque poet Angelus Silesius's "cherubinic wanderer"—a pilgrim who aspires to journey to God and arrives at an understanding of himself. An unhappy love and the experience of having been betrayed had thrown the former Latin scholar Knulp off course—and that was where he remained for the rest of his days: always on the periphery, aside from life's main thoroughfares. But this wayfaring gave him an insight into the transience and the care that he needed to show for even the smallest things. He learned not to miss experiencing the special moments, and realized that greater riches were not to be found on a person's brief passage through life: "If something beautiful were to remain constantly the same for all eternity, that would delight me for sure, but I would also view it with a more dispassionate eye and think: you can see this anytime, it doesn't have to be today."[75] Experiencing moments of happiness to the full was the yardstick that Hesse postulated in the middle of the First World War for a person's life to turn out well—and that was such a tantalizingly down-to-earth and civilized position that it sounded to jingoistic patriots like a deliberate subversion of the national war effort. So when one dies, does everything then come to an end? In this way, at least one was not dying some hero's death for the Fatherland: "When all is said and done, every person has their own life entirely to themselves and cannot have it in common with others. And you notice this when someone dies. There's a period of wailing and mourning, which lasts for a day, or a month, or a year, but then the deceased is dead and gone, and his coffin might just as well be occupied by a homeless and unknown journeyman."[76]

Knulp the outsider, who is beyond the comprehension of those who subscribe entirely to the prevailing order of things, nevertheless feels not the slightest hatred toward such people. He loves them in a way that you love something that you have irrevocably put behind oneself—and that is only still precious to you by virtue of being permanently distant.

The conversation that the dying Knulp has with God at the end of his wanderings is truly magnificent; it is also a final judgment on his life, and concludes with a lenient sentence, indeed virtually an acquittal. For the accusation of one of his former classmates, whom he now encounters working as a stone breaker, that he could have become something better in life than a hobo, reflects Knulp's silent and fearful self-reproach: "You had greater talents than others and yet you've made nothing of yourself."[77] That is the image that the world has of him. And isn't it actually correct? No, the freezing Knulp hears God say, it isn't true:

I could not have used you if you had been any other than the way you are, and I needed to give you the spur of homelessness and wandering, otherwise you would have just stayed put somewhere and spoiled my game. You wandered the Earth in my name, and your function was to repeatedly instill a little yearning for freedom into people living settled lives. You cut capers in my name and let yourself be ridiculed; and through you, I too was mocked but also loved. You are my child and my brother and a part of me, and there is nothing that you have tasted or suffered that I have not tasted and suffered along with you.[78]

And so, alongside the knowledge that God always resides in things that are smaller and more inconsequential and disregarded—an insight that binds Hesse to Saint Francis—there also remains, as a summary of Hesse's pantheistic mysticism, the author's own brilliantly playful, boastful, and sovereign declaration of identity with Knulp: this holy fool is so close to me that I could also be him—and at certain times even wish dearly to be so.

Monte Verità: Putting Life as a Child of Nature to the Test—Abstinence and Asceticism, but No Release from a Bourgeois Existence

Hesse felt ever more keenly that he was trapped in the wrong life. He did not want to go on living like this. But as a married successful writer with a country house, a wine cellar, a garden, a wife and children, what was he to do? Simply run away? He certainly could picture himself leading a Knulp-like existence on the open road, making his way south. But he discovered that he had become embarrassingly accustomed to a life of comfort. Would he even now be capable of tearing himself away from his wine cellar? He was aware that he was drinking and smoking too much. His health was suffering, and his drinking didn't help his depression. He decided to go off on a rest cure. He wanted to try living healthily—maybe this would also help stimulate new ideas?

He gave voice to his predicament on July 31, 1907, when he was already right in the middle of an effort to turn his life around at Monte Verità, the sanatorium located on the hill of the same name (Mount Truth) near Ascona: "The onset of my thirtieth year, in which I now find myself, triggered a major crisis for me, which at first had to do with physical illness, a rest cure, and a slow healing process, but then began to affect me mentally too. If a young person who has hitherto had a great lust for life suddenly renounces good eating and drinking, and cigars and coffee, he doesn't want to do it under duress, but instead to formulate a corresponding philosophy."[79]

Robert Landmann, who became co-owner of the Monte Verità sanatorium in 1923 and sold it to Baron Eduard von der Heydt two years later, recounted the history of this colony of dropouts in his memoirs *Ascona—*

Monte Verità: In Search of Paradise. It is the story of a series of idealists imbued with the values of Count Leo Tolstoy who, as soon as they attempted to put into practice the theory of how to reform their lives, became embroiled in power struggles—a clash in which pragmatists were pitted against fundamentalists, an all-too familiar scenario from the history of the Church and political parties. Every community that has become an institution and constitutes itself through exclusion produces outsiders. Every institution gives rise to heretics. In theory, this loose collection of dropouts, ranging from vegetarians of various degrees of strictness to anarchists and sun worshipers, naturists and practitioners of meditation, were perfectly well aware of such pitfalls. They wanted to replace conventional society with a community of like-minded people—but what form should such a community take, especially one that also shunned money as a practical element of social intercourse? The atmosphere of love that they aspired to create quickly degenerated into hatred, and the zealous adherents of the true doctrine immediately turned into persecutors of all kinds of revisionists. Before long, one was seeing traitors and charlatans everywhere among the ranks of one's adversaries. Relationships of personal dependency became the dominant factor, like in a sect. People denounced and disrespected one another, and one person would try to get another banished from "Mount Truth." This mechanism started to operate immediately after the founding of the commune, which saw itself as a beacon colony for a new, truthful mode of living. And presently, money suddenly regained its importance.

The founders of the colony were Henri Oedenkoven and Ida Hoffmann—both of whom came from wealthy backgrounds, and who had espoused the principle of "back to nature," a mixture of anticapitalist sentiment and a utopian vision of a state where the sun was worshiped. According to them, nature cured all the evils of civilization! This idea of these reformers encapsulated the essential mood of the age—fear of the hegemony of technology and the Moloch of the metropolises. The question of a new beginning took on great urgency in a period hallmarked by terrible industrial pollution, poor hygiene, gloomy urban courtyards, tuberculosis, and child labor. How might it be possible to live and work healthily? Or at least in not such an alienated way as hitherto, trapped in the body-hostile dogmas of the Church and exploited by capitalism. This meant vegetables instead of beer, horticulture instead of working on a conveyor belt, sunny hills in place of basement flats, and a naturist's joy in air and light rather than the unhealthy pallidness of a body hidden away in shame. Workers' sports clubs also discovered naturism, and all questions of nutrition at this time were highly political.

The *plein air* painters of the Barbizon School in France (ca.1830–1870) had already entertained the dream of an artists' colony in the south, and Vincent van Gogh and Paul Gauguin also found—albeit for a very short time—their "southern studio" at the Yellow House in Arles.

Ida Hoffmann and Henri Oedenkoven had the vision that this kind of life should be open to all people. But the notion of salvation for humanity that this entailed immediately assumed an ideological dimension. In her memoirs, for example, Ida Hoffmann wrote that their shared aspiration had been "not only to rid themselves of the detritus of life from humanity but also to bring humanity salvation."[80] In this statement there is also a hint of that militancy which would soon repel Hesse, who arrived at Monte Verità in April 1907 in a state of high expectation. Moreover, because of the many visitors who were drawn to "Mount Truth," the owners had started charging an entrance fee of 2 francs to everyone who wanted to come in and look around—and who hoped, among other things, to catch a glimpse of the notorious naked people wandering about.

Meanwhile, in his memoirs, the Ticino writer Johannes Vincent Venner, who was also a great connoisseur of the wines of this region, described how the reformers who gathered at the Monescia Hill (the real name of Monte Verità) dug out the old vines there. Granted, these had already been destroyed by an infestation of phylloxera. Even so, it was understandable that he would not necessarily warm to these "prophets with long white beards and straggly hair" who now took possession of the hill. He continued: "We shrank ever farther away from this truth, you, my green Monescia Hill, and I. Our final refuge was in the tumbledown mill on the high road to Ronco. . . . The sounds of the new prophets' axes falling came ever closer and soon drove us even from there."[81] It is fascinating to learn that, until his death in 2003, Hermann Hesse's son Heiner would live in this very same mill—he too living the life of an unassuming hermit, though in old age he had completely dedicated his life to preserving his father's work.

Venner mourned for the Ascona that he loved. It played the same role for Locarno as Fiesole did for Florence. Nor did his melancholic mood lift even when he occasionally got to taste the fruits of the old Monescia Hill: "From time to time, when the mood is good, old Quattrini fetches a bottle of your legendary Nostranus from the farthest recesses of his café, and we drink it together in celebration and in blessed remembrance of you."[82]

In 1909 Hesse's friend, the Austrian graphic illustrator and novelist Alfred Kubin, wrote a book entitled *The Other Side (Die andere Seite)*, as enthralling as it was dark, about the kind of utopia that already contains within it the seed of a dystopia, like in Franz Kafka's story "In the Penal Colony" ("In der Strafkolonie"). In Kubin's novel, the children of the sun, in their great striving for a new world, only succeed in becoming once more the prisoners of an abstract human objective. For Hesse, the month he spent at Monte Verità was an object lesson that would make him thereafter a vehement opponent of any ideology that claimed to have as its goal the greater happiness of mankind. It was all right to impose asceticism upon oneself as a test; but as a constituent element of a large, heterogeneous community, it inevitably became misanthropic or not infrequently even genocidal. The anarchist poet Erich Mühsam initially took a sympathetic view of the Monte Verità project but increasingly came to cast a skeptical eye on it, asking what kind of saviors and preachers advocating a new life these people were: "I know how they puff themselves up as 'original thinkers' with their little bits of philosophy, though in actual fact they are as alike one another as if they'd been traced."[83] Their little foibles, which could even be construed as endearing, took on a dangerous character when they were sold to the world as its path to salvation. Instead of letting people run free in nature, the list of proscriptions only grew and grew, as Mühsam remarked: "I would like to mention one particular gentleman on account of his peculiar foible; not content with being a consumer of raw vegetables and a teetotaler, he even spurned eating grapes. He justified this by pointing to his principle of absolute chastity. Grapes, he maintained, had an effect on the genital nerves, for even the ancient Greeks celebrated the feast of Dionysus in conjunction with that of Aphrodite. I cite this merely as an example of the kind of justifications that you can hear being trotted out here on a daily basis by all manner of people for every conceivable stupidity."[84]

And so Hesse stepped into this scene of folkloric-looking "children of nature" in order to gain some sort of distance from the self-indulgent lifestyle that he had begun to view with suspicion. At the time, his new house, one might even say villa, was being built in Gaienhofen. Had he betrayed his ideals? It was to try and find that out, and to gain a clear head once more, that he came to stay at Monte Verità. Immediately after his arrival, he wrote in a letter that he was living in a wooden hut in the middle of the countryside and was enjoying the peace and freedom. He also said that he was living a life of strict abstinence and eating vegetarian food, something that came very easily to him here.

Hesse wrote a number of fascinating observations about his sojourn at Monte Verità, which was more like an expedition than a rest cure. One essay, which he published in the magazine *März* in 1908, was entitled "Among the Crags: Notes from a Child of Nature." He came to the sanatorium with the best of intentions, but these could not eclipse his own experiences: "The things I wanted to learn and experience here I have in fact already found. I have become acquainted with loneliness and misery, I have gone back to a primitive existence and witnessed an awakening of my dormant instincts. When I arrived and put my clothes in my rucksack and began my course of treatment, naked except for sandals and a hat, I had some very enterprising and joyous thoughts. I sang happily to myself as I set off on the first afternoon of my stay to gather some foliage for my camp bed."[85] But in much the same way as his hat was soon blown off his head and was lost forever over a cliff edge, so his idealism too quickly evaporated. He got so badly sunburnt on his very first day there that his lobster-red skin blistered. He contracted a fever but didn't even have a proper bed in his wooden hut, just a hard stone floor to lie on. Driven by a raging thirst, he dragged himself to a stream, and tried to combat the sunburn by burrowing into the earth. After a few days, he had got over the worst effects, his skin had started to peel, and even his appetite returned, so that—now clothed in leaves to protect himself against the sun— he went in search of berries in the wood. His summary sounds quite downbeat: "To be sure, I convinced myself that a regeneration of our people and their entire way of life might be possible through a fruitarian diet and embracing naturism. But I hadn't come looking for such insights, and I count them among my corporeal experiences. I haven't had any spiritual ones, however."[86] Even so, he would retain his love for nude rock-climbing forever after—even letting himself be photographed doing so. In these images, Hesse the author struck a very natural pose as a nude model. Later on, whenever the temperature permitted, his children would also play naked in his garden. Nevertheless, the pompous self-importance of various "turnip-green apostles" regarding their pure doctrine of vegetarianism quickly got on his nerves. From time to time, Buddhists would also visit Monte Verità; perhaps, Hesse speculated, they might be more relaxed. Hesse was keen to explore their worldview.

He never returned to Monte Verità, however; presumably its owners and occupants were not best pleased by his reports, since he treated these lifestyle reformers in a way that fanatics hate to be treated, namely ironically. One of the finest, most scurrilous, and yet at the same time most liberating of Hesse's stories goes by the title "Doctor Knölge's Demise" (1910). In it, a harmless vegetarian who is drawn to the idea of leading a healthy life in harmony with nature arrives at the fictional "Life-Reform" colony—but instead of the laid-back atmosphere he expected to find, he encounters stressed-out ascetics who appear to know no other topic in life anymore beyond their own nutritional rules and their vehement defense of them. He finds himself all at sea among the various vegetarians, vegans, fruitarians, and others at the colony. All he can see there is a "kind of vegetarian Zionism. . . . Priests and teachers from all churches came there, along with false Hindus, occultists, masseurs, believers in the healing properties of magnetism, magicians, and faith healers. The only vice displayed by most of these people, who had gone off the rails in Europe or America, was one that was characteristic of so many vegetarians—a marked aversion to work." Little wonder, then, that Doctor Knölge, who is so little inclined toward fanaticism, is ultimately clubbed to death by one of the "children of nature," who lives in a tree like an ape (a figure modeled on the former army officer and later naturist Karl Gräser).

Gertrud, or the Eroticism of Music

> I play no musical instrument myself, though I do sing and whistle a lot. But I always need music, and it is the only art form that I admire unconditionally and regard as utterly indispensable—something I cannot honestly say of any other.
>
> —Hermann Hesse, letter to Alfred Schaer (1913)

The question of the possibilities of love was something Hesse carried within him throughout his time at Gaienhofen. Maria Bernoulli was no longer acting as a muse, inspiring him to write; on the contrary, she had increasingly become a burden to him. She did not want him to bare his soul in his writing, considering it vain. Couldn't they just be content living together in the countryside, far removed from the noisy world, and tending their garden? Hesse now realized that he had never desired any such thing. Nor did it help when his wife played the piano in the evening, even if it was Chopin, whose music otherwise had the capacity to lift him out of the everyday humdrum and transport him to another sphere. But when Mia played it wasn't for him anyway. She was more wrapped up in herself than he had supposed—and he couldn't find any way to reach her anymore, plus he felt ever less inclination to do so. He preferred to take refuge at his desk, or in a glass of wine, or to go off on his travels. Yet he knew that this was just putting off the decision as to how he should live as an artist in future, and what inner yearnings he should heed. He and Mia just went on living parallel lives—in truth, there never had been any intimate connection between them.

This insight was debilitating, but it caused him to think about the nature of love. In *Rosshalde* he would continue such musings in a stylistically altered form, and combine them with the question of how firmly an artist should entrench himself in bourgeois life. Indeed, could an artist be wedded to anything other than his work?

Gertrud was the title of the book in which Hesse attempted to reflect the crisis of his existence as an artist yet also as a father of a family and a husband. Outwardly, everything seemed to be going smoothly: Hesse was successful. But inwardly he felt he was increasingly dried-up and trapped in the wrong life. An existence in a gilded cage. Samuel Fischer—who as far back as 1903 (!) had talent-spotted Hesse as an author who typified the ethos of his publishing house—had been keen to keep him tied to Fischer Verlag. The contract Hesse had signed ran for five years and committed him—who was always reluctant to be tied down—to letting Fischer publish three out of every four books he wrote over that period. To guarantee this, Fischer paid Hesse the sum of 150 marks per month as a loyalty bonus, over and above any royalties he earned from the sale of his books. The contract—which was extremely unusual in its terms, and not just for its time—was subsequently extended on many occasions, to the advantage of both the author and the publisher, as the print runs were always very high. In 1913 Fischer told his author that he had already paid him 18,000 marks extra. Yet some of Hesse's works—in a clause that the writer had insisted on—did not form part of this contract, leaving Hesse free to decide who should publish them. Accordingly, he gave *Gertrud* to Albert Langen, who also roped the author into his pet project for a South German (and hence explicitly anti-Prussian!) cultural journal—the magazine *März,* for which Hesse not only contributed articles but also acted as joint publisher.

As a novel about an artist, *Gertrud* is a self-portrait by Hesse, though in it he plays various roles. Hesse treated the contradiction between the inner and outer person, a topic that was now assuming ever greater urgency for him, by playing it out through two characters, an introvert (the composer Gottfried Kuhn) and an extrovert (the singer Heinrich Muoth). It is a question of what role art, here in the form of music, plays in the lives of two people whose self-sacrifice it ultimately demands. Art takes the life of Muoth, a drinker, gambler, and womanizer, while granting the other man, Kuhn, fulfillment in love. Here Hesse is trying to lend tangible form to Nietzsche's opposition between the Dionysian and Apollonian principles. Kuhn only manages to write a single opera during his lifetime; Hesse too had attempted to write for the stage, but its nature always remained a closed book to him. "Bianca" was the name of the libretto that he prepared for the Swiss composer and conductor Othmar Schoeck. It was never made into an opera—and this failure only heightened Hesse's deep mistrust of the theater and opera.

The title character, Gertrud Imthor, appears here as the kind of idealized vision that Hesse had already created in the figure of Elisabeth. Gertrud is a symbolic figure who, as Hesse notes, is also at the same time a "stimulant" to Kuhn.

In *Gertrud* only one thing seems absolutely clear for Hesse: true love must be like music, seizing hold of a person's inner life and permeating their everyday existence. For brief moments it can cast a spell over a person, but the impression it leaves is long-lasting—perhaps permanent. But Hesse also felt that, in order to give this subject matter truly convincing expression, he would have to write the text like a musical composition. This was a task he could not solve—and one at which he ultimately failed. In truth, *Gertrud* as a whole is not one of Hesse's strongest books; for long stretches it reads like a potboiler, and in terms of both plot and characters, for all Hesse's best efforts, it never fully succeeds in emerging from the shadow of cheap sensationalism. The worst thing that could happen to Hesse, as regards his own conception of himself, comes to pass: the story remains superficial. He was aiming for the exact opposite—to link the essence of love with that of music. All told, Hesse rewrote *Gertrud* three times—accordingly, three completely discrete manuscripts, which have only the most basic outline in common, appeared between 1906 and 1910. Of these, Hesse ultimately submitted the final one for publication, and even then not without reservations.

As Hesse was working on the novel, the image of an acquaintance from his Basel days kept obtruding ever more deeply into the portrayal of the title figure. Hesse never managed to bridge the gap that existed between them. Despite this, or perhaps precisely because of it, this image of a love that remained unattainable for him is now very vivid in his mind: Elisabeth LaRoche. A woman he had long worshiped from afar, yet about whom he knew little. She was a pure projection of his desires. A madonna who was solely there in order to be transfigured. Small wonder, then, that in all three versions, the character of Gertrud is never fully fleshed out and remains a rather pallid construct. For Elisabeth—who showed no interest in Hesse, being unhappily infatuated with another man—likewise remained a rather formless figure to the writer. Hesse knew no more about her than we do. This is revealing insofar as he was quite consciously playing with the motif of the unrequited nature of true love—which seen in this way remains a purely monological affair. And so we encounter Elisabeth in the first version in the guise of Gertrud Chevalier, in the second as Gertrud Flachsland, and in the third and final iteration of the novel as Gertrud Imthor.

The problem of the book resides in its very structure. In his youth, the musician Gottfried Kuhn allows himself to be talked into a dare by a girl whom he wants to impress. He meets with a terrible accident on a toboggan ride and is crippled for the rest of his life, thereafter evoking pity from women rather than feelings of love. And so music becomes the only way for Kuhn to express his unfulfilled love. He meets a singer, the Don Juan-like figure Heinrich Muoth, who ruins women with his reckless way of treating erotic encounters as nothing but sexual conquests. Gertrud also falls victim to Muoth.

The third version, which Hesse finally submitted, is written in the first-person form. It is an easy read, and consequently was a great success. But some critics were still rather disappointed. They had expected something different from Hesse, and it was conjectured—not entirely unjustly—that he was trying to present himself to the book-buying public as a brand that the reader would find unproblematic. Indeed, *Gertrud* could easily be pigeonholed as a novel under the category "unhappy love" without irritating anyone too much. This bothered Hesse, who had to admit to himself that this book was too much of a "confessional" piece: "it sets forth its worldview too directly rather than letting this shine through the actual narrative." And in a letter to Theodor Heuss, who had voiced the view that Hesse had made too few demands on himself when writing *Gertrud,* the author gave the following response on November 17: "What you don't know is that I labored long and hard on the 'tone' of this work *Gertrud,* whose flaws I sadly recognize only too well." There was no helping it, Hesse was fully aware; he had not pulled off what he had really set out to demonstrate with *Gertrud:* namely, that pure love and pure music are one and the same thing. He felt as though he had failed.

He could not go on writing in the same vein that had made *Peter Camenzind* such a success—or he really would have sunk to the level of a mere popular novelist. In a letter of December 29, 1908, to Helene Welti, Hesse revealed the invidious situation in which he had been placed by the enormous success of *Peter Camenzind.* His readers would not forgive him, he told her, if—as he had already done in *Beneath the Wheel*—he altered his style again: "Firstly, they don't understand that I have to some extent weaned myself off florid words and grand phrases since writing 'Camenzind' and that I consider that a sign of progress."[87]

And yet, he also asked himself, ought one first to lead a different life in order to be able to write differently? Where should his path lead next: into the world or out of it? To the outside or the inside? Hesse was at a loss—and it is telling that those passages in *Gertrud* that express Kuhn's perplexity over how he can live as both an artist and a bourgeois are among the strongest in the book, precisely because they were not "crafted" but drew upon the glaring contradiction at the heart of Hesse's own life: "I had no wish to be another person, I wanted to remain in my own skin, even though it was often too restrictive for me. I began to feel power within me ever since my works began to have an effect, however understated, and I was on the point of feeling proud. I had to find some kind of bridge to other people; somehow I had to be able to live alongside them without constantly being the underdog." Hesse was basically summarizing his life as an author up until then. And he knew that he had arrived at a dangerous point: the point of success. And so, as he embarked on his thirtieth year, he found himself already beset by melancholy: "Of all the forms of fame, the sweetest is that which does not yet look upon great successes, which can as yet excite no envy, and which doesn't set you apart from others. You walk around with the feeling that you're being looked at every now and then, and name-checked and praised, and everywhere you go you encounter friendly faces and catch sight of well-known people nodding cheerfully at you, while younger ones greet you with respect. And you constantly have the secret feeling that the best is yet to come—as happens to all young people until they realize that the best is already behind them."[88]

He found himself at a crossroads, then. He was gripped by the fear that everything might already be slipping away from him. What was he still capable of? Hesse ran through the situation in his mind, but could find no solution. Then his alter ego in the book was given a piece of advice that he must surely have given himself frequently over this same period: "Just for once, take some time to think more about others than you do about yourself!" Was this sound advice? Could he refrain for a spell from pursuing what he had recognized as his calling in life? His wife had asked of him—and society demanded it of him, too, like it was self-evident—that he should be a good writer and an exemplary bourgeois citizen at the same time. And outwardly that was exactly what Hesse was during those final years at Gaienhofen.

His second and third sons were born, his earning power as a professional wrier was enviable—so what was he lacking? It is at this point that we realize that the fickle singer Muoth, who cuts such a clichéd figure in the book, is also an alter ego of Hesse—the Steppenwolf in embryonic form, as it were. Here was someone—albeit still outside the first-person perspective—who was well acquainted with the dark and compulsive, the disharmonious and destructive realms from which every sweet and harmonious tone in art inevitably derives. One cannot have the beautiful without also accepting the risk that it will be destroyed—the beautiful and the terrible grow from one and the same root. Even though it is still concealed here in the clichéd portrait of Muoth, this is the self-portrait of Hesse an author: "I knew him only too well, the headstrong melancholic who was accustomed to indulging his whims and never making any sacrifices, a person who was directed and pulled this way and that by dark impulses and who in moments of reflection looked upon his own life as though it were a tragedy."[89]

Furthermore, something else was changing here almost imperceptibly—Hesse's image of nature. It was no longer simply a place of refuge and the idealized alternative to the alienated civilization of the metropolises—above all it was deeply ambivalent. Hesse had grown weary of nature; he needed a break from it. This is also apparent in *Gertrud:* "Fate was not kind, life was capricious and cruel, and there was no goodness or reason to be found in nature."[90]

This was a new insight, and it would have ramifications for the way that Hesse wrote henceforth. For the most part, the reviewers of *Gertrud* failed to spot this. They were too exercised by the conventional narrative style, which made them suspect that this was just a simple imitation of his earlier *Peter Camenzind.* Somewhat disgruntled, Hesse registered this on November 28, 1910: "My 'Gertrud' is having a strange old time of it with the reviewers. Alongside some uncritical praise, there's also strong evidence of a backlash among the gentlemen of the press, who loudly proclaim an author a genius until they grow tired of that and then suddenly turn to pronouncing him a complete idiot." These criticisms were emanating from Prussia, of course, which he found intolerable at the best of times, but then suddenly in his anger he also began clutching at anti-Semitic clichés: "I'm particularly amused by the antics of the clever Berlin Jews, who don't think much of me, but who at least have to grudgingly applaud my German prose. These people, whose grandfathers mostly spoke far better Polish than German, still find it curious that a person should be as happy and naturally at home in his native language as he is in the air of his homeland."[91] Here Hesse was responding to criticism like a second-rank German nationalist regional writer. But even in the very next paragraph of this letter to Conrad Haussmann, he admits that there is not much truth in his claim to be "happy and naturally at home" and that he was actually far from operating as freely "in his native language as in the air of his homeland." In fact, Hesse was at that time in the midst of a crisis, of which *Gertrud* was only the first serious symptom: "I'm finding writing difficult; in fact, I've spent the whole of today carting slurry about! Though this is by no means my favorite form of physical exertion, at least it's preferable to and healthier than poring over books the whole time, something I now keep to a bare minimum. It ruins my eyes and over the long term robs you of all freshness in your own work."[92] For him, there was nothing to indicate that he would ever regain this freshness. Might it happen through that love that sounded like music and brought life into a new rhythm? Nietzsche had determined that without music, life would be a mistake. The texts that Hesse would write over the following years strive to mirror this new music in language and hence to convey an essential truth about themselves.

Moreover, Hesse's view of Jewish intellectuals soon changed, as the standard-issue anti-Semitism of the period gave way to a conscious focus—against the background of nationalistic hate propaganda after the outbreak of the First World War—on the philosophy of the unconscious, on psychoanalysis, on mythology and the fairy-tale form, whereas the nationalistic spirit of the age regarded psychoanalysis as a Jewish invention, something sordid that delved into the realm of sexuality (which was assiduously kept under wraps by the bourgeoisie), and that even liberated the androgynous and the homoerotic from the stigma of being regarded as mental illnesses. For Hesse, these very fundamental questions would constantly play a role in the consultations he had with his analyst, Dr. J. B. Lang. That led to insights which Lang shared with Hesse in a letter of January 22, 1918, after he had read a book by Ignaz Goldziher entitled *Der Mythos bei den Hebräern und seine frühe geschichtliche Entwicklung* (Myth and its early historical development among the Hebrews): "Up until now, I had still labored under the delusion expounded by Houston Stewart Chamberlain [the British son-in-law of Richard Wagner; a virulent anti-Semitic philosopher] that the Jews are and always have been a creatively impotent people. Here I have found this delusion comprehensively refuted, and all of a sudden everything became crystal-clear to me and I discovered connections I had never realized before that helped me to understand ancient European mythology and to comprehend many dreams from a new and fruitful standpoint."[93]

For Hesse, who went on to marry the Jewish art historian Ninon Dolbin (née Ausländer) from Czernowitz (modern Chernivtsi, in Ukraine) in 1932, the problem of assimilation always also had something to do with his own self-image regarding his nationality. As a Jew, must one be so very keen on becoming a German? This question was posed by one who always had deep reservations about his own German-ness, and who finally—after 1945—declared all forms of nationalism to be harmful.

★   ★   ★

Gertrud therefore already contained several pointers as to how important music was and would continue to be for Hesse. Time and again, he would return to the mystery that he believed to be inherent within music.

In the 1913 sketch "Old Music" ("Alte Musik") he described his attendance at a concert in Berne, where music appeared to be the sole placeholder for the love that was missing in his life:

> Grey rain was falling steadily and gloomily outside the windows of my isolated country house, and I felt disinclined to pull on my boots again and walk the long and muddy road into town. But I was on my own, and my eyes were hurting from long hours of work, and from all the walls of my study the gold-embossed books gazed down grumpily at me, promising nothing but difficult questions and obligations, and the children had long since been put to bed, and my little fire in the grate had gone out. And so I made up my mind to go out after all, and dug out my concert ticket, tugged on my boots, put the dog on a chain, and set off in my raincoat out into the mud and the wet.

On his way to hear the music, what he leaves behind him is pure sadness. But then this muddy evening journey he takes through the suburbs becomes one leading to a new inner life, to a kind of jubilation that can only be triggered by a love enlivened by a transcendental spark: "From a country house hidden behind dark hedges came the sound of a piano playing. There was nothing more beautiful and wistful than to walk alone like this across fields of an evening and hear music coming from a solitary house; it instantly put me in mind of everything that was good and lovable, of home and lamplight, of pleasant soirées in quiet rooms, of women's hands and of old-fashioned domesticity." There came to Hesse a whispered yearning for what he was missing most: love that was like music and that lent life that heightened sense of expression that people look for in togetherness and that in the main is so swiftly stifled by everyday concerns. The story then goes on to recount his arrival at the minster, and the moment of fulfillment: "Suddenly there comes a high, strong note from the organ. Swelling, it fills the immense space, it becomes the space itself, completely enveloping us. It grows and relaxes, and other notes now come in to accompany it, and all of a sudden they all flutter away into a precipitate decrescendo, twisting, hallowing, showing a hint of defiance and finally coming to rest, subdued, in a harmonic bass."

To India: An Escape into Exoticism

> I even learned to make fun of India, and I swallowed the bitter
> pill of realizing that the soulful, questioning, questing, im-
> ploring look of most Indians is not an invocation of deities
> and salvation at all, but simply a plea for money.
>
> —Hermann Hesse, *Aus Indien* (*Reports from India,* 1913)

Hesse's journey to Ceylon, Sumatra, and Singapore (a region referred to in German at the time as Hinterindien, "Far India") was many things—a personal reaffirmation of his family's missionary origins, and a way of transcending European Christian horizons, but above all it was an escape from the confines of domestic life. His third son, Martin, had been born on April 26, 1911, and less than eight weeks later Hesse was aboard the passenger liner *Prinz Eitel Friedrich* of the Norddeutscher Lloyd shipping line. He was also leaving Europe because Italy as a place of southern promise no longer held the allures that it once had for him at the beginning of the century. Now he was going in search of the true South, a genuine alternative to Europe, which he identified as having reached the end of its potential—even before historian Oswald Spengler expounded his doctrine of the life cycles of civilizations in his famous work *Der Untergang des Abendlandes* (*The Decline of the West,* 1918). The ship set sail from Genoa on September 4, and by September 8 Hesse was casting a disdainful eye over the scene as they docked at Naples: "In the evening, a boat came alongside with kitschy folk singers and they set about practicing their customary musical-ethnographic prostitution in return for money."[94]

Hesse traveled with a growing distaste for European politics, and sensed that things were drawing to a close there—but what new things were to come, and from where? Looking back at this time in 1922, Hesse wrote: "I had not grasped the spirit of India yet, nor found what I was looking for. I was still searching. That was why I fled from Europe back then, for there was no question that my journey was an escape. I fled from it and found myself almost hating it—for its gaudy tastelessness, its fairground atmosphere, its hustle and bustle, and its crude, foolish hedonism." Did he imagine that by taking a voyage by steamship he would find the "real India," a place he hoped would be the source of a spiritual revival—possibly not even in India itself, but in Singapore or Sumatra? And how did he even know what constituted the "real India"?

From the very outset, his expectations did not seem to be very high. In any event, a constant undertone of irritation pervades his "Diary of the Journey to Indonesia," which ran to the middle of December 1911. He was traveling as though in a European time capsule, visiting places where colonialism cast its ugly shadow. At root, that was nothing new to him; he was well aware that untouched idylls and zones where "primitive" life still went on unaffected could no longer be found in any part of the world. Hesse basically expected from his journey little more than that it would put as great a distance as possible between himself and Gaienhofen. He was tired and tense, a fatal combination that was only exacerbated by the climate: as early as September 14 he noted: "Increasing heat, the sea is growing calmer. Diarrhea as a result of too much booze (red wine) in the evenings, unbearably hot in my tuxedo." He managed to get some sleep at night only by taking barbital. The days spent at sea were anything but relaxing. He remarked on this not in his diary but in one of the travel supplements he wrote, which he worked up by combining with various notes he kept during his trip and published retrospectively under the title *Aus Indien (Reports from India)*: "Whenever people weren't sitting at table or in company in the evening, there was a sad bleakness and a subdued look on everyone's face—that languid, apathetic expression you see in all those who are frequent travelers, combined with the weariness and nervous febrility that seem to adhere to white people in the tropics . . . all the faces were eerily faded, with just a handful of children, Portuguese, who were running about cheerfully."[95]

He still felt that he was out of place, and the English-style food served at dinner was not to his liking—at every step he could feel Europe breathing down his neck. His companion on the voyage, the painter Hans Sturzenegger, could do little to help. Even the Leutholds, a married couple he met on board and with whom he remained lifelong friends, could not tear him away from his feeling of being in a time capsule, something he noticed most clearly with regard to the crew members, who, no matter where the ship was at any given moment, remained at all times on board the vessel. Hesse did not feel at home here, but neither did he feel like he was abroad, or in the "totally alien" environment of the South.

The tropical climate did not suit him at all, as a result of which he cut his trip short, forgoing the opportunity to visit the Malabar Coast, where his mother had been born. He could not muster any strength or enthusiasm to embark on any great expedition worthy of the name. On Ceylon

(Sri Lanka), amid a litany of complaints about bad hotels, worse food, importunate street traders, even more importunate beggars touting for tips, and apathetic Europeans, he climbed the highest peak on the island, Mount Pidurutalagala (2,518 meters). On the Chinese steamship *Maras* he traveled on to Singapore, where he promptly boarded a vessel returning to Europe. By Christmas he was back in Gaienhofen, none the richer for his experiences, only poorer through having been disillusioned once more. A profound feeling of emptiness now set in.

The entries in his travel diary trail off into banalities and generally end with a reference to the barbital that he found essential to snatch even a few hours' sleep. His "Kandy Diary Entry"—one of the few significant literary accounts of this trip—describes what it was that made this trip into such a catalogue of mishaps. He went in search of genuine treasure and only found counterfeit gold. This was because he came as a tourist with no knowledge of the real lives of the indigenous people. Accordingly, he was exposed to the sometimes exotic, and sometimes extremely filthy and ugly, surfaces of life in these regions, which had already been culturally deracinated: "Ceylonese Buddhism is an attractive phenomenon to photograph and write features about, but beyond that it is nothing more than just one of several poignant, painfully grotesque forms in which helpless human suffering expresses its misery and its lack of spirit and strength."[96]

In the run-up to his journey, Hesse had already clashed with his publisher Samuel Fischer over the "marketing" of Southeast Asia. In July 1911 Hesse inquired whether Fischer might pay him a travel subsidy, despite telling him that he couldn't promise to deliver anything publishable in return. Fischer was generous, offering him 4,000 marks, which he told him he was free to retain even in the event that he wrote nothing. But if he did, then Fischer required that he publish it first in the *Neue Deutsche Rundschau,* the Fischer in-house magazine, and consider the 4,000 marks as an advance, at a rate of 40 marks per page. Hesse now felt compelled to deliver something, and sent Oskar Bie, the publisher of the magazine, a selection of his travel reports, which really were quite strikingly dull; unsurprisingly, these failed to excite much enthusiasm among the editorial staff. Oskar Bie duly offered to print just *one* of these texts, which offended the author. He sent Fischer his 4,000 marks back. Fischer tried to placate him, telling him that he had been given the money free of any obligation to provide work in return. Once more, he transferred the money to Hesse; he did not want this affair with the *Rundschau* to jeopardize their extremely successful collaboration.

Yet Hesse was still bothered by the unfinished notes on "India," and so, on the basis of his diary, he wrote a compact collection of travel texts that take on a quite different scope than the pages of his diary, which constantly revolve around the same bleak daily routine. *Aus Indien* was published by Fischer in 1913 and was an instant success.

The significance that the East would continue to have in Hesse's work was already foreshadowed in *Reports from India*—albeit under negative auspices. However, the real encounter between the self and the unfamiliar, the truly fruitful interplay of internal and external, would attain its fully accomplished literary form only in *Siddhartha*, in *Die Morgenlandfahrt (Journey to the East)*, and finally—where it achieves great synthesis in space and time—in *Das Glasperlenspiel (The Glass Bead Game)*. What occurs here in *Reports from India*, though, far removed from Europe, is the account of a decline.

The reorganization of the world according to the dictates of imperial colonial policy destroys the spiritual basis of every civilization. Hesse stated as much here with all the bitter virulence he could muster. For even in its mildest and most inconspicuous form, this still represented an ongoing act of wanton destruction, as he wrote in "Indische Schmetterlinge" ("Indian Butterflies"): "For this destruction proceeds in an extremely human, friendly, and cheerful manner, there's no slaughter involved and not even any exploitation, but instead a surreptitious, gentle corruption and moral execution."[97] In such a situation—in the midst of decline—where were the forces for a genuine revival supposed to come from?

Butterflies: The Deceptive Play and the True Promise of Beauty

> We seem nowadays to be infinitely far removed from any ability to revere nature in the devout sense of searching for unity in multiplicity, and are unwilling to confess to this child-like primal urge, and make light of it when someone reminds us of it.
>
> —Hermann Hesse, "Über Schmetterlinge" "On Butterflies" (1935)

Hesse, however, did discover something instantly fascinating in Southeast Asia: butterflies. Here, for once, fantasy did not change into reality (and

lose its allure in the process), but instead the reality itself was so excessively rich in inventiveness that it outstripped any flight of the imagination. Might this beauty have the capacity once more to transcend all those
vile calculating expediencies that currently governed the world? With
seemingly playful grace and ease, butterflies overcame the chasm between
the Nature and Art. What a perfect symbol for poetry! Arising as they did
from a "gentle creative sensuality," they had the power to fascinate the observer. But here too the dictum held true that you already had to have the
butterfly inside yourself in order to recognize it in nature as that heightened counterpoint to which nature itself—transcending itself, as it
were—had given birth. Consequently, these "heraldic beasts of the soul"
were more than just collectors' items, with their wings pinned and kept
behind glass. Their tantalizingly lazy mode of flight could not be preserved.
Their beauty was living—in other words, in the here and now, or nothing.
That was why they were also symbols of transience. No pleasure except that
of watching them flutter past could be gained from them without destroying
them. They thus carried within them both the principle of the moment as
well as that of eternity. Because of this, Hesse described them as "the festive, bridal, at one and the same time fertile and ephemeral form of that
creature which was previously a sleeping pupa and before the pupa stage a
voracious caterpillar." Once again, we swiftly find ourselves back with
Hesse's idol Goethe, and his eulogizing of metamorphoses. Accordingly,
Hesse's 1935 essay "On Butterflies" begins by going back to basics. Here
a pantheism that was present from the outset combines with the experience he gleaned from his initial encounter with psychoanalysis—a discipline he dubbed "the philosophy of the unconscious": "Now, whether we
prefer to behave in a pious and modest manner or in an impertinent and
arrogant way, and whether we choose to either mock or admire early
forms of belief in the animation of nature, the fact remains that our actual
relationship to nature, even where we only still consider it as an object of
exploitation, is precisely that of a child to its mother. Furthermore, no new
routes have ever been added to the few ancient paths that are able to lead
a person to bliss or wisdom."[98]

The new wisdom is therefore at the same time ancient wisdom. And
yet, with regard to butterflies—which, like flowers, were for Hesse "a fa-
vored piece of creation, an especially valued and effective object of
amazement"—this artificially heightened form of nature can also be placed
in a completely profane context. For even the butterfly does not exist free

from the machinations of time; it too is a commodity, albeit an exotic one. Hesse portrays this experience in a drastic way, when he writes of the old royal and priestly Ceylonese town of Kandy: "Walking through the town involves an exhausting and shocking running of the gauntlet through the hyenas of the tourist industry."[99]

What would become of tradition, and things that were precious and valuable and vulnerably beautiful, in a world that was becoming increasingly uniform and more and more geared to a pure profit motive?

This question was one legacy for Hesse of his journey to Southeast Asia, a trip that not only disappointed him but also engendered in him feelings of aversion, even disgust. Unlike a humorous and high-spirited piece he wrote about the hunt for the tiger moth *(Chelis maculosa)* commonly known as the "Alpine Bear" *(Alpenbär),* a rare species that inhabited the Alpine uplands and kept successfully hiding from its would-be captor, one always fears the worst for the butterflies that appear in Hesse's sketches of India. They would not, one senses, survive long in the coming world of pure utility, tireless efficiency, and sordid commercial interests. That is the unspoken conclusion that emerges from "Indian Butterflies": pure resignation and a hitherto unknown irritation regarding his own role. For here Hesse pictures himself, not, as he had done hitherto, as a writer on the side of the threatened species and as an outsider, but as being on the side of the sinister rulers of this world—as an accomplice in the universal business of wiping out jewels that had up to that point been shining preciously in secrecy. He did not find his way out of this dilemma of the threatened deadening of his own perception: "I learned to look past the prettiest little girls with their sad black Indian eyes, I learned to rebuff with a frosty glance white-haired great-grandfathers who looked like saints, and instead I got used to a faithful retinue of corruptible people of all kinds, whom I found I could keep in check with imperious hand gestures and curt commands."[100]

Similarly, Hesse's story "Robert Aghion" of 1912 also concerns butterflies as symbols of both a deceptive beauty and genuine though indefinite promise. Here we encounter a missionary who travels to India to follow his calling, not least because of the native butterflies there, but who is confronted by the ugly colonial reality of the "mission to the heathens." Heathens? Might it not rather be the case that the ancient culture of the indigenous people was actually superior to that of those who came here to convert them? Hesse here took his family background in missionary work, combined it with his travel experiences, and created a narrative that for the first time posed the question of religiosity from a viewpoint that was no longer Christian.

Asia became a significant crossroads in Hesse's life. Here there occurred for Hesse something that one might, borrowing from Nietzsche, call a "re-valuation of all values": "The whole of the East breathes religion, in the same way that the West breathes reason and technology. The spiritual life of the Westerner seems primitive and hostage to every twist and turn of fortune when compared to the shielded, sophisticated, and trusting religiosity of Asians."[101] He then goes on to make an even more acerbic point when he writes that no import from the East could possibly rectify the "weaknesses of the West." "Rediscovering the art of living spiritually and of holding spiritual property in common" will, he maintains, become an existential question for European civilization. However, Hesse is uncertain about what the implications of this might be for religion: "Whether religion is something that can be surmounted and replaced is a moot point. Yet never more abundantly than among the peoples of Asia has it become clear to me that what we lack most profoundly in the West is religion or its substitute."[102]

6

A NEW BEGINNING IN SWITZERLAND
AND THE FIRST WORLD WAR

The Welti House in Bern and the Stench of Death

> Moving out is no pleasure, in fact I'd go so far as to say it's awful. But things have two faces, and however unpleasant it may be to have to clear a house, I find it just as pleasing and enjoyable moving into another one.

> —Hermann Hesse, "Moving House" (1912)

As early as May 30, 1912, Hesse wrote about his plan to move from Gaienhofen to Bern. He gave the following reason: "I had exhausted Gaienhofen, and there was no life there for me anymore."[1]

Remarkably, even at this early stage he was talking about the Welti house in Bern. Hesse was a friend of the painter Albert Welti and his wife. At the end of May he learned that Welti wanted to give up his house in Bern. His wife had died the previous year. Hesse had visited Welti several times—staying for a whole week in 1908—and had been struck by the unique atmosphere of the property on the Melchenbühlweg:

This certainly gives me food for thought. As far as I can call the house to mind, it might well suit us despite the fact that most of the rooms are small. I do worry about it being cold, though; the house is also in a poor state of repair. If only one could carry out a few improvements in return for a slightly higher rent or some other form of remuneration, I would take it. The house needs to have running water and a bathroom installed, and a gas supply too if possible, and various other things could also be improved.[2]

The house did not even have electric light. Instead, just as in Hesse's childhood home in Calw, illumination was provided by petroleum lamps. Hesse dithered about taking it; for sure, the house and garden had a romantic setting, but the rudimentary level of comfort reminded him of his first temporary accommodation in Gaienhofen. Inwardly, his whole being was yearning for a change. Perhaps he might actually find it easier living together with Mia and the children somewhere else—a notion that Hesse had up till now shown great virtuosity in sidestepping. "I'm all agog to see how things turn out with the house in Bern! It would be a real shame if nothing came of it. Bern is the only city that I instinctively have some confidence in." However, in the following passage of this same letter, he reveals that he is still involuntarily on the run: "and in any event my wife, who doesn't always find it easy with me and the children, might well feel happier there. As for myself, a bit of roaming around and rootlessness will always be part of my life."[3]

He wrote to Conrad Haussmann, his fellow editor of the magazine *März,* to tell him that Bern would also be a good choice because people would leave him in peace there. It was a town with good schools, friends, music, and beautiful natural surroundings. "And above all: my wife would feel happy and at home there, meaning that I'd feel more justified and have a clearer conscience about shutting myself away, going off on my travels, and so on."[4] During this period, from late May into early June 1912, Hesse was greatly preoccupied with the idea of moving to Bern and taking possession of Welti's "charming, somewhat dilapidated house and grounds on the far outskirts of the city."

But before he had a chance to speak to the painter about his intentions, Welti died suddenly on June 7. The news came as a great shock.

Now he and Mia had to decide very quickly whether they wanted to move into the house. The principal aim of uprooting themselves and moving to Switzerland was to save their marriage, which was on the rocks. Mia wanted to return to Switzerland, but not to Basel. Only recently, a fast railroad connection to Bern had been built, meaning that it was now connected to the wider world, a far from unimportant consideration for Hesse. But then they began to get cold feet about moving into the Welti's house: "We found ourselves balking inwardly at the thought of taking possession of the house straight after them; the whole idea had a whiff of death about it. And so we set about looking for other accommodation in the vicinity of Bern, but we couldn't find anything we liked."[5]

★   ★   ★

So they decided after all to pursue their original plan; the house on the Melchenbühlweg was lying empty for the time being, but they would have to move fast. Initially, they rented out the villa at Gaienhofen. Hesse did not get an exact impression of how "pleasing and enjoyable" it would be to move into an old house, because he was scarcely present during the move: "Between moving out from the house by the lake and moving in, in Bern, I took off for a few days to get some peace and quiet."[6] He went to Grindelwald on a "fact-finding trip," a phenomenon that was apparently well established even then.

There is something spooky about the way Hesse anticipates this scene in a foreword that he wrote in 1917 to accompany a monograph of Albert Welti's paintings—with Albert Welti as the main protagonist: "In our very first conversation, we got onto the topic of changing house and the process of moving, and I confessed my deep fear and loathing of such operations, which I just don't feel equal to, but I also added that I was reassured to some extent because my wife had long ago promised me that, should necessity require it, she could manage a house move all on her own. On hearing this, Welti shot me a twinkling, combative look from his bright blue eyes and cried out: 'What, are you really such a coward?!'"[7]

Hesse should have let the case of Welti be a warning to him: a native Swiss, he had enjoyed his happiest time as a painter and graphic artist in Munich, where he had been a protégé of Arnold Böcklin—thereafter he moved to Bern after being offered a monumental project that would ensure his livelihood for years to come. His task was to cover an entire wall of the main assembly hall of the Bern Federal Palace with frescoes. As it turned out, though, the project only brought him ill fortune and ruined his health. Hesse's introduction to Welti's posthumous book—in the penultimate war year of 1917—sounded uncommonly patriotic. Holding up this native Swiss to be the epitome of a German artist, as he did, was surely in part an insurance policy for this German writer resident in Switzerland who regularly suffered accusations of a lack of patriotism. But there is clearly something deeper going on behind his portrayal—in the sense of his Alemannic Avowal—when he adds that "a primal and feral power of the life of dreams and desires, indeed a strikingly demonic touch, was present" in Welti. What he meant by this was that here was a person who would not subjugate himself to any official role or bland system, someone who followed his own vision of art and who was therefore only German in the sense that the writer Novalis was, whose character Heinrich von Ofterdingen followed the lure of the blue flower of longing, unfazed by any external attempts to appropriate his art. In addition, his talent was completely untrammeled; this was no academician but an autodidact, and what's more a wild-growing one: "a kind of dilettante and interloper, and this character was precisely and admirably suited to the elemental raciness and wildness of many of his whims and fancies."[8]

When Hesse finally arrived at his new house in Bern, which this time was only a rented property, he was met with a gratifying sight: "I found my wife hard at it among craftsmen and laborers. Work had already progressed so far that, at a pinch, one could sleep and eat in the house."[9] In addition to the Hesse family with their three children, the house and extensive garden were also home to the Weltis' orphaned dog, a wolfhound by the name of Züsi.

The following year, on April 22, 1913, Hesse gave his first account of their new hometown in a letter to Otto Hartmann: "Everything you might have heard about the pride of the Bernese is not something just plucked out of thin air, though it may well be exaggerated. The Bernese still represent the most conservative aristocrats in the whole of Switzerland, a community made up of former lords, military leaders, and diplomats, who have rather grumpily withdrawn from politics in recent times. They are haughty, for sure, but also genteel and self-contained, and so there's nowhere where it's easier to keep yourself to yourself than here."[10]

And yet before long, hints arise in Hesse's notes pointing to something that Hugo Ball would later get right to the demonic heart of in his monograph on Hesse: "You can't spend an undisturbed night in a haunted house. You'll be tracked down by the unredeemed souls who roam around there."[11]

In his essay "On Moving to a New House," written in 1931—by which time he had already relocated several more times—Hesse recalled the Welti house, albeit from the embittered end of the period he spent in Bern. This was the house where he lived for the duration of the First World War and where his family finally disintegrated. And it was from here that he finally departed—alone—to Montagnola, and into an uncertain future. "It was something of an omen that this new life of ours should have begun with the death of both of the Weltis . . . only several years later did my wife tell me that, from the very outset, she had often felt afraid and oppressed in this old house, which like me she had initially seemed so enchanted by, and had been gripped by the fear that she might meet a sudden death or encounter ghosts. Now, slowly, the pressure began to mount that would change, in part also destroy, my life hitherto."[12]

Rosshalde, or the Problem of the Married Artist: Martin's Illness

The book *Rosshalde* represents a leave-taking: the author Hermann Hesse, as people had known him up until then, quits the stage. This novel, which Hesse started when he was still living in Gaienhofen and finished in 1913 in Bern, marked a transitional stage in the writer's work. Kurt Tucholsky identified it as one of the first: all of a sudden a different strain becomes apparent in the narrative form—the conventional narrative would be gone in Hesse's later works.

There is something disjointed and implacably demonic about the novel's character Veraguth—Hesse's alter ego in the guise of a figure in crisis. He is a painter who must decide between his art and his family. And ultimately he genuinely does come to a clear decision.

Rosshalde follows on seamlessly from *Gertrud*. The sense of crisis evoked in that work endured even in the pretty Welti house in Bern, which was too steeped in an atmosphere of finality (death!). Indeed, it had only deepened by this stage. Whereas the milieu in which it played out in *Gertrud* was music, in *Rosshalde* it is painting. It has often been remarked that Hesse Hesse's doppelgänger compositions reflect Nietzsche's dichotomy of the Dionysian and Apollonian. In every creative process, the unchained ecstatic element and the sober artistic one always form a whole—albeit an entity of contradiction. This process was evident in a traditional form in what we might call Hesse's "pre-psychological" novels. The opposing principles of Kuhn and Muoth in *Gertrud* are here represented by Veraguth, his wife, and two sons on the one hand, and on the other to an unannounced visitor, the traveler Otto Burckhardt, who makes the painter aware of how untenable his life has been thus far. Yet *Rosshalde* also did not bring Hesse any relief—he felt that he was, as in *Gertrud,* simply pouring new wine into old vessels, and that if he was going to break through to a new form of narrative, he would have to shed his old skin. He knew that he had to change his life. But how to achieve this? Did he not have a responsibility for his wife and his three sons?

Martin, the youngest son, was born in 1911. In an interview recorded shortly before his death, Hesse's second-oldest son, Heiner, revealed: "My father couldn't stand this child!"[13] He was referring to Martin, who fell ill with meningitis and had behavioral problems. The very presence of Martin—who would in later life take some wonderful photographs of his father—disturbed Hesse. Eventually, according to Heiner, Hesse presented Mia with the brutal ultimatum that either she remove this child from the house or he would leave himself.

In the summer of 1913, Hesse wrote to Alfred Schlenker: "That novel you were asking about has been finished for some while now, though it didn't go well."[14] And in a letter to his doctor in Badenweiler—which Hesse had previously visited for a rest cure while working on *Rosshalde*—he confided that he had learned a lot in the course of this work: "and what's more it helped me overcome and understand a number of personal problems, though I'm not sure whether it will be of any significant use to others."[15] For Hesse, *Rosshalde* had become a vital document of self-reflection, a testament to his inner crisis. Not a great novel, maybe, but rather a sketch of a decision. The author had to leave behind his previous life, relinquish what had been important and familiar to him. On November 20, 1915—by which time Hesse had long since been scapegoated as an enemy by the nationalistic wartime press in Germany—he told Stefan Zweig; "I'm delighted that you like Knulp in particular! Alongside *Rosshalde* and some poems, it's one of my favorite works."[16] This was a truly inopportune confession on his part! But precisely for that reason, he was showing himself to be wholly incorruptible in his view of contemporary Germany. For the whole of his lifetime, this position was not negotiable where he was concerned: "Wherever hatred is being stirred up and people persecuted, you can count me out; I'm expecting a quite different future Germany and type of German-ness than most of the blowhards."[17]

Rosshalde became an intimate portrait of the failure of Hesse's marriage and of the inexorable disintegration of his family. It was also a leave-taking from the persona of the successful middle-class writer, whose *Peter Camenzind* had by 1916 already reached its ninetieth edition.

By this stage Hesse, like his character Veraguth, was walking through his house, his garden, and his workroom knowing full well that he had a long journey ahead of him but repeatedly putting off his departure.

Hesse's third son, Martin (1911–1968)

On the very first page of the novel, we read: "It was a shame about the beautiful manor house." Why was this so?—Because, it transpires, no one had ever been happy there. We are put in mind here of Hesse's villa in Gaienhofen or even the Welti house in Bern—the beauty of the place was no longer inspiring his work, and he felt exhausted and empty. Even Bern could not improve this situation—and it is hard not to associate his circumstances there with his portrait of Veraguth. He too lives semi-estranged from his wife, having retreated to his studio, and only enters the villa proper, which his wife has never gotten used to either, as a visitor. In this rift—which is never spoken of directly and which is nothing more than a state of profound alienation, yet for that very reason quite insurmountable—his elder son, Albert, is entirely on the side of his mother. And when the painter's old friend Burckhardt comes to stay and notices from the very first moment the wretched state of this marriage, Veraguth makes the following admission, which sounds very much like Hesse recapitulating the decade that he has spent with Mia:

> You know that I had problems with my wife from the very beginning. Things ticked along for a couple of years, not well but not badly either, and at that time perhaps we still might have been able to salvage this and that. But I found it hard concealing my disappointment and I demanded from Adele precisely what she was in no position to give. She never displayed any zest for life; she was earnest and took life very seriously; I should have

realized that beforehand. She could never take a more relaxed view of things and learn to use humor or levity to overcome difficulties. Her sole response to my demands and my moods, my impetuous passion and my ultimate disillusion was silence and patience, which often moved me but which really didn't help either me or her in the long run. If I was irritable and discontented, she simply kept quiet and suffered. . . . If I was with her, she maintained a compliant and fearful silence, and she treated eruptions of fury and joyous outbursts with the same equanimity, and when I was away from home, she spent her time alone playing the piano and reminiscing about her girlhood. I found myself increasingly in the wrong, and eventually had nothing further to give or to communicate myself. So I began to apply myself more and more to my painting and gradually learned how to entrench myself in my work like I was in a fortress.[18]

This exhaustive account, which is far more extensive in Hesse's diaries, arose from the need to say something about his marriage. Mia, however—and this was the root of the problem—felt no such compulsion. Time and again, Hesse uses the word *schwerlebig,* "taking life too seriously," when describing his wife. She had a complete lack of spirit and was a profoundly self-contained person, whom Hesse found as impossible to reach as his character Veraguth in *Rosshalde* does his wife Adele. After reading this description in his novel, Hesse's apodictic assertion in a letter to his father on March 16, 1914, that his difficulties with Mia had less to do with a "wrong choice" on his part and more to do with the problem of "artists' marriages" in general, appears more than questionable.

There was no getting round it—he had indeed chosen wrongly when he married Maria Bernoulli in haste and in so doing made not only himself but also her deeply unhappy. This was quite clearly a case of two people being a total mismatch for one another. It would take Hesse several more years to fully admit his error to himself and to draw the only possible conclusion from it—namely, that he should bring this ever more unseemly situation to an end. "Iris" was the title of a fairy tale that Hesse would subsequently write for Mia in 1918, when he was under the influence of psychotherapy conducted by J. B. Lang and his resolve to leave his wife and children was growing:

She was older than he would have wished for a wife. She was very idiosyncratic and it would become difficult to live alongside her and at the same time pursuing pursue his ambition, for she would hear nothing of it. Nor was she very robust and healthy, with the result that she found company and parties hard to take. Her favorite way of life was to be surrounded by flowers and music and reading a book, say, in peace and solitude, and waiting to see if anyone came to see her. She simply let the world pass her by. . . . He was often convinced that she was fond of him, but just as frequently it seemed to him she loved no one and that she was just tender and friendly with everyone, and desired from the world nothing but to be left in peace. He, though, wanted something else from life, and if he was to have a wife at all, then there would have to be life and noise, and hospitality in the house.

Then again, he already had a wife—though she brought him no "life and noise."

The metaphor that he chose in *Rosshalde* for the end of his marriage sounds almost sinister. Pierre, Veraguth's younger son, falls ill with meningitis. Pierre is the painter's last real connection with his wife. He really does love the boy. Large sections of the book consist of the painstaking description of the course of Pierre's illness—which ends with the boy's predictable death. For Veraguth this is a signal to follow his friend Burckhardt to India and leave the wrecked marriage behind him. Pierre is reminiscent of the figure of Echo in Thomas Mann's *Doctor Faustus* (for whom the author took his grandson Frido as a model), who also succumbs to meningitis in the story.

The incredibly bitter irony of the tale is this: Hesse's youngest son, Martin, really did come down with meningitis in March 1914, shortly after the completion of *Rosshalde*. However, unlike Pierre in the novel, "Brüdi" (the family's nickname for Martin) survived. The burden that her youngest son's illness placed on Mia was immense. In March, Hesse wrote to his sister Adele:

> For some time now, Little Brüdi has been phenomenally agitated, and recently he has also started suddenly waking up screaming at night, leaping out of bed, and suffering panic attacks. In the end, we began to get really scared, and now the lady doctor has declared that he has a nervous condition. He spends his days in complete isolation, with only Mia for company day and night, and is given bromide four times a day. Heiner has been quarantined at the Schädelins, and Mia has moved into the room with the lad, with the curtains drawn the whole time, and dares not leave even for a moment. She even eats her meals up there for the most part, and no one else is permitted to see Brüdi. This is supposed to go on for weeks![19]

Thus far, this is very much as any concerned father would have phrased things. And such a father would even perhaps—in order to give his over-burdened wife some respite—take a turn himself sitting by the bedside of his son as he fought for his life. But Hesse, as we know, reacted differently when he was confronted with troubles and pain: "For the time being, I will stay here to see how things turn out, but then I will probably go off somewhere in the interim and take my work with me." And indeed, in early summer—on his own, naturally—he set off on a journey to places where he had spent his childhood, including Maulbronn, the school that he had once left under such a dark cloud of shame. On his travels, he wrote to his father: "Little Martin's condition is stable now, maybe even a little better. Quite apart from the sheer worry, this whole business has been in-credibly difficult for Mia; every day, she hardly leaves the boy's side for so much as quarter of an hour at a stretch."[20]

When Hesse writes the following lines to Adele, shortly after the out-break of his son's illness, one gets the distinct impression that the worst thing about Martin's condition was that he had thrown his father's summer travel plans into disarray: "As far as our plans for the summer are con-cerned, I had originally intended to visit a small Italian seaside resort for a short spell and take Mia and Bützi [a nickname for Bruno]. Then a plan emerged to head off with the whole family and perhaps to rent a small farmhouse in the mountains (in Vallis) for two months and keep house there. I have no idea what will become of that idea now."[21]

In this situation, Mia herself lapsed into depression—and Hesse duly absented himself as best he could (and he was a past master at that!) from the unpleasant atmosphere of illness that pervaded his house. As early as April, he set off to Italy to stay near Florence.

Wilhelm Raabe: True Fame and False Celebrity—A Signal with Long-Distance Effect

> The newspapers of today and the modern literary marketplace know just as little about Wilhelm Raabe as they did in his heyday, around twenty-five years ago.
>
> —Hermann Hesse, *On Visiting Wilhelm Raabe*

Hesse mused on his relationship with fame in one of his most charming but also least-known texts: *Besuch bei Wilhelm Raabe (On Visiting Wilhelm*

Raabe). This visit took place in 1909 during a reading tour, when he stopped over in Braunschweig, where the then almost eighty-year-old writer was still living, as if caught in a time warp. Yet instead of finding the now-unknown Raabe to be a sad reminder of former celebrity, Hesse was on the contrary deeply and unreservedly in awe of the writer's understated eminence, which shone forth at one remove from the garish glare of current success. Granted, this glow of fame was not very strong—you had to look for it in order to notice it—but on the other hand it had an enduring power that stood above the vicissitudes of modish celebrity.

Twenty-four years later, in 1933, when the Germans were about to take leave not just of any literary finesse but also any last vestige of civilization, Hesse put pen to paper to describe this visit. The impression it had made was precious to him, yet the lapse of time militated against his memory. What he had actually experienced took on a mythical substance, in which reality and dream blurred into one another. This was difficult terrain for a writer who felt beholden to the yardstick of truth. What was true about reminiscing, what were its parameters? Did one require an external corrective, adducing dates and facts by way of comparison, or was the yardstick for the truth of these kinds of life-changing encounters an entirely internal matter?

At the start of his account, Hesse admits that he had never set much store by being acquainted with so-called famous men, with the possible exception of Knut Hamsun, whom he would have loved to have met when he visited the editorial offices of the magazine *Simplicissimus* in Munich. However, Hesse's future course was set from an early age: "I have never loved public life, and I never found it pleasant to live in an environment where I was known as a name and a brand; my life couldn't be private enough for me, and so I have never attended any gathering of so-called 'famous people,' be it at a salon, a club, a ball, or a banquet. I could easily find excuses to avoid such events, since I always lived way out in the sticks."[22]

But he was really keen to meet Wilhelm Raabe, whom he had already greatly admired before he discovered Gottfried Keller, Theodor Storm, and Jean Paul, when he was in Braunschweig. This proved to be more difficult than he had anticipated, as Raabe failed to appear in the wine tavern where he normally received visitors because he had contracted a cold. But Hesse's wish to meet him was conveyed to him, whereupon the old writer invited Hesse to come and visit him at home.

This was a journey into the secrets of creativity. To the great solitary one, who lived apart from society yet without in the slightest growing embittered. For Hesse the visit to Raabe was a beam of light that would light his way on his future path. He had retained a vivid image of the old man: "Slender and tall, and dressed in a long nightgown—there stood this amicable and yet majestic figure, and from a great height an old, lined, teasingly intelligent face gazed down at me in a very friendly and pleasant manner. For all that, though, it was still a fox's face, sly, artful, and enigmatic—the wizened countenance of a sage, mocking without any malice, knowing but well-meaning, wise with age and yet somehow ageless, an impression that was reinforced by his upright bearing."[23] It then becomes clear wherein a large part of the younger man's fascination resides: in Raabe, Hesse was meeting his grandfather's generation, the demise of which he had mourned as an irretrievable loss. He keenly felt the absence of their natural dignity, and their chivalrousness, in which authority and humor combined.

In front of him, therefore, stood one of the last examples of this so congenially outmoded type, whose *Abu Telfan* and *Die Chronik der Sperlingsgasse* he loved in equal measure. Yet it was a love with reservation. Raabe kept his readers at a distance; he didn't make it intentionally easy for them. "There was something confused and almost strange about his work which I found partly entrancing and partly off-putting, along with something North German, which was quite alien to me."[24] There resided in this great portraitist of the Germans between 1850 and 1880 both a dreamy fantasist and a harsh critic, and yet above and beyond this duality he remained "an ardent admirer of his fellow countrymen." It was this out-and-out paradox in Raabe's character that fascinated Hesse: Raabe was at the same time devout and skeptical—a derisive figure even, but one who was also given to devotion and admiration.

Then something quite remarkable happened. Something that rankled with Hesse and caused him to place a question mark over every future recollection of the event. They chatted for a long time and Raabe, for all his quietly smiling distance, listened intently to what the young man had to say. His visitor finally plucked up the courage to ask Raabe a question that he had been dying to ask him. What, asked Hesse, had he made of the poet Eduard Mörike, whom he had met forty years earlier in Stuttgart? In an affable but reserved way, Raabe gave Hesse to understand that he hadn't particularly got on with Mörike. Coming as it did from such a scrupulously polite person, Hesse took this to mean that Raabe had actually taken a thorough dislike to Mörike: "He had evidently been a sensitive man and probably somewhat thin-skinned. He smiled to himself and I gazed at him with intent fascination, for I could clearly sense that he had a very precise recollection of Mörike and could see him before him right now, and I would have given my eye teeth to have been able to see for myself the image that he had conjured up."[25]

And now came the extraordinary thing, the positively insoluble mystery that Hesse, after he had completed his wonderful text, observed with dismay and—without altering what he had already written—noted down in an afterword to the piece. This runs: "As I later found out, Raabe had testified unequivocally on several occasions that he had never known Mörike personally." What had happened here? Had Hesse simply, after all this time, imagined the conversation with Raabe about Mörike? Surely not—it had meant too much to him for that. Or hadn't Raabe perhaps made it sufficiently clear that he hadn't known Mörike personally and had just formed his impression of him from hearsay? Time leaves its marks on memory, to be sure, but it also erases things—in turn, other things can be overlaid with later experiences or changed by memories of subsequent events.

Can, then, the recollection of things that happened decades ago be anything other than a dream image of reality? Raabe himself had treated this question in his *Chronik der Sperlingsgasse:* "The bright, ever-changing, constantly fresh images in this giant picture-book we call 'the world' grow dimmer and dimmer to my old eyes; they become increasingly blurred and flow into one another. In a lifetime, I have arrived at that place where, as in the transition from waking to sleep, the experiences of the day just gone still swirl dully around the brain of the tired person, bit also where the dark, dream- and spirit-filled night is beginning to cast its shroud over everything, good and evil alike."[26]

Something that would continue to resonate throughout his life remained from the young, though already extremely successful, Hesse's meeting with Raabe: reverence—that example that one person can set for another, the most precious of all gifts. Hesse had been deeply impressed by the old man's aristocratic form of reclusiveness, which was as modest as it was dignified. If it was at all possible to withstand the ravages of time, or even to overcome them, then surely this was the only way to do so. His encounter with Wilhelm Raabe immunized him against the false criteria of the contemporary world, protected the renown of someone who was intent on sticking to his increasingly unassuming post against the false celebrity of the age, which was geared to stock-market prices, for "at every point where one has collaborated, even in the most inconsequential of ways, with this world where celebrities are manufactured, afterward one feels somehow abused and derailed."[27]

Outbreak of War, Summer 1914:
"O My Friends, No More of These Tones!"

There can be no question now of doing any intellectual work, the business of literature has ground to a halt like every other enterprise.

—Hermann Hesse, letter to his father, September 9, 1914

The outbreak of war found Hesse on his travels, as he revealed to Harry Maync in a letter of September 1914. For he had taken every opportunity to absent himself from the Welti house in Bern. In his biography of Hesse, Hugo Ball would elevate the situation in which the writer found himself that summer into the realms of a Dance of Death: "To put it bluntly: when war broke out the author Hermann was living in a state of morbid drunkenness, and of contradictory emotions that could no longer be separated; flayed by a dark dreamlike grief in which he was indulging himself and at the same time by the discord in his family life."[28]

In such circumstances, the war of course was an effective interruption of the eternally identical, hopeless humdrum of everyday life. Hesse was a German patriot and he was determined not to shirk his duty in this conflict. And so, on August 29, 1914, he voluntarily reported for duty at the German consulate in Bern, but his application for military service was turned down on the grounds of "extreme short-sightedness." In September he offered his services as a welfare officer for German prisoners of war at the German embassy in Bern, though he was less than clear about precisely what duties he expected to perform: "Unfortunately I do not have any practical skills or other educational qualifications to offer. I can write, and use a typewriter too, but I do not know any shorthand. I am not fluent in any foreign languages, although I do have a smattering of the sort of phrases you need when you're traveling."[29]

As he told his father, although there was little sign of the war in Bern, he had forebodings that dark clouds were beginning to gather over the daily lives of German émigrés in neutral Switzerland. As yet, these were just harbingers of all the difficulties that life held in store for the family: "We notice nothing of the war here except for the chronic lack of money. The fact that I have no prospect of earning anything more for the foreseeable future shouldn't be so important because I have some savings, but the banks are releasing virtually no funds, so we have to scrimp and save and are in a constant state of anxiety, though our worries are small in comparison with those who are currently controlling our destiny."[30]

However, those worries quickly grew, because inevitably he did not manage to keep his name out of the nationalistic frenzy of war jingoism.

In September 1914, ninety-three German intellectuals, literary figures, and artists had drafted a declaration that proclaimed the unity of German militarism and culture. "The German Army and the German People are as one," it announced. This public statement was directed above all at any attempt to position the preservation of culture in opposition to the barbarism of war. The "Manifesto of the 93" was, so to speak, a preemptive strike to take the wind out of the sails of any potential alliance of Europe's leading cultural lights against militarism. The signatories included, among others, the Naturalist playwright Gerhart Hauptmann, the Impressionist painter Max Liebermann, the physicists Max Planck and Wilhelm Röntgen, and the biologist Ernst Haeckel. And Thomas Mann wrote in his "Thoughts in Wartime": "Why should the artist, the soldier in the artist, not have praised God for the collapse of a world of peace of which he was fed up, so completely fed up?"[31] Hesse himself was not so very far from this position. In the diary entries he kept from August 1, 1914, onward, for instance, we find the following passage on September 11: "Morning in the garden. Bützi [Bruno] helped me and showed great zeal in rooting up all kinds of weeds once I'd told him that they were Russians, Serbians, Belgians, and so on."[32] Of course, half of what Hesse said here was in jest. But only half.

And yet his ultimate judgment on the war—from a similar intellectually conservative basis—turned on a decisive nuance, and a skeptical attitude began to predominate. The final entry in this diary, written on October 17, 1914—Hesse did not have the stamina for writing extensive diary entries of this kind, especially because half his day was taken up with writing letters—runs: "The growing phony-patriotic psychosis in

Hermann Hesse, pictured shortly before the outbreak of the First World War

Germany (the same is true of the enemy nations as well) mortifies and upsets me."[33]

He would never, though, come out so openly against the war as his friend Stefan Zweig, or Heinrich Mann or Leonhard Frank. Yet his conservative-nationalist and moderate position was to bring down far greater opprobrium on his head than that suffered by these out-and-out opponents of the war. Why was this so? It was because his position directly contradicted the "Manifesto of the 93"—for him war and culture were entirely separate entities. War might well be necessary—but that in no way invalidated the norm of culture, and not just German culture but that of Europe as a whole.

So, all Englishmen and Frenchmen were supposed to be his enemies? For Hesse things could not be that simple. Although he rejected, as his parents had done, England's hegemonic foreign policy and had only contempt for Anglo-Saxon mercantilist pragmatism, xenophobia was still alien to his nature. He was on the horns of a dilemma.

Fundamentally he supported Germany's role in the First World War, which he believed should be won with the utmost speed—yet he was repelled by the implications of the conflict for civilization. He found it impossible to keep these strong reservations to himself for long. What prompted him to take his first public stand was a series of caricatures entitled "Estheticism Abroad" published in the satirical magazine *Simplicissimus,* which lampooned the Swiss painter Ferdinand Hodler. The basic tenor of the piece was: Just look at this Francophile, this traitor to Germany in her hour of destiny! All Hodler had done was to comment that in shelling the cathedral at Reims, the Germans had destroyed something that belonged to the whole of humankind. Romain Rolland, who had settled in Switzerland and quickly made friendly contact with Hesse, responded to the attack on Hodler in a piece in the *Journal de Genève.* For his part, Hesse contributed an article to the *Neue Zürcher Zeitung* on November 3, with the title (taken from Beethoven's Ninth Symphony) "O My Friends, No More of These Tones!" This was an attempt to build a bridge between intellectuals—from Romain Rolland to Thomas Mann. His message was this: We must not relinquish our culture and our feeling for art! We artists needn't hate one another just because our countries' armies are at war.

Accordingly, he came out in opposition to any boycott against the culture and writing of "enemy" nations. The two realms of conflict and culture had nothing to do with one another—this was Hesse's preferred view of things. In this he was hitching his wagon to an outmoded image of warfare. Now it wasn't just armies that were pitted against each other; instead, the war had gripped entire nations, their media, sciences, and even the churches. War had permeated all walks of life and become a universal phenomenon, leaving no sacrosanct areas where the life of the mind could remain unaffected.

Even so, Hesse's text, which totally ignores the political realities of the day, is still interesting because it poses the question: What will become of civilization and of us as a European intellectual elite once this war is over? Leaving aside politics, what consensus will we still be able to find, and will we be unable any longer to talk in terms of "Europe's conscience"? This was a question that aligned him closely with Romain Rolland.

Such considerations anticipate for the first time the themes that Hesse later treated in *The Glass Bead Game:* What can the spirit do to counteract naked force, and how can the individual intellectual survive in a world that has been increasingly abandoned by any spirituality?

On October 25 he wrote to Conrad Haussmann: "The thing that troubles me most about the war right now is the brutality with which all those common spiritual values that transcend the political sphere are being scorned and spat upon."[34]

By writing "O My Friends, No More of These Tones!," he was trying to exert a moderating influence upon the omnipresent war hysteria. But in this inflamed situation, his suggestion that war must ultimately have as its objective a peace in which all the nations of Europe could live together once more was seen as treasonous. All that Hesse had done was to bring into play an approach that would basically be acceptable to all Germans—as well as to the French, British, and Russians—namely, that advocated by Goethe: "Goethe was never found wanting in his patriotism, despite the fact that he did not compose any national anthems in 1813. Yet his delight in German-ness, which he knew and loved like no other, was overtrumped only by his delight in humanity as a whole. He was a citizen and a patriot in the international world of ideas, of inner freedom, and of intellectual conscience."[35]

Hesse had underestimated the febrile mood in Germany, and the hatred that was directed against anyone who did not bellow along with the enraged herd but instead tried to strike a different note. It was this above all that incited the gutter press to attack him—this different tone, which refused to be swept along by a murderous blood-lust, preferring instead to inquire in measured terms about the core values that should govern a future world.

Hesse tried to pursue a dual track in his arguments, but precisely by doing so he only found that he fell between two stools. But he was genuinely conflicted, and he embodied within himself contradictory attitudes. He regarded the war as necessary and supported it, but his support was founded on an unconventional, and illusory, image of war—namely, war that would not destroy the whole of European civilization: "Let us honor every man who fights on the battlefield amid shellfire and gives his blood and his life! As for the rest of us, who want the best for our homeland and do not want to view the future with despair, we are charged with the task of maintaining a little piece of peace, building bridges, and trying to find new paths, but without in the process wading in thoughtlessly with our pens and thereby further disturbing the foundations on which a future Europe will be built." As if this weren't enough to provoke the warmongering yellow press, the article concluded with an appeal for reconciliation: "Precisely this disastrous world war should serve to drum into us more insistently than ever before the realization that love is better than hate, understanding better than anger, and peace nobler than war. Otherwise what would be the point of it?"[36]

The idea that the Great War was a disaster was at complete variance with the general mood of the public in Germany in the autumn of 1914. Hesse, who up until then had been rather pampered by the press, now experienced firsthand how the pendulum could swing. The wave of vitriol did not spare him. He couldn't understand it; after all, he hadn't insulted the troops in their trenches, and he had volunteered himself. All he had said was that in this war too, one should not lose sight of the fact that hatred could not form the basis of a future peaceful coexistence between European peoples.

This marked the beginning of Hesse's alienation from the Germans, which would ultimately prove to be irreversible. With his attitude—however inconsistent it may have been—he was an unwelcome outsider among the German populace. And he would remain so for a very long time. His relationship with his readers had been disrupted, and any kind of connection to them in the future would have a strongly distancing aspect to it, every association with them being based on a misunderstanding.

His poetry collection *Musik des Einsamen* (Music of the Lonely One), which he published the same year war broke out, was the music that would henceforth accompany all his writing. The war had found him in the same situation as everyone else, except that one thing distinguished him from most other people: his distinct lack of enthusiasm. And in the midst of a hysterical mob, a cool-headed, distanced individual rapidly becomes an object of hatred.

Thereafter he would heed the voices of only a handful of people, such as Theodor Heuss, one of the few people who dared to voice the opinion that Hesse's intentions were honorable. Or Romain Rolland, the French exile in Switzerland, whose experiences were similar to Hesse's—and who saw his like-minded neighbor as a kindred spirit rather than an enemy. Rolland dubbed the stance that Hesse took in "O My Friends, No More of These Tones!" a truly "Goethian attitude." The German press, though, branded Hesse a traitor. The *Kölner Tageblatt* accused him of being a "draft-dodger." For the majority of Germans, he was an "unpatriotic type who has long since inwardly knocked the dust of his homeland's soil off his boots."[37]

In her 1972 monograph on Hesse, Eike Middell points to a fundamental trait linking Hesse and Thomas Mann—namely, the "introversion of the war," the assumption that the honorable man in his innermost soul always remains a warrior, even when he carries no weapon. It is therefore not so very surprising that Hesse wrote a positive review of Max Scheler's *The Genius of War and the German War* in which he praised the "spirit of German youth's affirmation of the war." The war appeared in this context to both Hesse and Scheler as a manly and elemental force that a person should not shy away from: "The affirmation of war in general, not as a necessary evil but as a vital force, along with the affirmation of this war in particular, above all an affirmation of the war against England."[38]

Hesse calls Scheler's book a beautiful, inspired work that explored depths in order to lay bare the necessity of war:

> The fact that this is not about rivalry and different firm's signs, or percentages and exchange rates, but about something much more profound, about the downfall of a soulless capitalism made in England, and the realization that clandestine outposts of this enemy have already long since been set up in our own country and among our own people, agents with whom we shall have to deal just as thoroughly and unequivocally as we will with our cousins on the island across the sea—nowhere has this all been expressed with such clarity, or such well-grounded arguments, or so warmly and sincerely as in this book, which is the work of an inspired author to whom the outbreak of war represented a cleansing thunderstorm and a first bolt of lightning striking into the fog of a barren utilitarianism and illuminating it.[39]

Can the war really be an answer to a perceived vacuum of spirituality? But that was just one side of the contradiction that Hesse was unable to resolve and that plunged him ever deeper into the "crisis" that shackled him to the sinister Welti house for the remainder of the war. The demonic nature of circumstances thus advanced even further into the most intimate realms of his spiritual life. For the deep-seated contradiction he carried within himself regarding his nationality made him vulnerable to the incessant stream of hate mail that he began to receive from Germany, which imbued him with a lasting distrust of Germans until his dying day.

And yet all he had wanted to do was to defend the kind of German spirit that he enthusiastically affirmed and adored in such figures as Goethe and Mozart!

Following the celebratory tone he adopted in his review of Scheler's book, it would take less than a year for Hesse to admit his error—as here in a letter to Kurt Wolff written on December 30, 1916: "I really ought to recant the position I took on Scheler's book about the war. When I read it, it was my first real encounter with this kind of attitude, plus there was also the sheer enthusiasm of the writing. None of his ideas on time and history have stood up to closer scrutiny."[40]

In order to understand Hesse's position on the war, one needs to refer back to a primal force in his psyche: music! Eichendorff's line "Let us sing nonetheless!" (from his poem "Du liebe, treue Laute!") expressed what Hesse was attempting to defend in the midst of barbaric times—the strain of music that he had already identified in *Gertrud* as being inextricably bound up with love.

What does war do to people in the event that it does not kill them? It destroys their souls, and suddenly things that are uncouth and mediocre emerge triumphant. Every finely structured soul that refuses to be reduced to a simple friend-or-foe ideology is forced to suffer the steady and growing drumbeat of dull propaganda speeches. Hesse was certain that this should not be the standard we live by. In this so-called great time, only petty spirits thrived, as Hesse recalled with a contempt that was only thinly veiled by irony in his *Life Story Briefly Told* (1925):

> In a hospital for the war wounded I got to know an old maid who had formerly in happier times rented out rooms and was now performing nursing duties in this hospital. She explained to me with stirring enthusiasm how happy and proud she was that she'd been able to experience these momentous times. I found that quite understandable, since it had taken the outbreak of war to turn this lady's listless and purely selfish existence as an old maid into an active and worthwhile life. But as she explained her good fortune in a corridor full of soldiers wearing field dressings and all shot to pieces and crippled, running between rooms full of amputees and the dying, I could feel my sympathies shifting. However much I understood this old dear's enthusiasm, I could not share it and I could not applaud it. If there

was one such elated nurse to every ten soldiers, then this lady's good fortune had been bought rather dearly, I thought.[41]

Yet the problem of war in history was not to be solved for Hesse by simple rejection. He ranged far and wide in search of answers, and it is not always clear what his point is—as, for instance, in a letter he wrote to his family in Calw on December 15, 1914:

> As far as an intellectual response to this war is concerned, the best advice I know of comes from the old Bhagavad Gita. I'm thinking in particular of the lesson that the god Krishna imparts to a prince who is loath to go to war because he finds the whole enterprise cruel and pointless. Krishna tells him in no uncertain terms that he must do his duty as befits his station in life, and in the process he utters the splendid, quite Christian, and almost Lutheran dictum that everyone is required to do his allotted duty, and not someone else's, and that it is better to die in the course of fulfilling this task than to shirk one's responsibility.[42]

This demonstrates that Hesse at this stage still, like Ernst Jünger, had an image of himself as a "warrior," which was still conditioned by Protestantism. The point he was driving at here was dangerous, potentially even fatal. But what did he mean by "his duty"? This was the central question troubling Hesse—and the answer he arrived at soon after was "to obey his own self-will." He was committed to this responsibility with his life, and saw it as a solemn duty.

In a text of 1914 entitled "A Page from My Diary" we encounter, as it were, an existential, self-referential commentary by Hesse on the didactic Hindu poem from the *Bhagavad Gita* that he mentions in his letter to Calw. We sense here how Hesse attempted to justify each of his decisions, and his attitude to the prevailing political climate and the war, through conducting a dialog with spiritual authorities. Hesse's life was conditioned by his reading.

And so, on a scant one and a half pages of print, we find Hesse rehearsing a question that caused him profound pangs of conscience. He adduces the "wisdom of the most ancient orient" to help him determine what attitude he should take to the events of the summer of 1914. And this really does help:

I am testing myself. Am I pleased that war has broken out? No, never for a moment! Am I avoiding getting engaged in the war out of cowardice, or convenience, or is it the egotism of someone who is focused on other goals entirely? Yes, yes, guilty as charged.

Do I hate the enemy? Take pleasure in destruction? No. But do I exult when I hear a report that an enemy cruiser has been blown up? Yes, I'll admit to feeling a twinge, a frisson of pleasure—oh what the hell, I'm overjoyed, delighted.[43]

No, there is no neutrality here. But surely there had to be a position over and above the warring parties? This conflict was threatening to tear Hesse apart.

Working for the Welfare of Prisoners of War: Books in Wartime

Triumphalism, even in sentiment, was alien to Hesse. Just as his parents knew of no victorious deity but only a humble God, so Hermann had not the slightest feel for the kind of nationalism that could captivate others, indeed take hold of entire peoples and masquerade as a patriotic virtue. Hesse was not a person who was given to fanaticism. Even so, he took very seriously the question of duty in times of war.

Accordingly, the accusation that he was an "unpatriotic type" who was sitting pretty in Switzerland hit him hard. He was a German national (and remained so until 1924), he had immediately volunteered for war service—and now that he had only been assigned to the reserves due to his poor eyesight, he at least wanted to do something for captured German soldiers in order to help them to survive. And he knew from his own times of crisis what would help: books! Not the sort of books that celebrate heroic deaths, but those that deal with individual human beings and their hopes and sufferings. Working from Bern, and in collaboration with Richard Woltereck, professor of zoology at the university there, Hesse established an aid agency to provide books to captured soldiers. The day-to-day business of this aid organization, in which Hesse had the status of an acting imperial civil servant, resembled that of every other charity in the world: writing appeals for donations of money or goods. Hesse and Woltereck's special concern was collecting books to send to German prisoners of war.

Hesse published his "Letter to a Wounded Soldier" in 1914. This text demonstrates the extent to which Hermann Hesse, in his tireless efforts to make his own contribution to the war effort, marginalized himself from mainstream German society through his writing. Imagining himself responding to a lieutenant's inquiry as to "what reading matter he would recommend for educated wounded men," he began to ponder aloud about the "foundations for our future world."[44]

He proceeds in his reply to talk about the "simplification of thoughts and emotions, which all combatant nations have experienced over the past few months," and how this presented a challenge to those people whom Hesse refers to as "we intellectuals." To be sure, against the background of war, people needed to reassess what they believed in and knew, and to cast off some ballast. But what he then goes on to write runs directly counter to official war propaganda:

> By "ballast" I do not of course mean all things foreign, just as I do not consider everything German as being indispensable. No, we should not make the matter so easy for ourselves, nor do we intend to. We should not forget that, like us, many people in France, Russia, and England are deeply shocked and, with their innermost consciences stirred, follow the fate of nations, examine their own hearts and minds, and find themselves at one with us in their resolve not to let the momentous experience of war become some adventure but instead to heed the call of this desperate hour to all thinking people as if it were the call of God to those still slumbering.[45]

Hesse was already thinking about what Europe would be like after the war—and not at all in the sense of a peace imposed by a victorious Germany, but a peace that did not consist of coercion and subjugation. He was concerned about Europe's spiritual condition following the destruction of the old order that existed prewar. This was a grand vision that no doubt required the distance of someone viewing events in Germany from Bern, given that such speculation was taboo there. Hermann Hesse was thinking in terms of a reorganization of society, because "the man who today is standing shoulder-to-shoulder with me, or with my brother on the battlefield, cannot tomorrow, once the war has ended, simply revert to being some proletarian I pity from afar."[46]

And so he recommends to the "wounded educated man" two books that call for the old ownership structures to be overthrown: *Progress and Poverty* by Henry George, and *Land Reform* by Adolf Damaschke.

He certainly wasn't making himself popular among his former readers by recommending such texts. Because Hesse was not caught up in the hysterical war atmosphere that pervaded Germany, he had no idea that these kinds of intellectual speculations bordered on high treason there.

He patiently went on collecting books for the libraries of prisoners of war. Hesse himself spoke of more than a hundred POW camps in France alone that had to be supplied. He traveled to see potential sponsors and corresponded with colleagues. The Austrian philosopher Martin Buber, for instance, put up the funds to found no fewer than fifty Jewish reference libraries; Hesse later gratefully recalled Buber's generosity when sending him greetings on his eightieth birthday in 1958. In the autumn of 1915, he informed Colonel Borel of his intention to produce a magazine for POWs that would appear at regular intervals, the *Sunday Courier for German Prisoners of War.* He outlined his plans quite candidly: "I'm not going to present things from a patriotic angle, but solely from a human one, and in the way that I conceive of and wish to organize my paper, I see it as a means of popular education the like of which we will never get the opportunity to create again."[47] Hesse was successful in his request, and the *Sunday Courier* began to appear regularly from January 1916 on, and six months later was joined by the *German Internees' Newspaper.*

On February 17, 1917, Hesse was called up after all. Having been exempted from frontline war service because of his bad eyes, via the Imperial German Consulate in Bern Hesse suddenly received his conscription orders, which instructed him to "report for duty following his recuperation." There could be no question of any "recuperation" in Hesse's case, in fact, but nobody was interested in hearing this during the final, desperate phase of the war. It was solely due to the intervention of Richard Woltereck, his colleague at the prisoners' welfare agency, who pleaded Hesse's case in Berlin, that he did not end up being sent to the front. On July 7 he wrote in a letter that he had had to put all literary endeavor to one side, as it did not sit well with his "war work." The only things he could take any solace from for the time being were painting and drawing, which he had recently taken up: "The war has fundamentally changed my relationship with the world, as it has for everyone, but it hasn't politicized me. Quite the opposite in fact. The external and the internal worlds seem to be even more sharply divided than before, and my sole interest is in the internal."[48]

★   ★   ★

The Welti house increasingly metamorphosed into an office. Hesse wrote letters, packaged books, and received visitors there. Literary work was out of the question; for years he wrote just correspondence and pieces on current affairs, and reaped in return only one thing: new aggravation.

In a sense, Hesse suddenly found himself following precisely in the footsteps of Grandfather Gundert and of his parents with their Calw Publishing Union. He developed an extraordinary talent for organization. When he looked back on this period in his life some time later, it seemed to him to be shrouded in a gray veil of mist. Whenever the mist lifted for a few brief moments, he was astonished. In his short essay "Bücher-Ausklopfen" (Spring-cleaning my books; 1931), we read: "A few days later I chanced upon another, even more forgotten, even stranger and more remote stratum of my library. It contained publications from the war years, all of which I had been responsible for publishing and editing. These included newspapers for German soldiers being held prisoner in France, whose welfare I was involved in for the duration of the war. I unearthed back numbers—three years' worth—of the 'Sunday Courier for German Prisoners of War,' which I used to send several thousand copies of to France, England, Russia, and India."[49]

Hesse was indefatigable in his industriousness. Besides taking on this far too onerous burden of work, he also published a series of volumes of selected excerpts from other works, which were published under the imprint Publishing House of the Central Book Depository for German Prisoners of War, specially founded for this purpose. The sole criterion for selection in this twenty-two-volume series was that men interned in the camps should still have access to a voice of humanity. Many of Hesse's favorite authors were represented here, such as Gottfried Keller and Theodor Storm, as well as Thomas and Heinrich Mann and Robert Walser. Hesse the flayed Romantic appears here as an enlightener, a forerunner of attempts to establish a set canon of great literature, which subsequently became a very popular trend. Hesse himself took an initial step along this road with the Library of World Literature series he founded in 1926.

His position as an émigré German in Switzerland was anything but comfortable. On February 24, 1915, he described his precarious position in a letter:

> The Swiss army has been mobilized, which is a controversial matter except
> in time of war. As a result, the state has run up several hundred millions in

debt, the hotels are standing empty and some have even gone bust, and the best that Switzerland can hope to gain from all this upheaval is that it continues to exist and can pay back its debts. In short, although there's been no bloodshed here, the war has still managed to kick up a lot of fuss and bother here, and the animosity between people of German and French or Italian extraction often splits families right down the middle.

Internally Switzerland was undoubtedly a powder keg; the front between German and French culture ran right through the country. In addition there was great concern over which side Italy would join in the war. Could Switzerland survive this explosive situation? In these circumstances, Hesse's balancing voice, talking about a shared culture between the warring parties, was of immense significance for the Swiss policy of neutrality.

And yet even in Switzerland he found himself almost alone in the position he took. He kept aloof from radical antiwar positions as represented in Switzerland by the publication *Die Weissen Blätter*—and maintained a firm distinction between the front and cultural matters. However, it was clear where his sympathies lay when he wrote to Romain Rolland about the authors of the *Weissen Blätter,* describing them as "displaying the crassness of youth, though there are many upstanding and right-minded young men working there."[50]

Outwardly he continued to take a dual position: the German military must win the war, but the intellectuals of Europe should not allow themselves to be drawn in and seduced into hatred. Was this a realistic position? The main thing was that, for him, it was a pragmatic one, for when all was said and done he was also subservient to the Prussian War Ministry.

Yet a select band of kindred spirits knew what Hesse in his complicated situation had achieved for a future Europe. Romain Rolland, for instance, who lived near Hesse, noted in his diary in November 1914: "Because Hesse is resident in Switzerland, he is immune to being infected by what's going on in Germany. He addresses intellectuals, writers, artists, and thinkers and deplores seeing them taking part in the war with such bitter gusto."[51]

Stefan Zweig also described in his diary how Hesse's outward appearance had changed over this period, after visiting him on November 23, 1917: "His face has grown sharp, half boyish-looking and yet at the same time resembling that of an old, genteel scholar. A face from the paintings

of Holbein, German, severe, and astute. He speaks like a Swiss now. . . .
He's repelled by small talk and distrustful of former friends, and lives a
very isolated existence."

However, his "politics of conscience," which he formulated time and again
during the First World War while working from Bern, and which goes
hand-in-hand with Rolland's concept of the "conscience of Europe," already signals the beginning of a fundamental sea change in Hesse's work.
The collapse of old Europe becomes for him a prelude of global historical
proportions. In the spring of 1915 he noted in a letter that he regarded a
united Europe as just a preliminary stage in the history of humankind:
"The European spirit with its methodical way of thinking will initially
govern the world, but the culture of the soul and of deeper religious values
is the preserve of the Russians and Asiatic peoples, and over time we will
find that we have need of that also." Here we can see Hesse preparing to
make that transition he completes with regard to both his individual and
the supra-individual history of spiritual concerns in his novel *Demian*. The
direction of travel is already set: "It has become clear that nationalism is
not an ideal, now we have witnessed how morals, culture, and reason have
all become so seriously bankrupt among our spiritual leaders."

Hesse's patriotism had by now been subjected to a nonnegotiable proviso, which he never tired of explaining over the following years: "I will
happily be a patriot, but first and foremost I am a human being, and if the
two don't go together, then I will always side with humanity. Goethe once
said to Eckermann: 'You will always find xenophobia at its strongest and
most violent on the lowest rung of the ladder of civilization.'"[52]

A Salutary Glimpse into the Abyss: Meeting with
J. B. Lang and the Question of
Where the Analysis of Dreams Leads

> But each one is a gamble on the part of nature in attempting
> to create a human being.
>
> —Hermann Hesse, *Demian*

In 1916, Hesse's sense of being deeply ill at ease within his own skin became unbearable. It didn't suit him anymore; it had become too tight and

restrictive for him. A profound inner crisis was choking off his air supply, stifling him. Was should he do? Could he somehow shed his skin, and take on a new form—or would he simply drown in the maelstrom of time like so many others before him?

In March of that year, his father died in Korntal. What a happy life he had led in the service of his calling, without any significant external shocks, and able to follow that one voice which he trusted implicitly! Increasingly, Hesse admired his father for this calm certainty about how to lead a fulfilled life.

The situation in Bern became ever more oppressive. In addition, his wife's mental state was becoming increasingly difficult for him to bear. In the summer of 1917 she took another man into the Welti house, an unemployed person—Hesse was struck dumb with astonishment at her actions. Mia's behavior, which Hesse found quite inexplicable, was the result of an attempt to have herself analyzed. Hesse noted in his "Dream Diary of Psychoanalysis" for the year 1917–1918: "For the first few days after the start of the analysis experiment, Mia seemed very open and inclined to embark on a new, deeper relationship with me. But that has all come to an abrupt end once more." The reason for this was that the amorous impulse that had been awakened in Mia was now being directed at another person, that unemployed man, who was suddenly standing outside their door. He took up residence with them—and because he had no ration card, they had to share all their meager provisions with him. This was a truly bizarre scenario that Hesse found himself confronted by in his own house: "He [the stranger] sleeps in the house, and he spends hours on end having animated discussions with Mia; like she is basking in a newfound, blissful state of love she for the most part seems receptive to anything and everything—except for me, that is. Presumably she doesn't realize it herself, but it is remarkable how, without uttering a single word or displaying any aggression, she can still mange to convey how profoundly weary she is of me."[53]

It was like the first few months of their marriage, only now with another man in place for Hesse. In the evenings, piano music would reverberate through the house, but whenever Hesse ventured downstairs, the stranger was sitting next to Mia on the piano stool. During this period, Hesse noted, he couldn't bear to listen to any kind of music. Pretty soon the interloper wasn't even bothering to do a modicum of work: the firewood that he'd been paid to chop remained untouched.

Hesse's father shortly before his death on March 8, 1916

Hesse wasn't feeling jealousy, he remarked, just a sense of total impotence at being forced to witness how completely superfluous and unwelcome he had become in his own house. He would agree with Mia about almost everything, going along with her belief that she'd found a real treasure in this man: "Some day soon, this workman would be lying in my bed, washing himself with my sponge, and starting to order me about. What would I do then? Things aren't far off this even now: the fellow spends his time lounging around the house and getting paid for having my wife play the piano to him all day long."[54]

On July 26, 1918, Hesse finally reported to his therapist—and his utter bewilderment is still clear from his tone—"The man has gone, and my wife is much calmer and in her general conversation no longer exhibits any alarming signs or a sense that she is disturbed."[55]

All the same, the atmosphere remained tense. Mia showed a tendency to uncontrollable fits of rage directed against him, and over the following months one bizarre scene after another would ensue—for instance, when she threw all of her luggage out of a moving train while returning from a rest-cure or, as Heiner Hesse reported, tried to strangle her youngest son, Martin, while the balance of her mind was disturbed. Hesse knew he would have to act, but he was also aware that it would be hard to get Mia to agree to a separation.

Dr. Josef Bernhard Lang (1881–1945), etching by Gregor Rabinowitsch

Yet it was not just within his family that problems began to mount and threaten to overwhelm him; as he would later reveal in his *Life Story Briefly Told,* he was viewed with suspicion in Bern as an outsider. Admittedly, he would come to realize the full extent of this only in retrospect:

> I was living among diplomats and military men, and what's more I was socializing with people from a wide variety of countries, including enemy states, and the very air surrounding me was one giant web of espionage and counterespionage, of spying, intrigues, and political and personal machinations—and over all the years I was there I noticed none of this! I was sounded out, spied and snooped on, and depending on the particular time was looked upon with suspicion by enemies, neutrals, and my own compatriots, yet all this passed me by, and it was only much later that I got to hear this and that about it, and was at a loss to understand how I could have lived so untouched and unscathed in the midst of this atmosphere.[56]

Hesse felt utterly empty and burned out.

His condition was exacerbated by his certainty that in his father he had lost the only person who naturally and effortlessly embodied the principle of ordered stability within the chaos that was afflicting both the wider world and his own mind, and that his father's example was the only one that could bolster his spirits. He knew that he would never be able to follow his father's path in life; his inner demons were much too strong for that.

His crisis became acute, and a total nervous breakdown loomed. His headaches became unbearably intense. He was plagued by sleeplessness and panic attacks, along with dizzy spells and a debilitating feeling of enervation. He knew that he was seriously ill. A rest cure at the Sonnenmatt Clinic in Lucerne did little good, however. The specialists were unable to explain his condition. In purely physical terms, there were no grounds for his poor state of health. So his case was turned over to a psychiatrist—Josef Bernhard Lang. During that period Lang belonged to the circle of therapists around Carl Jung, and was a psychoanalytical practitioner specializing in the study of dreams.

The meeting between the two men had far-reaching consequences. Lang proved to be exactly the right person for Hesse to talk to at this threshold in his life. Lang had recently been looking into the history of gnosticism, the doctrine of two worlds—the material and the spiritual—which seemed tailor-made for Hesse's doppelgänger principle, and into the creation of opposing but related figures representing the divisions of an entity that was originally whole: for instance day and night, light and dark, and order and chaos.

The problem of the nature of God was no easy one; Hermann Hesse heard very contradictory sounding voices within himself, in which good and evil, reason and instinct, the godly and the satanic intermingled to generate a cacophony of sounds that to his ears did not produce a harmony. What demon was at work there? How could he ever turn this chaos into an order that he trusted? With the interpretation of dreams, an element is introduced into Hesse's stalled writing that clears a path for the "child's soul," within which a dual perspective is also inherent: paradise in competition with hell. Could he successfully lock away one part of the dichotomy—the evil, destructive principle—banish it like his parents had, and lapse into feelings of guilt if he failed? He had known for a long time that he was incapable of this. His route to the fairy tale and to painting was thus set. He had written fairy tales when he was a child, and he had drawn throughout his life, albeit only sporadically. But now it took on a totally different significance. It opened doors, behind which lay a world to which he had not yet had access.

In another sense, too, the encounter with J. B. Lang was a happy co-incidence. The psychiatrist admired Hesse and was keen to help him clear the obstacles that stood in the way of his writing. With Lang, "clearing away" was to be understood almost literally, for he was a sworn enemy of marriage, which he regarded as an institution that needed to be vanquished. All the same, he himself was married, and very erratic in his wishes and desires. This highly neurotic individual would ultimately end up as a patient in the institution where he had once been a doctor.

In Hesse, who nevertheless was an extremely depressive patient, Lang hoped after they met in 1916 to have discovered a friend who could help him become himself. Their recently published correspondence is astonishing. Within a very short space of time, a role reversal took place. Hesse, whose work with the prisoners' charity agency kept him busy in Bern every day, traveled to Lucerne once a week to see Lang. What was billed as therapy was almost certainly more of a conversation between men, but one that was beneficial, at least for Hesse. Inwardly, Lang was on the antibourgeois side, whereas Hesse would never quite relinquish the role of the bourgeois, although during certain phases of his life this was not much more than a mask. Hesse found in Lang a radical thinker who emboldened him to abandon everything that hindered him from following his true vocation. Lang told him that he should not allow himself to be imprisoned in a false bourgeois existence; he must, he urged him, leave his wife and children in order to fully realize himself. Lang was the most important source of support for Hesse in enacting this steadily growing resolution. Moreover, the death of his father brought Hesse's own beginnings vividly to mind once more.

Anyone wishing to know how he has become the person he is must turn to his childhood—and not just to those aspects that have been retained by his conscious mind, but also to those unconscious sources, his hidden desires and neuroses. This is what happened in the first twelve consultations between Hesse and Lang in May 1916, which were followed by another sixty sessions up to the autumn of 1917. As soon as his depression become more bearable, though, Hesse began to look with an artist's eye at the dream material that he and his therapist had brought to light. Before long he was master of the situation and Lang was his "assistant" who tried in vain to follow him into this realm of art.

For Hesse the encounter with Lang became a happy stroke of fortune, through which he found a path of salvation out of his existential and creative crisis. For Lang, however, the course of analysis became a decisive step on his path to self-destruction.

In the fall of 1917, in barely eight weeks, Hesse wrote the novel *Demian*. The sessions with Lang were an inner preparation for this creative act—one might almost say a process of gathering material for the book.

Who Is Demian?

Demian marked a transition. How could one process and get over something that lay far back in the past, right at the beginning of one's life in childhood? Individual psychological and mythical inquiries coalesce in this question. The challenge for the artist was to lend expression to the simultaneous act of leaving something behind and rediscovering it.

Hesse recommended to his publisher Fischer the slim volume that he wrote, as if in a frenzy, in September and October 1917 as the work of an anonymous, young, terminally ill author who did not have long to live and who therefore found it impossible to handle his own affairs. Fischer replied that he personally had not yet found the time to read the debut work of this author whom Hesse had discovered, but that his reader Oskar Loerke was full of praise for it.

Because Hesse here voluntarily placed himself in the role of the debutant author, he had to wait until June 1919 for *Demian* to finally appear in a modest print run of 3,300 copies.

Why did he name the main protagonist of this supposedly autobiographical tale, Emil Sinclair, after a revolutionary friend (Isaac von Sinclair) of the early nineteenth-century German poet Friedrich Hölderlin?

Hesse did not want to publish *Demian* under his own name because he was aware how groundbreaking the novel was. An element of recklessness was also doubtless in play here: Would the book be a success even if his name was not attached to it? The answer was a resounding Yes. Emil Sinclair was even awarded the Fontane Prize of 800 reichsmarks for first-time novelists.

This nom de plume was soon unmasked, however—not by Hesse's publisher or his reader, but the wife of the writer Otto Flake, who identified Hesse behind "Emil Sinclair." After Eduard Korrodi had written an article for the *Neue Zürcher Zeitung* a year after the publication of the book, entitled "Who Is the Author of *Demian*?," Hesse confessed in an interview for the magazine *Vivos voco*—and handed back the Fontane Prize that had been awarded to Emil Sinclair. The German-language literary scene had a scandal, but it did not affect the sales of the book in the slightest—on the contrary, the public would not have credited "old uncle" Hermann Hesse with so much playful and youthful exuberance.

"Emil Sinclair" became the new voice of a generation of youth who had lost their innocence in the trenches of the First World War. Hesse felt part of that generation with *Demian*. For who is this Demian? First and foremost the person responsible for the spiritual awakening of Emil Sinclair, a kind of soul-guide who is well-versed in gnostic symbolism and immediately recognizes the mythical bird Abraxas above the door of Sinclair's parents' house. A sign! Indeed, everything here is replete with signs, for the slim book is written in a form of secret code, very much in the style of *Steppenwolf*—which content-wise represents a direct extension of *Demian*, and where there is a door marked "Reserved for the Insane." So who were these lunatics in an age that was witnessing the collapse of the bourgeois world? Individuals who did not fit into the conventional scheme of things, outsiders, and people branded as heretics since time immemorial—those who carry the mark of Cain, which branded them as outcasts from society.

Demian tells the story of a birth which at the same time is also a death: *à propos* those metamorphoses of individuation, in which something always opens and simultaneously closes. Hesse noted: "The name Demian was not invented or chosen at random by me; instead I became acquainted with it in a dream, and it spoke so strongly to me that I made it the title of the book."[57]

The story has a structure that can hardly be recounted in rational terms. It turns away from external matters almost entirely and instead looks inward to tell the psychological story of a person growing up. Most of the figures that appear in this book are fragments of Emil Sinclair's own psyche, and by extension of the author Hermann Hesse.

Hugo Ball identified in the progression from *Hermann Lauscher* to *Demian* a consistent shift toward inwardness. Here a dream is recounted that no longer distinguishes between the waking state and the sleeping state.

And so Max Demian, Emil Sinclair's mysterious friend, becomes a "great seducer to life," in the words of Hugo Ball: "Through him there speaks a Dionysian voice, and an Apollonian responds to it. This, then, is the genesis of one of the strangest and most profound books in German literature: a Songs of Songs from a friend who carries the mysteries and traits of Providence in his enigmatic face."

There has been no shortage of suppositions about who might have been the model for Max Demian. Hesse's fellow pupil at Maulbronn Gustav Zeller or Gusto Gräser from Monte Verità have been suggested—however, these seem inadequate or even far-fetched attributions which ignore the fact that Hesse was portraying a general principle through this character. Hugo Ball called this the "daemon" that Demian represents for Emil Sinclair. If we understand "daemon" in the sense of that *Daimonion* which Socrates identifies as a person's inner voice—one that neither persuades him or her to do anything nor insinuates, but is exclusively there in order to dissuade or warn them off a course of action—then we arrive at a very modern translation for the figure of Demian—namely, the voice of conscience.

That was surely appropriate, and yet when one considers that, with the first three chapters of *Demian* ("Two Realms," "Cain," and "Among Thieves") Hesse entered into the gnostic mythology of Abraxas, we must also factor in a magical dimension—the connection between the Self and the world in a transformative moment. This immediate exhibition of the truth was a form of mysticism.

In a letter of December 12, 1917, J. B. Lang offered a hint that has hitherto been disregarded as to the possible identity of Demian. This occurs in the context of a discussion of the composer Othmar Schoeck and the "Umbrian principle," which Lang states that he cannot yet fully define. By this he meant the sphere of ideas within which Hesse and Lang were operating in the fall of 1917, the time when *Demian* was conceived and written: that same landscape that had given rise to Giotto's frescoes in the spirit of St. Francis of Assisi. The theme of music as the most elemental and most existential form of art is brought to the theme of painting, and in the process the ecstatic Dionysian and the pictorial Apollonian principles harmonize together anew, against the background of the globally historical catastrophe of the war and of Hesse's family drama. What can save him? Art? or only a new religion?

Hesse's understanding of art is broadened here by adding the dimension of a mythology that draws upon the unconscious both of the individual and of whole peoples. The fact that in his letter Lang discusses Goethe, who appears in the chapter "Eva" in *Demian,* shows how intensively Hesse was playing with the magical motifs of Goethe. Lang was the first person permitted to read the manuscript. He recapitulated: "Only *with* Homunculus, the child of personal knowledge, can Faust chance his creative descent into the realms of the Underworld, the place where he is first able to enter into an intimate relationship with Helen, the most beautiful woman of ancient times, who draws him toward the East and with whom he will conceive Euphorion, though in the end all that remains to him of their son is his clothes."[58]

In the figure of Sinclair-Demian we see the strong emergence of Hesse's principle of contrasting pairs, where a person can form a whole only in conjunction with his matching opposite. This creative relationship of the Dionysian (Demian) with the Apollonian (Sinclair)—which was for Hesse a kind of "white magic"—reveals friendship and creativity, eroticism and art. Pure visual forms of individuation. This is also a question of power, something that it is vital to contain within ritual in order to prevent it from serving base destructive purposes. Sinclair has allowed the boy next door, Franz Kromer, to gain power him, and Kromer torments him for it, standing for a form of "black magic," which always serves a banal end—namely, the pursuit of money and dominance.

Demian, the friend who saves him, the fellow pupil as a figure of enlightenment, appears here as a potentiality within Emil Sinclair to grow up, a draft version of his Self. Franz Kromer embodies reality as it is, that primitive and power-seeking type of "man of action" that the boy already finds unacceptable, and which was anathema to Hesse also. "Naturally the boy Kromer also lives out his urges. He does this on the basest level and will, if he doesn't ever raise his sights, end up either as a bank director or a convicted criminal."[59]

In the figure of Demian, Hesse created—in the Freudian sense—a kind of superego of Emil Sinclair. A game of identities. A glance into the mirror, which reveals both heaven and hell. Demian: the uncanny one.

I am a multiplicity of characters. A spectrum of images whose respective degrees of reality can never be proved. Confusions between dream and reality are therefore unavoidable, but also disastrous in individual cases, as when one kills a real person instead of a figment of one's imagination. How quickly can one become a criminal? The first text Hesse wrote after *Demian* when he arrived in Montagnola in the spring of 1919—by which time he knew he was in an even deeper crisis than ever—was *Klein and Wagner,* a Jekyll-and-Hyde story that represents nothing less than a (his!) fantasy of murder.

The old Pietist motif shines through, yet it is taken to the extreme in artistic terms. Man proceeds on his narrow way through life, with the forces of light and darkness competing for control of his soul. In such circumstances, can we expect the artist to play with the devil and get off scot-free?

In *Demian* Hesse liberated himself from the stigmatization of his parents' world of Christian symbolism by reinterpreting it in the sense of a philosophy of the Unconscious and thereby lending it a psychological dimension. The gnostic motif of the two realms is something that he had long since consciously developed as a form of expression—in terms of the doppelgänger motif—yet his conversations with J. B. Lang, who had embraced gnosticism as his worldview (which Hesse would not follow him in doing), deepened his instinct for the esthetic possibilities of such a central symbol as Abraxas. As we read, this mythical-gnostic avian god automatically invokes in us thoughts of the phoenix rising from the ashes of something on fire: "Anyone wishing to be born must necessarily destroy a world."

In *Demian* Hesse's ties to the world of his father, which seemed long ruptured, are in evidence once more—yet they now appear not as shackles but as something connecting in a positive sense. The gravestone of his father, who had died the previous year, had been engraved with the guiding motto of Johannes Hesse's life, a sentiment in which his son—in however different a manner, nevertheless in the same sense of individuation—also recognized himself: "The halter is severed, the bird is free." Hesse adapted this for the heading of the fifth chapter in *Demian:* "The Bird Fights Its Way Out of the Egg."

Abraxas appears here as a hermaphroditic creature, whose mysterious figure lends tangible form to the concept of metamorphosis. We live our lives on a straight course to death, and in our demise life begins again afresh. This bird is just as divine as it is devilish, a silhouette of the constant transformation of good into evil and vice versa, a play of light and shade.

So it was that Hesse's concept of reality changed fundamentally with *Demian.* To borrow Calderón's famous phrase, life is a dream. Or as Novalis, whom Hesse quotes in *Demian,* puts it in the novel *Heinrich von Ofterdingen:* "Destiny and soul are two names for a single idea." In other words: anything that happens to a person in their life is not chance but follows a plan ordained by fate that everyone carries within them right from the start. This is shown by the "mark of Cain" that those individuals who are different from most people carry on their forehead—the chosen ones who appear in the form of mistrusted or even despised outsiders. According to Hesse, Cain was someone who should be seen not just as a criminal but also as a person who resolves to carry out a deed that will change his life.

The erotic dimension that Hesse gives to the encounter between Sinclair and Demian is intriguing. Existing as he does under the sign of Abraxas, Demian is a thoroughly androgynous figure. Hesse also uses the figure to express an autoerotic attitude (let us not forget that Demian is his alter ego!), that of Narcissus, without whom no artist would ever create his works. Here that role-play with potentials of the Self is already being raised into the realms of the archetypal (C. G. Jung) and the unconscious (Freud). On January 26, 1920, Hesse sent a letter to J. B. Lang, and what he wrote only superficially has to do with the question of the pseudonym Emil Sinclair, under which *Demian* had first appeared, a game of hide-and-seek that was soon to be exposed: "Increasingly there are some troublesome signs that people are beginning to guess who the author is. I beg you not to fuel this speculation! I'm sure it will happen, but I'm sorry—I'd rather have remained anonymous. What I'd really like to do is to publish every work I write from now on under a new pseudonym. When all's said and done I'm not Hesse, but I was Sinclair, I was Klingsor, I was Klein, etc. and will be several other people."[60]

★   ★   ★

Above all, *Demian*'s significance for Hesse was that it set him on a path toward acknowledging the contradiction at the center of his life. The sources he drew upon were not clear and pure. The same thing happens to Demian the first time he falls in love with a girl, whom he calls Beatrice. Other than that, we learn very little more about her. The only thing that does become apparent is that this first encounter with the opposite sex passes him by without leaving a trace. But the resolution of the conflict of puberty—which for Hesse is not resolved with the passing of puberty but instead carries on!—is in no way a transformation of dark chaos into bright light, or of compulsive behavior into reason. Art makes no attempt to sever its roots in nature—and this nature has a dual aspect. On the one hand, growing and fruitfully attaining full bloom and beauty, while simultaneously being cruel and destructive. A cycle of birth and death. And it is the poet's lot to try to find a way to express this simultaneity and give it a form that is authentic. And so Demian begins to paint a picture of Beatrice, he dreams of her: "With a wildly beating heart. I stared at the sheet of paper, at the thick, brown hair, the half-womanly mouth, the strong forehead with its curious brightness (it had dried on the page to this color), and I felt an increasingly intimate sense of recognition, of recovery, and of knowledge." But then, on closer inspection, he experiences a shock, albeit mingled with a moment of bliss: "And gradually I began to get a sense that this wasn't Beatrice or Demian, but—myself. The picture did not resemble me, it's true—nor ought it to, I felt—but it did represent what constituted my life, it was my innermost being, my destiny, or my daemon."[61]

The figure of Eva in Demian represents a lover who at the same time should be a mother. For Hesse, too, his wife Mia was a kind of mother substitute, but without the erotic fascination that he portrays here in Eva. When creating Eva, he had in mind not only Goethe's "Descent to the Mothers" in *Faust,* part 2, but also Swiss anthropologist Johann Jakob Bachofen's myth of the "Great Mother." Furthermore, J. B. Lang, the psychotherapist and increasingly the friend who came to Hesse seeking advice, also makes an appearance in Demian, as Pistorius, the eccentric organist who guides Sinclair to his hidden Self, and whom he must also ultimately overcome in order to become himself.

Abraxas is also identifiable in the bird of prey, in the not only endangered but also at the same time dangerous Ego, which, in order to arrive at its own world, always has to destroy another. The cult around Beatrice finally reveals a stylization of love so extreme that it becomes an arid abstraction. Sinclair dreams of her, and her image transforms into that of Demian—and ultimately ends up taking on his own features. Even here, then, the way to love leads through a hall of mirrors composed of dream images (a Magic Theater!), where one thing changes into another. The opposite of all things is not only conceivable, but also capable of being lived out. This principle is embodied in Abraxas, the god of the living paradox: "Love was no longer a bestially dark impulse, in the way that I had fearfully experienced it at the outset, nor was it any longer the pious and spiritual adoration that I had offered up to Beatrice's picture. It was both of these things, and much more besides, it was an angelic image and Satan, man and woman in one body, human and animal, the greatest good and the greatest evil. I appeared destined to live this out, and it seemed my fate to taste this."[62]

Esotericism, Astrology, and Ghost Stories: Hesse Goes in Search of Magic and Magnetism

The author in crisis succeeded in setting free new forces, and in renewing himself with the help of his analyst. Lang, however, found Hesse assigning him more and more practical tasks, which he willingly took on. For example, it was Lang who eventually conducted negotiations with Mia's brother, who was responsible for managing her financial affairs, concerning how to proceed with the divorce. In all his endeavors, Lang was something of an esotericist, who aimed to reach great heights by means of gnosticism. Hesse took from him the things he found useful, even trying out astrology, which Lang took very seriously, and having a horoscope prepared for himself. This was the only one he ever commissioned, however.

In 1926 Hesse released under the Fischer imprint the volume *Pages from Prevorst,* with the subtitle "A Selection of Reports on Magnetism, Clairvoyance, and Spectral Apparitions, and so on from the Circle of Justinus Kerner and His Friends." The subject matter concerned the "Visionary of Prevorst" (a German woman in the early nineteenth century who experienced prophetic visions and dreams, and was treated by the local doctor Justinus Kerner), familiar spirits, recurrent premonitions of death, and the revenant spirits of the deceased. What was Hesse's interest in such phenomena? The remarkable coincidence of improbable circumstances takes on a particular quality in these stories, as does the existence of a form of knowledge that transcends what is governed by reason, that sense that points toward realms in which extraordinary individual occurrences become charged with a mythical significance. For Hesse this presented a route into the unconscious, into dream regions—a path he was beginning to explore in his discussions with J. B. Lang.

Were stigmatizations perhaps an expression of a hysterical constitution, and did symptoms of illnesses conceal within them general symbols of existence, for which one had to have a particular sense? Hesse was very open to these kinds of inquiries during this period. He got hold of a selection of late Romantic texts, which had already been published in 1831 under the title of "Pages from Prevorst." One of the contributors was a Franz Baader. These were texts from that phase of Romanticism when the movement began to take a turn toward things Catholic and restorative. Nevertheless, Hesse discovered within these writings a hidden spirit that had been ignored by science and technology: "Cases of the possessed, of clairvoyants and other mediums, and of other inspired individuals were commonplace at that time, or at least the interest shown in such phenomena back then was especially great. A contemporary of the Visionary of Prevorst was Katharina Emmerich, whose amanuensis and publisher was Clemens Brentano."[63]

At the same time as he was undergoing psychoanalysis, Hesse had a horoscope drawn up for him which he found extremely accurate, though that was no coincidence, since the astrologer was Joseph Englert, who lived in neighboring Lugano. This engineer was extremely well acquainted with Hesse's family circumstances. It was not that Hesse had actually expected the horoscope to provide him with answers about his life. These, he knew, did not lie in the stars. But he was intrigued by the technique of creating a horoscope, by the manner in which connections were made between the most general cosmic constellations and an individual's fate in life. That assumed a positively mythical dimension for him, in which one might discover first and foremost certain esthetic facets. In other words: Only someone who expected no answers from a horoscope could hope to actually discover something in one. It was not by chance that that horoscope-making engineer Englert makes an appearance in *Klingsor's Last Summer* as the "Armenian" and the "Stargazer," and in *Journey to the East* as the magician Jup.

★　　★　　★

Hesse was in no doubt that things signify not only themselves but also something hidden from us that has nothing to do with their manifest character. Hence his passion also for stories about ghosts and witches. What is the origin of these unseen forces that guide us in our lives, leading us toward certain people and then away from them again, and what is it that engenders love and hate within us? How can individual words take on such a life-changing, even world-changing, power? How can some words become magical spells—and what implications does that have for poets? If Europe is in terminal decline, what new entity is on the rise? Will there be any omens of this?

All these questions were burning within Hesse. Like Dostoyevsky had, he was gazing quite literally into a state of chaos. Yet something kept him from fully embracing esotericism: he did not believe in simple explanations of the world, or in the idea that the world could be improved. Sects were just as suspect to him as political parties. As a result, he remained an interested spectator who kept his distance, as he emphasized in the afterword to *Pages from Prevorst:* "Now I would like to note expressly that despite having had a lot to do with magical and so-called occult matters, I have never found any cause to adopt the faith of the spiritualists in any of its versions. . . . The tide of belief in spirits is once more on the rise today. However, what gave me the impulse to publish Kerner's ghost stories was not this, but instead the conviction that in the past these phenomena were considered more purely and profoundly than is the case nowadays."[64]

Yet Hesse increasingly distanced himself from the occultists—despite his great interest in the phenomena of life that cannot be proved scientifically—just as he had taken a distanced attitude to the "reformers" and "world-improvers" at Monte Verità, people he had originally viewed with sympathy. Every trace of fanaticism disturbed him, and any kind of practical application of an idea awakened the skeptic in him, the person who was adept at defending his solitude as the thing he prized most highly against the greedy, importunate nature of communities. He therefore made this clear to J. B. Lang also, who was plaguing him with his favorite topic of esotericism at the time. On June 5, 1922, Hesse wrote to Lang to congratulate him on getting so far in his study of astrology: "I really do envy you the doggedness with which you conduct such studies." And yet—the word "really" gives it away—this letter is a clear rejection of Lang's attempts at proselytizing: "I'm not familiar with those 'magic pages' that you wrote about, and in general I know next to nothing about the newest 'occult' literature. I've actually grown rather tired of these things, especially the crassness with which every sect makes its own specialty the main event and pronounces their symbols to be 'facts.'"[65] And in his very next letter he repeats this rejection, while at the same time making friendly efforts to include Lang in his take on things: "You're right, and like you, the thing I find off-putting about all these sects and religious and occultist foundations is the rigid system they espouse, plus the ambiguity of symbols is something that Europeans cannot easily take on board. Thus, things like anthroposophy come into being with some very appealing aspects but also weighed down with this Pharisaism and Catholicism."[66]

And yet precisely through his close contact with the astrologer and engineer Englert, something occurred that was of great significance for Hesse's subsequent writing: magic and transformation become decisive themes. In those years since starting psychoanalytic therapy and since his hostile reception in Germany as a traitor to the fatherland, his concept of reality had become quite different. In his *Life Story Briefly Told* of 1925, he would come to formulate the famous credo without which his work after *Demian* would be unintelligible:

> People claim that I have no sense of reality. The poems I write as well as the little pictures I paint do not correspond with reality. When I write I often forget all the demands that educated readers make of a proper book, and above all I really do lack any respect for reality. I deem reality the last thing that one need concern oneself about, for it is, tediously enough, ever-present, whereas more beautiful and necessary things demand our attention and care. Reality is something that one should under no circumstances be content with, and under no circumstances worship and revere, for it is accidental, the flotsam and jetsam of life. And it can be altered in no other way—this shabby, consistently disappointing and barren reality—except by our denying it and thereby demonstrating that we are stronger than it is.[67]

Being stronger than reality? That sounds like a self-destructive claim, yet Hesse means to denote by this, not open warfare against reality, but instead vanquishing one's adversaries by trying to charm them. If that doesn't work, his alternative is simply to make himself invisible to his opponent.

In this same essay Hesse admits that he often sees and feels that the connection between his inner world and the outer world comes about in a magical way, with the result that his life appears to him like some fairy tale.

A new sense of "being in the world" requires a new way of writing about it. And Hesse increasingly wrote about the inner world, because this was the real place where transformation occurred. Accordingly he turned toward "practical magic": "Now by means of magic I manipulated this reality according to my wishes and I must confess I took a great deal of pleasure in doing so."[68]

Nor did he just use harmless white magic, but also black magic. He played with the daemon that emerged from the abyss that he carried within him. As a result, an ironic distance enters Hesse's writing—as when he thinks he is being pursued by the emissaries of reality and finds himself in jail once more for having seduced a young girl. But here he proves that he has the capacity to enchant just as much with words as he can with paints. In the closing image of *Life Story Briefly Told,* he subjects his external existence to a magical exercise, which is the only way he can save himself from the world:

> Then I made myself small and stepped into my picture, climbed aboard my little railroad train and rode in the little train into the black tunnel. For a while, sooty smoke continued to billow out of the round hole, then the smoke dispersed and cleared with it the entire picture and I along with it.
> The guards remained behind in great embarrassment.[69]

Even during his time in his parents' house this connection with the occult existed, a fact that Hesse found himself reminded of when he read C. G. Jung's book *On the Psychology and Pathology of So-Called Occult Phenomena* in December 1917. He made the following observation in his diary: "Such memories resonated in our house as well. My grandfather was friends with Professor Schubert, who at the time was the most renowned Christian mystic and author of *The Dark Side of Nature.* Schubert's bust stood in the hallway of our house."[70] Nor should it be forgotten that the most important spiritual leader in his parents' lives, Johann Christoph Blumhardt (the Elder) in Bad Boll, was a famous faith healer and exorcist! Hence Hesse's knowledge of the "Visionary of Prevorst," who represented a phenomenon similar to that of the "lover of God" on whom Blumhardt practiced in his capacity as an expeller of devils. This young woman was reputed to be tormented by demons, who inflicted life-threatening injuries on her—and Blumhardt battled these for two long years with passages from the Bible. Then her attacks abated, her recovery was ascribed to Blumhardt's intervention, and he kept the "lover of God" on as his housekeeper for almost thirty years thereafter until her death.

Legends such as this played a key role in the Hesse household; his parents firmly believed in a form of possession by demons and in exorcism. For Hesse, however, who did not share their faith, it was a familiar atmosphere in which he was not unhappy to operate. Nor did he find it odd that his friend Hugo Ball began to take an interest in exorcism shortly before his death.

And even as late as 1960, on the occasion of a review of Ernst Jünger's *An der Zeitmauer* (At the Wall of Time), which he had read with great approval, Hesse still spoke of the "beautiful symbolic language of this noble art," by which he meant astrology. Jünger, Hesse maintained, had not "betrayed his belief in the value of astrological forecasts," despite the fact that he viewed the appearance of horoscopes as a sure sign of the decline of an age.[71] That sounds approving.

Demian was aimed at the generation of returnees from the First World War. It is a record of a self-liberation from a false self-image. The rebirth of the Ego in the affirmation of the paradox of the destruction and re-creation. Abraxas as a symbol of a rebirth that does not avoid danger but heads straight toward it—this is the strong signal from a person who is facing an uncertain future. As was everyone else, the whole of Germany, the whole of Europe.

Yet the writing of *Demian,* this renunciation in the spirit of Nietzsche of all cults of leadership and every ideology involving devoted followers, brought Hesse something that he precisely wanted to exclude through this creative act: for many people he himself now became a "leader," and those returning from the war to a land that had become alien to them felt like people bearing the mark of Cain, who only recognize one another. These comprised an explosive mixture of adherents of the extreme right and extreme left, and believers in a cult of fate, esoteric pacifism, esthetic self-stylization, and militant questing for an ideology. Hesse could feel himself to be misunderstood by all of these followers in their own different ways—and precisely that was the also a main theme of *Demian*.

Hanns Johst, who later became head of the "Reich Writers' Guild" under the Nazis, was one of these aggressive young authors. He reviewed *Demian* for the *Neue Rundschau* magazine—and likewise gave a signal, though his was by way of political action. During this immediate postwar period, the intellectual spectrum was taking shape: Johst was on the far right; Arnolt Bronnen flitted, will-o'-the-wisp-like, between right and left; Bertolt Brecht initially posed as an anarchist before assuming a position on the left. The motif of "patricide" was in the air, and Hesse, who was adamant that he stood alone and did not belong to any political party, and indeed who made it clear that it was his intention to transcend the political sphere as a whole, found himself swept up in these struggles. Yet Hesse acknowledged that the seething discontent that was being articulated so violently by these writers did deserve to be taken seriously; Hesse was someone who granted almost everyone the right to have their say and to have it heard, excluding virtually no one *a priori*.

Alfred Rosenberg was one of the few people Hesse ignored, and Rosenberg would subsequently hold this against him. In 1933 he sent Hesse his book *The Myth of the 20th Century* for review; quite contrary to his usual custom, Hesse gave no response. He reacted quite differently to Rosenberg's far-right colleague Johst. Hesse reviewed Johst's publications, beginning with the poetry volume *The Call of Roland* for the magazine *Vivos voco* immediately after the First World War in 1919. He submitted a brief, though friendly, piece in which he praised the authenticity of each of these young voices: "from his mouth there speaks the best of German youth, who marched off to join the war so innocently, so devoutly, and with such infatuation, and who now stand there so disillusioned, so perplexed, and yet who still have no choice but to search for some faith, some love, and some kind of future." Nowadays we can only read the final sentence of this review with a feeling of horror over what was to come, yet Hesse could not possibly have had any inkling of it: "He is right, and his spirit will triumph."[72] Should Hesse have excused himself for placing more confidence in young writers than they would subsequently prove to have merited? No, it was one of his best qualities that he was able to keep his vision unclouded for new talent that had the capacity to irritate and provoke, emanating as it did from genuine spiritual experience. He would retain this openness throughout his life and rarely put a foot wrong; he was often one of the first to discover books that others had paid no attention to. In the process he walked a tightrope across an abyss. However, there was no alternative to seeking out the spirit in its most dangerous places, for it was only there that anything significant arose. Even so, Hesse's innate sense for disastrous transgressions of the spiritual and mythical into the esoteric and the ideological saved him from aligning himself with any obscure doctrines. No, for all his readiness to be enthralled, Hesse the Romantic still remained a coolly detached observer. It was in this spirit that he wrote to Peter Suhrkamp on April 27, 1935, about Julius Evola's *Revolt against the Modern World:*

> This dazzling and interesting, but also genuinely dangerous author is a classic example of a certain mode of seemingly transposing esoteric learning into exoteric knowledge. Except in the process the purity of the categories really ought to be retained to some extent, whereas Evola, in a quite wild and dilettantish and domineering manner, muddles these all up. I largely share his exoteric basic view; for almost twenty years I have ceased to see world history in terms of some kind of "progress'" but instead, like the ancient Chinese, as the gradual decline of an order that was once divine. But the way in which Evola bandies about his superficial knowledge, sometimes dealing with "'real'" history, and at other times with pretentious occultism, is nothing but reckless. In Italy virtually no one will be taken in by him anymore, but the situation is different in Germany (see G. Benn, etc.).[73]

Exchanging Roles with His Therapist: The Uses and Drawbacks of Psychoanalysis for the Artist

At its start the correspondence between Lang and Hesse followed the conventional roles for doctor and patient. The first communication, dated April 1916, is very brief: "Dear Doctor! Camenzind here. I'll come and see you again tomorrow at 4.30 after we have skipped the consultation. No dreams. Kind regards, Yours H. Hesse."[74]

No dreams? That would soon change. Hesse sent Lang *Flute Dream,* a fairy tale that he had written in 1912, although it was, as he added in a note, "quite consciously made up, with no recollection of dreams." It anticipated many of the topics they would discuss in their sessions, regarding symbols of growing up or ways in which a person finds his true self. As a result, Hesse would formulate his new standpoint as a motto prefacing the introduction to *Demian:* "All I really wanted was to try and live the life that was welling up unbidden inside of me. Why was that proving so difficult?"

It was indeed difficult, but it was worthwhile opening himself up to his suppressed fears and his unacknowledged desires. These were a unique treasure trove, provided one knew how to exploit them as foundational material for new artistic forms. Lang attempted to follow him in this, sending Hesse his own dream chronicles and asking him to appraise them. He too had ambitions to be a writer—and it was no easy task for Hesse to explain to him that what he sent was little more than material for psychotherapy. Lang found it hard to accept this harsh judgment of his writing. A letter from Lang to Hesse in the spring of 1918 contains the surprising confession: "For me, you are the kindly father leading me toward art."[75]

Clearly on display, here, is an astonishingly swift reversal of roles. Hesse's crises are still there, but considering them now in different light, he writes something that goes far beyond a simple dream diary. Instead it is a modern myth concerning the never-changing difficulties of becoming a grown-up without killing the child one once was. And there is something more besides: precisely as a result of deep subjectivity, the symbolism in *Demian* raises it to the status of a very special record—hitherto unknown in twentieth-century literature—of an age cleft by a deep and violent rupture. Could the soul of Europe, badly damaged by war, ever be healed again? That struck the nerve of his readers in the aftermath of the First World War. On the very first pages of Demian, they found a succinct summary of the drama of their lives during and after the catastrophe:

> Admittedly, people today have less understanding than ever before of what constitutes a real living, breathing person; indeed, human beings, each of whom is a priceless, unique experiment of nature, are still being shot down in droves. If we weren't something more than unique individuals, if we could really be wiped off the face of this Earth by the simple expedient of a bullet, then there wouldn't be any point in telling stories anymore. However, each person is not just himself, he is also the unique, very special point, important and remarkable in every case, where the decisions of the world intersect, for one time only and never again in the same way. . . . Few people nowadays know what man is.[76]

Here, Hesse reaches new heights of questioning, delving deep not just into the unconscious state of the individual, but also into the subconscious regions of human history. With *Demian,* Hesse became modernism's myth-creator par excellence, a mystic with the capacity to lend literary form to the paradox of the eternal moment. "I was a seeker, and I still am, but I no longer search in the stars or in books; instead, I am beginning to heed the lessons of the blood coursing through my veins. My story is not a pleasant one, it is not sweet and harmonious like the made-up stories; it tastes of folly and confusion, of madness and dreams like the life of all people who no longer wish to tell themselves lies." This speech—which like Nietzsche's *Zarathustra* presented a great liberating blow, and which ascended from being a simple personal confession into the coldest regions of abandonment of the Self and descended into the most private structures of human coexistence—pained and frightened him, precisely because of its barely concealed prophetic nature, which like Nietzsche delivered a hard and skeptical slap in the face to any notion of leadership toward a new existence (the kind of messianic role J. B. Lang dreamed of!): "We can understand one another, but each individual one of us can only be interpreted by himself."[77]

The starting point of memory is when a person admits his own weakness and sets aside the triumphant image of his own biography. Thus, it is not a question of "I have triumphed," nor yet of "I was proved right"—but on the contrary, of "I have succumbed, I was horribly mistaken. And yet for all that, something has remained that is valuable, though it is something different from what I previously thought. I must first learn how to discover this valuable thing." This is the substance of *Demian.*

The story of Emil Sinclair's childhood and youth appeared new in every respect: the reality it conveyed was different from before and the way of writing about it was too. Hesse opened himself to this in his unconventional relationship with J. B. Lang. Behind this lay something more—and ultimately something qualitatively different—than the ruins of his self-image as an author, citizen, husband, and father of the prewar era. He now began again at the bottom of the heap, with all the anxieties of his childhood and his shame at not being like other people.

At the outset, for the child—and later for the adult—there are two worlds: that of childhood and that of adults. But that is a mistake. The two worlds are not those: instead, there is the world of normal, daytime people trapped in their humdrum existence, and the world of nocturnal dream-animals, who during daylight hours are regarded as useless or even annoying outsiders. But what is it that the nocturnal dreamers know, and that the rest of humanity has forgotten?

This perspective was neither new nor a discovery of psychoanalysis, but instead was a principal theme of Romanticism. Yet his conversations with Lang were the first time Hesse experienced detailed discussions of the intimate side of corporeal existence, in all its susceptibility to interference by prevailing norms. He had never before been able to speak so candidly about his difficult puberty, either to his parents or to his prewar readership, as he did in this letter of June 22, 1918, to J. B. Lang:

> After reading some medical histories, I recalled that as a child I suffered a long period of bed-wetting—at least until I was eleven years old—which nothing could cure. Likewise, whenever I was excited, especially when I was laughing, my bladder would often empty itself involuntarily. In addition, I also remembered that from a very early age (around seven years) I could sometimes evoke pleasurable sensations by playing with my genitals. What brought this all back to me was the fact that I remembered how once in Basel a family friend with whom I was walking down the street made me take my hand out of my pocket by saying to me: "Playing pocket pool, then, are you?"[78]

Important motifs in *Steppenwolf* are anticipated here: also, the Magic Theater as a realm of unconscious self-awareness, as a laboratory of dreams, is already laid out in *Demian*. And doesn't Demian sound in some passages like Harry Haller's alter ego, Hermine? For example, when he, in that quietly superior way of speaking he has—but precisely, in its motherly tone, indicating that he will tolerate no contradiction—insists like a good daemon, after the evil daemon Kromer has just walked past them:

> Look here, if you jump like that when someone appears who has never done you any harm, it will set that someone thinking. It surprises him, it makes him curious. Then that someone thinks to himself: it's remarkable how easily you get scared, and he keeps on pondering: people only get that nervous when they're anxious about something. Of course, cowards are on a

constant state of fear, but I don't believe that you're really a coward. Are you? Admittedly, you're no hero either. It's just there are certain things that scare you, and people you're afraid of. But that should never be the case. No, no one should never be afraid of people.[79]

This was the fear of a boy in puberty, whose familiar life has become alien to him, and who sees himself as cut off from the peaceful world of childhood by his sexuality, which appears threatening to him. That was something his parents were unable to help him with. They couldn't protect him, cast adrift suddenly as he was on the open seas of life. And something else also shone through this terror of the erotic: the fear of death. "My condition during that period was a sort of insanity. In the midst of our household's orderly, peaceful existence, I was living as timid and tormented as a ghost; I took no part in the lives of others, and rarely took my mind off my own troubles even for an hour."[80]

And that was exactly Hesse's condition in the autumn of 1917 when he embarked on his course of psychoanalysis with J. B. Lang: an artist who rejected the citizen, the husband, and the father as alien roles and who as a result was almost dying of a guilty conscience. On March 1, 1919, he wrote to Lang: "I continue to burn in the hell of my circumstances, and am watching my former existence crumble before my eyes, piece by piece, and can see no future. I have been living alone once more for several months, without my wife and children, and am clinging to the three consolations of my younger years: literary work, alcohol, and in the background the comforting thought of suicide."[81]

The first description of Max Demian sounds like a confirmation of what Hugo Ball wrote about Hesse: that as a young man, he was already old—and thereafter got progressively younger. There is no shortage of descriptions of this phenomenon in Hesse's work; indeed, it seemed that he was intent on illuminating every nook and cranny of this strangely alien and yet familiar figure: "This extraordinary pupil seemed so much older than he appeared; no one got the impression that he was just a lad. He moved among us childish boys like a stranger, with the poise of a man, a gentleman even. He wasn't popular, and he didn't take part in any of our games, still less our fights, and it was only his self-confident and decisive tone when he addressed the teachers that really impressed the rest of us."[82]

Hesse was skeptical and became even more so regarding Lang's deep involvement with esotericism. Consequently, over the following years he preferred to seek out the company of C. G. Jung. He even underwent a course of therapy with him, but both Hesse and Jung were well aware that after *Demian,* the writer had long since held the key to his own psychological recuperation in his own hands. He shared Jung's skepticism regarding the benefit of psychoanalysis for artists. And yet who could be expected to be more open to his hidden dark and destructive sides but also—in the most fortunate case—have the power to express them and assign to them a figure of esthetic value than an artist? According to Hesse, an interest in psychoanalysis was all very well—but what value did it have for writing?

Hesse's view—and in this he followed Dostoyevsky and Nietzsche, who had already displayed a past mastership in it—was that every artist should also be a psychoanalyst. He must divine the atmosphere a person inhabits, and sniff out what has hitherto remained hidden to him. The artist requires a positively Chekhovian talent for knowing humanity, which did not automatically mean that he had to be a philanthropist of the most general kind. No, without the ability to cast a malevolent eye on himself and others, the artist would scarcely be in a position to attempt to "gaze into chaos" (that is, into the unconscious), and without the benefit of distance, would sink into the maelstrom of destruction.

Hesse reflected on this subject in his essay "The Artist and Psychoanalysis" (1918). There is already a great deal of skepticism apparent when he writes: "Just as historical knowledge alone does not make a person capable of writing historical fiction, and the study of botany or geology does not guarantee a successful rendition of landscape, so the best academic psychologist cannot help you portray human beings." So, psychoanalysis remained an auxiliary discipline, an instrument that—in the right hands—could help enhance one's self-knowledge but did not automatically do so. Psychoanalysis applied to a vivid dream, the interpretation of the intuitive, most certainly did have the capacity to serve the artist as an impetus for his own creativity, but it could also bring about the opposite. For the secret of the mythical oneiric realm, in which all art has its origins, should never be demystified. In the interim, Hesse had gained a very precise impression of what it would be like to be fated no longer to shape his dreams into artistic form but instead to interpret them according to set patterns. The warning was loud and clear—he would do well not to ignore the danger that he identified for the artist in the discipline of psychoanalysis, should that artist lack sufficient strength to leave behind the analyst, who in a particular phase of his life had acted as a kind of soul guide, and to free himself from his state of dependency. This is exactly what Hesse undertook in *Demian;* he had absorbed psychoanalysis without abandoning himself totally to it, and he was well aware of the great danger of succumbing to that temptation in a crisis: "What psychoanalysis had identified and scientifically formulated was something that writers had always known about; indeed, the poet turned out to be a representative of a special kind of thinking that was at complete variance with the analytical–psychological mode of thought. The poet was the dreamer, whereas the analyst was the interpreter of his dreams. So, for all his engaged interest in the new field of psychology, was there any course of action left for the poet other than to continue dreaming and to heed the call of his unconscious mind?"

The answer to this question turned out to be unequivocal—no doubt also under the influence of the dream chronicles compiled by J. B. Lang, who failed to grasp why his writings could not be construed as literature too. What was it that made a person an artist? It wasn't his need to get his innermost secrets off his chest, but on the contrary his need to guard his secret even in the act of expressing himself, and imparting to it a permanent radiance in the form of a myth that would have the ability to constantly regenerate itself even after many years had elapsed. The poet is a seer, a sorcerer, a stargazer, a magician, a visionary—but always in the light of the effect his work has on the reader. For at the same time he is also a dispassionate engineer who meticulously calculates the workings of every *deus ex machina*—a perfect illusionist.

Artistry now therefore consisted in being simultaneously a confessor seeking the truth and a vaudeville act who knew how to entertain his public. The secret was laid bare, but for all that it did not thereby cease to be one: "No amount of analysis could ever make a person who wasn't already a poet and hadn't already intuitively sensed the internal structure and pulse of the inner life into an interpreter of souls. All he could do would be to apply a new schema, and perhaps in so doing momentarily bamboozle people, but he would never substantially augment his powers. The poetic grasp of mental processes remained, as it always had been, a matter of intuitive rather than analytical skill."[83]

Nevertheless, Hesse's experience in writing *Demian* showed that there could be such a thing as a fruitful symbiosis of art and psychoanalysis—and this interplay, he believed, was by no means new; rather, it was an "affectionate hearkening to the hidden wellsprings, and only then a critique and selection out of the chaos—this is the way great artists have always worked."[84]

Proximity to and Distance from Rudolf Steiner's Anthroposophy

Hesse wrote to J. B. Lang on January 21, 1918, about Rudolf Steiner: "Much of what he says accords very closely with the views that I have been formulating about the soul and personality over the past few years."[85] Internal and external, these were key terms for Hesse as they were for Steiner—and for both, the internal would become a force that increasingly molded and shaped the external. They were also in agreement over the need for spiritual themes to emerge of their own accord from nature, and in their general admiration for Goethe.

And yet Hesse's path took him via all the things that interested him—albeit only for a very short time—about the various theosophical, anthroposophical, and occultist tendencies of the time, before swiftly leading him on to the sources of Eastern thought:

> Through friends, I learned about certain writings, which at that time were called theosophical, and which were reputed to contain an occult wisdom. These works, some of which were weighty tomes, while others were scruffy little pamphlets, were all of a rather irksome nature, unpleasantly didactic and schoolmarmishly precocious. Granted, they had a certain idealism and unworldliness about them that I found not unsympathetic, but they also exuded a bloodlessness and a spinsterish wholesomeness that I found totally abhorrent. Even so, they engaged my interest for quite a while, and before long I had discovered the secret of their allure. These occult doctrines, which invisible spiritual guides allegedly whispered to the authors of these sectarian volumes, all pointed to a common provenance: namely, India.[86]

Rudolf Steiner, who while working in Weimar first published Goethe's scientific writings before moving on to the Nietzsche archive, appealed—especially from the early 1920s onward—to the educated middle-class elites, especially women. Taking as his starting point the magical conception of nature in Goethe, whose resistance to any simple "encoding" of nature comes through clearly in the polemical stance against Isaac Newton in his treatise on "Colour Theory," Steiner arrived via Nietzsche's atheism at a plethora of "-isms," among which were theosophy and anthroposophy. Yet the prevailing view among anthroposophists was not a straightforward fear of technology, or even a hostility toward it, but a remarkable euphoria over the potential within the realm of things that had hitherto been invisible; this could, however, quickly swell into hysteria. One need only think here of the invention of radio and the telephone, the transmission of voices through the ether—and the fantasies associated with these technologies regarding the afterlife. Steiner was a child of modern technology. His father was a railroad official, and the growth of a modern rail network, which relativized any distance to a degree never known before, became the formative fundamental experience of his life: "On the contrary, people reportedly saw Steiner's face light up and his eyes grow bright, even at the age of sixty, whenever he picked up his pen to write about railway technology, about the tracks that disappeared into the mountains, and the telegraph wires that connected the railroad with the rest of the world."[87]

Hermann Hesse, who had many friends in Switzerland from Steiner's circle, regarded such prophets with a growing sense of distance. He knew the game with dates of birth from his friend Joseph Englert, the runaway disciple of Steiner. Like Steiner, he hushed up his date of birth, and even the dates of letters were "disguised." J. B. Lang also had contact with Steiner, whose influence was growing constantly in the early 1920s. He developed his theories through delivering lectures to audiences. He would make personal appearance on an almost daily basis in German-speaking countries; eventually he was able to fill entire concert halls with his followers. When speaking he clearly had a hypnotic effect on his mainly female audience, whereas his writing was characterized by clumsy and long-winded phraseology. Very quickly, those of sharper intellect deduced from Steiner's theories, which were introduced with ever more bombastic-sounding names, that there was a considerable degree of rhetorical "smoke-and-mirrors" in this form of esotericism; these theories were basically endless reiterations of a blend of Rousseauesque "back to nature" ideology, a magical view of nature, and the latest para-psychological craze. "Holistic" was the buzzword of the anthroposophists, though no one could say precisely what it meant; nonetheless, its ardent devotees were captivated by the concept. In a letter of May 8, 1920, J. B. Lang told Hesse about a "eurhythmic performance involving Rudolf Steiner" in Dornach, a town in the Solothurn canton of Switzerland that was home to the "Goetheanum," the headquarters of the Anthroposophical Society: "There's nothing to interest us there, though: old and young maids performing some boring, mechanical physical exercises accompanied by Frau Steiner declaiming with empty pathos, and Steiner himself giving a sermon."[88]

Hesse certainly maintained contact with the Steiner circle. For instance, in 1921 he traveled to give a lecture in Stuttgart, where he gave a reading to the assembled workers of the Waldorf-Astoria cigarette factory. The factory was owned by the anthroposophist Emil Molt, who had been at school with Hesse and who in 1919 had also founded the first Free Waldorf School in Stuttgart. For this reason, Hesse was reluctant to speak openly about the sense of unease he felt around the anthroposophists, which was an unpleasant reminder of his experiences at Monte Verità near Ascona, where he had spent some time around the turn of the century in the company of nudist, vegetarians, fruitarians, and all manner of other "children of nature." What bothered him about these dropouts was their fanaticism, their sectarian militancy, which managed to turn every appealing idea into a rigid, intolerant ideology. Thereafter he had been intent on giving all reformist movements a wide berth. Nevertheless, he formulated his misgivings rather circumspectly in a letter of December 11, 1923:

> As it happens, I have several personal friends who are under Steiner's influence and who count themselves among his followers, whereas I myself am neither a friend nor a follower of his. . . . All the same, I would ask you to please treat this correspondence as a *private communication,* as I am publicly making every possible effort to avoid taking sides. I'm not doing that out of convenience, but from the conviction, or rather the certain knowledge, that the dispute about factions and principles is being conducted on a totally different plane from the matters that my own thoughts and efforts are focused on.[89]

Following one lecture by Steiner, which had taken place amid an "unbelievable crush," Hugo Ball, in a letter of January 18, 1922, aired his views on the nature of anthroposophy: "It was a disappointment, however. I had faith in personal magic and hung on his every word to try and divine his soul. Yet his linguistic energy really isn't so 'ethereal' (to use his own terminology). I am mystified as to what his success might consist of."[90] In his diary for the year 1920 / 1921, Hesse gave his own drastic assessment of Steiner: "his whole personality (his lecture tours, intense propaganda, financial foundations, personality cult, etc.) utterly and fundamentally contradicts what all religions throughout the world define as the characteristics of a saint and a flawless person."[91]

Hesse saw in Steiner the "opposite of a saint; a brilliant careerist"—and even refused to concede that Steiner was making a great personal sacrifice in undertaking his tireless program of lecturing to promote his cause. "Precisely this habit of working himself to death is a sign of ambitious zealotry, never a sign of a holy man."

Little is known about Rudolf Steiner's life: "He was the 'Great Master' and not a historically researchable individual,"[92] wrote one of his followers—a "guru" who was transfigured but never scrutinized, a "chameleon" who used the "dime novel" language found in a novel: "Let us continue to help ourselves from the department store of life-reform."[93] From the Waldorf Schools to biodynamic farming methods, an abiding principle was the *unio mystica,* which promised the unity of material and spirit, of body and soul, and of nature and culture. But an undifferentiated unity, a mysticism without skepticism, inevitably turns—for almost all practical philosophical intents and purposes—into incoherent esotericism.

Steiner's great synthesis of carnality and spirit, of body and psyche, nature and technology—indeed, this whole cult of anthroposophy as the "spiritual person's philosophy"—irritated Hesse, who was a champion of (gnostic) dualism; for him, two principles were always in conflict with one another, and body and spirit, spirit and carnality, were like day and night where he was concerned. Without the dark, the destructive side of the instinct-driven creature that was a human being, the enlightened side of reason and humanism could not exist. But the two cannot be reconciled; at best, the confrontation can resolve itself into a kind of parallelism, which in Hesse's work then regularly assumes the character of (contradictorily defined) doppelgänger figures.

★   ★   ★

With Goethe, the key thing was to find a balance between the degree of euphoria and the degree of abstinence. The definition of something good was what helped a person to survive one more day and perhaps in the process even find something like consolatory pleasure. In 1918 Hesse responded to a questionnaire about smoking, and in the answer he gave, his relaxed attitude to life where aspirations are concerned clearly shines through:

> Smoking is one of the pleasurable vices in which I have indulged ever since I reached adulthood. I have often given it up, on the advice of my doctor, and every time I did I was assured that after a short while I'd lose the habit and along with it my need or craving to smoke would also cease. However, that wasn't true; even spells of abstinence that lasted for months did not manage to kill my craving, so I started smoking again. Insofar as I could get hold of them, I had a particular liking for cigarettes from the Dutch East Indies; and now I find the best cigar after dinner to be a Brissago or one of those Toscani that are made in Ticino. I have never found a Swiss "cheroot" that I liked except the ones from Valais. I would happily subscribe to the view that people would do better not to smoke and should never get hooked on the habit, just as I would to any fine moral dictum. But it is up to each and every one of us as individuals to decide how to come to terms with the harshnesses of life and what creature comforts we'll employ to do so.[94]

"Zarathustra's Return": Nietzsche as a Role Model

> Only a few people have any inkling that the decline of the German spirit had begun long before the war.
>
> —Hermann Hesse, "Zarathustra's Return"

In later life Hesse noted that he wrote "Zarathustra's Return: A Word to German Youth" in just three days and nights in 1919. The conceit of the essay is that Nietzsche's Zarathustra mingles with the flood of bewildered people washing about at this period in history. He makes fun of them and mocks the seriousness with which they do things. But precisely in doing so, he becomes an enlightener who utterly debunks the new illusions, which are nothing more than the old attitudes that people have dragged with them from a now-vanished world that existed prior to the war. "You're

heading in the wrong direction!" he calls out to them—"Not toward yourselves, but away from yourselves!"

What are these thirty or so pages—a program, a pamphlet, or a polemic
against such things? This was a matter of complete indifference to Hesse;
the words just flowed out of him. The focus of the piece was the future of
Germany—and the incipient mistake of once more talking in general or
political terms, where in fact people really ought to be going back to basics and beginning by examining themselves.

The whole tone of the work, as well as the title figure, were borrowed
from Nietzsche. The essay appeared anonymously, with the somewhat
pathos-tinged byline: "By a German." The last book to be launched at
the German public under such an authorship had been a work entitled
"Rembrandt as Educator"—the art historian Julius Langbehn was
behind that anonymous publication. This was an embarrassing book,
which utilized the fear of science and industry to disseminate an intellectually lazy irrationality and an equally casual antisemitism among the
German populace—its basic thrust was that in a situation when there
are more and more losers from modernization, someone must be to blame!
Langbehn exploited this fear and at the same time discredited terms such
as "myth" and "mysticism."

Hesse took up the cue from Langbehn's book and attempted, like
Nietzsche, to exorcize from German subjects, who suddenly found themselves embroiled in revolution or counter-revolution, any fantasies about
changing the world or hankering after leadership figures.

Young people reacted vehemently to the application of Nietzsche's
critique to the Germans. In writing this, Hesse had touched the raw nerve
of the time. Many of those returning from the front, who had read their
Zarathustra, now felt themselves betrayed by the former elites of the Second
Empire. But whom should they follow? Hesse provided the answer in
"Zarathustra's Return": No one but yourselves! Don't ever again place
any faith in the promises of factionalists whose sole aim is to turn you into
vassals. That was the path to the next catastrophe: "You shouldn't worship
Zarathustra. You shouldn't imitate Zarathustra. You shouldn't wish to become Zarathustra! Within each of you there is a hidden figure who still
lies in the deepest slumber of childhood. Breathe life into it! . . . There is
no other God than the one that resides within you!"

★　　★　　★

In this slim tract, which has something of the character of a pamphlet, one thing above all becomes clear: Hesse's path inward, his withdrawal from the world of zealous striving, and his disgust at the political world with its parties and its lies. At a time when calls for action were coming from all quarters, Hesse insisted upon distinctions. The necessary deed was not the same thing as that unfocused, indiscriminate action that only accelerates the pace of disintegration. It is impossible to overlook the quasi-religious impetus, which was not just borrowed from Nietzsche but also indicates what was taking shape within Hesse: "The deed is light, which springs from a benevolent sun. . . . The deed is not mere doing, deeds cannot be devised or contrived." Then comes a piece of dialectical sleight of hand, which adumbrates Erich Fromm's *To Have or To Be?:* "Dear friends, our willed action, which is meant to approach the light via seeking and doubting and zigzag paths, this action is the opposite and the arch-enemy of the deed. In truth your actions are, if you will permit me this nasty term, cowardice." The argument that follows is a renunciation of any form of soldiers' revolutionary council, of the Spartacist League, and of any other of the sham organizations of the so-called world reformers, which were really only themselves symptoms of the decline. According to Hesse, what was needed was a new starting point. Here he introduced the provocative concept of "gazing into chaos" that so appealed to him in the works of Dostoyevsky. Destiny! "Destiny is earth, is rain, is growth. Destiny is painful. Yet what you call 'action' is really running away from the pain, wishing you had never been born, a flight from suffering."[95] A few years before the turn of the millennium, the German writer Botho Strauss, in his controversial essay "Goat-Song Rising" ("Anschwellender Bocksgesang"), presented a similar rejection of modernity's "relief project," which served to shake up perceptions of Western European civilization. Hesse's position was already a rejection of mass culture and that form of comfortable social democracy that pledged, slowly but surely, to improve everyone's lives in the sense of making them easier. But shouldn't it also be the aim of art to improve life too?

In response to this question, in the year before his death in 1956, Gottfried Benn would give a resounding No; Hesse was several decades ahead of him when he wrote: "The world wasn't made to be improved. Nor were you made to be improved. You were made to be yourselves. You were made to enrich the world with a sound, a tone, a shadow. Be yourself, and

the world will be rich and beautiful!'[96] Can it really be as simple as that?
No, Hesse argues, this is precisely not an easy task, but a difficult and protracted one—as shown in *Demian*. And then, when one has finally become
the person one ought to be, the question of "betterment of the world"
can be addressed once more:

> If the world has ever been improved, if it has ever been enriched by human
> beings, then this has not come about, not through reformers, but rather in-
> stead through true self-seekers, among whose number I would dearly love
> to count you. Those earnestly and truly self-seeking men who have no goal
> and purposes, who are content to live and to be themselves. They suffer a
> lot, but they suffer it willingly. They are happy to be sick, so long as it is
> *their* illness that they have to endure, one which that they have acquired
> as their very own. And likewise they cheerfully perish provided it is *their*
> death they are being allowed to die, the death that is theirs by right.[97]

With a defiant, almost violent gesture Hesse in "Zarathustra's Return" announces to the new era what he thinks of it: nothing. He has no time for
political action, or for the vision of a thoroughly technological, scientific
world that attempts to divest the individual of their dignity by making them
part of the mass of humanity and so robbing them of their solitude, the most
valuable thing that they possess.

In the final number of the *Sunday Courier for German Prisoners of War*,
which appeared at Christmas 1919, Hesse published an "open letter." He
knew full well how painful it must have been for thousands of German
soldiers who were still interned in camps to slowly be forgotten. The
postwar society had better things to do than worry about them. Everyone
was trying to gain a foothold in the new era and ensure that they and their
family got by somehow.

By this time he wrote this, Hesse had been released from his wartime
service and was already living in Montagnola—thereby ending the chapter
of his life concerned with the care of POWs. But the experience of the
conflict remained very much alive for him, when he warned the captured
troops who were still having to pay the price for the war:

> Don't let yourselves become embittered! Don't come away from this war
> with hatred and animosity or thoughts of retribution! Take nothing from

this conflict and your time in captivity except the realization that war, killing, and incarceration are inadequate and ugly instruments to which no one who has ever experienced them at first hand in all their dreadfulness can ever themselves resort. If there really is no other option, then take feelings of sorrow, shock, and despair from your experiences of the war—but not hatred, not enmity, and not a thirst for revenge! For with each of those feelings you render yourselves complicit in the war, and in the possibility of war! . . . It is a difficult injunction by Jesus that we must love our enemies, possibly too difficult. But at least not to hate the enemy, or to assign sole blame to him, or not to wish to hold him solely responsible for all the ills you have suffered—that is an essential requirement and a commandment for everyone who harbors any feeling within them for humanity and its future.[98]

And what about the philosopher Nietzsche? For Hesse, he was above all a person who knew how to preserve his solitude. And who for that reason—and that reason alone—had something worthwhile to say. And with the beginning of this text, the circle closes once again for Hesse. His statement on the contemporary age, which was also a declaration of belief in the fate of the German nation, thus went further along the road he had embarked on in *Demian* by embracing old-fashioned values:

> There was once a German spirit, a German courage, a German manliness that did not manifest themselves in the clamor of the herd or in mass enthusiasm. The last great spirit of that kind was Nietzsche, who, amid the sheeplike conformism and commercial bustle accompanying the rise of the German Second Empire, became an anti-patriot and an anti-German. In making my appeal here, I want to remind the intellectuals among modern German youth of him, and of his courage and solitude, and in so doing distract them from the outcry of the herd—whose current lachrymose tone is not one whit more appealing than the loudmouthed, brutal one it adopted during those "great days"—and point them instead toward a few simple, inalienable facts and experiences of the soul.[99]

However, Hesse's great turn inward did not just have to do with Nietzsche, whose Zarathustra figure he borrowed here, but also with Dostoyevsky, whose "gazing into chaos" opened the door to the subconscious for him. Nor did Hesse take his inward turn in purely psychological terms, relating everything to the individual, but as an artist casting his eye over an entire era.

Excursus: A Report from the Periphery—Dostoyevsky and Europe

> Every man for himself, everyone against you, and God on
> everybody's side. Of course, it follows from this that little hope
> remains for the individual.
>
> —Fyodor Dostoyevsky, letter to P. A. Karepin, August 20, 1844

The story of Dostoyevsky's mock execution in 1849 is a familiar one. He had been condemned to death for his closeness to the social revolutionary Nikolai Petrashevsky and his circle:

> Today, on December 22, they led us out onto Semyonov Square. There, our death sentence was read out to us. The firing squad shouldered their rifles, the staffs were broken over our heads, and we were dressed in shrouds (white shirts). Then three of us were tied to posts for the sentence to be carried out. . . . Suddenly there was a drumroll and the order to fire was suspended, the three men tied to the posts were led back, and a new proclamation was read out to us, to the effect that His Imperial Highness had deigned to spare our lives.

Although the execution had ostensibly been canceled, something in Dostoyevsky remained dead for ever after. He felt that he was living in a morgue, not just during his spell of four years' forced labor in the fortress at Omsk and his years as a soldier in Semipalatinsk, but also subsequently. He had lost all faith in civilization, in the social movements of the West, and the Enlightenment image of humanity. He saw himself exiled to the periphery of the vast Russian Empire—Siberia. Yet this periphery expanded into a way of life that the center had no conception of.

It did not take a sham execution and banishment to Siberia for Dostoyevsky to start to doubt exalted forms of Romanticism, especially the German variety. As a young man he had read Schiller and E. T. A. Hoffmann in both Russian and German, and the sentiment that the eighteen-year-old Dostoyevsky had written in a letter to his brother Mikhail on August 9, 1838, set the tone for the rest of his life: "I have a plan: to lose my mind.—Let people get enraged, let them try and cure me and make me rational again."[100] And indeed, there would be no shortage of attempts to make him see reason—though time and again he evaded this form of discipline. Or more accurately, something in him balked at it. An elemental feeling of freedom. For Hegel's philosophy of world history, Siberia was not even remotely a region that had any relevance—just like Africa. A non-place like this, located beyond the horizon of reason, caused Dostoyevsky a great deal of suffering. What was this concept of reason supposed to mean to him, banished as he was to Siberia, where he could identify no sign of it? It wasn't hard to lose one's rational mind when one knew that one's own suffering did not exist as far as Hegel's notion of world history was concerned. Something else was less easy: namely, to discover what it was that did lend weight to the individual's suffering in history.

More than 150,000 exiles—most of them banished for political crimes—lived in Siberia in the mid-nineteenth century. Omsk, with its fortress, was a desolate garrison town. A godforsaken place. This absence of God would become more and more of a theme for Dostoyevsky after his arrival in 1854, as an ordinary foot soldier, in Semipalatinsk, a settlement that was situated on the fringe of the Siberian steppe. There he made friends with the local public prosecutor, Alexander Yegorovich Wrangel, who was only twenty-one years old. Wrangel was a subscriber to the German newspaper the *Allgemeine Augsburger Zeitung,* and they also read Hegel together. Hegel made one brief mention of Siberia: "We must first of all discount Siberia, the northern slope of Asia. For it lies outside the scope of our inquiry. The whole nature of Siberia is such as to rule it out as a setting for historical culture and prevent it from attaining a distinct form in the world-historical process."[101] Dostoyevsky thus knew where he stood from the perspective of the world spirit: "beyond consideration."

The great paradox was that he had been condemned to death for espousing European ideas, but that very same Europa for which he had propagandized not only refused to recognize Siberia as a place of terror but even expunged it from its memory and the map of civilization. This was not the onward march of history in the growing awareness of freedom, such as Hegel had assumed would take place, but agonizing stagnation. A lack of freedom as if for an eternity, meaning that Dostoyevsky would only write one work here: *The House of the Dead.*

As he was working on this, something dawned on him that would completely shift his global coordinates: the experience from the periphery, the place where everyone inevitably ended up who dared to take a stand against the prevailing views of the age. Dostoyevsky knew that the stigmatizing shadow cast by institutionalized history on those whom it excluded was his own.

His view of history was the result of his intense interest in the various ways in which it could be written. Thus, he wrote to his brother Mikhail on February 1854 from Omsk, after his time as a shackled convict—on Christmas Eve 1849, a chain weighing five kilograms had been attached to his ankles—had come to an end and he was awaiting his transfer to Semipalatinsk:

> What I am really lacking (and they are extraordinarily important) are the works of the ancient historians (in French translation) as well as more modern ones such as Vico, Guizot, Thierry, Thiers, Ranke, and so on, and the works of the economists and the Church Fathers. Get hold of the cheapest and most robust editions you can and send them to me without delay. . . . But you should be aware, dear brother, that these books are essential for my life and sustenance, and my future lies in them! . . . Also send me the Qur'an, Kant's *Critique of Pure Reason,* and if you're also able to send me something not officially sanctioned, then make it some Hegel, especially his *History of Philosophy.* All my upcoming work has to do with this!

Hegel could only attain an understanding of life by raising himself above its arbitrariness, and above the sickness, pain, and death of the individual. He was incapable of recognizing anything that was beyond the grasp of reason. Yet history, like nature, displayed little in the way of rationality. Dostoyevsky wrote the following account of his journey as a shackled prisoner from Saint Petersburg to Omsk on an open sled in the biting cold: "It was a particularly dismal moment when we crossed the Urals. The horses and the sleds stuck fast in the snowdrifts. A snowstorm was raging. We alighted; it was nighttime and we stood around waiting until the sleds had been dug out again. All around us were snow and snowstorms; we were on the far frontier of Europe, with Siberia ahead of us, where an uncertain fate awaited us, and behind us the past—it was terribly sad, and my eyes filled with tears."[102]

In his *A Writer's Diary,* the section "Confessions of a Slavophile" contains the following passage: "I have in many regards purely Slavophilic convictions, although I am perhaps not a complete Slavophile." For Dostoyevsky, Slavophilia meant "that our great Russia will utter its new and healthy pronouncement, as yet unheard by the world, at the head of the united Slavic peoples of the entire world, and of the whole of European humanity and its culture."

However, he had not forgotten his former confederates—the Decembrists, the Petrashevsky Circle, Vissarion Belinsky, and Alexander Herzen. Dostoyevsky renounced neither his opposition to serfdom nor his contempt for censorship. His father had been murdered by his own serfs, when Fyodor was just seventeen, and he knew that the root cause of this lay in the inhumane conditions associated with this state of bondage. So what had he, the author of *Poor Folk,* been condemned to death for? The judgment of the court ran thus:

> The military court finds the accused Dostoyevsky guilty insofar as, after receiving a copy of a corrupting letter written by the literary critic Belinsky . . . he proceeded to read said letter out in March of this year to various assemblies in Moscow. . . . Furthermore, Dostoyevsky was present at the house of the accused Speshnev when the seditious work by Lieutenant Grigoryev entitled *A Soldier's Conversation* was read out. For the crime of failing to report the dissemination of the anti-religious and anti-government letter of the literary critic Belinsky and of the criminal work of Lieutenant Grigoryev, the military court has therefore condemned the serving Engineer-Lieutenant Dostoyevsky to death by firing squad. He will be stripped of his military rank and divested of all his property rights.[103]

So it was that Dostoyevsky's main body of work very nearly never came about. The fact that it was written is down to a person from whom one might least have expected it: Czar Nicholas I. He pardoned all those who had been condemned at this trial (officers and aristocrats to a man).

By 1859, however, when Dostoyevsky put in a request to leave the army on health grounds (he was suffering from epilepsy), he was an officer once more. He had been very fortunate.

Things in Russia were changing at that time. The democrats who modeled themselves on Western liberals were growing stronger and demanding respect for the rights of the ordinary citizen, as promulgated by the French Revolution. Serfdom was finally abolished. When the anarchist

Vera Zasulich shot and seriously wounded the governor of Saint Petersburg in 1878 because he had ordered the flogging of a political prisoner, a trial by jury found her not guilty. The prevailing mood was a euphoric feeling of freedom. The intellectual elite of Russia looked toward Germany and France, and aspired to bring backward Russia into line with the Western standard of civilization. But Dostoyevsky chose to align himself with the Slavophiles and against his former friends. Did he do this put of opportunism or because he was a broken man by this stage? On the contrary, he was motivated by experience.

His frequent trips abroad increased from 1865 onward, leading to a prolonged absence from Russia of six years. Having incurred huge debts, he was unable to return to Russia lest he be thrown into a debtors' prison. From 1869 to 1871 he lived in Dresden, where he wrote the novel *Demons*. He felt as though he was in exile—and his view of Europe had changed and become more sober. "I would rather be banished to Siberia than be marooned in Florence or Geneva!" he lamented. Unlike Turgenev, who accused Dostoyevsky of being on the cusp of becoming a German, Dostoyevsky once again turned his gaze on an institution that for him was a quintessential feature of his homeland: the *staretsdom* (hierarchy of elders) of the Russian Orthodox Church. These elders had a knowledge of the world that was more than simple worldly wisdom. But what a terrible inner turmoil inhabited the Russian soul! Eternally condemned to being half-European and half-Asian! Here, Dostoyevsky sensed, was something that the rest of Europe lacked and that only Russia could give him. The question of God lay at its very heart. He realized that the Enlightenment, and the culture it had ushered in, could not be undone. Nor should that happen—otherwise surely new wars of religion would loom on the horizon. God was not present in this world, yet didn't the very question of an absent God appear to be something that strengthened a religious feeling? The old God was dead and with him the superstition that came from ignorance. And attempting to comfort the oppressed by pointing to the life hereafter was finally a thing of the past.

Nietzsche saw in Dostoyevsky the psychologist of a coming age, and knew that the question of God would not die. Precisely because he does not exist, we need him. The mysticism evident in Dostoyevsky's late work has at its heart a paradox: Faith cannot banish skepticism from the world—but neither can skepticism banish faith. He planned a major book that would be his legacy, and which he intended to title *Atheism*. When it appeared in 1879, it was under the title *The Brothers Karamazov*. It has been the subject of fierce debate and discussion ever since.

For it was not just in the "Russian spirit" that Dostoyevsky saw a way forward for Europe; working equally strongly on him was the influence of someone whom one doesn't immediately associate with Dostoyevsky: Friedrich Schiller! Even as a child, the Russian writer had been fascinated by a performance of *The Robbers*. Consequently, many of Schiller's motifs found their way into *The Brothers Karamazov*. The father–son conflict in *Don Carlos,* for example, or the portrayal of his protagonists Ivan and Dimitri as figures resembling Karl and Franz Moor respectively from *The Robbers*. In his study of Dostoyevsky (1928), the critic Julius Meier-Graefe wrote: "Rather than provide the form or content for Dostoyevsky's work, Schiller supplied its whole impetus."[104]

And so Dostoyevsky remained a Slavophile for the time being. Every year, even after his return to Saint Petersburg, he would spend several months in Germany as soon as he could scrape the funds together for his travel, going to Bad Ems for a rest cure. A notorious gambler, he had already lost all his money in Wiesbaden. Nor was this the only such occasion; one time he even pawned his wife's clothes—and lost. He needed no lessons about the agonizing contradictions that go into making up a person. And just as the individual carries within himself the contradiction of being simultaneously an animalistic and barbarian creature, on the one hand, and a rational and civilized person, on the other, this tension is also inherent in entire communities. To have one without the other, Dostoevsky knew full well, would be disastrous. He had an overview of the entire gamut of people's bodies and souls, their tears and smiles—something to which Hegel was blind. This was an insight into the truth that derived from personal experience of suffering, a view from the periphery, cast by outsiders.

And it was in order to bring about a return of these outsiders to the map of Europe that Dostoyevsky became a provisional Slavophile, a European who could bring something from Europe's borders with Asia that the West appeared to have lost—a sense of the alien within the familiar, a feeling for the power of mythmaking as a necessary corrective to any pretense to reason, lest this mutate into an instrument of dominance of the center over the periphery.

★   ★   ★

But did such a viewpoint override Dostoyevsky's urge to attain civil rights and liberty? Certainly not—precisely the insufferable nature of feudal conditions (especially serfdom!) was what had driven him to make common cause with the circle of social revolutionaries around Belinsky in the first place. But simply being liberated from something was not enough to ensure that a person would become a human being. Dostoyevsky came to realize this during his travels through Switzerland, Italy, and Germany. The Germans, he wrote, had destroyed his nerves. In Dresden, Dostoyevsky abandoned his last illusions about enlightenment and rationality. He nevertheless remained opposed to any form of fanaticism or any triumphalist view of history: "By reality and realism I understand something quite different from our realist writers and critics' view. My idealism is more realistic than theirs. My God! If I were to recount all the things that we Russians have experienced over the past ten years in our intellectual development, how loudly the realists would clamor that this was pure fantasy! But exactly that is realism, and what's more a profound realism, whereas with them everything remains purely superficial."[105]

Gazing into Chaos: Hesse's Reading of Dostoyevsky

> I have long since stopped believing in Good and Evil, and instead take the view that everything is good, even what we call crime, filth, and horror. Dostoyevsky knew that, too.
>
> —Hesse, letter to Carl Seelig, spring 1919

Hesse saw himself corroborated most strongly by Fyodor Dostoyevsky in his view that reality was something that one should under no circumstances simply accept, not even in the name of reformist or revolutionary change; rather, the only way of looking at reality was to adopt a totally different concept of it, which basically amounted to a utopian exploration of its further possibilities. The first story that Hesse wrote after moving to Italy, the murder-dream *Klein and Wagner*, could not possibly have come into being without Dostoyevsky's *Crime and Punishment*.

In a letter written in the autumn of 1919 to Carl Seelig, Hesse described this transformation in the light of reading Dostoyevsky:

Formerly, under the influence of models such as Goethe, Keller etc., I as a writer fabricated a beautiful and harmonious and yet fundamentally untruthful world, by hushing up all the dark and wild things within me and suffering in silence as a result. Instead, the only things I emphasized and portrayed were "'goodness,'" a sense of the sacred, respect, and purity. That led to figures like Camenzind and the novel *Gertrude,* which suppressed a thousand truths in favor of conveying a sense of noble decency and morality. This state of affairs ultimately brought me, as a man and as a writer, to a state of tired resignation, where on my poetic lyre I could admittedly make sweet music on my poetic lyre which that wasn't at all bad, but which for all that was devoid of all life.[106]

Now that his bourgeois existence had collapsed, he claimed that he had begun, "sick and half-mad with suffering," to straighten himself out and to acknowledge "all the chaotic, untamed, compulsive, and 'evil' things" within himself. This new commitment to unsparing truthfulness had, he maintained, changed everything for him: "As a result, I have relinquished my earlier sweet, harmonious style. I had to seek out new tones, and to do bloody battle with all the unresolved and primitive urges within me—not in order to eradicate them, but to understand them and give them expression."[107]

If we finally abandon the lie fabricated by bourgeois order, an order moreover that had itself long been in a state of decline, then—and only then—will we have a chance, as individuals, to survive the downfall and heal ourselves spiritually. This attitude—the courage to look into the shadow that we cast ahead of ourselves as we move forward—would shape Hesse's writing henceforth: "The less we fight shy of our own fantasy, which in our waking hours and our dreams makes criminals and animals of us, the smaller the risk that we will actually fall victim to these evils and perish through them in reality."[108]

The work *Gazing into Chaos (Blick ins Chaos),* published in 1920 by the Seldwyla Press in Berlin, comprised three essays that Hesse had written the previous year. Two of these were on Dostoyevsky: "The Brothers Karamazov and the Decline of Europe: Reflections on Reading Dostoyevsky" and "Reflections on Dostoyevsky's *The Idiot.*" The other essay was "A Discussion of Avant-Garde Music."

Hesse denied that he had been inspired by the work *The Decline of the West* by Oswald Spengler (whom he certainly admired). When he first wrote about the subject of decline, in *Klingsor's Last Summer,* he maintained that he had not even read Spengler's work. In a letter of December 14,

1919, he explained: "What I call decline I really do also see as a rebirth. The 'Decline of Europe' for me is a process that I am living through in myself and that one might liken to the decline of the ancient world; not a sudden collapse but a slow, growing transition in people's souls."[109]

The two texts on Dostoyevsky form some of Hesse's most important self-reflections in the years following the First World War.

What did Dostoyevsky stand for? Somewhat in passing, Hesse gave an answer to this question in a letter to Theo Wenger, the father of Ruth Wenger and his future father-in-law: "for the intensity of a more primitive sex life."[110] This was an urgent topic in the conversations that Hesse had with his analyst J. B. Lang in the years when Hesse's marriage to Maria was breaking up, although Lang was suffering more severe marital restriction on his own sex life than even Hesse was at this time. Conflicting processes of formation and deformation were in operation. Each in his own way, Hesse and Lang both experienced this contraction at close quarters. For Hesse, his own self-image as an author also changed in the process. Despite the fact that he regarded the term "intellectual" as "a dreadful word,"[111] he provided what is possibly the most important contribution to the definition of the intellectual in postwar Europe. His model for this was, of all people, Prince Myshkin, the chief protagonist of Dostoyevsky's *The Idiot* and a genius of suffering. His "timid chastity," his complete "isolation" made him into a "magical person." For Myshkin, reality was something totally different from how those around him saw it: "In seeing and demanding a new reality, he earned their enmity."[112]

Something happened with Myshkin that the bourgeois world could not forgive. Hesse noted that he approached the borderline "where the opposite of each and every thought could also be seen as the truth." This disrupted the whole order of Good and Evil, and chaos ensued: "A mode of thinking that reverts to the unconscious, to chaos, destroys all human order."

This was exactly the same step that Hesse himself had taken and that he had deemed essential.

The "*Idiot*", if thought through to its logical conclusion, introduces the matriarchy of the unconscious, and annuls civilization. It doesn't smash the tablets of the law, it merely turns them over and shows us what is written on the other side.

The fact that this enemy of order, this terrible destroyer appears, not in the guise of a criminal, but as a kind, shy man full of childlike charm and grace, full of well-meaning innocence and selfless bonhomie, therein lies the secret of this shocking book.[113]

Hesse recognized in Dostoyevsky the person who in the terrifying moments before his "execution" became a prophet and who as a result was able to create figures like Prince Myshkin, who in the eyes of the world is little more than an idiot. We can also see in Hesse's reception of Dostoyevsky his Franciscan sympathy for suffering outsiders, for people institutionally condemned as heretics, people whom the existing system refuses to believe speak any truths. For precisely that reason, that system was also in a state of decline: "In Dostoyevsky, all agents of the new, the terrifying, and the uncertain future, all harbingers of an anticipated chaos are sick, dubious, put-upon figures. . . . All of them are depicted as people who have gone off the rails, as strange oddballs, yet without exception in such a way that, when confronted with their deranged nature and their mental illness, we feel something of the sacred reverence that Eastern people feel they should show to madmen."

It is evident that Hesse is constructing a bridge here from *Demian* to *Klingsor's Last Summer*. The god who embodies both good and evil, saint and criminal—a god who is at the same time a devil: Abraxas becomes a symbol for this deity. What is the upshot of all this for an intellectual in a future Europe? For this is the thing that truly concerns Hesse—the rebirth of the soul of Europe in the midst of the collapse of a survived world.

Hesse bars himself from seeking a way forward through political action. Such activity belongs to the external world, from which no genuine renewal should be expected. And what of revolution? Certainly, but only if that is synonymous with the rebirth of the foundering human being, the sinking civilization.

On March 11, 1919, Hesse had received an offer, by word of mouth, to join the government of the Munich soviet republic. Kurt Eisner had already been murdered in the city. At the root of this offer was a "misconception of my character," Hesse said in declining the offer. It wasn't political solutions that he was searching for, but rather that spirit which would be able, for the first time, to impart a meaning, a wholly new meaning, to any future political endeavor. But in the current situation—and the revolution in Germany had done nothing to change this—he was keeping his distance from politics, as he feared that any engagement in it might rob him of his creative impetus. Accordingly, he sent the following categorical reply to Johann Wilhelm Muehlon (a lawyer and diplomat intermediary of the Munich revolutionary government): "The state in particular uses its citizens in a most extraordinary way. Poets are employed as soldiers, professors as gravediggers, Jewish merchants as statesmen, and lawyers as journalists. And none of that has changed with the so-called revolution, it seems. The state, at least our state, is accustomed to the talentless flocking to its service and to being able to dispose of them in any way it sees fit. And as far as I'm concerned it can go on doing that." In discussions, he said, he hadn't been able to persuade anyone that tabling motions and implementing ideas wasn't his kind of thing and that he would cease to have any worth as a moral being if he was exposed to direct influence by people and political tendencies. And so, while it might sound appealingly fanciful for him to talk about a possible return to Germany, he felt a deep impulsion to explain himself: "I most definitely feel tempted to return to Germany and perish alongside you there in the general misery and bustle, but can really only see this as a form of suicide wish. My whole nature is pushing me in another direction."[114]

In "The Brothers Karamazov or the Decline of Europe" Hesse finally spelt out clearly what he meant by "decline": the "revaluation of spiritual values."[115] For Hesse, *The Brothers Karamazov* was a "mythical novel" that demonstrated the threshold on which Europe stood, a dream of humanity in which that "dangerous moment of floating between nothingness and the universe"—the customary sign of the dawn of a new age—revealed itself. It was in the light of this that Hesse interpreted the middle of the Karamazov brothers, Ivan—the one who came closest to the archetype of the Western European intellectual. This figure and his transformation, which seems hardly credible, possessed for Hesse a signal effect for the "Decline of Europe" that he was prophesying:

When he is first introduced to us, he is a modern, assimilated, cultivated person, rather cool, rather disenchanted, rather skeptical, and rather weary. But he grows increasingly younger, more ardent, more significant, more Karamazov-like. It is he who is the author of the poem "The Grand Inquisitor" and who is impelled from a cool rejection of, and even contempt for, the murderer whom he believes his brother to be to a profound awareness in the end of his own culpability, to the point of self-denunciation. And it is he who also most clearly and remarkably experiences a conscious process of analysis of his unconscious self. (Everything turns on this! It's the point of the entire cycle of decline and rebirth!)

In this way, Hesse—largely unnoticed by contemporary reviewers—arrived at a modern interpretation of *The Brothers Karamazov* in the spirit of Freudian and Jungian psychoanalysis: "The final book of the novel contains a very singular chapter, in which Ivan, returning home from his interview with Smerdyakov, sees the Devil sitting there and proceeds to sit and converse with him for an hour. This Devil is none other than Ivan's unconscious self, nothing other than the stirred-up content, long submerged and seemingly forgotten, of his own soul."[116]

"Hate Mail": Falling between All Stools

> This one-sided, pigheaded German-ness, which is taught from so many lecterns and pulpits, and which does not appear to have collapsed even with the end of the war, must now make way for an infinitely broader, more flexible definition of German-ness if Germany is not to remained isolated, resentful, and mournful amid the other peoples of the world.
>
> —Hermann Hesse, "Hate Mail"

With the outbreak of war in the summer of 1914, Hesse became a stranger to many of his readers. For the first time they became aware that his work was a mixture of half-inwardness and half-outwardness. Hesse's neutrality in political matters and his appeals for moderation were provocative in a period of national mass hysteria. His attempt to be a German patriot while still remaining a citizen of the world who refused to hate another human being just because he happened to be a Frenchman, an Englishman, or a Russian was not well received. He was particularly decried and resented for wanting to be one without renouncing the other. The common slur

that he was a naively unworldly writer was virtually tantamount to accusing him of cowardice.

It was this question of the national versus the international that made
Hesse a source of irritation for many journalists from the start of the First
World War. The sense of outrage over his conduct did not abate in the
1920s, and after the Second World War, prompted by his "Rigi Diary,"
culminated once again in a sustained cry of fury against the "traitor to the
Fatherland." As early as November 4, 1915, Stefan Zweig noted in his diary:
"Attacks on Hesse, because he is not Teutonic enough for the Teutons. His
response has been measured and elegant. He tells me he thinks he'll have
aged ten years by the time this war is over. Which of us won't?"[117]

Again Hesse found himself between two stools. He had sacrificed five
years of his life, between his mid-thirties and early forties—irreplaceably
valuable years in a writer's life—on a civilian variant of war service, in
attempting to preserve a little piece of culture and humanity for German
POWs. He had plenty of other things he could have done; he wasn't like
some lonely people who had found the war a godsend as a way of filling
their pointless days and who cared for mutilated soldiers in field hospitals
puffed up with pride and full of patriotic zeal. He had written with bitter
irony about the war as a measure designed to give point to some people's
existence. But for him, his work for the prisoners' welfare agency was
not a compromise; he took his service for those who had been forced to
suffer the consequences of war very seriously indeed. That came from his
Pietist and missionary background and from his Franciscan attitude to life.
Consequently, he was angered by a certain type of pacifism whose propo-
nents seemed primarily concerned with rhetoric. This was the root of his
1915 article "To the Pacifists." In this polemic, Hesse sounded almost like
the attacks of German nationalists against him. What was the point, he
wrote, in speaking and writing about the ideals of humanity when soldiers were bleeding to death on the battlefields?

In the pacifists' stance there was something that he found just as insufferable as those who spent their time writing paeans of praise to the war: their
smugness.

> Something wasn't right, there was something rotten, something inflexible
> and dead about this idealism, which sounded so pious and yet which passed

by bloody life so calmly and unconcernedly without paying it the slightest attention. All that stuff about peace, world peace and the brotherhood of man was all very fine and good, it was splendid, but it was a doctrine, it was words, it was a printed catechism. . . . When all's said and done, aren't you just people who are shirking your duty in the here and now because you see a more noble and convenient duty looming on the horizon for the day after tomorrow?[118]

Unquestionably, it was a contradiction: Hesse was firmly on Germany's side in this conflict, and wanted a German victory—but he did not believe that such a victory would do a thing to alter the downfall of Europe. The spirit of the warring parties on both sides had nothing in it that could genuinely form the basis for something new to grow—and nor did that of the pacifists. And he saw it as his task as an author to go in search of this new spirit—a spirit that was not merely a national, but international.

The pacifists, in their turn, were outraged by Hesse—they had assumed that he would be a political confederate of theirs. The nationalists were even more outraged that he refused to join in their hate of the enemy. "To the poet Hermann Hesse" was the title of a six-stanza hate poem which he received in November 1915. What he read when he opened it sounded like an incitement to murder:

> I can barely find words to express my hatred of you!
> You specimen, you worm; have you been totally abandoned
> By your spirit and sense of Germany's sanctity
> That you don't feel the sorrows of this time?
> . . . .
> Clubbing you down or running you through with a sword would be
>   too good for you, you poet!
> You just wait, someone else is coming to pass judgment on you.
> Without more ado he will pierce you to the marrow with
>   glowing steel:
> May your well dry up, and everything you do prove fruitless![119]

Thereafter, a deluge of insults was directed at him—he could try to explain his position all he liked, but it did no good; this was not a time for subtle differentiations. The German warmongering popular press had long since placed Hesse on the side of war traitors. For instance, in

Hesse mountaineering with his eldest son, Bruno, on the Schaafschnur above Lake Oeschinen in the Bernese Oberland region of Switzerland, 1905

November 1915 the *Augsburger Abend-Zeitung* carried a piece that expressed the new disaffection for Hesse that was coming from all sides: "A Hermann Hesse would be unthinkable without German culture, whereas it's easy to conceive of a German culture without Hermann Hesse." These same sentiments were voiced once again in newspaper editors' offices after 1933—in many cases by the same opinion-formers—demanding that Hesse be expelled from all German "cultural institutions."

During this period Hesse often had occasion to call to mind Nietzsche, whom an overzealous petit-bourgeois nationalism had decried as an out-and-out anti-German.

In 1921 he reacted to this never-ending hate campaign with a newfound acerbity. In the article "Hate Mail," he cited excerpts from the mail that came to him on a daily basis from Germany. The thing he found most appalling was that it was students in the main, young and not unintelligent people, who had made him their sworn enemy. And it was precisely they who had had been the target audience for *Demian* and "Zarathustra's Return"! And now he had to read things like this: "Your art is a neurasthenic-salacious wallowing in beauty, it is a tempting siren calling across still-warm German graves that have not even been filled in yet. We hate writers like this, for however often they might serve up polished works of literary art, all they are aiming to do is to turn men into women and to make us degenerate and internationalize us and pacify us. We are Germans and wish to remain so for all eternity!"[120]

Anyone who writes something like that must, Hesse decided, regard the artist as some kind of "functionary." "But as a symptom of the age we're living in, this reaction of modern German students to reading Italianized, pacifist writers and to their efforts to combat barbarism and promote humanity interests me."[121]

Speaking on the subject not only with no hint of pathos for the first time, but also with full antipathetic vehemence, Hesse voiced his opinion that it was the flag-waving, saber-rattling spirit of the "great age" that was rearing its head here once more, and, having just emerged from one catastrophe, was marching headlong into another:

> It is the spirit that is afraid of itself and that sees any temptation away from rallying round the customary flag as positively satanic, but which that conceals this inner cowardice behind noisy saber-rattling. The fact that this spirit has been permitted to masquerade as the German spirit and that for decades, supported by the regime of 1870, it has been allowed to trumpet its message to the outside world, has made those of us who hold no brief for this spirit and who see it as a bugbear, into internationalists and pacifists. For, not to put too fine a point on it, it is this phony German spirit that the rest of the world has, quite rightly, blamed for starting the war. And anyone who subscribes to it goes on being culpable for that crime.[122]

This drew up the battle lines unequivocally. Hesse was against the nationalists, and in their eyes he was henceforth—and remained—a traitor.

Little wonder, then, that he wrote a series of miniature Orwellian dystopian sketches, such as "If the War Lasts for Another Two Years" (1917) and "If the War Lasts for Another Five Years" (1918). In these a "prewar person" runs up against the logic of an enduring state of war. These are two different worlds that are incapable of comprehending one another. War has become a mechanized, permanent state of affairs, with bombs being dropped from free-floating balloons—with no specific target, purely because it is wartime. In the first of these pieces, the first-person narrator, who has just come home after many years traveling, gets caught up in the mill of bureaucracy. "Permit" and "existence authorization card" are the two principal terms in this little story, which makes it clear that the difference between combatant nations and neutral states has long since disappeared. This was an allusion to Switzerland and to Hesse's constant battle with Swiss bureaucracy concerning his residence permit. Dragged from one hearing to the next, the narrator wearily wonders aloud why they don't simply condemn him to death and have done with it. But for that, apparently, one requires a "death card," the fee for which is too high for a traveler. And so he finally asks an official how people can stand living like this. The answer he receives is this: "You are in a particularly bad position, as a civilian, and with no papers to boot! You see, there are very few civilians left now. Anyone who isn't a soldier is a state employee. That alone makes life much more bearable; in fact, many people are even very happy."[123]

And why should the war be so important that everything needed to be sacrificed to it, the traveler now asks, before leaving this inhospitable place for cosmic realms. The astonished reply comes back: "Why, the war is all we have!"

In "If the War Lasts for Another Five Years," Hesse carries this absurd situation to even further extremes. There comes to light a man who, living far off the beaten track in his house in the country, has heard nothing of the war. The only newspaper still being printed in the Kingdom of Saxony in 1925 runs the headline "The New Kaspar Hauser." The person who has been discovered is the seventy-year-old private citizen Philipp Gassner, who then, despite his food rations having been reduced as a result of his unsuitability for war service, still shirks his responsibility to sacrifice himself for the fighting men at the front (namely, by dying quickly of starvation). At the end of a specified time period, presumably as the result of a well-tended vegetable garden, he is found to still be in the best of health. This was also how Hesse saw himself in 1918. Much to the annoyance of some people, he was still alive. And not just as a civilian but as someone who was completely out of kilter with this "great time," governed as it was by the logic of war: "He had spent all these years outside the world that surrounds the rest of us! Just as he was absent from the world as a citizen, so was the life of his mind located outside our time and our world."[124]

A dream that could be dreamed only by someone who was wandering across mountain ranges? Certainly. But for the uniformed world around him, the "prewar person" was nothing but a curiosity. The University of Leipzig appears on the scene, wishing to acquire this unique living example of the civilian species; Gassner is "to be subjected to a thorough examination and if possible preserved for science."[125] And what of Hesse himself; what did he do with the "prewar person" who still resided within him?

On January 25, 1918, he recorded in his "Diary of Psychoanalysis" a dream in which he met an old friend (Ludwig Finckh) from his youth, during the time he spent at Gaienhofen on Lake Constance. This dream was symptomatic of Hesse's relationship to Germany—and Germany's relationship with Hermann Hesse: "All our attempts to reconnect and to revive our friendship ran into nervousness and resistance on both sides. In conversation, he kept harping on about patriotic topics, while I steered clear of them."[126]

His day-to-day existence in the shadow of the war became ever more oppressive for him. His money worries grew. As early as September 11, 1917, he noted: "For almost two years now I have been in a constant state of financial embarrassment. I haven't bought myself a new suit in over two years and am traipsing around in some very battered shoes."[127] The possibilities for changing reichsmarks into Swiss francs were very limited, and what he could scrape together wasn't enough to live on, as he wrote on February 12, 1919: "At the moment, I—who have a wife and three children to support—am only allowed to take out around 65 francs' worth of the money in Germany that belongs to me, while having no sources of income whatsoever here in Switzerland! The country of profiteers and braggarts has never been generous or even indulgent toward writers, and I don't like German officialdom any more since the revolution than I did before."[128]

If he was to survive in Switzerland, then, it would be crucial for him to earn money there—Swiss francs—and also to find patrons who could support him. At the beginning of 1919, he fell back on an idea that had helped him fund his first trip to Italy back in 1901. He prepared several handwritten manuscripts and decorated them with little watercolors in the hope of selling them. He wrote to the painter Cuno Amiet, who in 1920 took Hesse's son Bruno under his wing, acting as his foster father: "This year, I have produced a number of manuscripts with little drawings on them. Each of these manuscripts comprises 12 poems and a title page, in other words 13 pages in all, and will cost 200 to 250 Francs apiece.

Portrait of Hesse by the Swiss painter Cuno Amiet (1868–1961)

They will appeal to friends and collectors of fine books, curiosities, and the like, and I've sold a few already. I plan to donate the proceeds from the first few copies to the German prisoners' welfare fund, but need to sell the remainder for my own benefit."[129]

Shadows on the "Child's Soul": The Book Wall Collapses

> And I, on the other hand, I would always stand nearby out-
> side, alone and unsure, full of forebodings but with no
> certainty.
>
> —Hesse, "Kinderseele" (Child's Soul)

"Kinderseele" picked up on the themes already broached in *Demian*—that change is crisis, and that anyone who wishes to grow must have no fear of gazing into their own shadow. In this story, which Hesse wrote in 1918 while he was still living in Bern, the first-person narrator looks back on a sheltered childhood. The parental house is the place that anyone who wants to realize their potential must eventually leave behind. Hesse— albeit painfully—did so in good time, but now his father had died and his own family was on the brink of irreparable disintegration. For Hesse, it was time to take a different view of his own beginnings.

Despite the sense of being protected, which also was a form of helpless subjugation, his childhood was no idyll but instead the first step on his
path to becoming an outsider. The world lay like an alien and closed environment before the eleven-year-old boy; it was that world of reality, always viewed with suspicion by Hesse, to which Oskar Weller, the son of
an engine driver, belonged. Hesse however—and that was the terrifying
feeling of someone growing up—lacked the unquestioning sense of being
at home in the world, that stolid matter-of-factness of existence. The feelings of the child that Hesse described here were none other than those
that tormented the fourteen-year-old writer: "This life was accursed and
repugnant to me, a disgusting sham."[130]

The thing that drives the story's central character from the security
of his parents' world is a misdemeanor. Driven by his inner "demon,"
the boy steals some figs from a cupboard in his father's study. The story
describes him waiting to be found out, and the ensuing punishment.
Yet prior to this he has already experienced his true trial; namely, when
he sits in judgment on himself, hurling reproaches and damning accusations at himself and wishing in vain that he could undo everything
he'd done. It is his awakening conscience that tortures him here. He
knows he has done wrong, but he does not know why he did it. Now
he finds himself tormented by the knowledge, previously hidden from
him, of what he has the capacity to be: a criminal who gratuitously does
evil deeds.

And then it emerges, the vision that troubles and intoxicates him at the
same time—and we are unsure how much of it is a dream and how much
is reality, or where Hesse's own biographical details come into play. Presumably, over the course of his life, during the various phases of his fire
worship and pyromania, Hesse himself lost any clear sense of the boundary
between imagination and reality. "Sometimes I felt as though I would set
fire to our house: huge flames would beat their wings through the night,
houses and alleyways were consumed by the conflagration, and the whole
city became one massive blaze against the black sky."[131] And why did he
do that? "I have set houses on fire because it amused me, and because
I wanted to taunt and enrage you."[132] There is no explanation, at least no
rational one—it is simply a dark urge that reason and awareness of morality cannot always control. Those falls from grace completely isolate an

individual within a world that knows nothing of his dark secrets. "There was no criminal in our house except me."[133]

In this, the artist is more akin to the criminal than to the bourgeois citizen. In his propensity to find occasions to shock, undoubtedly. The extent to which all the things that concerned Hesse during this period after the end of the First World War found their way into "Kinderseele" can be seen from the inclusion of the motif of suicide. Suicide was an ever-present topic for him, a bit of freedom—and on several occasions during his lifetime, he tried it as an escape route from reality, though we cannot know precisely how seriously he intended do away with himself, or whether it was something of a relief to occasionally go through the motions of suicide without actually going through with it. In any event, he has his eleven-year-old protagonist in "Kinderseele" speak the following words: "I knew full well that you could take your own life. I also thought that I would surely do it myself one day, later, when things got really bad."[134] Less than a year after writing this story—by this stage he was already in Ticino—Hesse had arrived at the point where he only wanted one thing: to die.

Another story from 1918 anticipated the end of his time living in Bern. It was entitled "The Man with Many Books" ("Der Mann mit den vielen Büchern") and depicted the insupportable degree of his alienation from what he had once wanted to be. A terrible disillusionment had taken hold of him: "In all matters concerning learning and writing, those ancients had already had the best of it, with just a few worthwhile contributions coming later, from Goethe, say, and if mankind had made any progress whatsoever in the intervening period, then it was only in areas that were of no concern to him and seemed to him to be superficial and dispensable, such as building engines and weapons and in ways of changing living things into dead ones, and in transforming nature into figures or money."[135] Here, already, we encounter the same suicidal tone that the "Steppenwolf" Harry Haller adopts. The man in the 1918 story dreams that he is constructing a wall out of nothing but books. But then it suddenly collapses—and "behind the wall of books, he could see something monstrous, saw in the light and haze a huge chaos." He then finds himself shocked to the core: "He had been cheated, cheated of everything! He had spent his life reading, turning over page after page, he had eaten paper—and yet behind all this, hearts had been aflame, passions had raged, blood and wine had flowed, and love and crime had been going on. And he had been party to none of this at all; his domain had been one of thin, flat shadows on paper, in the books!"[136]

That was the feeling Hesse had at the end of his time in Bern: that his life had somehow passed him by. And that it would be criminal if things were allowed to continue in that vein. He had already decided to leave his old life behind. He had been living in the Welti house in Bern for almost seven years; all in all, it had not been a good time for him. In consequence, his summing-up of this period was also correspondingly downbeat: "Apart from that, I didn't find it especially hard taking leave of Bern. It had become clear to me that, morally speaking, only one way of living lay open to me now: namely, to put my literary work before everything else, to live entirely in this realm and not to let either the breakup of my family, or money worries, or any other consideration worry me in the slightest anymore."[137]

His involvement with the prisoners' welfare agency officially came to an end on April 15, 1919, and a few days later Hesse was traveling south, to Ticino. For the first few weeks there, he stayed in a small farmhouse in Minusio near Locarno, before moving on to Sorengo. On May 11 he rented four rooms at the Casa Camuzzi in Montagnola. His new life could begin. "I had my writing desk sent from Bern, but otherwise I managed with rented furniture."[138]

7

Making a Fresh Start and Falling to Earth in the South

Wandering: Yearning for Faraway Places and a Dream of Home at the Same Time

It's like in war, when people played the hero despite being all twisted up inside with fear! Dear God, what a pathetic ape and shadow-boxer man is—particularly the artist—particularly the writer—particularly me!

—Hermann Hesse, *Wandering* (1920)

Wandering gives us a snapshot of Hesse after he had finished writing *Demian.* In this collection of notes and sketches Hugo Ball sees the author temporarily recovering a degree of measure and equilibrium: "His feelings have crystallized, and make a tinkling sound when he disturbs them. Changing a single letter turns *Wanderung* into *Wandelung* ['transformation'] and that accurately reflects what's going on here."[1] The euphoria of recuperation brought on by his encounter with J. B. Lang had long since dissipated. *Demian,* that important document of his spiritual rebirth, which he had completed by the fall of 1917, was with his publisher Fischer but had not yet been released. After all, the author wasn't Hermann Hesse, but a debutant by the name of Emil Sinclair, and paper was in short supply after the war, especially for the first publications of unknown young novelists.

Hesse chose to remain incognito and bided his time. In the meantime, in a series of short pieces that were published under the title *Wanderung (Wandering)* in 1920, he presented a kind of summing-up of the parting of ways *Demian* represented for him. Something had to perish in order for something new to emerge. Once more, he rehearsed for himself the fundamental contradiction between the artist figure and the bourgeois citizen. For the first time, he committed to paper the feelings that his encounter with Lang had triggered in his life. He was painting and writing, and the harmonious blend of the two was what generated the poetry that enlivens *Wandering*. This work saw him departing for a realm where he felt so much at home—namely, an itinerant existence. It also represented a leave-taking from an alien world that had become a false homeland to him.

So, what is *Wandering*? For one thing, it is a book of affirmation after a long, agonizing period of rejection. Plus an act of faith after all the skepticism. Not belief in place of skepticism, but instead in the midst of it. Not a return to the old organized Church faith but instead a document charting the sense of devotion that resides within life itself and is life-affirming. A rebirth amid decline, an arrival during an act of departure.

In this book, parts of which had appeared previously during 1919 in the form of newspaper articles, Hesse transcended his personal experience of wandering and his individual crisis and turned them into a picture of the contemporary age. What was to become of the individual who has escaped the mass slaughter in the trenches of the First World War in a Europe that consisted of nothing but the victors and the vanquished of the greatest conflict that had ever taken place in the history of the world?

Wandering exudes a Romantic spirit that has not been consumed in the flames of patriotic clichés but that, by contrast, engenders a catharsis that derives from the piety of those who stayed true to their own inner law of conduct throughout the collapse of civil society. For such people, a new start was not to be sought among the ranks of the military and the politicians, who were just then busy drawing up new lines of demarcation. Through a simple hike across the Alps, from north to south, Hesse turned a world upside-down and set it to rights:

> How fine is it to cross these borders! The wayfarer is, in many respects, a primitive person, just like the nomad is more primitive than the settled farmer. The overcoming of a sedentary existence and the contempt for national borders make people like me the true heralds of the future. If only there were more people whose contempt for national borders was as heartfelt as mine, then there would be no more wars or blockades. Nothing is more petty than borders, nothing more stupid. They are like cannons, like

generals: just as long as reason prevails, you don't see anything of them and you smile at the very thought of them—but as soon as war and insanity break out, they become important and sacrosanct. How much these things became a torment and a prison for us wayfarers during the war years! The devil take them![2]

During the war, Hesse himself had experienced at first hand, and in a very traumatic way, the dread that borders might prevent him from traveling to and fro between his two homelands of Switzerland and Swabia, and the unbearable feeling of being penned in. This had happened in the fall of 1916, when he had been trying to get back to Bern after a trip to Germany, and had found the border crossing at Singen closed. With his fear of being cut off from the rest of the world, of being trapped in a place he wanted to leave behind, Hesse touched on a raw nerve of the age. Many of the men returning from the front felt that they were caught in limbo between the past and the future. What was left at the end of all the grand rhetoric of hollow-sounding words to which they had been treated? The answer was the individual, abandoned to face his pain, his sorrow, and his fear all on his own. What were men like this after? A period of peace and good fortune, which wasn't filled with lies and promises of great times ahead. They wanted to see, hear, and feel things for themselves. Not the whine of bullets, the screams of the wounded, and the death-rattles of the dying but instead to feel the gossamer breath of a summer breeze, hear the sound of birdsong, smell the aroma of a wood, and watch clouds drifting slowly by. As such, the text takes on a programmatic force when Hesse writes: "For such a long time I abased and mortified myself before gods and laws, which to me were just idols. It was my mistake, my worldly torment that in the process I did violence to myself and lacked the courage to take the path to my salvation. This way to redemption does not lead to either the left or the right, it leads to one's own heart, for it is only there that God and peace can be found."[3]

Who better to follow in this hour of need than a person who in seemingly hopeless times led by example and refused to be swept up in the great xenophobic game of hating the enemy en masse? And where might one find such a leader, who would not immediately proceed to make you his blindly obedient follower once more? The answer for Hesse was clear, as it had been for Nietzsche: the only voice worth listening to resides within our-selves. But is that the voice of one's own conscience or of God? Who could say?

Wandering was a testament to a form of freedom that promised to become essential. Hugo Ball remarked that this wayfarer in Hesse's work had al-most no dark side. That was soon set to change once again, but certainly these new texts radiated the kind of harmony that can only come from a great inner security. That said, Hesse's life at this time was anything but harmonious, and he himself was by no means sure of his way.

A wayfarer is someone who breaks free in order to become a new person, yet who only realizes while they are under way what they have left behind in doing so. You must have the urge to take everything with you and leave everything behind—only in this way can you stay true to yourself and experience your transformation as both a joy and a sorrow. For only the creature that struggles and breaks its way out of the egg with all its might is truly fresh and new. This is only a shell, it would seem, yet it also formed the limits to one's former life, which is now finally set to turn out quite differently. This was what drove Hesse south across the Alps. He wanted to rediscover his own world.

Everything that he wrote from now on, though, would act as a red rag to his enemies. He acknowledged as much in *Wandering:* "I am an admirer of unfaithfulness, of change, and of fantasy. I do not care to pin my affec-tions firmly to any particular spot on Earth. I only ever take what we love to be an allegory. If the love we feel should ever get stuck and turn into loyalty and virtue, then I begin to view it with suspicion."[4] "We knew it all along!" the nationalist press in Germany declaimed when the book ap-peared: "Just look at the kind of person Hesse is, who mocks loyalty and virtue!"

Hesse's confession here is informed by the self-willed obstinacy that we have already observed on many occasions. He does display loyalty, but to himself. Likewise he also obeys laws, but only those inherent within him. Never before and never again was Hesse such an unquestioning Nietz-schean as he was here. Never again would he walk so firmly in the foot-prints of Zarathustra, affirming his fate with every step, as he did on his north–south crossing of the Alps. This journey was more merely symbolic, though; it represented a key turning-point in his life.

How he longed to be an upstanding citizen, to have a homeland, and to be content in the location that fate had assigned him. But he found this impossible; something was always driving him on toward an uncertain future, to an unknown life that lay ahead of him. One time, as he was walking past a rectory, he imagined himself as the pastor there. He of all people, who in his youth had poured such scorn on theology! But even that attitude of his had changed by now: "It is, as I now know, a scholarly vocation full of charm and magic, it has nothing to do with such vulgar concerns as weights and measures, nor indeed with the vile business of global history, which is full of violent conflict, bombastic rhetoric, and base betrayal. Instead, it takes a subtle and delicate approach to inward, pre- cious, blissful matters such as grace and salvation, angels and sacraments."[5] Wouldn't it be wonderful, Hesse mused as he passed by, to live there and to gaze out at the wanderer, half pityingly and yet half wistful, as he tramped past on his dusty way? Yet wouldn't he be another person if he were ever to play the role of the settled pastor? Wouldn't he lie awake in fearful dreams, disputing with a thousand devils and frittering away his nights drinking heavy Burgundy? The initially dignified scene evaporates before his eyes—like every dream of having a worthy station in life, it is pure illusion. "On the other hand, I might keep my green garden gate firmly closed and have the verger ring the bells and let my calling as pastor and my village and the world go hang, and lie on my wide couch smoking and loafing about. At night, I'd be too lazy to take off my clothes and in the morning too lazy to get up." And so, while touching briefly on such topics as bourgeois fixity and the institutionalization of knowledge and faith, he proceeded step by step to conjure up the possibilities that had come his way during his life—and those that might still appear. Had he missed an opportunity? Should he have lived his life differently? Yes, though def- initely not by denying his own inconstant nature as a wayfarer but instead by enthusiastically embracing it and by living according to its principles. "In short, I wouldn't actually ever be the pastor in that rectory, but in- stead remain the same inconstant and harmless wayfarer I am now. I would never be a proper vicar but rather, on occasion, a theologian building castles in the air, and at other times a gourmet, or just a bone-idle good-for-nothing who can't keep off the wine, or someone obsessed with young girls, or a writer and a mimic, and sometimes a homesick wretch whose poor heart is filled with fear and sorrow."[6]

You can never be anyone other than who you are. The only thing you can do is decide to take control of your journey through life, to plow your own furrow—and to ultimately identify a goal that you have a realistic possibility of attaining. And yet all the paths that were left untrodden, and that opened up to you to no avail because they weren't your own, nevertheless (or precisely because of that) strike you in your mind's eye when you recall them as having at one time held real promise for you: "One day I will no doubt feel homesick for this rectory, which I only glimpsed from the outside and where I do not know a living soul, every bit as strongly as if it had really been my home, the place where I was a child and enjoyed happy times."[7]

Trees as the Most Ardent Evangelists of Pantheism

In quite an incidental way, *Wandering* is also one of Hermann Hesse's most poetic works. These are the thoughts and observations of someone on the move, traveling light, ideally so light as not to impair easy motion. Bourgeois and artist, home and abroad, faith and the meaning of life—all these topics are covered in just a few pages between hastily sketched watercolors and poems that, as is generally the case with Hesse, sound like hiking songs and whose principal value lies in their singability.

There then comes a song that expresses both a lust for life and the agony of death—both conveyed in one and same melody:

Transience

Leaf after leaf falls
From my life's tree.
O, life's dizzying round,
How you weary and sate me,
How drunk you make me!
Today's ardent glow
Presently abates.
Soon the wind will whistle cold
Over my brown grave.
The mother bends down

Over the little child.
Let me see her eyes again,
Her gaze is my star,
Let all else pass and be taken by the wind,
All that's mortal dies gladly.
Only the eternal mother remains,
From whom we came,
Her playful finger writes our names
In the fleeting sky.

The image of "life's tree" encapsulates the spirit of *Wandering*. For it is a shorthand expression of his religious creed—which is that of a mystic who harkens after God in the depths of his soul and who does not take the presence of the hereafter in the here and now to be a lie. And the mystic unmasks himself through characteristically paradoxical utterances—this certain knowledge that God reveals his presence in the world by concealing himself within it. The greatest entity always reveals itself through the smallest—and vice versa. This is a god of growth and decay.

The mystic is also a pantheist. God does not reside in Churches or dogmas—instead, he is immanent in every living thing. He is the power of transformation. Thus, individual letters of the alphabet come alive when the words that they compose take on a reality of their own, as in poetry. So it is with rocks, the Sun, the rain, and all plants and animals—they are all inhabited by something divine, the spark that gives them meaning and lends them a voice.

Trees were imbued with a very special significance for Hesse. Accordingly, the chapter in *Wandering* headed "Trees" is generally regarded—quite rightly—as Hesse's profession of faith:

> Trees for me have always been the most powerful evangelists. I revere them when they live in tribes and families, in forests and groves. And I revere them even more when they stand alone. They are like solitary people. Not like hermits who have absented themselves out of some weakness, but like great, solitary men like Beethoven and Nietzsche. In their highest boughs the world rustles, their roots rest in infinity; but they do not lose themselves there, they strive with all their life-force for one thing only: to fulfill themselves according to their own laws, to develop their own form, to rep-

resent themselves. Nothing is more sacred, nothing more exemplary than a fine, strong tree.[8]

As a result, Hesse maintains, it wounds the very soul when a tree is felled. The godlessness of a person is shown in his willingness to cut down a tree without feeling any great sorrow at having done so. When a tree has been felled, in the open wound of its severed trunk the growth rings tell of its ongoing struggle over many years with the cold, the wind, the sun, and the rain. They provide evidence that the tree, growing ever upward, attempted to form a link between the Earth and the heavens. This was why Hesse called trees "saints." "Anyone who knows how to speak to them, anyone who knows how to listen to them, can learn the truth. They do not preach learning and precepts; unconcerned by particulars, they proclaim the ancient law of life." And Hesse lets the tree itself explain what this ancient law of life is: "My task is to shape and reveal the Eternal in my smallest individual detail."[9]

Trees are plants in which a very particular form of architecture becomes apparent. An eight-hundred-year-old oak still carries within its memory the presence of the Gothic. The spreading plane tree becomes a living cathedral. It will grow right up to the sky—so long as it is given enough time. Because this is far more time than is allotted to man, he intuits in trees a secret knowledge that makes them superior to him. Yet to grow tall, a tree needs to have a firm footing in the earth.

Hesse's fascination with trees is also evident in the 1922 fragment "A Guest at the Spa." They are beautiful, and their beauty is not just ephemeral—although what remains precious to us forever is the brief moment in which we realize how magical their presence is: "They would still be beautiful tomorrow too, but right now they had that magical, never-to-be-repeated beauty that comes from our own soul and that, according to the Greeks, can shine in us only when Eros has cast his gaze upon us."[10]

When Hesse arrived in Montagnola and moved into the Casa Camuzzi, he was particularly delighted by the villa's gardens with its trees. The Judas tree that he so loved and that "blossomed magnificently year after year from the beginning of May to well into July, and whose red-violet pods had made it look so strange in the fall and the winter" he would ultimately lose, for "one night in autumn it fell victim to a storm." This was a heavy blow for Hesse, because its loss reduced the network of roots from which he drew his strength here and that for him represented a piece of—borrowed—homeland. Even worse was to follow: a hostile act of vandalism, which suddenly made the familiar seem alien, was perpetrated against another tree: "Klingsor's great flowering magnolia, which grew right in front of my little balcony, and whose huge, ghostly blooms almost grew into my room, was chopped down one day during my absence."[11]

Painting and Fairy Tales: The Magic of Colors and the Enchantment of Invention

Was there ever anything more perilous, more difficult, and more dispiriting than painting? Or more tricky and hopeless? Wasn't it a bagatelle, mere child's play, to write *Don Quixote* or *Hamlet,* say, in comparison to the far more presumptuous undertaking of trying to paint a magnolia?

—Hermann Hesse, "The Joys and Sorrows of Painting" (1928)

Wandering would have a lifelong resonance for Hesse. For the first time, he had written *and* illustrated a book! In 1949, in the piece "Hours at My Writing Desk," he would again invoke the magic of his illustrated books—works that he created on demand, perhaps a half-dozen every year. In 1917–1918, during his first tentative attempts at painting, he sold these manuscripts to raise funds for the prisoners' welfare agency. Having now finally arrived in Ticino, after the First World War, and in a period when he was desperately short of hard cash, he began work on similar manuscripts at the behest of wealthy collectors, mostly in Switzerland.

And so, if we were to cast a glance into Hermann Hesse's workshop at this time, we would see an artisan working at what he best loved doing: namely, retransforming the intellectual into the sensory. It quickly becomes apparent that he was an enemy of all abstraction, of everything that was simply born of obsessive willfulness; instead, he dedicated himself to forming a unity of material and dream, using his head and his hands in equal measure to lend it artistic form:

I open the cupboard and set about choosing a sheet of paper; sometimes I'm drawn to the smooth ones, sometimes to those with a rougher texture, and sometimes to fine watercolor papers. While searching on this occasion, I got a fancy for a very simple, slightly yellowish paper, a few sheets of which

I reverentially keep hold of. This is the same paper on which one of my most favorite books, *Wandering,* was once printed. The remaining copies of this book were destroyed by American bombs, wiping out the entire available stock, so for years now I have been buying up every copy I come across in secondhand bookstores, at any price, and today one of my few remaining wishes is that I might one day live to see it reprinted. This paper isn't expensive, but it does have a very special lightly absorbent porosity that gives the watercolors painted onto it a slightly faded, antiquated look.[12]

Painting was a redemptive expression of crisis for Hesse. Without psychoanalysis he would likely never have found his way to it. To begin with he found it difficult, in the same way that he had found keeping his "Dream Diary of Psychoanalysis" hard. From June 1916 onward, he had traveled every week from Bern to Lucerne to meet his therapist, J. B. Lang, at the Sonnmatt Sanatorium. He had already been receiving treatment for over a year when he started keeping this diary. On August 5, 1917, he noted in it:

In Zurich Dr. Lang and I agreed that I should start painting or drawing, and I also took it upon myself to work through as many as possible of the things that have come up in analysis—I'm attempting that here right now, and it's working on one level, but then again it isn't. Least of all with the drawing. All in all, my current condition is this: I live in an absence of thoughts and memories, a state that I would decry as idiotic in someone else; I spend my day doing trivial things, making it a priority to read my mail and the newspaper, and doing a bit of work in the garden. The occasional cigar and, in the evening, a glass of wine afford me moments of contentment. My condition is at its worst in the morning, when I find myself incapable of thought, and everything seems dull and repellent.[13]

And yet images now kept welling up inside him—in his dreams, of which he noted down fragments, and in the fairy tales that he wrote, where he addressed the theme of childhood that he had long forbidden himself to tackle. He recognized in the irascible character that his family had to suffer the child that he had once been: "At the age of around four, I was prone to terrible fits of temper, which in part I directed against myself."[14]

His struggles with the pencil also caused him to fly into frequent fits of rage. The short "Fairy Tale of the Wicker Chair" from 1918 makes reference to this. This portrayed a narrator figure who had been inspired by reading a book about a Dutch painter (Julius Meier-Graefe's 1912 biography of Vincent van Gogh). In this work, he learns that when bad weather prevented the painter from setting a foot outside to make his *plein air* studies, he would simply sketch a pair of old shoes or a wicker chair. And so the narrator, a would-be painter himself, also attempts to do this in his lonely garret studio. But he fails miserably—and Hesse reflected and exaggerated his own inability to make accurate copies in a dialogue between the wicker chair and the dilettante draftsman. The chair mocks the crooked lines the narrator commits to paper: "There's a thing called perspective, you know, young man."[15]

That proves to be the last straw for the impatient beginner, who has also tried and failed to draw a self-portrait, so he simply drops everything and walks away. The wise chair stays behind and breathes a sigh of resignation. "It was sorry that its young master had gone off like that. It had been hoping that a proper relationship might develop between them. It would have loved to have a word with him every so often and it was certain that it had lots of worthwhile things it could teach a young man. But all this would now unfortunately come to nothing."[16]

Hesse was deeply frustrated by his repeated failings. And by this stage, at over forty years of age, he was no longer a young man, either. He found he couldn't draw people, or chairs; in fact he was a very poor draftsman all round. Anyhow, he far preferred to dive straight into using color—but did he dare to do that, knowing as he did that Vincent van Gogh, say, had banned himself from using color for many years until he had forced himself to master the technical skill of drawing?

Here, then was yet another proscription that he had imposed on himself, another impediment to his fulfilling his desires. But in this instance it was the magic of a new beginning that helped him make a fresh start in his life. A sudden inspiration took hold of him and transformed what one could call a crisis into a process of growing self-awareness. A certainty inscribed itself upon his most secret, innermost self, as he would later formulate it in "The Childhood of the Magician" (1923): "The realm of freedom is also the realm of illusions."[17]

This process of delving far back into his childhood now forced him to confront the realization that it was still very close at hand. He was setting foot in that mythical terrain that he had once conjured up in *Peter Camenzind,* though at that stage he had done so without the experience of an aging

Hesse photographed on a walk in the Ticino region

author who was only now beginning—already almost too belatedly—to affirm his own early years. He descended deep down the mine-shafts of memory. And what he discovered there was not just of a personal nature but—and this is where his acquaintance with the work of C. G. Jung came into play—it also had an archetypal character. As a result, we encounter the following lines in "The Childhood of the Magician": "I was not raised by my parents and teachers alone, but also by higher, more hidden and more mysterious forces, including the god Pan, who appeared in the form of the statue of a small, dancing Indian deity, which stood in my grand-father's glass curio case." Subsequently this figure would frequently play a role in his works as a fetish, as the guardian of a portal into a magical di-mension of reality. There was something living in it which for Hesse rep-resented an antithesis to the world of the here and now.

So, there existed a cult of the disempowerment of reality! That meant that one could render oneself invisible in the face of prevailing standards and criteria. This notion, that there was a secret to which only a select few were privy and that later would form one of the central ideas of *Steppen-wolf*, found its earliest expression in "The Childhood of the Magician": "Fortunately, like most children, I had learned what is most valuable, most indispensable for life, before my school years began, taught by apple trees, by rain and sun, river and woods, bees and beetles, taught by the god Pan, taught by the dancing idol in my grandfather's treasure room."[18]

And so Hesse now took up painting before he had perfected the art of drawing. He just wanted to abandon himself to the joy of enchanting through the use of color. Hesse's aim here was not to imitate nature but to create a relationship between colors that would correspond to those found in the natural world. Hesse remained faithful to what he observed, he was a representational painter—even so, the fact that his pictures display an almost imperceptible shift toward a dream reality serves to emphasize the artificiality of what are ostensibly pictures of nature. They are therefore just as much archetypal images of the kind that were revealed to him during his psychotherapy as they are likenesses that sprang from his joy in looking at things. On August 11, 1917, he noted: "Yesterday I began to paint one of my earlier dreams, that is to say to create a color illustration of that subject. These little pictures are not deeply analytical, rather they show the accessible features of those dreams. My playful instinct invariably tends to veer toward things that are fully formed and intended and communicable."[19]

Hesse deliberately sought the company of painters. He found himself constantly fascinated by pictorial representation and the various different ways of achieving it. He was enthralled by the works of such artists as Albert Welti, Alfred Kubin, Cuno Amiet, Louis Moilliet, Gunter Böhmer, Ernst Morgenthaler, and Hans Purrmann. It was to the last of these that he dedicated this poem:

An Old Painter in His Studio

December light falls from the large window
Onto blue linen, rose damask,
A gilt-framed mirror talks to the sky,
A blue-bellied earthenware jug embraces the bouquet of flowers,
Multicolored anemones, yellow cresses.
In their midst, engrossed in his game,
Sits the Old Master, painting his own countenance
In the way that the mirror reflects it back to him.
Perhaps he began it for his grandsons.
A testament, maybe seeking a trace of his own youth

In the mirror's glass. But that is long forgotten.
That was just a whim, just a prompt.
What he sees and paints isn't himself; he carefully ponders
The light on his cheek, forehead and knee, and the blue
And white in his beard; he makes his cheek glow
And flower-pretty colors blossom out of the gray
Of the drapes and his old jacket,
He hunches his shoulders, exaggerates the size
Of his rounded skull and gives his full mouth
A tinge of carmine. Engrossed in this noble game
He paints as if he were painting air and mountains and trees,
Paints his likeness into imaginary spaces
Like it was anemones or cress,
Caring about nothing except the balance
Of red and brown and yellow, the harmony
In the interplay of the colors that radiates
In the light of the creative moment, beautiful as never before.

Painting gave Hesse a sense of inner fixity that writing never could; unlike writing, it was not just the realization of a thought in black and white but a form of meditation. Could there be anything more exhilarating than seeing the world in colors that one had imparted to it oneself? Anyone who paints has a more precise view of things—for the visually oriented Hesse this was a way of liberating himself from lethargy, and in the midst of a war, what's more. On May 26, 1917, he wrote to Alfred Schlenker: "I know that I can never be a painter, but even so the intense feeling of forgetting yourself by giving yourself over to the world of visual phenomena is quite an experience. This was the first time since 1914 that I completely forgot myself and the world and the war and everything for whole days on end."[20]

Painting was also a liberation in the sense of being a detachment from the dictates of reason, a way of immersing oneself in inanimate objects that speak to you in a totally different way: namely, directly. Here was that detachment from the "world as will" of which Schopenhauer had spoken—indeed, the growing affinity Hesse felt toward this philosopher was not least a result of the crisis he went through during this period. The increasing creative impulse to paint that had come upon him so unexpectedly had opened up new realms of the imagination. The possibilities of expression multiplied—and that proved to be a lifesaver to him during these years.

Painting became a bridge to the world for him just when other bridges were collapsing. Through painting his attitude changed from that of an observer deliberately keeping himself detached from the action to a new participation in worldly things. It was the sheer pleasure in forgetting himself in the interplay of colors and forms that gave him back to the world, not least because painting is always a subjective activity and this in turn brings childhood back into the picture, as an instinctive realm beyond the reach of the will. To this extent, painting was part of his therapy—yet it was also a new beginning for his writing, because it allowed him to take a different view of himself. Painting fed off similar unconscious impulses as dreams, as Hesse noted in his dream diary on August 12, 1917:

> Besides, all hell has broken loose again today. My brief recent upswing has dissipated, my dreams have abandoned me, as have all the good things, and to boot the weather is cold and rainy, so I am sitting here and freezing and getting furious about the children making noise in the room below. As far as they are concerned—that is, my wife and the neighbors—I have long been the oddball and crazy person who can't stop swearing. This obsessiveness of mine, which is ruining my family's life, comes from my total inability to live with other people. I see them all passing their days quite naturally full of the joys of life, and it's only me who finds every hour a torment. The really terrible thing, though, is that the more I think about when this dreadful state of affairs might have set in, the more I come to the conclusion that it must have been present even in my earliest childhood, only back then it was an exceptional occurrence, whereas now it has become constant.[21]

Painting became a means of learning to like himself again, and of regaining a lost harmony between his own nature and the things that must necessarily remain artificial about art.

Hesse used painting as a medium through which to protest about a particular form of modern life that Charlie Chaplin was later to caricature in his movie *Modern Times:*

> Just you try it one time; try giving a modern-day American, whose musicality only extends as far as owning a gramophone and who thinks that a well-polished automobile is an object of esthetic beauty—by way of experiment one time just give someone like that who is blissful in his ignorance

and completely undemanding a lesson in art and how to paint a flower wilting, and invite them to experience, like you do, this transformation of pink to light gray as the most vital and exciting thing and as the secret of all life and beauty. They will be astonished.[22]

Hesse wrote this in his post-*Steppenwolf* phase, in his 1928 work "Late Summer Flowers" ("Spätsommerblumen"). That was also a period when he turned to painting once more—and the fact that the line began to play a more important role than the plane in his watercolors demonstrated that he too, who was a self-confessed dilettante where matters of painting were concerned, was constantly trying to become a more complete person, in other words to experiment with new forms of expression. This meant that even technology suddenly became a potential subject for poetry, something that Hesse had long thought impossible:

The Painter Paints a Factory in the Valley

You too have a beauty about you, factory in the valley,
Even though you are a symbol and repository of things I hate:
The scramble for money, slavery, dismal incarceration.
Yes, you are beautiful too! Many is the time
The subtle red of your roofs
And your flagpole and flag and your proud chimney
Have delighted my eye!
So, hail to you too and well-met,
You sweet faded blue of mean dwellings,
Which smell of soap and beer and children!
Set amid the green of meadows and the violet of farmland
The little boxy houses with their red roofs
Have a cheerful look, cheerful yet also subtle,
Not unlike wind music, the oboe and the flute.
Smiling, I dip my brush in varnish and cinnabar.
Wash over the fields with dusty green,
But the red chimney stack shines more beautifully than anything else,
Set vertically in this absurd world,
Massively proud, as lovely as it is laughable,
The pointer on the childish sundial of a giant.

The transition from word to color is a matter of nuance, and ultimately the determining factor for the quality of a picture or a text is whether the

right rhythm has been found or missed. This musicality is the bridge between the two art forms, but for Hesse it always remained the overarching
theme: successful form was like singing to him, just as his often straightforwardly rhymed poems are a form of song that follows simple melodies. In
every creative endeavor—be it writing, painting, or making music (Hesse
had learned to play the violin at school)—an echo of Mozart's *The Magic
Flute,* Hesse's favorite opera, can be heard. The heart of that work, too, lay
in its primal scenes, to which Hesse kept constantly returning, where it is all
about transformation and remaining the same, about creating and being
created, about sensuality and asceticism, and the whole birdlike existence of
a person who refuses to be locked up in the cage of systems that are alien to
him, and yet to whom nothing is so suspicious as a lack of order.

But above all, painting was a form of self-defense, a shield of beauty
against a world that was becoming ever uglier. To him it was a new, fresh
language, in which he could express things that he had said too often in
written form like he was saying them for the first time.

The first exhibition of Hesse's watercolors was held in 1920 at the art
gallery in Basel, with another being staged by the Heller Gallery in Vienna
in 1927. A contemporary reviewer remarked that Hesse painted "with such a
lack of formal technique, directly from experience" in the manner of "Doua-
nier" Rousseau: "But whatever his technical methods, he is most decidedly
an artist, a creator, a person whose meager watercolors vie with the richest
nature and compellingly depict sights that he has seen and experienced."[23]

Hesse put it more simply: painting was his lifesaver. He confided as
much to Ina Seidel in a letter of September 12, 1925: "The plain truth of
the matter is I would have died long ago had it not been for the fact that,
during the most difficult period of my life, my first forays into painting
brought me great solace and saved me."[24]

Casa Camuzzi in Montagnola

> It was like waking from a nightmare that had plagued me for
> years, I eagerly imbibed freedom, the air, the sun, solitude, and
> work.
>
> —Hermann Hesse, "On Moving to a New House" (1931)

At this juncture in his life—he was forty-two years old—Hesse pressed
the restart button. And in his first few months in Ticino, this fresh start

really did seem to be imbued with a powerful magic. From May 1919 on, he gazed down from his penthouse apartment in the Casa Camuzzi over a southern landscape. The door to his balcony remained open most of the time from May to October. Hesse took a deep breath and inhaled the heady, sensuous aroma of freedom. And for the first time in years, he also found himself able to exhale to some degree.

Hugo Ball and Stefan Zweig both remarked on Hesse's affinity to Vincent van Gogh. And indeed, Hesse's first reports from Ticino had an effusive ring to them that was similar to van Gogh's letters from Arles. Both men were living their dream of a studio in the South (though there was snow on the ground when van Gogh arrived in Arles). Vincent van Gogh expressed his euphoria through flamelike brushstrokes on his canvases, while the equivalent for Hesse was a new ecstatic tone to his writing when he settled here on the southern slopes of the Alps. The adventure of freedom resonated in every sentence he wrote.

The established best-selling writer Hermann Hesse was now old hat. But this meant that there was lifted from his shoulders a weight that he had become increasingly unwilling to bear. He felt strong and healthy, and it was as if his fear of the future had been suddenly swept away. He sensed that he would be able to work here, that he could catch up for lost time—both where his writing and his life were concerned. On Casa Camuzzi, that "beautiful, strange house" where he would live for the next twelve years, he wrote:

> Granted, I owned absolutely nothing here, and didn't even live in the house proper, but instead just rented a small apartment of four rooms. I was no longer a head of a household and a family, a man with a house and children and servants who whistles to his dog and tends his garden; now I was just a little burned-out man of letters, a shabby and somewhat suspect foreigner who lived on milk and rice and macaroni, wore his old suits until they grew threadbare and who in the fall foraged for his supper in the form of sweet chestnuts from the woods.[25]

Was this finally, then, that place of refuge he had always sought? Now, after what he called the "great shipwreck," he believed he had found it. Casa Camuzzi was an historic building, an "imitation of a Baroque hunting lodge," an extraordinary palazzo, which Hesse loved and whose

Casa Camuzzi in Montagnola

architecture he found "comical." He especially enjoyed the panoramic view from his balcony over the landscape of Ticino. In the garden stood a Judas tree, "the largest I have ever seen." It was cold there only in winter—the house had no heating. As early as the start of September, Hesse began to worry about the falling temperatures, as he wrote to his benefactor Georg Reinhart: "If you'd like to treat me, then I'd ask you to send me a little electric stove, as I find myself at a great disadvantage in this regard in the winter. We have a 600-volt electricity supply here."[26]

However, this turned out to be a very inadequate solution to Hesse's heating problem, as evidenced by the short text "Conversation with a Stove" ("Gespräch mit einem Ofen"), which concerns a stove with the brand name "Franklin." Although it looks good and has a nice-sounding name, this proves to be a complete monstrosity of a stove, as it fails in its primary function by generating absolutely no warmth. Written in 1919, "Conversation with a Stove" is—like all of Hesse's short prose pieces—by no means lightweight but rather a parable of the contemporary age.

But how was it that an Italian-made stove should have an American name, anyhow? Hesse's answer is still characterized by irrepressible good humor (after all, it was only his first winter here) and by the charm of having embarked on a new phase in his life, and on this occasion at least, this helped him cloak the sense of deep cultural pessimism he felt at the same time:

> Cowardly people have folk songs glorifying courage. So it is with us stoves. An Italian stove generally has an American name, in the same way that German stoves mostly have Greek ones. They are German—and believe me, they don't warm one bit better than I do—but they are called Eureka or Phoenix or Hector's Farewell. They are very evocative. In the same way, I am called Franklin. I am a stove, but according to my brand name, I might just as well be a statesman. I have a large mouth, consume a lot, generate very little heat, and am very evocative. That how it is with me.

Hesse seamlessly portrays the clash between the attractive appearance and the sheer uselessness of "Franklin." A stove that can do nothing, and is a total failure, but which for that very reason introduces itself with such gravitas! We are confronted here with a sparklingly witty mental image worthy of Oscar Wilde, which in the shortest of narratives parodies the deeper meaning, the higher sense, that nobody actually goes looking for in a stove: "Where the whole of Nature is concerned, the oak remains an oak, the wind a wind, and a fire simply a fire. But for Man, everything is always something else, everything has a meaning and an association! To him, everything becomes sacred and a symbol. The act of killing is a heroic deed, a plague is the finger of God, a war is evolution. So how could a stove just be a stove? No, it is also a symbol, a monument, a herald."[27] And consequently, being thus embellished, there's one thing it doesn't need to be able to do anymore: namely, supply heat.

The apartment in Casa Camuzzi was uninhabitable from November through to March due to the cold. And so it was that Hesse, who had decamped to the southern slopes of Alps in search of warmth, found himself going back north every winter: to Basel and also to Zurich. Quite apart from having more in the way of urban infrastructure, from restaurants to the opera, those cities up there had a better grasp of one crucial thing: heating.

Dreams of Becoming a Murderer / Suicide in *Klein and Wagner*

> We need to be both: without the animal or the murderer
> within us we are nothing but castrated angels with no real life,
> and likewise things aren't right with us either without that
> constantly renewed desire for transfiguration, for cleansing, and
> for worshipping something nonsensual and selfless.
>
> —Hermann Hesse, letter to Carl Seelig, autumn 1919

Klein and Wagner, the first book Hesse wrote on the southern side of the Alps during the summer of 1919, was filled with feverish creative energy. It is a nightmare that gives furious vent to all the feelings of guilt of a husband and father who has walked away from his obligations.

In an essay written for the magazine *Vivos voco* in 1921, Hesse said of the genesis of this tale, which many of his former readers found deeply disconcerting: "The tale of a philistine who find himself catapulted into a world of adventure, into the sphere of uncertainty that he finds alien, evil, and dangerous and who perishes there, has been told on many occasions in our times (by me as well, in 'Klein and Wagner'). It is a symptom of the age we live in, a way of expressing our feeling of standing on the brink of chaos."[28]

The doppelgänger theme had already been treated by Dostoyevsky *(The Double)* and by Robert Louis Stevenson in *Dr. Jekyll and Mr. Hyde*. In Hesse's story, the clerk Klein embezzles money, abandons his wife and family, and goes on the run to Italy. Wagner is the imaginary murderer who inhabits Klein's psyche. His dark alter ego: the criminal figure. Here, Hesse very clearly follows the Freudian principle of the conscious ego and the suppressed subconscious. Yet one also senses that Hesse immersed himself in Dostoyevsky's world and had a good insight into the mind of the murderer Raskolnikov in *Crime and Punishment*.

Yet what can be done about an impulsive nature that knows only how to murder and destroy? Or is that just bourgeois prejudice speaking? Hesse lets the situation play out—yet he seems unsure whether it isn't in fact larger and more uncontrollable than he was prepared to admit. Maybe fate is actually playing with him, even as he imagines that he is the one who is playing?

After writing *Klein and Wagner* Hesse went straight on to write *Klingsor's Last Summer*. As early as June 1919, the summer heat in Ticino was positively tropical. By moving to the southern side of the Alps, Hesse had also left the German-speaking world, which further contributed to his feeling of living in exile. Although he soon mastered enough Italian to get by in daily life, unlike Rilke in Valais, who even wrote poems in French, for Hesse Italian remained very much a foreign language.

He was far removed from German newspapers, which in any event rarely had anything nice to say about him. He continued to review books for the Swiss *Neue Zürcher Zeitung*. He also wrote articles for *Vivos voco* (literally "I Call Upon the Living"); by this time Richard Woltereck had joined the magazine as Hesse's coeditor. But where space, landscape, climate, and language were concerned, things German were now at one remove, or so it seemed at least. Hesse immersed himself in a stream of storytelling.

But unlike other occasions in his life when he had taken off on a journey to try to forget the daily grind, this was not about escaping. This time he had gone away to find a clear perspective on his previous life, as he told J. W. Muehlon on June 14, 1919: "I am trying to survive and recover from my private breakdown and to attempt on a small scale what Germany as a whole should also do. Accept what has happened, not to shift the blame onto others, but instead to suck it up and acknowledge my fate. I'd be the first to admit that this is incredibly difficult."[29]

The weather in the south could rapidly turn unsettled, very much like Hesse's state of mind. In June it had been swelteringly hot. By the end of July he suddenly found himself sitting in cold and rain and at a loss how to finishing writing his hot-weather fantasy *Klingsor's Last Summer*. The painter Louis Moilliet, who appears in the novel under the guise of "Louis the Cruel," learned from Hesse about the abrupt end to the weeks of unseasonal heat: "the weather outside is filthily cold today." And suddenly the notes of depression creep into Hesse's voice again: "It's often very hard to endure this existence." As he was working on *Klingsor's Last Summer,* Hesse told his Swiss painter friend about the novella he had just completed, *Klein and Wagner*. Hesse was immediately aware of the very special significance of this story within his work as a whole, and that it was a threshold he needed to cross: "It is a long novella, the best I've ever written to date, and it represents a break with my previous mode and the beginning of something new. Granted, this writing isn't beautiful and refined, in fact it's more like potassium cyanide, but it's good for all that and it was essential. Now I'm writing a new story, and drinking wine into the bargain, as I find it intolerable to be without work or wine."[30]

The crisis wasn't over; it had just taken a brief pause.

Klein and Wagner possesses a threatening undertone, which has a sudden chilling effect on that euphoric new departure to the South. One cannot help but be reminded of Dostoyevsky's *Dream of a Ridiculous Man* or his *Notes from the Underground*. In it, we see a person attempting a new start in life in the South, with a new name, and yet he knows in his heart of hearts that this will not be a new beginning for him; he is a man on the way down. Was that also Hesse's condition when he arrived in Ticino? Certainly. And his manic high during the summer of 1919 was merely a prelude to a nervous breakdown—the heaviest he had ever suffered, which would debilitate him for months. It all had to do with his self-image, "namely, the murderer who lives in me as well."[31]

The story turns on Klein, that fugitive who so strongly resembles Hesse. During his flight to Italy he styles himself "Wagner." In choosing this pseudonym, Klein had in mind Richard Wagner, whose erotic and sultry music fascinates and repels him in equal measure. But all of a sudden he realizes that Wagner was also the name of a murderer whose deeds were all over the newspapers (the true case of a teacher who murdered his wife and children)—and his shock at this becomes a sentence of condemnation against himself. He too is just such a murderer, albeit only in his thoughts; he too could be this Wagner. Hesse wrote about this to Carl Seelig in the fall of 1919: "The potential to be a murderer is the one pole, while the opposite pole is his goodness and his calm acquiescence in his fate. . . . The murderer keeps reminding us loudly and insistently about our hidden depths, which are full of filth and dark, primal thoughts. The other impulse in us is toward cleanliness and transfiguration, but it also tends toward glossing over embarrassing things, and toward denying and hushing-up things that we find impossible to swallow."[32]

During this period Hesse certainly hinted to J. B. Lang that everything would be easier if his wife, Mia, who was plaguing him with her uncontrollable fits of rage, was no longer alive. Would her death have been a release for him? When he wrote to Lang, Hesse was thinking Klein's thoughts, as expressed in the novella: "Perhaps—it was perfectly possible— it had not simply been his aversion to his wife and his married life, an aversion that in the interim had assumed massive proportions, that drove him to leave home, but instead much more the fear that he might really one day commit this dreadful crime: murdering them all, slaughtering them and watching them lie in their own blood."[33]

Klein could hardly believe that he had entertained such a thought—and the fact that he gave utterance to it was proof positive for him of how urgently he needed a change in his life. But now he had freed himself from his wife and children—and together with his light pack of belongings he also took a guilty conscience with him on his journey south. In this landscape he could live at long last! "So, this South really did exist, it wasn't a myth. The bridges and cypresses were youthful dreams fulfilled, and the houses and the palm trees said to him: you're no longer in the old groove, a whole new chapter is beginning. The air and the sunshine seemed spiced and fortified, his breathing grew easier, life became more possible, the revolver more dispensable, and the need to wipe himself out on the railway tracks less urgent. Despite everything, it now seemed possible to attempt something. Perhaps life might be bearable after all."[34]

He met a young woman of the brash kind that he had always despised in his former life. Or had it been his wife who had despised them for him, acting on his behalf? Being in the South meant feeling your own sensual temperature rise once more, and leaving behind the false yardsticks of "decency." After all, given what he had actually done, let alone the sort of thoughts he had been having, he had long since ceased to be a "decent" person. He was a free agent and this girl, whose name was Teresina, suited him much more than his wife had ever done. "The South made life easier. It consoled you. It numbed you . . . he found that there was something primeval, cultivated, and yet primitive about it, a simultaneous innocence and maturity that was lacking in the North."[35]

Klein knew that his relationship to this girl Teresina would never be anything more than a brief, passionate affair. He didn't have much time— Wagner, the artist and the criminal, was sitting inside him, ready to pounce. Klein was constantly on the run from him, he couldn't live as a criminal! Hesse and Klein alike were caught in a trap: "He felt like a child who had been playing with matches and had set a house alight. Now it was blazing away. My God! And what had he profited from all this? Even if he traveled on to Sicily or Constantinople, would that make him twenty years younger?"[36]

Klein chooses to escape through death, and Hesse allowed himself six pages to depict this suicide, describing in detail the way in which Klein slips from a boat into the water and drowns. As he is sinking through the water, he senses his life rushing through him with an intensity he has never felt before. Here, the motif from *Demian* appears once again: "The world was continually being born and continually dying."[37]

Everything seems possible in the moment when one is prepared to relinquish one's life. "There was nothing in the world that wasn't just as beautiful, as desirable, or as exhilarating as its counterpart! It was blissful to live, it was blissful to die as soon as one was suspended alone in space."[38]

Was Hesse working here toward his rebirth in the South and did the philistine Klein only perish in order that Wagner (the artist and criminal) might continue to live? Or had Hesse already come to a secret arrangement with the idea of taking his own life? Did he regard this as inevitable, and did he even intend to commit suicide after he had soaked up as much of the southern summer as he possibly could?

Klingsor's Last Summer: Bacchanalian Flights of Fancy before the Breakdown

> It is late Romanticism which is keenly aware of missing out
> on love, on life, and on animality and which in one final surge
> attempts to reclaim youth; yet what it ends up doing is sur-
> passing it by virtue of all the mature wisdom of age.
>
> —Hugo Ball, biography of Hermann Hesse

Toward the end of the feverish summer of creativity in 1919, Hesse wrote to Georg Reinhart on August 31: "Yet times such as this have one good thing about them, one great blessing, as I have been discovering for myself these past few months: a passion and intensity of artistic endeavor such as one can never manage when one is feeling well. When you feel fragile to the very core of your being and sense that you can't count on being around for much longer, you summon up all your energy like an old tree that bears leaves one last time and tries to immortalize itself through its seeds before it is cut down."

It was as if Hesse had really and truly—and after a delay of twenty years—been kissed by that "fever muse" he had written about in *An Hour Behind Midnight,* and which his mother warned him was a "snake" like the one that slithered into Paradise. And here he was living it—that febrile state in which a person believes that they can achieve everything, and all at once. It was a creative ecstasy the like of which Hesse would never experience again! He was free and the war lay behind him, as did Bern and the constant pressure exerted by his family there. Everything dark was in the past, and the present was a blazing summer that burned with an intense heat, inside and out.

But for all that, he knew that he was no longer a young man, he could feel the toll that had been taken on his strained eyes and his aching joints and bones, where the first signs of gout, rheumatism, and arthritis were becoming apparent—not to mention sciatica. He had long since got used to drinking wine in quantity again, he was unsociable, and his mood swung from one moment to the next from friendly engagement to curt dismissiveness.

What's more, he wasn't actually a believer in upbeat moods and sensory stimulation. He thought they were more likely to prevent a person from working. He was old enough to know that. After all, as far as he was concerned, writing had always been a way of enduring all those things that otherwise could not be endured. It was cool and calculating work, a pure drudgery in the service of words. And yet this time, he did not deny himself the feeling of ecstasy, not least because he knew that it would only last for one summer. Precisely for that reason!

He spent most days, not writing, but outdoors enjoying the countryside around Lake Lugano, which enchanted him time and again. He painted with an insatiable delight in color and form.

In these circumstances, what could be more appropriate than to write the story of a painter who is getting on in years, whose senses are captivated by the burning summer, and who longs once more—for one final time—to taste the sweetness of youth, and who massively overtaxes his already dwindling powers, as if time held no dominion over him?

This was a pipe dream, for sure, which Hesse himself did not believe in his more sober moments, yet he was quite prepared to unhesitatingly devote his energies to it. He knew that these brief moments were precious. But he did this all against a backdrop of constant worry. He was afraid that this might really be his last summer; these mortal fears were the price he paid for his overstrained youthful willingness to start a new life. And so, in a letter of August 27, 1919, to his publisher Samuel Fischer, we find him giving instructions about what, in the event of his sudden death, should be done with his unpublished manuscripts, which for him were the artistically precious distillation of this chaotic period: "Every now and then I get the feeling that something could happen to me. In that event, I would ask you to take note of the fact that it is essential that the following books of mine be published: a book comprising three novellas, my latest revolutionary new works." The texts he was alluding to here were the short story "Kinderseele" and the novellas *Klein and Wagner* and *Klingsor's Last Summer* (he was still working on the last of these at the time). Hesse was fully aware of the significance of these texts, which for his work really were revolutionary from an esthetic point of view. They were all, so to speak, children of *Demian,* which had finally been published shortly beforehand. The authorship of this later work was still being credited, not to Hesse, but instead to a young, unknown, terminally ill writer by the name of Emil Sinclair.

In the preliminary note to the novella *Klingsor's Last Summer* we are told that the great creative surge of the painter Klingsor was his swan song: the last summer of the forty-two-year-old artist (exactly Hesse's age), in which his work broke through into a new dimension. Hesse called this "those free paraphrases on the forms of the phenomenal world, those strange, luminous and yet tranquil, dreamily tranquil pictures, with their crooked trees and their plantlike houses."[39]

Around this same time Hesse was asked to write the text for a monograph on Vincent van Gogh, a painter who had made a strong impression on him, especially in the account of his life by Julius Meier-Graefe (whom Hesse also greatly admired, despite the fact that he too had once had the misfortune of being in vogue, which he would be obliged to atone for forever after). Even so, he found himself unable to commit to writing a monograph on Van Gogh.

A phrase in Meier-Graefe's book struck a particular chord with him—and this duly reappeared in his own novella on Klingsor: "the myth of his life."[40]

And so the self-portrait of Hesse and the portrait of Vincent van Gogh merge together in a fairy-tale-symbolic manner to form—and this is the quite astonishing effect—a new and unexpectedly hard-edged realism. In a world that is entirely geared to utility, maneuvering, and dissembling, the artist becomes someone who founders. He is a fool in the eyes of that world, which regards itself as rational and sensible. Once again we see Hesse harking back to his own beginnings, to that little monograph on St. Francis of Assisi, which took it upon itself to retell the legend of the saint.

The very first page of *Klingsor* cites all the conjectures that might equally well have applied to either Hesse in his first summer in Ticino or van Gogh in Arles: "Some of his letters had contained premonitions or death-wishes. . . . Many maintained that Klingsor had been suffering from mental illness for months already. . . . But the anecdotal rumor that Klingsor had a great fondness for drink was better founded than such gossip. This inclination was certainly present in him, and no one was more candid about calling it by its name than Klingsor himself."[41]

If we want to delve down to the spiritual source of this story, then we should heed the words of Hesse's biographer Hugo Ball, who called Hesse the last knight from the brilliant procession of Romanticism and added: "He defends the rearguard. . . . He salutes the Sternbalds, the Schlemihls and the Taugenichts of this world. He carries all their wistful and joyous intonations in his blood; he has assimilated all their sky-blue and golden childishness."[42] And seldom did Hesse confess so openly to being a successor to the Romantic movement as he did in *Klingsor's Last Summer.* Novalis had introduced the magical teacher of poetry Klingsohr (spelled with an "h") in his novel *Heinrich von Ofterdingen;* this character performs the role of a seducer to a life of fantasy and to fairy-tale-like transformation, and his temptations have an enduring effect. Hesse willingly follows this cicerone in the "Southern realms" of life here—in the full knowledge that the twentieth century will be dominated by machines and science and that the decision to lead a life defined by poetry goes beyond an individual's powers.

A heightened state of existence carries within it a divine spark, but the boundless sense of the possible which that entails—and which forms the sole basis of poetic inspiration—at the same time erodes a person's capacity to withstand the demands of real life; it makes them ill, and to the extent that their poetry begins to live, they are led toward death. That is the paradox in which, since the time of Novalis, Hesse saw the Klingsor figure inextricably caught—and his prospects of encountering a reality that was favorably disposed toward poetry had only grown progressively slimmer with the passage of time. But the utopia was alive and well for all that—and Hesse found himself fired up by it in the Ticino summer of 1919. And so he found himself subscribing wholeheartedly to these sentiments from *Heinrich von Ofterdingen:* "Without dreams we would surely grow older sooner, and so we may see dreams, if not as directly sent from heaven above, at least as divine gifts, as friendly companions on our pilgrimage to the holy sepulchre."[43]

Like Novalis, Hesse followed his dream, and for him it was his only route to recovery—even if it cost him his life. Only poetry could over-come life—and a false life at that! Thus, through every form of order there shone a beneficial chaos—and yet for Novalis, poetry was something, as he had his magician Klingsohr say, that must be "pursued as a rigorous art form." An artist must not only be prepared to labor at his work, above all he must yearn to gain self-fulfillment by living through his art. His lan-guage is "a microcosm of symbols and sounds."[44]

Novalis's work set a whole new course for poetry, presenting nothing less than an inversion of the customary definition of reality; the dream world was now real, and reality unreal. In order to live a poetic life—that is, a nonalienated existence—a person needed to follow their dream and only that.

The symbol of such Romanticism was the "blue flower" *(die blaue Blume).* In *Heinrich von Ofterdingen* it embodies the "magic wand of the soul," that heightened feeling of living to which a new world reveals itself—and where the internal trumps the external. Everyone already carries within them-selves their own Arcadia, all he or she needs to do is to discover it. This idea also became a guiding principle for Hesse. Everything is given over to poetic form, which must above all be light and comprehensible. Yet this by no means precludes it from assuming fragmentary characteristics, for the material must shine in its very own original atmosphere: "Only an un-forced composition can make the richness of invention comprehensible and charming; set against this, even simple symmetry has all the unpleasant dryness of a set of numbers. The best poetry is very close at hand, and not infrequently an unfamiliar object its favorite subject matter."[45]

Musing on such things, Hesse lived through his first summer in the South, a brief but intense state of ecstasy whose finite nature he was aware of every second—indeed, that was what made it so precious. But he was enough of an artist to always view himself with an appropriate measure of detachment, in the same way that one observes an animal that has suddenly been released into the wild from an enclosure. This was an undeniably paradoxical situation: wonderful and yet also fear-inducing—however, one could forget this as long as the sun kept beating down with summery intensity, and there was sufficient wine to hand, along with girls who did not always remind him that he had long ago ceased to be a young man. This could all come about only through a new enchantment of his own life, an enterprise he eagerly embraced: "A magical outlook on life was always close to my heart, I have never been a 'modern' person and always considered Hoffmann's *The Golden Pot* or even *Heinrich von Ofterdingen* as far more worthwhile pieces of literature than all the histories of the world or of nature (whenever I read such works, I always regarded them too as delightful confabulations)."[46]

For Hesse the southern summer became a flaming reality and a symbol of the brief period that still remained to him. He was intent on creating a body of work that would succeed in showing a "gaze into chaos" in the Dostoyevskian sense: "However long they were, the hot days blazed up like burning flags, and short, sultry moonlit nights were followed by short, sultry nights of rain, which passed as swiftly as dreams and were crowded with dreams, and the shimmering weeks rolled by feverishly."[47]

This was a ruinous rapture, which hit Hesse at an untimely moment and which his aging body could endure only for brief moments at a time. Was it even a slow form of suicide amid all the ecstasy he was experiencing?

His body sent out signals, and Hesse was enough of an inveterate chronicler to record this: "Perhaps, if only one could really sleep for a succession of nights, get a proper six to eight hours' worth of sleep, one might be able to recuperate, and one's eyes would become obedient and patient again, and the heart quieter, and one's temples wouldn't ache all the while. . . . No, no human being could endure this flaming life for long, not even Klingsor, who had ten lives." And then the rapture suddenly turned to a deep depression and the hunted feeling of dread that the summer might draw to a close before he had managed to create something that would live on for a while beyond his death: "It will come to an end, already much energy has been spent, much eyesight expended, much life bled away."[48]

Like Klingsor, Hesse knew that if he wanted to work on at all for a while, he could not live like an aging man who was already plagued by various frailties for which he had to make allowances. But what did "a while" mean, when the Here and Now was overwhelming him with a hitherto unknown intensity? His fear about the days he had wasted grew, and in the long term he could not block out memories of earlier upswings in mood that had all been followed by severe crashes. There was only one way out: to throw the last log into the fire to try to generate even more heat. Hesse shows us all that, the completed arc of Klingsor's life, even in the preliminary note. Before the novella proper even begins, it has already been narrated to the end. That is one of the devices through which Hesse manages to write such a densely packed tale, immersing the reader from the start in shimmering heat and impending thunderstorms.

Klingsor's Last Summer is therefore also the thing that Marie Hesse had suspected all those years before on the basis of *An Hour Behind Midnight:* an erotic dream, a sexual outburst so powerful that it—for the first time in Hesse—also irrupts into the work, where it sets about destroying all previous templates with an archaic and chaotic force. That was the music of the apocalypse: the only thing that could follow an erotic force that broke out with such unconditionality. During this summer Hesse felt the presence of Eros and Thanatos more powerfully than he had ever done before, and realized how great the affinity was between destructive energy and the creative force. Happiness and fulfillment and death and annihilation grow from the same root of human nature. And Hesse undertook an experiment to discover how far that nature could be stimulated before he lost the ability to shape this mighty chaos of energies and give it artistic expression.

Here, then, we can see his changed relationship to eroticism. Previously he had foregrounded the ideal of a "desireless love," the contemplation and adoration of the beautiful woman who inspires, or of the motherly figure who protects. In Hesse's earlier works there are depictions, wonderful in their indeterminate confidentiality, of brief glances exchanged in railway carriages and on balconies—invariably the image of women there is a promise whose fulfillment is not remotely sought after. Hesse folds the image within himself, carries it away as a possession that keeps on working inside of him. Such a glance is enough to fill his day with a special atmosphere, which he had to be careful not to destroy through any importunate attempt to approach the woman in question. This art of erotic allusion becomes a constant feature of his writing thereafter. An aura that turns an everyday situation into a special one.

Hesse on a walk near Carona

In *Klingsor's Last Summer,* though, a sexuality that is not about allusions and atmosphere suddenly breaks out of Hesse with unforeseen violence. This is demonstrated most clearly by Klingsor's dream. It lays bare the primitive, the elemental, sexual, and primal force in which all art is rooted. For, as we learn in his *Life Story Briefly Told,* art begins when a person casts off all abstractions and abandons himself to the "primitive pleasure of creation."[49] And that describes Klingsor's dream too:

> He was lying in a forest and had a redheaded woman on his lap, while a black-haired woman leaned against his shoulder and another knelt beside him, holding his hand and kissing his fingers, and everywhere, all around, were women and girls, some of them still children, with long thin legs, some nubile, some mature and with the signs of awareness and of fatigue in their mobile faces, and all loved him and all wanted to be loved by him. Then war and fury erupted among the women . . . they all fell upon one another, each one screaming, each tearing, each biting, each hurting, each suffering pain. Laughter, cries of fury, and howls of anguish rang out intertwined and tangled, blood flowed everywhere, nails dug bloodily into plump flesh.[50]

A primal battle of the sexes, an orgiastic scene in which the author makes himself the object of desire. A reverie in which the pubescent pipe dream of sexually possessing a woman (or womanhood as a whole) so to speak explodes in the knowledge of its sheer futility. In Harry Haller's "Magic Theater" in *Steppenwolf*—Haller is a descendant of Klingsor—the slogan bandied about is: "All women are yours." Which is tantamount to saying: None of them are yours, your woman is just a deceptive pretense.

In a letter of July 24, 1919, to the painter Louis Moilliet, Hesse recounted the bacchanalian days he spent in the environs of Montagnola:

> There were many beautiful and magical days, and at night the moon raced like a mad thing across the sky and before you knew it, it was morning again, and you crawled home and discovered your waistcoat was covered with red wine stains. We were also in Carona, where we saw the cannon-balls and violet Mount Generoso again, and that lovely girl Ruth was running around in a little flame-red dress, accompanied by her aunt, two dogs and an unfortunately insane piano-tuner—a marvelous menagerie of people! The whole party ended up in a dark grotto, hanging in the air some-where up a steep slope, with lit-up trains roaring past below, and there was a lot of kissing of girls and tree trunks, it was beautiful and terrifying.
>
> It's through little pleasures like this that one can delight one's poor heart and make the long journey through life seem much shorter. Unfortunately, though, my eyes have been really bad and hurting me for the past three weeks.[51]

Here, in his description of an excursion to Carona (which finds its way into *Klingsor's Last Summer* as the chapter headed "The Day at Kareno") we also find the first mention of Ruth Wenger, daughter of the writer Lisa Wenger and her manufacturer husband; five years later, Hesse would marry Ruth. In addition, two of the many dogs (and other animals) with which she surrounded herself, much to Hesse's displeasure, are also present during this excursion—here, they did not appear to have bothered him.

An earlier tale that we might see as the prototype of *Klingsor's Last Summer* is the short story "The Painter" ("Der Maler") of 1918. In this story the artist, Albert, who finds himself disillusioned with the world, becomes a recluse. He turns into an eccentric, a semi-idiot. Hesse portrays his plight thus: "With the kind of pictures he painted, he could not achieve the success or impact he yearned for."[52] He goes abroad to live, and in time the world forgets about him. On one of his long, aimless walks, though, he suddenly starts to look at the landscape differently. Something resonates in him—"deep within his soul, he felt an old song from the time of legends swelling up." And he begins to paint as if he is enraptured: "Never again did he find himself thinking 'Why am I doing that?' He just painted. He did nothing any more except observe and paint." When word gets around that he is painting again, people think he's gone crazy, especially because he refuses to show the pictures to anyone. He shuts up his apartment, gives the key to an acquaintance, and sets off on his travels. During his absence, people get to see the paintings and find them works of sheer genius, and when he comes back from his trip, incognito, there is a man posted outside his door and he has to buy an entry ticket. He finds the interpretations that have been assigned to his paintings very odd; they have nothing to do with the rapture of seeing that he painted them in. And so, still unnoticed, he leaves the city again, never to return: "He still painted a lot of paintings and gave them lots of names, and was happy doing so; but he never showed them to anyone."[53]

In this story—written in the year before he moved to Montagnola— Hesse expresses an ideal without which his life in Ticino would be inexplicable.

It was the dream of a place of refuge, which he had dreamed so often, that erupted from him here with such unexpected force. A new life!

It began with him writing and painting like Albert, without questioning why he was doing it. What a joy it was to once more engage in something that was as natural as breathing, and not to have to give directions but instead surrender oneself to the rediscovered creative rapture. And to embody this idea, Hesse did not just pick any name, but *the* name that epitomized Romanticism: Klingsor.

In the course of his creative rapture, the magician Klingsor does not transform himself into the guise of another person—but always into himself, into one of his many possibilities. Klingsor, wrote Hesse, had ten lives, all of which had to be tasted to the full.

When he first set eyes on Casa Camuzzi, Hugo Ball, who soon became one of Hesse's closest friends in Ticino, could not help but be reminded of the Villa Rufolo in Ravenna, where Wagner found the model for Klingsor's magic garden in his opera *Parsifal*. It had the same overflowing southern fecundity, which then ultimately wraps itself up in the secret of unrealizable desire. Like the Villa Rufolo, Casa Camuzzi even had a little balcony looking out onto the neglected garden—for once not a garden for family use, but a rampant, jungle-like park. For Hesse, this was to become "Klingsor's Balcony."

Hesse's musical language in *Klingsor's Last Summer* also reminded Hugo Ball of Wagner's *Tristan und Isolde*.

> It has a deep note of sorrow and all the torment of a love that is inseparable and indistinguishable from death. And what is truly remarkable is the sultry, rampant, cooing tone of this final novella in the set, this anxious lamenting over transience, this plunging into the abyss and this rekindling from the depths, this chromaticism of languishing and voluptuous sounds that build to a crescendo and then recede: each in their own way, they are both maestros—the one from Ravello and the one from Montagnola. A *furioso* of passion breaks all boundaries and threatens to burst apart the idyllic landscape and then races to its conclusion in self-abnegation and tender infatuation.[54]

The most important factor is this: Klingsor's newly rekindled enthusiasm for something that he has been doing for a long time—for *too* long, it some-times seems to him—has its most significant root in the sudden affirma-tion of the fact that he is completely at odds with the world as it exists, and with the false criteria it sets for being considered important or famous. Should the world (or posterity) be the judge of which of his works were a success and ultimately what value his life had as a whole? Now—in the midst of the "music of doom" *(Musik des Untergangs)*—he can laugh about it all; this world of false standards does not concern him anymore.

All of a sudden he understands such things. Louis the Cruel, a fellow painter and a Gauguin-like character, comes to visit: "Louis was a legend." What follows is another grandiose monologue in which Klingsor expli-cates to Louis the course of events in this declining world:

> "It occurs to me that the only two painters our good country can boast of are sitting together here now, and then I get a horrible feeling in my knees as if the two of us were cast in bronze and standing here hand in hand on a monument, you know, like Goethe and Schiller. After all, it's not their fault that they're condemned to stand there for all eternity holding each other's bronze hands and that, little by little, they come to seem so embar-

rassing and abhorrent to us. It may well be that they were perfectly decent fellows; years ago I read a play by Schiller and it was pretty good. And yet this is what has become of him now—he's become a monument and is forced to stand beside his Siamese twin, with their two sculpted heads in relief, and you see their collected works standing on shelves and hear them analyzed in schools. It's awful. Just imagine a professor a hundred years from now preaching to his students: '*Klingsor,* born in 1877, and his friend Louis, nicknamed The Glutton, innovators in painting, who liberated art from naturalistic color, and on closer inspection the works of this pair of painters fall into three quite distinct periods!' Honestly, I'd rather just throw myself under the wheels of a locomotive right now."

"It'd make more sense to throw the professors under it instead!"

"There aren't any locomotives that big. You know how small-scale our technology is."[55]

Here Hesse shows us Klingsor and Louis—and in the process also himself—in a conversation between two truly free spirits. It is a rejection of everything officiously self-important or stultifyingly academic, and of a reality that has been institutionalized and bureaucratically managed. Here, once more, we can see Hesse's radical Protestant spirit in all its immediacy, which is in a state of constant revolt, even against its own points of fixity; this is akin to the attitude of, say, the seventeenth-century Lutheran theologian Gottfried Arnold, whose *Impartial History of the Church and Heresy* (1699–1700) was a church history based entirely on the viewpoint of heretics as unbiased witnesses to the truth. Yet all visible history is the history of decline!

Only invisible history, to which those who have been marginalized and excluded from visible history—namely, the heretics and outsiders—bear witness, provides a living testimony to the truth.

The fantasies that Hesse imagined his two painters dreaming up here in their cups and declaiming to the summer night sky unleashed a further storm of violent reaction in Germany—something that the writer had expected after his earlier experiences. But this was quite intentional on his part; in the meantime, Hesse began to take secret pleasure in scandalizing the German petit bourgeoisie and their conservatism. In his *Life Story Briefly Told,* he recalled his "harmless remark about the famous poet Schiller, whereupon every last South German skittles club declared me a desecrator of the Fatherland's shrines."[56] This is further evidence of the new ironic tone adopted by Hesse—a far cry here, therefore, from the clichéd view of him as a whispering romanticist of pure inwardness. Though he indisputably was both a late Romantic and a poet of inwardness, he conveyed this not through whispers but instead by means of a humorous voice satirizing the poses struck by German spirituality. The relationship between Hesse and the Germans was one of deep alienation, very much like that of Heine in the previous century—yet it was also characterized by just as much unspoken affinity. But what is new here is the offensive attitude with which Hesse—like Nietzsche—carefully preserved a secret sense of his very own Germany amid all his anti-German protests. Accordingly, his "contrition" is very provisional when he continues, in sarcastic vein: "For several years now, however, I have managed not to say anything that desecrates national shrines or causes people to turn crimson with fury. I regard that as some kind of progress."[57]

In approaching Romanticism through the religious forms of Pietism and Catholicism, the writer Hugo Ball, Hesse's first biographer, arrived at a highly contemporary view of this artistic movement, which in its yearning for another life created some remarkable syntheses of esthetics and religion. As a result, Ball's interpretation of *Klingsor's Last Summer* is a high point of his slim, highly intimate volume on Hesse, which combines self-reflection and an insight into Hermann Hesse's life and work in a way that has never since been matched. It was Ball who spoke of a "Klingsor German"—the poetic counterpart, so to speak, of the popular myth of the "Rembrandt German," as promulgated by the nationalist art historian Julius Langbehn. According to Ball, Hesse's painter Klingsor was a "self-portrait of the dying Romantic."[58] This prompted the further question: Will he be reborn—and if so, when?

Ball also highlighted the fundamental contradiction at the heart of the novella. The painter Klingsor paints the "music of doom." This also corresponds to the self-image of Vincent van Gogh, who felt he could see music and hear light when he was painting. The paradox reveals a form of mysticism. The direct perception of the essence of things! It also reminds us of Nietzsche's dichotomy of the Dionysian and the Apollonian. Music as the most ecstatic of all the arts here combines with the graphic sensibility of the painter. Hesse, who was highly visually oriented but who often had to stop himself from looking at things thanks to the pain in his eyes, now set about, through his painting and drawing, to compose a kind of music that was not a grand Wagnerian opera but rather a song by Franz

Schubert: Hesse walked on summery paths with "Winterreise" ("Winter's Journey") in his heart. In Arles, van Gogh also soon found himself dreaming once more of the North, of coolness, and of colors that were not bleached out. Likewise, Swabia was weighing heavily on Hesse's heart even as he drank large quantities of wine and celebrated the freedom of sensual ardor. He could not rid himself of this gravity and become insouciant in a southern way. As a consequence, the summer that had been such a great and powerful dream finally drew to a close—in *Klingsor,* we see it fading and declining toward the fall. Hesse could not and would not forget all the things he had experienced and suffered since the publication of his youthful work *Peter Camenzind:* his rise to success as an author, the endless world war, the incessant insults directed at him by German nationalists, and the drama of his marriage. His soul was no longer intact, it was damaged, and his work henceforth was one long struggle to give expression to this damaged state.

The Hesse biographer Ralph Freedman concurs with Sigmund Freud in regarding all artistic endeavor as a form of sublimation of a person's carnal nature. There is undoubtedly some truth in this, but it does not seem to explain art itself. Hesse actually dealt with the arguments of psychoanalysis within *Klingsor's Last Summer*—posing the question of whether art was a substitute for "missed life, missed animality, missed love" and reacting vehemently to this objection that he himself has raised, which to him (in the guise of Klingsor) sounds like nothing so much as a cheap excuse: "But it really isn't so. It's altogether different. We overestimate matters of the senses if we regard the matters of the mind merely as paltry substitutes for missing sensuality. Sensuality isn't worth a jot more than spirituality, and it's the same the other way around. It's all one, everything is equally good. Whether you embrace a woman or create a poem, it's the same. So long as the main thing is there, the love, the ardor, the passion, it doesn't matter whether you are a monk on Mount Athos or a man about town in Paris."[59]

Klingsor's Last Summer became the centerpiece of Hesse's work. Everything he wrote hereafter would march to the same rhythm as this novella—including far larger and more wide-ranging works such as *Siddhartha, Steppenwolf,* and above all *The Glass Bead Game.* Nowhere else did Hesse fid such an appropriately fairy-tale-like way of portraying his own psyche as he did here. The myth of the magical king Klingsor, who in his declining months paints his most beautiful, and yet to the public his most disconcerting, paintings, would carry his work henceforth through all the phases of incomprehension and rejection it encountered. With *Klingsor's Last Summer* Hesse succeeded in reconciling the contradictions that once threatened to tear him part. A man of duty and an anarchist, an idler and a workaholic, a moralist and a libertine, a wise man and a lunatic, and intellectual and a child of nature. It was only as a result of this successful reconciliation, not only in writing but also in painting, that Hesse was able to make a fresh start and to locate a space within which his writing could operate in future, after he had finally delivered the *coup de grâce* to his Bern existence with *Klein and Wagner.*

This fairy-tale, fundamentally magical dimension required not only that Hesse withdraw from the world but also its exact opposite: that he immerse himself in a world into which he could enter only as an individual and not as a collective or party. When a stranger brings Klingsor greetings from friends in Paris—by this stage it is the fall and he has done what he had to do—and this visitor tries to engage Klingsor in a little conversation, the painter remains distant and barely answers. The guest is an unwelcome disturbance. Then, as they are taking leave of one another, Klingsor suddenly lays his hand on the man's shoulder: "'Thank you,' he said slowly, with effort. 'Thank you, dear friend. I'm working, I can't talk. People always talk too much. Don't be angry, and give my friends my regards. Tell them I love them.'"[60] This sounds as Protestant as Chekhov's exhortation at the end of Uncle Vanya: "We shall work without rest!" As for the finished painting, "he showed it to no one"—thus restoring a dimension of secrecy and concealment to a world that consisted of pure obviousness and was sinking into banality.

Even so, the urge to express himself remained. The discrepancy between the life of the work and that of the author could be overcome only in rare moments, before the two diverged from one another once more. Continuing to live thereafter was not easier but harder. In *Klingsor's Last Summer* there suddenly appears one of those sentences that give the indeterminate tone of the novella an unexpected everyday grounding: "Are people who write so many letters happy?"[61] That struck certain notorious chords in Hesse's own life, notably the drudgery of writing letters, which other authors (not Thomas Mann, but certainly Gottfried Benn) rigorously shunned; an enormous number of letters, no fewer than 44,000, came to light in Hesse's estate after his death. The question in the novella sounds like someone who wanted to be alone yet who was never able to be so.

*   *   *

It was the classic situation of an author who had crossed a boundary and could now no longer go back. This too became henceforth one of the abiding themes of Hesse's work that was first anticipated in *Klingsor's Last Summer*. There the "astrologer," the "Armenian" (a figure modeled on Joseph Englert), whispers to Klingsor, who at this juncture has styled himself Li Tae Pe: "You have struck up the music of doom, you sit singing in your burning house, which you set fire to yourself, and you are very unhappy about it, Li Tai Pe, even if you drain three hundred cups a day and drink toasts with the moon."[62]

Li Tae Pe (or Li Bai), the figure whose persona Hesse assimilates here, was an eighth-century Chinese poet. His poems, which are written in a simple conversational tone, clearly form one of the stylistic models for Hesse's own verse. This Li Tai Pe was a mythical figure to Hesse's taste. The atmosphere around Li Tai Pe sets the whole tone for *Klingsor's Last Summer*. This poet was appointed by an emperor with a feel for the arts to be a court advisor, so making his position unassailable. Yet the poet enjoyed the pleasures of wine and intoxication and took pleasure in disrupting the established order, which for him was just as dubious a gift as the status of a successful bourgeois author was to Hesse. The early twentieth-century writer Klabund wrote the legend of Li Tai Pe:

> Li Tai Pe dragged the emperor's robes through all the gutters of the province and in the evenings, drunk as a lord, had others pay homage to him as emperor. Or, dressed in the emperor's clothes, he would deliver rebellious speeches to his drinking companions and the assembled public. He died in a state of inebriation when he fell out of a boat one night while crossing a river. Legend has it that he was saved by a dolphin, which carried him out to sea and, as angel-like spirits descended from the sky to look after him, took him away into the wide blue yonder of immortality.

Like Hesse, Klabund was also using the ancient Chinese poet as a guise, in order distance himself through fantasy from the contemporary reality of the First World War (his book of poems based on the work of the Chinese writer appeared in 1915). One of the poems in this volume, "Auf der Wiese" ("In the Meadow") is very much in the spirit of Hesse's Klingsor:

We lie in the blossoming lap of the meadow's fringe
And drink a cup, and then another and another.
When I am drunk, like an open gate in the wind, I croak:
"Go home and fetch me my guitar!
And then leave me alone in the little boat of my intoxication:
I want to wake up with a young poem in my arms."

Here we see the same dual movement that also pervades *Klingsor's Last Summer:* namely, an attempt at rejuvenation when death is already in sight, in a state of creative intoxication that acts just like wine.

A memorable conversation takes place between the artist and the astrologer. Hesse would sustain the theme of magic right through to the "Magic Theater" of *Steppenwolf.* In the novella, Klingsor asks the astrologer if the latter can do anything to guide his stars differently. The astrologer replies that he cannot guide them, only interpret them. The Armenian tells him that it is down to Klingsor himself to redirect his fate and that there is a freedom of the will, which is called magic.

"Why should I practice magic when I can practice art? Isn't art just as good?"
"Everything is good. Nothing is good. Magic dispels that worst of illusions which we call 'time.'"
"Doesn't art do that too?"
"It tries to. Is your painted July, which you have there in your portfolio, enough for you? Have you annulled time? Are you without fear of the autumn, of the winter?"[63]

Hesse was incapable of answering this question of what significance art has for life. It does not prevent people from falling ill and dying—but perhaps it can help them bear this inevitable fate more easily?

At times he believed this, and at other times not. After he had completed *Klingsor's Last Summer,* Hesse fell into a deep depression. What he really wanted to do was to summon up one last remnant of Klingsorian euphoria and follow his character into a death that was the natural corollary to the completion of his work. But was Hesse's own work also at an end? Or was it not instead the case that a completed fragment such as this novella formed a far more fitting capstone to the former life that he now found unlivable?

Emmy Hennings and Hugo Ball read *Klingsor's Last Summer* in May 1921; Hesse had given it to his new friends to see what they made of it. Ball wrote to Hesse, who was visiting Zurich at the time: "We read *Klingsor's Last Summer* with deep devotion, on the quietest of all Sunday afternoons. The village trumpeter was blowing away for all he was worth and the hens in the garden were cackling in a very Indochinese way. It is a fiery book full of color and sun, even death has a fever. But it shouldn't be the last summer."[64] Emmy Hennings found that astrology, which was practiced by their mutual friend Joseph Englert and had now found its way into the Klingsor novella, tended to create an ironic distancing effect, for she wrote to Hesse about the "stars" that she saw rising up above the fields on one of her evening walks: they were fireflies. "Looking at them, I made some astonishing progress in my understanding of astrology. People have a powerful influence on the stars. There is only the one constellation: a yearning for omnipotence. And with that all the stars fall to Earth."[65]

Hugo Ball told Joseph Englert that Hesse's *Klingsor* was a "very febrile book," but that it contained one very beautiful, calm poem. Acknowledging that Hesse was quintessentially a poet, Ball went on to pronounce, "Poetry is his health."[66] The poem in question was that great declaration of consent to the necessity of his own death in order that life, the "eternal mother," might live on:

> Leaf after leaf falls
> From my life's tree.
> O, life's dizzying round,
> How you weary and sate me,
> How drunk you make me!
> Today's ardent glow
> Presently abates.
> Soon the wind will whistle cold
> Over my brown grave.
> The mother bends down
> Over the little child.
> Let me see her eyes again,
> Her gaze is my star,
> Let all else pass and be taken by the wind,
> All that's mortal dies gladly.
> Only the eternal mother remains,
> From whom we came,
> Her playful finger writes our names
> In the fleeting sky.

Yet even if Hesse appeared to have resolved for himself questions of existence in a cosmological context, in private his worries were mounting once more. The matter of his wife and children, Hesse was to learn, had been settled only provisionally. Mia had followed him to Ticino, and had purchased a house in Ascona—she failed to grasp that he had separated from her once and for all. She shouted at him over the telephone; sometimes her hatred for him knew no bounds, while at other times she realized—or so it seemed—that the only bond there could now be between them was the children they had had together, and not their married life as a couple. Hesse now found himself on the receiving end of another of her psychotic phases. It is a moot point whether she really was afflicted by schizophrenia at this time—something that Heiner Hesse was still vehemently disputing in his old age, maintaining that his mother had only suffered bouts of severe depression. In any event, Hesse suddenly found himself confronted by all the unresolved issues of his former life, which he thought he had left behind him.

In mid-September 1919 he attempted suicide by taking an overdose of opium, which, as he later wrote, he had stockpiled for just such an occasion. Was opium an effective way of killing yourself? Perhaps he hoped he would slip imperceptibly from narcosis and dreams into death? In actual fact, the opposite was the case, as he wrote to J. B. Lang: "I am still suffering from the effects; in my state of stupefaction I couldn't help but vomit everything up again, and after lying there for 12 hours in a daze, I now keep staggering, half-drunk and with stomach pains, between my sickbed and the toilet."[67]

He had now embarked upon the decade of the "crisis" and of *Steppenwolf.*

Siddhartha: The Indian Way?

Of course, its Indian and Brahmin milieu is all just scene-setting, and with Siddhartha I don't mean to portray a Hindu, but man in general. For all that, though, this scene-setting is more than just a theatrical backdrop.

—Hermann Hesse, letter to Fritz Gundert, March 12, 1923

Hesse had overtaxed himself in decamping to the South. The great summer that had given rise to his rush of creativity had already been infected by the virus of skepticism. Every summer draws to a close sometime, but where was he to draw strength to withstand the long winter that was looming? With *Klingsor's Last Summer* he had solved the problem through an orgiastic frenzy of creativity. When the summer was at an end, so was Klingsor. But he, Hermann Hesse, had remained behind and did not know how he might now make another fresh start—in a situation where none of his familiar problems, not even that of his own self-image as an Alemannic author whose spiritual homeland lay somewhere between Germany, Switzerland, and Nirvana, had been resolved.

Admittedly, though, Nirvana might have been an opportunity for him to rid himself of all the ballast he was dragging around with him—his twilight existence in Switzerland, for instance, where he was half-domiciled and half a guest and exile, and his role as public enemy number one of the German nationalistic press, for whom his anti-ideological pronouncements had made it easy to tar him as someone who delighted in running down his own native country. Inwardly Hesse had never managed to disengage himself from the German problem—preferring as he did to look beyond nationalistic concerns and asking himself how things might transpire if, after the humiliation of the Versailles Peace Accords, the Germans were to develop a new national sense of identity. But as it turned out this national self-consciousness only became even more excessive and militant, drowning out the last vestiges of humility and reflectiveness in the German intellectual elite. Hesse knew that he remained an outsider, and an author who was successful and misunderstood in equal measure—and yet he had no intention of ceasing to try to make himself comprehensible to his readers.

And then suddenly the form of an Indian myth suggested itself to him—although the subject matter had nothing whatsoever to do with India. Or rather, it concerned India only inasmuch as it concerned the whole world when Hesse began writing about his long pilgrimage to himself. He veered from one mistake to the next and yet found himself incapable of not going on, not continuing to write. "Become the person you are"—this motif from *Demian* had by no means vanished: quite the opposite in fact—the urgency to do so had only become greater, since *Demian* was not a solution either, only an interim stock-taking on a path whose ultimate destination appeared more uncertain than ever to Hesse in the fall of 1919.

One thing alone was certain, and this became the leitmotif of this remarkable myth of the Brahmin's son Siddhartha, who sets off on a journey to try and discover the truth about his life: Place no credence in those who teach wisdom, for you can only attain wisdom through your own life and your own sacrifices. By contrast, if you follow the former path, all you will ever be is at best a good student, who in turn becomes a teacher who has nothing to impart about his own experience—except for knowledge that is of little value.

That insight undoubtedly had more of Nietzsche's Zarathustra about it than of Buddha. "Don't follow me, follow yourself." For it was not a question of renouncing the Self but precisely about finding it. This was a very Western line of thought. The only things that were to be left behind were the idols that feigned a truth they did not possess. This also included smashing false self-images. Individualism that had disconnected itself from the totality of things was an aberration. The Enlightenment image of humans as the masters of nature was a lie. Siddhartha finds himself faced by a series of pure graven images—all of which he must destroy in order to become himself. That was Hesse's task, and he did not feel at all equal to it.

And so, in view of the helplessness he felt and having also dared at the same time, following Dostoyevsky's lead, to gaze into chaos, all he could do was utter a ritualistic phrase of self-encouragement that sounded like a trite saying yet which—if taken in the serious spirit in which it was offered—was also a warning to the world not to write him, Hermann Hesse, off too soon. At the very least, he was still cultivating within himself a spirit of danger when he had his character Siddhartha, the helpless pilgrim who constantly and despairingly keeps missing out on penetrating to the truth, mutter the mantra to himself: "I can think. I can wait. I can fast."

Hesse wrote the slim first part of what is in total a very slim book during the period from December 1919 to the spring of 1920. It comprised around thirty pages of text. This was the end of the short sensual flight of fancy in the South and of the brief upsurge of his creative powers. Now, as he himself remarked, he was living like a snail, slow and frugally. In August he broke off work on his new manuscript, only finally finding himself able to complete it in the spring of 1922 (a year and a half later). When he did so, it was again in a frenzied bout of writing over just a few weeks.

What prevented him initially from continuing to tell his story of Siddhartha? He first had to live through it in order to be able to then recount it. When he broke off writing his manuscript, he knew that he was in the same situation as his character: he had burned all his bridges behind him, had shunned all his former teachers, and had no roots in any community. He was alone with his crisis, with no faith in anything that might save him: no mission, no confession, no party or academy. No ideology—and also no strength to save himself. All he had was a dark pit of depression and the daily struggle to brace himself against the undertow that was trying to drag him under. And yet he had the continuing urge to write something, and the unwavering discipline to keep the creative spark alight, be it in the form of letters, reviews, poems, fairy tales, or feature articles. And in between doing this to also go out walking, drink wine, and paint. Painting above all was an important activity, because it countered his inner turmoil with something harmonious. But simultaneous with the undimmed joy he experienced in the act of seeing, the pain in his eyes increased to an almost unbearable intensity.

This, therefore, as Gottfried Benn also acknowledged, was the basic situation underlying the genesis of *Siddhartha* that we need to appreciate. Against the wishes of his father, Siddhartha leaves his parents' house in order to join the Sramanas, a caste of ascetic wandering monks who live in the forest. These Sramanas are remarkably similar to the wood-dwellers of Monte Verità, whom Hesse lived among during one of his early crises, until the fanaticism of these raw-food eaters, vegetarians, and vegans of all stripes finally forced him to take flight—back into the unhealthy world. In the same way, Siddhartha also leaves the Sramanas, and as a result finds himself standing alone with his skepticism. He doubts everything and believes in nothing—a very modern figure who is not unlike Hesse during the first years he spent in Ticino.

It is tempting to assume that in *Siddhartha,* Hesse was continuing what he had begun with his *Reports from India,* the account of his journey to Southeast Asia in 1911. In a letter to Alice Leuthold on July 26, 1919, however, he stated that this voyage was of only minimal significance for the picture he formulated of India:

> You assume that a certain spiritual affinity I feel for all things Asiatic must be the result of my short trip to India. That is not so. For some years I have been convinced that the European spirit is in decline and that it is sorely in

need of returning to its Asiatic origins. I have revered the Buddha for many years and have been reading Indian literature since my early childhood. Later on I gained a more intimate knowledge of Lao Tzu and other Chinese writers. My trip to India was just a little adjunct and illustration to these thoughts and studies, nothing more.[68]

Hesse wrote *Siddhartha* in the form of a legend, which Henry Miller would later claim the author had in all probability chosen in order to upset "the intellectual ossification of those literary Philistines who always know so exactly what good and bad literature is." But surely all readers who embark upon *Siddhartha* find themselves pulling up short and asking themselves what kind of extraordinarily stylized and studiedly mannered language it is that they are reading, all the more so because it is written from a distancing third-person perspective reminiscent of Bertolt Brecht's early "didactic plays" *(Lehrstücke).* Except that nothing is being taught here other than the insight that any lesson must ultimately be subsumed within real life if it is to be at all fruitful.

All the while that Hesse was working on *Siddhartha*—only to then break off because he sensed that he did not yet know the answer that he would subsequently be required to provide—he remained the coeditor of *Vivos voco,* a magazine that discussed the spiritual state of postwar Europe. It was a forum for debating the decline of the West, along with questions of individualism and avant-garde art, plus collectivism and political revolution. The question of communism also required an answer. Writers like Kisch, Becher, and Lukács had pledged their allegiance to the Communist Party and saw art henceforth as an integral part of the ideological struggle. Not long after, the League of Proletarian Revolutionary Writers was established, which saw itself as the executive organ of the playwright Friedrich Wolf's thesis that "Art is a Weapon." During this period Hesse saw himself increasingly caught between the opposing fronts of right-wing and left-wing politics. Nationalists and Internationalists vehemently denounced one another as traitors to the Fatherland—but in Hesse's view, all of that missed the essential question that now needed to be asked, namely, what spirit could now guide Europe out of the crisis in which it found itself, and above all where might that spirit ultimately lead?

When Hesse finally wrote to Georg Reinhart on July 9, 1922, to tell him that he had at last completed *Siddhartha,* he added: "and even though I am not at all happy with it, I do feel nonetheless that I have managed to formulate in it a certain new Indian-meditative ideal for living for our age."[69] This letter coincided with news of the assassination of Walther Rathenau on June 24, 1922, after he had served just four months as foreign minister of the Weimar Republic. A few weeks prior to this, in a letter to his sister Adele, Hesse had joked that, in signing the Treaty of Rapallo, Rathenau must have secretly sold the sun to his Soviet counterpart in the negotiations, Georgi Chicherin, "because there's been no sign of it since."[70] There was real substance behind Hesse's joke—the notoriously bad weather that summer had forced the sun-worshipper Hesse to champ at the bit. But all Hesse was doing here was picking up on general talk that had been doing the rounds; however, the hints of dim-witted militancy that also blew his way—which tried to whip up a campaign of political hatred from the same material that had furnished Hesse with a dubious witticism— shocked and appalled him. For many Germans the Weimar Republic was one big sales event for the victorious powers, and Rathenau, who really had no negotiating position to speak of at the treaty talks, gave his murderers from the extreme right-wing Organization Consul (one of whose organizers was the author Ernst von Salomon, who harbored dreams of a "national revolution") the opportunity to style themselves as martyrs in the struggle against a Jewish–Bolshevik global conspiracy. All of this was also part of the background to the writing of *Siddhartha,* as Hesse explained later in the same letter to Georg Reinhart: "Rathenau's death didn't exactly surprise me, though it did greatly sadden me. Several years ago, when he started writing on matters that directly concerned our times, I engaged in correspondence with him. The kind of thinking, or rather the complete lack of thought and the uncouth saber-rattling, that killed him is exactly what I have been fighting against and pillorying all these years, and unfortunately German universities are a stronghold of this stupid and hateful thoughtlessness."[71]

To counter this, therefore, he presented an Indian legend, which had no pretensions to being an allegory of contemporary circumstances in Germany but which nevertheless treated the same fundamental problem: namely, that of an intellectual and spiritual reorientation following the complete collapse of the old system of values. This related both to Europe as a whole and to the poet who had moved into the southerly light of Ticino and who regarded himself as an escapee from the question of how he might lead a correct life. In this regard, Siddhartha was a spiritual brother to Hesse's own feeling of helplessness. All the old tablets of the law had been smashed, and falsehood had been exposed as such—but how did that help? All the old rituals made no sense anymore: "The ablutions were good, but they were water, they did not wash away sins, they did not heal spiritual thirsting, and they did not dispel the heart's fear. The sacrifices and the invocations of the gods were admirable, but was this all there was? . . . But where were the Brahmins, the priests, and the sages, or the ascetics who had succeeded not only in knowing this most profound knowledge but also in living it?" Like Hesse, Siddhartha stood helplessly at the beginning of his own psychoanalysis. He was looking for someone to lead him out of his crisis. He wanted to learn how to feel *atman,* the primal inspiration of life that inhabits all things, working within him. "Where were the adepts who had learned the skill of bringing indwelling within *atman* out of the realm of sleep into that of wakefulness, who had made it an intrinsic aspect of life at every turn, in word and deed? . . . He had to find it, that primordial spring within one's self, he had to take possession of that! Everything else was just a vain quest, a diversion, an aberration."[72]

And now began that long pilgrimage to himself, which was also a pilgrimage to the world in order to find the place within it that appeared to have been assigned to him. Now, through the vehicle of Siddhartha and Indian mythology, Hesse was resuming the wandering existence that had been familiar to him since childhood through the Gundert branch of his family. Yet through his reading of Schopenhauer, he now had a new perspective on such an existence, which broke with the cognitive optimistic outlook of the Enlightenment. Hesse knew that in this book he could only commit to paper what he had directly experienced. Yet he felt so much disgust both with the world and with himself. The only thing that would help was to renounce the world and mortify the flesh—this was the insight he had his character Siddhartha arrive at, mirroring his own attempts to embrace such an attitude in the winter of 1919–1920. And so we read: "He ate only once a day and never cooked food. He fasted for fifteen days. He fasted for twenty-eight days. The flesh fell away from his thighs and cheeks. Fevered dreams flickered from his dilated eyes, and the nails grew long on his shriveled fingers and from his chin a dry, straggly beard sprouted. His gaze became as cold as ice when he encountered women; and his mouth twitched in contempt whenever he had to walk down a street among people dressed in fine clothes."[73] In such a condition, a person believes that they have totally renounced the world, and that because they know it they are entitled to despise it. It is remarkable to see how the spirit of Hesse's earlier monograph of St. Francis of Assisi reasserts itself here, albeit with a very different accent—far more skeptical and devoid of that love of humanity that Saint Francis never lost but that Siddhartha holds to be an illusion. He wants only one thing: "to become empty, empty of thirst, empty of desire." To wither away, and when the old Self is dead, to finally learn all the secrets of life that hitherto remained hidden from it. Yet that too proves to be a false path, indeed the very worst of all aberrations!

Siddhartha is a book concerning the recovery of individual experience in place of external knowledge, which has caused so much harm in the world! In this process, the path of sacrificing one's own Self and of ascetic depersonalization may be an important exercise, a transitional phase where one may not remain: even this role, as a student, must be shattered once more. Hesse, the autodidact, had retained a sure instinct for what knowledge might be useful or harmful to him in any given situation. Thus, from his description of the first Sramanas whom Siddhartha sets eyes on, we already know that he will never fully be one of them: "three gaunt, faded men, neither old nor young, with dusty and bleeding shoulders, almost naked, scorched by the sun, cocooned in solitude, alien and hostile to the world, misfits and scrawny jackals in the world of men."[74]

Sramanas—those ascetic itinerant preachers who have honed the technique of meditation, not to mention that of manipulation, to a fine art—would also have been a fitting description for prophets who were arguing over the future of the European spirit: all those party strategists, professors, journalists, and academics, though admittedly not all of these could necessarily have been said to have a propensity to asceticism. Yet what all of them certainly did share was that entourage mentality which demanded that the masses subjugate themselves to their leaders. Alongside the hegemony of technology, which was robbing the individual of his or her right to autonomy (while at the same time ostensibly expanding it), this represented an increasingly offensive emergence of a collectivism, which from the left wing followed the model of Bolshevism, and from the right was beholden to the ideology of the national ethnic community. Both were equally suspect in Hesse's eyes. Accordingly, he portrayed Siddhartha as marching under no party's banner, not even that of the Buddha himself, to whom Siddhartha's friend and companion Govinda becomes slavishly devoted at the very first opportunity. Siddhartha's encounter with Gautama (the Buddha) is somewhat reminiscent of Dostoyevsky's legend of the Grand Inquisitor in *The Brothers Karamazov*. Siddhartha's concern—and in this regard he was like Jesus—was not with doctrinal matters, or dogma, or about one institution sharply demarcating itself from others and declaring all apostates to be heretics, but instead with the *atman,* the living spirit within all things.

The great time of leave-takings thus commences. After taking leave of his father, the Brahmin, Siddhartha soon parts company with the Sramanas, the itinerant monks. Govinda is astonished by this, but Siddhartha, in his confrontation with the oldest of the Sramanas, shows that he is more than a match for him—he is already superior to them, though this is of no importance to him: "What I have learned up to now from these Sramanas, O Govinda, I could have learned faster and more easily elsewhere. I could have learned it, my friend, in any tavern in the whores' quarter, among wagoners and dice players."[75]

The ultimate goal was Nirvana, the liberation from all worldly bonds, and the complete absence of desire as the most perfect form of enlightenment. But Siddhartha doubts that a Sramana, however zealous he may be in his asceticism or however well versed in every meditation technique, could ever attain Nirvana.

Even at this early stage, he senses that, in order to attain a remarkably lifeless life, it is too simple to merely wish to mortify the flesh, or to let the Self, and with it the world, atrophy. The answer does not lie therein. One cannot escape oneself, one cannot with impunity simply transform one's life into a doctrine. One had to overcome the Self, for the sake of one's own Self. One had to resist the temptation by giving in to it. One could overcome life only through living, not through mortification of the flesh. This is the paradoxical insight that Siddhartha arrives at in the first part of the novel. He departs and leaves his old life behind and yet all he wants is one thing—to return home. However, the way back is barred to him. His meeting with Gautama was also too important for him to allow him to do that. In this encounter with the Buddha, he learns that Gautama genuinely does tread his own path and hence is enlightened. Nothing would be more false, however, than to wish to follow him on this path—you have to travel the route that is assigned to you personally. Yet how can one find out which one that is? This is how the first part of *Siddhartha* ends. Siddhartha has been liberated but only in the form of falling into a bottomless abyss. "No other teaching will seduce me, since this man's teaching did not seduce me. The Buddha has robbed me, thought Siddhartha, he robbed me, and yet he gave me even more. He robbed me of my friend, of the person who once believed in me and now believes in him, who was my shadow and is not Gautama's shadow. But what he gave me was Siddhartha; he gave me myself."[76]

Siddhartha knows that he is attending his own birth, but he does not know if he will survive it. These are the steps that one is required to take on this path to self-discovery. Yet one never knows whether the steps that one has just taken with great effort and sacrifice are leading upward or downward. For even the steps form part of the great cycle of life.

Siddhartha is an attempt to synthesize Eastern and Western thinking, as represented by Buddha and Heraclitus. Hesse was searching for a "European Nirvana." He tried repeatedly—right up to his death—to formulate exactly what this meant. The final large-scale attempt to answer this question—in a series that began with *Siddhartha*—would be *The Glass Bead Game*. In a preface to the Japanese edition of *Siddhartha*, which was published in 1955, he wrote: "Nowadays, it is no longer a question of trying to convert the Japanese to Christianity, or Europeans to Buddhism or Taoism. We have no desire, nor should we, to convert or be converted; instead it is incumbent upon us to open ourselves up and expand our minds. We no longer regard Eastern and Western wisdom as mutually hostile forces engaged in a power struggle, but as poles between which a bountiful life oscillates."[77]

The impulsion to write this story was twofold: Hesse's deeply personal self-reflection about the meaning of his own life, an attempt to overcome his existential crisis at being a father, a husband, and a writer—yet at the same time it is also a treatise on the future of Europeans. Regarding history, this was already a way Hesse could lend meaning to meaning-lessness, by devising a figure of thought that transcended European in-tellectual history and, in accord with Hegel, vehemently refuted any suggestion that history might be meaningless:

> I do not believe in any religious dogmatism or in a god who has created humans and enabled them to develop their expertise in killing one another with a progression of weapons from stone axes to nuclear arms and to be proud of such progress into the bargain. And so I don't believe that this bloody history of the world has any "meaning" in the plan of some superior divine ruler, who has thereby devised for us a destiny that is heavenly and magnifi-cent but unintelligible to us. Even so, I do have a faith—a knowledge or intu-ition about the ultimate meaning of life that has become instinctual for me.[78]

Hesse saw his postulated dictum "Be yourself" as forming the decisive bridge between Eastern and Western thought. A synthesis for sure, but one that was not susceptible to being institutionalized and that could be re-voked at any moment. Creating this synthesis remained a constant task, and furthermore one that constantly needed justification:

> As I understand it, Nirvana is the return of the individual to the undivided whole, the liberating step behind the *principium individuationis,* or, to couch it in religious terms, the reversion of the individual soul to the universal soul, to God. It is another question whether one should yearn for this re-turn or not, and whether one should do so on Buddha's path to enlighten-ment or not. If God casts me out into the world and makes me live as an individual, it is then my task to get back to the universe as quickly and easily as I can—or ought I not rather to fulfill God's will by casting myself adrift (in Klein and Wagner I called this "letting oneself fall"), and by atoning with him for his inclination to split himself up into individual beings once more and to live vicariously through them?[79]

In *Siddhartha,* Hesse rehearsed his Protestant perspective through the vehicle of Eastern thought. Protestantism requires no institutions of dogmas, it is a direct form of spirituality pertaining to life itself. But doesn't this Protestant path lead to an overtaxing of the Word, insofar as it is com-pletely devoid of all external ritual? Hesse was deeply beset by doubt on this matter, all the more so because he now had, in Hugo Ball, a close friend who was a champion of Roman Catholicism; although Ball was decidedly undogmatic, he did have all the zeal of a convert.

Hesse was under enormous pressure at the beginning of the 1920s. The profound crisis in his relationship with his readers, especially those in Germany, ultimately had its roots in his relationship with himself. What was his standpoint as an author in this age characterized by political battles, hatred, and ideology following the First World War, which Germany had lost? Moreover, most Germans did not accept the defeat. Many believed that conspiracy and political intrigue had brought them low. And a person like Hesse was particularly suspect to them. After all, he lived in Switzerland, knew nothing about the daily woes of life in Germany, and still gave himself airs as the orchestrator-in-chief of a European conscience, in cahoots with Romain Rolland, the emissary of the enemy, whom he called his friend. Hesse was in a difficult situation. He felt himself misunderstood, and he did not know whether or how he would ever make himself understood to the Germans. Or indeed whether he should even bother trying. In a letter of February 10, 1956, he wrote the following about his long journey promoting the idea of "Be yourself," a task he would never abandon:

> For anyone with a more than average sense of their own individuality, life's major struggle resides in the fact that their journey through life is impeded by many moral and other obstacles and that the world prefers us to be acquiescent and weak rather than headstrong. In these circumstances, everyone must decide for themselves, according to his own strengths and needs, to what extent he will submit to convention or defy it. If he chooses to turn a deaf ear to convention, and the demands of his family, the state, and his community, he must do it in the knowledge that he does so at his own risk. There is no objective measure of how much risk a person is capable of shouldering. One has to atone for every excess, every transgression of one's own boundaries, and one cannot go too far in either waywardness or conformity without being punished.[80]

And so, in the spring of 1920 Hesse left Siddhartha standing on a riverbank, having made many departures but as yet still with no certainty of arriving anywhere. Hesse himself had no idea whether he would ever manage to reach the far bank. Yet it is precisely this unknowingness that

lends *Siddhartha* the character of a self-exploration with an uncertain outcome. "He felt that this had been the last shudder of his awakening, the
last pains of birth. And without more ado he strode out once more, taking
swift and impatient steps, no longer homeward, no longer to his father, no
longer looking backward."[81]

During the year and a half Hesse needed in order to live out what he
now intended to write about, the prosaic nature of current events in Germany bore down upon him with full force. Hesse found himself adopting
the polemical tone that was directed at him from Germany. He reacted to
nationalism, and to that particularly German self-righteousness that always
sought scapegoats for defeats the nation had brought upon itself, with just
as much irritation as he did to the bureaucratic spirit of the universities.
Thus, in a review of *The Speeches of Buddha,* which he contributed to *Die
neue Rundschau* in October 1921, he wrote: "There is a whole swathe of
nervous German professors who fear something like a Buddhist inunda-
tion and a decline of the intellectual West. Rest assured, the West will not
collapse and Europe will never become a Buddhist empire. Anyone who
reads the Buddha's speeches and converts to Buddhism as a result may
well have thereby found some kind of solace for himself—yet in place of
the path that the Buddha might show us, all that person has opted for is an
emergency exit."[82]

This uncompromising, self-confident tone conceals the fact that Hesse
himself was searching for just such an emergency exit. Around the same
time, in November 1921, he wrote to Carl Seelig: "I am living here in my
old fashion, doing battle with my demons; I've done a lot of new things,
but haven't written anything for a year."[83]

But in May 1922, in a letter to Lisa Wenger, came the sudden news:
"I am just putting the final touches to *Siddhartha,* it's finished."[84]

Where had this sudden creative surge come from? An encounter succeeded in building bridges between Christianity and Buddhism. Hugo
Ball—until 1916 a Dadaist artist in the Cabaret Voltaire in Zurich, and
now a disciple of Nietzsche who had converted to Catholicism—who was
engaged in studying the problem of intellectuals and the Byzantine, yet
who also took an interest in demonologies and exorcism, inspired Hesse
to take his unorthodox religion seriously. Ball's wife, Emmy, appeared
to Hesse like a fairy who had been damaged by the daily struggle for
survival.

In February 1922, shortly before Hesse wrote the second part of *Siddhartha* over a few weeks, his cousin the Japanologist Wilhelm Gundert paid him a visit. He gave Hesse the final impetus to finish *Siddhartha*. In recognition of this, Hesse dedicated the second half of the novel to him, while the first was dedicated to Romain Rolland.

But his ability to finish *Siddhartha* was facilitated not just by external confirmation but also by Hesse's own constant rethinking and experiencing of the problems of the journey through life, which he saw as a process of building a decisive bridge across the river that appears to separate the Self from the world. This great act of affirmation, nevertheless, contained a great deal of negation and brought the pathos of changing the world back down to a human scale by applying a faint touch of irony, as he revealed in a letter to Emmy Hennings: "In the end, my Siddhartha learns his wisdom not from a teacher but from a river that makes a funny roaring sound and from a kindly old halfwit who smiles all the while and is secretly a saint."[85]

The ferryman who becomes the key intermediary, the translator between the two worlds, is called Vasudeva. Siddhartha meets him right at the beginning of the second part, after that "last shudder of his awakening" in which Hesse had left him at the end of the first part. Now he had, so to speak, reawakened, and the ice that had once held him trapped had melted—and so we read the very first sentence of the second part as a revelation: "Siddhartha learned something new every step of the way, for the world had been transformed and his heart was enchanted!"[86]

Or could it be that this is just the illusion of someone who believes he has found something that one can in truth never find but only seek? Whatever the case, this powerful, life-affirming beginning is lent weight by having been wrested from a state of deep depression. Hermann Hesse had no intention of letting himself be booed off the stage. He had by now adjusted to the fact that his writing had the capacity to excite not only love but also hatred. A new sobriety becomes apparent: he develops a hard carapace against the world. This, then, was another key function of *Siddhartha,* serving him as the kind of refuge that his second homeland Switzerland would never be for him; for now, the country was a welcome long-term provisional arrangement that had nothing romantic about it. The hateful responses to *Siddhartha* that now instantly kicked in—no longer to Hesse's surprise—showed the parlous situation in which he found himself and the image that a not-inconsiderable portion of the German press now had of him:

> But this latest work reveals something worse than just a weakness. Hermann Hesse's compatriots are bleeding and starving to death, and are being tormented by Fate in the fiery furnace of their own and foreigners' guilt and are crying out to Heaven—For pity's sake, I am not expecting Hesse to start writing polemics! But if he has pretensions to being a poet and not just an esthete, not just a paltry man of letters, surely something of this age's outcry, or the anguished lament of his people ought to strike a chord in him, and some sign of greatness, depth, and ultimate human sympathy become apparent in him. It is with a profound feeling of bitterness that one watches him lounging about on the shore of some southern lake or other, brewing weak Indian tea for his friend Rolland—an equally dead husk of a figure. What do we mean to the Hermann Hesse of today, what does he mean to us? No writer can part company with his people in this most bitter and yet deeply vibrant of times and do so with impunity.[87]

The final sentence of this critique of *Siddhartha,* which appeared in the magazine *Die schöne Literatur* (Belles Lettres), summarizes the situation. It shows how short a distance there is between being venerated and pilloried. Yet both these states were part of that external world to which one must never surrender oneself or one's most precious possessions—one's hopes and dreams.

In addition to Hugo and Emmy Ball, who moved into the neighboring village of Agnuzzo in September 1920 and who quickly became his most important contacts, it was also Hesse's meeting with C. G. Jung that strengthened his resolve to supplement the first part of *Siddhartha,* that of negation, with a second part, that of affirmation. Jung was skeptical about applying psychoanalysis to artists. He regarded J. B. Lang as being largely unqualified in this matter—and the brisk, almost curt, tone that he adopted when he met Hesse, who by this stage was even more tightly wrapped up in neurotic isolation, appears to have helped Hesse more than all the sympathetic understanding he had been shown hitherto for his personal dilemma. Hesse had consulted Jung for the first time—over an entire week—as early as February 1921, and returned to see him for a second time in June of that year. On 28 June, he wrote in his "Zurich notebook": "He has sent me away with the maxim: 'Desire to do (consciously) what you (instinctively) long to do!'"[88] And the following day Hesse noted: "My last visit to Jung. We speak about my having virtually no dreams any more. He tells me that I don't need any . . . and that patients often ask him how they should 'solve' this or that problem. Jung tells them that they shouldn't be seeking to solve it, but rather just to have a crack at it, to grapple and struggle with it. Problems aren't there to be 'solved'; they are pairs of opposites that between them produce a tension that is called life."[89]

This attitude was by no means a new one for Hesse. It impelled him— after *Demian*—to give poetic expression to the contradictory doppel-gänger nature that he knew resided within him. Yet his narrative stance here, and hence his way of formulating questions here, was totally different from in the earlier novel. Unlike his approach in *Demian,* in *Siddhartha* Hesse does not just present the story as a process of someone "becoming oneself" or simply as the account of a person attaining self-awareness— indeed, there is no hint of a psychoanalytical motive here—but as a question of being, as a way of determining one's purpose within the context of a suprapersonal crisis of meaning. The perspective here is no longer that of the first-person narrator, but of a third person. Hesse wrote a myth about an individual who gives up trying to find the truth, to besiege it in an Enlightenment-like way until it capitulates in the face of his dogged determination—no, instead Siddhartha learns that one has to give up something of oneself in order to gain something. Not in the sense of a transaction from which everyone can profit, nor in the sense of a self-castigation as practiced by the ascetic Sramanas, still less as a pathos-laden ideology of sacrifice—but instead in the sense of the grateful acceptance of the gracious gift of life in all of its often brutal and unjust contrariness. Every doctrine contains its own inherent contradiction, with which it struggles. For this reason, doctrine is never the way to wisdom. Only when one recognizes that a thing constitutes a whole only when combined with its opposite is one on the path to wisdom. Nor can one ascend to a state of wisdom by one's own efforts. Rather, one is raised up to it (or abased, which amounts to the same thing), and if one becomes party to wisdom, one cannot count that as a personal success. Instead, it is a gift that one must prove oneself worthy of.

Does that mean that all one has to do is wait for the right moment? It was not just a question of that, as Hesse explained: the *vita activa* and the *vita contemplativa* stand in a very sensitive relation to one another, which must constantly be rebalanced. He would come to summarize this in 1956: "The flaw in our questioning and complaining is presumably this: namely, that we desire to have something given to us from outside that we can only attain within ourselves, through our own dedication. We demand that life must have a meaning—yet it has precisely as much meaning as we are able to impart to it."[90] This led him on to formulate the idea of an elite, a secret society, the invisible realm of the league of those taking part in *The Journey to the East* and finally to *The Glass Bead Game*—the "monastery for free spirits" that Nietzsche had in mind and that Hesse affirmed and rejected in equal measure: "In short, wanting to improve humanity is always a hopeless task. That is why I have always built my faith on the individual, for the individual can be educated and is capable of improvement, and according to my faith it has always been and still remains the small elite of well-intentioned, dedicated, and courageous people who are the guardians of all that is good and beautiful in the world."[91]

Siddhartha's path to recuperation begins on the far bank of the river. He turns his attention to things that, as a Brahmin's son and a Sramana, he formerly contemptuously overlooked: life in all its beautiful and vile materiality, and sensuality, which likes to adorn itself and then gives itself to the person who buys it the most expensive jewelry. The world of optimized pleasure! One cannot appreciate its insipid aftertaste until one has first tasted it.

And so, surreptitiously, this book turns into a treatise, which ultimately has Siddhartha living by the precepts that the narrator sets for him. For example, the guiding postulate for the second part of the work is this: "Both ideas and the senses were fine things, behind both of them the ultimate meaning lay hidden, both were worth heeding, and it was worthwhile to play with both of them, neither despising them or overrating them. The secret voice of the innermost essence could be heard in both of them."[92]

And so, on the "far side" of the river, the fugitive Brahmin's son and runaway Sramana Siddhartha and the fugitive husband, father, and German best-selling author Hesse both become acquainted with a sensuality neither of them knew before. Maria Bernoulli had been more of a mother substitute, whereas Ruth Wenger could have been Hesse's daughter. Ruth was the model for Kamala, the courtesan whom Siddhartha meets and whose skillfully managed sensuality opens up to him, for a while at least, new worlds—namely, those of free and playful eroticism. At this point another guiding precept becomes clear to Siddhartha: "You are the first woman to whom Siddhartha has spoken other than with downcast eyes. Never again will I lower my eyes when I encounter a beautiful woman."[93]

For obvious reasons, Kamala maintains close contacts with influential men, and this becomes the subject of the chapter "Among the Child People." These are the representatives of visible, temporal order, of trade and gold. Siddhartha enters the service of the merchant Kamaswami and proves successful in business matters. All manner of material pleasures are now showered upon him—and he appreciates them. There is no reason for him to scorn life's comforts and material success. Only fanatics do that. Yet equally one should not let oneself become the prisoner of prosperity—one must remain inwardly free and ready at any moment to renounce it.

In the end, therefore, Siddhartha remains inwardly different from the child people. "Maybe people of our kind are incapable of love."[94] Is this because, Hesse let his character Siddhartha speculate, he treats love like an art form, and only permits love to exist within the boundaries of art? It is that tiny yet irrevocable distance from all external matters that brands Siddhartha with the same "mark on the forehead" that was mentioned in *Demian.* An outsider who will never belong to anyone other than himself.

And once again Siddhartha becomes someone who disappoints others and who leaves them behind to go off on his travels. But this time he knows what he is looking for, and he is following an inner voice that is not susceptible to any blandishments.

In his "1920–1921 Diary," which has the subtitle "Following an Illness," Hesse described both the crisis into which he fell while writing *Siddhartha* and its resolution:

> It all began so beautifully, the book flourished on a nice straight line, and then all of a sudden it was all over! In such cases, the critics and the literary historians generally talk about a diminishing of powers, about the atmosphere

petering out, and about loss of concentration—just consult any biography of Goethe with its idiotic remarks if you want confirmation of that!

Now, in my case the matter is quite simple. In my Indian novel everything was going swimmingly so long as I was writing what I had actually experienced: the mood of the young Brahmin who was seeking the truth, who torments and mortifies himself. But once I had finished with Siddhartha the ascetic and sufferer and attempted to portray Siddhartha the victor, the affirmer, and the conqueror, I found I couldn't go on anymore.[95]

And this was how things stood with Hesse for the whole of 1920, which he would later call the most unproductive year of his life—which wasn't actually true, as he himself conceded: "Although I work the entire day—I study, keep up my diary, read and write any amount of letters, read new books, paint and draw—all that is mere preparation, getting myself in the mood, it's far from being proper concentrated work in the form of literary creation."[96]

Yet for all that, he was keeping busy, and it would be presumptuous to claim that his reading and reviewing of books, the countless letters he received and responded to, and his frequent walks and bouts of painting did not represent creative endeavor. But in 1920 only *Siddhartha* counted where Hesse was concerned, and he did not add a single line to the novel over this period. That made him ill. Or was he just coincidentally ill, and was something in him working toward recuperation? The first entry for July 1920 in the diary that he kept during this period begins:

All I have been doing for weeks and months is lie in bed, because it's so cold, and because if I don't the wood wouldn't last for the winter, and because one has more dreams lying in bed, and also because one really ought to go easy on oneself and take care not to drive yourself to an early grave and generally fall into despair and to have done with everything. Today, the shutters are open and I can see that it's summer and that there's no point in me lying in bed any longer. Today of all days, when I'd planned on taking my own life, it's summer, and Polly the parrot is sitting on the window sill and singing, and in the trees beneath the window the ripe cherries are shiny and black. Just a few hours ago, before I went to sleep for what I thought would be the last time, I made a resolution that I would, come what may and whatever the weather was like, get out of bed, have a shave, put on my boots and go into town, and visit the grubby shops in the Via Triombo where you can buy an antique revolver for 40 liras. But now that I've been woken by Polly's voice, and the sun is high and hot in a clear blue sky and there's no more snow to be seen, and the sun-drenched floor is warming my feet, I've completely forgotten my decision, I've let it drop and I'm watching it fall and sink, like in a pond, where it joins all the other things, all the other resolutions and other matters I've cast into oblivion and that I'll one day recall and retrieve from the glassy green depths.

So, the Earth and the Sun are turning for me once more.[97]

This is the same point of utter exhaustion and disillusionment that Siddhartha finally reaches when he is with Kamala and the child people. Once more, it was a mistake to believe that he was on the right path. Once again it was just one more mistake in his life, which had been full of such errors. But as a consequence, had it all been in vain?

The way to that form of Nirvana that was more than just some folkloric pose, more than an acquired (in other words, purely external) simulation of wisdom, led via a nervous breakdown, via searing pain, and via utter despair. This emptiness is a torment—and Nirvana means enduring such a state, affirming that essential inner chaos without trying to impose some abstract order upon it or to keep it at bay. For life is not abstract. And so we see Siddhartha already fleeing from his life of material prosperity that had offered him every conceivable pleasure, even the courtesan Kamala's mastery of the art of love. For it all tastes stale and flat to him; indeed, it disgusts him. And so he finds himself back at the river once more, this time on the far bank, yet still in the same crisis as before, which had merely been silenced for a while by external activity: "I had been full of haughtiness, always the smartest person, always the keenest. Always a step ahead of everyone else, always the knowledgeable and spiritual one, always the priest or the sage. His Self had taken refuge in this hieratic persona, this haughtiness, this spirituality; and there it sat and grew, while he thought he was killing it off through fasting and penitence."[98]

And there at the river is the ferryman Vasudeva once more. Siddhartha now recognizes in him his true teacher—the man who constantly shuttles between the two banks of the river, a translator in the elemental sense. He remains with the ferryman, though not as his pupil—for this aspect of himself Siddhartha has already, to quote the Romanian–French philosopher Emil Cioran, "killed outright" within himself—but as his assistant. Working at his side, he gets to know the river: "Among the secrets of the river, however, he saw only one today that captivated his soul. He saw that the river flowed and flowed relentlessly, and yet it was always there, always and for all time the same and yet every moment new."[99]

The same river in which a person cannot bathe twice, which is always the same and yet at every instant is different, became for Hesse a key connecting element between the Eastern and Western spirit: Heraclitus and Buddha. Something caught in a state of constant flux yet which eternally remains the same.

Mirrored in the river is the problem of time: its mystery, its relativity. It cannot be turned back, but perhaps it might be suspended momentarily? In a state of meditation, say, or of ecstasy? These were questions with which Hesse was preoccupied, and not just regarding his own life. Where does childhood go when we are grown up? What becomes of all the time that has passed, which after all was filled with life? This is where "Chronos" (clock time, sequential time) becomes "Chairos," that special moment in which time can metamorphose. That meaningful moment in which a secret that is hidden in time reveals itself—manifests itself!—for a brief instant becomes that sanctification of the moment which is defined by the term "Chairos." Hesse now extrapolates from the question of individual fate to a general allegory of history. This is why the narrative of *Siddhartha* is presented in the form of a saint's legend.

This has a polarizing effect. In truth, there are some irksome passages here—especially at the start of the second part—written in a style that is in danger of slipping into cliché. Some of the images teeter on the brink of cheap sensationalism. Hesse appears loath to wean himself off his favorite word from his early writings, *hold,* "lovely," and his attempts at writing erotic scenes descend into the most awkward schoolboy prose: "Looking up, he saw her smiling face full of desire and her narrowed eyes pleading with longing."[100] It was thanks to sentences like that that Hesse had to suffer the jibe that he was a writer of kitsch. Was that fair? Of course not; the fact remains no one could rival Hesse in his ability to treat complex problems in a language that was in part irritatingly conventional and that displayed no ambition to be iconoclastic, while at the same time never remotely suggesting to his readers that these were simple questions under discussion. However artificial an image might be in detail, this takes nothing away from the authenticity of the depiction as a whole. What might be the root of this? At all times, one gets the impression that there is someone writing here who is quite literally writing for his life! A confessor who does not pretend to have found a way out of the labyrinth of life—and who nevertheless does not give up looking for it. Stylistically too the novel is fraught with contradiction. After the trite image cited above of a "smiling face full of desire" and "eyes pleading with longing," there immediately follows one that is anything but easy to digest, which the reader runs into quite unexpectedly, as it were, and which conceals more than it expresses. This is the moment of disillusionment, when the cheap allure of the merely sensual falls away from Siddhartha: "All the enchantment vanished from the smiling face of the young woman. All he saw now was the moist gaze of a female animal in heat."[101]

When Hesse spent his "year in the wilderness" sick, or rather pronouncing himself sick while lying in bed, he was fully aware of the task that he had set himself in *Siddhartha:* to learn patience. Patience toward his mentally ill wife, Mia, whose problems continued unabated and continued to occupy much of his time; patience with his three sons, who were living in residential schools or with acquaintances and whom he presumed had come to hate him in the interim; and patience with the German public. He had no patience with the nationalists who had declared him, as author of *Vivos voco,* to be a sworn enemy whom they proceeded ever openly to pillory as a traitor to the Fatherland:

> In the meantime, German nationalist students from dueling societies continue nonstop to send me their brave hate-mail, full of bile and lofty indignation, and all I need to do is read one of these letters, one of these obsessive, forced, nasty letters by these little puppets, in order to realize quite how healthy I am, despite everything, and to realize quite how much I annoy them, how much I infuriate and trouble them, and how my writing must still have the capacity to speak to people's sense of danger, thought, intellect, understanding, ridicule, and fantasy. But what a sad place the intellect, or rather the complete lack of intellect, must be which gives rise to the kinds of views and letters that they churn out![102]

Siddhartha also learns to wait, and over and above this to recognize that there is nothing a person can do to help others find their path. Siddhartha has a son, who not only does not want to live the same life as him but who despises him almost to the point of hatred. He runs away and wishes to have nothing to do with his father. There can be no more wounding pain for a father. Only now does Siddhartha learn the second part of his life lesson, after having previously only appreciated the first part, that of a son who takes the liberty of departing. Siddhartha now learns firsthand about slighting a father's attempts at rapprochement and simply rejecting out of hand his wisdom—and with it the long traditions of his lineage—as totally irrelevant, but this time from the position of the snubbed old man who cannot get through to the young man.

That was how Hesse now felt toward his own sons, while knowing that he had behaved in exactly the same way toward his father. Here it was not a question of guilt, but instead the natural progression of different generations. His sons would in their turn become fathers, and they too would eventually become old men hoarding a treasure of wisdom in which, apparently, no one has the slightest interest anymore.

A Gautama, an enlightened one, Hesse knew, would be somebody who was able to accompany what came from deep within with a smile and full of approbation. He also knew that he himself was not such an enlightened one.

The messages that he had to impart to others were always of a prosaic nature, but life-tested for all that: "Whenever a poor person has told me his life story, I basically find I can say nothing but: 'Yes, that's sad, life is often sad like that, I know, that's happened to me too. Try to grin and bear it, and if nothing helps, then drink a bottle of wine, and if that does no good either, then be aware that you still have the possibility of putting a bullet in your brain.'"[103]

Eike Middell has written that, in *Siddhartha*, Hesse was trying to broach a question similar to the one Alfred Döblin had posed in his books: namely, What becomes of a good person in bad times? Yet in Hesse this question is tangential to what he regards as the irreducible dual nature of humanity: to be good and evil at the same time, The world is merely a mirror of this dichotomy.

This becomes clear from a long poem entitled "Media in vita," which Hesse wrote in his diary on February 15, 1921:

How fine are property and money!
How fine it is to scorn property and money!
How fine to turn away from the world in renunciation!
How fine to burn with desire for its pleasures!

Upward to God, back to being an animal,
And all around are brief flashes of good fortune.
Go where you will, be a person, an animal, a tree!

And what message does Siddhartha—whom Govinda, his once-disloyal companion and eternal alter ego and pupil, finally attests has himself become a Gautama, an enlightened one—have to impart that was worth undertaking such a long pilgrimage for?

> But today I think: this stone is a stone, it is also animal, it is also god, it is also Buddha, I do not venerate and love it because it could at one time turn into this or that, but rather because it has long since been, and always will be, everything. And it is this very fact—that it is a stone, that it appears to me in the here and now as a stone—that makes me love it and see value and purpose in each of its veins and pits, in its yellow, in its gray, in its hardness, in the sound it makes when I tap at it, in the dryness or moistness of its surface. There are stones that feel like oil or soap, and others that feel like leaves, and others like sand, and each one is special and prays the Om in its own way, each one is Brahman, but at the same time and just as much it is a stone, oily or soapy, and this is the fact in which I take delight and see as wonderful and worthy of worship. But let me speak no more of this. Words cannot do justice to the hidden meaning. Everything always becomes slightly different, and a bit distorted and slightly foolish, the moment it is put into words. And that is also good, and pleases me a lot. It is perfectly fine with me that what to one man is precious wisdom to another always sounds like foolishness.[104]

Here Hesse is not far from Hugo von Hofmannsthal's findings in his famous *The Lord Chandos Letter;* but Hesse combines the crisis of modernity with the atmosphere of those ancient Asiatic texts that stood on his grandfather Gundert's bookshelves. Was Hesse's relationship to India simply the continuation of that projection which German Romanticism had first used to come to an understanding of itself? That would be an unjust claim, for Hesse felt a strong inner affinity to Indian and Chinese wisdom; this fact is also demonstrated by the books he chose to review during this period, a task that he in no way considered to be a secondary or uncreative substitute for working on his own writing. When Hesse read and discussed books, he found himself in the thick of the problem that had become an existential question for him.

How independent can a person become of their surroundings and of tradition without in the process ceasing to be part of a culture? How can one take the path from the outward life to the inner life without entirely relinquishing external existence?

Ralph Freedman has claimed that *Siddhartha* is a missionary book in the best sense of the term. Did he perhaps mean by this that it is a thoroughly anti-missionary work? For it most decidedly is that: completely undogmatic, anti-fanatic, and anti-ideological. It goes in search of the common roots of all humanity—and everywhere runs up against the same fundamental conflicts of autonomy and alien control, of tradition and modernity. So why did Hesse take India as his setting?

Hesse, who throughout his life was a patient answerer of letters, even those sent to him by readers he didn't know at all, gave a response to precisely this question when writing to a Miss Berthli Kappeler on February 5, 1923:

> I consider certain maxims from the New Testament, together with some from Lao Tzu and some of Buddha's sayings, to be the truest, most pithy, and most vital utterances that have ever been said and made known on this Earth. Nevertheless, the Christian way to God has been obscured for me by my strict and pious upbringing, by the laughable nature and petty quarrels of theology, by the sheer boredom and yawning barrenness of the established churches, and so on. So I sought God by other routes and soon found the Indian route, which I naturally found a close affinity with, since my forbears, my grandfather, father, and mother all had intimate ties to India, spoke Indian languages, and so forth. Later I also discovered the Chinese path through Lao Tzu, which was a truly liberating experience for me. Of course, in addition to and at the same time as this quest, I was also engaged in no less intense a study of modern approaches to such problems by Nietzsche, Tolstoy, and Dostoyevsky, but the deepest insights I found were in the Upanishads, in the writings of Buddha, in Confucius, and in Lao Tzu, and then, once my old aversion to the specifically Christian form of truth had gradually subsided, also in the New Testament. Even so, I remained loyal to the Indian path, though I do not necessarily view it as being better than the Christian one. I did so because that Christian presumptuousness, that monopolizing of God, and that exclusive claim to rectitude that began with St. Paul and that runs through the whole of Christian theology, was deeply abhorrent to me, and also because the Indians, with the help of

yogic methods, have far better, more practical, cleverer, and deeper forms of seeking the truth.[105]

It was this form of lived spirituality that Hesse was also driving at when he told Fritz Marti that he did not agree that, in writing *Siddhartha,* he was moving from literature to philosophy; instead he saw it as a "kind of renunciation of the value of speculative thought."[106]

On August 10, 1922, he wrote to Romain Rolland outlining who he had in mind as a negative example, as an impending calamity, when he considered a path to his own truth that was free of hatred: "Over there in Germany, the intellectual mood has something anarchic about it, but also something religious and fanatical, it's the kind of mood that would prevail at the apocalypse and the ensuing thousand-year reign of Satan."[107]

As a result, in September 1922 he also let Romain Rolland persuade him to appear at a congress held in Lugano, Switzerland, organized by the International Women's League for Freedom and Peace. There, he read the conclusion of *Siddhartha*—which as expected only succeeded in sowing incomprehension and alienation among most of the delegates. All the same, he did receive enthusiastic encouragement from Kalidas Nag, a history professor from Calcutta. He understood that Hesse—fully in the spirit of Schopenhauer—had imbibed Buddhism as spiritual sustenance and reworked it. And he found that much closer to his way of thinking than any foreigner simply converting to Buddhism.

On February 10, 1923, Stefan Zweig also got to hear from Hesse about the other, not easily communicable, dialectics of proximity to and distance from Buddhism that impelled him to write *Siddhartha*. It was ultimately a question of the mythical imagery that forms the core of any religious attitude to the world: "The fact that this imagery is still going round in Indian garb in 'Siddhartha' does not mean that the Indian aspects were still important to me. On the contrary, it became possible for me to portray this Indian setting only once it had begun to diminish in importance for me, just as I always find I can depict those things in life that I am just taking my leave of."[108]

To many contemporary readers, *Siddhartha* appeared merely to be flirting with the exoticism of the East. In light of this, the parable that was applicable to the whole of humanity was largely overlooked, as Hesse complained in a letter of April 6, 1923, to Romain Rolland:

> With no book hitherto have my personal friends left me in the lurch so much as they have with *Siddhartha*. Hardly any of them have taken the trouble to write so much as a line to me about the book. . . . You are right: among my colleagues, there are very few who are capable of savoring and understanding *Siddhartha*. Where public criticism is concerned, up till now I have heard nothing except expressions of respectful embarrassment . . . well, at least I have been able, with *Siddhartha,* to repay some of the debt I owe to India, and I believe that I will probably never need these Eastern garments again.[109]

The mythical form of *Siddhartha* thus remained a one-off experiment, although its theme would accompany Hesse on his onward journey.

Vivos voco: The Magazine as a Propagandizing Tool

> I was a co-founder of the journal, but have no connection to
> it anymore; the enterprise is failing due to high postage costs.
>
> —Hermann Hesse, letter to Rudolf Trabold, spring 1923

Many of Hesse's texts that were more than just daily newspaper feature articles—namely, his often short prose pieces that were just as atmospheric as they were reflective and that to call just "notes" would be to sell them short—show him to be a typical magazine writer. The magazine form resides somewhere between a newspaper and a book, and extends things of daily interest beyond that time frame without making any grandiose claims that the subjects it covers have everlasting value.

Thus, the magazine exemplifies the quiet death of being forgotten that is suffered by all written matter—but in a particular manner that nowadays seems completely antiquated, being consigned to oblivion quicker than a book but slower than a newspaper. It occupies the intermediate realms of the mind, serving the needs of both daily use and poetic self-sufficiency.

Hesse complied with those requirements. Like *März,* the South German anti-Prussian cultural magazine that he had once written for, *Vivos voco* was also a forum that aimed to serve several purposes at once—and yet that operated within the restricted parameters of its scope and effective duration. Together with Richard Woltereck, whom he knew from the prisoners' aid agency, Hesse founded *Vivos voco* as a space for voicing the "conscience of Europe," a term borrowed from Stefan Zweig's famous description of Romain Rolland. Hesse wanted to reach out to Europe's youth, especially students, and to those many young people who had been sent straight from the classroom to the battlefield and who now, in their mid-twenties, were already spiritually deformed survivors.

How could one create a common Europe comprising parties that had formerly faced one another as enemies in war, and what would be its presiding spirit? The spirit of reconciliation had to be a key ingredient, for sure, if one did not want to slide straight back into the next conflict!

Hesse had no idea of the scale of the enmity he would stir up through his work for *Vivos voco*. His previous, somewhat casual position statements on contemporary political issues had earned him the hatred of nationalist groupings whose broad agenda was revision of the terms of the Versailles Peace Treaty. Hesse also believed the Versailles settlement to be unjust, but he thought that it was not the right time for the Germans to be making demands. Defeat in the war should, he thought, prompt a different, deeper, and more serious reflection, generating ideas for a future Europe and for a new spiritual and cultural order! He was sure that a hysterical revanchism would be the wrong answer to the downfall not just of the German monarchy but also of the whole social order that existed in Europe prior to the war.

With *Vivos voco* Hesse provoked hatred from the circle of German nationalists of whom his old friend Ludwig Finckh was a textbook example. The basically hostile standoff between Hesse and nationalist opinion continued, and over the ensuing years Hesse made no bones about who was to blame for Germany's prevailing misery. Thus, in a letter to Finckh in March 1926, Hesse stated: "It seems to me that intellectual Germany has not experienced the war at all, otherwise after all those terrible years it couldn't start singing the old tunes again and gazing out into the world all blue-eyed and innocent. In my view Germany has not just lost the war, but is also to a large extent guilty for starting it, and its intellectual attitude and public opinion during it, first and foremost the stance of the Kaiser, was stupid and dangerous and has only been partially corrected in the meantime by the miserable state we find ourselves in."

The moralizing and didactic tone of *Vivos voco* had a polarizing effect. The magazine announced the formation of a "youth movement and educational reform" with the aim of putting up for discussion "everything relating to the future of Germany": "We want to attempt to find a clear direction and identify guidelines in the chaos of the youth movement and the reforms of schools and universities. Above all, it is vital that young people themselves be enlisted to assist in this task."[110] As formulated by Hesse and Woltereck in the first issue in October 1919, this was the stated aim of the magazine, which was published in Bern and Leipzig.

Vivos voco, the genesis of which was still entirely in the spirit of the prisoners' aid agency, looked forward to a time of freedom for Germany, not as a victorious power but as a vanquished one. That was, the two editors maintained, not the worst position from which to try to make a genuinely fresh start and instigate correction and reform. And so Hesse wrote in an essay he published in the magazine entitled "Thou Shalt Not Kill": "If we try to identify the interim stage of human development that has been attained in fulfillment of the spiritual demands that have been set by the religious leaders of humanity since Zoroaster and Lao Tzu, then we must say that humans nowadays are still far closer to gorillas than they are to being men."[111]

Hesse had no inkling of the storm he would unleash with such appeals. For the students at whom *Vivos voco* was primarily directed were for the most part of a German nationalist persuasion, and students from the traditional far-right dueling societies became Hesse's principal enemies. And precisely because Hesse never took a direct political stance in the magazine, preferring instead to simply promote a "conscience-driven politics" and always trying to shift discussion of patriotism, nationalism, and political party affiliation onto a superior plane—namely, that of the spiritual well-being of Europe—he became a bogeyman for adherents of many different party factions.

Hesse was already viewing postwar Germany from within and without at one and the same time—distancing himself from Germany had become vital to his survival. Seen from the perspective of Ticino, the contemporary circumstances in Germany, with all its heated debates, appeared far less important than they did to the protagonists there. As he wrote to Georg Reinhart on November 26, 1919: "The reason I don't want to go back to

Germany has to do with my work and my spiritual existence. I am in close touch with Germany and know for sure that if I started living there again, I would find it impossible to stay away entirely from politics for any length of time. But that would run completely counter to all the aspirations I have for the intellectual task I have set myself in my work."[112] In saying this, Hesse had effectively already taken leave again of this form of propagandizing, and this time for good.

The Girl Ruth: Eroticism and Marriage

She was easy on the eyes. A young girl from a solid bourgeois household, slender, elegantly dressed, usually wearing a hat or a headscarf and cradling in her arms one of the lapdogs that she so adored. Yet for all that she was not coquettish, but instead enthusiastic in an indeterminate way, and had in her eyes the expression of a fairy-tale figure, normally an all-too-ephemeral visitor in the everyday humdrum.

This was exactly what Hesse had been seeking. This image inspired him when he met her for the first time on July 22, 1919—during that excursion to Carona, where the Wenger family had a summer house, the Casa Costanza. His first summer in Ticino and the sight of the girl Ruth; all this helped generate that atmosphere of languid heat that pervades *Klingsor's Last Summer.*

The artist in him was reborn through his discovery of sensuality and of the free play of eroticism. Hesse described his first encounter with Ruth Wenger in the chapter in *Klingsor* entitled "A Day at Kareno." Ruth became the "Queen of the Mountains," and the Villa Costanza was transformed into the "Parrot House."

The Wengers were a family of stainless-steel goods manufacturers. Ruth's father was the proprietor of the Coutelier Suisse cutlery factory, which also produced the famous Swiss Army penknife. Her mother, Lisa Wenger, wrote books and became well known in Switzerland for her novels *Die Wunderdoktorin* and *Der Rosenhof.*

Hesse, who had very few acquaintances in Ticino, instantly felt at home in the company of this family. He felt a particular affinity with the worldly-wise Lisa Wenger. By contrast, Ruth floated before his eyes like an erotic dream. The twenty-one-year-old enchanted him with her naturalness.

Only later would he come to admit to himself that it was also a naivety, which made it difficult, and eventually impossible, for him to tolerate her around him for any length of time.

In 1975 Ruth Wenger, who by then had long since been called Ruth Haussmann (after her divorce from Hesse she married the actor Erich Haussmann), wrote her recollection "My Love and Marriage with Hermann Hesse," which began with a paragraph that smacks of bitterness: "I have kept silent for almost fifty years. Including saying nothing about the fact that all biographies of Hermann Hesse have ignored, erased, and completely expunged the significant role that I played in this writer's life." Her bitterness was only set to increase, for her forty-page text, which she was commissioned to write by the publisher of the work *Hermann Hesse in Eyewitness Accounts,* was deemed to be malicious defamation by a divorced wife and ultimately not included in the published volume.

This was a mistake, as would subsequently become clear. It helped ensure that, right up until her death in Weimar in 1994, at the age of ninety-two, Ruth Wenger felt ignored and misunderstood as the second wife of Hermann Hesse. Publication of the correspondence between Hesse and Ruth Wenger was blocked by Ninon Hesse (the author's third wife), which prevented editors from discovering the intimate details of this non-marriage. In the interim, Ruth Wenger's account finally appeared as an appendix to *Love's Heart,* the published correspondence between Hesse and his second wife, which came out in 2005. Much of it accords closely with the letters, or helps fill in some of the gaps they leave. There is no doubt about the credibility of her recollections; the only thing is question is Ruth Wenger's judgment concerning the possibility of a lasting relationship with Herman Hesse. For instance, when she writes that Hesse's later friendly resumption of contact with her after years of silence "cannot erase my memory of that tragedy, which derived from the fact that two people, who in mind and spirit were absolutely made for each other, should end up unable to live with one another thanks to the self-centered nature of one and the great sensitivity of the other."[113] But were they really "made for each other in mind and spirit"?

On August 5, 1919, Hesse wrote Ruth a first, brief letter. Could she perhaps send him a picture of her, he asked? Perhaps in return he could offer

her one of his watercolors, which he took the precaution of declaring unworthy as a gift in exchange, since they were too dilettantish. For as a
daughter of the *haute bourgeoisie,* Ruth Wenger had a fully rounded education in the arts. Not only did she paint, she was first and foremost an
accomplished singer.

Hesse was enthralled, but also—as a man in his mid-forties who was
in a complicated relationship with his mentally ill wife and his three sons
by her—extremely wary. As a result, very little happened at first. Hesse
was caught up in the feverish bout of writing that gripped him in 1919,
and Ruth Wenger responded to his overtures with palpable enthusiasm
only when she felt that Hesse was beginning to take her seriously as a budding artist.

There then ensued a mutual misunderstanding. He had sent her a watercolor, and she responded on December 22, 1919, informing him that it
was already framed and hanging on her wall: "But why didn't you write
anything to accompany it? Or ever write anything at all to me, for that
matter? I can only conclude that your entire friendship with me was based
solely on the pleasure you took in my pretty face."[114] She was well aware
that she had a pretty face. But that wasn't enough for her. And so she told
Hesse: "I'm working hard at the moment. I cannot give up my struggle to
achieve something through my art." In these words of a woman a quarter
of a century his junior, Hesse heard something speaking to him that also
played a decisive role in his own life. Only later would he realize that she
had meant something quite different—and his disappointment when he
did was profound.

Ruth Wenger was no artist. Throughout her life she remained just a
musically gifted daughter of a respectable family. Nor was she soulmate for
such a complex and problematic character as Hesse, who at the time was
suffering the torments of serious writer's block. But precisely for that reason
he found the thought of Ruth a kind of refuge from his troubles.

She also proved to be the lightning rod for all the repressed eroticism
that had played no role in his life up to that point. As he was plunged into
the deepest crisis of his life in 1920, all those things that he had discussed
with J. B. Lang began working within him—such as the insight that a
person should not deny himself his sexual desires, and that they constituted the basic impulse behind all creative activity. And so Hesse wrote to
Ruth in the summer of 1920:

You told me recently with a tone of regret that you meant no more to me than any other girl. As far as erotic matters are concerned, that is true. As Klingsor, I see nothing in you except a pretty girl. But as Sinclair, I see in you a person whose fate is very close to my heart and who needs my support from time to time.

Dear Ruth, sensual love still lies in the future for you, like a beautiful garden of dreams. For me, though, it is a cup from which I have drunk many times, and the drink it contains is no longer a sacrament. A year ago, when we first met, I felt justified in thinking that you were too young and possibly also too good for Klingsor. . . . You are looking for more than just a lover in me, and yet you would lose all that as soon as I became your lover. And I too would gain nothing by it except a cup brimming with lust, which is beautiful but which I can do without. In any event, I must soon bid farewell to all such cups.[115]

From the very beginning, then, there was an imbalance between them where a physical relationship was concerned. At first Ruth paid no attention to that: "Physical love was irrelevant; I was content for him just to sit opposite me in his white summer suit."[116]

What did the poet, the fugitive family man and husband, hope to achieve by flirting with young women? In actual fact, this was nothing but the belated attempt by a man who had married a much older woman when he was still very young, and who was now standing on the threshold of old age, to gain more experience in love. What's more, Hesse had another sweetheart in 1919, one on probation so to speak: Elisabeth Rupp, who admittedly was thirty years old, but still very young in comparison with Hesse.

Like Elisabeth Rupp, Ruth Wenger was part of Hesse's fresh departure to southerly climes, the atmosphere of which he conveyed, and also dissipated, in a number of texts. So unique and intoxicating was this new start in Montagnola that he found it impossible to preserve the initial euphoria over the long term; and the ecstasy was followed not only by disenchantment but also by a deep crisis of self-understanding as an author. Ruth could not understand all this; after all, her mother Lisa was also a successful writer and did not torment herself and others like Hermann Hesse did!

Ruth did not know that she was merely filling a gap in Hesse's erotic biography. Not even Hesse could fully admit this to himself; as a rule he found himself attracted to older women, as, indeed, he was to Lisa Wenger, because he found them to be more understanding of his inner turmoil than younger women, whose love had so little of genuine devotion about it. Balzac had once written that young women only wanted to validate themselves in love, and in contrast to older women had nothing to give.

Ruth Wenger was the kind of young woman who with artless calculation made one man after another fall in love with her. It was all a game to her! A spoiled girl from a privileged background could pick and choose what she wanted for herself—both in art and in erotic encounters. In both realms, this activity never went beyond the stage of dilettantism. Did Hesse really fail to notice how little true understanding he could count on from the twenty-one-year-old Ruth? At the outset, that was doubtless precisely what fascinated him: her totally unspiritual aura, and the impudent child of nature in her, who could also be affectionate.

On July 10, 1920, he wrote to his former psychoanalyst and friend, J. B. Lang: "You can rest entirely easy as regards my relationship with Ruth. My recent role as her protector was a natural one, which devolved to me unwittingly. Apart from that I behave toward Ruth as I do to all women—sensuality remains just a game, and I only allow it to take the upper hand when the woman clearly demands it, and Ruth doesn't, and indeed young women in general rarely do so. So, she is a companion, with whom I socialize in the kind of flirty manner I like to adopt with girls."[117]

At this stage Hesse had no idea that Lang of all people would fall head over heels in love with Ruth. Lang, a married man, began wooing her with an intensity that bordered on insanity, so that even Ruth, who had led him on, started to find his behavior "extraordinary"—for instance, when she was forced to witness Lang losing his composure entirely, becoming enraged and shouting and raving; on this occasion Hesse was finally able to calm him down only with great difficulty. The psychoanalyst also increasingly became a very troublesome case for Hesse to deal with, not least because of Lang's obsession with Ruth, who in all her customary naivety noted retrospectively: "By now I had grown into a very pretty girl and was extremely attractive to men, especially important or famous men."[118]

Yet another person would fall for her charms in this summer of 1919—namely, the Basel painter Paul Basilius Barth, about whose highly

Hesse with Ruth Wenger, ca. 1920

idiosyncratic behavior Ruth wrote: "Barth caused some dreadful scenes, kneeling down in front of me one time and begging me to marry him."[119]

Also with Hesse, a volume of whose poetry she owned and whose presence immediately entranced her, right from the outset it was little more than a frivolous erotic game between two people who wanted to enjoy a carefree life. Yet Hesse, despite his intention to give it a try, was simply not cut out for a laid-back attitude to life.

Was Ruth merely a pretty plaything for the deeply neurotic Hesse, who was beset with all manner of worries and no longer in the first flush of youth? No doubt that was part of her appeal, yet when Ruth's father asked Hesse whether that was all she meant to him and demanded, if this were the case, that he should leave his daughter in peace, and if not, that he should marry her without more ado, Hesse reassured him how serious he was about Ruth and that he would of course marry her as soon (and here he was playing for time!) he had obtained a divorce and been granted Swiss citizenship.

On March 9, 1923, he wrote to Lisa Wenger, his future mother-in-law, with whom he felt he had a relationship much more intimate than he did with Ruth, about his impending divorce from Mia. His tone was ominous: "All these things that one does for the sake of others, against one's inner sense and judgment, aren't good, and will some day have to be paid for dearly. But that's life—you have to pay for things two and three times over, and so I will set about my task even though I don't believe it is right."

He took a gloomy view of the future—an unusual attitude for a bride-groom. In mid-June 1923, on the final day before Hesse was due to leave Baden, where he had spent five weeks on a rest cure, he told J. B. Lang: "Meanwhile things have been going badly for me. I've contracted rheumatism and sciatica, and on top of all that the rest cure and living in a hotel have made me depressed. Admittedly, I've got other things preying on my mind, too, concerning my remarrying (but let's keep that to ourselves!)."[120]

Applying for Swiss citizenship, getting divorced, and assembling all the necessary paperwork for a new marriage are customarily onerous bureaucratic procedures with an uncertain outcome. But Theo Wenger helped smooth Hesse's path in these matters. In July 1923 Hesse was divorced from Mia and was granted Swiss citizenship, for which his future father-in-law paid several thousand Francs.

Hesse was caught in a trap. He had pledged his word, but every fiber of his being rebelled against the sheer insanity of getting married again—and moreover to a pampered girl who lacked any experience in life. Once again Lang was the recipient of his bitter complaints, on December 13, 1923; by this stage Hesse was staying with Ruth at the Hotel Kraft in Basel, and it was dawning on him that he was in a serious predicament: "I'm having a truly miserable time; aside from serious misgivings about the wedding, I have also had to try and reacclimatize to city life, and my sciatica is troubling me too, and if all that weren't enough I have also been involved in an endless rigmarole with no fewer than six bureaucratic departments about my marriage papers, which still aren't quite in order." The pressure on him was mounting, and the tension was beginning to tell on him. Wasn't he far too old for Ruth? "The thing that bothers me most is sexual dysfunction, though things are getting easier in this regard than they were at the beginning, when Basel and the whole situation there were making me quite desperate. The wedding is due to take place in a few weeks' time." He talked about Ruth like she was a child who just happened not to be pestering him right now: "Ruth is very sweet and sends you her fondest greetings, and has made some really good progress with her singing."[121] In her memoir, Ruth Wenger states that Hesse told her even in the period prior to the marriage that he could no longer have sexual relations with her because he was suffering from an infectious disease. Yet he also insisted that Lisa Wenger should also be informed about this, which Ruth registered with astonishment.

And so Hesse agonized over his suitability for marriage—to no avail, because he was already too deeply committed and at the crucial moment had assented rather than demurred.

However, his love affair with Ruth—it really amounted to not much more than that—was long since over by the time he got divorced from Mia in order to marry his young girlfriend. The only side effect that was of significance to him was his regaining of Swiss nationality, which he had had as a child and which his parents had renounced in favor of becoming citizens of Württemberg after settling in Maulbronn. But now he had been resident for more than ten years in Switzerland without interruption—and furthermore never intended to return to Germany. And he knew full well that, in order to be able to remain indefinitely in Switzerland, one had to be a Swiss national. Theo Wenger paid for the divorce—although he threatened on several occasions not to also pick up the tab for all the incidental costs arising from this separation. Hesse was alarmed—what was that supposed to mean? And immediately he started playing the deeply injured party with Lisa Wenger and Ruth, who couldn't possibly stand for such shabby treatment by some disgruntled industrialist. Whereupon the women of the family persuaded the old cutlery manufacturer to pretty much apologize to Hesse for not having written him a blank check for his divorce costs!

Yet it was no longer a question of Hesse and Ruth Wenger simply going through a rocky patch in their relationship—this had long since come to a dead end. Ruth amused herself in her somewhat superficial way, which Hesse could not abide, and he in his turn was completely unsociable, something the young woman could not put up with under any circumstances. As a result, letters between them became increasingly like the one Ruth wrote to him on April 13, 1923, in which she stated: "My dear friend, your behavior toward me showed such a total lack of love, trust, togetherness, or friendship that I believe it impossible for us to build any kind of bond between us, let alone a marriage, on that basis. . . . Were you aware that every word I uttered, even completely innocuous remarks about the weather, profoundly irritated you?"[122]

Hesse knew that he was committing a huge folly in going through with this marriage. He could sooner have imagined marrying Ruth's mother, Lisa, if she hadn't already been married to the patriarchal Theo Wenger, but never their daughter Ruth. When Theo Wenger was away on a rest cure in Baden, Ruth wrote to Hesse in a very unbridal tone: "Already I am almost a widow, less than nothing."[123] Hesse ought never to have married this perpetual girl, who was only interested in her dogs, and who could spend weeks obsessing over the purchase of a new Affenpinscher, which she would then proceed to dress up with a huge, fashionable ribbon tied around its neck and add it to her collection of playthings. Her mother only just managed to dissuade her from buying a monkey. While Hesse was on his Baden rest cure, she accompanied her sister and brother-in-law to Munich, from where Hesse received a letter that began: "You'll miss out on letters from me, I'm afraid, but you can imagine how packed our days are here."[124] He could imagine only too well; he knew his flirtatious fiancée, who incessantly made other men fall in love with her and who reported blithely from Munich: "How lovely the shops are here!"[125] Her taste in music seemed very conventional, too—at least, after attending a concert by the conductor Hans Knappertsbusch, she remarked: "He's very young, an unmusical greenhorn!"[126] Yet if one listens to the recordings of this "unmusical greenhorn," it is astonishing how fresh they still sound even today. Otherwise, Ruth's entire interest in the world was summed up in remarks like this: "I never saw so many men, and many of them are handsome."[127] Why Hesse had not long since run a mile from this person who was superficiality incarnate was a mystery. Perhaps he harbored a secret ambition to be able to compete successfully with the droves of young and handsome men who swarmed around the girl Ruth? But undoubtedly he also felt a sense of obligation, more to Ruth's parents than to her personally, from which he felt unable to withdraw—especially because he had given his word. And he was loath to give Theo Wenger, who already viewed him with suspicion and even contempt, the immense satisfaction of finding him in breach of promise.

★   ★   ★

Still, several women were in awe of Hesse—Hugo Ball's wife, Emmy Hennings, for instance, who had already, like her husband, led an exciting past life. Once an author and a leading light of the German bohemian world, she had suffered a dramatic social descent into destitution! However, in between her drug abuse, prostitution, and time in jail, she and her husband became deeply devout Catholics. The Balls knew a thing or two about the demons to which creative people were prone. In January 1924 Hesse wrote quite openly to Hugo Ball: "There's a funny side to all this, too: you have a wife who is enamored of poverty and adventure. And I, who am a great admirer of abstemiousness and monasteries, as an old man have gone and taken myself a wife who would gladly sacrifice several ideals in exchange for a pair of pretty shoes and a cute dog."[128]

What a deep sense of disenchantment this must have generated in Hesse, yet this had been inevitable from the start. On February 17, 1924, Carl Seelig received the following very matter-of-fact communication: "I've now been married for several weeks and I've spent almost the entire winter in the city, though without actually living any differently from how I did otherwise. I drifted about the alleyways pretty much unmolested and unnoticed, and I lived just as self-contained a life as I was accustomed to." Hesse then added the laconic observation: "We are not living together. In the spring I plan to go back to Montagnola and live there on my own, apart from having her come to stay for short visits."[129]

So, a marriage according to the parameters of a hermit, in other words a nonmarriage? That can be seen as deeply unfair to the much younger and less resilient woman. Set against this, Rainer Maria Rilke's announcement, on getting married to Clara Westhoff, that one person in their marriage had been appointed to guard the other's solitude, sounded almost sensitive.

Ruth had no idea, indeed could not have known, what marriage meant in terms of daily routine, especially marriage to an artist. Hesse, on the other hand, knew only too well.

He was determined—indeed, knew that it was essential for him—to avoid this daily routine at all costs. He was well aware that marriage as a bourgeois institution was not just a one-off symbolic proof of love, but a permanent, practical everyday institution. Conducted in mutual solidarity, if one was lucky. But that, Hesse suspected, was very unlikely to be the case here. They were separated by fundamentally different perceptions of the world.

Hesse instructed his future wife under what conditions he would be prepared to marry her: primarily, that they had to lead separate lives. When necessary, they could visit one another, to have tea together or something similar. One wonders why she didn't immediately say no to this nonsensical arrangement, which could only be made by two people who shared a mutual degree of disillusionment and had nothing left to lose.

Perhaps Hesse's fame dazzled Ruth and she genuinely believed that she could share in this as his wife. This was a classic girlish way of thinking. Even fifty years after the event, she was still capable of writing, with undiminished amazement: "Every woman who is in love thinks of the state of marriage as two people living together under their own roof!"[130]

However, as was only to be expected, her image of Hermann Hesse rapidly changed. He was a moody man who regarded her as a disruptive nuisance. A person with a demonic side, which she did not understand and had not suspected. Hesse could not be bothered to play the affable family man; he was struggling with his work, which was in crisis. And in such circumstances, any creator tends to act unjustly. He worked hard, grappling with intractable material that refused to take the form he wanted. And what did Ruth do all the while? She was living in a comfortable three-room apartment in the Hotel Kraft in Basel, where Hesse was only an infrequent visitor from the start. He took every opportunity to absent himself. Small wonder, for Ruth already had plenty of company: "I was constantly surrounded by dogs, a cat, and a parrot and I even once rented an extra room because I was keeping two Aesculapian snakes in a crate."[131]

When Hesse also arrived in Basel in the fall of 1923—he was taking refuge from the winter in the poorly heated Casa Camuzzi—he took up residence in a different wing of the Hotel Kraft, "a wonderful Biedermeier-period room with two windows looking out over the pleasant bank on the Grossbasel side of the river."[132] All that was at the expense of Hesse's father-in-law, as Theo Wenger was only too well aware. It had always been a costly business being the father of a daughter, especially when she was married to a writer. Despite his success (the Fischer publishing house was just then printing the fiftieth edition of *Demian!*), hardly any of the money that he earned in Germany arrived in Switzerland, being whittled away by the effects of inflation and an unfavorable exchange rate.

They had hardly been married any time when Ruth suddenly fell sick. Her symptoms were tiredness, fever, and chest pains; the diagnosis was at first pleurisy, and then tuberculosis. Ruth was forced to stay in bed for whole days at a stretch—in all, her illness lasted for over a year. Hesse was irked. He suspected that this illness was Ruth's way of getting back at him. He wrote to his sister Adele: "I must say, I find it quite remarkable that, precisely at the moment when I was finally about to put my foot down over Ruth's passivity toward me, it takes on the form of this illness, so that Ruth is now, for at least a year, relieved of any obligation to look after me. How curious!"[133]

Around this time Hesse found that he could no longer bear Ruth's pseudo-intellectual attitude toward art, whose purpose she believed was personal edification and self-improvement in the context of a comfortable lifestyle. For him, writing demanded deadly seriousness, and regarding art and writing in such a way made them the very opposite of pleasant pastimes. Art was more than just constant, strenuous work: it was an unceasing struggle to lend expression to tormenting inner contradictions and the demons of the creative mind.

Ruth was a dilettante in several realms. At first she had taken up painting. In her memoir, she wrote: "However, over time, painting began to bore me, though I did fall in love with my painting instructor."[134] Eventually she settled on singing lessons, and had just made her first advances in this when Hesse first met her.

Yet it turned out that singing wasn't quite the right thing for her either: "At root, I was not musical, although I did feel spiritually drawn to music. But I should have realized that, however talented I might have been, I could never have shouldered the enormous burden of performing in public. For even as a child I fainted away in fear whenever I was called upon at Christmas to perform a piece I'd been practicing on the piano, though the only people present were my parents, my sisters, and the servants." Accordingly, she did everything from a position of superfluity, and never from one of deprivation or the pressure of having to earn money through art as a professional skill. Her dabbling in art angered Hesse because it did not arise from an inner compulsion. Instead this kind of application of art to life was typical of the superficiality of wellborn daughters schooled in the fine arts. Everything was studied in a half-baked way and only up to the point where it started to become difficult, to hurt. And so we read of her life in the Hotel Kraft: "I immersed myself in literature and pictorial volumes about the Biedermeier and Empire periods, and ultimately knew almost enough to become an antique dealer."[135] It was this "almost" that really enraged Hesse and made him, a constantly irascible and morose neurotic at the best of times, positively aggressive toward his wife. But was her nature a surprise to him? After all, he knew all about Ruth by the time he finally married her, more than four years after they first met.

As a result, he started to avoid all contact with her.

Furthermore, his extremely heartless and egotistical reaction to the onset of Ruth's illness also reveals another aspect of his character: his complicated relationship with health and sickness. He himself felt thoroughly unwell. He was suffering from gout, sciatica, headaches, and pain in his weak eyes. And he knew that had something to do with the way he lived. In large part his poor state of health could only be explained psychologically, which was not to say that his pains were purely imaginary, just that it is no coincidence that certain people suffer certain illnesses at certain times. This would become an important theme of his "Psychologia Balnearia," which became famous under the title *A Guest at the Spa*.

In her recollection "My Love and Marriage with Hermann Hesse," which presents, not a proper reckoning with Hermann Hesse, but merely a retrospective attempt to understand why they could not live together, Ruth Wenger spoke of Hesse's way of presenting himself as a "drinker" and a "wastrel." He was neither of these, she maintained. Never in all the years they knew one another did she see him drunk, and he tended to steer clear of any sexual encounter, even in their marriage.

> He was an ascetic, that was his predominant character trait. He was surely aware of that himself, otherwise how could he have let so much time pass without using it in the pursuit of love? Why did he need so young and passionate a girl as his lover? He had no need whatsoever of the love that I was prepared to give him. . . . Although he loved me, I never experienced any outpouring of spiritual or physical love from him. He understood nothing about love, either spiritual or physical. He expressed his love in little terms of endearment, calling me *Pünktchen* or *Pünktlein* [little dot], *blaue Stern* [blue star], and most often *Rehlein* [little roe deer].[136]

Yet something of the demonic nature of the artist, of which she remained oblivious during their time together, must have dawned on her in the intervening decades. What she identified in the years of their marriage was the

Ruth Wenger, Hesse's second wife

beginnings of the Steppenwolf persona, full of self-loathing and disgust at the world, an outsider who shunned bourgeois society, its values and norms. In this, she was no companion to him, no support, but instead merely an extra burden in her gastronomic attitude to both life and art.

Even fifty years later she would recall his petty incivilities and his quirks and the fact that he was suddenly no longer presentable: "Hesse didn't wear his gold velvet suit anymore, but an unprepossessing dark gray suit instead. His gray wool socks sagged down over his shoes and the collar of his shirt hung round his neck like a shapeless poultice. All the magic of his former slender and graceful appearance had vanished."[137] She was particularly disturbed by the "sullen silence" he lapsed into to signal his displeasure at one of Ruth's animated chats with, say, her "charming brother-in-law." The smallest things could trigger serious resentment. Hesse felt himself completely misunderstood by his young wife; and reading her memoir it becomes clear that she never had even the beginnings of an understanding of his character: "Furthermore he was completely un-biddable, and there was something unapproachable about him. When he was in a difficult frame of mind, I would venture to say that Hesse had an inhuman aura."[138] He was not warm, or cheerful and pleasant, but for the most part outwardly cold and deeply withdrawn—and she could not tolerate that. Yet in this marriage, right from the outset, she had never been an equal partner, as she noted bitterly: "We never slept together in the same room. Yet this subject was not discussed, like it would naturally have been in a normal marriage. Hesse ordered, arranged, and organized things, and I simply obeyed."[139] And yet there was within Hesse a secret hankering after solid petit bourgeois foundations for his life, which of course he had to destroy over and over again—and there was also something within him that made him the enemy of all bohemians and demanded a rigid, everyday sense of order. In a letter to Walter Schädelin dated May 30, 1912—in other words, long before Hesse's "Steppenwolf period" of the 1920s—we read: "Yes, I love the philistine (whom I could not endure even for a single day in reality), because I envy him the firm foundations of his life, in the same way that I envy healthy, robust, happy people their appetites, their regular sleep, and their laughter. Stability is the whole name of the game."[140]

"Piktor's Metamorphoses"

Hesse wrote a fairy tale for each of his wives; the one for Ruth was entitled "Piktors Verwandlungen" (Piktor's Metamorphoses). It was composed in 1922, when Hesse was already looking back on what it was about the girl that had first enchanted him. The story concerns Piktor, a figure easily identifiable as Hesse himself. Piktor sees life in all its colorful variety flowing past him; he is in paradise, and the snake urges him to make a wish, quickly, or he will miss his chance of good fortune. And so Piktor wishes to be turned into a tree—not a bad choice when one considers Hesse's reverential attitude toward trees. The tree takes no further part in the colorful hurly-burly of life; it grows tall with its branches and leaves and is rooted in the cool depths. It is happy: "Gradually he learned to see with tree-eyes. Eventually he gained the power of sight and was sad." The reason for this was that everything around him was changing, with new things springing up all around. "He, though, the tree Piktor, constantly remained the same, he could not transform himself anymore. Once he realized this, his happiness evaporated; he began to age and took on that increasingly haggard, earnest, and distressed look that one can see in many old trees. . . . As time passes, and they no longer possess the gift of transformation, they lapse into melancholy and waste away, and their beauty vanishes."[141] Here, then, is Hesse's self-portrait as a man who feels exhausted and empty and is approaching old age with a stoical attitude. Could there be one final new possibility of enchantment? At this point Hesse introduces a fairy tale within a fairy tale, which recounts how the unhappy tree Piktor, whom the colorful world is passing by, does not have to be a tree any longer. His tree-life, which has become a torment, with its premature renunciation of all joy and sensual delight, can be remedied only by an extraordinary encounter. A new enchantment. But where was this to come from?

This was a fairy tale for Ruth, yet it was dedicated to this moment of reawakening as a man: "One day a young girl strayed into that region known as paradise; she had blonde hair and was wearing a blue dress. Singing and dancing, the blonde girl walked beneath the trees, and up till then had never even thought about wishing to have the gift of transformation. . . . When the tree Piktor saw the girl, he was seized by a great longing, a yearning for happiness such as he had never felt before."[142] This girl enchanted him with her youth. This new tone, and the creative upsurge it signified, can be clearly identified in the chapter "The Day at Kareno" in *Klingsor's Last Summer*. Hesse had Ruth to thank for that.

Yet many critics have identified a note of parting in the tone Hesse adopts in "Piktor's Metamorphoses," a sense of someone already moving on. For instance, it sounds a little too fairy-tale-like when he writes: "Now everything was good, the world was in order, and now for the first time he had found paradise. Piktor was no longer an old, sad tree, now he sang aloud: 'Piktoria, Viktoria!'" He felt that he had been transformed by this encounter and this time it was the "proper, the eternal transformation." But in truth Hesse was actually too clever and undoubtedly also already too old for such absolute statements, which are more the domain of youthful and naive temperaments. Yet if one reads on to find out what Hesse was really driving at, this metamorphosis suddenly appears in a quite different light.

One gets the impression almost of vampirism at work here, for his transformation from a half-person into a whole one is not about someone else but about himself—he has absorbed the girl Ruth within himself. On the face of it that sounds beautiful, but in fact it is gruesome, for he has exploited the gift she gave him as a means of rejuvenation, so to speak. That is now inside him, whereas Ruth herself as a separate individual is superfluous. The deeper underlying cause of the irresolvable alienation between them, therefore, was the fact that Hesse had assimilated her spirit as

Caricature of Hesse as a gardener, by H. U. Steger

sustenance for himself. Ruth, on the other hand, occasionally adorned herself with his fame. And that very quickly became intolerable for Hesse, trapped as he was within his agonizing doppelgänger neuroses.

For Hesse, an expression of the androgynous Adam figure, was more than just a modern solipsistic Narcissus; he was a mystic, a sorcerer, a magician, who combined with himself inwardness and outwardness, the Self and the world, and man and woman: "He became a deer and a fish, he became a human and a snake, a cloud and a bird. But in each form he was complete, he was a pair, he had sun and moon, man and woman within himself, and flowed as a double stream through the world and stood as a twin star in the heavens."[143]

"Twin star" had long since ceased to be one of those endearments he applied to the loved one that Ruth momentarily represented for him; it denoted himself, Herman Hesse as a singleton, yet in a new form, a higher state of perfection, which was more "oriented to the world" than his previous one.

And yet, he acknowledged ruefully, his former existence as a tree, his life as a stoic who shared in the "tree of life" in his own quiet way, had not been such a bad one after all: he had grown tall, towering above all others and yet remaining inconspicuous at the same time, and drawn to the colorful and changing shadow-play that flitted by beneath him as a purely esthetic phenomenon, but otherwise fundamentally unimpressed by it.

On 1920, Hesse wrote a tree poem that, like many of his lyrical texts, is not terribly compelling in its form (simple "versification," to borrow Gottfried Benn's term), yet despite certain sentimental elements it does tell us a great deal about Hesse in this phase of his life:

Pruned Oak

Oh oak tree, how they have pruned you,
Now you stand there strange and oddly shaped!
You have suffered a hundred times over
Until you had nothing left but defiance and will!
I am like you, I will not sever my connection
To my mutilated and tormented life,
And every day I raise my brow anew to the light
Out of all the indignities I have suffered.
What in me was once mild and tender
The world has ridiculed to death.
But my being is indestructible.
I am at peace and reconciled.
Patiently I grow new leaves
From boughs split a hundred times.
In spite of all the pain and sorrow
I am still in love with this crazy world.

The Garden—a Blossoming Estate, an Alternative World, and a Place for Bonfires

> There is no summer that does not feed off the death of the previous one.
>
> —Hermann Hesse, "In the Garden" (1908)

In Hesse's work there is no demarcation between the poetic and the profane, or between the utilitarian and the merely beautiful. This is a hallmark of the pantheist, who can find evidence of God everywhere, not just in those places where he is ritually worshipped, yet it also denotes the petit bourgeois concerned with working everything out exactly. On February 22, 1927, Hesse wrote to Annette Kolb when he was toying with the idea of moving to Badenweiler, where she was also living: "How does one do that, though—become a neighbor? It requires all sorts of things that I am totally incapable of doing: buying or even building a house, purchasing furniture for it, including beds and curtains, and dealing with banks and local authorities. But above all it requires someone who can maintain order in the house, and do all the cooking and cleaning and so on. I've been wanting all these things, including a bathtub and a small garden, for the last eight years, possibly only because I always had them before and they struck me as perfectly natural." In the same letter he then went on to make a revelation about his marriage to Ruth Wenger that bordered on self-incrimination: "I even let myself be seduced into my second marriage, simply in the mistaken hope that this might be a circuitous way of getting myself a little house and garden, etc., etc."[144]

Hesse was fond of presenting himself as an impractical man who required the help of others to even cope with everyday life. There was a degree of play-acting in this, and he made a habit of dramatizing his situation. The question remained of whether he was capable of being a diligent gardener. Then again, who said that a gardener even had to work in his own garden—isn't every garden a little slice of paradise on Earth, a spin-off of the Garden of Eden? Living in a garden meant constantly gazing at beauty and being in the midst of it. This was not an idyll, but an interplay of the forces of fire and water! In a garden, demons were banished and forced to submit to the cycle of the seasons.

The writer, who was often described as a straw-hat wearer, particularly liked making bonfires of twigs in his garden. He never tired of gazing at the flames as they went about their work, changing all the while. But what about the rest of the work that is necessary in a garden, leaving aside this element that he found so mesmerizing?

The type of garden that Hesse loved, he was well aware, was a phenomenon in danger of dying out, a last bastion against the industrial noise and pollution that was being spread by the growing uniformity of life. The kind of place where plants still simply flourished of their own accord! In the meantime, however, the garden had also long since become an infiltration zone for machine culture, which replicated the scenario of industrial conveyor-belt noise on private plots, as electric—or even worse, petrol-engine-driven—lawnmowers, hedge trimmers, and circular saws of all kinds carried the "music of doom" into even the last refuge of silence. Where and when could one peacefully burn twigs in one's garden, as Hesse's third wife Ninon Dolbin (whom he often jokingly called "charcoal-burner") loved doing?

From the very beginning Hesse's love of the garden was always with the proviso that he did not wish to cultivate all aspects of nature. The garden according to his way of thinking would be a place where all manner of fantasy, even the most demonic, might be given free rein: the Garden of Eden *with* a snake. For only the snake can engender knowledge. Conversely, from the outset he shunned the idea of the garden as drudgery or any concept of useful horticulture. In a letter he wrote as a boy to his parents when he was incarcerated in the asylum at Stetten in 1892, we read: "I hate working in the garden, and since I have been here I have only been out into the garden a few times, though I'm really 'supposed' to go there daily."

Hesse has provided wonderful descriptions of what the garden meant to him: a burden he cheerfully bore, to the end that it might ultimately blossom and bear fruit. Thus, for him the garden was not just a symbol of human existence, it also became the model for his work as an author, a school of seeing and sowing, and of the happy balance between the *vita activa* and the *vita contemplativa*. The garden was also in a very direct way a spiritual location, where things that had once been sown transformed themselves, through numerous metamorphoses, into things that could enchant even gardeners with their extraordinary beauty.

One had to have sufficient time to let things grow and to intervene at the right moment to stop the garden from turning into a wilderness, one had to water the garden and constantly prune back vigorous young shoots to keep them in proportion to the rest of the garden. One had to weed and be sure not to miss the optimal moment to harvest. Creating beauty was also a form of work, albeit one that natural growth naturally facilitated. Organizing the interplay of the natural and the artificial was also the task of the author, who approached his manuscripts in the same way as he did his garden.

In his sketch "In the Garden" ("Im Garten") of 1908, Hesse created a reflection of his world in miniature. In it, he revealed himself as a not particularly exemplary gardener, a dilettante in directing and organizing nature. In the first spring, the garden lay there, still covered with patches of snow, as a "quiet, expectant world." But instead of immediately getting down to practical work, as other garden managers, life's "professional gardeners," would have done, Hesse the gardener was himself only just waking up to his new life and shaking the frosty stiffness of winter out of his limbs. Accordingly, he portrayed himself as a Johnny-come-lately of a gardener—"We dilettantes and slackers, we dreamers and hibernators, find ourselves once again surprised by the advent of spring and observe with dismay all the tasks that our hardworking neighbors have already done, while we were idling away our time blithely in pleasant winter dreams. Now we're embarrassed, all of a sudden time is terribly pressing, and as we run to catch up with neglected jobs and sharpen our shears and dash off urgent letters to the seed merchants, half-days and whole days once more pass by unproductively."[145]

Little dramas unfolded daily in gardens as well. They were not just refuges and sensual mirrors of the world, places where we could conjure up beauty through fantasies of the natural world, or flee from the banal utilitarian world, but also living proof of the fact that beauty can only exist in conjunction with ugliness, and good with evil. Part and parcel of his attitude to gardening was praise of weeds and of the little pests that plague the garden—from the irritating mosquito to the mole that undermines even the most manicured lawn and covers it with little mounds of earth. They too belong in the garden, as Hesse well knew:

> Nature is unrelenting. It allows you to charm certain things from it, and seems to let itself be outsmarted now and then—but then it only returns to claim its dues all the more severely . . . among plants too, there are good and bad families, savers and squanderers, proud hardy plants and parasites. There are plants whose way of life is philistine and homely and others that behave like profligate lords and bon viveurs; just as, among us humans, there are good and bad neighbors, friendships and animosities. There are plants that germinate and live and die wild and untamed and beyond all measure,

and there are some poor, disadvantaged plants that waste away piteously
and lead a pale and difficult existence.[146]

Every garden therefore carries within it a distant echo of the first
garden, of Paradise. In terms of the individual, this first garden is synonymous with childhood. The child expects something from life, which it
stands at the beginning of; it expects everything in excess! The artist, in
Hesse's case the writer, is like that child, which the gardener awakens
within himself every year in the spring. He is on a quest for the beginning, for the first word with which he can begin a text, in which those
sentences will be reflected that were important to him as a child. The
Danish author Herman Bang's famous words in the novel *The White
House* (1898)—"O days of childhood, I want to recall you"—allude to
this garden of childhood, in which everything still seemed possible in the
sheer exuberance of a fresh start: good as well as evil, the beautiful as well
as the ugly.

Later, after one has made this fresh start for the thousandth time and
made oneself a past-master at repetition (the opposite of a routine!), one
realizes that the ever more original beginning is nothing but a nostalgic
picture. It can only be preserved through the exercise of fantasy by constantly recreating it afresh—in order that we might once again, on the basis
of the picture we have conjured up, expect everything, at least for a brief
moment. These gardens are beautiful fulfillments of all the things that
are possible in the world—and at the same time places from which to
repulse the world: "The way the poet carefully picks and positions and
selects his word in the midst of a world that could easily be destroyed
tomorrow, that is exactly the same as what the anemones, primulas and
other flowers growing on all the meadows do. They grow in the midst of
a world that night well be covered tomorrow by poison gas; they carefully
form their lamellae and calyxes with five or four or seven petals apiece,
smooth or serrated, with everything precisely positioned and as beautiful
as can be."

The 1924 story "The Lost Penknife" ("Das verlorene Taschenmesser")
shows the author as a garden laborer and a garden artist at the same time,
a man who, like all cultural critics schooled in Rousseau, asks how one

might cultivate nature without destroying it. The garden answers this question for him.

His lament about the lost penknife is a lament about the transience of life in general, the inevitability of our death, and about the way we gradually relinquish all our cherished objects and customs. The knife was a memento, which was so much a part of the narrator's life that its loss now grieves him: "And that knife was one of the very few objects that had up till now survived all the changes in my life and accompanied me for decades through all the upheavals."[147]

Until the very last, the knife had not only performed useful services in the garden, but it was also a symbol for long-distant past hopes that once attached to the garden. Some of these were in vain, while others were fully realized, albeit in ways that were very different from how he had envisaged them all those years ago.

How lovely it is that there can exist an object that has survived many changes and yet still holds a future within it! "I did not imagine that, out of all the lovely things I had when I was young—my house and garden and family and homeland—this knife would one day be the only object that I still had in my possession."[148]

And now, thanks to his carelessness, he has also lost this knife, which was so precious to him. Like Balzac, Hesse knew that life consists of expended wishes. What remains is an excess of melancholy, an awareness of the dwindling of the time left on this Earth and hence also a contraction of the future. By contrast, one's recollection of things that are irretrievable grows—yet with the passage of time even this awareness gradually recedes in the aging brain.

Nonetheless, there is hope for the author and the gardener alike: successful form wrests moments of eternity from the transient instant! But for Hesse the gardener, that knife is also a sign of rootlessness, of his lack of a homeland, and of his destiny as a wayfarer. He also ponders the thought that, in extremis, one can plunge a knife into one's own heart, and in the process he does not fail to cite "Goethe's excellent advice to sentimental individuals contemplating suicide."

A knife affords its owner freedoms regarding the pressures of life—even if a person is "only" then compelled to use it to prune branches in the garden, it is already an indicator of his heroism in the face of life, especially if he has "a little bonfire lit in one corner of the garden." This penknife also testified to Hesse's uneasiness with his own existence, and the aspect of it that could not be satisfied—namely, the Steppenwolf side of him: "But I did not mention to a soul that remaining here in this life had lost its meaning for me and that my dream of happiness and contentment in this house had been a false aspiration and needed to be buried."[149]

By this he meant his life in Gaienhofen, but can we also say that it was wholly inapplicable to his time in Montagnola? His great distress at the loss of the knife would appear to refute this.

8

THE AWAKENING OF STEPPENWOLF

Common "Flight Out of Time":
Hesse's Encounter with Hugo Ball and Emmy Hennings

It would turn out to be possibly the most important encounter of his life. Hugo Ball was a kindred spirit, such as one meets only once in a lifetime, and Emmy Hennings likewise impressed him in a way that he could never have imagined he would be impressed by a woman.

It touched the vital raw nerve of his existence as an artist. Might there be some kind of salvation for him after all? And what price must he pay for it? Should he cease being a writer who documented his own crises, an approach that really only succeeded in dragging him further down into the maelstrom of self-destruction?

Hugo Ball had been living near Hesse during the period he spent in Bern. At that time Hesse knew nothing about him—indeed, did not even know his name. Ball had a slightly different recollection of Hesse at this time, as he revealed in a letter of 1934: "He belonged to a small, radical group of people opposed to the war, yet although he knew my name at that time, he regarded me as nothing but a rather laughable sentimental and bourgeois writer."[1]

★   ★   ★

On December 2, 1920, the two writers met at the house of Joseph Englert, an engineer, a lapsed disciple of Rudolf Steiner, and an enthusiastic astrologer. Around this time Hesse was paying frequents visits to Englert in Casserate; topics in which they shared an interest were stars, magic, and the occult. Even so, Hesse kept his relationship with Englert somewhat distant. They spoke extensively about religion and also discussed the main points of Hesse's essays on Dostoyevksy. However, Hesse was wary of the way Englert projected himself. Since his time on Monte Verità, he had an instinctive aversion to such esoteric figures, fanatics obsessed with order and with a predilection for forming sects. Thus, in a letter of May 25, 1927, to Georg Reinhart, after conceding that Englert was a "pleasant, upstanding fellow who is clever and very useful in many ways," he added with a hint of reserve:

> But I do believe Englert has something of a tendency to compensate for feelings of inferiority, and this forces him to constantly play a role to some degree. To his worldly-wise acquaintances he presents himself as a ascetic, to the more superficial among them he comes across as the knowing occultist, and in front of Protestants he appears as a Catholic. For his second marriage (in other words, the one before last) he pestered the Catholic Church right up to petitioning the pope, and then went and broke it off anyway. Mind you, I don't hold all this against him, because I have never taken his religious side—that is, his dabbling in Catholic ritual and his supposed piety—at all seriously.[2]

Hesse's observation of the masquerades his friends indulged in was clear-eyed and sober. And yet everything about someone like Englert that he found implausible he accepted without demur in Hugo Ball and Emmy Hennings right from the outset—and this would remain the case throughout his life.

There was something fateful for Hesse about this first encounter with Ball and Hennings in Englert's house. If he had not met them, his *Siddhartha* would not have been completed—or at least not in the form that we now know it—there would have been no *Steppenwolf*, and Ball's posthumous influence on such works as *Narcissus and Goldmund*, *The Journey to the East*, and *The Glass Bead Game* would not be apparent.

It took only a short time after this first meeting at Englert's for their relationship to blossom. Two days later Hesse dropped by the Balls's house in

Agnuzzo, not far from Montagnola, as if he were just passing, as Emmy Hennings recalled: "He had painting kit with him, including an easel and a folding stool, and showed us his watercolors, which we found charming. He said he'd just dropped by to say hello and to look us up, but on this occasion he stayed for over twelve hours." This was unusual for Hesse, who normally guarded his solitude like a precious commodity. He only left their house after midnight, when he had a long walk back ahead of him. Emmy Hennings noted the conversation she and Hugo Ball had after Hesse left that evening:

> "At eleven I thought, perhaps he isn't planning to leave at all and will stay overnight with us, and maybe even stay tomorrow too if there's nice weather, and so on."
>
> "It would be nice if you'd been right. Still, he might stay over with us some other time."[3]

All three of them shared a single wish: namely, to see one another again soon. What was the reason for this strong impulse? Hugo Ball and Emmy Hennings had both, independently, fallen in love with Hermann Hesse on the spot. There is no other way of putting it, even though this doesn't adequately describe the entirety of the triangular relationship that began at this point. Hermann Hesse, who cannot have failed to notice that the two of them liked him as a person and admired him as a writer, did not react by shunning them; instead, for the first time in a long while, he felt that he was being understood and regarded with sympathy. Nothing could help him in the deep crisis into which he was plunged at the beginning of the 1920s. Yet even the fact that Emmy Hennings found it impossible to conceal her confusion at Hermann Hesse's sudden appearance did not frighten him off from intensifying his contact with the Balls.

Did there exist in Hesse—in whose texts such a major role is played by the androgynous, a prime example of this being the dual figure of Hermann and Hermine in *Steppenwolf,* who represents the division of the Self into a male and a female side—a homoerotic tendency, which manifested itself at the very least through bisexual behavior? According to the ideal, this kind of bisexuality would have accorded entirely with Hesse's conception of himself—and yet in his life, where eroticism was concerned, men played a smaller role even than women. Like Rilke, Hesse was of a narcissistic personal temperament, with the result that all his experiences, even the erotic, were played out within himself, while the external world was at best only a trigger to his desires and never either the principal basis or the ultimate goal of those urges.

Homoeroticism was also a theme, albeit peripheral, in his "Dream Diary of Psychoanalysis" of 1917–1918. Hesse proceeded anyhow from the assumption that people had a fundamentally hermaphroditic nature, which manifested both male and female traits—for him this did not present a problem, nor was it a concept fraught with feelings of guilt. On August 6, 1917, he observed, vis-à-vis his dreams: "What is remarkable is how in these dreams naked men appear time and time again; yet the only figure toward whom I detect any erotic resonances is Schoeck. In reality, Schoeck is discreet and prudish."[4] Othmar Schoeck was a composer whom Hesse had befriended, feeling that his compositions had a close affinity to his poems.

With regard to the fact that Hesse repeatedly saw no problem in becoming friends with men who more or less openly displayed their homosexuality, it seems clear that he did not feel any erotic interest in them. Similarly, in the encounter with Hugo Ball, who had had homosexual relationships in the past, the erotic played no role in their intense friendship. As for Ball himself, who was instantly fascinated by Hesse as a man, he had only just committed himself to an ascetic lifestyle—Hesse met him in a phase when he was to all intents and purposes on the way to becoming a kind of monk who sought death in life in order to find life within death. It was a similar story with Emmy Hennings. Emmy took Hesse's fancy, but in a very particular way—she was simply more interesting to him than other women he had met.

The course was thus set for an extraordinary *ménage à trois* characterized by strict abstinence and a positively ascetic discipline on the part of all three. This was undoubtedly the secret to how their intimate connection lasted so long.

To understand their special relationship, we first need to turn our attention to the lives Hugo Ball and Emmy Hennings led before they met Hesse. For, like Hermann Hesse, in 1920 they too stood at a point that could easily have signaled their demise. All three of them felt themselves to be in a state of crisis from which they suspected they would probably not be able to extricate themselves by their own efforts alone. They were all obliged to seek help from outside, though they were loath to have this appear in the slightest way external.

All three were on the run from their former lives. They had no idea how the future would turn out. They were banking on the mercy of a spirit of salvation, on true friendship.

If one looks at photographs from this period, one sees a woman with a resigned set to her mouth, which appears almost embittered, or in any event has something hard about it yet which at the same time seems hungry for life in a guilt-laden way. Emmy Hennings was a childlike and naive creature who had aged far too quickly, and who had become worldly-wise and calculating in a detrimental way as a result of false expectations and external circumstances, which at the same time had left her deeply humiliated. As a result, she came across as both shameful and frivolous. She was like a figure from a film by the Danish director Lars von Trier— simultaneously a saint and a whore. Beside her in the pictures is Hugo Ball, mostly in shirts buttoned up to the neck, resembling the shirts worn by Hesse but on Ball they looked more severe and monastic. He was an individual seeking salvation with unqualified seriousness, and inspired by this to lead a saintly life, although this former Dadaist artist and offensive social critic was well aware that this would make him into a ridiculed outsider.

So what was the common bond between Hugo Ball and Emmy Hennings in 1920? The blows that fate had dealt them over the war years just past had knocked all the exuberance out of both of them, and life weighed heavily on them. Their conversion was not meant rhetorically, but was vital to their survival. Praying together was the only point of fixity they could still identify in an age driven by a frenzy of destruction.

They were also bonded with Hesse by common spiritual themes: the demonic and exorcism; libidinous urges and asceticism; the sacred and the increasing banality of mass culture; the task of the intellectual between social criticism and the timeless evocation of meaningfulness; the monastic life, religion, and atheism; the question of the cultic in religion, action, and contemplation; the idea of the artist as narcissist; Protestantism and Catholicism; the role played by sacrifice for faith; guilt and atonement; the

An excursion to Carona. From right to left: Hugo Ball, Emmy Ball-Hennings, Hermann Hesse, and an unknown female friend

creation of heretics by institutions; the neuroses of modern humans; pantheism and mysticism. The role of myth in the writing of history, the forgotten Middle Ages and the hidden treasures of Romanticism, self-realization and self-abnegation—the circle of themes was vast, but between the two men, everything they discussed was at the same time always very personal. This was not like a debate between academics; no one was attempting to win the other over in the way that converts and adherents of a particular ideology do, but instead they talked about their experiences, confessed their dreams and fears to one another. By turns, each listened or stayed silent, sparing his interlocutor by refraining from asking questions or demanding responses and merely enjoying his presence. It was a kind of brotherhood that grew up between them, with the inclusion of Emmy Hennings as a sister—and all three of them felt inwardly strengthened by this relationship. For all three were people who had been damaged by the outside world, refugees from false ways of life, and seekers after God in a godless world.

Hesse had just completed *Klein and Wagner,* that tale of his criminal alter ego on the run, while around the same time Ball was writing his essay

"Flucht aus der Zeit" ("Flight Out of Time"). Ball described Hesse after their first encounter as a slender, youthful-looking man "with sharp facial features and the demeanor of a sufferer."[5] Emmy Hennings, who tended to fall in love with men of monastic appearance, instantly fell for Hesse's morbid allure.

The two men were also alike in the fact that, in order to plow their own furrows, they had been forced to defy their fathers' authority. Hugo Ball's father was a leather trader and a shoe salesman. It took a nervous break-down for Hugo to finally be allowed to finish high school and study—and not to have to follow his father into the leather and shoe trade. There then followed many unstable years of searching, in which he disappointed and left behind all those who thought they had got the measure of him. But Hugo Ball himself did not yet know who he was, and was still searching. After a year of university study, he abandoned the dissertation he had begun to write on "Nietzsche in Basel" and went into the theater, studying to be a director at the Deutsches Theater in Berlin and becoming a dramaturge in Plauen and at Munich Comedy Playhouse (Lustspielhaus), which at his instigation was rechristened the Munich Chamber Theater (Münchner Kammerspiele). His family, meanwhile, had disowned him, and he staked everything on a career as a playwright. His play *Michelangelo's Nose (Die Nase des Michelangelo)* found favor with the publisher Ernst Rowohlt. He met the renowned German playwrights Frank Wedekind and Franz Blei, and embarked on a homosexual relationship with the Expressionist poet Hans Leybold, with whom he founded the magazine *Revolution* in 1913. When war broke out, Ball volunteered for military service, but was not called up due to his poor health. His lover Leybold went off to the front as a lieutenant in the reserve—where, after a short time, he shot himself. Ball was deeply shocked.

Emmy Hennings's life had begun in similarly straitened, only even poorer, working-class circumstances in the North German city of Flensburg. The daughter of a longshoreman, she entered the bohemian demi-monde of Berlin in 1910, where she quickly made a name for herself as a man-eating femme fatale with her radically short blonde haircut and extravagant style of dress.

Before she arrived in Berlin, she had attempted to realize her dream of entering the world of the arts by working at the Flensburg municipal theater. This naive aspiration of a working-class girl led her to fall for a typesetter by the name of Joseph-Paul Hennings, who was a fan of the theater; however, as soon as they were married and she had a child, he locked her up at home. Their son died the following year, whereupon Emmy rebelled against her wretched circumstances by contracting nervous paralysis. She joined a traveling theater troupe, fell pregnant again in 1906 with her daughter Annemarie, whom as soon as she was born Emmy entrusted to her mother back in Flensburg to bring up, while she went back on the road with the theater.

She wrote theater pieces, and performed in cabarets and bars—without much success. She started taking drugs and spiraled down back into poverty; she also fell into prostitution, fraud, and theft. In Munich in 1915 she was jailed for stealing from one of her clients—a low point from which the only way was downward into the gutter.

At this point she received a prison visit from Hugo Ball. In 1910, when she had been ill with typhoid fever, she had converted to Catholicism; in Ball she found someone who was keen to return to his Catholic roots. From the very beginning, this truly remarkable relationship was conducted in the spirit of Catholicism. It was a case of a drowning person trying to save another from the same fate. Emmy had a single mission: "I wanted to be a little bringer of solace, and he was receptive to receiving it."[6]

Together, after the end of her jail term, they traveled to Zurich, though here too they were kept under surveillance as suspicious and dangerous subjects. On July 14, 1916, they were at the forefront in presenting the "First Dada Evening" of the Cabaret Voltaire; other artists involved in this groundbreaking "happening" included Hans Arp, Richard Huelsenbeck, and Tristan Tzara. The program promised music, dance, theory, manifestos, poetry, paintings, costumes, and masques. The dance routine was a "cubist dance," for which Ball devised the choreography and designed the costumes. He also read out the first manifesto of the Dadaist movement at this event. In 1918 Ball published a novel, *Flametti or the Dandyism of the Poor*, based on his time in Zurich. As early as 1916 he said that the aim of the Cabaret Voltaire was to "transcend the war and fatherlands and recollect those few independent individuals who espouse different ideals."[7]

That mission statement accorded closely with Hesse's position during the First World War. He too wanted to see an alliance of European intellectuals that would look beyond the warring parties' formation of hostile fronts and keep alive a shared spirit that would form the basis for a new order in postwar Europe.

Soon after, however, Ball and Hennings did something that seemed quite inexplicable to all the couple's friends—they withdrew to Lake Lugano, and left behind all "-isms," which they decried as "bourgeois nonsense." Worse, Ball renounced their most famous creation: "The Cabaret Voltaire is useless, bad, decadent, militaristic—you name it. I want no part of it any more."[8] Friends suspected the influence of Emmy Hennings behind this abrupt change of heart. But in actual fact the couple were fully in agreement that they were looking for peace and quiet beyond the rat race of the city, a haven where they could write. Moreover, they planned to make a serious attempt to live out their Franciscan ideal, and so moved into an isolated hut, taking with them only writing materials, a few provisions, and a goat; they also had in tow a young likeminded acolyte, the writer Richard Glauser. He was primarily drawn to Hugo Ball, but soon left their little group and moved on. Bärbel Reetz, Emmy Hennings's biographer, has suggested that Emmy had a liaison with the young author behind Ball's back, which prompted Ball to drive Glauser away. After the death of her mother in 1916, Emmy had to look after her nine-year-old daughter, Annemarie, for the first time; the child moved to Zurich to live with them.

In 1920 Hennings contracted a life-threatening bout of the Spanish flu. She and Ball made a snap decision to marry. Their economic situation was disastrous, far worse than Hermann Hesse's, who by this time was forced to live in Switzerland on a tenth of his former income, but fortunately found patrons quickly enough, who supplied him with regular injections of cash. Georg Reinhart initially sent him 200 francs a month, a sum he later doubled.

Money was a subject on which Hesse could not afford to be indifferent—his commitments to Mia and the children were too great, and in addition his life as a spa guest, which was about to begin, did not come cheap. On July 26, 1917, in his "Dream Diary of Psychoanalysis" he mused on his "dependent and inhibited relationship with money." He despised money, "while at the same time hoarding it like a miser; I've also frequently stolen it."[9] This was a surprising piece of self-incrimination. In any event, where money matters were concerned, Hesse was far more enterprising and resourceful than Hugo Ball and Emmy Hennings, a couple who really were total idealists and ascetics, and who time and again were quite literally faced with utter destitution. Henceforth, Hesse would often beg his friends—not always successfully—for cash to give to Ball.

In 1922, in a private confession, Hugo Ball officially returned to the fold of the Roman Catholic faith; presumably his wife Emmy was also the driving forced behind this. Ball was strongly under her influence—though Hesse too was fascinated by this deeply conflicted individual. In December 1911, for instance, he wrote to Lisa Wenger: "This woman Emmy is a small, delightful child, whom Our Dear Lord has, for some strange reason, allowed to be exposed to all manner of suffering and all the vileness of the world, and who would have found all that unbearable if little miracles had not kept happening along the way, and if someone had not shown her kindness."[10]

There is no doubt that Hesse saw a kindred spirit in Emmy. He, who repeatedly portrayed himself as a hybrid of bourgeois citizen and criminal, here found himself facing someone who really had spent time in jail. He was well aware that it was often merely a matter of good fortune that he had avoided that same predicament himself. He felt that he had sufficient destructive energy within himself to commit a major act of arson or to kill a person. This amalgam of anxieties and secret desires would find expression in *Steppenwolf*. For Hesse—who in the summer of 1921 resumed his course of psychoanalytic therapy with C. G. Jung, praising his intellect and his character—Hugo Ball embodied a step beyond his own individual psychology. Hesse compared the process of psychoanalysis as having to walk through a "fire," which "caused me a lot of pain. That's all I can say about it."[11] The path he had embarked upon with Jung led him on to study myth and legend—and also ultimately to religions in their various forms. And on this double journey of discovery of the Self and the world, Ball was an important fellow traveler. In March 1921 Hesse noted in his diary:

> I went to visit Hugo Ball again yesterday. He and his wife are wonderfully feisty people; they live in a state of poverty and primitiveness that is positively classic, without a word of complaint. It is a crying shame to think that Ball, the author of *A Critique of the German Intelligentsia,* and such a mas-

sively erudite, esteemed, and significant man, might soon be forced to set aside his great work and go earn a crust in a factory or an office job. He suffers all this without demur, but we friends of his should try and stave off this situation for as long as we can.[12]

At the time Hugo Ball was on a journey *ad fontes,* back to the roots of the Christian faith in his research into the Church's early thinkers. In "Flight Out of Time" he wrote: "Yesterday, during a discussion with Hesse, the true nature of Saint John Climacus suddenly dawned on me. It was clear to me that people even back then must have known about psychoanalysis; they just had another name for it. The Therapeutae, whom Philo of Alexandria mentions, were quite evidently psychoanalysts, only they used different forms of interpretation and the therapy they offered was inextricably bound up with exorcism."[13]

Hesse had already studied and written about the Catholic saint Francis of Assisi, who at the same time had also been considered a heretic by his church. He was also very concerned with the problem of institutionalized forms of faith, and the different Protestant and Catholic forms of ritual observance—albeit from a pantheistic standpoint, which in its rejection of denominations was akin to the "atheistic mysticism" of Fritz Mauthner. In January 1921, in the midst of the troubles he was experiencing in completing *Siddhartha,* Hesse noted in his diary on this topic:

The reformed Puritan faith demands a sacrifice of the Self that few people are capable of, and even those few who are cannot always manage it, only in rare exalted moments. The sacrifice of my individuality, my desires, and my aspirations is something that I can only do occasionally and imperfectly; yet donations, adorations, wreath-laying, dances, and genuflections are things that I can manage anytime, and on the right occasion even these apparently external, crude, and mechanical sacrifices can become one internally with my offering-up of myself. Catholic worship can be conducted at any moment; all the Catholic priest needs to do is put on his vestments in order to immediately become a priest—Lutheran worship, on the other hand, contradicts itself and dispenses with consecration, and the Protestant pastor has to demonstrate through long, laborious sermons that he is a priest, and yet no one believes him. In this way, every religion that styles itself as reformist initiates its adherents into an evil cult of feelings of inferiority.[14]

Hugo Ball pursued his ideal of a monastic existence. The perfect monk should speak and act as though he were already dead, he claimed, for such a person was already dead as a human being and had anticipated his own death. This standpoint of death as being that of "perfect disinterestedness" was, Ball maintained, the prerequisite of all philosophy. This was also the starting point for justifying the value of asceticism for saintliness. In 1921 he told Hesse about his deliberations on the subject of how the early Christian monks regarded the human soul: "Modern humanity's sickness stems from the fact that its clarity about Paradise has been buried and perverted. It is now essential that we restore—through obedience, tears, shame, renunciation of our habits, and through all manner of self-denial and solitude—the 'spaces' within which the concept of Paradise might undergo a revival.—Judging from all that I know about modern analysis, this is just about the diametrical opposite of what is being taught nowadays. Today, rather, asceticism is held to be responsible for all inhibitions."[15] Ball's thesis effectively proposed an expansion of the time frame of the history of ideas and of the soul, and showed the *vita experimentalis* as deriving from far more remotely distant sources than previously imagined, sources that suddenly took on an urgent topicality, and that also prompted inquiries into the nature of the Self. And a deep thinker on the subject of "self-will" like Hesse, who had already successfully resisted any form of domestic indoctrination, had keen antennae for whether someone was trying to convince him of some apparently unassailable truth or to make him into an adherent of an ideology of whatever kind—or conversely whether a person was simply setting forth his own way of thinking and acknowledging the internal conclusions that he had reached. Only in the latter case was it possible to have a conversation about questions of faith as the spiritual bases for existence.

Even so, Hugo Ball could not seriously have entertained any hope that he could make a Catholic of Hesse, however willing Hesse was to discuss the topic; Hesse's own experiences with religious denominations as a form of prison for religious feeling were still too raw for that. On July 23, 1915, Hesse wrote to Ball after reading his essay "Religious Conversion": "The question about conversion is one I have also asked myself. I do not think it likely that I could ever become a Catholic. Instead I will continue to live in the misery of a life without purpose, center, and community, in the firm belief that even enduring the most 'senseless' sufferings through to the bitter end must still ultimately somehow amount to an existence in a divine sense."[16]

In his diary of 1920–1921, Hesse touches repeatedly on the question of the conflict between the urge to live and a longing for death. In the figure of Siddhartha this conflict found a resolution in the eternal cycle of life and rebirth. Hesse had such great difficulties with *Siddhartha* because he was grappling with the deepest of all the crises he had experienced hitherto regarding his self-conception as an artist. Even as he did so, he knew that he could never overcome this crisis, only acknowledge it and give it creative expression:

> To craft a work, patiently and diligently, and lovingly, be it a poem, a painting, a novel—while the whole time life rolls by, growing richer, fuller, more diverse by the hour—and one is expected to stick to one's gossamer thread, to keep spinning away at one's work, this one, single, poor thread, and is expected daily and hourly to hold back or dissolve the flood of tears, views, and ideas in order that one might keep harping on at the single, thin melody, in which one has captured not even one-thousandth of what one wanted to! This urge to creativity is terrible, terrible and magnificent, and from one work to the next, from one attempt to the next, it becomes ever more difficult, more fateful, more dedicated, more furious and more ardent. . . . There are reputed to be artists who love their finished works—how is that possible?[17]

In the light of this, observing Hugo Ball working on his *Byzantine Christianity* was an eye-opening experience. Here was someone at work who, both in the topic he was covering and the way he was treating it, could not hope to achieve great success with the general public, but who was nonetheless imbued with a great seriousness and sense of purpose.

So what were Hermann Hesse's reasons for writing? This question arose now in his mind with a force hitherto unknown as he observed the spiritual exercise that was Hugo Ball's writing. His example prompted him to delve deeper, to find a different way of combining his biographical details with words, spirit, writing, and ritual. With the death of his father in 1916, he once again felt a closer affinity to Johannes Hesse's religious horizon of understanding. His father was a person who often appeared unintelligible and forbidding to those around him, even his son. And yet he did provide a template for a meaningful life guided by the spirit.

Hugo Ball's ideal of asceticism suddenly caused all the concepts and ideas that had shaped Hesse's childhood, which he had been obliged to keep at arm's length in order to be himself, to loom unexpectedly large in his life again. At this stage, he was not standing on the threshold of converting to some religious denomination; that was far from his thoughts. But he was now intent on settling the question of the artist's relationship to religion:

> If one construes writing as an act of confession—and that is the only way I can conceive of it at present—then art reveals itself to be a long, varied, and tortuous route, whose aim is to express the personality of the artist's Self so comprehensively, and to explore all its diverse ramifications and divisions so thoroughly, that this Self is ultimately unwrapped and laid bare, ransacked and all spent, so to speak. It would then be time to explore higher things, supra-personal and supra-temporal matters, and in the process art would be surmounted and the artist would be ripe to be canonized. The function of art, insofar as it concerns the artist as an individual, would therefore be exactly the same as the function of religious confession, or of psychoanalysis. This was the meaning of all of Nietzsche's later writings, or Strindberg's books of confessions, or Flaubert's chronicles.[18]

Art as a form of personal avowal ultimately turns into a confession. But does that therefore condemn it to silence—does the artist have to sacrifice his art to make this act of confession? This was another of the questions that was dealt with in *Siddhartha*. The insight offered there was clearly that the artist was someone who overestimated the significance of his work if he exclusively sought to justify his own position through his art. But was asceticism a way out? Like his character Siddhartha, Hesse too left the Sramanas behind, choosing instead the path to life, not the one that led to the monastery and to self-abnegation. He could not sacrifice his role as an artist, despite frequently believing that this was precisely what he ought to do:

> If I had grown up in a respectable religious tradition, for example as a Catholic, I would probably have stuck to the faith throughout my life. But an ineluctable feature of my background and makeup is that I come

from a tradition that, while intensely religious, was also thoroughly Protestant and sectarian. And that is no coincidence—this is what I wanted, I chose this background for myself, I landed myself in it, together with this denomination, and this encumbrance with a spirit of sectarianism and reformation, and just as at the hour of my birth, Saturn and Jupiter and the Moon stood in alignment and could do nothing other than this, so my devout Pietist father and the Protestant baptismal font stood ready for me.[19]

Hesse continued to tread Siddhartha's path, alone with the spirit of God that he had to bear—with his own spirit, which became his passion.

But scarcely had Hesse and the married couple grown so close to one another that they had started to discuss intimate questions of faith than Hugo Ball and Emmy Hennings suddenly left for Germany, even though they had already paid the rent for their house in Agnuzzo for months in advance. At the time, Hesse was absent on a book tour to the Waldorf-Astoria cigarette factory in Stuttgart, at the invitation of the factory owner, Emil Mont. The news of the sudden departure to Munich of his new friends came to him quite unexpectedly. To be sure, the couple's financial troubles were dire, but would they be any less so in Munich?

The fact was that Hugo Ball needed to be near to a major library, like the one in Munich, in order to finish his book about the major saints; this work, *Byzantine Christianity,* was the primary reason for their sudden departure from Switzerland. Ball had asked the manufacturer Charles Brown for financial support for this project, to the tune of 300 francs a month, but when Brown turned him down, Ball and his wife immediately packed their bags and left.

Another flight, then. Possibly also from too close a proximity to Hermann Hesse? Whatever the case, both Ball and Hennings wrote to Hesse to reassure him that they were missing him terribly. And Hesse too— particularly after Joseph Englert had also moved on—now felt very isolated in Montagnola: "It's so sad that you're no longer here. After I came back from Stuttgart, it took me eight days to pluck up the courage to go over to Agnuzzo, and there were your house and garden, bathed in sunshine!"[20]

Emmy Hennings wrote back to Hesse, addressing him as "Dear Shepherd's Song" ("Liebes Hirtenlied"), but after he replied very formally, beginning his letter "Dear Frau Ball," she quickly let this term of endearment drop. Hugo Ball was disenchanted with Munich despite the fact that he could visit the library there on a regular basis: "This city, which once seemed so lively to us, is losing its charm day by day."[21] Emmy Hennings had never liked the place anyhow, and was already itching to get back to Ticino, as Ball was at pains to inform Hesse: "She treats this city like it is a personal affront to her, and refuses to face up to the idea that the Ticino dream might be at an end."[22] In Munich both Hugo Ball and Emmy Hennings had the opportunity to give readings of their works, which even received positive reviews. And yet they felt increasingly suffocated by the city's atmosphere; two such outmoded figures as them simply did not fit there, especially in this period, as Hugo Ball already suspected: "There is something indefinable in the air. It's like being inside a diving bell. It must be the war cemeteries that don't allow you to take a single breath of fresh air."[23]

Living in Munich was extremely difficult, and the anonymity of the metropolis only made their misery all the more humiliating. At first the married couple could not even find a place where they could live together. Emmy moved into a room that she sublet in the Schwabing district, Hugo found a place in Bogenhausen, and Emmy's daughter, Annemarie, was entrusted to the care of nuns.

In the spring of 1922, Emmy Hennings was obliged to take up work as a washerwoman in order to make ends meet. At the same time her volume of poems entitled *Bright Night (Helle Nacht)* was published. In the summer Ball completed his *Byzantine Christianity*—so there was now no further reason to stay in Munich. Hesse meanwhile had also finished his *Siddhartha,* and invited the Balls to visit him. He managed to obtain funds— some 5,000 francs—from Theo Wenger and H. C. Bodmer to pay for Ball and Hennings to move back to Ticino, and so in October 1922, a year after they had left, the Balls found themselves reinstalled in their house in Agnuzzo. And because Hugo Ball had also found supplementary employment as a music transcriber, this meant that they could face the future a little more confidently.

However, *Byzantine Christianity: Three Saints' Lives,* which was published in 1923 by Duncker und Humblot in Munich, was not a success. It appeared that there was no audience for a work that took an essayistic approach to speculation on the nature of religious belief. In the eyes of academic and Catholic theology, this work was the obscure product of an outsider and quasi-convert to the faith, which could be safely ignored. And to the majority of potential readers, the book's subject matter alone must have seemed eccentric and old-fashioned. Nonetheless, the book was accessible to anyone who was prepared to immerse themselves in the kind of mystical language that had set poetic standards ever since Angelus Silesius's "The Cherubic Pilgrim" of 1657. At first glance the lives of such saints as John Climacus, Dionysius the Areopagite, and Simeon the Stylite could not be farther from our contemporary existence. However, this first impression is deceptive, for it is precisely by virtue of the fact that they are untouched by modern times that they have something to say to us.

How ought one to live? This question is an eternal one. In *Byzantine Christianity,* Ball wrote the following: "The tranquility of the saint is like a whirlpool in the depths, which devours everything that desire has swept into its sphere of influence. His prayer is the fullness of the abyss itself. And just as that prayer can dissolve into death, so too can it dissolve into life, when the whirlpool, which has consumed all the water within itself, returns and merges into the general flow."[24]

This mystical form of expression was translated into twentieth-century language by authors close to Hesse such as Fritz Mauthner and Gustav Landauer. Landauer, who was a member of the Munich Räterepublik (Workers' Soviet), the short-lived revolutionary government of the Bavarian capital established after the First World War, and was murdered by the forces of reaction, wrote about this phenomenon in his book *Skepticism and Mysticism* (1903), and his views closely accord with not just Ball's but also Hesse's understanding of language at its natural root:

This, then, is how things stand: our world is a picture that had been produced with some very poor materials, namely our paltry senses. Yet this world of nature, in all its speechlessness and ineffability, is immeasurably vast compared to our so-called worldview and compared to what we idly call or perception and expression of nature. For language is just a picture of a picture. Because all language had arisen through metaphor and evolved by means of metaphors. Our senses only inform us about what we perceive, in other words the things that we can grasp with our minds and our language. But our nerves know more about what affects them than we owners of those nerves suspect and than our conscious self knows and can capture

in words. The world is without language, and "anyone who truly understood it would also be rendered speechless."

For just a moment here we glimpse a door left open, leading to *The
Glass Bead Game*. Indeed, it sounds uncannily similar to that novel when
Landauer continues: "And so, from now on I will simply invite people to
play whenever I wish to embark on an attempt to discover the world—
which most decidedly does not reside out there in the world of objects—
in the innermost core of our most hidden nature, within the individual,
and whenever I want to descend into the mine-shafts of my Inner Self in
order to extract from myself the paleontological treasures of the
Universe."[25]

The circle thus closes. Hesse pointed to Ball's book, which was such
an important source for him, on two occasions to try and explain what
was so especially beautiful about it. The first time was in a review for *Die
neue Rundschau* in 1923: "This language is his secret, this language that
originates from the spirit of that early Christianity, which sounds impersonal and timeless and which constantly names the unnameable and yet
which also constantly has resonating within it a knowledge of ineffability."[26]
Like Mauthner, Landauer, and Hesse, Hugo Ball was also a modern mystic
who knew that the bridge between speech and silence is often a stam-
mering, in which the truth reveals itself to the initiated. The second occasion on which Hesse was moved to put pen to paper about *Byzantine Christianity* was in 1924, in the pages of the magazine *Werkland* (the new name
of *Vivos voco*), so strongly did he feel about his friend's book, which was
rapidly sinking into oblivion and incomprehension. Here Hesse stated that
Ball was intent on venturing farther down the "path leading inward." And
it is certainly true that the book has a jarring tone. It evokes the paradoxical
concurrence of faith and skepticism, and is as religious as it is atheistic. In
this juxtaposition of the sacred and the heretical, a defining characteristic
of modern mysticism becomes apparent: the *kairos,* the transcending
moment in a world that does not recognize any afterlife.

"Ball's book is as devout as the naive tract of any venerator of saints,
but at the same time it is informed by a sensitive, alert spirituality that is
almost stretched to the point of irony. A pure, clear air blows around his
carefully, faithfully and almost impersonally composed structures, creating an atmosphere of purity akin to that in books of the Early Middle
Ages."[27]

On the Spa Guest, or the Modern Artist as a Neurotic

Sciatica is no joke.

—Hermann Hesse, letter to Emil Molt, June 26, 1923

Matters concerning the body remained a problem for Hesse. This was ex-traordinary, given his closeness to the advocates of naturism soon after the turn of the century, and his predilection for naked climbing trips, on which he even allowed himself to be photographed. At the height of summer in Bern, his sons Bruno, Heiner, and Martin would walk around the whole time in the garden with no clothes on—Hesse loved the natural life, fresh air, and the sun. It seemed incredible, therefore, that he of all people should find himself caught in an insolubly difficult relationship with his own phys-ical being, most particularly his sexuality.

First and foremost, Hesse had a neurosis about any form of physical contact. He could only stand to be around other people for a short time, and any bodily intimacy quickly gave way in him to an insurmount-able urge to distance himself. Even as a young man, he admitted that he could not bear any physical act of love. It was in discussion with his analyst J. B. Lang that he first broached the issue of this phobia.

On September 21, 1917, he jotted down some notes in his diary about his experiences while on a rest cure that he had taken at the Sonnmatt Sanatorium in Lucerne the previous year. To his own astonishment, he had not found this at all unpleasant:

> I have always enjoyed being massaged, and precisely that feeling of being tickled, even violated, which I have experienced repeatedly in my dreams, I often find really stimulating. When you're being massaged, you can enjoy physical stimuli and activity while having to remain passive yourself. That's the beauty but also the slight perversity of it, and the Romans were particularly partial to it. My nudity and the sight of my penis remind me of the sensitivity that always made me very averse to appearing naked in public. Some time ago, this was joined by a feeling of uncleanliness and flac-cidity in my genitals, which also manifested itself externally; at least, an army medic at a military inspection three years ago definitely noticed it.[28]

The *Psychologia Balnearia or Glosses of a Spa Guest in Baden,* to cite the original title of the story *A Guest at the Spa,* was a slim volume. Some Hesse biographers completely disregard this work, sandwiched between *Siddhartha* and *Steppenwolf*, or give it only a very cursory treatment before moving on. For example, Eike Middell speaks of the "banal account of the spa, which is given in a rather sedate and homespun way."[29] In actual fact the tale is a quite unexpected stroke of genius. For it represents a declaration of self-healing by the neurotic artist Hesse, couched moreover in terms of the kind of sophisticated humor that he so admired in Mozart's opera *The Magic Flute*. Here Hesse practices the art of magic in a playful and ironic fashion that is completely devoid of any pathos. And all of a sudden we see the blossoming of a new spirit, which skips lightly over the dark periods of depression and transforms them into the base material for playful poetic creation. It would be as unjustified to call such a work superficial as it would be to attach that label to Mozart's fairy tale about the birdlike Papageno.

What, then, is the nature of that neurosis of the intellectual and spiritual individual in the modern age, from which Hesse diagnosed himself as suffering? It consists basically of a disintegration of the spirit and the senses. These are powerfully related to one another, and yet, as Hugo Ball wrote, in Hesse they were caught in a state of "intense hostility" to one another. Given that the spirit and the senses could not be separated and yet could not attain any measure of harmony, there arose in Hesse that doppelgänger motif, which is evident in his writing from his earliest texts to his late works. Although Hesse was fully aware of the inadequacy of this dualism, it nevertheless forms the basis for him of every genuine unity, which is not merely stated but lived: "I have the misfortune, you see, of always contradicting myself. Reality does that all the time, but the spirit shouldn't do that, and nor should virtue."

The roots of this neurosis, this state of imbalance in the soul into which the artist here lapses, surely lie in the immoderation of his defense—demanded from him by his parents' lack of understanding—of a profoundly serious mode of writing that struggles to convey ultimate truths in words. How long this wound remained unhealed is revealed by a letter of Hesse's to his sister Adele in 1926 concerning the tenth anniversary of their father's death; a turn of phrase in her previous letter to him had incensed him:

> In your letter, you write about the period around Papa's funeral, "there wasn't just a wonderful atmosphere at that time, there was also strength."

Now look, Adisle, I can't go along with you in drawing such fine distinctions, and in fact your tone reminds me a little of our parents. It often happened that Papa or Mama would speak very approvingly about a poem or a piece of music, but with a rather telltale smile, and then they'd always add that it was naturally *"just"* an atmosphere, *just* beautiful, *just* art, and at bottom not nearly as important as such things as morality, character, will, ethics, etc. This doctrine of theirs has ruined my life, and I will have no further truck with it, not even in the pleasant, mild form of your letter. No, if your experience of Papa's death was of a wonderful "atmosphere," then I'll refrain from adding any "just" to that assessment, but simply gratefully accept that atmosphere as an experience.[30]

There is no higher truth, no superiority by virtue of believing in the correct faith! Against the hostility toward art displayed by his parents, Hesse here proclaims his allegiance to Nietzsche: Only fool, only poet! But this confession had long since taken its toll, in the form of illness, depressions, and neuroses. For the sick world regarded itself as healthy! That put anyone who was furnished with a particularly sensitive nervous system in the situation of being seen as insane amidst all this madness. There are hints of the Steppenwolf already evident in the figure of the spa guest. In a letter of June 26, 1923, to his friend, the anthroposophist cigarette manufacturer Emil Molt, Hesse explained how he saw the connection between sickness and a person's mind:

You ask whether my complaints do not in large part also stem from "psychological" causes. But my dear old friend, have you never read a line I have written, then? Otherwise you would surely know that I not only concur with psychoanalysis in regarding all illnesses of the "nerves" as being purely psychologically conditioned, but that I also consider all physical ailments of any kind, even a broken leg or pneumonia, as being no less engendered and dictated by the psyche. I have nothing new to impart or to learn on this subject. I recognize the most deep-seated cause of my entire life's malaise only too well—it resides in the fact that in my boyhood, a stage of development that was meant to be filled with life, my entire disposition, and all my aspirations and attempts at self-improvement were directed purely toward things spiritual and poetic, and that with the passage of time I came to see ever more clearly that this had made me into an outsider with no prospects in the contemporary world. If this weren't the case, I could churn out my books just as wantonly as you do your cigarettes.[31]

The *Psychologia Balnearia* are therefore a series of accounts by an outsider, not quite written from Dostoyevsky's point of view in *Notes from the Underground,* but instead from the comfort of a spa hotel—and from the perspective of someone labeled as a neurotic. The artist can no longer be a bourgeois, but even worse than this he is finding it increasingly hard to be an artist, since his words refuse more and more to coalesce into a coherent work, which would then anyway just become a product among many— more or less successfully marketable—products for sale in a material society.

Furthermore, the connection to Casanova, the "typical impulse glutton," as Stefan Zweig called him, still held good for Hesse the spa guest. As early as 1906 he had written a story—admittedly a rather weak effort, ignoring as it did the fundamental contradiction in the character—entitled *Casanova's Conversion (Casanovas Bekehrung).* Thereafter, however, he avoided engaging specifically with this subject matter. In the essay "Casanova: A Study in Self-Portraiture," written in 1928, Zweig tackled this same topic, identifying the figure of Casanova as playing a key role in Hesse's life problems (and indeed in those of all artists):

> That is the eternal tragedy of the spiritual man, namely that he, yearn though he may to fulfill his calling by experiencing to the full all the sensuality that life has to offer, nevertheless remains shackled to his task, a slave of his workshop, fettered by his self-imposed duties, and tied to order and earth. . . . Generally speaking, every true artist only ever creates that which he failed to experience firsthand in his own life. . . . The irresolvable paradox is that men of action and epicures have more experience to report than any writers, but lack the creative means to do so—while conversely, creative types are obliged to fabricate, because they have seldom had enough real experiences worth reporting.[32]

The two pages plus that Hesse devotes to the introduction to *A Guest at the Spa* are among the most farcical and maliciously ironic pieces he ever wrote. Basically, he says here in his own words the same things that Stefan Zweig wrote about Casanova. He consigns not only himself but also the entire spirit of his age to a rest cure. Hesse, who first came for a cure in 1923 at the Verenahof in Baden (where he subsequently returned for many years), makes observations about that same spiritual type identified by Zweig, to whom he ascribes a "certain skeptical piety," a "highly intelligent form of anti-intellectualism," an attitude that is cultivated by the title figure of Hesse's story:

> We spa guests and gout-sufferers are particularly intent upon smoothing over as many of life's rough edges as we can, taking a relaxed attitude, and not cherishing any great illusions, and instead nurturing a hundred small, harmless illusions. Unless I am very much mistaken, we patients in Baden are especially in need of knowledge about the antinomies, and the stiffer our joints become, the more pressing is our need for a flexible, two-sided, bipolar way of thinking. Our sufferings are undoubtedly sufferings, but they are not of that heroic and picturesque kind that entitles the sufferer to regard them as being of earth-shattering importance without in the process losing face.[33]

The spa hotel was run by two brothers, to whom Hesse would subsequently dedicate *A Guest at the Spa.* Dr. Josef Markwalder was the resident physician, whom Hesse would subject to the test of a discussion at the start of his cure concerning why the pains a person suffered from having sciatica, gout, or rheumatism did not completely correspond with the actual stage the illness was at. Could it be, Hesse inquired, that psychological factors were also at work here? The doctor passed the test of a grilling by someone who was clearly a neurasthenic, which is also described in *A Guest at the Spa,* with flying colors. Henceforth Hesse felt that he was understood on this "Magic Mountain"—and even accepted that his condition steadily continued to worsen over the ensuing weeks of the course of treatment. In his letters, especially those he wrote to Hugo Ball, Hesse spared none of the details of the day-to-day business of the rest-cure regimen, many of which he also incorporated directly into the story manuscript. In May 1923 Ball received the following news: "Every morning at around 6 A.M. I immerse myself in a mineral bath, which is run at 37°C and which I stay in for a good half hour, and afterward I drink a glass of sulfur-water from the source, which I actually like the taste of." Hesse also painted a picture of Baden for Ball, describing it as a small town situated in the Limmat Valley, in parts still Gothic and medieval. A typical little spa town, in which none of the spa guests wanted to appear to be ill: "Everyone walks around the streets very slowly, supporting themselves on sticks, and many of them are limping, though everyone is desperate to conceal their sciatica as much as they can. When I'm out in public, I too make out that I'm someone who's only passing through and who's just looking round Baden for pleasure. The upshot of all this is that there's an atmosphere of artificial jollity and gracefulness, while secretly the spas cause us grievous pain, and the hotel bills even more so."[34]

The tribulations of the treatments were made up for by sumptuous meals—for which Franz Xaver Markwalder, the hotelier and brother of the chief physician, was responsible. Hesse noted ironically that this was a fine way of providing people suffering from metabolic disorders with a surfeit of indigestible food—but that it was all part and parcel of being a prestigious spa hotel.

Hesse's spa guest was the prototype of the kind of neurotic urban dweller who would later become the stock character of Woody Allen's movies, a person who had no wish to be any other way—not a priest or a prophet, or a statesman or a general—who is prepared to acknowledge his totally unmelodramatic existence, no hero bursting with good health and blinkered against all misgivings about his character, but a person who is always the first to testify against himself and who is his own severest critic. Toward the end of the first part of the course of treatment—he would return to Baden for the second installment in the fall—Hesse wrote to Hugo Ball that he had become so lame and palsied "that I often think it's not worth the trouble of transporting this bag of bones back to Ticino."[35]

On the whole he felt unwell, and he found the nightly dining rituals a nightmarish ordeal; he was not a big eater at the best of times, and here he was faced with an endless succession of courses, "while in between people tell one another their life stories, but I only ever play the mute listener, because I'm living just as hermit-like an existence here as I do in Ticino." The cure—despite or because of its tiring effect—also had its positive sides, and Hesse found himself coming back year after year to the Verenahof spa hotel; the Markwalder brothers became his friends, and were great admirers of his writing. Hesse noted with pleasure that the hotelier had placed an order with him for an illustrated edition of "Piktor's Metamorphoses." One thing that warrants scarcely a mention in Hesse's notes was that his younger brother Hans was also living in Baden at the time, where he was employed in a lowly position as a bookkeeper for the Brown Electric Company. Hermann Hesse tried several times to secure a better post for his brother, but Hans had long been a broken person inwardly who was beyond any help.

His future wife Ruth Wenger visited Hesse at the sanatorium at the end of May 1923. She was traveling around extensively during this period, and on this occasion had come directly from Munich. She rhapsodized about the shops and all the handsome young men there. She had also bought herself another dog, an Affenpinscher this time, which she told Hesse about at great length. Ruth's head—and by extension Hesse's too—was buzzing with pets' names: from the Affenpinscher Tilla through the kitten Lilith and the parrot Coco, not to mention the two snakes. "Cleopatra is about 90 centimeters long and Barrabas is about 1 meter 10."[36] Thank goodness that she hadn't gone ahead and bought an ape, having been warned that they gave off a very pungent odor.

For his part, Hesse refrained from regaling his young future wife with accounts of his physical state, which struck him as being that of an old man. Instead he wrote to her, "It's not the physical side of things that bothers me, in fact I'm happy to have aches and pains provided I know there is hope of them being cured." He also chose to highlight his unsavory fellow guests at the hotel in his letters to her: "But my spirit and my nerves have gone to the dogs; for almost three weeks now, I have been sitting here feeling lonely, mad, and wretched—surrounded the whole time by a bunch of fat, sated, corpulent, plump, and florid bourgeois types. Their presence is soul-destroying and is driving me to distraction."[37] Doubtless it wasn't as bad as Hesse painted it, and even Ruth made mention of the pretty waitresses at the hotel whom he found so pleasing. Furthermore, Hesse would not have returned here regularly, year after year, if his disparaging description had really been true. Yet here too he was leading a double life: while the shy recluse was suffering, the successful bourgeois writer, which he remained in spite of all the self-incriminations suggesting the contrary, was enjoying all the attention he got.

Hesse wrote the *Psychologia Balnearia or Glosses of a Spa Guest in Baden* in a kind of frenzy of creative activity in the fall of 1923 after his first two says at the spa hotel in Baden; it was printed privately in 1924 in an edition of 300, and was published by Fischer a year later under the title *A Guest at the Spa.* He hadn't worked in such an intense way since writing *Klingsor's Last Summer,* he told Georg Reinhart on October 29, 1923—it had been a joyous if also exhausting experience after the agonizing stagnation of writing *Siddhartha,* which was now finally behind him.

The motto of the book in the *Psychologia Balnearia* came from Nietzsche: "Idleness is the beginning of all philosophy." However, in *A Guest at the Spa,* although the attribution to Nietzsche is retained, the quotation is subtly changed to "Idleness is the beginning of all *psychology.*" This was what the book turned on: a reconvalescent withdrawal from the great battles of the age, a retreat into an illness that had its distinct advantages as a place for fostering self-awareness. Switching from being an active participant to an observer could even take on some unexpectedly entertaining traits, for without the "art of idleness," to cite the title of a short essay of Hesse's, we would only be half-persons and would miss hearing and seeing the most important things.

That was Hesse's dilemma—he was expected to play along in any given context: to masquerade as a poet, even though inwardly he had long since gone beyond that and yearned to be something else, something he was not yet able to be: a sage who would punish his age by staying silent. The spirit was sustenance for the body, and the body needed to consume the spirit in order to live. This was no momentous event, but administered at regular intervals, it was as vital as the supply of calcium for building bones. "My relationship to the so-called 'spirit,' for example, is exactly the same as it is to eating or drinking. At times, there is nothing in the world that attracts me so strongly and seems so indispensable as the intellect, as the possibility of abstraction, of logic, and of ideas. Then again, when I have had enough of it and feel the need for its opposite, everything to do with the intellect disgusts me as surely as if it were food that has gone off."[38]

Here, for the first time, Hesse was taking a sovereign overview of his depression and his nervous state of overexcitement, which had for years now been the subject of psychoanalysis and therapy. This represented an impressive recapturing of the artistic standpoint vis-à-vis himself. His conclusion: I am far less sick than the contemporary age! This insight forms the basic tenor of these glosses, in which he characterizes himself as "an outsider from the family of schizophrenics, though not one who needs to be locked up." To phrase the question another way, what would this world be without the madmen running around in it, provided that they do not constitute a danger to the general public, or at least not more of a danger than that posed by the forces which are imposing uniformity and monotony on the world under the pretext of public benefit? "That other more complex question about the justification of the psychopath, that dreadful, shocking question as to whether, under certain temporal and cultural circumstances, it is not more dignified, more noble, and more appropriate to be a psychopath than to conform to these temporal circumstances by jettisoning all one's ideals—this terrible question, this question posed by all discriminating minds since Nietzsche, I shall leave untouched in these pages; in any case, it is the theme of almost all my writings."[39]

This was the first time that Hesse as a writer had publicly come forward and laid bare the schizoid foundation of his writing—namely, his compulsion to present a "stereoscopic viewpoint" (to borrow a phrase from Gottfried Benn), to create doppelgänger figures. Here was the peaceable, sociable Herr Hesse showing himself to also be an evil neurotic, who wished every noisy neighbor dead (the "Dutchman" in *A Guest at the Spa,* for instance!). Hesse answered the question of how one could possibly endure this Dutchman, this disgustingly robust and noisy contemporary in the adjoining room, by stating that one had to learn to love him in the same way that only through love could one tame an evil demon that resided within oneself. This short work is a very wise book, but is also very playful in a wonderfully uninhibited way in its pithy and witty malice. With it, one can do magic and make from the agonizing half-Self a whole person, though naturally a contradictory one. How might that happen? It is a magical process, which one can only learn from a distance (idleness!). Some people must first fall ill in order to get well again. This is the point at issue here:

> I would like to find expression for duality, I would like to write chapters and sentences where melody and countermelody are both apparent at the same time, where unity stands beside every multiplicity and seriousness beside every witticism. . . . I would consistently like to demonstrate that beauty and ugliness, light and shade, sin and saintliness are opposites only for a fleeting moment, and that they are continually merging into one another. For me, humanity's most exalted utterances are those few sentences in which this duality has been expressed in magic signs, that handful of mysterious sayings and parables in which the great antitheses of the world are simultaneously recognized as a necessity and as an illusion.[40]

If one reads *A Guest at the Spa* as the diary of a mystic surrounded by the banality of mass culture, then we are suddenly confronted with the question of the sacred. Hesse was in search of it in this godless world, which his contemporaries took to be real though in fact it is wholly unreal. Yet Hesse was well aware that certain truths had to be hidden from public view, and that one had to "work one's way up to them" in private. One of the high points of this slim chronicle concerning the sickness of the contemporary age and the possibilities of healing it is the encounter between the spa guest and writer with another guest at the spa, an envoy of that world that was so certain of itself, and whose manifestations the writer so despises. This is a joyous expulsion from his inner life of the world as it presents itself to him. A charmingly contemptuous sleight of hand toward those importunate exponents of the real world, who with their broad buttocks and fixed opinions constantly made life difficult for the spirit. Hesse encapsulated all this in a speech simply addressed by one spa guest to another:

> You exist, dear Sir, that I cannot dispute. But you exist on a plane that in my view is lacking any spatial or temporal reality. You exist, I may say, on the level of paper, of money and credit, of morality, of laws, of intellect, of respectability. You are a space-and-time companion of virtue, of the categorical imperative, and of reason, and for all I know you may even be related to the Thing-in-Itself or to capitalism. But you do not have the sort of reality possessed by every stone or tree, every toad and every bird, which I find instantly convincing. My dear Sir, I may approve immeasurably of you, and respect you, I may doubt you or give you the benefit of the doubt, but I find it impossible to experience you, and utterly impossible to love you. You share this fate with your relations and esteemed next of kin, with virtue, with reason, with the categorical imperative, and with all of humanity's ideals. You are magnificent. We are proud of you. But real you are definitely not.[41]

Hugo Ball, who was one of the first people to read the *Psychologia Balnearia,* immediately wrote about it to his wife, Emmy, who was staying in Florence at the time: "These are 'self-observations.' The author appears in person as Herr Hesse in the text, which covers some seventy printed pages—highly precisely formulated and surprising in how far removed they are from his other work. In places, he draws attention to himself in a way that we have not thus far seen from him. That will do him good, we've said as much many times, though probably not in the bourgeois press."[42]

Knulp in His Luggage: "Journey to Nuremberg"

> Among the rules of life formulated by many wise men, there
> is this maxim: Live every day as if it were your last. Well then,
> who on Earth would spend his last day breathing in soot, lug-
> ging suitcases, squeezing himself through station turnstiles, and
> performing all the ludicrous contortions that are part and
> parcel of a train journey?
>
> —Hermann Hesse, "Journey to Nuremberg" (1926)[43]

The travel essay "Journey to Nuremberg" is what we might call the intermediate link between *A Guest at the Spa* and *Steppenwolf.* A provisional return to Germany from the end of September to the middle of
November 1925, and also a trip to revisit the places of his childhood and
youth. On November 16, Hesse wrote about Nuremberg: "The old city
with its medieval and Gothic buildings has been entirely driven to the
wall by industry and uncommonly loud traffic noise, and can no longer
breathe. I have never seen so clearly that we have produced nothing to
compare with these works of the old culture and that the only thing
left for us to do is to completely destroy them with our utterly soulless
technology."[44]

Hesse knew that this journey was special before he even set off on it:
he could savor in it the excitement he had once felt at being on the move
and his yearning for faraway places, and could conjure up the eroticism of
travel. Although he would subsequently return to Germany on several occasions, this trip was an unusual journey into a kind of retrospection that
the spa guest, whom he had long since become, would carry on into *Steppenwolf.* Yet it was also part of Hesse's continuing focus on his own first
steps, which had begun with *Demian* and *A Child's Soul.* Hesse found himself confronted by the alarming prospect of turning fifty, beyond which
he could not imagine a continued existence, and this only strengthened
the tone of taking stock and summing-up in his writings. What had become of his boyhood friends in the interim? And what would the places
he had known as a child now look like? There are long periods in life when
one is preoccupied with looking forward, discovering one's own identity
and what one is capable of—without feeling the constant need for reassurance in one's own origins. But there then comes a time when precisely
that becomes important: namely, looking back, meeting people whom one
once knew—and whom one has not seen for many decades. Hesse was

Hermann Hesse in 1925

now at that point in his life where he was starting to look backward more than forward.

It was only fitting that Hesse should have carried the third tale from the *Knulp* trilogy *(Das Ende)* with him in his bag as reading matter. Since he had been living in Ticino and felt, in his new chosen home, that he was also in the foreign country of his choice—in other words, since he had moved from living north of the Alps to their southern slopes—he had lost that urge which had regularly driven him south prior to the First World War. *Wandering* had been his final testament to this yearning while also being a melancholy celebration of his leave-taking from it.

He had agreed to travel to southern Germany and see Swabia again—but he embarked on his journey with very mixed feelings. Even so, he did not cancel, despite entertaining this as a possibility right up the very last moment. He knew that he had changed since the First World War, since he had become a hate-figure for German nationalists. But he had also simply grown older, more awkward, and more comfortable—and at any rate certainly more dedicated to solitude.

And so we can already catch a glimpse here of the notorious Steppenwolf, the avowed outsider, embarking on a journey into the past.

There was something within him that proved greater than all his abhorrence of the inconveniences of travel. He himself could not put his finger on what that something was—and sensed that, in order to find out, he would have to go to Germany. Hesse, who like his three sons was now a Swiss citizen, was deeply preoccupied with the theme of the inscrutability of the German character; the intensity of his treatment of this subject was matched possibly only by Thomas Mann. Yet his initial concern was with the journey's daily practicalities that he would have to shoulder if he wanted to get to its magic: "Much as I liked the idea of seeing an old friend who would be delighted by my visit, I am nonetheless a comfort-loving person who abhors journeys and crowds, for whom the idea of a long trip on small, remote country roads held little attraction. No, it was not friendship or even politeness that caused me to make that promise, there was more to it than just that; behind the place-name 'Blaubeuren' there lurked a charm and a mystery, and a welter of reminiscences, memories, and enticements."[45]

In Blaubeuren, according to Hesse, there was a monastery school like the one he had attended in Maulbronn, plus it was the setting of Eduard Mörike's legendary tale about the spring called the Blautopf. It was also the heartland of the Swabian Pietism that made him what he was, and was steeped in that flavor of romanticism, whose magic he now wanted to recapture—even though inwardly he was now very distant from it.

Hesse crossed the border into Germany in order to make his peace with those places he had once quit in rebellious mood. He wanted to encounter the landscapes, towns, and people of old. He had put off this trip for a long time, and now he felt compelled to go. And to the best of his ability he steeled himself against the disappointment that he fully expected to feel.

What resulted was an account of his Nuremberg journey, the charm and intellectual weight of which has been persistently misjudged right up to the present day. Yet even at the time, the critic Hans Sahl identified "a heroic form of humor" in this work, which he called the "humor of the suffering man." Without this apposite characterization, which Siegfried

Unseld also quoted in an essay that recognized the high literary status of this travel report, Hesse's *Steppenwolf* would not be comprehensible as a testimony to extreme despair with an ultimate homage to "humor as a survival mechanism."

This report of his journey affords us a glimpse into the workshop of the author Hermann Hesse, in addition to being an acknowledgment of his neuroses and his physical handicaps (notably his constantly painful eyes!), which he nevertheless defied in order to ultimately produce a body of work so extensive that many people have quite justifiably asked how a single individual could possibly have achieved such a workload. Hesse's answer to this would have been: by living life at his own rhythm and by defending the idleness that was so vital to his ability to write with all the militancy that he could muster. Accordingly, he put pen to paper to describe his trip—and his feeling of being provoked by a spirit of the age that was solely geared to utilitarianism is plain for all to see:

> As for myself, I believe that no decent and hardworking person would shake hands with me if he knew how little value I place on time, and how I can squander days and weeks, even whole months, and the kind of nonsense I waste my life with. No employer, no office, no rules prescribe when I must get up in the morning or when I am to go to bed at night, no deadlines are set for my work, and it makes not the slightest difference whether I take an afternoon or a quarter of a year to write a poem of three stanzas.[46]

After this introduction, his announcement of what, in spite of this—or precisely because of it—he still has time for, comes as something of a surprise: "To be sure, I have time to do nothing, but I have no time for trips, or being sociable, or fishing or other pleasant things—no, I must always be close to my workroom, alone, undisturbed, and ready at any moment to get down to work if I need to."[47] So, in the interim, Hesse had also added travel to the list of major disruptions to the idleness he deemed necessary for achieving a high rate of work productivity, and whose tranquility was not to be violated by anybody or anything. Particularly not by traveling around doing book readings!

In the 1913 text "An Evening with the Author," Hess had already described the absurd scene of an author reading his work in front of an audience: a unique form of humiliation, he felt, for a little recognition—stemming mainly from sheer misunderstandings, no doubt—and a small appearance fee, which would maintain the writer on his orbit around the modern world, revolving like some anachronistic curiosity whom anyone who deigned to pay the entrance fee had the right to laugh at or to treat with contempt, in the main both at the same time. Of course, people expected a different sort of author, this was simply a mistaken choice. What the public wanted was someone who could regale them with amusing anecdotes, and maybe even throw in a song or two—in any event, not someone reading out his poems! The humiliation of the evening that Hesse portrays here already begins with the visit of a bitterly disappointed secretary of a literary society to the "cost factor," that is the author, before the event: "He complained that the advance sales of tickets had been very poor, and that they would barely cover the cost of renting the room, and then proceeded to ask me if could see my way to accepting a smaller fee."[48] The author, who already feels guilty despite himself, throws the man out. But when he enters the auditorium, what little courage he has left deserts him: "There were about twenty rows of chairs, of which three or four were occupied. Behind the small podium, someone had pinned up the society's banner. It was dreadful."[49] At the very moment he starts reading, from the room below

> there suddenly erupted the din of a beer-hall band, complete with bass drum and cymbals. I was so enraged that I spilled my glass of water. This splendid joke elicited a great collective belly laugh from the audience.
>
> After I had read three poems, I glanced up at the room. I was confronted by a row of grinning, baffled, crestfallen, and angry faces gazing at me, and about six people got up, visibly in distress, and walked out of this uncomfortable event. I would have loved to join them.[50]

The same feeling of unease haunted him, more than ten years later, as he set off on his Nuremberg journey. And so the author went on the offensive, determined to make his status as a fool crystal clear, against the soulless machine culture. Hesse lay down naked, so to speak, on the avenue of spitefulness—yet what he had to say was also designed to lay that avenue bare:

> I could also mention that my time-wasting is not simply due to laziness and a lack of organization, but is a conscious protest against the craziest and the

most sacred dictum of the modern world: Time is money. In and of itself, this sentence is perfectly true; one can easily transform time into money, just as one can easily convert electric current into light and heat. But what's crazy and vulgar about this most idiotic of human dicta is simply this, that "money" is unqualifiedly regarded as having a supreme worth. Permit me to omit self-justification. Despite all proofs that might be adduced to the contrary, I am in fact a time waster, a contented and work-shy person, not to mention some of my other vices.[51]

Kurt Tucholsky once wrote that Hesse was a completely humorless writer—a slur repeated by many others since. They all presumably omitted to read *A Guest at the Spa* or "Journey to Nuremberg": these works bear witness to a truly Nietzschean sense of humor, directed against the world of virtues, diligence, and measurable success. All of it downright lies! If you can manage it correctly, it is perfectly possible to derive quite some entertainment from observing the human comedy from the perspective of an outsider. But you can also forego that, since the monotony of activity has something quite exhausting about it.

So, are we to see Hesse exclusively as the loner, the solitary one? Not without a measure of smugness, some critics have pointed to Hesse's many—and in many cases carefully cultivated—relationships with his patrons, his extended rest cures in Baden, and the invitations he accepted to comfortable houses or castles to prove that Hesse was dissembling in this matter, and that he was not alone all that often, and hence could not have been lonely. There is more than a hint of extraordinary hubris in these critics' attempt to sit in judgment on a person's inner attitude to his surroundings. Hesse himself gave the following account of the difficulty of integrating oneself into society, on the occasion of his six-week trip to southern Germany: "In no art am I such a dilettante and tyro as in that of sociability, but none enchants me more than the kind I can practice in those rare hours when I find myself in sympathetic surroundings."[52] A piece of Solomonic wisdom from a person who once had a sign attached to his garden gate reading "No Visitors, Please!" No, the company of others was a real torment for Hesse—though he did not want to put it so bluntly for fear of alienating a series of very helpful patrons. By way of explaining his social withdrawal, Hesse described himself as an "outdated person,"[53] a confession that he reiterated on this journey. Swabia seemed truly like his homeland on this trip, and he was happy to declare his allegiance to it—this was also an olive-branch to those readers of his who were still mourning the demise of the writer of *Peter Camenzind*.

Melancholic feelings were therefore permitted on this trip: "Everything was redolent of home, of Swabia, of rye bread and fairy tales, and once again I was amazed at how little this wonderfully lively and truly remarkable landscape is known to modern German painters."[54]

His meeting with those who had been fellow pupils of his at Maulbronn also passed off harmoniously. Hesse's declaration of love to the old Swabia included all the people from the period of his childhood and youth. He had already reconciled himself with his parents, more so with his father than his mother, both of whom by now were long dead.

Hesse, who was averse to any form of association, found common ground with the former Maulbronn pupils in the fact that back in the day they had all stood on the threshold of their adult lives and had in the meantime long since become old men. Even fickle Steppenwolfs found the cockles of their hearts momentarily warmed by such thoughts! "And how touching and funny it is each time to find that people whom one knew in in their early youth do not change in the slightest!"[55]

Nevertheless, "Journey to Nuremberg" is not a sentimental trip down memory lane: it holds the past up against the present, but if the present then appears to be nothing but decay, is the person who establishes that fact necessarily a hopeless Romantic? Absolutely not, as this work, Hesse's rejoinder to *Peter Camenzind,* the novel with which many people still identified him, demonstrates. In this, he reveals that he is completely unreconciled with his own beginnings, and without a doubt judges himself far too harshly. Perhaps, more than the book itself, which along with some flaws also had many good points, he had something else in mind, as he suggests to his readers in "Journey to Nuremberg":

> A reader whose acquaintance I had made greeted me enthusiastically as the author of *Peter Camenzind*. So there I stood and grew red in the face; what was I to say to the man? Should I tell him that I could no longer remember the book, that I hadn't re-read it in fifteen years, that it was frequently confused in my memory with *The Trumpeter of Säckingen?* And that it was not the book itself that I detested, but simply the effect it had had on my life—to

be precise, that its totally unexpected success had impelled me toward a career in literature, from which I had not, despite all my most desperate efforts, ever managed to extricate myself?[56]

The confusion with *The Trumpeter of Säckingen* (a sentimental epic poem by the nineteenth-century writer Joseph Victor von Scheffel) is of course an instance of Hesse's mischievous playfulness—as is his assertion that he made "desperate" efforts to escape from a literary life. Yet the image of him as a sentimental regional writer—something he had never been, even back then, but which many people wrongly deduced from *Peter Camenzind*—had been fostered precisely by that book. Thereafter he had spent decades trying to refute in his subsequent writing this false image of Hermann Hesse.

On his trip, he visited Augsburg, Ulm, and Nuremberg. In Nuremberg he found himself at an absolute low point. "It was all so desolate."[57] In this city, it seemed to him that he was "ninety years old and on my deathbed," and his only desire was to be buried.[58] The evil eye in him came to life. Secretly he had expected this Gothic city to yield all manner of wonderful things, such as encounters with the spirits of E. T. A. Hoffmann and Wilhelm Wackenroder, but he now found himself shocked by the banal reality of a modern metropolis:

> I saw a truly enchanting city, richer than Ulm and more unusual than Augsburg, I saw the churches of St. Lorenz and St. Sebald, I saw the town hall and its courtyard with that incredibly charming fountain, but everything was completely hemmed in by a big, inhuman, bleak city of business, drowned by the roar of engines, and surrounded by motor cars snaking their way through the streets, with everything quivering imperceptibly to the tempo of a different time, an age that no longer knew how to build fan-vaults or erect fountains lovely as flowers in the quiet courtyards. Instead, everything seemed just about to collapse within the next hour, for it no longer had any purpose or soul.[59]

The soullessness of modern life was one abiding impression, but "fountains lovely as flowers" was another. The persistence with which Hesse continued to use the Biedermeier-era word *hold,* "lovely," from his earliest to his very last books, once again comes across as irritating here. Indeed, it is not at all uncommon (and not just in his poems either) to find Hesse's generally clear-sighted and skeptical gaze taking refuge in seductively harm-less verbal images like this.

Perhaps it was precisely the sight of the stark contrast between old and new, as he sat here in a Nuremberg hotel with "overactive steam radiators that could not be turned to cool the whole night through" and the im-possibility of "keeping the window open due to the noisy traffic in the street,"[60] that stimulated in him the idea of a "big-game hunt for automo-biles," as described in *Steppenwolf.*

By contrast, the story strikes a conciliatory note at journey's end in Munich, where he visited the chamber theater and watched comedian Karl Valentin's play *The Robber Barons at the Gates of Munich.* Here Hesse, the notorious hater of theater, was enthralled by Valentin's comic drama. He found in it exactly kind of sophisticated humor he had been searching for—the art of the absurd—a motif that would then duly reappear in the Magic Theater in *Steppenwolf.*

Several years later Hesse attempted another book tour, this time to Tübingen and Stuttgart—with a similar outcome. Before he set off in No-vember 1929, he complained: "I find traveling a dreadful ordeal; no one realizes the high price I have to pay for giving this sort of book reading."[61]

Hesse kept a diary of this journey as well, but only filled in six pages of it—repeating the same disappointments wearied him. Even the begin-ning of this trip was dreadful: a cold hotel room in Tübingen with no heating. His mood also sank below zero there, and he was caught in the undertow of negative thoughts. Adding insult to injury, this took place in the very town where he had once, while working in Heckenhauer's book-shop, dreamed of his future as a writer. And now the future was here—and could not be more dispiriting: "I am ill and old and I have made nothing of myself; Sadly I gaze at the alleyways where I was once young and full of high ideals."[62]

Now, for his irritable bowels, he was obliged to take opium as a tran-quilizer and in order that he might get some sleep. He ran into people whom he had known in his former life. It is touching when things and people that have survived in his memory suddenly step straight back into the present, such as when he comes face to face with Sonnewald, his old mentor from the bookshop. Emil Molt, his fellow pupil at the Latin school in Calw, and now the proprietor of the Waldorf-Astoria cigarette factory, also makes an appearance at his book reading, as do his sisters Marulla and Adele.

Hesse read some excerpts from *Narcissus and Goldmund,* a work that had already been published in the *Die neue Rundschau* and that would appear the following year in book form. "Once again, I found the reading far too stressful, I really must pull myself together, I'm exhausted. . . . Afterward we went to the 'Alte Post' inn, and everybody ordered food and wine, and proceeded to chow down and laugh, happy to be able to forget Goldmund again."[63]

He sent his new partner, Ninon Dolbin, the following downbeat assessment of the lecture he gave in Stuttgart, after the one in Tübingen: "It was all futile." He was particularly bothered by the post-reading sessions in taverns, where a sudden sense of relief generated an atmosphere gravitating toward loudness and jollity that was wholly out of keeping with the reading he'd just given: "Now everyone set to ordering wine, beer, schnitzels, salad, and ham; I sat for half an hour between guzzling people, quiet and alone, with nobody even offering me so much as a glass of wine, nor did I have the energy and the elbows to push my way through the throng and order one myself from the overworked waitresses. So there I sat for half an hour before slinking out, putting on my coat and walking home. Nobody noticed I'd gone." Nevertheless, he conceded that the reading hadn't gone as badly as the one in Tübingen.

Even if one takes his oversensitivity into account, who could dispute Hesse's own very gloomy summary of these events? "You read out your poems, concentrating as hard as you can, and then someone taps you lightly on the shoulder and you look around and see everyone else tucking into schnitzels and sausage, and you're sitting there feeling so lost and dispensable that it chills you to the marrow."[64] Hesse could never come to terms with this realization, which for him pointed up the situation of the author in modern mass culture.

The Prologue to *Steppenwolf*

The "Steppenwolf" had been resident in Hesse ever since he had plummeted from the high-flying euphoria of *Klingsor's Last Summer.* His mental preparation for the novel began with his essays on Dostoyevsky. Prince Myshkin, the title figure of *The Idiot,* provided Hesse with a moral template for his character. Before Hesse positively dashed off his novel *Steppenwolf* in December 1926, he had already made a number of false starts.

Even this sense of failure, this self-exposure in an incomplete fragment, forms part and parcel of the character of Hesse's main protagonist, Harry Haller. As early as 1922 Hesse—very much in the style of Dostoyevsky—wrote "Tagebuch eines Entgleisten" (Diary of a man who has gone off the rails), which remained only a sketch. This fragment makes clear the extent to which Hesse's thinking was influenced by the Gnostic motif of two kingdoms: the conflict between light and darkness, God and the devil, spirit and material, and good and evil. However, Hesse gave the doppelgänger motif a different slant in *Steppenwolf*. The central theme was now no longer that of the criminal and / or artist, on the one hand, and the solid bourgeois citizen, on the other; instead, the decline of the West was set against a spiritual principle with the power to overcome the crisis, a new form of transcendence. However, this did not make that crisis any less existential for the individual:

> I hurl it away, my life, so that it shatters into a thousand tinkling pieces; I, an aging man, fritter away my hours and days like a student. I try my utmost to live simply from day to day, with no past and no future. But the Other, that second person within me, sharpens his pen; he finds the idea of living day by day unbearable, he needs his line of descent, he thirsts after a future, and he screams urgently for context and continuity. From one hour to the next, he attempts to nail down, to document this dizzying whirl of life as it trickles away, and to frame it and hang it on the wall of eternity.[65]

What a call for salvation from all the problems of his confused existence! Day after day, he continued his wholly indecisive struggle for survival, on the sunny side of life in Ticino. He wrestled with the difficulty of how to overcome his inner turmoil. The practical and the metaphysical problem of life come together in a way that seriously afflicts him, and become inextricably intertwined within the realm of eroticism. In the preparatory sketch to *Steppenwolf,* Hesse enunciated not only Harry Haller's problem, but also the problem of all gender relationships comprised of the contradiction between sexual attraction and moral scruples, between momentary fascination and the swift onset of tedium, or even disgust.

Hesse's own erotic biography was likewise characterized by this inhibition toward acting in sexual matters: "From my first crushes as a schoolboy, I was a fatalistic, a poor, timid, shy, and unsuccessful lover of women: All those I feel in love with seemed too good and too exalted for me. As a boy, I never danced or flirted with them, never had any little dalliances, and throughout a long marriage that made me deeply dissatisfied, although I have loved and missed women, I have in truth avoided them."

When Hesse wrote that, he was still married to Maria Bernoulli. But at the very moment he was committing these thoughts to paper, something was happening in his life that was decisive and unfamiliar to him and that deeply unsettled him: "And now, when I have started to grow old, suddenly there are women at every twist and turn, who have come to me unbidden, and my old shyness has vanished. Hands find my hand, lips my mouth, and I'm starting to find garters and hairpins lying all over the place in my house." And then suddenly—with a piece of narrative artifice—a second person suddenly appears within the Self, a second perspective:

> And in the midst of this rather crammed and frantic love life, in the midst of reading little *billets-doux,* amid the scent of hair and skin and powder and perfume, I know, or rather someone within me knows exactly where all this headed, where all this is leading. He knows: all this ought to be taken from me, this chalice too should be drunk dry and refilled over and over again until I'm sick of it, this most secret and shameful desire should be sated and die away, and that I ought soon to leave this Paradise for which I yearned for so long, with the realization that this Paradise was merely a tavern, which one eventually leaves, jaded and bereft of memory. This is how it is, and so I will drink from this lukewarm chalice and expunge the dream of this desired goal too, which I harbored for such a long time.[66]

Here we see someone unable to rid himself of the person whom he has become—despite the fact that he desperately wishes to without more ado. In the very moment when everything that he desired for so long literally falls into his lap in abundance, he realizes that he doesn't actually want it.

A case of fulfillment at an inopportune moment—and in fact, such inopportune moments invariably dog the German intellectual who wants to learn the art of living (by whom Hesse undoubtedly means himself). This passage is a prelude to Hesse's unsparingly ironic portrayal of himself as a someone who thwarts himself—a fitting description of the Steppenwolf, who is driven forward and pulled back with equal force. Half-human and half-animal—and, of course, half-god too.

On August 8, 1925, Hesse announced to Georg Reinhart that he had completed a new book—mentioning it somewhat in passing as a reprise of his *Life Story Briefly Told,* which he had written earlier that same year. Not without a certain mischievousness, he described the book's genesis as having been prompted by the fact that "in all probability I will soon be taking myself off to the hereafter—life has just become far too onerous to me of late." This melodramatic announcement was half down to Hesse's absolutely hopeless state of depression during this period, but also half a rehearsal for the figure of his alter ego Harry Haller, this suicidal type (again, a borrowing from Dostoyevsky), who has set himself a deadline of his fiftieth birthday to decide whether he should go on living or kill himself: "I do not know whether the fantastic book about the 'Steppenwolf' that I am planning will ever be written. It is the story of a person who, funnily enough, is suffering from the affliction of being half-wolf, half-human. One half of him likes such simple things as eating voraciously, drinking, and killing, whereas the other enjoys thinking, listening to Mozart, and so on. This causes some upsets, and the man is in a bad way until he discovers that there are two ways out of his predicament—either kill himself or begin to acquire a sense of humor."[67]

One person who did neither of those things in that same year 1925 was a painter *manqué,* who as a result of his attempt to stage a putsch in Munich two years earlier had been sent to prison and who now published *Mein Kampf,* the manifesto of the Nazi movement: Adolf Hitler. The pseudonym Hitler used in his early days of political agitation was "Herr Wolf." Hesse too, when he was writing *Steppenwolf,* liked to go by the name Wolf. In these two men, who could not have been more different where their views on nationalism, war guilt, violence and politics, Jews and the Aryan race were concerned, we find a reflection of that basic problem that Hesse was grappling with in *Steppenwolf:* namely, that there is a criminal lurking inside each and every one of us, ready to pounce. It is a question of commuting the murderous energies, the destructive and impulsive urges within us, into something that does not have a devastating impact on the external world. Through art, for example—a route from which Hitler was debarred.

Anyone who unlocks the dangerous innermost recesses of the human soul must steel themselves to witness a scene like those in paintings by Hieronymus Bosch. Hesse played out within himself this conflict between nurturing and destructive tendencies, and effectively kept it in check by giving it visual artistic form. By contrast, a fanatic and ideologue like Hitler ended up visiting all the filth within his psyche upon the outside world, and what's more doing so, perversely enough, in the name of cleanliness and hygiene.

A Genius of Suffering and Humor: Harry Haller and the Apotheosis of the Outsider

> I am living the life of an outsider, and have turned my back on the contemporary intellectual world (as represented by Keyserling etc.).
>
> —Hermann Hesse, letter to Richard Wilhelm, June 4, 1926

Steppenwolf is the story of a man who is almost fifty years old. An intellectual who has thought and written about the hidden side of his contemporary age, an outsider filled with a loathing for the world and self-disgust. His crisis is an identity crisis, both inwardly and outwardly. This existence on the lip of the abyss, this life on the razor's edge, constantly aware of death as an option—that was Hesse's contribution to the theme of the intellectual. Here again, Hugo Ball was an important inspiration. For the failure of intellectuals who did not follow Nietzsche in setting a example but instead were just themselves symptomatic of the demise of community and the collapse of all intellectual systems of order was an abiding theme of Ball's—from *A Critique of the German Intelligentsia* through *Byzantine Christianity* and on to a planned work on forms of the demonic and the phenomenon of exorcism. Similarly, the monograph that Ball began writing in honor of Hesse's fiftieth birthday treated the question of how the thinking person might survive in the modern world.

Hesse's situation at the start of the 1920s can be illustrated by an example: the devaluation of his property in Germany. This became for him a threatening symbol, which he tried to laugh off, but his laughter was tempered by alarm at all the potential absurdities that could arise when history rode roughshod over the individual and his small attempts to secure his existence. He had just finished writing *Siddhartha,* which in a letter to Ludwig Finckh on September 10, 1922, he called "the most concentrated of my books," when he lapsed once more into a deep psychological trough of depression. What was the point of still working, he speculated, when "for years I have had no income or remuneration for all the work I have done"?

Indeed, Hesse found this particular matter very hard to get over—his sale of the house in Gaienhofen in 1912, an affair that now turned into a painful devaluation of his past. The business could only be completely concluded at this late juncture: "I recently received payment of the second tranche owing for my house in Gaienhofen, the full price for which I have now irrevocably lost. The princely sum of 15,000 marks in outstanding mortgage payments on it. The present owner now has a house, while I have enough money from the proceeds to go out for three dinners."[68] For after conversion and taking into account the rampant inflation of the period, 15,000 marks in 1922 were equivalent to just 37 Swiss francs. Hesse had a good opportunity here to practice the gallows humor that his character Harry Haller subsequently has to learn: "All these funny things often make me laugh, I don't take them seriously and I'm actually happy not to have a house anymore." Much the same thing happened to Hans-in-Luck [the eponymous hero of a Brothers Grimm fairy tale that is an ironic inversion of the "rags to riches" cliché]. Yet living in Switzerland, Hesse did not exactly feel like Hans-in-Luck, especially when he cast his eyes over the border to Germany: "Over time, almost all my friends in Germany have abandoned me. . . . From time to time I still get the odd poem or essay printed in German journals, but this is a reckless enterprise, since the postage costs me more than I receive in fees."[69]

If one were to try to sum up the content of *Steppenwolf* in a sentence, then perhaps this might be apposite: it is a chronicle of self-knowledge on the verge of self-destruction. A highly intimate contribution to the problem of nihilism, the revaluation of all values that Nietzsche had prophesied for the twentieth century. Hesse refers to this in the preface, and his words sound very much like those of Dostoyevsky, specifically Prince Myshkin in *The Idiot:* "I recognized that Haller is a genius of suffering, that he had cultivated within himself, in the manner of many of Nietzsche's sayings, a brilliant, unlimited, terrible capacity for suffering. At the same time I realized that self-loathing rather than a disdain for the world was the basis of his pessimism, for however mercilessly and disparagingly he talked about institutions or people, he never excluded himself; he was always the first person whom he hated and negated."[70]

A kind of romanticism that has been put through the filter of Nietzsche's metaphysics of the artist is evident here. Hugo Ball appended to his remark that Hesse was the last knight from the magnificent pageant of Romanticism the question: "But will he suddenly wheel around, this knight, and mobilize a new front?"[71] The story of Harry Haller as the Steppenwolf is the biographical documentation of this sudden about-face. To stick with the military metaphor: with *Steppenwolf,* Hesse opened up a new front. Against what? No longer merely against the bourgeois ideal of art, or lazy humanism or nationalism, say, which he despised. Against all of that, certainly, but now in addition against himself.

Yet even so, in Hesse's own words we risk misunderstanding this product of a crisis, this chronicle of a person for whom only a breath of air prevents his immediately doing away with himself, if we only read it from Harry Haller's perspective. In 1942 Hesse wrote a new afterword to the novel, from the viewpoint of his work on *The Glass Bead Game,* which right from the outset is astonishing in its optimistic tone. By then Hesse had overcome the crisis of *Steppenwolf* and was able to point to the two competing perspectives of the book—that of Harry, the destructive self-hater on the verge of suicide, and the second viewpoint, which reveals itself to him at the end of the work, in the Magic Theater scene, when he is simply derided for his tragic murderer's pose. This is the perspective of the operators of the Magic Theater, which also crops up in *Journey to the East* and finally culminates in *The Glass Bead Game*—a supraindividual perspective, which, as it were, transcends Harry Haller's despair: the laughter of God. In his 1942 afterword, Hesse referred to "all those passages in the book dealing with spirit, and art, and the 'immortals,' which posit a positive, cheerful, suprapersonal, and supratemporal world of belief in opposition to the Steppenwolf's world of suffering, with the result that although the book does give an account of sufferings and distress, it is in no way ultimately the book of a despairer, but that of a believer."[72]

Hesse wrote this in retrospect, from the perspective of someone who had escaped from just such a crisis—and in his words one can sense the spirit of saintliness that so fascinated him about Hugo Ball at their very first meeting. Accordingly, in this belated afterword, the author insisted that the story of the Steppenwolf "certainly portrays an illness and a crisis, but one that ends, not in death or destruction, but, on the contrary, in a recovery."[73]

Yet these matters were not so clear to Hesse in the years from 1922 to 1927, when he appeared to be trapped in a state of self-disgust and a downward spiral of destructiveness. At this point it seemed entirely uncertain whether the crisis would be followed by recovery. Decline and death seemed just as likely. And it was from this uncertainty that *Steppenwolf* derived its internal tension—the author who wrote this work really had no idea how he ought to live his life properly. He did not even know if he would make it to his fiftieth birthday.

Hugo Ball, who wrote a small monograph on his friend for the Fischer publishing house, which was due to be published simultaneously with *Steppenwolf* in the summer of 1927, was an eyewitness to Hesse's enduring crisis. Hesse had set himself a deadline of his fiftieth birthday. He still wanted to try to hold out up to that point, and decide on the day whether he would go on living or die. The motif can be seen in the "Treatise on the Steppenwolf," the booklet that is given to Harry Haller in the novel. At the same time it was Hesse's own stance toward a future in which he could place no faith. As a result, what Harry Haller has to say on the subject has a very autobiographical feel:

> If for some reason or another he was going through a particularly bad patch; and if in addition to his customary bleak, solitary and turbulent life, he was suffering some special pain or loss, he was now able to respond by saying to the pain: "Just you wait two more years, then I'll get the better of you!" And then he would take profound delight in imagining all the cards and letters of congratulation that would arrive on the morning of his fiftieth birthday just as he, certain in the knowledge that his shaving razor wouldn't let him down, was taking his leave of all pain and closing the door behind him. Then the gout in his joints, his depression, and the headaches and stomach pains would just have to make their own arrangements.[74]

He meant that seriously, he who already had tried to kill himself on several occasions during his lifetime. To have the prospect of death clearly in sight, and to admit the possibility of suicide, was liberating for him. He knew full well that it was a distinguishing characteristic of the kind of person who would take his own life that, in the event he did kill himself, he would not be doing it by chance or out of an inability to cope with life. On the contrary: he had the strength to live with the constant prospect of death before him.

The Steppenwolf Harry Haller was one of those potential suicides who in life were already dead where their surroundings were concerned: outsiders who had opted out of the great competition for power, money, jobs, or bourgeois honors, despite doubtless belonging to their country's intellectual elite, albeit one that was invisible to the majority of people.

Life in Ticino had changed too, with motorized mass tourism now dominating the scene. What was landscape prior to the First World War had now become a built-up suburb of the city of Lugano. The magic of the place had evaporated, as Hesse wrote in his 1928 prose piece "Rückkehr aufs Land" (Back to the land), where he adopted his absurd Steppenwolf tone:

> Year on year, the number of cars grows, the hotels get fuller, and even the last, most good-natured old farmer feels driven to fight back by putting up barbed wire against the flood of tourists who are trampling his crops. And in this way one meadow after another, one beautiful and tranquil forest-edge after another, is lost, either becoming a building site or being fenced in. Money, industry, technology, and the spirit of modernity have long since taken control even of this landscape, which not so long ago was still magical, and we old friends, aficionados, and discoverers of this landscape are consigned to that category of uncomfortable, old-fashioned things that need to go to the wall and be exterminated. The last of us will eventually hang ourselves from the last chestnut tree in Ticino the day before it too is uprooted at the behest of a property developer.[75]

On October 13, 1926, Hesse sent his friend Hugo Ball the following advice regarding the monograph he was about to write: "Inasmuch as a biography of myself has any point at all, it must surely be to show that the personal neurosis of a cerebral individual, which is incurable yet which he has overcome after a fashion, is at the same time symptomatic of the soul of the age."[76] At the time he wrote this he was at the end of his tether, while also having to provide for Mia and his children. Rather too much ballast for a solitary Steppenwolf, who would have dearly loved to embrace his loneliness and to turn it into the truly accomplished solitude of a hermit, but who was prevented from doing so by the world around him. All attempts that he had previously undertaken to escape from the bourgeois world had failed. Hugo Ball, who became a kind of confessor for Hesse, learned from his friend: "I am just finishing work on my 'Steppenwolf,' preparing the transcript for my publisher, and that's holding me together for the moment, but when I'm done with that I hope I have the courage to slit my own throat, because life is truly unbearable for me, and that also manifests itself in my constant physical sensation of pain."[77]

Hugo Ball had come directly to his task from writing his *Byzantine Christianity,* which treated the lives of major saints who had also been regarded as heretics. He approached Hesse's life and work from the same standpoint. And this kind of approach via forms of religiosity, which at first sight looked really unconventional, gave rise to an image of the author Hermann Hesse that simultaneously revealed his secret and concealed it once more. The art of this kind of biography is that of the *legend,* which nonetheless, in its combination of myth narration with the recounting of a life story and a spiritual vision, achieves an unexpected actuality.

In this respect, Hesse's *Steppenwolf* and Hugo Ball's monograph on Hesse treat one and the same theme: the soul biography of the modern intellectual.

Ruth Wenger would later claim that Hesse refused to allow publication of a chapter in the monograph that Ball wrote about their marriage. That is not true. Firstly, Hugo Ball did not hold her as high in his estimation as she perhaps imagined (and as Emmy Hennings's attempts at friendship might have led her to believe), meaning that he did not even feel the need in the first place to include Ruth Wenger in the biography, and secondly, at a very early stage in his work on the monograph, Hesse had given him to understand how his two marriages should appear in the book. On October 13, 1926, he told Ball: "My first marriage is far enough in the past that, if you feel the need to mention it, you can do so briefly. But I'd rather you didn't discuss my second."[78]

The novel *Steppenwolf* is to a certain extent a reduction of *A Guest at the Spa* to its most basic tenets, the "deeper and broader counterpart"[79] to that work. One might also say that *A Guest at the Spa* is the humorous version of *Steppenwolf,* and of that crisis undergone by Harry Haller—in whom Hesse portrayed himself as a person foundering—which in the end turns to his recovery. Hesse always regarded *A Guest at the Spa* as one of his most important and cherished books, no doubt also because of the light touch he brought here to his treatment of the theme of the outsider.

Yet *Steppenwolf* was also an account of the Moloch that Hesse saw the modern metropolis as being, a location that he had long avoided—without, it must be said, ever really knowing city life. Furthermore it was a winter book, written in those months when Hesse found it too cold to remain in the unheatable Casa Camuzzi. He spent the winters of 1923 and 1924 in Basel, the latter winter in a small furnished attic apartment at number 7 Lothringer Strasse, which was owned by a Fräulein Ringer. This place became the setting for the writing of *Steppenwolf;* it was here that he wrote the preliminary drafts.

We are immediately put in mind of the stench of cleanliness and well-ordered petit bourgeois life, which strikes Harry Haller as so domestic and yet at the same time so insufferable. The only thing he can do is sit down on the steps, facing that famous monkey puzzle tree, which for Hesse became the quintessential symbol of domesticity, alongside pot-plants and entrenched views about life. It is lovely and peaceful here, but he, the Steppenwolf, is a homeless drifter, a spectator on life, who just once happens to sit down on a flight of steps in front of unknown people's apartments to take a brief rest and breathes in the aroma of this alien yet familiar lifestyle. It smells not only like floor polish and boiled vegetables, it also smells of childhood and the mistaken belief that one can ever find a place in this world that one does not immediately feel compelled to leave.

For the two following winters of his Steppenwolf period, 1925–1926 and 1926–1927, Hesse lived in Zurich, where Alice and Fritz Leuthold had put an apartment at his disposal, at number 31 Schanzengruben. This was where, in December 1926, he began writing the final version of *Steppenwolf,* a task he completed in January 1927.

Steppenwolf is a test of Nietzsche's dictum "Without music, life would be a mistake." But what music, that is the question. Hesse had often spoken in terms of the "music of doom," yet music as such was a medium of rebirth, and for the resurgence of lost melodies. What were people listening to? Music on the radio as a diversion, or Mozart's *Magic Flute?* The year 1927 also saw the premiere of the first talkie: Al Jolson's *The Jazz Singer.* Mozart and jazz, the saxophone and the soprano—that became the music of the age, the rhythm that transformed the dissonances of modern life, of the machine culture, into a form of expression played on the most diverse instruments that was as intimate as it was universal. And while he was living in Zurich Hesse, the non-dancer, attended masked balls for the first time in his life and learned how to have fun. For a person who was raised in the Pietist tradition, amusement was a sinful word. And so, with the passage of time, what was doubtless quite harmless and banal amusement began to take on traits of the demonic, behind which Hugo Ball, who carefully observed Hesse, was in turn the inspiration.

Hesse could only throw himself into enjoying nightlife with a Protestant bad conscience. Also, as an aging man, he instantly stuck out like a sore thumb. This was the background to his so-called "Crisis" poems, which were originally intended to directly follow the prose text of *Steppenwolf* as a kind of epilogue. But Samuel Fischer, who had been immediately captivated by the novel, was dead set against this idea, as he disliked the poems. And it is true that this act of self-exposure lacks artistry, giving the poems a hint of the embarrassing that cannot be overlooked. Hesse was missing here his confessional tone, of which he customarily had such an assured command. His "Crisis" work was a piece of doggerel born of sheer desolation and self-accusation.

Thomas Mann, to whom Hesse sent a copy of his collected poems, which had been published in a limited edition of 1,000, when responding also took refuge in discreet irony, a tone he used only very rarely with Hermann Hesse—and with him, this was always a sign that he felt affected in an unpleasant way. Accordingly, he acknowledged receipt of the gift to Hesse on January 3, 1928, in the following terms:

> Dear Herr Hesse, I thank you for honoring me by sending me these poems; I know the atmosphere they evoke won't be to everyone's taste. But you may rest assured that I will understand them, inwardly, despite the fact that my metabolism is physiological. The charming appeal of your hypochondria and your fundamentally youthful yearning to "cut loose" have touched my very soul, as is often the case with your work. One finds oneself getting ever more jaded and choosy where reading matter is concerned, and unable to get on with most of it. But your *Steppenwolf* was a breath of fresh air for the first time in ages, and really taught me the meaning of reading again.[80]

In this way Mann, too, prompted by Hesse's having sent him his "Crisis" verse and notwithstanding the brevity of his own reply, ultimately drew a clear qualitative distinction between Hesse's treatment of the same theme in prose and poetry, by emphasizing how successful he had found *Steppenwolf.*

Much to the relief of Thomas Mann, no doubt, the novel, which indeed is not a novel in the classic sense, only contains two poems. The spectrum of different facets of personality that unfolds in *Steppenwolf* through a surreal constellation evidently impressed Mann, because he later wrote that Hesse's boldness in this novel vis-à-vis formal experimentation easily rivaled that of James Joyce's *Ulysses.*

However, the following poem, one of the two in *Steppenwolf,* is remarkable for the directness of its tone, which actually pays very little attention to form. This is what lends it its very particular effect:

> I, Steppenwolf, trot to and fro,
> The world is lying deep in snow,
> The raven from the birch tree flies,
> But nowhere a hare, nowhere a roe!
> I really am so fond of roe,
> Would that I could find one, though!
> I'd take it in my teeth, my hands,
> It is the best thing in the land
> I would cherish the lovely beast,
> And on her tender thighs I'd feast,
> I'd gorge myself on her red blood,
> Then howl all night, a lonesome flood.
> A sweet, warm hare would fit the bill;
> And sate me with my nightly fill.
> Am I then to be deprived
> Of things that might cheer up my life?
> My tail fur is growing gray.
> And now I'm plagued with failing sight.
> Years ago my dear mate died.
> And now I trot and dream of roe.
> I lope along and dream of hare.
> I hear the winter night winds blow.
> I cool my burning throat with snow,
> And to the devil my poor soul bear.

Here we see the Steppenwolf as a sexually driven older animal, who makes no attempt to poetically transfigure his carnality but instead announces that he will live it out, without further ado. We see a figure roaming through the night, looking for someone to satisfy his lust. Never before had Hesse confessed these desires so directly.

As a result, critical voices were raised against this kind of poem, which had no further pretensions to be art, but instead was raw confession. Hesse sent the following, rather testy reply to Heinrich Wiegand on October 14, 1926, in response to his criticism of the "Crisis" poems:

> The one line in one of my poems that you have lighted upon as being rather conventional is actually one of my favorites. And in fact if you read Eichendorff, it is far more noticeable how he positively conceals himself behind a whole façade of formulaic expressions, because the constant urge to display originality was such anathema to him. Compared with Eichendorff, who used the device of a naive folk song to say the most incredible things, I find your esthetically unimpeachable poets such as Stefan George and his ilk, with their exquisite, novel rhymes and their precisely measured syllables, frankly silly, though at other times I am also capable of enjoying and admiring their work. As for myself, I cannot count myself among them—I gave up any ambitions to be an esthete years ago and consequently I'm not a writer of poems, but of confessions, in much the same way as someone who is drowning or has been poisoned isn't bothered about his hairstyle or the modulation of his voice, but simply shouts at the top of his lungs. You are quite right, my dear friend, to reprimand me for that, but you can't stop a man from yelling for all he's worth in his death throes.[81]

That was Hesse's classic Steppenwolf tone during these years, expressing the pathos of his distance from all those around him, even from the few friends that he still had. There s can be no doubt that this was a conscious decision of his, and was meant seriously, as Heinrich Wiegand was to learn: "Now I have long since given up trying to please anyone here on Earth. I'm just content that I've still got a few friends left, who in some cases are the same people as my harshest critics."[82]

Things went badly for Hesse in the Zurich winter of 1926–1927—or to be more accurate, things went badly for one part of him: namely, the part that tried to keep working, to be creative, and to give his life some structure. The other part of him, the Steppenwolf-like one, set its face against this Nietzsche-inspired, Apollonian attempt to create, devoting itself instead to dissolute Dionysian behavior in the form of orgies of drunkenness. In his New Year's letter to Hugo Ball on January 2, 1927, he confided that he would have given a great deal not to have had to experience this new year. "I am finding the *taedium vitae* ever more stifling. At present all I do day after day is sit at the typewriter with sore eyes and aching, arthritic hands, trying to produce a clean copy of the prose *Steppenwolf* . . . the work itself brought me no pleasure and now I'm positively sick to the back teeth of it."[83]

In addition to his perennial problems in motivating himself to write, he also found himself oppressed by domestic worries. For one thing, difficulties had arisen over the education of his three sons, who did not really know what they wanted to do with their lives, and for another there was Ruth, who was growing steadily more estranged from him. Things couldn't go on like this, Hesse sensed, when he wrote to his wife on December 5, 1926: "I am very sorry to hear that your life is so empty and unfulfilled, and that you find it impossible to say anything about it, and that after such a long time the only news you deem worthy of telling me is your purchase of a new dog."[84] Two weeks later, he prepared his mother-in-law, Lisa Wenger, for the fact that his marriage with Ruth would in all likelihood not survive the following year; he expressed his deep regret at this, since he had always felt very close to Lisa Wenger as a motherly friend. Now, for the first time, he openly admitted to her the serious error he had committed in entering into this union in the first place: "I really do consider that I have jeopardized our friendship by having made the cardinal mistake of changing our status from that of friends to relations. I now cannot imagine that this relationship will last forever—Ruth walked out on me eighteen months ago. And I fervently believe and even hope that Ruth is healthy and young enough to one day fall truly in love with another man—a man to whom she can feel genuinely committed."[85]

There was a reason behind him questioning his marriage, which only existed on paper, openly like this, for the first time—the blossoming of his relationship with Ninon Dolbin, which had until quite recently only been conducted through letters. Born in the Ukraine, Ninon had first written to Hesse at the age of fourteen; she was a great admirer of his poetry. And now that they had met and begun to see more of one another, she seemed to have fallen in love with him. A new problem with women loomed on the horizon for Hesse. That was the worst thing he could imagine: he found the prospect of entering into binding relationships with other people hard to take. This too was down to the heretic and the mystic in him, who shunned anything that threatened to formalize and institutionalize a living feeling—be that the established Church or the institution of marriage. This extreme self-centeredness was narcissistic. But in this, Hesse was far from being an exception among artists.

During the divorce proceedings his dispute with Ruth took on an ugly aspect, for which Hesse blamed his wife. It took a long time for him to forgive her behavior. On April 27, 1927, the marriage was formally annulled, with the judgment of the civil court of the Canton of Basel citing, of all things, one of Hesse's own characterizations of himself in "Journey to Nuremberg" as damning evidence—what treachery to call a literary work as a prosecution witness against its own creator! In the passage in question, Hesse referred to himself and others like him as "hermits, oddballs, insomniacs, and psychopaths."

Four days before the divorce was pronounced, Hesse wrote Ruth a kind of farewell letter, in which he spoke of the "sham marriage" that was now being dissolved, again "on sham grounds": "You claim I destroyed so much in you. But in truth I destroyed nothing except the image that you once had of me. In many ways, all I have done over the past two years is destroy myself."[86]

The atmosphere was so toxic that—yet again—he announced in May, with an eye to his milestone birthday on July 2: "The only thing I wish for my fiftieth birthday is that I won't live to see my fifty-first."[87]

No sooner had he arrived the previous November in Zurich, where he would write the final draft of *Steppenwolf,* than he sent Stefan Zweig a devastating snapshot of his mood: "I am writing nonstop in an unfavorable environment. I only moved here in the first place to spend part of the winter here, and am sitting among half-unpacked trunks and still haven't reacclimatized to the noise of the city." The problem of the content of *Steppenwolf* now spread out to encompass concerns about its external form too. This revealed the overriding insecurity of an author who, to quote from Gottfried Benn, was approaching those regions where the aging process starts to become a special problem for artists: "It is not just the problem of a man who is beginning to grow old and who has to taste the difficult years around fifty, above and beyond this it is the problem of an author who has begun to regard his profession as dubious and almost impossible because he has lost all sense of his roots and his purpose. This feeling has been steadily growing in me since the war, and seven years of solitary living in my village in Ticino haven't helped."[88]

Yet Hesse's life in Zurich wasn't entirely composed of suffering, as he often liked to make out; he was also fond of going out on the town. He learned how to dance and plunged into Zurich's winter nightlife, with its bars where the demimonde plied its trade. The high point was an erotically charged carnival. Hesse saw himself as some old uncle from the provinces who had come on a visit to the city. He felt his years amid all these bright young things. He gave a thumbnail sketch of the kind of man he was: one who was at the same time sensually aroused yet skeptically distant. He was afraid of young women, whom he also rather despised for their carefree lifestyle (the eternal burden of his Pietist upbringing again), but above all he was utterly fascinated by their playful erotic allure.

It was now a question of putting this confusing, kaleidoscopic situation, the inner chaos he felt, into a convincing literary form. Hesse knew this would have to be as fresh, as ecstatically charged and yet dispassionately disparate as the unfathomably permissive nightlife on the streets of the city, which he was now getting to know as part of the metropolitan bohemian set, albeit at least ten years too late. And suddenly he found himself facing some totally new challenges: "I made only modest progress with my dancing, and now I've had my six dance lessons. The Boston or the Blouse (or however you write it) is still causing me a lot of problems, and I very much doubt I'll ever be able to get the hang of it. On the other hand, I think I've mastered the foxtrot and the one-step about as well as one might expect from an elderly gentleman with gout."[89]

Hugo Ball was treated to a description of Hesse's dangerously high-spirited lifestyle over this winter, which culminated in a frenzy of writing. During this period Hesse not only flung *Steppenwolf* out at the world as a record of his hatred and disgust, but also attempted to overcome this gloomy mood by adopting a superior, divine, positively Mozartian demeanor. On February 22, 1927, when the manuscript of the novel was long since complete and Hesse was already giving public readings from it, Ball received the following account:

I'm back in the old routine once more and the day before yesterday I even found myself foxtrotting and tap-dancing again at a big masked ball, complicated by the fact that on that same evening I had to give a reading of *Steppenwolf* at the Psychologists' Club. So there I was, working as a poet and bard until ten o'clock, when I put my feet up for half an hour, only to reappear at half-past eleven at the ballroom, feeling a distinct lack of get-up-and-go. So with my first mouthful of champagne I took something for my headache. Gradually, the girls around me began to blossom so beautifully that I warmed up and had a couple of dances until, all of a sudden (just like that time when I had the flu), I felt heart palpitations and had to sit down. But over the course of the evening, the music seeped back into my bones, and this old man, who really could do with taking it easy, was back on his feet again, dancing and kissing, and suddenly it was morning, and the musicians packed up and left, the chairs were being stacked on the tables, and the trams were noisily and pointlessly clanging their way along the streets. At half-past seven, I finally went to bed, where I dozed for an hour but then felt the urge to get up and wash my face, but that was when my heart really started to play up, thumping away and causing me really unpleasant pain. So that day wasn't exactly sparkling, but today I'm back in the land of the living, and although I'm not dancing, the pain has at least gone away.[90]

What was the true state of affairs, then—the longing for death, born of boredom and disgust, or the good humor with which Hesse now increasingly approached the entertaining aspects of life? The answer is: both. In virtually every letter he wrote during this period, he managed to include an announcement of his impending death, yet it was invariably delivered in a teasing tone. It was the gallows humor of someone who really had, in all seriousness, set himself a deadline to end it all.

And so Hesse reeled his way through the nightlife of Zurich:

But when the carnival is over I will do away with myself, out of sheer despair that I was such a massive chump and squandered my whole life. I was a proper dunderhead to have spent thirty years agonizing over the problems of mankind but without the slightest idea of what a masked ball was. I thought that everyone was pretty much like me. If only I'd known how simple, stupid, and nice my fellow human beings were, I could have saved myself a whole heap of grief. But what sort of friends must I have had, who let me go around like that for decades without saying anything!

Hesse's rather desperately hedonistic tone here already has a smell of death about it. Whenever he described his Dionysian revelries in Zurich, he seemed certain that they would be followed by retribution. That was when he really came across as a runaway paterfamilias from the provinces, who was ready to drown himself in all the amusements the big city had to offer. Even Emmy Hennings, who had an intimate knowledge of the cynicism of pleasure that was bought and paid for, was shocked by Hermann Hesse's behavior. This was not the person she had revered as the prophet of a new spirituality, this was a self-loathing person with a death wish, for whom any old dance merely for entertainment was one and the same as the dance of death: "Dear God, if only I could remember the name of that beautiful, beautiful girl yesterday! I must dance another foxtrot with her and that lovely dance that they quite rightly call the 'joy-step.'"[91]

Yet Hesse's interest was by no means simply in his own personal amusement right up to the bitter end, but instead—and this was one of the two perspectives offered in *Steppenwolf*—in portraying an interwar period that seemed hell-bent on dancing itself to destruction.

The highly neurotic individualist found here the kind of intoxication that he had hitherto gotten only from wine; now it was embodied in an ecstatically pleasure-seeking community, which included women! A frequent companion on these outings to attend the masked balls of the carnival period was his friend the psychoanalyst J. B. Lang. Hesse, the misanthrope, found it all splendid:

> I had never known the experience, not even when drunk on wine, of losing one's individuality and simply being absorbed into a crowd. This desire, this wine-fueled rapture, this camaraderie, sexuality, warmth, and music was a wonderful feeling for which I am very grateful.
>
> Of course, it seemed rather odd to me to be staggering home through Zurich at around eight in the morning, in broad daylight with the city already bustling. But it was a good feeling, and the slight increase in pain from my gout that it brought on is a small price to pay.—What a pity it's all over![92]

The End

The flame that lured me through the pain
Of frantic pleasure has flickered and gone out.
My rigid fingers scream with gout,

And suddenly I'm in the wilderness again.
Recoiling from the shards of luckless revels,
Glutted, exhausted, disappointed, I,
Steppenwolf, have packed my bag. I'm going
Back to my native steppe to die.
Goodbye to sparkling, smiling masquerades,
Ladies too lovely, too ingratiating.
Behind the suddenly fallen curtain,
I know the old familiar dread is waiting.
Slowly I go to greet the enemy.
Harried by anguish, with laborious breath
And pounding, apprehensive heart,
I wait, wait, wait for death.

The Magic Theater: Big-Game Hunting for Automobiles

The time was past when one could walk on country roads all the way to
Italy. And yet it was actually only a quarter of a century that had wrought
such radical change in Europe. The First World War provided the catalyst
for technology to develop at a pace quite unimaginable up to that point.
Stefan Zweig called this phase of universalization of life "monotonization,"
and Hesse likewise saw the individual becoming the object of a machine
culture. He had already expressed his fears on this score in a letter to Hugo
Ball on November 5, 1921: "The Germany of today has become a kind
of America, you have to hustle and bustle to stop yourself from going
under—but then things seem to go pretty well."[93] But this sense of well-
being was only superficial. Many things may have functioned better than
they did before the war, it was true, but the spiritual substance of the
culture had been ruined—Hesse and Ball were in full agreement about
that. Hesse's "Crisis" poems give us an insight into his thoughts on this
matter. We have already touched upon their dubious artistic quality, but
their value as biographical documents is beyond dispute. For instance,
we find the following lines in the poem "Battle of the Machines" ("Die
Maschinenschlacht"):

The machines attack us furiously,
And bellowing squash us against the concrete walls
Run us down, drive over our heads and hands.
They are strong as devils, but woe unto them!

All they consist of is reason,
That makes them stupid and shallow, and these bovine beings
Know nothing of foolishness or love, or dreams or music or fantasy!

This attack by machines on the life of the imagination is followed in *Steppenwolf* by a counterattack, launched by the partisans of self-will, the notorious pedestrians of life, who insist on proceeding at their own pace and defending their own rhythm of life. Thus, in the section of the novel relating to the Magic Theater, we see a door being opened on which hangs a sign reading "Tally Ho! A-Hunting We Will Go. Big-Game Hunting for Automobiles." Behind this door lies the world of big-city traffic, that automobile apocalypse of noise and exhaust fumes that for Hesse had become the scene of a militantly Rousseauesque critique of modern culture. He conceives of this utopia of total mobility from its murderous endpoint: "Cars, some of them armored, were racing along the streets, hunting down pedestrians, running them over and mangling them to a pulp, or crushing them to death against the walls of houses. Straight away I realized that this was the war between humans and machines that had long been prepared for, long awaited, and long feared, and had now finally broken out."[94] The depiction of the scene is cold and distanced but has an expressive power worthy of a painting by Georg Grosz or Otto Dix. The coolly descriptive gaze captures the state of anarchistic uproar. The signal for the downfall of a degenerate culture. But Hesse also remains a dispassionate observer when he describes the posters calling for people to rise up and "finally put an end to the plump, well-dressed, and perfumed plutocrats who used machines to squeeze the fat from other men's bodies, to them and their huge fiendishly purring automobiles. Set the factories ablaze at last, make a little room on the crippled Earth, and depopulate it so that grass might grow once more, and something resembling woods, and meadows, and heathland, and streams, and moors might emerge from the dusty world of concrete."[95]

And so it comes to pass that the convinced pacifist Harry Haller is seized by the blood-lust of this massacre.

This too is one of the compartments that the outsider carries within him: the guerrilla fighter. He allows his blood-lust to be fueled by the general distress, and begins ambushing cars by sniping at them: "I saw how a joyous desire for destruction and murder burned so brightly and righteously in all their eyes, and these wild red blooms began blossoming in me too no less joyously, growing tall and fat. And I cheerfully joined the fight."[96]

This episode serves to lay bare the nature of the Magic Theater: it is an experimental stage for world history, as it appeared to Hesse in the 1920s—an assemblage of radical ideologies, in the clash between which a massive bloodbath was already looming.

Gustav, Harry Haller's old boyhood friend, who in the meantime had become a professor of theology, suddenly appears at his side and—shooting all the while at cars and their occupants—begins to wax lyrical about his destructive fantasies. "Kill your neighbor before he can kill you!" his motto might well run. It is all-out war, not just between humans and machines, but between spirit and ideology, between love and indifference. A wallet containing visiting cards is found on one of the victims

> "Taking one out, I read on it the words 'Tat twam asi.'"
> "Very amusing," said Gustav, "but it makes no difference what the people we are killing are called. They just poor devils like us; their names are immaterial. This world has to be destroyed and us with it. The least painful solution would be to submerge it under water for ten minutes. Come on, back to work!"[97]

This, then, is humanism in action, as espoused here by a theologian, who is no doubt of a patriotic bent. This is what all those fine words—about reason and progress, about necessity and going to war for the Fatherland, about a chosen class or race or nation, and about fighting a war now to ensure peace later—have brought people to. Who cannot help but call to mind here gulags, Auschwitz, and the atomic bomb!

The Magic Theater thus affords us an insight into the laboratory of extremisms.

It turns out that even a member of the educated classes, a former academic friend of Harry's who is now a German professor—with all his (now purely ornamental) erudition, which culminates in a hideous plaster bust of Goethe on the dresser in his study—is collaborating in the great downfall. Harry Haller visits this professor, who wastes no time in informing him that he must have an evil namesake, a traitor who has renounced his Fatherland! All this forms part of the stage scenery of a world of the past that is in decline.

By contrast, the Immortals who populate the Magic Theater—Mozart in the guise of a saxophone player, for instance!—are the only reliable figures in a world that has long since betrayed all its humanist principles.

The Brave New World of modernity—as portrayed by Aldous Huxley in his eponymous novel of 1932—is first and foremost one of deception and manipulation. And also of total surveillance. Where can one as an individual still emigrate to, where can one hide from the advancing tsunami of uniformity?

The Magic Theater is a hall of mirrors in which one can not only lose one's own way but also shake off one's pursuers! You step into another form of reality—and you are saved, just like the painter in prison who steps aboard a train he has painted himself and rides away to freedom. Anyone in the Magic Theater who has not learned to play in this way, remains unfree—this is the lesson that Harry Haller has to learn. Distance yourself from yourself, observe yourself from an ironic viewpoint!

This novel about an interwar period, as reflected in the personal crisis of its fifty-year-old author, has continued to appeal down the decades to new generations of young people struggling to come to terms with puberty. Without a doubt, there is a great deal in *Steppenwolf* that might lead a person to become a refusenik, a rebel, or a dropout. But this also runs the risk of the book being misunderstood, something that Hesse feared. In was with this in view that he wrote retrospectively to Horst Dieter Kreidler in October 1955: "I often have cause to get a little annoyed at schoolboys reading and enthusing over *Steppenwolf;* after all, the fact is that I wrote this book shortly before my fiftieth birthday. But of course it's simply not true that all I wanted to put across was some theme like 'the problems of the 50-year-old,' and in general I have never had such clear thematic–theoretical purposes in mind when writing any of my books."[98]

That was a smokescreen on Hesse' part, however, for "thematic–theoretical purposes" came to occupy an ever larger part of his work, as Hesse himself noted in a piece he wrote to mark his fiftieth birthday, entitled "Crisis—A Diary Fragment." In this, he remarked on the poems of that name, which he originally called his Steppenwolf poems, and which at this point in time were just as important to him as the prose text of the novel: "In my life, periods of great sublimation and of asceticism aimed at spiritualization have always alternated with periods of devotion to naively sensual, childlike, and foolish things, as well as to things that are insane and dangerous . . . I was better versed in matters spiritual, broadly speaking, than I was in the sensual; in thinking or writing I was able to hold my own with a selection of prominent contemporaries, yet in dancing the Shimmy and the art of being a man of the world, I was a barbarian."[99]

In this respect, therefore, doors in the Magic Theater marked "All Girls Are Yours" are not merely dreams of a pubescent boy, or a fifty-year-old, they are extensions of reality. Behind these doors, the bounds of what is possible are tested—in the imagination. The figure of Hermine in the novel is quite clearly Hesse's alter ego. This reveals an androgynous dimension in his conception of the erotic. There is a fleeting hint at an incest motif. Everyone has something of the opposite sex within them and must embrace that reality. For instance, there is the handsome Pablo, who is a picture of superficial beauty as presented by human nature, but also a transformative figure composed of that musical base material of which Mozart was also made. A world of mystery and magic caught in a state of permanent flux—and would it not be the highest form of fulfillment to attain for himself the status of a fellow magician in this world?

And so Hesse wished for a release from the fatalistic aspects of his life, a life that had thus far stood in the shadow of the vicious Pietist circle of gilt and pangs of conscience. He kills Hermine, who taught him how to dance and enjoy erotic love and who is now lying there naked and sleeping, exhausted from her lovemaking with Pablo. In stabbing her, he is fulfilling the task she set him—in the only way he is capable of grasping. And yet it is as though he has also killed half of himself in the process. It is a judgment upon him: "My whole life had been like that. What little happiness and love I had known was like this rigid mouth of hers: a touch of red painted onto the face of a corpse."[100]

Yet at this stage in his writing Hesse was not prepared to allow so much pathos; this was not a judgment upon him, in fact, but only a self-accusation demanding that he be given the death penalty.

However, Mozart and the Immortals have other plans for him: he must first learn how to live and to love. This has been something that Harry–Hermann has hitherto, in his intellectual ivory tower, arrogantly disregarded: "life's damned radio music." His sole defense against this has been scathing cultural criticism: "And indeed, to my indescribable surprise and horror, the devilish tin horn now immediately began to spew out that blend of bronchial mucus and chewed-up gum which the owners of gramophones and the subscribers to radios have conspired to call music."[101]

Of all people, it is the great and revered maestro, the divine Mozart, who is called upon to teach Harry this lesson:

> When you listen to the radio, you are hearing and seeing the primal struggle between idea and appearance, between eternity and time, between the human and the divine. . . . The whole of life is like this, my little one, and we must allow it to be so; and unless we are complete asses, we laugh into the bargain. People like you have absolutely no right to criticize the radio or life. Instead, try learning how to listen first! Learn to take seriously what is worth taking seriously, and laugh at the rest! Or have you yourself perhaps already found a better, more high-minded, intelligent, and more tasteful way of doing things?[102]

Hugo Ball's Death

Hesse's mood was worse than his actual situation. *Steppenwolf* was published punctually—and made an immediate splash; Hugo Ball's monograph was also completed on time. But two things that now happened in swift succession were to alter Hesse's outlook on life. The first was that the lover whom he referred to in his letters as "a Viennese girl"—Ninon Dolbin—now began staying with him more often, and for longer spells, than before. The second was something that Hesse had not at all anticipated. In June, he wrote Hugo Ball a letter of thanks for his monograph: "I really must congratulate you on this book, and myself as well, even though I don't share your opinions at all points, and despite the fact that I am a bit shy and don't like to see myself as being the focus of discussion." A few events in what he called Ball's "second-best book" had been incorrectly dated, he told him, but that was of no account; the most important thing was that it tied in directly to his best book, *Byzantine Christianity:*

> Only now do I see how correct you were not concentrate on the banal basic story but instead to write the legend of this life of mine, and to unearth its magic formulae. . . . Some of the things you say shame my modesty. But because you have once more shown yourself in this book to be a master of real poetry, and of searching out hieroglyphs and ideograms, may I say how delighted I am to find that I have been properly understood on precisely

this essential point by one of the few people I consider my soul-brothers in this art form. I hope that you are also pleased with the finished book and that it will continue to bring you joy.[103]

As it turned out, this wish of Hesse's was never to be fulfilled. On June 18, 1927, he was still introducing Ball to those readers who had only got to know about his work through his Hesse biography in the following terms: "He is the poorest of church mice that I know, and has for many years rarely experienced a month when he hasn't had to scrimp and save in order to pay the peppercorn rent for his primitive proletarian apartment and to buy a couple of loaves of bread. . . . He is a kind of ascetic holy man, though less in the Indian manner and more like a saint of the early Christian Church."[104]

In a letter to Walter Schädelin on June 28, Hesse speculated on the reasons for his special closeness to Hugo Ball. They were both, in their own way, misunderstood authors, and that created an unspoken bond between them: "Both as a political and as a religious writer he has remained misunderstood in a truly tragic way, and found his most serious misrepresenters and opponents taking his part. Right now, he is critically ill."[105]

Fate continued to deal a cruel hand to Hugo Ball. For Hesse, the news came as a shock. Three days before Hesse's fiftieth birthday, at the celebrations where Hugo Ball was due to be the "chief guest of honor," his friend was rushed into hospital. He underwent an operation on Hesse's birthday.[106] The following day, Emmy Hennings wrote to Hermann Hesse: "Hugo is already a doomed man, a sad and hopeless case."[107]

In his turn, on July 25, Hesse informed friends about Ball's state of health: "Yesterday Hugo Ball was transported back from Zurich, where they had operated on him and removed half his stomach. He is now lying in bed and in a good recuperative mood, but for the present he doesn't know quite how serious his condition is; in medical terms, he is terminally ill. I went to see him yesterday and today, and his welfare will be my chief concern for the time being."[108]

Hugo Ball was suffering from stomach cancer. He died on September 14 and was buried two days later in the cemetery at St. Abbondio. His friends Lang and Englert also attended his funeral. Hesse noted: "He was borne to his last resting place by a bunch of heretics, and I walked behind his coffin over to the church of St. Abbondio in the storm and the rain carrying a tall candle."[109]

On September 18, Emmy Hennings again got in touch with Hesse, at whose house she had spent the evening after Ball's funeral: "My dear, good friend Hesse, it was so lovely to spend Friday evening with you, although the path to your house was darker than it had ever been. A storm was blowing, it was pouring with rain, and there was lightning, and our Hugo was spending his first night alone beneath the earth and no longer in my arms like he had been in the final night of his life."[110]

Hugo Ball's death, which Hesse experienced at close quarters, had a decisive effect on him. It cured him of his own morbid fear of death. On the day of the funeral, he wrote an elegy to his friend. Addressing the deceased directly, it ran:

> You were a model for us. In the rigor of your thinking, in the strictness of your sense of linguistic responsibility, in your unremitting service to the word, in your conscious struggle against the tendency of our age to negligence and irresponsibility in thought and speech, you were for many years a shining example to us, which spurred us on and comforted us in many an hour of despondency, and which in many an hour of weakness looked admonishingly over our shoulder. In your presence, it was impossible to get away with a shallow platitude or a piece of grandstanding pseudo-intellectualism.[111]

Hesse mourned the passing of Hugo Ball, who lived a life in the service of the intellect and who was "spurned by the world." On September 21 he wrote to Volkmar Andreae to tell him that he had lost in Ball "the only person who was a genuine spiritual soulmate to me, who completely got what I was talking about, and with whom I could discuss spiritual matters in real depth. I will not find his like again. He was the only one of my friends who not only enjoyed my company and gave me a sympathetic hearing, but who also understood me and fundamentally grasped my need to think in the way I do and the entire way I go about things."[112]

At this point, Hesse appears to have taken to heart Ball's equable nature and his affirmation of life in the face of great sacrifices and to have used his friend's death to lift himself out of his midlife crisis and to force himself to really grow up for the first time. This was certainly how it sounded from a letter he sent in the immediate aftermath of Hugo Ball's death, in which he replied to a young fellow writer's question regarding his vocation:

> For as long as you çan take it or leave it, as long as there is still a way back, you should consider nothing as being cast in stone. It's true that you might now and then experience a faint premonition of the dread and of the terrible sacrifice that is required of us, and you will flinch at the thought. But if you still want to carry on despite all that, you will get used to the dread, and ultimately it will become the strongest thing spurring you on. For some people find it impossible to live without dread and the proximity of death, and it's all the same to them whether they seek that in real life or in their minds. But I have already said too much![113]

At this juncture, the points were switched for Hesse's later writings, sending him off on a track that he had already embarked upon with *Narcissus and Goldmund,* and that would now continue on through *The Journey to the East* and *The Glass Bead Game.* It seems that his late work began promptly with his fiftieth birthday.

Two weeks after Hugo Ball's death, Emmy Hennings left Ticino; she could not bear living on her own there amid all the places like Agnuzzo that she associated so inextricably with her late partner. She traveled with her daughter, Annemarie, to Baden to recuperate in the Verenahof, where she wrote almost daily to Hesse. On October 12, Hesse himself arrived at the hotel to take his annual rest cure.

All Just an LSD Trip?

Hesse was annoyed that the mythical dimension of *Steppenwolf* was largely misjudged by his readership. In a fragment from the papers he left behind, we read the following: "For short moments I realized that terms from myth such as chaos and creation, and terms of rational discourse such as prehistory and evolution, at root denoted, not a succession, but instead a simultaneity and interlinkage. The primeval world was not older than the Here and Now, it had not ceased to exist:—The primeval world and the present day coexisted."[114] This was the deepest significance of the Magic Theater: its suspension of time, the sense of "mystical union" it entailed—a union of potentiality and actuality in the form of a collage.

Misunderstanding of Hesse's work seemed predestined. In his own late writings at the end of the 1940s, in works such as *Ptolomäer* and *Radardenker,* Gottfried Benn further developed the kind of hallucinatory style that Hesse had pioneered in *Steppenwolf;* Benn referred to this as his "orange style," a kaleidoscopic form of narrative that reflected a surrealistically unbounded reality.

Timothy Leary, however, understood that "hallucinatory" aspect of the Magic Theater differently—and his interpretation had major ramifications. In a 1963 essay—one of the key founding documents of the American counterculture—Leary picked up on Hesse's admission that *Steppenwolf* was not a book of despair but "the story of a believer." A telling phrase in the text by Leary and his co-author Ralph Metzner referring to Hesse as a "master guide to the psychedelic experience" encapsulates their reading of Hesse's work as a by-product of drug-taking. *Steppenwolf* and *Siddhartha* were expressly recommended by Leary as a supplement—a spiritual embedding, so to speak—to tripping on LSD.

Nowadays we may be tempted to smile at the truly naive psychologizing appropriation of Hesse by the drug scene of the 1960s, but at the time this way of reading a text was revolutionary. Hesse, who had died in 1962, would doubtless have reacted with total incomprehension to Leary's apodictic categorization of the Magic Theater: "It seems clear that Hesse describes a psychedelic experience, a drug-induced loss of self, a journey to the inner world. Each door in the Magic Theater has a sign on it, indicating the endless possibilities of the experience."[115] This equating of the positing of multiple realities, if only as sheer potentialities, in Hesse's work, with the simple experience of such multiplicity under the influence of drugs is somewhat presumptuous to say the least! Leary's description of Hesse an "esoteric" from the "psychedelic brotherhood" reduces the author's deadly earnest questioning of the future of the spirit within a reality that was becomingly increasingly hostile to it to the trivially pretentious level of a state of altered consciousness. And so the manipulation of the "master guide to the psychedelic experience" for the perfect drug trip culminates in the following instruction, couched in the innocent language of a guidebook: "Before your LSD session, read *Siddhartha* and *Steppenwolf.*"

Sound advice, no doubt; certainly one would not be in a fit state to do so afterward. To be sure, we are free to read Hesse in all kinds of ways and with any agenda in mind, however offbeat it may seem. But the strong suggestion here is that Hesse must have had experience with psychedelic drugs.

One might even come to the conclusion that the Magic Theater section had been written during an LSD trip. But nothing could be more far-fetched than this trivializing assumption! Hesse took a dim view of consciousness-altering drugs and regularly took recourse to wine and often tobacco as stimulants. Furthermore, there were certain times in his life when he felt that even these went beyond the bounds that his fragile health could tolerate.

Even Leary was ultimately forced to concede that there was no evidence that Hesse ever took the drug mescaline. The fact that, shortly after writing *Steppenwolf,* Hesse called Thomas De Quincey's *Confessions of an English Opium Eater* a "pathological book"[116] in his introduction to it in his Library of World Literature series should have been a pointer to Leary that Hesse always gave mind-expanding drugs a very wide berth.

In this, he was following firmly in the footsteps of Baudelaire, who indulged in alcohol yet who in his 1860 work *Les paradis artificiels* (Artificial paradises) categorically repudiated the sort of substances that Leary referred to as "psychedelic drugs": "If we assume for a moment that hashish turns you into a genius or at least makes you more clever, then what the consumers of hashish forget is that it is in the nature of the drug to sap a person's willpower, with the result that it gives with one hand and takes away with the other; in other words, that it furnishes a person with a heightened perception but at the same time robs him of the ability to benefit from it." It is hard to imagine a sharper rejection of opium and hashish than Baudelaire delivers in these sentences from his essay: "Anyone who takes recourse to a poison *in order to think* will soon find themselves in a position where they cannot think without taking poison. Can you imagine the dreadful fate of a person whose crippled imagination can no longer function without the help of hashish or opium?"[117]

The Expressionist Walter Rheiner followed the Romantic Charles Baudelaire in his outspoken animosity toward the drug that that already taken control of him. In his work *Kokain* (Cocaine) he dared to look into the abyss of destruction. The poison destroyed not only his brain, nervous system, muscles, and internal organs, but also his sensory perception and his mind. Rather than opening up worlds, it closed them off, or even worse caused first them and then the Self to collapse. Rheiner died in 1925 at the age of thirty from an overdose of morphine. Rather than finding himself party to new insights hidden from the rational mind, Rheiner the addict, who was no longer able to grasp anything but instead found himself being swept powerlessly to his death, was tormented by visions of sheer terror: "The poison that was his destiny spread out over the whole city like some huge animal, covering the horizons and his entire being: inescapable, a 'Charybdis sucking the dark water down.'"[118]

The ecstasy that Hesse was seeking was of a quite different nature: the cold ecstasy of creative production. And if, as we may reasonably assume it was, the Magic Theater was actually meant to be a model of psychoanalysis, then Hesse constructed it here with the sole purpose of playing with it, restoring to it the ironic distance—totally lacking in the writings of Freud and Jung—from the products of the subconscious. A Nietzschean stroke of genius designed to reclaim the power of interpretation over himself—and a wholly original contribution to the theory of the Superman!

Creative ecstasy required one thing above all: sober concentration. When all was said and done, nothing was such anathema to Hesse as the unsought "outing" as a Steppenwolf. Did everyone harbor a Steppenwolf within their own breast? Hesse could only laugh bitterly at this suggestion: "The breasts to which those who uttered these words customarily pointed were the highly respectable breasts of society ladies, of lawyers and industrialists, and these breasts were covered by silk blouses and modern waistcoats. Each and every one of us, according to these liberal-minded people, was perfectly well acquainted with the feelings, desires, and sufferings of the Steppenwolf, and each of us had to struggle to suppress them, and so each of us was in actual fact himself also a poor, howling, ravening Steppenwolf." Here Hesse was reacting to a trend that he had never foreseen or thought possible: the Steppenwolf had become fashionable, and people now saw it as the in thing to accuse themselves of harboring this kind of abyss of untamed wildness within. Claiming to have a touch of the social outcast was attractive—and safe: doing so didn't mean having to give up all your credit cards and go back to the wild! And so the cult of the Steppenwolf culminated in kind of appropriation of the concept by the solid bourgeoisie—a familiar phenomenon since the reception of Nietzsche. This entailed placing the dangerous precedent on a pedestal, defusing it like a bomb by subjecting it to solemn speeches, and finally burying it under a heap of laurels and lavish praise. Hesse reacted against this process with bitter irony: "One evening over a glass of whisky, one of them even suggested founding a Society of Steppenwolfs."[119]

Hugo Ball had called the Steppenwolf a "mythical beast," which had risen from the depths of European intellectual history, while the literary critic Hans Meyer (in his book *Steppenwolf and Everyman*) discreetly suggested what the key might be to the understanding of *Steppenwolf* which American youth culture had failed to grasp. The problem was, in Mayer's view, that that culture had very much created "its own Steppenwolf," who was not a fifty-year-old German intellectual profoundly at odds with himself and the world, but instead a young American, almost still a teenager, who was kicking against the norms and rules of his parents' generation with a mixture of coolness and nihilism and in the process casting a sharply critical eye—the outsider's viewpoint of Harry Haller—over the age he was living in: like Holden Caulfield in J. D. Salinger's *Catcher in the Rye*.

On the events that unfold in the Magic Theater, Hans Mayer remarked: "Moreover, one senses from these visions, which belong very much in the neighborhood of Picasso and his treatment of the war and the Minotaur themes, that even in the forms he used and even back then, Hesse was anything but a tame epigone and late Romantic but instead a passionate, embittered and despairing artist of his time." He then added a comment that already pointed in the direction of Thomas Mann's *Doctor Faustus:* "Besides, *Steppenwolf* is first and foremost a German book. Or rather: a work of fiction *offering a critique of conditions in Germany.*"[120] There are good reasons for seeing in *Steppenwolf* the late offspring of the magic mountain of German Romanticism. This archetypal story of going out into the world on a mission and retreating from it, of ardent and wistful poeticism and rational and cool distance, of clear purpose and losing one's way, would in the not too distant future find expression in Hesse's work under a new title: *The Glass Bead Game.*

Two examples of interesting experiments related to Hesse's soaring popularity in the culture of protest are the screen adaptations of *Siddhartha* (1972, dir. Conrad Rooks) and *Steppenwolf* (1974, dir. Fred Haines). Hesse did not think much of film versions of his novels, but then again—unlike his literary hero Franz Kafka—he had a very low opinion of cinema in general (and likewise of the theater, except for his own Magic Theater). He also took a very dim view of paperbacks—much to the dismay of his young publisher Siegfried Unseld, who then went ahead and defied the author's veto and in the 1970s brought out a series of paperback editions that made Hesse into the most successful German author bar none worldwide. There was little to object to in this—an author who brings a book into the world must ultimately let it go its own way; he cannot hope to stipulate, after his own death, how and in what form it should be presented to the reading public. The same applies to the—perfectly legitimate—transgression of Hesse's proscription against filming. And indeed, the results of this were remarkable: both films in their very different ways found a means of visually conveying the fundamental intellectual problem that lent both books their narrative tension in the first place.

Neither of the movies, however, was a commercial success, which speaks to their artistic quality and also testifies to the fact that a large proportion of that readership who bandied the name Hesse about in conversation in the 1970s did not remotely know what to make of the issue of intellectual self-discovery that was being shown here on screen. Timothy Leary had done all too thorough a job in generating a very soft-focus picture of the poet-rebel.

Fred Haines, who with his stars Max von Sydow and Dominique Sanda shot a movie of *Steppenwolf* that comprehensively flouted all cinematic visual conventions (producing almost a film collage!), especially through his use of a highly artificial clip esthetic, also wrote an essay titled "Hermann Hesse and the American Subculture." There, Haines observed: "However bizarre it may appear to Europeans, and particularly to Germans, that the most devoted and eager readers of Hesse are to be found precisely in the midst of the most power-threatened and materialistic civilizations, they can perhaps comfort themselves with the thought that Hesse is far more likely to destroy America than America Hesse."[121]

9

Hesse's New Female Companion, Ninon Dolbin, the Organizing Principle in His Life

In Zurich, of all places, in March 1926—during Hesse's wildest phase as a habitué of nightclubs—the spark was ignited between them. That would have consequences, of which Hermann Hesse, unlike her, probably had no inkling. They had already known one another for quite some time and had likely even met one another once, in January 1921. Ninon Dolbin, born Ninon Ausländer in Czernowitz (now Chernivtsi in Ukraine), was thirty years old by the time of their encounter in Zurich and had been longing for this moment to come for much of her life. Yet what she visualized as the greatest fulfillment of her life's dreams may also have spelled doom. For her, for him, perhaps for both of them? Or would seeing things in this light be a misrepresentation of the facts?

When she was fourteen years old, in 1910, Ninon sent her first letter to the poet she so admired. Ninon Ausländer was a pupil at the high school in Czernowitz, which was actually a single-sex school for boys in the manner of that period. However, she was granted special permission to attend the institution; as the daughter of the attorney Jakob Ausländer, president of the local lawyers' association, she was extremely ambitious. She was keen to study, and the solid bourgeois home she came from fully supported her and her sisters Toka and Lilly in their ambitions. At school, Ninon always sat in the front row of the class, alongside two other girls. At the start of lessons, the girls were the last children to be led into the classroom, and were the first to be escorted out at the end, when they would spend their break times shut away from the boys in a separate room. As nonboarders, they were also required to pass exams every year—a considerable hurdle for girls at that period. Yet unlike Hermann Hesse, Ninon Dolbin never gave any indication that she had suffered in any way at school, and she appears to have passed her high-school graduation exam with ease.

Czernowitz was situated on the farthest fringes of the Austro-Hungarian Empire, but the Jewish elite there thought very much in European terms. They regarded themselves as modern, and traditional Jewish customs and ritual played no part in these enlightened circles. The fact that Ninon's father was a devout Jew who attended the local synagogue and dutifully observed all the festivals of the Jewish calendar was treated by the family as something of an idiosyncrasy. Ninon, a "daddy's girl" who had rather a difficult relationship with her mother, recalled:

> We regarded our father's piety as an endearing weakness that we graciously indulged. When, on the eve of the most major Jewish festival, he emerged from the temple, his kindly face looked even more benign than usual, with a glow radiating from it that seemed to spread benevolence over all it surveyed. He sat at table with us while we ate our evening meal, and all we ever wanted to know from him was how he could stand the fasting. We asked him whether he was hungry yet and whether the smell of the food wasn't getting to him, and whether you could hear people's stomachs rumbling in the synagogue—all in all, fasting was a subject of endless fascination to us.[1]

The family also celebrated Christmas with a Christmas tree, as Ninon's father took the view that the children needed it. The Hasidic sect of Eastern European Judaism and its "crazy praying" was deeply alien to the educated middle-class ethos of the three sisters: "We did not love the race to which we belonged—its violent temperament, and all the jerky, extravagant movements really put us off; from our earliest childhood, we had learned how to move in a restrained way and to speak in muted tones—while those who attended the synagogue all abandoned themselves to their passions, and we found all that sobbing and moaning and the sing-song noise of the prayers truly repellent."[2] For the young girl Ninon, Czernovitz was "Little Vienna" and it was her dream to move from the periphery of the Austro-Hungarian Empire to its very heart. She set her heart on studying in Vienna!

The first letter she sent to Hermann Hesse—a piece of fan mail, certainly, but also a love letter, or perhaps more accurately a letter of amorous devotion—was remarkable for one peculiarity: it contains no opening address line! She still retained this odd habit by the time they met in 1926. After the first night they spent together, she sent Hesse a letter, likewise with no address line, in which she explained it in the following way: "'Dear Ninon' you write, and it sounds so simple and natural, but I cannot name you in return, just like the Jews are forbidden from uttering the word Jehovah."[3] This sums up how she regarded Hesse at the beginning—a beginning that lasted precisely sixteen years, from 1910 to 1926: "a wonderful being and a monstrous one too." The chosen poet as God.

And to her, he would remain a mixture of wonderful and monstrous being: in their day-to-day existence primarily a monstrous being, even an outright monster. But as an author, even beyond his death—for forty years, in other words, until her own death in 1966, he would remain her God, albeit a Janus-faced deity, a simultaneous combination of good and evil.

The first occasion on which she began a letter to him with the address "Dear Hermann" was in May 1927, by which time she had already suffered several severe disappointments. The Hermann Hesse whom she regarded as such a great figure could also behave in a very petty manner—and most of all could be very cold and dismissive. So we see that after they had spent their first summer together (though in separate apartments) in Casa Camuzzi, her mode of address had declined by October 9, 1927, to the positively blasphemous abbreviated form "L.H." (standing for "Lieber Hermann").

★   ★   ★

In 1910, when the fourteen-year-old Ninon had finally summoned up the courage to write to Hesse, her letter had the tone of someone who already knew that she was were thereby throwing down a challenge to her own destiny. The unusually stern attitude that would subsequently be the source of such great pain to her was already in evidence here: for all the devotion she felt toward the godlike object of her admiration, she could not bring herself to deny her own feelings and thoughts. No, Ninon Ausländer was not simply a fan in search of an idol to worship, or to put it more bluntly, a servant in search of a master. It was not out of weakness that she was seeking to get close to the famous author, but rather the opposite: she had the audacity to ask him to engage in conversation with her.

Accordingly, she was at pains to inform Hesse right at the outset what kind of letter it definitely was not. She also did not mince her words over the sort of response she was not seeking from him: "I am fearful of receiving one of those amiable and banal little missives that poets are in the habit of sending to young girls. But in the way that everyone thinks of themselves as an exception and hopes to be treated as such (and even this belief is stereotypical), so do I as well, and little by little I convinced myself that I should write this letter. 'Ultimately,' I thought to myself, 'I won't receive the little missive I so fear, but instead—instead—.'"[4] Although she did not go on to say exactly what she was hoping for, it is clear what she meant: she wanted to have him, the poet as a living person physically in front of her; to stand beside him, and be with him was her dream. This was far from being just a teenage fantasy. Ninon was imbued with a deep certainty that she would retain for her entire life: "The things that endure are created by the poets"—a high-minded sentiment on the primacy of literary creation variously attributed to Hölderlin and Goethe.

For Ninon, poetry was the only form of reality worth living for—this was her abiding conviction even at the age of fourteen. Unlike Hesse, who at the same age already knew that he wanted to become a poet *or nothing at all,* she felt no vocation to become a writer herself. Yet that only made her all the more certain of the key role that poetry would play in her own life. As a reader, as someone totally immersed in the poetic vision: "O how I envy poets! They can say what they feel, they can put into words the 'deepest pain, the highest joy.'"

She wrote the letter after reading *Peter Camenzind*. In this work she encountered something that would become a decisive factor in her life.

And she felt a compelling urge to talk to the author about this rite-of-passage experience of hers.

She was captivated by the tale of a person leaving his little village and setting out into the wider world to seek his fortune. Indeed, she found the idea so captivating that she refused to believe in his failure and his ultimate self-resignation to returning to a narrow little life in the provinces. He couldn't just give up on his quest! She sounded almost outraged. Reading these lines of hers, one thing becomes crystal clear: Ninon was desperate to tread in Peter Camenzind's footsteps—but, unlike him, not to turn back when she was already halfway to her goal.

She had been given the novel as a present on her fourteenth birthday—and even on her sixtieth she would still recall how she had gotten to know Hesse intimately on her birthday forty-six years previously, at the moment when someone pressed a copy of *Camenzind* into her hands.

She did not receive a reply to her first letter to the author. Yet no reply, she figured, was better that the vacuous response she had feared, and so she wrote him another, albeit a year later, followed by another a year after that, on August 2, 1912—letters at yearly intervals; she had learned how to restrain herself. And it was to this third letter that she finally received a reply from Hermann Hesse.

On February 1, 1913, Ninon wrote back, thanking her poet-idol for his response. The way in which she presented herself to him, as so single-minded, must surely have perplexed him: "Never, ever have I gone to bed at night without a sense of dissatisfaction at myself, at my achievements."[5] Before long the correspondence between them became more frequent. By the fall of 1913, and as per her plan, eighteen-year-old Ninon was living in Vienna and studying medicine. That summer Hesse had invited her to come and see him in Bern, as she and her mother were passing through Switzerland on their way to Lucerne. However, her mother vetoed this detour to meet Hesse.

And so the friendship between the author and his reader remained confined to correspondence for the time being. In Vienna, as was only to be expected, Ninon showed herself to be an eager student; in her very first letter from there to Hesse, she proudly announced that she was already being allowed to perform dissections. But she was also going to art galleries, taking an interest in the work of Sigmund Freud, and attending lectures by the writer Karl Kraus. She had a particular interest in painting, having already informed her parents in Czernowitz that she refused to take piano lessons and would rather be given instruction in drawing instead. She also scotched the idea of dancing lessons—she had no time for all those accomplishments that were traditionally deemed to be an essential part of a woman's education. She had no intention of becoming one of those typical daughters from a good household who would study for a while and take an interest in a whole variety of things—only then to get married and set to work learning how to become a wife and mother.

"I hate women!" she would sometimes be heard to exclaim. She wanted to make her mark in the world of men, she meant to prove herself in that forum, and there was only one man she could imagine herself acting as an assistant to—Hermann Hesse—and even then only because she had chosen him as the writer who would have the most decisive effect on her life. After the outbreak of war, she increasingly began to doubt her choice of profession; in 1916, in addition to carrying on her university studies, she worked as an auxiliary nurse at several hospitals in Vienna. The things she saw there made her decide to give up medicine (after three and a half years), and from 1917 onward she studied art history instead, in the course which she also had occasion to visit Paris and Berlin. She fell in love with Berlin for its fast pace of life, in diametric opposition to Hermann Hesse, for whom the German capital was the epitome of an abominable Moloch. Two years later she married Fred Dolbin, a flamboyant character of many talents who was twelve years her senior. He had already had a successful career as an engineer, and was now working as a newspaper cartoonist; in this capacity he became one of the leading caricaturists of the 1920s. In 1921 Ninon began writing a doctoral thesis, on the work of the sixteenth-century French goldsmith Étienne Delaune—a topic that did not truly captivate her, because in her eyes she was dealing here with the creations of a fundamentally derivative talent. What she was really looking for was an original genius who posed important questions and who as a consequence had to endure major life crises. The image of Hesse was no doubt in her mind at this time. In 1926 she wrote him a letter summing up how she saw the world and herself up to the death of her parents (her father died on Christmas Eve 1919, and her mother of septicemia resulting from an insect bite in 1925):

Ninon Dolbin at the time of her first personal acquaintance with Hesse

I was a terribly spoiled child and turned into a spoiled woman, I don't mean where material things are concerned. . . . A real cat that wanted to be stroked and fondled all the time. There was certainly more than a touch of lazy self-satisfaction in my forthrightness. When my mother died, I sensed the loneliness that would come. And now it has indeed come, now I am completely thrown back on my own resources and quite alone. The world now has a very different face, and I need to take a wholly new perspective on things and grasp them all afresh.[6]

One might be tempted to think that Ninon always had only one aim in mind: to win over the poet of her life. Yet if one reads her letters following their first erotic encounter on March 21, 1926, it becomes evident that she was far from being merely a calculating person. Over and over again, these letters are proclamations of love of the most genuine and touching kind, which in their poetic tone must also have greatly delighted Hesse. On March 24, already on her way back to Vienna, she wrote: "You're quite right, it's terrible to be sitting on a train—I am so full to the brim with thoughts and feelings that I want to run around or scream, but instead I'm sitting here hunched up in a corner and thinking of you. . . . Did you know that—that a person's heart can literally ache with happiness? I'm in such pain— . . . You are a mighty tree and I am a little bird sitting in the shadow of your branches and leaves."[7] In reply, Hesse sent her a bundle of books, some photos, a watercolor, and a poem. Perhaps something of an overkill response to such an intimate letter? Nevertheless, Ninon was enchanted and replied: "It is so beautiful to be filled with you. It is a painful to know that you are tormenting yourself. When your head lay in my lap, it was like I was holding the Crucified Christ."[8] Yet at this point Hesse appears to have become a little spooked by what was happening. He had had a few love affairs in Zurich, but nothing serious—and he was trying to lighten up somewhat and to take life in a more entertaining light. And although he found that he was only able to do so intermittently for short spells, it was still a step in the right direction. It did not suit his current frame of mind to be swept up in the grand passion of a young woman. On March 29 he wrote to her: "I want to come to you—everything is drawing and driving me to you." She underlined this sentence in his letter. But then he continued: "O, how your letter pained me."[9] It seems as though Hesse was doing all he could to distance himself at this point, though we can only deduce this from her reactions and from what Hesse conveyed to third parties, because his letters to her prior to 1927 currently remain inaccessible. Ninon ended her reply to him in a manner that sounds almost defiant: "You—I will kiss your hurting eyes (it pains me to hear that they are hurting!)—I will belong to you, and perhaps you will sleep by my heart, my love. Yours—Your, Ninon."[10] Again, she underlined the word "sleep." The next morning, before she posted the letter, she added a postscript, which reads like a deliberate reinterpretation of a piece of unequivocally bad news into good tidings:

> How good that that dreadful day yesterday is now past. Your letter paralyzed me for several hours, I lay there unable to move a muscle, and my mind was turning endlessly in circles—enough of that, I will spare you the details. . . . You wrote me a letter that made you sound like you're 95 years old, like you're always saying—it was so cold and clear and prudent—but that's just not like you! But precisely all those things that you actually are—young and old and cold and ardent and God and devil—that's what makes you wonderful.[11]

Ninon had made up her mind that she wanted him—and she was not going to be deterred by even the chilliest of rebuffs.

Hesse vehemently resisted the idea that Ninon should give herself to him so completely. Fortunately for him, he was still married, and so was she.

To be on the safe side, in May 1926 he asked J. B. Lang to draw up a horoscope for Ninon. Hesse appears to have taken this form of astrological forecast as more than just playful whimsy. Lang duly provided him with an exhaustive horoscope that reads like a piece of friendly encouragement; Hesse could happily go ahead and form a liaison with Ninon Dolbin. Though according to Lang, who could not resist dabbling in the occult, he should proceed cautiously all the same: "For me, one thing is clear, namely that you should exclude from the outside the biological side of eroticism, in other words that you should refrain from having children." Lang went on: "There are many hindrances in the way of your erotic self-realization, but you will eventually learn to live out this part of your being as perhaps only very few mortals can."[12] Had he read all that in the stars, or more likely extracted the basic gist of it from the many years of discussions that they had with one another? Whatever the case, the union between Hesse and Ninon Dolbin would indeed remain childless, despite the fact that she was only in her early thirties and desperately wanted to have children. Hesse, we may safely assume, did not need the astrological advice of his old friend to persuade himself that he didn't want any more offspring.

The swift blossoming of Ninon's relationship with Hermann Hesse came at a time when she had just begun to chart a quite different course for her life. After drifting apart several times thanks to his many extramarital affairs, she had just been reconciled once more with Fred Dolbin and had resolved not to leave him. Dolbin was to some extent a substitute for her dead father, who had been the most important person in her life and whose absence, for all the purposeful self-motivation she otherwise displayed, still rendered her helpless. And yet this man Dolbin still did not quite fit her image of a man who on the one hand represented an unequivocally protecting power and on the other was so in need of help himself that he could and must sacrifice himself for her. Dolbin was naturally jealous of the morose Hesse, who paraded his many woes to the world like an accusation.

Dolbin had once seen Hesse like that at a book reading, and had also sketched him looking grumpy. He called Ninon's credulous relationship to Hesse nothing more than "idolatry." Other friends also warned her against forcing herself on Hesse; she was throwing her life away, they told her, and surrendering herself to the moods of a constantly dissatisfied man, who in addition was well on his way to becoming an old and ill man. Didn't she want to be more than simply his career? She willingly took on this sacrifice; it was the price, she reckoned, for the great happiness she had experienced through him, as she exultantly but still understatedly wrote in a letter of May 7, 1926:

> I would so love to write you a letter without words, consisting of just some lovely, radiant melody that will delight you, just as thinking of you, of your existence, delights me! I can only experience things that are already fully formed; I do not have the capacity to give form to things I have experienced. The thought of you glows within me, I preserve it in myself, I cannot impart it to anyone else. . . . Sometimes I can work calmly for a couple of hours as though nothing had happened, and then all at once my heart stops because I can suddenly feel that you exist—that's so lovely![13]

Ninon was not to be deflected from her love for the poet: In the spring of 1927—Hesse had been legally divorced since April 26—she traveled to Baden to meet him. He had already told her several times in no uncertain terms that he wanted to remain single. *Steppenwolf* was behind him, and he was on his annual rest cure. Moreover, he was in a bad mood, as he usually was between books. He wrote to Ernst Morgenthaler about Ninon's sudden invasion of his peace: "At the moment there's a woman from Vienna here, who arrived out of the blue because she is fond of me. But despite the fact that I like her too and find her quite pleasant company, I don't know what to do about her. So here I am, stuck in this drastic situation and not in the best of humors."[14]

Hesse's cool and unfriendly manner, though, made no impression on Ninon. Not when it came to her mission of saving a poet, and a kindred spirit at that! Ninon was prepared to make any sacrifice—and Hesse ultimately accepted it, albeit reluctantly, while at the same time making it perfectly clear to her that there could be no question of them living together. At best they could lead a parallel existence, with her permitted to be there for him when he had need of her, but also required to disappear when he didn't. It would become a hard and exhausting task for her to distinguish between Hesse's two rapidly changing frames of mind—not to mention a thankless one, for after all, Hesse had not summoned her to him, and he would threaten time and again to simply dispense with her assistance. And yet for both of them, closeness was ultimately not something that they could achieve despite the distance between them, but precisely only through maintaining such a distance. This distance was for Hesse the air that allowed him to breathe freely. He had always been very wary of human contact and at certain phases of his life was simply unable to stand anyone being near him.

Was all this so very surprising? It is not uncommon for authors to want to interact with their surroundings only in writing; that is at one and the same time their passion and their profession. And Ninon, who had lived out her love for Hesse over sixteen years solely through correspondence, was likewise not unfamiliar with communicating with Hesse only in written form—a state that was set to continue even when they had long since been married and were living under one roof. Their day-to-day communication with one another was conducted by means of "house letters," like in a Trappist monastery, where one has to stay silent most of the time and jot down essential communications to one's fellow monks on pieces of paper.

This was the way in which Hesse managed to tolerate the presence of another person in his vicinity; he had to be sure that he wouldn't suddenly be spoken to. And Ninon willingly agreed to all these conditions. Four years later she was divorced from Fred Dolbin (with whom she would remain friends); he had never stood any chance against Hermann Hesse.

A Choleric Type and a Misfit: Trying to Tame the Intractable Hesse

Hesse reacted with extreme annoyance to any disturbance. Very soon Ninon would come to learn this for herself, after she made the mistake of moving several books from their original positions. Via "house letter" he angrily reprimanded her:

> Ninon, yesterday I was rather surprised at how badly you took my wish to retain control of my right of disposal over my own books. . . . Life for me now holds almost no pleasures any more, in fact I am living in Hell. You,

however, are fortunate enough to have some better relations with life, and living with me means a great sacrifice to you, I'm sure, compared to which such trivialities are of no account. As far as new books are concerned, I will make some arrangement that will satisfy you. Pretty soon, though, I won't have any books any longer, and so we won't have any occasion to be nice or nasty to one another (5 o'clock in the morning).[15]

How was it that Hesse believed himself to be "living in Hell," one might well ask, when he had a female friend who loved him more unreservedly that any before her, and who had placed her life entirely at the service of his needs? And what does he mean when he says that he will soon have no more books? His note sounds positively hysterical.

Yet Ninon had one weapon that neither Maria Bernoulli nor Ruth Wenger had at their disposal. Primarily she put herself entirely at the service of Hesse's requirements—and his moods—because it was first and foremost the author Hermann Hesse whom she loved, even when Hermann Hesse the man hurt her feelings, as in the unpleasant business with the books. However, such things did not make her abandon her single-minded mission, and she refused to be broken by his boundless egotism. Her response was to construct defensive walls of silence around herself, including in the matter noted above. She simply failed to give any response to his house letter and remained invisible. That only made the choleric Hesse even more furious. Another letter followed, the contents of which sounded no less unjust:

> Dear Ninon, it's a great pity that you are making a matter of principle out of the fact that I believe I have a right to dispose of my own books as I see fit, and measuring my love for you by the degree of "couldn't-care-lessness" that I am prepared to show regarding my library and my work. . . . If you had been a guest of Stifter's or staying in the Rose House in his novel "Indian Summer" or in any number of other houses where books are held in some regard, you would run up against the same outlook, namely that a friendly willingness to lend books out should not be equated with a total abandonment of all order.[16]

Hesse was making it clear that Ninon did not have equal rights to make free with his library just because she was living in the same house. She was a *guest* in his house as far as he was concerned, and if he saw fit to lend her a book, it would only be at her specific request and even then only reluctantly—for nothing was so dear to him as his books. Hesse had no intention of sharing his life, and for all his agitation, he chose his words carefully here. They were not living together, but side by side—and so it would remain. Ninon had long understood this principle. And the enormous feeling of euphoria she felt at now actually being near the author and man she so adored swiftly turned to one of great despair: "I know that nothing belongs to me." When a woman like her said such a thing, she did not simply mean material possessions.

In January 1928 Hesse and Ninon traveled together to the mountain resort of Arosa. Ninon regarded it as her success that, after eleven years in which he had taken no winter vacation, she had managed to persuade him to go on this trip. For Hesse had become extremely contrary: he had less and less tolerance for the business of packing suitcases, train journeys, and staying in hotels—he simply lacked the excess of energy that was required for such things. At least, that was his customary excuse for his inertia.

Accordingly, he would later write about this first skiing holiday in a long while that everything had begun very badly in Arosa, just as he had feared: he had heart murmurs and a mild fever and felt very agitated. But after a short while, he went on, these symptoms had abated and he had started to ski again like a young man. It was undoubtedly from this second phase of their stay in Arosa that a photograph has survived, showing Hesse wearing sunglasses, ski boots, and a hat and sitting on a bench, filling the frame in such a patriarchal and contented manner that Ninon is squashed into a narrow strip at the edge of the photo. She gazes out at the camera with an ambiguous expression that was typical of her: half offended because Hesse treated her like a secretary, but also half contented that she had succeeded in getting him there in the first place.

And it was as his secretary that Hesse would introduce Ninon to his two sisters when they journeyed on to Swabia after the ski trip. This was a grand tour that would take them first to Blaubeuren, Maulbronn, Göppingen and Calw (the places of his childhood) and on through Weimar to Berlin, the metropolis that Hesse so detested. In the capital he went to see the horse races at Karlshorst, an event that so thoroughly bored him that he would write the next day: "I have forgotten everything that happened yesterday."[17]

Hesse on a skiing trip to Arosa with Ninon Dolbin and Gottfried Bermann Fischer in January 1928

By that time Ninon had already taken a train alone to Paris, via Amsterdam—while Hesse flew back from Berlin to Stuttgart with Lufthansa. She wrote to him from the French capital about visiting museums, going to concerts, and strolling about the streets and spending time in cafés; meanwhile, he was sitting in Zurich and missing her more as a secretary than as a lover. In a letter of April 14, he magnanimously and somewhat condescendingly conceded to her that she was of course allowed to go on such a trip on her own:

> It's only natural and proper that you're spending some time away, and that you will continue to go away every now and then in order to keep your life in shape and not lose yourself here with me, and I'm pleased that you're enjoying Paris and other places and will presently come back here to be around me. . . . I often find myself missing you, that's only natural, and you've also taken away my eyes, which would otherwise have read so many letters and books for me, which I must now try and read for myself with the help of Fräulein Kaegi's spectacles.[18]

That doesn't exactly sound like a declaration of love, and indeed any such declarations that were made in this strange alliance were all on Ninon's side. Hesse, by contrast, celebrated his solitude, and it remained unclear, no doubt quite deliberately so, whether Ninon should also feel included within this: "But what I often missed recently, and continue to miss, are contemplation and quiet, a good atmosphere for working and withdrawal from the world."[19] Anyone else would have thanked Ninon, for she had been happy to accompany him on his trip in the rather demeaning role of secretary, but not Hesse. He simply took the view: thank goodness it's finally all over, it was terribly nerve-wracking. If one takes another look at that photograph taken in Arosa a few weeks before, it tells a quite different story: Hesse is sitting contentedly next to Ninon, not *with* her. The thing that he lacked was the slightest ability to see a woman as a friend; for him, there were only fleeting love interests and of course the all-determining image of his mother. He wrote some remarkable things on this subject, which he had never before expressed so forthrightly, in the work *Narcissus and Goldmund,* which he was working on at this time.

Ninon was ready to make sacrifices, but she was not helpless. Alongside silence, she also had another weapon she deployed to ward off Hesse's gloomy ill-temper: a brilliant and witty turn of phrase, delivered with understated or obvious irony. Hesse was deeply impressed by this propensity of hers. For it was not just he who was intent on preserving distance in proximity; Ninon wanted to do so too. And so, over time, she adopted a playful tone when reacting to his repeated reproaches that she had disordered his library, with a "house letter," say, which she couched in terms of a formal contract: "Ninon takes the liberty of inquiring whether she might take the following books with her to Zurich: 1) Wells's 'A Short History of the World,' vols. 2 and 3, 2) Freud's 'Civilization and Its Discontents,' 3) Kafka's 'The Great Wall of China.' She asks that any refusal be put in writing, should Hermann not wish to lend her the books; a simple 'no' will suffice. Hermann may say or write 'yes' as he prefers."[20] In responding in this way, she channeled Hesse's neurotic resistance into a kind of game—and in such circumstances even Hesse found it hard to refuse.

Ninon had read all of the books Hesse had written, and knew them almost by heart, including *Steppenwolf,* and was well aware of the biographical kernel of his writing. She came to live with him in order to help him, to bring some happiness into his life, which he was always complaining had become an almost unbearable burden. But she was shocked to discover that Hesse did not want to be saved and put up stiff resistance to any interference in his life. She was there for him around the clock, at his beck and call—and yet he still persisted in claiming that his life was a living hell.

However, his description of his winter quarters in Zurich in December 1928 did not sound remotely hellish: "My life here is quite quiet and tucked-away. I get up at around 10 A.M., sit reading my correspondence until 2, when my lunch is brought to me, and later Ninon comes to see me and reads to me for two or three hours, then in the evening I eat alone once more at home—yoghurt and a banana—and if possible do a bit more work."[21] That must have been an arduous task for Ninon, having to read to Hesse for several hours a day—whenever Hesse read his poems out in public on a few occasions every year, he was exhausted for days afterward.

Hesse's Third Marriage and the Move to Casa Rossa

> I have often said so: a writer is in many ways the least demanding creature on Earth, but then again in other regards he requires many things and would much sooner die than do without them.
>
> —Hermann Hesse, "Wahlheimat" (Adopted home)

For all his complaints, Hesse spent twelve—extremely productive—years living at Casa Camuzzi, the final four of these living simultaneously together and apart from Ninon, and within calling distance of her. For they occupied separate apartments in the building. Hesse lived upstairs in the right wing of the house, while Ninon's quarters were on the ground floor, in the left wing, where it was cold, dark, and damp—a far less salubrious place to live than Hesse's admittedly unheated but certainly sunny apartment.

In 1930, after acting as the writer's servant and secretary, Ninon thought the time was ripe for her to insist that Hermann Hesse marry her. As things stood, she wrote to him, the only formal sign that a couple were an item was marriage—this appeal to duty and the proper order of things sounded like Hesse's mother. Ninon knew that a merely insistence on bourgeois convention would not cut much ice with Hesse, so she allowed him a degree of inner latitude in the marriage arrangement that she was demanding: "It need not mean anything or change anything between us. It's all about how we appear to the outside world. After all, we're not living on the Galapagos Islands, and here my position in the world is all wrong."[22] Otherwise how could she face Katia Mann, who had also for many years acted as secretary for her husband Thomas, but who when she stopped performing her public role at the end of the day could revert to her wholly private position as his wife? Hesse recognized that this situation was undignified for Ninon in the long term—especially when they were no longer living in separate apartments in Casa Camuzzi but had moved in together into the newly built Casa Rossa. There too, although there would be as much distance as possible between them, with each keeping to him- or herself when they wanted to, the fact remained that they would still appear in public as a couple. Hesse was skeptical, knowing what marriage meant and also well aware that in his past two attempts at wedlock he had cut anything but an ideal figure. So, should he go through it all again? There is no record of Hesse's reply to Ninon's demand that he marry her; all we know is that not long afterward Ninon wrote to Fred Dolbin to inform him that the subject of her and Hesse was now off the table.

Yet in spite of that, they did indeed get married the following year. What had prompted this change of heart in Hesse? The event went hand in hand with the construction of the new house, Casa Rossa. Left to his own devices, Hesse believed, he would never have even attempted this move—he had grown accustomed to the arrangement of spending the winter in Zurich and the summer in Casa Camuzzi, and in between going to Baden for a rest cure.

He had felt very much at home in Casa Camuzzi; it was a fairy-tale-like palazzo that truly suited him. However, he received an offer that he could not refuse:

> We were sitting in the "Arch" in Zurich one spring evening in 1930 and chatting, and the subject turned to houses and building, and there was mention of that occasional yearning I felt to own my own place. At this, my friend B. suddenly burst out laughing and announced: "Well, you

The Casa Rossa in Montagnola

shall have your precious house!"—I took this to be a joke on his part, the kind of thing one says over a glass or two of wine. But it turns out he was serious, and the house that we playfully dreamed of back then is now a reality, in all its great size and beauty, and it's mine to use for the rest of my life.[23]

It was Hesse's friend and patron H. C. Bodmer who had the house built to the writer's specification and then placed it at his disposal. He even wanted to donate it to him outright, but Hesse refused. As usual on such occasions as moving into a new house, Hesse was absent when the time came to take occupancy. Ninon and Hesse's son Martin dealt with all the practical arrangements.

Bodmer's negotiations to purchase the 11,000 square-meter south-facing plot of land with a view across Lake Lugano as far as Porlezza went on for months. Already fearing the worst, Ninon wrote on June 3, 1930, to Emmy Hennings from her clammy and dark ground-floor dwelling in Casa Camuzzi to tell her, "So, it looks like I'll be staying in my moldy castle after all, and the fungus will start growing on my body."[24]

But when Ninon set her sights on something, wheels were set in motion: plans were drafted and rejected, with Ninon project-managing everything and ensuring with an eagle eye that what was drawn on the blue-prints actually took real shape on the extensive building lot.

In the meantime Hesse had parried a second attempt by Ninon to get him to marry her; this time, we do have a record of his reply. He was alarmed at the prospect of moving into the new house, and especially the increasing inevitability of having to marry Ninon. In the summer of 1931 he wrote to her: "I need a space within myself where I can be completely alone, and where no one and nothing else may enter. Your questions threaten that space. You are swifter and cleverer than me in asking and expressing things and in setting out your innermost feelings in clear intel-lectual terms. I am much slower and more ponderous in that regard; in addition to my life, I also have to somehow find a way of saving my writing from impending chaos. Several times recently you have disturbed the natural tempo in which my soul exists."[25]

In June 1931 Ninon asked Fred Dolbin for a divorce, which was duly granted in September. In the fall Hesse then reluctantly married her—or rather, she married him. The pressure she had exerted on him had simply become too great. H. C. Bodmer, his wife, and Katia Mann had urged Ninon to persist and to refuse to continue her unworthy—though for Hesse clearly convenient—existence as the writer's secretary in the new house. And so, before Hesse set off that year on a rest cure in Baden for his rheu-matism, he noted that the wedding would "take place here in a civil service at the registry office, with no additional celebrations."[26]

Ultimately, then, he had felt obliged to legalize his relationship with Ninon, who had become indispensable in many areas of his life: reading to him for several hours in the evening, proofreading manuscripts, domestic chores, and fending off visitors, to name just a few. When all was said and done, he was getting older and more frail, and even though he made no effort to accommodate himself to Ninon's needs and desires, he still wanted to recompense her for always being there for him.

And it was roughly in this vein that Hesse also informed his friends that he was planning to marry for the third time—or, as he put it, "let himself be ensnared again by a woman." Ultimately, this woman, who was also "very nice" (Hesse had used the same phrase—*ganz lieb*—of Mia, and said something very similar about Ruth, too; he evidently couldn't think of much more to say about his wives), had made herself so useful in organizing the new house. Hesse rewarded her for her diligence by marrying her—and then proceeded to keep her at arm's length as before.

This was almost as Rilke had imagined things when he married Clara Westhoff (a grave mistake, as Rilke must have intuited from the outset) and saw the ultimate aim of their life together as being that one should act as the guardian of the other's privacy. In Rilke's case this unworldly construct, which derived from the spirit of a Romantic artistic ideal, was over and done with within a year, whereas Hesse and his wife spent the next few decades living according to this scheme. Could this have acted as a role model for pronouncedly eccentric characters? Certainly, Jean-Paul Sartre and Simone de Beauvoir followed this template, living in two separate apartments.

And the new house did indeed contain two apartments; that was Ninon's concession to Hesse's accustomed lifestyle. There were times, which could be quite protracted, when he did not want to see anybody. She accepted that, and the house was built accordingly. There were two entrances and two staircases, and the two apartments were linked only by a single door between the bathrooms in the upper story. This area was off-limits to anyone else, and only Ninon was allowed to cross over and bring him his mail—punctually—every morning. He was served breakfast at nine o'clock by a maid, although she had to make sure beforehand that he was in the bath and not in his room when she entered it—Hesse was especially averse to seeing anyone straight after getting up each morning.

All the utility rooms, such as the kitchen, the dining room, the guest rooms, and the library where Hesse had Ninon read to him in the evenings and listened to music, were in Ninon's part of the house. From there she organized the entire household—not without a certain resistance, for she had, after all, studied art history and was not just a housekeeper—with great determination and meticulous attention to punctuality and cleanliness around the house. The domestic staff feared her. Several of them quit immediately after taking up their posts, because Ninon treated servants with the same rod of iron as had been customary in grand bourgeois households in Czernowitz during her childhood around the turn of the century. She refused outright to have vacuum cleaners or any other labor-saving devices in her house, which would have been entirely suitable in such a large building. Brooms had to have short handles, so anyone using them was forced to bend down to get a better view of the dirt that needed sweeping.

*   *   *

Casa Rossa therefore became a castle, with Ninon in charge of the draw-bridge. Even old friends came to realize this, as she set out the times when they were allowed to visit. She kept a close eye on anyone who came to talk to Hesse, and if the conversation seemed in her opinion to be veering in the wrong direction, she would bring it back on track. Several guests were greatly angered by this, seeing Ninon as a Cerberus guarding and dominating Hesse, albeit with his collusion. Yet the relationship between them wasn't as simple as that. Ninon had placed herself entirely at the disposal of Hesse and his neuroses. He remained her lord and master, whose moods she tolerated, whom she looked after, and whom she shielded from the outside world. And Hesse was content to let this happen; he realized that he had lived for far too long as the Steppenwolf, and now things around him should be more organized and comfortable. However, the key question was: Was this conducive to his work as a writer?

All anarchism and any dark, demonic element now seemed to have disappeared from his writing—anyone reading *The Glass Bead Game* can immediately sense this. The very fact that Hesse spent eleven years working on this novel—whereas his previous works had almost all been dashed off in short, ecstatic bursts of creative activity interspersed with periods of deep depression—speaks volumes about how his perception of himself had changed. He knew full well that the "Glass Bead Game," the quest for places of refuge for the spirit in profoundly unspiritual times, would be his last great theme. Anything that came after that, presuming there was anything at all, would be nothing but marginalia.

And what of Ninon, who had no wish to abandon her own interests, particularly in ancient Greek mythology, but found she had no time to pursue them? Katia Mann had advised her to take some time for her own pursuits and not to sacrifice everything to running the household. Ninon rhapsodized about Katia's support for her in a letter to Fred Dolbin: "I can take or leave Tommy [Thomas Mann]," she wrote there, rather condescendingly, but then continued: "I have grown so fond of Frau Mann—I cannot tell you how delightful she is."[27]

At root, Ninon felt she had been forced into a corset of a false existence, something she would come to feel ever more keenly and find increasingly oppressive. This explained her growing sense of bitterness and her first thoughts of suicide, which arose after just a few years and which would keep recurring forever thereafter.

Hesse also found himself prey once more to his old depressions in Casa Rossa, and here too, as he had done several times before in his life, he was repeatedly assailed by thoughts of taking his own life.

Ninon was also beset by melancholy; she was oppressed by the memory of her sister Toka's suicide, by the death of her parents, and by living with Hesse, who lectured her yet who remained a god to her. A malevolent deity, perhaps? Ninon, who liked to compare herself to the Greek goddess Hera, could also be a malevolent deity herself. And so it was that two people who both in their own ways were trying to resist the destructive sides of themselves came to live together under one roof. It was a daily struggle, although they both attempted to encourage their playful side—with the games of *boccia* they played in the garden, for instance, for which Hesse organized proper competitions. On other occasions in the evening, when they had had enough of reading, they would play board games like Halma or Nine Men's Morris. They had no other choice: if they had not repeatedly transformed the deadly earnest and the great incompatibilities of their lives into play, their lives would have become pure hell.

And they succeeded—this union of two potential suicides would endure for over thirty years, and at crucial moments the one would be there as a support for the other.

Their move to the comfortable Casa Rossa, as a result of which he no longer needed to decamp to Zurich every time winter set in, made it unequivocally obvious: Hesse had by now become an old man. He would spend long hours sitting in the garden next to a small bonfire and watch the grey smoke rising up to the sky—he no longer felt the need to prove anything to the world, or to keep on turning out new books. He had found a settled abode—his last, as he well knew—and the time of searching and restless wandering was now over. He immersed himself in the tranquility of his garden and appeared to confirm that cliché that he was a straw-hat wearer who no longer cared about what was going on in the world. And yet this period of untroubled repose and refuge would turn out to be very brief—barely two years, from their taking occupancy of the house in 1931 to the Nazis' accession to power in Germany in 1933. In time, the consequences of this catastrophe would also shake the tranquil life of Casa Rossa to its foundations.

★   ★   ★

So, Hesse was now married for the third time and was living in a beautiful house with a fine garden. An idyll? At this juncture, the eighteen-year age gap between himself and Ninon began to make itself felt. In intellectual terms Hesse was disinclined to take seriously his young wife, who had, he must have thought to himself from time to time, insisted on throwing herself at him like a literary "groupie." As a result, he continued to lecture her from on high and to find constant fault with her.

Yet the real tragedy of this was that, if Hesse had ever been able to take a woman seriously intellectually, then Ninon Dolbin would have been an ideal candidate. But this he could never do, and nor would he learn to do so over the thirty-five years they lived with one another. The simple truth was that Hesse never thought of women as potential friends whose intellect would count for something with him. The sole exception was Emmy Hennings, whose intellectual ingenuity he admired, just as he also felt an affinity to the criminal turmoil in her past life, including her prison sentence for robbing a client while working as a prostitute. His tendency toward most women—including his three wives—was to dominate them from a distance, or even worse, as Ninon Dolbin's biographer Gisela Kleine has written, to hurt them "as though from some inner compulsion."[28] In this matter Ralph Freedman was wrong when he claimed that, except for his two sisters, toward whom he behaved like an overbearing head of the family, Hesse had never "taken a domineering role"[29] toward women, including his three wives. That said, it was his fundamentally neurotic and irritable personality that impelled him to do so rather than any need to openly assert a "leadership role."

At certain phases in their relationship, Hesse tormented Ninon with a kind of psychological terror: accusations, intemperate self-accusations that then turned into endless reproaches of her, and little everyday irritations that were blown up into abstruse generalizations. All this points to a fundamentally psychopathic streak latent within Hesse's character.

In any event, he was fully aware that he was just as incapable of constantly being around other people as they were of being around him. Hadn't he also warned Ninon about this side of his personality? He had also thought of every conceivable safety mechanism to try to maintain some distance between them. After a short time together, it became clear that Ninon was deeply wounded by the way he treated her.

On moving from Vienna to Montagnola, she abruptly broke off writing her doctoral dissertation—after seven years' work on it. Hesse told her: "Just drop that rubbish and don't bother about it anymore!" And Ninon's first thought had been to rejoice that she was finally free of the task. But she also abandoned all her own attempts at writing—as she did with all her manuscripts henceforth. The only important things now were Hesse's texts. Hers were, and would remain, nothing but "rubbish" that she didn't need to bother about any longer. And why would she anyway? The answer was too self-evident to need saying. But in her heart of hearts Ninon knew it had been a mistake to renounce her own ambitions, and thereafter—right up to the year Hesse died and beyond, until her own death—she would take every available opportunity to go off on her own on study trips abroad to Italy and Greece. And Hesse learned to let her have a free hand in this.

Ninon could have been his daughter, but in actual fact became a substitute mother who looked after him and patiently put up with all his moods. Before long she suddenly began to appear plump and aging on photos, just as Mia had done. She aged quickly at his side. Yet for all that, Ninon managed to carve out an important position for herself in Hesse's everyday life: that of a moderator of the outside world. Some people maintained that Ninon often made it impossible for them to have a real conversation with Hesse, because she always interposed herself, whereas others took the view that she frequently defused his often combative attitude toward visitors. At such times, despite being eighteen years his junior, she would suddenly come across as far more mature than him.

Claims that the inhospitable Hermann Hesse possessed a "genius for friendship" relate first and foremost to his books, not to relationships with real people. Little wonder that he could become extremely irritable when anything unforeseen disturbed his quiet dialogue with books: namely, a third party who was just as passionate a reader as he was—Ninon! Hesse was beside himself with rage: anyone who dared to make free with his books without permission would feel the full weight of his righteous anger. But the fact that Ninon removed books from his shelves that he would later look for in vain would often have a quite plausible reason that should actually have made him more conciliatory toward her: she was planning to read them aloud to him because of his bad eyes. She had also increasingly taken to reading books that Hesse had been sent to review, digesting the contents and giving him a summary of what she thought of them. In 1929 she started to keep a record of all the books she had read to Hesse on long evenings spent together: they totaled some 1,500! One is reminded of Nietzsche, who, thanks to an eye condition similar to Hesse's, expressed a wish to have a "reading machine"—in the shape of his companion Lou Andreas-Salomé, whom he was even prepared to marry if need be.

A Reader's Passion: The Library of World Literature

> There are no Hundred Best Books or Authors! There is no such thing as generally applicable, irrefutably correct literary criticism!
>
> —Hermann Hesse, "Dealing with Books"[30]

Hesse's 1929 essay "A Library of World Literature" is, as one might expect, not a canon or a list of those books that everyone ought to know. Hesse showed himself here to be a passionate reader, and a lover of any book that helped people lead more meaningful lives. Yet all persons had to discover for themselves what that actually entailed; there was no ready-made instruction manual one could follow.

This was of a piece with Hermann Hesse's general attitude to the written word. In his eyes it was a magic spell, which opened up new worlds both externally and internally. The written word was a spiritual legacy of that kind of mysticism that the Pietism of his childhood had also dealt in. To Hesse, it appeared completely without question that every word should have its own reality. And a poetic word was the antithesis of a word that was merely used as an instrument for achieving particular ends, because it already contained its own end within itself. Here, Hesse was defining something that would come to preoccupy him in the ensuing phase of his writing career: the ideal of education within an increasingly "monotonized world" (Stefan Zweig). Accordingly, this essay, which has the characteristics of a manifesto, commences as follows: "True education is not education for any purpose; like all striving for perfection, it carries its purpose within itself. Just as striving to attain physical strength, dexterity, and beauty serves no ultimate end, such as making us rich, famous, and powerful, but instead is its own reward . . . so the striving after 'education,' that is, after improvement of the mind, is not an arduous journey toward any definite goal, but an exhilarating and fortifying broadening of our consciousness, an enrichment of our potential for life and happiness."[31] In this respect, "true education" was, Hesse maintained, always both "a fulfillment and a stimulus."

Regarding books—specifically, their life-enhancing capacity and their ability to build bridges between yesterday, today, and tomorrow, the inner and outer life, the real and the ideal, and the body and the mind—Hesse became an evangelist of a secular spirit, which nevertheless still had a transcendental spark in it, and which in his own finite existence touched upon a little piece of immortality. He was not concerned with reality but with the mystery of life, which consisted at one and the same time of nature and spirit. This inherent contradiction culminated, at best, in the growth of civilization, at worst in barbarism. It was necessary to look the danger of the self-destruction of the individual and of the whole squarely in the face; such a danger was part and parcel of the claim to truth. That was why this could not be achieved simply through avid reading—the decisive factor was always real life.

Hesse, the passionate reader who could not live without books, nevertheless harbored just as large a degree of skepticism toward the written word. For everything that was written ran the risk of having no life thereafter, of being nothing but an assemblage of dead letters. It was his Franciscan sympathy for poverty, including poverty of the spirit, that led him to see books differently than the educated bourgeois elite did. Books were alive like trees or clouds in the sky, they were our companions on that journey that ended inevitably in our death. But the key question was, Do we perish in our entirety, or does something of us live on—perhaps in the written word? For Hesse, true education, of which proper reading formed an integral part, must lead to inner growth. But proper reading is the same as proper living: one can only learn this art if one does not imagine one knows what it consists of in advance. One must always be open to new discovery, like a wayfarer who cannot see his goal but instead carries it within himself.

That was also Hesse's basic attitude where books and reading were concerned. What a person reads, or how much he or she reads, is only of secondary importance. The only really important thing was that one should always begin reading with a genuine sense of expectation, with complete immersion in the magic of the moment.

In espousing such a—thoroughly Goethean—belief, he knew that this already made him an outsider who would be ridiculed as just another late Romantic. And yet it remained an article of faith for Hesse that without books' capacity to make us relive our past lives and engage in new experiences, we would be all the poorer.

The conclusion of "A Library of World Literature" is dedicated to "The Secret Life of the Christian Middle Ages." In this, Hesse was aligning himself with what Hugo Ball had posited in his work *Byzantine Christianity:* there is a hidden body of knowledge that is accessible only to the initiated. Hesse had already hinted at this in *Steppenwolf,* when he wrote that the Magic Theater was "not for everyone." In *Journey to the East* and *The Glass Bead Game,* he would repeatedly pose the question about the monastic principle and being one of the chosen few. In the essay "The Magic of the Book" (1930), he stated his position plainly:

> And so we see: although the intellect has apparently been democratized and the intellectual treasures of an era seemingly belong to every contemporary who has learned to read, in reality everything important happens in secret and undetected, and there appears to be a clandestine priesthood or cabal living underground, which from its anonymous seclusion directs people's spiritual destinies, which disguises its emissaries, who have for generations been equipped with power and explosives, and sends them up to Earth with no legitimacy whatsoever, and ensures that public opinion, which is so pleased with its state of enlightenment, never notices any of the magic that is going on right under their very noses.[32]

Monasteries and religious orders were the places where this spirit was handed down through generations, in and for the world, but hidden from the eyes of the majority of people. According to Hesse, it was only through the agency of the chosen few, to whom words spoke in a special way—not in the sense of conveying information, but through their rhythm, their sound, and their music—that readers were able to become themselves. Whether a person who reads experiences a world that is hidden from others who do not read is already settled in the first encounters with the written word: "The child proud of learning its alphabet will soon master reading a verse or a saying, and then its first little story, and its first fairy tale, and while those who are not destined to be readers soon content themselves to practicing their ability to read on the news and financial sections of their newspapers, the select few remain forever bewitched by the strange miracle of letters and the words (each of which was once a charm, a magic formula)."[33]

Hesse saw writing as an elemental form of expression. Life wrote itself into our faces. And nature could also write, according to Hesse, achieving this feat without the use of any pen, brush, paper, or vellum: "The wind writes, as do the sea, the river, and the stream, animals write, and the Earth writes, for instance when it wrinkles its brow somewhere and in doing so blocks the course of a river or sweeps away a mountain or a town."[34]

This conception of writing had ramifications for the text that any author wrote and the books that he published. Things themselves were encapsulated within words, they were so to speak captured in their naming and endowed with a magic which then proceeded to transform them into something that could not be found in real life, but which had to be invented. Not only the speaker or the writer but also the person being addressed recognized themselves in words as in a mirror, but it was a magic mirror. And in his dealings with words, Hesse showed himself throughout his life to be that *Lauscher*—that eavesdropper—to whom he gave his own Christian name in his eponymous early tale. Hesse listened intently to the natural sound of words, because it was in their nature to impart something—though not everyone could hear it. And so for the author this interplay between contemplation and action became a matter requiring immense exertion, a fact that was rarely recognized from the outside: formulating ideas in words was hard work, because every word that was placed differently also changed the reality that the words carried within themselves. Gottfried Benn addressed this very subject in one of his finest poems, "Satzbau" ("Sentence Construction"). And Hesse himself noted in his 1929 essay "Reading in Bed":

> My acquaintances and reviewers of my books are almost all of the opinion that I am a man without principles. These less than perspicacious people have inferred from some observations and some passages or other in my writings that I lead a free and easy life with no strings attached. Because I like to lie abed for a long time in the mornings, because I permit myself

the odd bottle of wine amid all the hardships of life, because I don't receive visitors or pay calls on anyone else, and from various other trivialities, these poor observers conclude that I must be a weak, lazy, and dissolute person who has no backbone, who is unable to commit to anything, and who leads an immoral, rootless existence. Yet they only say this because they find it irritating and presumptuous that I happily embrace my habits and vices and that I don't try to hush them up. If I wanted to pretend that mine was a well-ordered and bourgeois way of life (which would be an easy thing to do), if I wanted to stick an eau-de-Cologne label on the wine bottle, and if, rather than tell my visitors that they were a downright nuisance, I was to make out that I wasn't at home, in short if I was prepared to live a life of pretense and lies, my reputation would be sky-high and my first honorary doctorate would no doubt soon be conferred on me.[35]

Everyone loves with the words, the sentences, and finally the books that suit their lifestyle. And Hesse's word-perambulations closely accord with his journey through life to a place of refuge from the world where he, the notorious outsider, could feel safe from the intrusions of the contemporary age. Not because he did not take that age seriously, but precisely because he did—in this, he was like the monks with their eternally identical rituals, which were ultimately all just a hymn in praise of the gift of the spirit-filled moment in the face of eternity.

In consequence, his relationship to his profession as a writer was just as distanced as his relationship to his environment and also to himself. Should one live from words? Apart from his early years, Rilke largely absented himself from the daily journalistic routine. By contrast, throughout his life Hesse wrote book reviews and short features for newspapers. He therefore knew what he was talking about when he criticized the "journalistic age" in *The Glass Bead Game*. Yet his feeling of distance, the need he felt to stay silent and to keep his views on what he had read, seen, or thought about to himself without immediately firing them off into the public domain in exchange for a fee, increased with every year that passed. He preferred to express this wish in an offhand and matter-of-fact way (after all, being an author was a way of life!) rather than load it with pathos, but even so what lay at the heart of this was a concern for the nature of the word and a desire to protect it from devaluation through inflationary overuse. The following passage from "The Magic of the Book" shows Hesse at his most confessional, laying bare his role as writer:

Life is short, and in the hereafter, no one will be quizzed on the number of books they managed to write. For that reason it is foolish and harmful to waste time on worthless reading. In saying that, I am not even thinking primarily of bad books, but above all the quality of the act of reading itself. As with every step and every breath we take in life, we should expect something from reading, and we should expend some energy in order to reap redoubled energy in return, in other words one should lose oneself in order to find oneself again all the more surely.[36]

Making a living in language and from language was also associated with asceticism and sacrifice. The soil needed to remain fertile, and bad husbandry had irreparable consequences:

We should approach books not like anxious schoolboys approaching forbidding masters, or indeed like wastrels approaching a bottle of liquor, but instead like mountaineers nearing the Alps and warriors entering the arsenal, not as refugees or people jaded with life but in the way that good-hearted people would approach friends and helpers. If only things were like this and happened this way, barely more than a tenth of what is now read would be read, and we would all be ten times happier and richer. And if it led to our books no longer being bought, and if that in turn led to us authors writing ten times less, that would by no means be a bad thing for the world. For things are no better where writing is concerned than they are with reading.[37]

Notwithstanding the fact that Hesse worked time and again for newspapers and sold feature articles and book reviews as often as he could to papers like the *Neue Zürcher Zeitung* because his income in Swiss francs was otherwise so meager, he himself admitted that he hardly ever read newspapers, except for when he was on trips—say, in hotels, when there was nothing else at hand, as described in the virtuosic little text "Reading in Bed." A paper like that, picked up just once a year, must have seemed very odd. The kinds of reports they thought important, and the things they expended all that newsprint on!

Whenever Hesse broaches the topic of writing, one can immediately sense the inner tension, and the immense energy that only temporarily discharges in wonderfully trenchant formulations. Over the course of the years, he produced a whole series of texts on the subject of writing, books, and libraries. Every one of them seems old-fashioned and written from a position that appeared strikingly outmoded from a contemporary perspective and precisely for that reason of a vibrant intensity. That was Hesse's actual theme: his spirit was rejuvenated over and over again by the magic of the word. So where would all this writing, reading, continuing to write once more in order to be read again ultimately lead? Hesse's response to this question is decidedly that of the mystic of language, a man who knew the works of Gustav Landauer and Fritz Mauthner as thoroughly as those of Schopenhauer and Eastern philosophy, and it is no coincidence that he sounds as crazy as Mozart in the Magic Theater when he writes the following about the final and highest stage of reading—and of wisdom: "That's the way it is: the reader of the final stage isn't actually a reader any more. He scorns Goethe. He has no need of Shakespeare. The reader of the final stage no longer reads a thing. What's the point of books when he now has the whole world within himself?"[38]

Hesse the autodidact, who had acquired all his learning from books that he had chosen himself (in this, he was in good company with other important authors, such as Thomas Mann), knew that anyone who motivates themselves to read, reads differently than someone who is simply working their way through a program of compulsory reading. The self-starting reader seeks answers for his life in all the books he reads, and he expects every new volume he embarks on to open up fresh horizons. Books to him are the food of life, one might even say an essential means of survival. Yet alongside this function they also have an intrinsic value as beautiful objects with which he likes to surround himself. He recommends certain books (and follows his own recommendations in stocking his own library), at the very least identifying favorite books that he will read over and over, and will have rebound several times—or, should he possess an aptitude for handicraft (as Hesse did), rebinding them himself. In this way, the book collector becomes a co-creator.

The best way of organizing a library and how to handle antiquarian volumes were themes that Hesse was fond of airing his views on—repeatedly, and far into his old age. For one thing may be said about him with certainty: he was a thoroughgoing bibliophile, although this never caused him to lose himself in a world of paper. To him, books were the substrate of human existence, the best of all conceivable domestic companions, whose presence was never disruptive, in marked contrast to those frequently importunate visitors who deprived him of precious time in which he could have been reading and writing. For Hesse, therefore, a library was ultimately also a piece of nature: it grew of its own accord, and its owner was called upon to do little more than look after it and live in it. Thus, when he wrote about the organizing principle of a library that embodied the antithesis of any kind of externally imposed set of rules, he was actually referring to his own collection of books: "I know of a private library containing several thousand volumes, which are organized neither alphabetically nor chronologically, but where the owner has instead has determined the juxtaposition and hierarchy of all the books according to purely personal preference—and yet so organically has the whole place been arranged and so sovereign an overview does he have of his entire collection that he can effortlessly pick out any particular tome that someone has asked him to lend them."[39]

A Biography of the Soul, or Kitsch on Demand to Suit a German Pipe-Smoker's Sensibility? *Narcissus and Goldmund*

How was Hesse to proceed in his writing after producing a work like *Steppenwolf*? Its concentration of disgust with the world, on the one hand, and, on the other, of euphoria at overcoming the world had run its full course and could have no sequel. A new book required a new start, and it had to be radically different from *Steppenwolf;* it needed to surprise the reader—and yet still be instantly identifiable as a book by Hesse. Hesse wrote *Narcissus and Goldmund* under the direct influence of Hugo Ball's death. He could still feel the ripples of the aftershock of this terrible event. Just a few months earlier, Ball had still been working on his biography of Hesse.

In his later years Ball had been a strict ascetic, one of the few German intellectuals worthy of the name. Hesse had repeated occasion to evoke the memory of his friend—for instance, in a letter to his former classmate Otto Hartmann, who had made disparaging remarks about Hugo Ball's book on Hesse:

> It's a pity that you were disappointed by Ball's book, at least in part. That's just the way it is, and I can't deny that I find it hurtful. But why am I so pained? Not because Ball was some oversensitive child—in fact he was a very brave and upright person who wasn't remotely given to feeling sorry

for himself—but because he was one of the classic examples of the fate that befalls most of the responsible, genuine intellects among the German people. They are ignored, and left to die in penury while the only people who are accepted are those who can't hack starvation and who dutifully return to the fold to work as editors and professors or in some other respectable role.[40]

This raised the problem of maintaining friendships in light of the opposition of spirit and sensuality, and reason and impulse. Thomas Mann spoke of a "secret of identity" in regard to this—by which he meant the mass of contradictions that form the basis of every creative achievement. In his new work, Hesse was not concerned—or concerned only coincidentally—with sustaining a plot. *Narcissus and Goldmund* was a experimental setup investigating the oppositions of impulse and asceticism and reason and sensuality and showing the contradictory way of life of the spiritual individual, who struggles with his work and hopes that it will live on after his death.

The Eros principle within the creative individual has something universal about it, it cannot be restricted to the relationship between man and woman—especially not within the framework of the institution of marriage. Narcissus and Goldmund can in turn be understood as two sides of a contradictory whole. If one bears in mind that Hesse's main concern (as in *Steppenwolf*) is with a story that displayed out internally rather than externally, then Narcissus and his alter ego, Goldmund, are clearly facets of the personality of the author himself.

If one had to give this book a heading summing up its content, then perhaps it would be this: "How Ought One to Live?" The book itself provides the answer: by constantly striving afresh to reconcile these two sides of the contradiction and to bring them into a friendly relationship with one another. "Friendship" in this context means first and foremost harmonizing one's own extremes—through the very act of creativity itself. Yet in Hesse the question also constantly arises of the possibilities of friendship between two people who are seriously grappling with this question of how to live properly. This was a form of spiritual affinity, for sure, but what role did eroticism play in it?

When one considers how hard Hesse found it to take women seriously in intellectual and artistic terms, then one becomes aware that a whole series of unconscious impressions were at work here, which virtually compulsively steered Hesse in the direction of men whenever he spoke in terms of friendship. And if one now relates this question of Eros to friendship between men (or also to the relationship between teacher and pupil), one comes very close—as Hesse was fully aware—to identifying a homo-erotic self-image. Yet that was precisely what Hesse was keen to avoid suggesting. For him, there existed an eroticism of friendship that he was intent on preserving from any such facile, shorthand interpretation. Not because he shied away from the sexual sphere—indeed, he had explic-itly treated this topic several times—but because he regarded this kind of unconsidered explanation as a misunderstanding that obscured the true sources of creativity: "The idea that these friendships, just because they happen to be between men, are completely free of eroticism is a mistake. I am sexually 'normal' and have never had any physical love relationships with men, but to conclude from this that my friendships with them were totally un-erotic seems quite wrong to me. The case of Narcissus is particularly clear. To him, Goldmund does not just mean friendship and art, he also signifies love, sensual tenderness, and things desired and taboo."[41]

Narcissus is the strictly rational spirit and later abbot of the monastery at Mariabronn, while Goldmund is by contrast the restlessly wandering crea-ture of the senses who is forever seeking the love of women, and who later discovers the artist within himself. To use Nietzsche's terminology, this is a meeting of the Apollonian, formative principle with the Diony-sian, ecstatic principle. Two sides of the same coin, to be sure. But for that reason this dichotomy, which also exists between civilization and nature, appears no less difficult to reconcile. Or if it is at all reconcilable, then maybe only on a higher plane—namely, that of a spirit that does not take a hostile attitude toward the senses but instead sees them as a constituent element of itself? Must a person who thinks necessarily therefore cease to observe? Were ideas somehow exclusive of the image?

Hesse leads his reader to frame such questions. Goldmund returns from his wanderings around the world to the monastery from which he had once run away. He had spent his time moving from one woman to the next without ever really getting to essential truths. In his first attempts to express artistically what he had experienced on his travels, things that he had seen firsthand mingled with deeply hidden mental images that he had always carried within him (his mother!). From his experience of mass plague deaths, from pogroms of Jews through the murder of two people (in self-defense) by his own hand, to waiting for his execution—all of this flowed into the image of the Virgin Mary that he finally produced for the monastery. This stage also sees the emergence of the stark contradiction between Narcissus and Goldmund, and their conversations undergo a transformation that brings both of them to the state of self-awareness that they have been seeking from the beginning. This is a love, but one that, once it becomes universal, also entails death, indeed proves itself through death.

Narcissus recognizes himself in the figure of Goldmund, and vice versa—this is the "mystic union," the *unio mystica,* that Hesse has Narcissus explain to Goldmund: "If, instead of escaping into the world back then, you had become a thinker, you might have wreaked havoc. For you would have become a mystic. To put it succinctly and rather crudely, mystics are thinkers who cannot detach themselves from images, and who are therefore not thinkers at all. They are secret artists: poets without verse, painters without brushes, musicians without notes. There are some extremely gifted and noble minds among them, but they are all without exception unhappy men."[42] We may reasonably assume Hesse to be characterizing himself here: fated to be a hybrid of a thinker and a man of sensory pleasures—the artist, whose ultimate goal was not art but the living spirit, in other words has become nature.

In large parts, *Narcissus and Goldmund* is neither a story nor a novel: it is a treatise. This trait would subsequently come through even more strongly in *Journey to the East* and *The Glass Bead Game.*

The backdrop to the tale is medieval, though this is little more than stage scenery. Hesse gave his abbot Narcissus the unmistakable characteristics of his friend Hugo Ball, while modeling Goldmund on himself. The principal theme is what one might term "the communion of souls," and more broadly the spirit's potential within an unspiritual world. This internal subject matter makes the book a powerful read—however, its narrative quality is far inferior to anything that Hesse had written since *Demian.* This contradiction of strength and weakness haunts *Narcissus and Goldmund* to the present day. Yet one need only think of an incontestably important writer like Balzac, who was nonetheless capable of repeatedly writing, in novels such as *Le Peau de Chagrin* or *Père Goriot,* passages that are no better than the sort of thing one encounters in dime novels. This is an integral part of the mystery of being an author—those passages where one lays oneself open to charges of shallowness.

The stereotypical feel of chapter 8 of the book is especially off-putting. It describes Goldmund's arrival during his journey around the world—the sole purpose of which was to learn from women—at a castle inhabited by a knight and his two daughters, Lydia (aged eighteen) and Julie (sixteen). This is the occasion of that famous scene in which Goldmund goes to bed with both girls, but because both are haughty girls who are jealous of one another, he ends up as the dissatisfied third party. The narrative is very weak here, with descriptions of "imploring" looks of love, people "beaming" with contentment, their hearts "jumping for joy" or being "heavy in a lovely but painful way," and other such turns of phrase the author should have been embarrassed to write. Similarly, on both occasions when Goldmund kills a person, the description of the act descends into pure pulp fiction. Does Goldmund actually learn anything on this journey of his about women? Perhaps only that they all want to get intimate with him on the spot without wasting any words, for as long as he is young and handsome? And that they no longer desire him once the signs of his arduous wandering life begin to tell in his appearance—or more precisely, at the moment when something resembling a thought crosses his pretty face, which up until then was programmed to register nothing but lustful pleasure? Love is so simple, all you need to do is pay women a couple of empty compliments and they surrender. That had also been Hesse's experience at the round of masked balls in Zurich, while Harry Haller had similarly given himself over to pleasure in his own morose, unworldly way. But it was a different story with Goldmund, who is a direct descendant of the vagabond Knulp and Peter Camenzind, yet who this time does not renounce art in order to return to the hometown inn, or of Hans Giebenrath, the high-strung monastery pupil in *Beneath the Wheel;* likewise, Goldmund knows better than to drown himself.

The construct appeared so simple: in each of his fleeting love affairs, Goldmund is looking for the reflection of his mother, and even more the image of his great-grandmother Eva. This future sculptor intently studies people, especially women, and learns that cries of pleasure and the cries of people giving birth or dying all sound much like one another: archaic. Hesse was on the search for archetypes.

Goldmund completes his apprenticeship with Master Niklas, and feels he has an artistic calling, not like a master in the sense of someone with full mastery of a skilled trade, however, but as a kind of visionary. Hesse painted into Goldmund's features all his fear of false attachment, routine, and institutionalization. He had no time for fame and worthy positions.

One striking feature of *Narcissus and Goldmund,* which sold more than forty thousand copies in its first year of publication (though only sixteen in the Dutch translation!), is its affinity to death. Hesse positively revels in Baroque images of transience, and offers powerful portrayals of the plague and mass mortality. A pogrom of Jews is also described—it is an astonishing fact that *Narcissus and Goldmund* could still be purchased in Germany right up to 1941. For what Hesse pillories here as an outrage was official Nazi state policy.

After returning to the monastery—where he creates two final works and goes on one last, disagreeable excursion into the world of the senses before his death—Goldmund has a very revealing discussion with Narcissus. For the year 1930, this was a visionary passage:

"One question, Narcissus: did the monastery ever burn Jews?"

"Burn Jews? How could we? There are no Jews around here."

"Quite right. But tell me: would you have been capable of burning Jews if you'd had the chance? Can you imagine that as a possible scenario?"

"No, why should I do that? Do you take me for some kind of fanatic?"

"Don't get me wrong, Narcissus! I mean, can you conceive of a situation in which you would give the order for Jews to be killed or give your consent for it to happen? After all, so many dukes, mayors, bishops and other lords have issued such orders."

"Well, I would never give an order of that kind. But I can easily imagine a situation where I would have no choice but to look on helplessly while such an atrocity took place."

"So, you would suffer such a thing to happen?"

"Certainly, if I was powerless to prevent it. . . ."[43]

At which an agitated Goldmund exclaims that in that case the world is a living hell—to which Narcissus replies: "Certainly, the world is no different."

★   ★   ★

Leaving aside such scenes of violence, in its external form Hesse regarded this book as a kind of olive branch to the German "pipe-smoker's sensibility," which could read this work and lose itself in a sentimental reverie of the Middle Ages. But to see the book as nothing more than that would be a misunderstanding, as not only the passages describing the pogrom bear witness. For however thoroughly conventional the narrative form of the work, which often comes close to being trash literature, the internal complex of problems it treats is highly nuanced and uncompromisingly sharply delineated. Yet to Hesse's dismay, this aspect was scarcely noticed by reviewers and even the readers for the most part eagerly lapped up the truly banal outward plot, where Hesse not very inventively simply depicted a string of Goldmund's seductions of women.

What he really meant to show, however, was a never-ending Dance of Death. No sooner has something come into being than it is already on the road to decay. The oscillation between lust and apathy cannot save a person from the fate of annihilation toward which every human is heading. When Narcissus asks how art has benefited him, Goldmund replies: "It is the overcoming of the transitory. I saw that from the fool's play, the dance of death that is human existence, something survived and endured: works of art. They will undoubtedly perish some day too; they will burn or crumble or be smashed to pieces. Even so, they outlast many human lives, and form a silent empire of images and holy relics beyond the fleeting moment. To be part of that endeavor brings me happiness and solace because it almost succeeds in making the transitory eternal."[44]

Art between Eros and Thanatos, that it is the theme of *Narcissus and Goldmund,* along with the questing for a higher vantage point, so to speak, set above the simple run of natural events.

This novel saw the first appearance in Hesse's work of that particular concept of "spirit," which admittedly only Narcissus (the archetype of Josef Knecht in *The Glass Bead Game*) calls by that name; Goldmund, on the other hand, speaks of the "original image," by which he means his mother, whom he can only picture in his mind's eye as a distant, mysterious apparition. Here, Hesse was on the same wavelength as Goethe's (and Bachofen's) invocation of archetypal "mother" figures. But it has also been pointed out that Hesse also effectively produced a model of psychoanalysis in this text: Narcissus and the Unconscious; Narcissus as the midwife at the birth of Goldmund's self-recognition.

Here too the principle that Hesse had never before called so clearly by name becomes apparent: namely, that friendship between men begins where the love of women ceases.

Many of these same themes would run through Hesse's subsequent texts: Should a monastery be specially built to house free spirits, in order to give them protection from the outside world? Was there a need for a secret society of initiates who could save the world from its downfall? Such questions would pervade *Journey to the East* and *The Glass Bead Game.*

Ninon had been taken aback by the close association between love and death—which here sounds almost like a yearning for death—the first time she entered Hesse's bedroom at Casa Camuzzi in April 1927. Even during the train journey she took to Vienna the next day, she could not get out of her mind the curious quotation that she had seen hanging on the wall there—and that would later find a place in his studio in Casa Rossa. At first she could not see the point of this strange saying, but the longer she spent in Hesse's company, the more she came to realize how appositely it summed up his innermost being. The quotation was attributed to Jalal ad-Din Muhammad Rumi, the thirteenth-century founder of the Sufi order of "whirling dervishes": Hesse had copied it and illustrated it with one of his watercolors:

To be sure, death puts an end to life's misery,
And yet life shudders when faced with death.
In the same way that a heart shudders when facing love,
As if it were threatened with death.
For the awakening of love means
The death of the Self, that dark despot.[45]

Taken literally, this was an incantation designed to ward off love. Anyone who gives himself to another surrenders himself. And that was precisely what Hesse wanted to avoid doing at all costs, even fleetingly.

Hesse had himself clearly recognized his form of acute fear of contact, which also entailed a phobia toward love. In this he was not shunning the sexual sphere, as he clearly explained to, among others, his sister Marulla after she told him about a female friend's repugnance at a series of banal sexual encounters she had been through: "Her resistance to what she calls erotic liaisons are the customary old maid's objections commonplace among anthroposophists and other sects. This refusal to recognize the act of physical love is responsible for generating most neuroses and for giving rise, in most cases, to a general hypocrisy—noble in appearance but very damaging in its effects—in other spheres of life, such as patriotic or political matters."[46]

And when *Narcissus and Goldmund* addresses the question of the sources of creative activity and the overcoming of death, we can see from Hesse's strikingly unsuccessful descriptions of the act of love that the autobiographical principle governing his writing means writing about not just about the things he had experienced but also about what he had missed out on in his life. Above all, writing for Hesse was a substitute for life!

He wrote the following in his diary in July 1933 on his lack of ability to surrender himself completely to love—something he did not regret but instead embraced wholeheartedly:

> I tend to admire that powerful ability to love, indeed almost to envy it, in much the same way as I was always the one lost in admiration for the women who have loved me, and with a bad conscience too, for their ability to devote themselves entirely to a single person seemed to me to be something ineffably strong and beautiful. However, this was something I could admire but was incapable of imitating. I simply don't have the strength to commit myself to an object of love; instead, such an object has never been a material one for me, never a person or a people, but instead something beyond the personal—God or the Universe, or humanity at large, or the spirit or virtue or the concept of "perfection."[47]

When he came to read through the manuscript of the novel in its entirety, Hesse was pleased with his effort. And when the book was published, most of the reviews were positive, and yet he still felt he had been misunderstood. He hadn't intended to depict a flight from the present into the Middle Ages, but rather: "In this book, I have expressed the idea of Germany and the German nature that I have had in me since childhood and confessed my love for it—precisely because I find everything that is specifically 'German' nowadays deeply hateful."[48]

Thomas Mann, who tackled the same theme, defended Hesse's book to others as "a beneficial piece of German-ness from outside Germany," and in a questionnaire in the magazine *Das Tage-Buch* concerning the best books of 1930, cited it as one of the books written by "the older generation of writers" that he had liked best (a subtle qualification given the old-fashioned form of the work). Mann wrote in his review that it was "a wonderful book in its poetic wisdom, and its mixture of German-Romantic and modern-psychological, indeed psychoanalytic, elements." Yet all he wrote to Hesse personally was a postcard, in which he thanked him "for the admirable *Goldmund,*" adding in the next sentence, "Here's hoping your health improves!"[49] Had Hesse by now become so old and harmless that one could just fob him off with a few pleasantries, like it was already his obituary?

Hesse's intention was clear: he wanted to transform the Magic Theater into a magic landscape of the soul. Cast a spell over the iron snake of the machine culture before it crushes you in its coils! Unfortunately, he lacked the esthetic means to do so in this novel. And so all that really remained of this badly written tale was the convincing intention, which stands isolated and apart from the work. He had stated in his "soul biographies" that his main concern was that great monologue in which "a single person, precisely that mythical figure, is seen in its relations with the world and with its own self." Except that in this case, that attitude had led to the overpowering plot becoming a mere backdrop. Fritz Böttger has said about certain passages of his "fairy-tale novel": "These are raw and naive fairground images, gaudy in their coloration, but also doll-like, as if someone was playing around with hundredweights made from cardboard."[50] The passage he was referring to above all was the one where a rapist is murdered by Goldmund—at whom the girl he saves, Lene, then gazes "radiantly":

> In a frenzy, Goldmund kept squeezing until the other man let the girl go and slumped limply in his arms; continuing to choke him, he dragged the feeble and half-dead man a short distance along the ground to where a grey, rocky outcrop rose up out of the ground. There he hauled his defeated adversary upright, heavy though he was, once, twice, three times against the cliff face and smashed his head against the jagged rock. When the man's neck was broken, he cast the body aside, but his fury was not yet sated; he could have kept on torturing the man a good while longer.[51]

In a letter to Christoph Schrempf in April 1931, Hesse revealed what he had intended to signify through Goldmund's long journey to find himself: "That Goldmund achieves through art what he could not manage with women: that is, to lend spirituality to the sensual and thereby to attain beauty."[52]

That is the agenda of every *unio mystica*. Applied practically, however, it throws a familiar light on Hesse's problem with love.

Entry to the Prussian Writers' Academy and Resignation

> In being a member of the academy, I am acknowledging the Prussian state and its method of governing the intellect, but without even being a citizen of the empire or of Prussia. This dissonance is what bothers me most.
>
> —Hermann Hesse, letter to Thomas Mann, February 20, 1931

Hesse was anything but a committee writer. As a simple representative of literature he felt completely out of place in any academy, quite apart from the Prussian Academy with its headquarters in Berlin! Where art was concerned, it was always best if the state paid no attention to it—so he found the whole idea of the state acting as a sponsor of the arts deeply suspicious. As a result, he had from the outset no ambitions to be inducted into the literature division of the Prussian Academy of the Arts. While other authors hoped to be invited to join, he fervently hoped that he would not.

In 1926 a literature section was added to the Prussian Academy of the Arts. Six Berlin writers and eighteen authors from other parts of the German Empire were to be elected for the inaugural working session of the new division.

Robert Musil, who was not one of those chosen, used a memorial address marking the death of Rainer Maria Rilke at the end of 1926 to lampoon the composition of this institution:

> A little while ago, an academy of literature was founded. With—Ludwig Fulda at its head! Regarding its composition, one can only say that the significance of the writers who were excluded or who ruled themselves out easily outweighs that of its members. Naturally, I am pretty familiar with the inner and external worth of my Apollonian colleagues and I also have a fairly good knowledge of the various movements and circles, and the current trends in taste into which contemporary German litera-

ture is divided; but I have found it impossible to find an objective criterion according to which this collection of academicians could have been assembled. . . . Now, I don't want to say anything unpleasant about Ludwig Fulda. He has spent his life abusing the German language and the human gift of freedom of thought, but he was blissfully unaware of doing so. For 25 years he was as reliable as a thermometer, so that instead of having to waste words describing his writing, all one needed to say was, it's just like Fulda. Maybe that still means something today. In which case, instead of expending lots of words writing to the Academy of Literature, I can apply this critical criterion and simply say: There's a lot of Fulda in this—august body![53]

Hermann Hesse was also invited to play a part in the academy. He declined, citing as a reason his Swiss citizenship, of which the Prussians were clearly unaware. The Impressionist painter Max Liebermann, the president of the Academy of the Arts, assured him that this would not be an impediment. Consequently, Hesse no longer had any grounds on which to refuse this honor. On November 9, 1926, he gave in and duly accepted: "As a result of this clarification, it would be my great pleasure to accept the nomination and am greatly honored to henceforth be a member of your distinguished academy."[54]

This made him a foreign member of the institution, though he had no intention of ever being active on behalf of this academy. Any form of membership made him feel trapped. On March 9, 1927 (by which time Hesse had been a member for exactly four months), Oskar Loerke, a fellow academician, received the following letter from him:

I would give my eye teeth not to be a member anymore. Even the form that was sent to me, like I was applying for a position on the Prussian state railway, was dreadful, and all the statements issued so far by the literature section strike me as sad and laughable. When I was first informed of my election, I thought I might be able to bow out politely and without causing a scandal, by alerting the Academy to the fact that I wasn't actually a German citizen but a Swiss national and therefore couldn't accept their nomination. But when this reason for declining was declared invalid, I accepted, just for a quiet life and so as not to seem impolite.

But now he had only one thing on his mind: "If you can possibly think of a decent way, for whatever reason, in which I might be able to effect my withdrawal, please do let me know."[55]

The Academy of Literature behaved like any other institution—its principal concern was with itself, and its preferred method of resolving internal divisions was intrigue. Within the largely bourgeois Academy, especially under the presidency of Thomas and Heinrich Mann, a number of authors increasingly coalesced into a "popular bloc"—they included Wilhelm Schäfer and E. G. Kolbenheyer. Debates raged over terminology: Should they now call themselves an association of poets or of writers? Although Hesse never attended its meetings in person, instead keeping abreast of developments via the published minutes of its proceedings, he had a deep aversion to all this pompous academic posturing. What was wrong with wanting to call yourselves poets rather than writers? Was it somehow reactionary to be a poet, and were writers therefore more modern and progressive? Poets had some relation to the mythical that made them suspect in the eyes of those who wanted to disengage themselves from the term "poet." At least Hesse knew which side he stood on in this argument, which came to a head in the fall of 1929, and wrote to the Academy accordingly: "I fully concur with Herr Kolbenheyer, yet without sharing his wish to maintain the previous fiction that our section was concerned with things that had to do with the concept of the Poetic. Since reading the proceedings of the section, I have always been under the impression that it really had nothing to do with 'poetry,' and that 'poetry' was actually an outmoded and risible concept to most of the opinion-formers among our members." He then immediately took the opportunity of announcing his resignation: "Firstly, I would like the section, in choosing a new name for itself, to honestly admit to its true leanings—and secondly to give those members who do not share those leanings the opportunity to resign from the section without any scandal. I for one would be very grateful for such an opportunity."[56] It was not a good move for Hesse to ostensibly place himself in the same camp as Kolbenheyer—these nationalistic authors meant something quite different when they spoke of "poetry." Hesse soon realized his mistake.

Thomas Mann was irritated by Hesse's stance—could he really be of the same opinion as people like Kolbenheyer? But all Hesse had been trying to do was to find a quick way of extricating himself from the Academy; as of November 10, 1930 he duly ceased to be a member. Yet he was well aware that he had been misunderstood by all sides and was now frantically busy issuing explanations in order to regain his only rightful position— namely, one of his own choosing. All his explanations, however, only served to stir up further disapproval; just as in the First World War, Hesse was caught in a trap of nationalism and patriotism, and all his attempts to articulate his position publicly only met with incomprehension.

The more he sought to clarify where he was coming from, the more he simply confirmed his enemies' prejudices, and so, he noted, the "only official affiliation I ever let myself in for during my entire life" ended in tears. He had gone out of his way to try to keep himself out of everything external, particularly these mundane political wranglings, and to carve out for himself his own tailor-made intellectual realm (that of *Journey to the East* and *The Glass Bead Game*)—one that transcended any political context—and now he found himself brutally embroiled in these ideological controversies. He did not mince his words; his language was clear and unequivocal, as in his letter of November 1930 to Wilhelm Schäfer, one of the folkish-nationalist writers in the Academy. Hesse had known Schäfer for a long time, and even admired him as a strange oddball. And yet precisely here lay the fault line that separated Hesse and those who saw themselves as "German poets."

Hesse addressed his letter to Schäfer because the latter chaired the Academy's meetings at that time and on November 4 had suggested that less active members might be permitted to resign from the organization. Hesse lost no time in informing Schäfer that he accepted this offer:

> I wish the section nothing but the best, and have no rational grounds for leaving. It's just that I am finding the atmosphere too oppressive. Among other things, I get the impression that, should another war occur, the Academy will throw far too much of its weight behind those 90 or 100 prominent figures who will set about lying on behalf of the state to the people on all important matters affecting their lives, just as happened in 1914. Now, I don't pretend to wield any special authority in such political and moral questions, but I do demand and require that *I personally* have the freedom to go my own way and follow my own ethical code. These lead me inexorably out of the Academy, just as they have led me out of several easy affiliations in the past.[57]

★   ★   ★

However, his departure was not meant to appear like a public declaration; Hesse was keen to avoid causing a stir: "I'm sure you don't seriously imagine that my resignation will cause the section more than just an unpleasant moment. Members will say 'Oh well, that Hesse was always a damnably oversensitive and unsociable fellow,' and that will be that. That's how I see things panning out."[58] But Hesse was wrong in this assessment, for he was an author of such stature that both warring camps in the Academy wanted him on their side. So they began wooing him, assuring him that everything had just been a misunderstanding!

Schäfer was the first to respond to his letter and attempt to persuade him to stay. However, as he wrote to Heinrich Wiegand on February 7, 1931: "On receiving my reply, he decided to resign. So I too decided to leave, but entirely on my own initiative and wholly unconnected with the resignation of several others, which only happened *after* I had already quit."[59] Now, though, Hesse found his name publicly linked with those of E. G. Kolbenheyer, Wilhelm Schäfer, and Emil Strauss, and as a result he came under fire from Thomas Mann, who in an open letter proclaimed that the Academy, having taken cognizance of the resignation of several of its members, now needed to act: "Henceforth, it will be incumbent upon the Academy to defend intellectual freedom regardless of which intellectual tendency is being persecuted."[60] Did this imply that intellectual freedom also required defending against Hesse? Thomas Mann tried to get Hesse to rescind his resignation, which had inadvertently come across like a very deliberate snub.

But Hesse was now free of the Academy and did not wish to make the same mistake twice. He was no educator of the nation, nor did he aspire to be a representative of poetry—all he wanted to do was write. As early as 1928 he had stated very clearly that he did not feel he had any vocation to be a "leader": "My books lead the reader, but only then if he is willing, to a point where he can identify the sheer chaos behind the ideals and morals of our age. If I wanted to 'lead' him any further, though, I would be living a lie."[61]

And yet, as he wrote to Thomas Mann on February 20, 1931, he knew how awkward the situation was when even Heinrich Mann was talking indiscriminately in terms of the "gentlemen who have resigned." Again, as he had done once already to Wilhelm Schäfer, he now issued to his friend Thomas Mann a kind of declaration of principle regarding the Prussian Academy, which stressed his conception of himself as a German (more precisely a South German or better yet a Swabian or Alemannic) author who was resident in Switzerland: "Between ourselves, my personal attitude to the whole question is broadly speaking this: I am mistrustful toward the current state, not because it is a new or a republican entity, but because in my view it is neither new nor republican enough." This highly principled democratic stance, which was worthy of a Gottfried Keller, demonstrates how absurd it is to associate Hesse in any way with the poets of folkish nationalism. That said, where the truth of art was concerned Hesse went along with Nietzsche in placing no faith in popular majority decision—nor yet in those determining the spirit of an age.

Hesse's rejection of the Prussian state was also the root of his disquiet at being a member of a Prussian academy. The outsider Hesse had also felt uneasy in other academies, but never so totally like a fish out of water as he did in Berlin, of all places: "I can never quite forget that the Prussian state and its ministry of culture, which is the Academy's patron, is at the same time the body responsible for German universities and the dreadful spirit that presides there; and I cannot help but see the attempt to bring all the 'free' intellects under one roof in the Academy as a convenient way of keeping these often uncomfortable critics of the status quo in check."[62]

It was nine months before Thomas Mann responded to Hesse's position statement. He replied that he in no way wished to be an accomplice of the Prussian state's tendency "to try and govern the intellect."[63] He stressed that his reply was a private letter, but did not engage at all with Hesse's declaration. Instead, he proceeded quite pragmatically to explain some possible ways for Hesse to regain entry to the Academy. It was his "favorite dream," Mann wrote, that he might be able to woo Hesse back to the Academy. He had stated as much at their last meeting, and his intention had been "warmly applauded" by every one of those present, he told Hesse.

Mann deployed all of his considerable diplomacy to try to win Hesse over—above all, he said, if Hesse were to rejoin, this would represent a "truly gratifying step for the Academy in rectifying the public misunderstanding" that had attended his departure. Plus, Mann went on in a somewhat blackmailing tone, surely Hesse would welcome it

Hermann Hesse, pictured around the time when he was writing *The Glass Bead Game*

too, while adding that he was well aware of Hesse's aversion to anything "social and official, which is always inherent in corporative literary matters." We may well wonder whether Hesse laughed out loud when he read the following sentence of Mann's letter: "Basically, none of us are much inclined to things academic and binding, and it is only out of a sense of social duty expected and inculcated by the age we live in that we nonetheless heed such a call."[64] Thomas Mann, disinclined to perform official duties—surely not!? Mann was every inch an Academy man, whereas Hesse was not—and fundamentally they both knew it. Yet Thomas Mann saw it as his collegial duty to try to lure Hesse away from his insular outsider's existence, at least where the Academy was concerned. But did he intuit in his heart of hearts that precisely this outsider's role was so precious to Hesse that he would not be persuaded to rejoin even by a personal plea from Thomas Mann?

Hesse immediately responded with an emphatic "no" that must have left Mann in no doubt. But he added something that would presently lead both him and Mann to sense that they had an intense spiritual affinity with one another. Hesse had a deep mistrust of the Weimar Republic:

This unstable and spiritless state arose out of the vacuum, out of the exhaustion following the war. The few fine people involved in the [1919] "revolution," which was actually nothing of the sort, were slaughtered with the approval of 99 percent of the populace. The courts are unjust, the civil servants indifferent, and the people completely infantile. . . . In short, I find myself just as alienated from the mentality governing Germany at present as I did in the period 1914–1918. I see developments taking place that I regard as totally senseless, and whereas since 1914 and 1918 the general attitude of people has shifted slightly to the left, I find that I have been driven far to the left, to the extent that I can't bring myself to read a single German newspaper anymore.[65]

So it was that Hesse drew a definitive line under the episode of the Prussian Academy of Literature. Yet also for the academy itself, it would not be long before a chapter of its history came to a conclusive end; barely a year later, in common with all other institutions in the Third Reich, it would find itself disbanded and Nazified.

Travel through Time to Magic Lands: *Journey to the East*

> We journeyed toward the Orient, but we also traveled into the Middle Ages and the Golden Age; we roamed through Italy or Switzerland, but from time to time we also spent the night in the tenth century and dwelt with the patriarchs or the fairies.
>
> —Hermann Hesse, *Journey to the East*

With the book *Journey to the East,* Hesse continued his quest to discover the secret of the spiritual person who had forgotten neither how to hear and see, nor how to feel and yearn—a quest that he had first embarked upon in *Steppenwolf.* It is—as we might well expect—a journey through an inner space that reveals itself to be a labyrinth. It is a game with appearances that deceive—the hall of mirrors, the masks, the doppelgänger, and the Magic Theater all reappear here.

Basically, the story of the "League" of travelers to the East, bearers of arcane knowledge in a world increasingly devoid of mysteries, is an anticipation of an inner emigration, which Hesse himself embarked upon with this slim work, and would never leave again. The first-person narrator identifies himself as a "violin player" and a "reader of fairy tales." And it soon becomes clear that this journey is one into the depths of a library; it is a tale written by a passionate reader about the things he has encountered in his reading, as well as about his experiences in life—the story effaces the boundaries between reality and the imagination.

The Glass Bead Game would subsequently develop and flesh out all the motifs that Hesse first applied in *Journey to the East.* The novel finally took shape as the reflection of a way of life that Hesse had been cultivating for over a decade. Was it a new priestly caste that felt called to preach to us about the commandments we had more or less forgotten? The restrictive guardians of an order that seemed caught in a process of unstoppable erosion? Or was it, on the contrary, those who looked like troublemakers, terrible anarchists, who had put themselves outside of all rule-bound systems and been declared heretics by every doctrine that hallowed institutionalization? This also broached the question of humanism—and whether it was enough to simply defend it against any form of nihilism. At least since Nietzsche, the moral landscape had become more complicated. Dreams were accompanied by nightmares, and the notion of man as a rational being had now to be supplemented by a recognition that he could just as easily embody irrationality. The meaning of life was not just something that that one could simply find and then defend against all doubt—doubt had long since become a legitimate part of a meaning that every person first had to find for themselves. And according to Hesse, everyone had to do this on their own—there was no overarching meaning, no God, and no humanism that could carry a person through all the perils of life—one had to bear every burden oneself and settle everything with oneself alone. That was surely the sense of this journey—which, as always with Hesse, was a journey to find oneself. So, what of the League, the fellow travelers on this quest? They all wear masks, and are not what they seem.

The League was an imaginary collection of pure loners who only ever met each other in disguise. They were united by one thing: the knowledge that appearances are deceptive and that words lie. And for this reason the act of "treachery" represented by the apostasy of the Eastern traveler H. is an integral part of his journey, during which he is deprived of everything that he considers significant in his own conduct, and on which he could rely when he threatens to sink into a slough of depression and inactivity. But the truth is, no one except himself can endow him with this significance. The recurrent conclusion is that nothing should be expected from external agency: no instructions, no meaning, no mercy, and no salvation. One is required to sense everything within oneself.

In taking recourse to the story of the League—as in *The Glass Bead Game* also—Hesse searched for correspondences in the history of the Church. In doing so, he came across an identical pattern that kept recurring down the ages: the true saints of any period were those who were regarded by their contemporaries as heretics!

In the guise of the violinist and fairy-tale narrator in *Journey to the East,* Hesse took upon himself the role of the chronicler of the League. As a naive piece of presumptuousness, this was naturally an absurdity! An attempt by an individual to write the invisible counterhistory to the visible history: namely, the story of that secret elite who regarded themselves as having been specially chosen to survive the coming apocalypse. In other words, the true history of the spirit within the inexorable unfolding of the story of decline!

This motif was ever-present in Pietism—and in the period after *Steppenwolf,* Hesse recognized its topicality. As such, he slipped into a role similar to that of a Gottfried Arnold, the German Lutheran theologian who had already played a central role in forming Goethe's conception of religion. The young Goethe's conclusion after reading Arnold's monumental 1699 work *An Impartial History of the Church and of Heresy* was that anyone was free to discover their own religion, something he had henceforth set about doing with relish, as he later recalled in the tenth book of his autobiography *Poetry and Truth.*

According to Arnold, truly impartial people are those who bear witness to the truth as individuals. The institution of the church—indeed, any form of power, irrespective whether it derives from tradition or from dogma—is part of the history of decline. What was now required was a return to the original, unmediated spirit of religious belief. Especially the word—and in particular the written word, which claimed for itself a truth that it denied to others—had been a deeply corrosive influence on the original spirit. That is the magical point of that league of Eastern travelers, whose secret journey to the experienced truth ran, not from place to place, but instead through the ages to that original source, which was not simply there for people to stumble upon but which instead had constantly to be reproduced afresh. And in an era of demystification, this could only be achieved through an intense and new act of re-enchantment!

Nonetheless, the chronicler's work had to be carried out—even though its ultimate worth could not be guaranteed. The author had to transgress every border, beyond which there was no going back for him. It was no coincidence that Alfred Kubin (with whom Hesse corresponded)—the most extraordinary of the German Surrealists, who were a rare breed, and author of the spooky dystopian fiction *The Other Side*—drew the title page for the first edition of *Journey to the East*.

This, then, was not a journey conducted in bright sunlight, and those undertaking it were not some privileged elite. Quite the contrary: they were damaged and stigmatized individuals, who were now intent on following only one call—that of their dreams. Their traveling companions were all people whom the march of time had somehow left behind. They came from books, or from the neighborhood, and were figures as hopeless as Joseph Englert, who had in the meantime achieved success as an astrologer but made himself risible in the process, or Ninon Dolbin, who could have earned a doctorate in art history but instead chose to run Hesse's household and make herself truly indispensable as his reader!

So, a unique procession of fools! And yet for the traveler H. these were the only people who counted for anything on this mission that no one had sent him on. His still-living or long-dead companions, of whom one could expect one thing above all in return for their effort to show themselves worthy of the mission: that ridicule which had already been heaped on Harry Haller in the Magic Theater in *Steppenwolf,* and yet which then had the effect of liberating him.

So, what remained to be done? Without any hope of moving on, simply to serve the imaginary League! Nothing could be more wrong than the assumption that this League was a dropouts' commune, or a sect, or a grouping agitating for a different way of living. The opposite is in fact the case, for the ideology that a desire to change the world can be put into practice can only be escaped by absenting oneself from all groups and shunning all leaders except the one that one carries inside oneself. In doing this, one strengthens one's inner world against the external world's urge to destroy. Is this tantamount to escapism? Certainly it is that too, for attacking is not a mode at the spirit's command (for Hesse that would be mere journalism, a symptom of terminal decline); all reflection, instead, arises from setbacks and defeat.

★   ★   ★

It would be consonant with Hesse's own conception of himself at the start of the 1930s to claim that he had completely renounced the esthetic ambition to write literature. Or, as he confided to Heinrich Wiegand as early as November 14, 1926, that he was no longer writing poetry, "but only confessions, just as a man who is drowning or has been poisoned is not bothered about his haircut or modulating his voice but rather just yells for all he is worth."

Hesse stated as much right at the outset of *Journey to the East*—it was thus an open secret, known to all except those who obdurately refused to see it: "The exalted level on which our deeds were accomplished, the spiritual plane of experience to which they belong, might become relatively more comprehensible to the reader if I were permitted to disclose to him the essence of the secrets of the League. But a great deal, perhaps everything, will remain incredible and incomprehensible to him." There then followed a call to action that sounds like a pointer to the works that Hesse would go on to write in his old age: "One paradox, though, must be accepted—namely, that it is necessary to continually attempt the seemingly impossible."[66]

Journey to the East, which was published in 1931, was Hesse's answer to the demise of the bourgeois world. It asked which of those things that were important to us we might be able to salvage from the destruction. And how we might do so. Here the game became deadly earnest for the first time. If we had any ambition to preserve the great diversity of artistic and cultural treasures that humanity had produced, we would achieve this first and foremost by remaining open to flights of fancy ourselves, so that we might recognize the reality of magic and enchantment and accord greater significance to myths and folk fairy tales than we do to the daily stock-market reports. The true elite, the community of the initiated, was therefore that of dreamers! On November 24, 1931, Hesse wrote to his nephew Carlo Isenberg: "I am somewhat saddened because I did not intend my 'Journey to the East' to be read as some pleasant piece of whimsy, but as a serious profession of faith, even as an appeal to attitudes that run counter to those of our age. Of course, my enemies, the people of fashion and the journalists, will gain a great deal of ghoulish pleasure in seeing my fairy tale as further evidence of a new 'flight' from the modern world on my part, though in actual fact it is not a flight but a fight to the death."[67]

Above all, though, it was a pilgrimage, a questing after truth, as ultimately symbolized by the long and arduous route taken by the travelers. A quotation from Novalis acts as the travelers' lodestar: "Where then are we heading? Ever homeward."[68]

First, it was also a journey through Hesse's previous work (he would continue this trend in *The Glass Bead Game*)—characters that he created exist on a par with real people: "My friends the poet Lauscher and the artists Klingsor and Paul Klee; they spoke of nothing but Africa and the captured princess, and their Bible was the book of the deeds of Don Quixote, in whose honor they resolved to make their way across Spain."[69] This long procession also included Louis the Cruel (from *Klingsor's Last Summer*); Ninon, "the foreigner" (a play on her maiden name of Ausländer), whom he "met and loved"; Jup the magician (the astrologer Joseph Englert); but also E. T. A. Hoffmann's character Archivist Lindhorst from the story *The Golden Pot* (the Travelers to the East are a nod to Hoffmann's "Serapiontic Brotherhood"), who recognizes Mozart in his disguise as the musician Pablo.

In this way Hesse fashioned a setting for his work that is uniquely dreamlike, yet at all times it also possesses an oppressive actuality, like the recurrent nightmare of the author that he had never really had a vocation to be an author! How can one begin to write, and moreover about the most arcane questions of human existence, when one knows what a long procession of at least equal-rank, but in most cases far superior, intellects one finds oneself in?

What hubris to even dare to put pen to paper, to add to the overabundance of writing with one's own superfluous contribution. The first-person narrator, who finally finds himself in a situation similar to that of Harry Haller in the Magic Theater, finds himself face-to-face with the "Immortals," whose sole response to his proposition that he write a "History of the League" is a gale of scornful laughter.

However, Hesse did not intend this to signify that the modern author is in a hopeless crisis, but instead that the author must remain susceptible to decisive correction—he may write, indeed he must write, but from the position of an initiate. That was the path that now led him on to *The Glass Bead Game,* and permitted this work itself to resonate down the years. If we surrender ourselves to the reality of the dream, then the spirit of all ages will find exile within us.

Leo, the servant, is the real leader of the League on this pilgrimage—precisely because he remains a servant. He is a precursor of Joseph Knecht, the "Magister Ludi" of *The Glass Bead Game,* who embodies the idea of service in his surname (the archaic German word *Knecht* means "servant"). This is the secret of the spiritual elite, which forms the final objective of this journey through time. Leo is also a part of the author himself, his own leader whom he carries within him. And the court of the League, which sits in judgment on him, and over which Leo presides, therefore represents a process of self-judgment. And in accord with this, Leo's summarizing verdict on the author, H., who has succumbed to hubris in seriously intending to write a history of the League, does not simply condemn or exonerate him: "Brother H. was led to despair in his test, and despair is the result of every serious attempt to understand and vindicate human life. Despair is the result of every serious attempt to go through life with virtue, justice, and understanding and to fulfill their requirements. Children live on one side of despair, the awakened on the other side. Defendant H. is no longer a child and is not yet fully awakened. He is still in the midst of despair." Is this a hopeful conclusion? Yes, because Leo continues with his summing-up: "He will overcome it and therefore go through his second novitiate."[70]

Yet for Hesse this salutary exile of the pilgrims, in which they do not abandon their mission but actually discover it for the first time, was also cause for skepticism and for the gravest concern regarding the global political situation in the early 1930s. He wrote to his son Bruno on this subject in late 1931; the tone of this letter echoes the soulless prose generated by history as a mechanized process of destruction:

> What we see occurring in the world today is one of the final stages in the breakdown of the capitalist economic system, which has passed its zenith and lost its meaning and is now giving way to something new. In all probability, that new thing will be communism, which in and of itself I do not find unsympathetic. It would be wonderful if property and inherited wealth could be abolished at a stroke in all countries and if the 90 percent of humanity that are currently going hungry were no longer ruled by the other 10 percent who have plenty. But before that can happen there will of course be any number of transitional stages, some of them bloody, and we will see the coming and going of White and Red Terrors and the like.[71]

Let nobody therefore say that, in constructing the fairy-tale scenario of his *Journey to the East,* Hesse left the hard facts of the contemporary political landscape out of the reckoning. The opposite is the case—*Journey to the East*

represents a way of overcoming this and remaining creative in spite of everything. Or as H. in *Journey to the East* admits: "I either had to write the book
or be reduced to despair; that was the only way of saving myself from nothingness, chaos, and suicide. The book was written under this pressure and
brought me the expected cure, simply because it was written, regardless of
whether it was good or bad. . . . While writing it, I was like someone delirious or crazy, surrounded by three or four people with mutilated bodies—
those were the circumstances in which the book was produced."[72]

On the Pleasure of Self-Made Poems, Even Bad Ones

> In its genesis, a poem is something quite unambiguous. It is
> an unburdening, a call, an outcry, a sigh, a gesture, a reaction
> of the living soul through which it seeks to either ward off a
> surge of emotion or some other experience or to become
> conscious of it.
>
> —Hermann Hesse, "On Poems"

On November 3, 1930, Hesse gave an unexpectedly brusque response to
an inquiry from the University Library of Vienna about the future of lyric
poetry: "The future of lyric poetry would be all the better the less universities concerned themselves about it."[73]

Hesse's terse reply gave vent to his general aversion toward all forms
of academic endeavor—especially when it touched upon something that
in his eyes was as intimate and personal as the creation of poetry.

Naturally, Hesse was well aware of the contempt in which the German
Studies departments of universities held his poems—but what concern was
it of theirs how he spent his time? For him, there was nothing more personal than his relationship with verse. With its self-paced sentence melody
and a quite unique linguistic rhythm, it helped him get through the day—
in his view, any more information about how he wrote poems was neither
necessary nor possible. Only in the matter of painting did Hesse admit to
dilettantism as frankly as he did to the question of the point of writing
poetry. It was sensual wordplay, which instilled him with a delight he was
loath to see ruined by overanalysis. Later he would repeatedly comment
on what made for a good or a bad poem—and confess that the older he
got, the harder he found it to tell the difference: "Whenever I read other
people's bad poems, I always found it easier to identify the weak passages,

and was more ruthless in cutting or correcting them than I would have been with my own."[74]

Kurt Tucholsky hit the nail on the head when he called Hesse's verses "movingly bad"—though he did identify in them an honest and genuine voice, which does not necessarily save them but at least points to that background where they would always remain anchored for Hesse: as a recollection of his Pietist upbringing. In this setting, poetry had to be edifying, and in praise of God. Although Hesse disengaged himself from that background even in his early *Romantic Songs,* much to his mother's annoyance, for him some aspect of what constituted a poem still had its origins in this milieu: a song that one should sing for one's own edification, or also to lend form to one's suffering.

The plaintive tone about the vanity of all human endeavor derives from Protestant hymns. Even the self-accusatory element in these is an expressly Pietist trait. Generally speaking, in Hesse's writing, as the subjects he treated changed, so too did the form—though curiously enough this does not apply to his poems; they stand aside from all the developments in his work, sounding exactly the same in the 1950s as they did around 1900.

The "fever-muse" of his early writing, which so incensed his mother that she saw her son as already being in the clutches of the devil, is also evident in the poetry, particularly his "Crisis" poems, but it nevertheless appears in a strikingly conventional, almost staid form.

Writing poetry was a daily ritual for Hesse—like letter writing. Except that many of the poems are nothing more than rhyming exercises concerning mundane events. From his first forays into verse, which appeared in 1896 in the journal *Deutsches Dichterheim* (German poets' home) to his last poem, which he completed on the eve of his death on August 8, 1962, he continued to write these daily verses—in total over 1,400.

He never regarded them under the aspect of art—but always in the context of life, or more precisely, the context of his own life. They were in large part rhymed notes, nothing more—nor did they pretend to be.

An everyday exercise, in other words. Writing poems rather than praying became a test of the singability of the profane daily routine. And often enough the inconsequential event, some observation in the garden, would reveal an unexpectedly poetic content. Hesse's poems were like the songs of a wayfarer, and not infrequently were imbued with a sentimental atmosphere. But does that divest them of any real worth as poetry, as has often been claimed?

Poems such as "Ravenna," "Steps," "In the Mist," or "Creaking of a Bent Branch" are works that will endure; they are the fruit of an untiring effort to express experiences and observations, regardless of the fact that this form of "address" verse had become obsolete long before Gottfried Benn pronounced it so. Hesse cared little about such things—his poems had no pretensions to being modern. They were part and parcel of the unchanging inventory of his life and were avowedly old-fashioned.

What do we mean by such terms as "unmodern" and "formally deficient" anyway? Hesse set no store by objective criteria where such intimate forms of expression as poems were concerned. He regarded poems as wholly personal mirrors of the soul.

He wrote that he no longer presumed to judge whether a particular poem was good or bad. If the person who wrote it found it necessary to have done so, wasn't it then otiose to pass comment on it? No sooner had he formulated this question in his own mind than it took the form of an emphatic declaration: "Who on Earth would want to assess the esthetic quality of people's nighttime dreams, or the suitability of our hand and head movements, gestures and gaits?"[75]

Poetry is the realm of magic spells, those words from which everyone secretly expects something. What kind of words those are in detail can only be discovered by someone who tries out their effect: "Reading bad poems is an exceedingly short-term pleasure, as one quickly tires of them. But why bother reading them at all? Isn't everyone capable of writing their own bad poems?—Well, just go ahead and do it, and you'll see that composing bad poems is much more exhilarating even than reading the most beautiful of all verse."[76]

10

The Looming Presence of the Third Reich

Debates about Politics and Communism

Far back on December 23, 1918, Hesse had written to his sister Adele: "My hope for the future is that more noble sentiments will replace the dying feeling of nationalism."[1] One of these new forces, which had emerged onto the scene under the banner of internationalism, was communism, a doctrine that found many followers among intellectuals after the First World War—sensitive intellectuals like Georg Lukács and important Expressionist poets like Johannes R. Becher joined the Communist Party and set about spreading its ideology. Hesse was not antagonistic toward communism, but at the same time was by no means as unreservedly supportive of it as, say, his son Heiner would later become—something that would lead to vehement disagreements between father and son. Hesse's basic position was clear and consistent. In a letter of June 19, 1919, he formulated it as follows: "My endeavor is all on the side of the spirit, not practical action, and hence not political engagement either. I increasingly see a connection between current events and the thoughts that I had even prior to the war about the European spirit and the demise of Europe. It is this line of thought that I am pursuing."[2]

This attitude was all-pervasive in Hesse's thinking and is key to an understanding of his work. In his essay "Confession of a Poet" of 1927, for example, we read:

> We place no credence in any of the ideals of the current age—not those of the generals, nor those of the Bolsheviks, nor those of the professors, nor those of the factory owners. But we do believe that man is immortal and that his image is capable of recovering from every distortion of it and of emerging purified from every kind of hell. We do not seek to explain our age, or to improve it, or to instruct it, but we do mean to reveal to it over and over again, by laying bare our own suffering and our dreams, the world of images and the world of the soul. Some of these dreams are terrible nightmares, and some of these images are fearful specters—but it is our duty not to prettify them or to deny them.

To be sure, Hesse put no faith whatsoever in the solutions put forward by politics—just as he in general kept the world of the simply practicable very much at arm's length. Time and again, he was asked which side he was on. And his answer always remained the same: on his own side. Nor did this detached attitude derive from any disinterest or cold indifference toward social concerns on his part, quite the contrary. But was the stance that he took toward the Nazi regime a responsible one; and leaving aside whether it was a shrewd position to adopt, was it also what the circumstances of the time required? On September 29, 1933, Hesse aired his views about the situation in Germany in a letter to Joseph Englert, in which he also conceded that many of his friends found it baffling that he had not clearly taken sides or made common cause with the anti-Nazi opposition:

> Many are the times I have felt like joining their ranks, but the urge soon passes. Where good does protesting do? What's the point of writing witty essays about Hitler or the German talent for acting like subalterns? What's it got to do with me? I can't change a thing. What I can do, though, is offer a little succor to those who, like me, strive in everything that they think and do to undermine the whole filthy business of striving after power and political supremacy, and who want to create islands of humanity and love within this sea of infernal slaughter.[3]

The sentiments Hesse expressed here came from a different place than the realm of everyday politics. But did that make him any less decisive in his attitude? He was speaking here like Saint Francis of Assisi would have spoken, and surely no one would have suggested that the thirteenth-century saint's lack of political action made him into a tacit accomplice of despotism, an accusation that some people leveled at Hesse after 1945.

Hesse's position was perfectly consistent: it was the same attitude of searching that informed his writing of *The Glass Bead Game*. And the key questions it posed were: What comes after the demonic has run its course, and how is the spirit (that is, a mode of living that transcends our simple daily existence) to survive in such volatile times? Hesse's clarification of his position vis-à-vis communism, Nazism's most implacable adversary, should also be viewed in this same context. He was well aware that his sons Heiner and Martin had close links with the communists, and he was also concerned to try to explain his position to them. His attempts to do so were variations of the stance that he had already enunciated in a letter of April 9, 1929, to Heinrich Wiegand, who later, in the spring of 1933, became the first of a string of refugees from Nazi Germany to turn up at Hesse's door in Switzerland. Hesse had been angered by negative criticism of him in the Social Democratic Party newspaper *Vorwärts* (Forward), and gave a correspondingly testy response:

> I cannot tell you how much I regard this official attitude of socialism as incorporating and caricaturing all the very worst traits of Germans (which makes the good ones among them all the more laudable): banality and anti-intellectualism, a lack of any feeling for their own national traditions and for their own language, the laziest ignorance, a profound lack of education, and on top of all that a tendency to be gossipy, smug know-it-alls! . . . I have nothing but contempt for German social democracy, which has done nothing to either bring about the revolution or to exploit it effectively, but has simply been content to squat like some stupid, fat heir on the corpses of Liebknecht and Landauer and other such figures— people whom it did its damnedest to oppose, hate, and sabotage, just like it does every true spirit. In my thinking, I am far more of a socialist than, say, the entire editorial board of *Forward* (since 1914, I've taken to referring to it as *Backward*); I am a socialist in the sense of a person like Landauer.[4]

According to Hesse, in the hands of party politicians, where the class struggle was concerned, there was no "uniqueness, no personality, no tragedy, in other words fundamentally no artistry."

If there was one thing Hesse was determined not to be, it was an agitator who dressed political solutions up in fine words. For him, that would have been tantamount to a betrayal of his purpose as an artist.

On no fewer than three occasions in 1931, he would begin writing his essay "Letter to a Communist." For Hesse was a confessor; he wanted people to understand him—even in areas where he would not have much popular support. The difficulty for him lay primarily in explaining that he supported communism but that as a writer he could never be a member of the party. He was, he stated in his "Draft of a Letter to a Communist," not only supportive of communism with his "heart" but also with his "head." "I have always rooted for the oppressed rather than the oppressor, and in every trial my sympathy is with the accused, not the judge." And where cool reasoning was concerned, a big thing arguing in favor of communism was that "the capitalist economic and social model is all played out; its seriously ailing and on the verge of collapse."[5]

But aside from the fact that he was incapable of aligning himself with any party and "approving political programs lock, stock, and barrel," there was also another factor, a decisive one, that made it impossible for him to become a communist: "My second reason is my profound hatred of violence."[6]

This was Hesse's private credo, the essence of his self-conception as an author; it was totally non-negotiable and could not be co-opted to serve any cause, even when that cause was utterly convinced that it was the sole just course of action: "'So what good does your service on behalf of the spirit do if it doesn't directly and wholeheartedly devote all its efforts toward improving the world and enhancing the dignity of human life?'— Every political party poses questions like this to representatives of the spirit. But they are out of place and unanswerable."[7]

This was what he told his sons as well. Anyone who wanted to become a communist and engage in the class struggle not only had to be prepared to be killed but also to commit murder themselves!

Hesse knew full well that humanity would be the poorer in the absence of ideals. And he not only accepted that his sons felt a strong sense of unease in the midst of soulless capitalism, he also encouraged them to channel that unease into a clear repudiation of the status quo. He had written as much to Heiner in 1930, when his son had completed an apprenticeship as a window dresser at the Jelmoli department store in Zurich, which belonged to Hesse's friend and artistic patron Fritz Leuthold. Heiner had rebelled against the injustices he encountered in the world of work, and the insufferable atmosphere in this temple of consumerism. Hesse found it quite understandable that Heiner should now regard himself as a socialist: "But even the best and most noble principles cannot make a person a more worthy individual than he truly is. I don't judge people by the views they hold but by their character."[8]

And so Heiner went off to gain experience among the communist class warriors and instead of dressing shop display windows decorated those of party branch offices. This was a mistake, as he later realized (once again, his father had known better), but a mistake that it had been necessary for him to make—at least it was an attempt to plow his own furrow in life.

At the beginning of 1933, Hesse wrote a poem that he saw as an answer to the question of why he had not espoused the communist cause:

Refusal

Better to be killed by the fascists
Than to be a fascist oneself!
Better to be killed by the communists
Than to be a communist oneself!
We haven't forgotten the war. We know
How heady it is when the drums start beating.
But we are deaf, we aren't swept along
When you seduce the people with that old drug.
We're not soldiers or idealists any longer.
We don't believe that "German values
Will cure the world."
We are poor, we've been shipwrecked,
We have no faith in fine slogans any more,
The ones you used to whip and spur us into war—
Yet your slogans too, Red brothers, are evil spells that lead to war
    and gas!

Your leaders are generals as well,
Who command and yell and organize.
We though, we hate that,
We refuse to drink that moonshine any more.
We don't want to lose our hearts and minds,
Or march beneath red or white flags.
We'd rather perish alone as "dreamers"
Or die by your bloodstained fraternal hands
Than revel in some partisan show of power
And fire on our brothers in the name of humanity!

On March 19, 1933, Hesse replied to a lady reader to whom he had sent this poem at the beginning of the month and who now, at the time of his writing, had thrown in her lot with the fascists:

I don't want to pick holes in your patriotic enthusiasm for Germany. After all, you say it yourself: the people's role is to be happy and not to worry about the guiding spirit, whereas the spirit is there to blossom from the people and then quickly wither. Yet that's precisely why it is the duty of us spiritual types to stand alongside the spirit and not to sing along when the people start belting out the patriotic songs their leaders have ordered them to sing. . . . The Germans don't require much in the way of freedom, they are born servants and soldiers—but to have as little freedom as they do right now isn't good for any people.

Was he speaking here from the position of an outsider? No, because all this affected him too, since neutral Switzerland, as he was well aware, only continued to exist in the lee of a very provisional peace and by the grace of Nazi Germany. There was a constant whiff of danger in the air, detectable even in Montagnola—along with the fear that the entire world might be set on fire by this disastrous German nationalist euphoria, as he informed this lady from Germany, who had succumbed first to his poem "Refusal" and then to the National Socialist movement: "And I beg you, please do nothing that would help the Brownshirts take control of Switzerland too. Otherwise you could easily witness the spectacle of myself and other friends of yours being put up against the wall to the sound of a cheering mob and shot dead. And I feel sure that would sadden you a little."[9]

Discussion with Thomas Mann about the
German Character: The Year 1933

In February 1932 the Hesses and the Manns met in St. Moritz to go skiing, a passion that Hesse—thanks to Ninon—had rediscovered. Despite the business with the Academy, or perhaps precisely because of it, Hesse and Mann were getting on better than ever before. There was a new closeness between them. This much is evident from their correspondence during 1932, in which the looming shadows of 1933 are already apparent, though these are misinterpreted (by both men) in a wholly unsuspecting way. What, then, was the basis of this mutual affinity? To some extent it resided in their shared renunciation of the dark (and very German) Romanticism that had found its final expression and reached its zenith in Hesse's writings in the figure of Harry Haller—as it had beforehand in Mann in the subject matter of *The Magic Mountain.*

In March 1932 Hesse had written to Mann: "My origins are maternal."[10] Bachofen's concept of matriarchy remained an important intellectual coordinate for him, and the dichotomy of the paternal and maternal principles had just as formative an influence upon him as Nietzsche's opposition of the Apollonian and the Dionysian. Of particular importance to him was the dual nature, the hermaphroditic character, of all living things, which incorporated within itself the polarities of a contradiction. Thomas Mann, who understood Hesse perhaps better than anyone regarding his simultaneous propensity to faith and skepticism, had no wish to accompany him down this Faustian "descent to the realm of the Mothers"—that is to say, to a hidden and constantly newly creative nature. But it was precisely in this reservation of Mann's, which he now formulated while corresponding with Hesse, that he touched upon a point that the latter had also arrived at in *Journey to the East* and in his preparatory work on *The Glass Bead Game.* No mysticism, no sanctimony, and above all no hymns to the German character as a chosen people! They were of one mind on this. Mann had tackled this same theme when considering the work of Richard Wagner. The other front at which they stood shoulder to shoulder was in their common rejection of all trite faith in progress, and in pushing back against the growing hegemony of sociology over art, which manifested itself particularly in the form of an ideological appropriation of art by the communists, who wished to see it merely as one weapon among several in the class struggle.

Thomas Mann formulated his intellectual position as follows:

I do not have the right—plus it would be a kind of snobbery on my part—
to openly take the side of the maternal and the "Queen of the Night."
Between ourselves, even nowadays you find yourself in some terrible company if you choose that path, and it is my aversion to such company that
has led me to choose the lesser evil of acquiring for myself a reputation as
a dry, humanitarian rationalist. In truth, my works are a play between cherished and ironized opposites—and indeed, generally speaking, this space
between polarities seems to me to be the true realm for the free play of art
and irony.[11]

Hesse too trod this same—postclassical, so to speak—path during this
period. Did that make them both more clairvoyant regarding the impending calamity that was about to befall Germany?

In February 1932 Hesse wrote to Ludwig Finckh, his old friend from
their time as neighbors on Lake Constance, who now presented a very nationalistic and conservative face to the world, to inform him that the
looming fascist terror was

the precise consequence, very carefully nurtured by German politics over
the past few years, of everything that has happened in the Empire in the
public domain since 1914, and even before. Eventually, even Germans,
however uncomfortable it may be for them, will have to learn to feel
responsible for their Empire and its policies, and realize that you can't
conduct politics either through poems or via simplistic patriotic intoxication, and that they share the blame for wars that we have fought and lost
and for revolutions that have been staged or have failed to materialize, etc.
Until then, it cannot be the responsibility of the German spirit to cultivate
patriotic Romanticism, for all its many attractive aspects. Instead, it must
keep a close eye on the Fatherland and view any manifestation of nationalism with extreme distrust.

Thus far Hesse's letter is a remarkably clairvoyant diagnosis of the situation, but what then follows sounds almost like tempting fate, sum-
moning up the coming catastrophe, the magnitude of which even Hesse
cannot possibly have foreseen: "The world moves forward, not backward,
and someday Germany too must join this onward march of progress.
And maybe the path to that lies through that stupid ass Hitler."[12]

Hesse was wrong in this assessment. For one thing, Hitler was not a stupid ass—that underestimated the danger he posed—but more importantly neither was he any kind of staging post on an onward progression. The only path that led via Hitler was one culminating in death and destruction.

Here Hesse indicated that it was essential to abandon any nationalistic thoughts. Likewise it is a key tenet of *The Glass Bead Game* that we should start to adopt a quasi-cosmological perspective and thereby conceive of a new world that requires the demise of the old one. Was this a reckless game with the Apocalypse? Not really, given that Hesse already found himself thinking in terms of other temporal contexts, and his concern was with the new founding of a spiritual culture following the collapse of the existing one, a demise that—in whatever way in came about—he still believed was inevitable:

> It is cold in the world when you have no fatherland and no power to which you can cleave and alongside which you feel destined to triumph or suffer. Yet some of us have to live in this cold world nonetheless in order to lay the groundwork for a new atmosphere. . . . If only Germany had a halfway decent and genuine form of communism, I would put myself at its disposal. But where is such a thing to be found? Whether it be about communism or Hitlerism or whatever, thinking and wishing is false, however; it is sentimental and unproductive. A lot of things still need to die for the grass to grow once more.[13]

For all his contempt for Hitler, whom he could only see as a caricature, prior to 1933 Hesse still tended—and in this he was by no means alone—not to take him and the threat he posed to the world seriously, as evidenced by a letter to his sister Adele from the beginning of March 1931: "I hope it never comes to this, but if Hitler should really end up at the top of the heap, we would certainly lose everything—not just our money and our security but all our spiritual and moral certainties too. And yet we can be sure that the buffoon will soon break his neck, and I do fervently wish that this happens to him, this brainless stage Teuton!"[14]

Thomas Mann could also sense the changing atmosphere in Germany. On December 22, 1932, he wrote Hesse a letter to accompany his return of the hate mail from German nationalist students that Hesse had sent him to peruse. In it, he recounted his own experiences in this regard:

> Last summer a young man from Königsberg even sent me a scorched copy of the popular edition of *Buddenbrooks,* because I had dared to voice criticism of Hitler. He attached a note (anonymously) saying that he would like to force me personally to finish the job. I didn't do that, but instead carefully collected up all the charred fragments, in order that they might one day bear testament to the mental state of the German people in 1932. I do believe, however, that we are over the worst. We appear to have passed the peak of this madness, and as we grow old we can still look forward to some happy days ahead.[15]

Ten days after Hitler's seizure of power, on January 30, 1933, Thomas Mann delivered a lecture in Munich entitled "The Suffering and Greatness of Richard Wagner." By April the power of the Nazis was already so firmly entrenched in German cultural life as well, that the municipality of Munich, newly designated as "the city of Wagner," lodged an official protest against Mann's lecture. Thomas Mann de facto suddenly became a "non-person" in Nazi Germany.

Hesse studiously avoided any relationship with Wagner's music; in clear contradistinction to Thomas Mann, his musical ideal tended rather toward Bach, Mozart, and his friend Othmar Schoeck. Fundamentally he took the view that Wagner had created the soundtrack to Hitler: bombastic in its presentation and bodying forth into sheer self-indulgent excess: "You know that I am very much in agreement with your disparaging and critical comments on Wagner's theatricality and megalomania, whereas your love of his music in spite of that strikes me as honest and touching, to be sure, but very hard to comprehend nonetheless. Quite honestly, I cannot stand him."[16] Hesse had no time for Wagner's Romantic attempts to conquer musical summits—this was another thing linking Hesse and Nietzsche, who admittedly idolized Wagner to begin with, but whose musical instinct later led him to reject the composer's overplaying of the Romantic ideal of art (with Bayreuth as a temple to the arts!).

In the same letter to Thomas Mann, Hesse set out what implications these developments in Germany would have for them both: "But I can see a way out of all this for you and for us, a path leading out of things narrowly German and toward the European, and from the current to the timeless. In this regard I do not believe that the collapse of the German republic and of the hopes that you placed in it is unbearable. Something has died here that was never properly alive in the first place."[17]

Undoubtedly he had a European vision in mind. For him, the German nation-state had increasingly become something that should be consigned to history—and yet it is clear that he was (still) failing to recognize the cataclysmic threat that Hitler's Third Reich posed for the entire world. Yet Hesse was all too painfully aware of his own isolation. Henceforth, Mann and Hesse began to feel increasingly like two relics fretting over whether they could even make themselves understood amid the new ideological battles that were raging, with their thoroughly nuanced and contradictory intellectual positions. And to whom, to what public audience, would they address their concerns now that Germany had begun to comprehensively seal itself off from the rest of the world?

Thomas Mann was a guest in Montagnola on several occasions in March and April 1933; he appeared shaken by developments in Germany and was eager to discuss them with Hesse. Hesse noted in early April: "Meanwhile, Thomas Mann has come to visit us often, and I am delighted to see that he is slowly getting over his first serious bout of depression. We spent half the day together on many occasions."[18] And Thomas Mann wrote to Hesse on June 2, 1933: "I miss the opportunity of discussing things with you."[19]

After the war and the award of the Nobel Prize for Literature, for which Hesse largely had the persistent intervention of Mann on his behalf in Stockholm to thank, Hesse wrote the following observation about Mann on July 20, 1950: "Though I may seem to him to be a somewhat rural and harmless little brother, he does nonetheless have a very good feel and appreciation for the curious center around which I revolve."[20]

Thomas Mann left Munich in September 1933 and moved to Küsnacht on Lake Zurich. Even so, his continuing proximity to Germany bothered him, as he confided to Hesse even before his move, on June 2: "I'm feeling very uneasy about German-speaking Switzerland nowadays."[21] Furthermore, a publication ban was imposed on German émigrés to Switzerland, so that authors in exile (such as Kurt Kläber with his novel *Red Zora and Her Gang*) were forced to publish under pseudonyms. Kläber called himself "Kurt Held" in Switzerland. This would not have been a workable solution for Thomas Mann—he felt neither safe nor happy in Switzerland, and moved to the United States in 1938.

Hesse, though, could not imagine himself living in the United States. For one thing, he spoke no English (nor did Thomas Mann to start with, though he learned it), and for another he did not feel like a citizen of the world to the same extent as Mann. Nor did he have two children—as Thomas Mann did in Klaus and Erika—who positively forced him to take a public stand against the Nazis. Although Hesse's son Heiner, a staunch communist, urged his father to openly align himself with those who opposed Nazism and German émigrés, Hesse was loath to take this step. His situation was difficult, since neutral Switzerland outlawed any form of public demonstration of opposition to Nazi Germany.

Hesse wrote to Mann as he was preparing to embark on a book tour to the United States at Whitsun 1934 to tell him: "I don't envy you your trip to America," and added: "But fortunately you are more resilient than me and, unfortunately, better educated than this hermit, so you will easily be able to cope with it."[22]

Hesse too felt insecure in Switzerland. What protection could the country offer him and what would happen if German troops were suddenly to occupy Zurich, in the same way as they ultimately "reclaimed" Vienna for the German Empire with the *Anschluss* of Austria in 1938. He noted with alarm the activities of the Gestapo in Switzerland. Several hotel owners who had publicly expressed concerns about the new political circumstances in Germany and their effects on the kinds of visitors they were receiving suddenly disappeared. Gestapo kidnap and death squads were regularly entering Switzerland—and Hesse knew that he would be easy prey for them. And wasn't he also now married to a Jewess? According to the Nuremburg Laws passed in Germany in 1935, his marriage with Ninon was now considered an indictable offense of "racial defilement."

Hesse thus found himself in a bizarre situation. He was living with Ninon in the dark shadow of reports of deported or murdered friends and relatives from Czernowitz. His nephew Carlo Isenberg (the son of Hesse's half-brother Karl Isenberg, who died in 1937) was a close friend, with whom he had published, among other titles, *Pages from Prevorst*. Carlo, a church organist and composer, visited Hesse in Montagnola for two weeks in 1934 and gave his uncle a crash course in the history of music. He also made an appearance as the character Carlo Ferromonte in *The Glass Bead Game*. As of January 1945 he was listed as missing in action at the front.

Carlo had a sister, Marie—and during his book tour through Germany in 1929 Hesse had made a note of a visit to see her: "Trip with Adele to Korntal to see Marulla, and then all of us headed off to Ludwigsburg, where we spent the afternoon until 6 o'clock with Karl, Carlo and little Marie, all very jolly, drinking coffee and wine, and Marie very boisterous."[23]

This niece Marie would end up committing suicide in the spring of 1945, after having killed her three children. The background to this tragedy was that her husband, Walter Hees, an SS *Standartenführer,* had belonged to Heinrich Himmler's inner circle. A chemist by training, Walter headed up an SS forensic institute and played a key role in the technical implementation of mass extermination by means of gas chambers after the Nazis decided to go ahead with the "Final Solution." He was present in person at the tests of the first mobile gas vans, in which victims were asphyxiated by exhaust gases; dispassionately, he logged how long it took them to die and the appearance of the corpses. His justification for taking part in this experiment was that the "test subjects" who were herded naked into the gas vans would have been shot anyhow. Hesse was presumably unaware of the extent of his niece's husband's involvement in Nazi war crimes—though he would surely have been informed by his relatives in Germany of Walter's role within the SS leadership apparatus. For him and Ninon, it must have been a dreadful thought that they had within the family a principal perpetrator of the mass extermination of Jews.

As became clear in 1933, Hesse's distance from Germany could not have been greater—and yet the hate campaigns against him, which had begun when he called upon the European intelligentsia in the First World War to refuse to engage in nationalistic hate propaganda, were still all too present in his mind (indeed, they had never ceased). He was attacked from all sides—by the warmongers and the opponents of war alike—for voicing his aspiration for a Europe-wide alliance of artists and intellectuals that would, as it were, place itself above the events of the war. He had no desire to lay himself open to this kind of abuse again—not out of cowardice, but

because he could not see the point of such an enterprise. In mid-1933
Thomas Mann received a letter from Hesse:

> The letters I receive from the Reich, from supporters of the regime, are
> very odd: they all are all written in what appears to be a blazing passion,
> and they praise in grandiloquent terms the unity, indeed even the "freedom"
> that prevails in Germany today, yet in the next line they go on to furiously
> condemn the pack of vermin that are the Catholics or the Socialists, who
> are going to get what's coming to them now. There's an atmosphere of war
> fever and pogroms about them, delirious and heavily intoxicated, there are
> echoes of 1914 but without any of the naivety that was still possible then.
> This will bring a lot of bloodshed and more besides; it reeks of evil. Even
> so, I still find myself moved by the innocent willingness to sacrifice them-
> selves that many of them display.[24]

And so the process that began with the hate mail started up all over again.
An uncontrolled nationalism, which was now bolstered by an anti-
Semitism that had been made into a state doctrine, now had Hesse in its
sights. Why should he of all people be spared the Nazis' wrath when even
Gottfried Benn, who had initially shown sympathy for their cause, was
now being pilloried as a Jew, thanks to his surname. The same sort of accusation was flung at Hesse by *Ludendorff's Fortnightly,* a magazine founded
by the former Prussian general and Nazi supporter Erich von Ludendorff
(1865–1937), which had as its strapline: "At the Sacred Wellspring of
German Might." Ludendorff's Nazi agitators accused Hesse of being a
typical "mongrel" and summarily declared that his arch-Protestant mother
had been a Jew. Hence his "un-German" stance of dividing his loyalties
between nations, an act that stabbed German fighting men in the back.
"What's Hermann Hesse up to now? Unlike Löns, Gorch Fock, or Walter
Flex, he is not serving Germany with either his blood or his verse—
instead, he says he regards the 'popular enthusiasm for war . . . with a sense
of alienation and horror.' He left his homeland and moved to neutral Switzerland."[25] On one level, the opprobrium that was heaped on Hesse's head
here was truly laughable, but on the other it was deadly serious.

★   ★   ★

Hence, it was more than a simple "Not in my name!" statement that once more made Hesse into a special case—someone who refused to align himself either with Nazi fellow-travelers among artists, or with those who had emigrated. How could one confront such a power, which was blind with fury and in which the intellect was completely powerless? How did the mechanism whereby the masses were manipulated in this way operate? This was the principal question that preoccupied Hesse now: How could a person retain his spirit in times such as these?

Even many of the nationalist-minded authors, among whose number he had erroneously been counted during the dispute over his leaving the Prussian Academy, did not actually thrive under the Nazis. Unless they also openly allied themselves with them politically, that is, like Hanns Johst, for instance. The Nazis had no time for opportunists, only faithful acolytes who were fanatics like themselves. Neither Gottfried Benn, who in 1933 had helped organize the Nazification of the poetry section of the Academy, nor other authors who had hoped to gain favor from the Third Reich were welcome any longer. As Hesse wrote to Thomas Mann on March 18, 1934, "even a really harmless lecture by Kolbenheyer would be banned by the police now."[26] Later in this same letter, having remarked on "how serious things are," he added an observation whose drastic tone is in stark contrast to his usual studied reticence: "I really don't know what I would wish for or command if I was called upon to make global history just for a minute—I almost think that I would have France march across the Rhine and cause Germany to lose a war that it could in all likelihood win within a couple of years."[27]

Who could dare to indulge in the same flights of fancy as Hesse, who was fond of styling himself as the Hermit of Montagnola? Even so, his publisher was situated in Berlin. Samuel Fischer died in 1934—which only exacerbated the already tense situation for Hesse. His income, he told Thomas Mann on March 21, 1935, had dwindled so badly over the past two years that he was considering whether he ought to switch publishers. But, he added, he did not want to be disloyal to Fischer. Thomas Mann, a Fischer author himself, had also said as much previously.

In the interim, the business had come under the control of Fischer's son-in-law Bermann Fischer, who found himself in such a difficult situation that Thomas Mann asked himself whether a publisher of this kind even had a future in Germany anymore:

It seems ever more doubtful whether keeping faith [with Fischer] is even going to be possible for very much longer. How do things stand in the country and will there be any real point in being published there? Until recently, I too was determined not to allow myself to be cut off from my German public for as long as I could possibly manage it. But I confess that my desire to sever all my connections with this terrible country has grown stronger over the past few weeks and months, and even in material terms it would be better if I did so. Is there even the remotest probability that Fischer will be able to hang on?

There was a steady increase in the level of official anti-Semitism. Irrespective of whether they were authors, translators, or publishers, all "non-Aryans" were barred from operating any longer in Germany. "So why would they make an exception and allow Bermann to continue 'poisoning the people'?" [28]

The Shadow of Nazi Germany: Daily Life in Montagnola

> I am absolutely clear where I stand—it's the place I've always occupied, a solitary one, associated with no group or political party.
>
> —Hermann Hesse, "Letter to a German Scholar" (December 1938)

By 1933 Hesse had already been living in Switzerland for twenty-one years without interruption (plus he had also been resident there as a child and for several years as a young bookseller). Suddenly he found himself thrust once more into the role of standard-bearer for the hopes of those who yearned for the advent of new German spirit of whatever kind, a movement embracing various different groups opposed to the cabal of criminals in government in Berlin. He was aware of this and fearful of it, too, suspicious that others would force him to play a role that was not of his choosing. He wrote the following terse note to Thomas Mann in March 1935: "We had a reasonably quiet winter, but with the coming of spring now, the stream of visitors has resumed, and I'm convinced that one or two of them looked like spies."[29]

Hesse was living well at Casa Rossa, where his wife Ninon was now managing the household affairs, albeit in a fashion that kept on driving the domestic staff to quit. Ninon was indisputably the mistress of the house, even though she continued to bear the brunt of Hermann Hesse's volatile moods. In January 1933 Hesse noted that for some time he had been harboring a plan to write a new book—but that he lacked the energy to get on with the task "because I am getting old, because I'm living too well and comfortably, and because with every day's correspondence and such like I am compelled to play the incredibly busy, famous man."[30]

In May of that year, he remarked that he had "no literary ambition any more."[31] And yet with Hitler's seizure of power, the balance was shifting. For from one day to the next, Hesse increasingly became the first port of call for refugees from Germany. And he—the person who could not even bear Ninon to be constantly around him—took them in, and even allowed some of them, like Gunter Böhmer and Peter Weiss, to use his old apartment in Casa Camuzzi.

Back on March 20 he had informed André Gide that this was the day on which his "guest bed was ready and waiting for the first refugee from Germany."[32]

This first displaced person from Germany was Heinrich Wiegand, the communist and music critic from Leipzig, with whom Hesse had corresponded extensively.

Just a few months later, on March 8, 1934, Hesse reported to Thomas Mann that he had passed on the greeting which Mann had sent Heinrich Wiegand shortly before. However, the circumstances of life and death could change quickly in these troubled times: "Not long ago, Wiegand, who was beset by worries and had suffered a number of disappointments but who nonetheless began work on a new novel, died quite suddenly in Lerici after an illness of only one day. It was only about a year ago that he first turned up at my door as a refugee from Leipzig and was my guest for a spell, and now for the past three weeks we have had his wife staying with us, who doesn't know where she should go now."[33]

Hesse complained during this period about "terrible letters from Germany"[34] and resolved that anything he had to say henceforth as an author already in his mid-fifties should be his legacy—a spiritual last will and testament bearing witness against an unspiritual age. Over and above this, though, it should also be a symbol for the path a person who wanted to set an example should take through the changing times.

This broached the question of posterity and the methods by which intellectual wealth could be bequeathed. In the form of academies, perhaps?

A sketch of Hesse by Gunter Böhmer, 1939

Or through a republic of intellectuals, that kind of "monastery for free thinkers" invoked by Nietzsche? How far should the spirit be oriented toward life, and conversely to what extent should it shun it?

Hesse pondered over the matter of asceticism and the history of monastic orders. At the end of 1933 he told Thomas Mann: "As far as my eyes will permit me, I am reading the biographies of 19th-century Pietists."[35] He had found his way to the subject matter that his grandfathers on both sides and his parents had dealt with their entire lives. What testimonies of genuine faith could there be when institutionalization into churches and the channeling of true belief into rigid dogmas only served to warp this and ultimately turn it into its opposite? Shifted into the secular realm, this dilemma also suddenly became the abiding theme for Hesse's own life: How should the intellectual conceive of his duty toward his age if he aspires to be anything more than a state-sponsored functionary? How was a free spirit to avoid the fate of being denounced? Was it possible for him to evade being institutionalized—in either academies or universities? All of this would entail choosing, as Hesse had done, the path of the outsider.

The writing of *The Glass Bead Game* began to shape his days. He had already drafted a foreword to the novel in 1932, comprising the Pietist preliminary studies to "The Fourth Life of Josef Knecht." This now became a kind of apocrypha for *The Glass Bead Game*. Hesse abandoned this again after he had written a second version. These two drafts of "The Fourth Life of Josef Knecht" only appeared in 1965 in Hesse's "Unpublished Prose Works."

One thing was clear: in the midst of the catastrophe in Germany, the effects of which he could not escape, Hesse selected as broad and far-reaching a setting as he could for his new book, which he sensed would be his last major work.

The Glass Bead Game became a form of Platonic dream, which offered him a place of refuge over the next ten years. It was not just a wide-ranging work, but—to an even greater extent—an attempt to link his own biography with a universal intellectual history in such a way that a depiction of particular era would reveal an image of all ages and conversely that his own face would be reflected over and over again in the most diverse periods.

Hesse also took note of what Thomas Mann was doing; at the time Mann was writing *Joseph and His Brothers*—a myth about the emergence of that Western culture which the principal ideologue of National Socialism, Alfred Rosenberg, had recently brazenly reinterpreted as an "Aryan legend" in his book *The Myth of the Twentieth Century*.

Hesse also knew that he had to pursue myth into the world of symbols whose humane dimension appeared in a world threatened with destruction. He wrote to Thomas Mann about the latter's *The Tales of Jacob* (the first of the four parts of *Joseph and His Brothers*), which he had just read:

> Given the modern conception of history and historiography, I have naturally grown very fond, right down to the tiniest detail, of that quiet, gently melancholic form of irony with which you ultimately treat the problem of all history and every desire to recount stories, without for a moment ever relinquishing your own efforts to write the sort of historiography that you have recognized is fundamentally impossible. Though in many regards I am of a different disposition to you and have been schooled in very different things, I find precisely this aspect very sympathetic and familiar: undertaking the impossible, even though one knows one is thereby actively shouldering a tragic burden. Another thing about this book was that its

calmness came as a very welcome relief in an age crammed to bursting with idiotic topicality![36]

This was nothing less than an expression of Hesse's his own perception of himself, which also became the prime mover for his work on *The Glass Bead Game*. He remained resolute in his determination not to let himself become embroiled in political action against Nazi Germany, or to be misused as a mouthpiece by Germany's new rulers. It would be inaccurate, however, to see Hesse merely as acting as neutral as his adopted country Switzerland. His internal defensive attitude was quite unequivocal; he knew that it was a question of showing a spiritual way out of the catastrophe.

It was brought home to him on a daily basis that his situation was complicated. He outlined his predicament to his old friend Joseph Englert on September 29, 1933: "Since the spring I have had hundreds of Germans come and visit me, refugees and vacationers alike, supporters and opponents of German Fascism, people of almost every social rank, and I myself have such close ties to Germany (the very closest economically, it being my main market, as well as spiritually through both the language and literature and my closest relatives and friends, who are still living there) that I am essentially entirely oriented toward it."[37]

He felt a growing sense of responsibility for those people, especially the young ones among them, who made the pilgrimage to Montagnola to seek his advice and support. Some of them, like Heinrich Wiegand, were already refugees from Nazi Germany. Gunter Böhmer, who was just twenty-two at the time, was another escapee from the Reich; Hesse was immediately enchanted by him, and before long Böhmer was reading and drawing and working in the garden alongside Hesse.

Hesse's constant companionship with his "painting and gardening brother" only served to heighten Ninon's uneasiness at the state of their marriage. What was she, in actual fact? A housekeeper and reading machine—and now she even appeared replaceable in those roles. She could not hide her jealousy, and felt that she had already been half-usurped from her scarcely privileged position at Hesse's side. The fact was that he could never see women as true friends and far preferred having intellectual exchanges of ideas with other men—and this was precisely what hurt Ninon's feelings; after all, she herself had intellectual horizons that went far beyond the business of frugal housekeeping.

★   ★   ★

As a result, the atmosphere in Casa Rossa became toxic—the "house let-ters" from this period merely reflect their quarrels over trifling matters. But the more serious issue that lay behind them was that Ninon felt un-happy at Hesse's side, and unsure what she meant to him, or even if she meant anything at all. Even as early as October 1932, Hesse had written her a letter in which he told her that, if he had been away at war and she found herself at her wits' end wondering how she'd manage to bring up four children on her own, "or if there was no bread for the next day and no money in the house, you couldn't possibly look more gloomy, anxious, and downcast than you do now, often for days at a time."[38] And he com-plained about her "fanaticism" when it came to running the household, especially where the furniture and the parquet flooring were concerned. Ninon's response to this attack on October 11, 1932, was remarkable; though fundamentally extremely angry, she resorted here to a kind of irony, yet it brought no pleasure to either the writer or the reader of the following lines: "My dear, beloved Hermann! How could you of all people doubt that my greatest and indeed my only pleasure resides in living with you and in being your lover and life companion!" That sounded dangerous—revealing quite how disillusioned she had become over the past six years—especially from the moment when she no longer dared even to discuss her feelings openly with him! The letter continued: "How could you possibly think, as you suggested in your letter, that I see my life as some kind of slavery! And you the cleverest man on the planet! What must the merely clever think when the cleverest of them all can be so badly wide of the mark!"[39] This, then, was the prevailing tone at Casa Rossa—prudently confined to letters; the couple rarely spoke and when they did, they weren't candid with one another. But on the subject of the parquet flooring, Ninon still had a key point she wanted to make: "As regards the parquet flooring and the food, I can only apologize. The fact is, I couldn't care less about either—I've lived for long enough in unpleasant and dirty rooms, and I don't have a sophisticated, pampered palate. You in particular are a real object lesson in loyalty in the very smallest of matters—but if your loyalty is only grudging, then of course I deserve a sound thrashing."

But then she gave a hint at the real reason for her deep resentment. She felt cut to the quick, though in all likelihood Hesse gave little thought to the root cause of this: "Certainly, I have no desire to nurture this condition, after all it's not remotely enjoyable—but it's a reaction to internal experiences—it is a layer of ice that surrounds me, isolating me and offering me some sort of protection. I first felt this way after Papa died, this sense of numbness, and I had the feeling that it was protecting me and stopping my heart from breaking."[40] So, was she feeling that her heart was about to break in Hesse's presence?

There is a self-portrait of Ninon as the goddess Hera. In it, she appears like a grim, dangerous deity ready to go to war, or as she herself put it "like a zombie." Or is it just a portrait of an unhappy wife determined to deprive others of the zest for life that she herself has lost?

In any event, this image has a depth and power all its own—it speaks more to Ninon's talent than to any bad character. It is a form of unsparing self-accusation revealing the destructive side, the demonic aspect of a woman who has realized that she will only ever be important to Hesse in external and not internal matters. It reveals a complete self-knowledge on her part, and that was more than Hesse was ever able to achieve in his own pictures. That said, he did not pretend that this was his aim when he painted.

For the time being, Ninon went traveling, first to Italy—ironically, this trip was subsidized by Mussolini's Fascist government, enabling her to visit Florence and Siena and resume her studies in art history. While there, she kept a kind of travel diary, which she sent to Hesse in her letters. However, she was never able to fully suppress the doctoral candidate in art history within her, with the result that she frequently became bogged down in the sheer volume of the subject matter she was discussing, on which she wasn't confident enough to take an individual viewpoint. It was this shortcoming in her own style that she deplored above all.

In the meantime, Hesse set about organizing a private relief organization for refugees. He continued to take in escapees from Germany, while also attempting to set up contacts with both the Swiss authorities and his own patrons—yet all the while managing not to give the outward impression of being an enemy of Germany. Naturally, he was still coming under pressure from several quarters, including his three sons, to abandon his reticence to openly criticize Nazi Germany. Hesse responded to this pressure in a thoroughgoing manner, indeed the most thorough way he knew how as an author: by writing *The Glass Bead Game*.

In a letter to Rudolf Jakob Humm in March 1933, Hesse wrote: "I know the siren call that is exhorting us to join the masses and get involved in the actual struggle, and several times I have come very close to following it."[41]

He went on in this letter to say that he had been completely on the side of the November Revolution of 1918 and that he had some close friends among German leftists. However, precisely the experience of the world war had made him realize that social injustices could not be rectified through violence and that he could therefore not lend his support to such movements, "not even socialist ones, not even attempts at change that seem welcome and just. For it is always the wrong people who end up getting killed, and even if it were the right—right-wing—ones: I just don't believe in the improving and expiatory power of killing, and while I do acknowledge that the escalation of the political struggle between parties to a state of civil war has the force of decisiveness behind it, and the moral tension of an Either–Or situation, the fact remains that I have renounced violence plain and simple." Above and beyond this refusal, Hesse also laid down that article of faith here that would carry him through the ensuing twelve years of Nazi dictatorship and the Second World War: "The world is sick from injustice, for sure. But it is far more seriously sick from a lack of love, humanity, and a sense of fraternity."[42] He too, he told Humm, had undergone a long journey and many changes in his own life: "It may well be the journey of a Don Quixote, but come what may it is undeniably one of suffering and acknowledging my guilt, which has left me with a very sensitive conscience."[43]

Work as a Reviewer on *Bonniers Litterära Magasin* in Stockholm: Attacks on Hesse by the Nazi Editor Will Vesper and the Émigré Georg Bernhard

> This is all just a little part of the quiet struggle that we are conducting for the soul of Germany; for instance, in Fischer's review I am now the only German critic who reviews and sometimes even recommends books written by Jewish authors.
>
> —Hermann Hesse, letter to his son Heiner, January 19, 1935

On the face of it, it was an offer that was tailor-made for Hesse. It came to him in Switzerland from Sweden—in other words, from far beyond the realm of Nazified newspapers and of the German exile press. *Bonniers Litterära Magasin* was the leading Swedish literary journal, published in Stockholm. The magazine asked him to become a reviewer, providing a twice-yearly roundup of new German literature that would subsequently appear in Swedish translation.

Hesse was an avid reader, and reviewing books was a bread-and-butter job for him. His circumstances in Germany had also changed; although he had not been proscribed outright, he was not greatly in demand either, meaning that he could no longer write for daily newspapers and was only being published by *Die neue Rundschau*. From 1934 to 1942, selected chapters of *The Glass Bead Game* were published in this journal, the Fischer in-house literary magazine, in a total of nine separate preprints.

Hesse was grateful for the offer to write about German literature in a forum that was outside Germany. On January 15, 1935, he wrote back to the editors of *Bonniers* to accept—and his reply is the credo of a reader who was passionate about everything to do with books: "My literary criticism is thoroughly positive in nature, rather than polemical. Generally speaking, my guiding principle is this: Acknowledge anything that is good and spread the word about it, and simply ignore anything that is substandard!"[44]

Hesse also had need of the money, as he admitted to his sister Marulla in February 1935—"I'm on my uppers again, not for the first time"[45]— before thanking her for sending him ten marks. Hesse had found that this was the only way of getting hold of royalty payments from Germany that were still owing to him, mostly for reprints. Official channels would entail these being paid into frozen accounts, inasmuch as they were foreign money transfers. So he had arranged for some of them to be paid to his sister instead, who then forwarded them on to him.

In his next letter to *Bonniers Litterära Magasin,* on January 25, 1935, he had several corrections to make to his first contribution, however. First and foremost: "The title 'Letter from Germany' must be changed. Instead, we could call it 'German Letter on Literature.' The title you suggest would give the impression that I lived in Germany, whereas I actually live in Switzerland and am Swiss in my political outlook."[46]

Was this just a precautionary claim, to which Hesse could then later appeal in the ensuing campaign that was directed against him as an alleged "traitor to the Fatherland"? Yes and no. It was indeed a safeguard for him to be able to maintain that the jurisdiction of Goebbels's propaganda ministry and the Reich Chamber for Literature ended at his Swiss citizenship. Of course, he was, like few other authors, preoccupied with the theme of national identity—only Thomas Mann was comparable with him in this regard. In this respect, too, Hesse was a—very German—visionary of an International of the spirit! Accordingly, he was quick to tell the Swedish journal editors what he understood by modern German literature:

> So, of course I do not simply count as "German literature" the work that is being produced within the Reich, but also the writings of all Germanophone peoples, including German-speaking Switzerland and Austria, and now and then I will also cite books published by Germans in exile. My attitude toward the current social and political situation in Germany is that of every Swiss person and European, but I am a German author and my sphere of operation is Germany, and for that reason I am trying to keep working there, insofar as that is possible without making any concessions to the current regime. There is a spiritual Germany that at the moment is condemned to almost complete silence, but that lives on all the same and whose survival I am actively working for.[47]

This all sounds contradictory—"German author," "a spiritual Germany," "Swiss in my political outlook"—but this was the dilemma in which Hesse found himself caught at this time. Hesse sold a total of almost half a million books in Germany between 1933 and 1945, whereas his sales were just 35,000 in Switzerland over the same period.

The kind of books he reviewed were a red rag to the new Nazi regulatory bodies charged with watching over German culture. For instance, he recommended the works of Franz Kafka (he was one of he first to "discover" him), Moses Maimonides, Ernst Bloch, and Alfred Polgar. His position as a maverick who cared nothing for political battle-lines made him the target of vehement polemics—just as it had done in 1914 with his essay "O My Friends! No More of These Tones!"

The chief spokesman for this polemic, which was aimed at destroying Hesse, was Will Vesper, editor of the National Socialist magazine *Die Neue Literatur* (The new literature). Ironically enough, Vesper had been Hesse's predecessor at *Bonniers Litterära Magasin,* but his highly partisan right-wing contributions had led to his dismissal. Now Vesper hit back—advancing what he thought were discussion-ending arguments that must surely lead to Hesse's writings being proscribed, if not to the author being interned in a concentration camp:

> He insults the whole of new German literature in casting aspersions on writers working in Germany today—even those who were writing long before the change [i.e., before Hitler's seizure of power]—for being nothing but careerists. Furthermore, he refuses to discuss any of them in person, young and old alike. He acts as though Germany, the new Germany that is, has no writers, and as though the new German writing was the work solely of careerist chancers. In doing so, he betrays current German writing to the enemies of Germany and to international Jewry. Here we can see the depths to which a person can sink when he has grown accustomed to sitting at the tables of Jews and breaking bread with them. The German writer Hermann Hesse has taken over the treacherous role of the Jewish criticism of yesteryear.[48]

Vesper thus painted Hesse as an enemy of the people on the side of the Jews, Bolsheviks, and sundry other enemies of Germany!—That was a potentially fatal accusation. Even so, Hesse reacted as if this were nothing but a misunderstanding that needed clearing up, and as if this were a realm in which enlightenment and reason could still achieve something. But he instinctively did what was surely the only correct thing he could do in his situation—he simply declared himself to be outside the sphere in which Vesper's attacks had any validity; in other words, he refused to be treated like German writers who were citizens of the Reich, who could be forced to toe the party line (or silenced).

And so he issued position statements—first of all to *Die Neue Literatur* itself. He stated that he refused to tolerate these "shameful slanders, and in this I am supported by the Swiss Writers' Association, of which I am a member"—and turned Vesper's accusation on its head: "In saying what you do, you are damaging the already very poor reputation of Germany and its literature abroad—which I, a foreigner, am devoting all my efforts to enhancing, through my reviews both for *Die neue Rundschau* and for *Bonniers Litterära Magasin*."[49]

So, Hesse now found himself in the Nazis' firing line after all. Even in July 1933 he had been able to write to Thomas Mann to express his relief that he had "remained unmolested" by the powers that be in Germany, and that they must have just forgotten about him. This was not the case; Hesse was far too important a figure to the Nazi cultural functionaries for them to forget him. On no account did they want to see him join the ranks of the literary émigrés.

And indeed, this did not happen, though the dissociation was not at Hesse's instigation; instead, it was parts of the émigré press that launched personal attacks on him.

Initially the Fischer publishing house was the target of their polemic. The publisher Gottfried Bermann Fischer was fighting to keep the business afloat. For his pains, he was violently attacked by Leopold Schwarzschild in the Paris émigré magazine *Das neue Tage-Buch* (The new diary), who accused him of being a "protected Jew of the National Socialist publishing industry"—an absurd claim, given that Bermann Fischer himself was forced to emigrate shortly after, taking a number of his authors (who in any case were *personae non gratae* in Nazi Germany) with him to form the basis of a refounding of the press abroad. The rights to Hesse's works, however, were not released by the Nazi authorities and so remained with the "Aryanized" rump of the Fischer empire, now run by Peter Suhrkamp, in Berlin. Schwarzschild wrote that he "strongly suspected" the negotiations about moving the Fischer publishing house abroad "of being quietly orchestrated by the Propaganda Ministry in Berlin."

Hermann Hesse, Thomas Mann, and Annette Kolb protested in the strongest terms at this insinuation. The émigré journalist Georg Bernhard (formerly of the *Vossische Zeitung*) then wrote a leader on this open letter of protest by the three authors in the German-language *Pariser Zeitung,* in which he denounced Hesse and Kolb as "figureheads of the Third Reich." He also accused Hesse, in his capacity as an employee of the *Frankfurter Zeitung* (which he was not), of being complicit in Joseph Goebbels's propaganda offensive to deceive the outside world over what was happening in Germany.

Was Hesse really just a "fig-leaf for the Third Reich"—another charge that was leveled at him by Bernhard? On January 24, 1936, Hesse, angered by this libel, responded to Georg Bernhard:

I should like to point out to you, just in the event that you have not forgotten your service to the truth amidst all your struggles, that your statements about me are in flagrant contradiction of the facts. . . . Struggling is a fine thing, but it can easily taint one's character. We know that during the First World War the army reports from the combatant nations were all equally a pack of lies. It would be unworthy of the German exile community if you were also to employ such methods in your struggle. When all's said and done, what are you fighting for?[50]

Hesse was harder hit by this attack by the émigré press than he was prepared to admit. It did, though, confirm him in his belief that one needed to transcend the purely ideological and political confrontation if one wanted to retain any semblance of spirit and dignity in the insanity of world history.

It pained him that the émigré community should so misunderstand him. After all, wasn't he keeping his house open to refugees from Germany? Hadn't even Bertolt Brecht and Peter Weiss (who would end up living at Casa Rossa for a spell) visited him, and all the time more kept arriving, to whom he tried to offer both advice and practical help? This was something that no amount of leader articles, however fiercely combative, could achieve. In January 1936 Hesse wrote to Gunter Böhmer: "At present I am used to the post bringing me letters and newspapers in which I am pilloried by one side for being a traitor to the people and a cowardly emigrant, and by the opposing side for being a stool pigeon of Dr. Goebbels."[51] He told Klaus Mann: "In the war, while Herr Bernhard was busy writing passionate leader articles, I saw a few writers not just talking the talk but standing up to be counted as well, including people on whom Bernhard cast aspersions, like Annette Kolb and Romain Rolland. My friendship with them both was the only good thing to emerge from those dreadful war years for me. . . . Where the Fischer publishing house is concerned, I would like to add that my intervention on Bermann's behalf was just someone stepping in to help a friend being attacked by robbers."[52]

Hesse's work for the Swedish literary magazine, which had begun in March 1935, came to an end in September 1936. He suddenly found himself in a situation where his neutrality was being doubted by all sides. And there was no question that he was caught in a dilemma that was tantamount to a trap for him: he was a Swiss national whose publisher was in Berlin. He was still one of the best known—and most widely read—of all German authors. That couldn't be achieved in Nazi Germany without a certain amount of careful maneuvering, as, for instance, was also the case with Gerhart Hauptmann, Ricarda Huch, and Erich Kästner: under a pseudonym, Kästner wrote screenplays for the state-controlled Ufa studio (notably for the 1943 film *Münchhausen*).

Hesse knew that he had to devote himself now to writing his major work *The Glass Bead Game,* and that it would be a false move for him, for as long as he could not decide to likewise become an émigré writer, to dissipate his energies on political journalism.

But having been resident in Switzerland since 1912, ought he now to move to the United States, like Thomas Mann? Emigrating would not have befitted his position as a Swiss citizen—but on the other hand it would have been in accordance with his situation as an author of the Fischer publishing house in Germany. But could he simply leave Peter Suhrkamp and his German readers in the lurch—since that was definitely what provoking a ban on publication of his works by emigrating would amount to? Hesse was well aware that in the contemporary age, it was not so simple to oscillate between the different parties, who would presently be warring parties, without bringing blame down upon his own head. And yet in writing *The Glass Bead Game,* he found a way out for himself that was more than just a simple escape—namely, by putting forward a spiritual alternative in an age of barbarism.

Thomas Mann, who at this juncture was still in Küsnacht, learned of Hesse's intentions in a letter of March 12, 1936:

> The great disappointment that my thirty years of working as a reviewer have brought me, insofar as I have earned nothing but brickbats from both sides, the Germans and the émigrés alike, in response to my well-meant and often incredibly demanding work—this sense of disappointment has shown me how much my role as a well-meaning reviewer of German literature has also been a form of escapism on my part, an escape from having to look on impotently as current events unfolded, and also an escape from my writing, from which I have been separated for the past two years by a

widening vacuum. . . . Our work as writers is an illegal activity nowadays, since it is performed in the service of leanings that are an affront to all the warring factions and parties.[53]

Undoubtedly, Hesse was here articulating a position of retrenchment, but emphatically not one of capitulation. Rather, it was a reconsideration of his innate role as a writer.

In adopting this position of neutrality, he was certainly laying himself open to attack—and the fact that Nazi cultural policy rewarded his reluctance to openly criticize the Third Reich only made the whole matter appear all the more dubious. And yet what possible course could he have chosen in 1936 that would not have left him vulnerable to attack?

In May 1937 the head of the Reich Chamber for Literature issued a confidential communiqué that read as follows: "Contrary to conflicting reports, I hereby expressly confirm that, in agreement with the Reich Minister for Popular Enlightenment and Propaganda [Joseph Goebbels] and the official Party review board for the protection of National Socialist literature, I have on various grounds come to the opinion that the writer Hermann Hesse should henceforth not be subjected to any more attacks and accordingly that no steps should be taken to prevent distribution of his works."[54]

Was this good news for Hesse—even supposing that what it said was true (the passage of time would show that it was not)? Hesse's growing unease at being a widely disseminated author in Nazi Germany was unmistakable. Hesse described the situation appositely, in a letter of February 5, 1936, to Thomas Mann as "a poison-gas atmosphere between the opposing fronts."

The plain fact was that anyone in such an exposed position as Hesse who wished to continue to be tolerated in Nazi Germany had to pay a high price for it. For one thing, it required signing a "Declaration of Aryan Heritage," which Hesse received on March 15, 1935, and to which he responded as follows: "I am therefore not signing the declaration, not because I am not an Aryan, of course, but because this unreasonable demand runs counter to our Swiss sensibility and outlook."[55] Yet Hesse need not have added "of course" to his unequivocally clear rejection of this request, which would have outraged any fair-minded person—for there were plenty of people who weren't Aryans yet were decidedly German for all that, such as his wife, Ninon.

Hesse knew that these were not abstract discussions that were being conducted here; in the background were always a sense of threat and possible persecution, and he lived in a constant state of fear. In extremis, Switzerland would not be able to protect him. Although the authorities in Berlin had decided "on various grounds" (to quote their ominous-sounding formulation) not to place him on the list of generally undesirable authors, certain of his books were no longer published—notably *A Library of World Literature,* which contained many names of writers whom the Nazis would immediately have put on the index of proscribed books. And although *Beneath the Wheel* and the anarchic-decadent *Steppenwolf* were not officially banned, they were still frowned upon.

Awkwardness between Germany and Switzerland— Hesse's Ongoing Attempt to Remain Politically Neutral and to Point the Way Forward Spiritually—Suicide of His Brother Hans

Swiss–German relations day to day, which in the past few years had not been without their bureaucratic inconveniences, now became even more unpleasant. However, Hesse had experienced difficulties dealing with the German tax authorities even before 1933, as he told the institution that had asked him to sign the Declaration of Aryan Heritage: "However, I have had the experience that your official bodies do not abide by many of their promises and agreements. For example, your government signed a treaty with Switzerland over double taxation, according to which my royalties, which are liable to tax in Switzerland, would be tax-exempt in Germany. Even so, according to a recent statement broadcast on the radio, I discover that, quite contrary to all law, I am to have ten percent foreign transfer tax deducted."[56] Such were the irritations, the effects of the Third Reich, that Hesse experienced even in Montagnola. In view of the concentration camps and the Nazis' political and racial persecutions, all this comes across as very petty—but at root all Hesse was doing was what any normal person might do on a daily basis: measuring the promises of a government against its actions. And in so doing, he came up against, in microcosm, the same disconnect between propaganda and fact that was fast becoming apparent in Germany itself, albeit on a quite different scale.

Hesse expressed his basic awareness of everything that was going on in his 1938 essay "Letter to a German Scholar": "We underlings are now not only busy bleeding and complaining about what possessions of our have been smashed or stolen, partly out of sheer willfulness and partly out of greed, we also have other, in part very demanding functions, such as to cater for armies of impoverished refugees—the prisoners of war welfare organization where I once worked for three years and occasionally thought was really hard work, was a picnic by comparison."[57] Thus, Hesse was constantly engaged in delineating his own position, even in his replies to letters from Germany, some of which must have been framed in such a way as to try and provoke him. For instance, someone wrote to him on January 19, 1939, from London, claiming he defended National Socialism in England while not believing in it in Germany. What did this correspondent want from Hesse? Hesse deigned to give even this letter a response, though his reply was unequivocal: "Just open your eyes for a moment to the unspeakable misery that is filling the world, and to the untold suffering that those people whom you defend have visited upon the world, without themselves meeting any violence or resistance."[58]

During this period, misery lay heavily upon Hesse like a black cloth. In late 1935 he suddenly received news of the death of his younger brother, Hans. That same Hans whom he had found so annoying during his youth, and who had seemed too weak to withstand the external world's attempts to break him. Hans the dutiful son, who had always done what any authority figures—be it his parents, or teachers, or bosses—had required of him. A person devoid of any self-confidence. Hesse had always treated Hans with undisguised contempt, an attitude that had had consequences when they met again as adults at the resort of Baden near Zurich.

Hans, by then married, was working in Baden as a bookkeeper in a factory; Hesse, meanwhile, visited the city at least once a year for several weeks to take a rest cure at the Verenahof spa. He and his brother would meet on these occasions, though their interactions remained stiff and formal. There was no closeness between the siblings.

And then the most shocking thing occurred. Whereas Hesse had announced time and again throughout the 1920s that the only way out he could see was suicide, but then managed to somehow carry on after all, Hans really did take his own life. At the time, Hesse also happened to be in Baden; he was informed about the sudden disappearance of his brother and immediately wrote to his sister Adele. Hans suffered from depression and increasingly also from a persecution complex. Hesse feared the worst.

What he thought must have occurred had indeed come to pass. He recounted the sequence of events to his cousin Fritz Gundert: "And so he left home on the morning of November 27, but never appeared at his office. A search was immediately set in motion, people came to find me at the hotel and we looked high and low for him for a day and a half. . . . He was eventually discovered on the second day—he'd evidently been dead for some hours, after slashing his wrists with his penknife."[59]

The death of this always somewhat cowed, disturbed person, who had been broken "beneath the wheel" of life affected Hesse much more than his brother's inconsequential life had ever been able to do. Someone had taken the path that he had always envisaged for himself! Hesse remarked on his brother from the perspective of his neighbor in Baden: "Hans found it uncomfortable and embarrassing to have a brother who was far too intellectual and famous, etc. for him and, as I found out later, he went out of his way to conceal that he was my brother."[60]

Now, though, the demise of his brother, who hitherto had not meant a great deal to him, prompted him to write the surprisingly extensive text "Memories of Hans," which recounted their shared childhood and offered some thoughts on his brother's character and his inevitable failure in life.

However great a distance Hesse kept from his family, whenever he wrote about them, whether his father or his two sisters, Adele and Marulla, he always did so in a very empathetic way. These texts bring them vividly to life. And now Hans also became one of Hesse's subjects, this little clerk who took his life in such an ostentatious way, opening his veins like Seneca had done, although, unlike the Roman philosopher, not among a circle of friends and pupils but all alone, hidden from prying eyes. The only family member whom Hesse refused to remember fondly was his mother, the person to whom he had been closest in his childhood and youth. The fact that his mother had done all she could to snuff out the budding author in him had made her his enemy, and the scars still remained. Furthermore—unlike his father, whose awkward Pietist scholarliness had long made him a very remote figure to Hesse—it also precluded the possibility of any later rapprochement between mother and son. The person who suffered most from this deep rift was Hesse—and also to a great extent all the women he then went on to marry.

A Summer Guest: Peter Weiss

Hesse was someone who took a strong interest in other people,
and much of what is important about Hesse's work is not contained in his actual artistic endeavors but in his relationships
with other people, a major characteristic of Hesse that emerges
from his correspondence.

—Peter Weiss, interviewed by Peter Roos in 1979

Hesse in Ticino increasingly became an assembly point for exiles, who
came seeking moral support from him and often practical help as well. One
of them was Peter Weiss, the son of a Hungarian textile manufacturer and
a Swiss actress, who had grown up in Berlin and Bremen and who emigrated to the Czech town of Varnsdorf.

He was a keen painter and writer, but saw few opportunities of advancing his career in Czechoslovakia, particularly in the absence of any
ardent champions of his work. Accordingly, in January 1937 the twenty-
year-old Weiss wrote to Hesse, sending him samples of his work and asking
for his opinion of them: "I don't know anybody, because I always mess
things up with people straight away; or I am disappointed because I expect too much of people in advance. . . . So, I'm searching for my path in
life but can't find it. I write, but I have no idea whether it's good or bad—
because I only read it to myself. . . . I am only writing to you because I
know so much of your work—and because I consider you the real master
of the art."[61]

Hesse found it hard to resist this kind of flattery. He felt great sympathy toward outsiders like Weiss, and so he replied immediately. The head
of the letter that Hesse sent back to Weiss was decorated with a sketch that
Gunter Böhmer had done of him. Hesse told Weiss that he was prepared
to champion his work: "Perhaps you could try sending a publisher a selection of your pen-and-ink drawings, mentioning my name, and inquiring
whether he might occasionally have things he'd like you to draw, like a
book cover or text illustrations. A publisher I would recommend in particular is: Dr. G. Bermann, the son-in-law of my old publisher S. Fischer."

Hesse then went on to give the young man a piece of advice which at
first sight seems astonishing, but which on closer inspection tells us something about Hesse's own career as an author: "The main danger for you, I
think, is the state of isolation you're living in. At your age, you can't endure that for very long without damage. Find someone who can be your

friend, be frank with him about yourself and your artistic endeavors, and pay attention to his reaction; he absolutely does not need to be a genius."[62]

The response to this advice by Peter Weiss—who signed himself "Peter Ulrich Weiss"—was very adolescent in its directness: he announced without more ado that he would come and visit Hesse that summer, as part of a walking tour that he was planning to undertake around the Ticino region. Hesse was so taken aback by this that at first he did not reply. Yet despite this rather brazen act of inviting himself (which Hesse was getting used to now, anyway, on a larger scale), Hesse gave the young wanderer a warm welcome and allowed him to stay in his old apartment at Casa Camuzzi. Looking back, Weiss recalled that summer: "He invited me to come and eat, I was permitted to be present when he played music in his library, I went out into the garden with him to play *boccia* . . . and I discussed my future plans with him."[63]

Ninon sent soup over to Casa Camuzzi for Weiss when the young man fell ill—so he didn't have to cook anything, just warm up the soup, the shrewd housewife advised him. Meanwhile, Hesse wrote to the other young artist who regarded him as "the master"—Gunter Böhmer: "I have another young painter living at Casa Camuzzi once more, and again it is one who frequently corresponded with me for a year or two beforehand, but at the moment he's on his vacation and will return to the academy in Prague."[64] This was true, though Weiss was reluctant to go back; he would rather have stayed in Switzerland, but that was not so straightforward, as he would discover the following summer, when he repeated his journey (this time accompanied by Robert Jungk and Hermann Levin Goldschmidt) and attempted to stay longer than before in Ticino. However, this kind of extended stay was only permitted by the Swiss authorities if it was part of a course of study. Weiss was told that he would have to enroll somewhere to study or alternatively give the name of a painter who was teaching him.

Hesse now began to build bridges for Weiss by writing to his friends, including Alfred Kubin, to tell them about the great talent of this young painter and writer. Naturally, the exchange of letters between the twenty-year-old Weiss and the sixty-year-old author also focused to a large degree on what it meant to live as an artist. Hesse responded to Weiss's concerned inquiry as to whether it was permissible to simply concentrate oneself and ignore the outside world by telling him that this "egotism of the artist, which spurns all business and politics and wishes to do nothing except play games" was indeed allowed: "Ah, this is the most harmless form of egotism in the world—how peaceful and beautiful that world would be if there were no other sort! Stick to it!"[65]

He commissioned Weiss—in return for a fee—to illustrate some of his stories, including *Childhood of the Magician,* and gave the completed manuscripts to his friends as gifts.

In this period Weiss was completely entranced by Hesse, calling him "the old magician" and proselytizing to his friends about a new Romanticism. The landscape he walked through was an integral part of this new esthetic: "At that time, Ticino was still undeveloped, with extensive chestnut woods and wilderness areas. We strolled though this landscape. Past ruined buildings and into small villages, and the whole atmosphere of the place was steeped in the freshness of nature."[66]

Some of his friends from this period were amazed at the changes Weiss would later undergo in Sweden (above all under the influence of Brecht). Max Barth, for instance, recalled: "Peter was completely separate from the émigré community. He wasn't interested in politics. . . . No one could have imagined that he would one day be writing political dramas expounding political doctrine in a crude Marxist manner that relied in part on the techniques of the old theater of agitprop."[67]

Contact between Hesse and Weiss grew less frequent. They sent one another pieces they had written and photos—and Weiss made just a single attempt to really excite Hesse's interest in one of his projects: on June 23, 1944, he asked him to write a contribution for the catalogue of an exhibition of he was planning to organize. Weiss wrote: "You have always been a champion of youth and so it would be nice if we could have a few words from you for our first issue, which is due to be published in the fall."[68]

Hesse sent the following reply: "I'm afraid I cannot comply with your wish that I should write something for your magazine; I've never written anything on commission and besides I've gone into complete retirement over the past few years."[69]

The next time Hesse heard from Weiss was in 1961, and once again there was a specific purpose behind the contact. Weiss's *Leavetaking (Abschied von den Eltern)* was just about to be published by Suhrkamp and he was hoping that Hesse might write a review. Although Hesse once again could not be persuaded to oblige, he was pleased that Weiss, whose early career he had promoted, had written such a good book, which he included in his recommended "books of the year" for the magazine *Weltwoche*. In addition, he put Weiss's name forward for the Hermann Hesse Prize (whose first adjudicator, Friedrich Sieburg, he had angrily turned down due to his Nazi sympathies, thus prompting the appointment of another). In 1962 this prize was awarded for the second time (the first winner the previous year had been Martin Walser), but despite Hesse's personal recommendation, it did not go to Peter Weiss.

The Lead-up to *The Glass Bead Game*

> One should interrogate in detail every aspect of a book that strikes one as important rather than query what is not in it. That would be an endless task.
>
> —Hesse, letter of December 8, 1955

If there had not been a pronounced oneiric dimension to Hesse's work, there would have been no Magic Theater and no *Glass Bead Game*. Even the Magic Theater was already a kind of place of judgment on himself. Ultimately that was the only form, after numerous transformations, in which he could conceive of the theater. A kind of counter-theater to the public fair of mass culture, a realm that sought to absorb authors as well. A theater of the mind, a fantastic counterweight to the unimaginative outside world. It also invariably took the form of a rigorous self-interrogation, which escalated to self-condemnation.

For inasmuch as Hesse continued to regard all forms of virtuosity with deep suspicion, this was especially true of the theater, that place where people put themselves on display, and which was home to a particular strain of vanity whose constant pursuit of publicity condemned it to superficiality. This ascetic attitude toward any type of virtuosity had a great deal to do with the "forbidden path" that Hesse was repeatedly warned about in his Pietist childhood as the road to perdition.

In many respects he had managed to energetically liberate himself in later life from this upbringing—whereas in others he had not. Thus, he continued to feel uneasy about the theater—this also included fulfilling requests to him to make public appearances in the form of readings, lectures, and interviews. For Hesse these were more than just an irritation, as he feared that he would taint himself and damage his reputation as an author by engaging in them.

This theme of the Magic Theater from *Steppenwolf* found its way into *The Glass Bead Game*. Here, the constant switching between internal and external worlds blended Hesse's life story with reflection and mythical reenchantment. This imbued the work with a particular tone—that of a "biography of the soul," or historiography in the form of a myth. Hesse here recounts the journey of his main protagonist, Josef Knecht, the "Magister Ludi," through time. Knecht passes through the same stations in life as Hesse had, from the Latin school to the elite academy at the monastery in Maulbronn (which is rechristened "Waldzell" here, though Knecht sometimes calls it "Mariabronn"), until he finally attains the highest position in the order of administrators of the Glass Bead Game. This is basically the same path trodden by Hans Giebenrath in *Beneath the Wheel*—only this time with a positive outcome. It is an educational utopia about a highly gifted pupil who is recognized as such and supported by his tutors and ultimately himself comes to epitomize the ideal teacher.

The Glass Bead Game turned into an extraordinary book, on which Hesse worked for a decade, from 1932 to 1942. Though Hesse vehemently rejected the term "inner emigration" after 1945, because it was used polemically by the writer Frank Thiess against Thomas Mann and other German writers who had emigrated, he himself had survived the worst period of the Nazi dictatorship in the inner "exile" of his *Glass Bead Game*. This was a spiritual alternative world full of symbols, which he wrote himself into. In this, it was very reminiscent of Ernst Jünger's secret book of resistance against Hitler, *On the Marble Cliffs* (*Auf den Marmorklippen,* 1939).

So, what did *The Glass Bead Game* have that was lacking in the slim volume *Journey to the East?* The journey in this later work became like a treatise, and was undertaken with a pedagogical purpose. In *The Glass Bead Game* the Magic Theater, which lives on in both books, loses more and more of its disenchanting character, its motif of being ridiculed—both in a Mozartian and a Nietzschean sense—because one had taken a phantasm to be real. Here it has become just another part of a larger myth.

Thus, for the most part one would search in vain for humor or (self-) ironizing distance in *The Glass Bead Game*. At all times, the desire to create a major work that would become the writer's legacy is very much in evidence. But does that diminish the importance of this deeply unconventional book? Certainly not, though readers must be prepared to adjust to the fact that they are entering a realm of saints' legends, almost of the kind that Hugo Ball presented in his final works. Hesse took Goethe's vision of a "Pedagogical Province" very seriously—as he had every reason to, during this period.

What, then, did this novel hope to achieve? It was an attempt at an overview of the whole of history up to that point, Hesse's own as well as that of humankind. Might it be possible, he speculated, to take his own beginnings, his childhood and youth, along with all former epochs of civilization and fold them together into the present? The clever artifice of *The Glass Bead Game* was that the novel supposedly consisted of papers that were published after Josef Knecht's death. This was a device that Hesse often used in order to create a sense of distance, and to begin with a tale whose end we already know. The outcome is therefore not at all undecided, since we know all along where it is headed. In addition, *The Glass Bead Game* is narrated from the year 2200; thus, we find ourselves already looking back on a future that still lies ahead of us. This gives the work a surreal dimension and also anchors its central theme—the soul's journey through the ages—in its very structure.

To attempt to describe the whole panorama of *The Glass Bead Game* or to comment in depth on its philosophical motifs would be far beyond the scope of this biography. The analogy of the secret society of the *Turmgesellschaft* (Tower Society) in Goethe's *Wilhelm Meister's Apprenticeship* was just as clear as the work's affinity to Thomas Mann. Around this same time, Mann was writing his last great work, *Doctor Faustus*. Hesse and Mann had by then grown very close as a result of their exchange of correspondence. Among their shared concerns was the question of how knowledge and experiences that have been acquired with much effort and pain by individuals and entire peoples can be passed on to future generations. And what form should spiritual matters take in this? It was clear that there was an urgent need for a protected space beyond the clutches of barbarity. But it was just as clear that all institutionalization of the spirit would only ultimately lead once more to a kind of scholasticism and dogmatism and hence finally to a destruction of the living spirit. That held equally true for all institutions, be they schools, universities, academies, churches, religious orders, or masonic lodges.

Could there ever be, then, a "monastery of free spirits" like the one imagined by Nietzsche? Any such institution would be a living contradiction, an avowed paradox of a school of wisdom that everyone knew could not be taught—though this was far from indicating that one should ever abandon the perennially inadequate attempts to establish such a place.

Who were the elite, and how should they live? Here, once again, Hesse arrived at the answer that he had repeatedly been giving since *Peter Camenzind* and his acquaintance with Saint Francis of Assisi: the true saint is one who openly admits that he is a heretic at the same time!

It is an interesting question as to how Hesse even arrived at the kind of science fiction setting, with its future-oriented summing-up, he adopted for *The Glass Bead Game*. It seems safe to assume that, when writing the book, Hesse called to mind the shock he had experienced at the age of fourteen when reading Edward Bellamy's *Looking Backward from 2000 to 1887*. And even though the classical tone of the work—which in places sounds all too pastoral and convinced of its own superiority—may sometimes come across as downright staid, we should not forget that this late work of Hesse's, with all its strengths and weaknesses, still derives from the spirit of Romanticism.

In depicting a life lived (or an act of survival) in the labyrinthine passages of inner space, the novel belongs in tradition of German fiction, stretching from E. T. A. Hoffmann's *The Mines at Falun (Die Bergwerke zu Falun)* to Franz Fühmann's *In the Mine (Im Berg),* which has at its heart the motif of plumbing the depths of the soul.

In the depths, one can escape the clutches of the surface, the superficial! *The Glass Bead Game* is this kind of "mine of the soul" as well. Treasures may be hidden down below, but it is also a place where, far from the eyes of the creatures of the daylight realm, the night, the dark side can be cultivated and where, in the multitude of hidden passageways and caverns, knowledge and tradition can be experimented with.

Seen in this light, *The Glass Bead Game* is a laboratory of creativity. A questioning ultimately of the lighting conditions of day and night, respectively, and of the relationship between the surface and the depths. The demarcation between dream and reality is just as difficult to determine here as that between yesterday, today, and tomorrow, and between the potential and the actual.

The consistency of Hesse's ongoing act of self-perception is astounding: all of the underlying principles of *The Glass Bead Game* were already set out in the 1900 text "Romanticism and New Romanticism." There is a remarkable connection here to Maurice Maeterlinck, whose work *The Life of the Bee (La Vie des Abeilles)* fascinated Hesse in its symbiosis of fact and poetry, which shunned all external categorization and any form of hard-and-fast definition: "He stylizes, he composes, and he adorns his fictions with the free capriciousness of a Brentano or a Hoffmann. But he only does this ostensibly; he has also learned to see and portray things realistically, but that isn't immediately apparent because he talks almost exclusively about invisible things."[70]

The borderlines between the inner and outer words are as fluid as those between day and night. In the twilight all things visionary are transformed—the gaze turns more inward and becomes correspondingly more poetic. In this way, Maeterlinck wrote a wonderfully natural book full of deep empirical knowledge about bees. It is not a work of nonfiction, but instead a fiction that aims to tease out all the science associated with the subject and that tries to fathom the true nature both of bees and of the author who is writing about them. The end result is a highly symbolic work that immediately puts one in mind of *The Glass Bead Game.*

In Maeterlinck's work, the talk is always of dualities: of decidedly real bees, as described in any reference work, but also of bees as poetically stylized symbols. The dream of a bee as dreamed by long-forgotten flowers on one of the last afternoons of the summer. If we are not alive to this touch of magic, we as just as unenlightened by Maeterlinck's book as we would be if we read *The Glass Bead Game* in the same unimaginative frame of mind.

Each realm mutually enhances the other—the discovery of nature and its transformation through poetry, which for Maeterlinck was a form of dream in which the metamorphoses of living things were immanent. Hesse was fascinated by this positively surreal approach to a theme that in his eyes had become the modern application of the kind of dream esthetic Novalis had envisaged. In the first chapter of the book, Maeterlinck stated:

> It is not my intention to write a treatise on apiculture, or on practical bee-keeping. Excellent works of the kind can be found in all countries, and it would be pointless to write them afresh. . . . Nor do I mean to write a scientific monograph . . . or convey the findings of new studies and obser-vations. I will say hardly anything that those who already have some knowledge of beekeeping do not already know. . . . I will confine myself to recounting the facts as accurately as if they had appeared in a practical manual or scientific monograph, only I will relate them in a somewhat live-lier fashion than such works would permit, arrange them more harmoni-ously together, and blend them with freer and more mature reflections. Anyone who has read this book will not instantly be in a position to manage a hive; but he will know more or less all that can with any certainty be known of the curious, profound, and intimate side of its inhabitants. Nor will this be at the cost of what still remains to be learned.

When he pondered and wrote about "Romanticism and New Roman-ticism," Hesse was just twenty-three years old. But with this essay he was setting foot on a path that would eventually culminate in *The Glass Bead Game:* "The spirit of Novalis is to discover the profound laws governing all life and to see the reflection of the eternal even in a beehive."[71]

Maeterlinck was skeptical regarding the possibility of acquiring new knowledge, because we remain encumbered with the old uncertainties: "Beyond the appreciable basic facts of their life we know very little about bees. And the longer we keep them, the more conscious we be-come of our profound ignorance regarding their real existence; but at least such ignorance is better than the other kind, which is unconscious and complacent."[72]

But was this Hesse's sole aim? Perhaps he created his last major work—as exhaustive in its scope as it is magnificently obscure in the miniatures it contains—just in order to demonstrate to us that "such ignorance" actually amounts to a very great deal? He was suitably cryptic when answering the question as to what the Glass Bead Game actually was: "The Glass Bead Game is thus a mode of playing with the total contents and values of our culture; it plays with them as, say, in the great age of the arts a painter might have played with the colors on his palette."[73] He likened the Game to a "giant organ," which through the deployment of its various manuals, pedals, and stops was capable of producing a kind of global music ("the entire intellectual content of the universe")—a secret language that only the initiated (the travelers to the East!) could understand. Hesse therefore also spoke in terms of "the runes of Novalis's hallucinatory visions."[74]

Those visions went very far back, as far as Plato's *Republic*—which was a republic of scholars, in which the philosophers were kings and the kings philosophers. Yet Hesse, like Hölderlin, viewed with suspicion philosophers who were also at the same time poets. Even so, one motif that is absolutely central to *The Glass Bead Game* is undoubtedly a philosophical one: the dialectic of master and slave from Hegel's *Phenomenology of Spirit*. This presents a struggle between different forms of consciousness—in which the slave, as the dependent consciousness that is compelled to take action, ultimately overcomes through that very action the ruling yet passive consciousness of the master. With the result that the slave takes the place of the master—and the wheel of history turns ever onward.

In contrast to Hegel, Hesse does not allow his "slave" who triumphs over the "master" (i.e., all forms of power) to rule or to become the new master—for a lifetime of servitude represents the only possible way of living. Anyone who aspires to rule, on the other hand, is fated to perish.

An Alchemistic History of the World: What Does a Critique of the "Age of the Feuilleton" Mean?

Nothing would be more wrong than to take the Glass Bead Game as a sophisticated form of entertainment for the educated classes. To obviate such a misunderstanding and to make clear that what he was attempting here, quite to the contrary, was to save bourgeois culture, Hesse wrote in his introduction to the book a critique of the "Age of the Feuilleton."

Yet this had its pitfalls and traps, since he ascribes the concept to, of all people, a literary historian—for Hesse, the most despised group among academics (a body of people in general whom he viewed with suspicion)—and what's more one by the name of Plinius Ziegenhalss.

A true counterpart to the loyal German Serenus Zeitblom, the narrator in Thomas Mann's *Doctor Faustus!*

Of course, science has no time for feuilletons, since writing these requires wit and the ability to express oneself trenchantly and to distill complex relations down into a reduced form that is comprehensible and convincing. Alongside offering observations on the current age, Hesse's short prose writings such as "The Art of Idleness" also gather together notes on books Hesse has read—thus making it perfectly possible to describe these essays as feuilletons. An author who has no opinions on things is at best a custodian of an alien spirit, a bookkeeper or archivist. Thus, the "critique of the Age of the Feuilleton" that Hesse places in the mouth of Plinius Ziegenhalss actually runs counter to Hesse's own self-image, or at least characterizes this critical attitude as being just one of his many facets. Likewise, one is astonished by the further claim that the Glass Bead Game derived from a combination of music and mathematics. Mathematics as the key to a universal, language? To be sure, there are the Pythagoreans, who imputed a magical significance to numbers—yet skepticism still remains. This skepticism increases still further when Hesse (still speaking through Plinius Ziegenhalss) writes that the Glass Bead Game is ultimately an invention of *musicology.* This leaves one in a state of utter confusion, for hitherto—unlike Thomas Mann, who had Theodor Adorno tutor him in the basics of the twelve-tone technique—Hesse had not been notable for displaying any special interest in music theory, or in mathematics for that matter. Quite the opposite: Hesse was very doubtful about what could grow from abstraction. In his view, only more abstractions, never life itself. It would be Josef Knecht's alter ego Plinio Designori who came to embody all these reservations of the living spirit toward its dead form.

Thus, the "critique of the Age of the Feuilleton" appears to be more a part of the problem than its solution. This seems a reasonable assumption, given that Hesse found himself caught between all fronts in the 1930s. He shared Oswald Spengler's diagnosis of the impending decline of the West, he was no supporter of the Weimar Republic (which he actually did not know at all well, never having lived in it), and above all he was a sworn enemy of the bourgeois entertainment industry, the misuse of the intellect for the purposes of fashion and pandering to the spirit of the age, and everything that was readily marketable.

Gottfried Benn came to a similar judgment in a radio lecture of 1931 entitled "The New Literary Season." Art and literature, Benn maintained, should not serve any purposes, particularly not those that promote themselves as embodying benevolence. "Anyone who wants to organize life will never make art and is not entitled to count themselves among artists; from the point of view of the artist, creating art, whether it is the falcons in ancient Egyptian reliefs or the novels of [Knut] Hamsun, means excluding real life, restricting it, even fighting against it, in order to stylize it."[75]

As well as despising the bourgeois industry of art and literature production, Hesse also took a dismissive view of functional art deployed for sociological purposes or as part of the class struggle, as represented by the work of Friedrich Wolf, Egon Erwin Kisch, and Johannes R. Becher. But above all he was concerned that he should not be identified as a follower of the folk literature movement.

Yet the Nazis were using dictatorial methods to govern Germany. Anyone who still possessed a scintilla of culture and humanity had to be permitted to take cover and hide from this spiritual barbarism. Open resistance, by contrast, struck him as being futile. Hesse believed this to be one of the demands of the émigrés, who, with their militant sloganeering, would achieve little or even the opposite of what they intended.

In this respect, *The Glass Bead Game* is also a place to overwinter when there is a cold climate outside. This is the realm where the maskers appear—*The Glass Bead Game* is applied Magic Theater, in which one is only recognizable as oneself to the initiated.

This stoic withdrawal into a kind of exile, which can also be a protective place in which to cloister oneself away from the violence of the prevailing political world, became the setting for *The Glass Bead Game*. Here one can test out the various possibilities of slipping away from the world unnoticed while still retaining some of the valuable things that human civilization has produced.

This was more than just an experiment, this was an act of self-defense by someone who felt challenged and who knew that too much public exposure could have fatal consequences for himself and Ninon. *The Glass Bead Game* reflected Hesse's extremely tense life predicament as he asked himself what kind of world his children and grandchildren would live in.

In one ruled by the Nazis? Or one in which the Communists called the shots?

The old bourgeois world was passé, and would never come back, he was certain of that. But to find out what still remained intact and what new possibilities there might be—this was the purpose of this kaleidoscope of different ages and locations, all of which revolve around a single question: namely, What will become of the spirit and who will preserve it? Does an elite have the capacity to stave off the end of an era, or is it instead precisely their task to recognize the inevitable before anyone else and to understand it from the perspective of what will come after?

At least the "critique of the Age of the Feuilleton" is constructive criticism, framed in the same way that Hesse unfailingly framed his book reviews—recognizing that anything that is of value needs to be understood on its own terms and preserved, and that it is not worth even engaging with the rest, which is all just scribbling for profit. Thus, we are presented with the following thoughts about the "Age of the Feuilleton":

> Such tags are pretty, but dangerous; they constantly tempt us to a biased view of the era in question. And as a matter of fact the Age of the Feuilleton was by no means uncultured; it was not even intellectually impoverished. But if we are to believe Ziegenhalss, that age appears to have had only the dimmest notion of what to do with culture. Or rather, it did not know how to assign culture its proper place within the economy of life and the nation. To be frank, we really are very poorly informed about that era, even though it is the soil out of which almost everything that distinguishes our cultural life today has grown. It was, according to Ziegenhalss, an era emphatically "bourgeois" and given to an almost untrammeled individualism.[76]

Do we want to entrust ourselves unconditionally to the judgment of a Plinius Ziegenhalss here? It is a harking back to an era that is long past—Hesse's present day, in the moment when all bourgeois freedom came to an end and the dictatorship promised a great age, the Third Reich! As a result, mere traces have to be read, and testaments to this extinct era of "individualism" collected. From this broad overview, an image then emerges that one might call the myth of an era, the legend of the "Glass Bead Game" passed down through the changing ages. And Hesse opted to individualize the elite theme in the best bourgeois sense, by accompanying the figure of Josef Knecht, the Magister Ludi, the master of the Glass Bead Game, on his journey through various ages and regions.

Is knowledge teachable—and if so, to what end? After all, Hesse was an autodidact who knew the difference between learning that is essential for life and superfluous ballast!

Hesse started to write the introduction to *The Glass Bead Game* at least four times. That shows how important the concept and the spiritual objectives informing the book were to him. The first draft of an introduction that he later abandoned, dated May/June 1932, covered eight pages and had the title "On the Nature and Origin of the Glass Bead Game." This version is prefaced by the motto that also appears in the fourth draft, although in that final version a Latin translation has been added by one "Franz Schall," a device designed to emphasize that the fantastic character of the Glass Bead Game stretches far back into history. The motto, which is attributed to a certain "Albertus Secundus" (a name that calls to mind "Albertus Magnus"—a renowned thirteenth-century German theologian—but is in fact Hesse's own invention) runs as follows: "Nothing is harder, yet nothing is more necessary, than to speak of certain things whose existence is neither demonstrable nor probable. The very fact that serious and conscientious men treat them as existing things brings them a step closer to existence and to the possibility of being born."[77]

It becomes a question of the individual's imaginative capabilities as to whether "certain things whose existence is neither demonstrable nor probable" can be conceived of and thus made vividly present. Anyone who engages in an activity with utter devotion also assists at its birth. The opening "quotation" is an open assertion that what follows is magic: magical acts that involve translating into history worlds from inside the writer's own head—or, as Hesse wrote in the fourth (and final) draft of the introduction: "It represented an elite, symbolic form of seeking for perfection, a sublime alchemy, an approach to that Mind which beyond all images and multiplicities is one within itself—in other words, to God."[78]

The thesis of terminal decline is present even in the first draft of the introduction, "namely the thought that not only our civilization is in its dotage and can no longer produce any more efflorescences but also that the whole spiritual and moral framework of our life is rotten and decaying and in danger of imminent collapse."[79] This was very much in the same vein as Oswald Spengler's doctrine of the cyclical nature of civilizations, and was premised upon a diagnosis of Europe's decline and fall.

Likewise, this first draft also already contains the concept of the Age of the Feuilleton, by which Hesse meant his contemporary age in 1932, a period that, in the account of the history of the Glass Bead Game, already lies more than 150 years in the past. In this first draft, Hesse traces it back to a card game for the educated elite supposedly devised by a certain Chief Accountant Klaiber from Frankfurt in 1935; and although this figure Klaiber disappears again in the later versions, the prognosis of decline still remains.

Hesse intended the diagnosis of the Age of the Feuilleton to indicate that education was something that led directly to the quiz show—that the intellect was becoming nothing but a parlor-game entertainment:

> Now, Klaiber's little educational card game was very much of a piece with this "feuilletonistic" age . . . with the passing of Klaiber's generation the bourgeois feuilletonistic enterprise of the intellect had reached its final nadir: the things that were being written or presented in lectures, newspapers, and books around 1950 fell far short of even the very modest standard of what had been produced in 1930. Simultaneously with the childishly undisciplined playing-around practiced by Klaiber's generation, the production of derivative literary endeavors, derivative pieces of music, and derivative paintings by the art industry reached record numbers; it was as if Europe was trying to prove to itself, in one final effort, that its culture could still be creative.[80]

In other words, during this epoch of bourgeois society, education became simply an ornament. The counter-reaction was not long in coming, however. What ensued was a new, ascetic repositioning of culture by small (sectlike) groups as a form of *discipline;* at the same time, a belief was fostered in the superiority of those groups.

What are we to make of this? It would appear that the Nazi struggle to establish their own Third Reich provoked on the opposing side an apocalyptic urge as represented by the medieval theologian Joachim of Fiore's millenarian theory of the "three ages"; according to Joachim, the "third kingdom" would be the kingdom of God!

Hesse's aim was to set up this notion of the dawning of a new "Kingdom of the Spirit" in opposition to the concept of the Third Reich, which had been entirely colonized by the Nazis. However, this was never expressed openly but instead put in the form of myth and legend. The symbols should speak to the initiated. Broadly speaking, this was also the position of the "Confessing Church" established in Germany by Pastor Dietrich Bonhoeffer during the Nazi period (as distinct from the "German Christian" movement, which supported Hitler's regime).

Up to late 1942 Hesse hoped to be able to publish *The Glass Bead Game* in Germany (prior to this, it had appeared in the magazine *Die neue Rundschau* in nine installments). He attempted to play with the Nazi censors and at the same time thereby to demonstrate the mechanism of the Glass Bead Game. This is the reason the novel constantly operates on such a high symbolic plane, and rehearses that secret language of the travelers to the East which preserves everything that Hesse regarded as precious both in his own life as well as in that of the whole of humanity.

In *The Glass Bead Game* Hesse was attempting nothing less than to liberate the "German spirit" from its perversion under the Nazis. The time was ripe to do so, because there seemed to be no end to National Socialist hegemony for the foreseeable future and because the SS were casting themselves as the nation's elite, as a quasi-religious order of the elect, with strict hierarchies and secret rituals. Hesse's order of Glass Bead Game players embodied a competing ideal of education, which cultivated the "Pedagogical Province" in the spirit of Goethe's *Turmgesellschaft* from *Wilhelm Meister's Apprenticeship*.

In Castalia (the fictional setting of the novel), what is demanded is not blind obedience but instead the complete, albeit very strict, autonomy of the individual players of the Glass Bead Game, who are all, to a man, also travelers to the East. A decisive factor here is the spirit's renunciation of any exercise of power, which effectively puts a Romantic-skeptical spoke in the wheel of Plato and Hegel. Instead, music and meditation are presented as a route to self-fulfillment. When treated in this way, the myth became subversive in an enlightened way.

★   ★   ★

The decadence of the bourgeois era, which was originally conceived as an emancipation from authority, culminated in all-pervading lack of seriousness. This, then, was confronted by a new seriousness, which saw the increasing absence of order and authority as a shortcoming, yet this seriousness had two faces that had to be distinguished from one another: "Thus those struggles for the 'freedom' of the human intellect likewise happened, and subsequently, in the course of the aforementioned Age of the Feuilleton, men came to enjoy an incredible degree of intellectual freedom, more than they could stand. For while they had overthrown the tutelage of the Church completely, and that of the State partially, they had not succeeded in formulating an authentic law they could respect, a genuinely new authority and legitimacy."[81]

In *The Glass Bead Game,* Hesse sent this "genuinely new authority" off on a journey—in the shape of his protagonist Josef Knecht. Was he a true teacher of his students? Hesse, the school dropout and notorious naysayer to authority, speaks here of the attempt to devote all of his energy "to preserving for the future a core of good tradition, discipline, method, and intellectual rigor."[82]

Thus becomes apparent the basic outline of *The Glass Bead Game:* the creation of a subversive spirituality that, reaching beyond the current disastrous situation of the spirit, might provide for it a place of refuge from which it could in the future become active once more. Something must remain indestructible, even when everything round about was lying in ruins! This is one way to read *The Glass Bead Game,* though there are also other ways—the multiplicity of possible interpretations lies in the book's very nature.

In the light of the *vita activa,* Hesse regarded *Homo sapiens* as *Homo faber*—as a working man, that is, albeit in the sense of a craftsman. And in *The Glass Bead Game* Hesse presents the full gamut of a society constituted on the basis of craftsmanship—though here, too, he offers a dual perspective, which factors in the influence of the *vita contemplativa.* Combined with craftsmanship, this results in the figure of *Homo ludens,* as exemplified by Josef Knecht. In Latin, the term *ludus* denotes both "play" (in a general sense as well as in that of a drama, offering a view to the extended stage of the Magic Theater) and "school."

This linking of play and education, of purposelessness and the pedagogical, of edifying entertainment and serious instruction, becomes a paradox that engenders the higher form of unity Hesse saw as the purpose of all human endeavor—and idleness! The base of all creativity, which obeys its own rhythm! Accordingly, a key exercise in the Glass Bead Game consists of writing several fictional lives, which are set in different ages. Hesse has Knecht compose three of these: "The Rainmaker," "The Father Confessor," and "The Indian Life." However, a fourth life set in eighteenth-century Swabia and of particular interest to Hesse due to its Pietist milieu, Knecht never wrote.

Music forms the soul of the Glass Bead Game, while also serving as a model. Thus it reveals itself as having a sonata form: a theme is executed, then appears to recede—only to return again in a modified form. True harmony does not exclude disharmony but instead cancels its out. In this respect, therefore, *The Glass Bead Game* may also be read as a musical score.

This kind of music was different from the "music of doom" that accompanied the collapse of all order and authority—it was the music of what were, for the time being, only small circles of people, but it augured a new beginning.

The Glass Bead Game captured man in his creative potential—both as an individual and as a species: a masque that comprehends the game as a distancing medium promoting (self-) perception.

Unlike his adopted country, Switzerland, Hesse laid not claim to a state of neutrality for himself. His concern, rather, was to be literally *impartial,* to transcend partiality. This form of impartiality, which raises itself above the purely political, was for Hesse the sphere of the greatest possible intellectual radicalism.

Hesse's stance was a result not least of his intensive reading of Pietist writers. In addition to Friedrich Christoph Oetinger and Johann Albrecht Bengel, eighteenth-century Swabian Pietists whose works were greatly admired in Hesse's parents' house, he also took on board writings that were more in the tradition of radical Pietism, such as Johann Arndt's *The Four*

Books of True Christianity and *Garden of Paradise;* Angelus Silesius's *The Cherubinic Wanderer;* Thomas à Kempis's *The Imitation of Christ;* and Gottfried Arnold's *History and Description of Mystical Theology* and *Impartial History of the Church and of Heresy.* These works all turned on broadly the same issue: restoring the original spirit of the origin of Christianity, and bearing witness to the saints, who themselves bore witness to the truth and as a result were declared heretics by the established Church in its history of decline. This structural element of the Church was already recognized by sectarian Pietism with its mystical marginal figures: institutionalized faith was always constituted through acts of exclusion.

So it was that Hesse stubbornly positioned himself in the no-man's-land of global politics: firmly on the side of the individual, over whom the mechanism of grand politics, which exhibited all the symptoms of decline, forever rode roughshod.

As a result, the path of *The Glass Bead Game* leads inward. We enter the interior of the world, as it were, a world inside the mind, a form of Magic Theater yet one that is now conceived in terms of the history of the world—and once again it is Gustav Landauer who points the way with his indissoluble blend of skepticism and mysticism: "The path we must tread in order to commune with the world does not lead outward but inward. We must once again come to realize that we do not simply perceive parts of the world but that we ourselves form an integral part of the world. Anyone who could understand a flower in all its complexity would have understood the world. So then, let us turn our gaze inward once more, then we will have discovered the universe incarnate."[83]

In the chapter of *The Glass Bead Game* entitled "The Legend," we experience the demise of Josef Knecht, which is brought about by the exuberant youthfulness of Tito, the son of his old antipode Plinio Designori, for whose education Knecht has been made responsible. Only through the example of his death can he impart to Tito a quality that his soul has been lacking thus far: humility. Tito hounds Knecht into visiting a high mountainous region that is harmful to his health and then challenges him—though he is already suffering from giddiness and heart murmurs—to a swimming race across the icy waters of a highland lake. Without considering the implications, he leaps into the freezing water.

This spells the end of Knecht, and Hesse recounts the episode with a vital freshness that is otherwise lacking in a work that generally comes across as highly contrived:

> The lake, fed by glacial waters so that even in the warmest days of summer one had to be inured to it, received him with an icy cold, slashing in its enmity. He had steeled himself for a thorough chilling, but not for this fierce cold that seemed to surround him with leaping flames and after a moment of fiery burning began to penetrate rapidly into him. After the dive he had risen quickly to the surface, caught sight of Tito swimming far ahead of him, felt bitterly assailed by this icy, wild, hostile element, but still believed he could lessen the distance, that he was engaging in the swimming race, was fighting for the boy's respect and comradeship, for his soul—when he was already fighting with Death, who had thrown him and was now holding him in a wrestler's grip. Fighting with all his strength, Knecht held him off as long as his heart continued to beat.[84]

Hesse completed *The Glass Bead Game* in late 1942, when the Nazi regime was at the height of its power, and sent the manuscript to his publisher, Peter Suhrkamp. Suhrkamp was required to present the manuscript to the Propaganda Ministry for its approval. The officials there immediately took against the work and—after Suhrkamp spent seven months in fruitless negotiations with them—a publication ban was finally issued by the Rosenberg Bureau (the official Nazi body responsible for formulating cultural policy). This ban definitively made Hesse a proscribed author in Nazi Germany. Likewise (under the pretext of a paper shortage), no reprints of his other books were permitted after 1943.

Hesse's principal work, which he had very deliberately written for readers in Nazi Germany, was thus left hanging in mid-air.

Hesse felt a failure, at rock bottom. In November Peter Suhrkamp brought the manuscript of *The Glass Bead Game* back to him in Montagnola. In a letter to his son Heiner, Hesse described Suhrkamp's outward appearance as shocking; he had by then grown so skeletal that Hesse barely recognized him from their first meeting at Bad Eilsen in August 1936.

Under the circumstances, Suhrkamp had done all he could to get the book published, but the censorship authorities only approved books that benefited the "life and death struggle of our people"—in other words, nothing but anti-Semitic and militant works. The fact that *The Glass Bead Game* was informed by a very different ethos did not escape the censors.

Hesse now offered the manuscript to the Zurich publishing house of Fretz & Wasmuth, who published it in the fall of 1943 in a print run of three thousand copies, which were only intended for distribution within Switzerland. In 1946 Suhrkamp was finally able to publish the German edition of *The Glass Bead Game*. Despite its hugely complex structure and its challenging theme, it became a worldwide best-seller; thus far some two million copies have been sold.

Hesse wrote to his son Martin on December 3, 1943, about the role that *The Glass Bead Game* had played in his life: "Although I made life almost unbearable for myself during this period, firstly through tying my entire existence and life's work to the publisher in Berlin, and secondly by marrying an Austrian Jewess, on the other hand in all the many hundreds of hours that I spent writing *The Glass Bead Game,* I encountered nothing but a totally pristine world which I could inhabit, completely free of all immediate concerns."[85]

This gives the impression that Castalia might have been very close at hand for Hesse—in the form of his study at Casa Rossa, which only he was permitted to enter.

The Clockwork Mechanism of Time: Hesse and Ernst Jünger

As he grew older, Hesse's distance from everyday concerns steadily increased. This was not from weakness or inconsistency, but quite the opposite: in this, Hesse was going the way of all travelers to the East and Glass Bead Game players. Their aim was, of necessity, to have an internal effect beyond their death and to make themselves invisible to the outside world even prior to their death.

The alternation between the endlessly repetitive round of hustle and bustle with its destructive consequences—never-ending wars and all the specious everyday things that were deemed important—Hesse could now endure only in a magical–mythical form. And was such a state any less substantial than the hysterical clamor of the daily news? Was it not rather a way of saving oneself from such things?

He gave vent to his views on this subject in a letter of July 6, 1943, to Karl Kerényi: "Yet as one gets older, one is less and less touched by one's surroundings, one is heading toward a realm of timelessness, and what's more mostly via the past, with the result that very little of the present remains, and one has absolutely no interest in the future. The nice thing about being like this nowadays is that, in such a state, one is not remotely curious about either war news or debates about what will come afterward, nor can one get agitated at what one reads or hears in the papers or on the radio."[86]

The mining analogy certainly held good for the Glass Bead Game, but it was also an airy, insubstantial game, a symbol of the transparency of all things spiritual. A tower clock of the kind that Hesse got to know during his apprenticeship with the master mechanic Heinrich Perrot in Calw, but here pointing toward the surreal: a timepiece that transcended the merely mechanical and machine-like. The craftsmanship evident in this creation revealed itself to be an art form that eavesdropped on nature and showed it from a hitherto hidden side. This magical clock indicated the age of time, as it moved on from one era to the next!

This explains Hesse's late fascination with Ernst Jünger, and the great respect he showed toward his novel *An der Zeitmauer (At the Wall of Time)*, which was written in much the same spirit as Hesse's great work. Hesse wrote in 1960: "To get straight to the point: this is an extremely clever and good book, which I read with the kind of pleasure you experience when you see your own feelings and thoughts confirmed by a more competent person. Though this is by no means to claim that that I already had all of Jünger's principal and basic thoughts myself. The book is a study of the unease in modern humanity, especially in the West."[87] That was also the theme of *The Glass Bead Game*—and the two authors were also linked by their common insight that the "present hour of history was the end of an era," that basic certainty that the golden age was long past and that its resurrection must remain a nebulous dream.

Over the preceding decades, Hesse had already commented several times on Jünger, though always with a great deal of reserve. For instance, on April 20, 1942, he wrote to Luise Rinser: "He is one of those writers who certainly love the spirit but who feel no love or fellowship toward nature; he shares this trait with many great writers such as

Schiller, for example, but I find them also fundamentally alien and suspicious."[88]

Jünger and Hesse also had certain basic tendencies in common. We have already had occasion to mention Hesse's inclination toward pyromania, and Jünger too had been fascinated by fire from an early age. In the earliest letter of his that has survived, written to his mother in 1902 when he was just seven years old, we read: "Dear Mama! We were very pleased to receive your letter. Fritz would like a big box of lead soldiers on horseback. And I would like a gun and a saber." Jünger would go on to elevate Karl Marx's rhetorical inquiry as to whether Achilles could possibly co-exist alongside gunpowder and lead-shot into a mythically heightened concept of fire. Only in fire would human beings truly experience themselves, he wrote, in allusion to Heraclitus.[89] This was very much akin to Hesse's conception of fire.

Yet they also shared another passion—or perhaps it might be more accurate to call it a weakness or a foible. In Jünger's great esteem for astrology—"the beautiful symbolic language of this sacred art"—Hesse recognized a kindred spirit. Two authors who cultivated a dual perspective in their work found themselves enthralled by astrology's capacity to simultaneously examine both the closest and the most distant things. Likewise, for both of them natural science was also a cosmological picture where that which from a human perspective was born and died, and rose and declined, had for millions of years been trapped in an eternally identical cycle.

In August 1950 Hesse wrote the following appraisal of Jünger's *Radiations (Strahlungen)*, as his diaries from the Second World War were called:

> Extremely accurate, very good and sharply formulated observations, the product of a well-bred, highly disciplined and truly sovereign talent, far superior to the other talents of his generation. However, there are also a lot of unpleasant things to swallow in the book: for instance how the German officer [Jünger] in occupied Paris is keen not to let slip any opportunity to acquire money and good connections, the descriptions of him buying antiques and rare books and of his hobnobbing with the French literary avant-

garde, and how he attends an execution by firing squad and then, with well-washed hands, goes to a high-society gathering to drink champagne and talk about noble things—for us antebellum types, all this has something deeply worrying and also distasteful about it.[90]

In *An der Zeitmauer* Jünger expounded his vision of a "world state"—a concept with which, at root, Hesse was greatly in sympathy. He found himself especially in tune with Jünger's challenge to the reader to "see himself and all his actions and sufferings as also being determined by the Earth and the Cosmos,"[91] his departure from all foregoing history and his willingness to enter a "cosmological" context, and expressly professed his allegiance to Jünger's perspective, which was determined "no longer by history, that is, human history, but by the history of the Earth."[92]

We may draw conclusions from this for our understanding of *The Glass Bead Game*. Certainly, Hesse displays an astonishing degree of sympathy in the following assessment of Jünger's work:

> To what extent Jünger's writings and prognoses have been proved "correct," or what valid points may have been adduced against them from this or that standpoint, is of no concern to me. The debate about all this is just so much literary hot air. It is enough for me to have shared in Jünger's vision and spent many fruitful days in its company. His fine body of work has instructed and corrected many of my misconceptions in the realms of natural science and technology, in which I was very backward. In human and moral terms it has not changed me, but it has certainly fortified me beneficially.[93]

What was Hesse driving at here? Hesse the former Steppenwolf and later traveler to the East, and from now on a master in the Glass Bead Game, yet at the same time the first apostate of this all-too-virtuosic art, recognized himself in Ernst Jünger's "forest travelers" and "anarchists," in much the same way that Gottfried Benn's "radar thinkers" and "Ptolemies"—all modern Stoics, to a man!—were familiar figures to him.

He too was one of the "Old Men of the Mountains," whose distance from the people who inhabited the plains appeared to have become insuperable. A person who had become divorced from the prevailing times here below. A yesterday's man who was lost to the present, but who had potential for the future—a comic figure, not unlike Don Quixote.

Hesse's Debt to Goethe

The human spirit

Is like water:

It comes from heaven,

It rises to heaven,

And to Earth

It must again descend

Ever changing.

—Johann Wolfgang von Goethe, "The Song of
the Spirits over the Waters" (1779)

Without Hesse's constantly renewed encounter with the works of Goethe, he would never have written *The Glass Bead Game*. Goethe was Hesse's guiding star, and not just in his later years.

The affinity of the ideal state of Castalia portrayed in *The Glass Bead Game* to Goethe's "Pedagogical Province" has often been remarked upon—yet one gains a proper understanding of Hesse's connection with Goethe, which is anything but a conversation between "classicists," only when one appreciates that he was also able to view Goethe in a way that was wholly untrammeled by illusions. Hesse's attitude was a combination of unconditional admiration and harsh disapproval. Goethe embodied everything that he himself was striving for, but also everything that he rejected.

One first needs to disengage Goethe from the ideology of the "Faustian"—the aggressive man—which the nationalists had pinned on him, as Hesse stressed in a letter of February 4, 1933:

Western man, and especially his stupidest and wildest, most belligerent form, namely "Faustian man" (in other words, the German who has made virtues out of his inferiorities simply by shooting his mouth off), loves fighting and is full of praise for it, and regards conflict as a virtue; there's actually something childishly charming and moving about that. As long as farmers' sons keep slugging it out with one another out of an excess of youthful vigor, or even kill one another, that's all just so much child's play. But when organized (in other words, Nazi) mobs start doing the same, it looks a whole lot less pleasant.[94]

★   ★   ★

Hesse regarded Goethe as if he were looking into a mirror and always seeing a double face. In Steppenwolf, he had already informed readers what he thought of that side of Goethe as represented by a classical plaster bust, when he portrayed Harry Haller having an audience with Goethe in a dream sequence. In Hesse's view, this old Goethe still controlled the world from his Weimar museum, complete with "a large decoration adorning his classicist's breast." Thus began a sustained attack on the representative of a classicism who had long since become nothing but an ornament and prey to any and every possible misuse by the unimaginative: "You are too solemn for us, Your Excellency, and too vain and pompous and not sincere enough. . . . For decades you have acted as if the accumulation of knowledge and the writing and collecting of letters, indeed as if your entire existence in Weimar in your old age, were just a way of immortalizing the moment, which after all you could only mummify in order to spiritualize nature, which in the end you could only stylize into a mask."[95]

And yet then the stiff old dignitary suddenly showed himself to be the indisputable genius that he truly was. He had, he claimed, undoubtedly overestimated the value of time, for in eternity there was no such thing as time; eternity was a mere moment, just long enough for some fun.

And so it is that two kindred sprits come together in their magical conception of the world, for all of a sudden Goethe is transformed; or, more precisely, he rejuvenates himself in a dangerous way: "And in fact there was no serious word to be had anymore with the man; he danced joyfully and nimbly up and down, and first made the primrose shoot out from his star like a rocket, then made it grow small and vanish. As he was showing off with his dance steps and his figures, I was forced to reflect that at least this man had not neglected learning how to dance."[96]

Here, then, we see the kind of identity between the sage and the fool that Cervantes first introduced to the world, yet which was largely a closed book to German professors—the childish and playful aspects of genius, which Hesse admired in both Mozart and Nietzsche. Intellect should not aspire to gravitas, since only deceased things displayed an unchanging, dead exterior; by contrast, anything that was alive was constantly in a state of flux and was capable of metamorphosing into even the most unprepossessing and ludicrous forms.

And so the evil trickster that Goethe has now become proceeds to show his dream-visitor Harry Haller a small box containing, on a cushion of dark velvet, a tiny woman's leg, "bent at the knee, with the foot extending downward, ending in a point with the daintiest toes." Haller is enchanted and reaches out to seize the leg when all of a sudden he becomes suspicious that it might in fact be a scorpion. The one thing he is certain of is Goethe's laughter, his "unfathomable dotard's humor," which makes him feel inferior.

This was Hesse's assessment of Goethe in *Steppenwolf.* In *The Glass Bead Game* he appears as the "old music master." This was an allusion to the fact that Goethe had been exploited by many people for their own ends down the ages. As a corrective, therefore, at the request of Romain Rolland, in 1932 Hesse wrote an essay entitled "Gratitude to Goethe" for an issue of the magazine *Europe* devoted to the great German writer. This was a kind of manifesto that it is thoroughly justifiable to see as a prelude to *The Glass Bead Game.* In it, Hesse revealed that Goethe was by no means the writer he enjoyed reading the most—he preferred Novalis, Jean Paul, or Eichendorff—but that he certainly was the author with whom he had had most "intellectual debates and intellectual disputes." No other writer, he continued, combined so many disparate, indeed, so many contradictory, elements in his work. Goethe hid himself behind the mask of the great ambassador of literature. According to Hesse, the true countenance of the author of the *West-Eastern Divan* was "a Chinese face."

Reading Goethe always entailed setting him against a concrete temporal background. The spirit both of Goethe's work and of *The Glass Bead Game* did not hover above the catastrophes of the real world, but lay hidden within them, ignored and distorted. The key question was how to revive this sprit in its original form: "I have struggled with Goethe over many years and allowed him to become the bane of my intellectual life, him and Nietzsche. If the world war had not broken out, I would have thought the same thoughts a thousand times over with the same vacillations. But the war did come, and with it arose the old German problem of the role of the writer, the tragic fate of the spirit and of the word in German life, more painfully than ever before."[97]

For Hesse, Goethe's spirit transcended national borders and had a beneficial effect in times of patriotic fervor, when even renowned intellectuals "suddenly began writing like subalterns."

What had immunized Goethe against deploying the spirit of his work for polemical, bellicose ends—as, say, Hegel or Schiller had done? Goethe resolved his inner contradictions publicly—at all times the light is in conflict with the dark, reason with impulse, and science with magic. When Goethe addressed questions of culture, he did not abandon nature—and it was this and, even more so his wisdom—that made him so significant in Hesse's eyes. To anyone who attempted to brand him as a classicist, Goethe would immediately reveal himself to be a Romantic, an exponent of *Sturm und Drang,* and he likewise countered with lucid reason anyone who planned to press him into service for their own ends as the creator of "Faustian man." In sum, Goethe could not be pinned down. Nor was he of much use as a role model in a purely pedagogical sense, given that he lost himself increasingly in esoteric learning, was vain, and in his old age cut a very pompous figure and drank excessive amounts of wine. For that reason, Hesse believed, it would be best to ban Goethe in schools.

In 1924 in a remarkable essay entitled "Goethe and Bettina," Hesse demonstrated that he had no intention of turning Goethe into any kind of cult figure or idol. Instead, what fascinated him was "the whole purposeful absurdity of Goethe's life."[98] The way in which, with great clear-sightedness, he laid bare the loss of poetic substance in the aging Goethe testifies to the great affinity and sympathy he had with this author, to whom the world had assigned a role that put him head and shoulders above the rest. And he played this role dutifully. Not, however, without permitting himself flights of fancy into offbeat preoccupations (his philosophy of nature, for example!). His gradual diminution, the dying of one who had had an intimate relationship with so much in life, though never with death, was not recounted by Hesse as the story of a defeat, but as a progressive humanizing process in all its facets, including those of reason, morality, and most particularly religion. And the flashes of spirit that then unexpectedly shine through the wine-fueled haze of self-righteousness are all informed by his awareness of the unavoidability of being part of the great cycle of nature. For Goethe this insight was not general but intensely personal. Did he, then, become a stoic in his old age? For Hesse, who had in mind the Magic Theater, the journey to the East, and the Glass Bead Game, Goethe undoubtedly was that—yet at the same time also the very opposite, with the same intensity or lack of it: "And it is the secret of the older Goethe that he, that quaint, stiff old man in his excessively large shell full of junk and things he had collected, still managed like some Chinese sorcerer to generate all around him, far and wide, that magically ambivalent atmosphere, that Lao-tzu-like air, in which activity and idleness, creativity and suffering are no longer distinguishable from one another."[99]

Hesse thus identified in Goethe that mysterious, dangerously seductive "allure of the hermaphrodite," who combined within himself every conceivable dichotomy, even that of gender. Here was another instance of the *unio mystica,* like that invoked by Jakob Böhme with his "androgynous Adam." In Hesse's view, this was proof positive of the "deadly, uncanny, and positively unearthly agency of a towering genius."[100] What kind of people are such geniuses? "Are they affirmers? Are they even humans anymore? Most certainly—they are all affirmers of life and affirmers of nature, but deniers of themselves, deniers of the human within them. The more 'perfect' they become, the more both their life and their work tend toward disintegration, straining toward an anticipated distant possibility that no longer bears the name of human, but at best superhuman—a new form of existence of which no one need be ashamed anymore, and of which nature could be proud."[101]

Here Hesse was clearly reading Goethe through the filter of Nietzsche, and without a doubt that was the most radical and modern of all readings of this writer—in addition to being one that showed Hesse himself as being a dangerous thinker!

Hesse also admired Goethe the lyric poet, yet his friendly and respectful evaluation consciously avoided any hint of a hallowing, adulatory tone, as, for example, when he writes that Goethe produced "an almost monstrous mass of poems,"[102] all too conscious as he was that the same could be said of himself. His selection of thirty poems by Goethe, in the introduction to which he made this remark, naturally include those verses with which Hesse felt a special affinity. Among them is "Wanderer's Night Song (I)":

> O you who are from heaven,
> Who calms every pain and sorrow
> And who fills the heart that is doubly wretched
> With double refreshment,
> I am weary of striving

The view from the Casa Rossa

What is the purpose of all this pain and longing?
Sweet peace!
Come, o come into my breast!

Wherein, then, did Hesse believe Goethe's wisdom resided—that wisdom which not only accompanied him on his path through life but also, in spite of all his assertions of distance, guided him on his journey? It lay in the affirmation of the dual existence as a game of life that constantly transcended this world and entered cosmological realms: a fervent celebration of the paradoxical. This will to synthesis was in permanent conflict with the tendency toward disintegration. The cultivation of mutually opposing forces became for Hesse the ideal for his own passage through life. Commensurate with this was Hesse's statement in his 1949 essay "Goethe and Nationalism":

Almost every statement about Goethe, however accurate and well-substantiated with quotations it may appear to be, still yields the surprising realization, if one turns it on its head and twists it around, that the exact opposite is fundamentally just as valid and correct. To Germans, he was the foremost classicist and anti-Romantic, and yet at the same time, for the literatures of many non-German civilizations he was the great innovator and figurehead of what they understood as Romanticism. To the devout Christians of his time, he was an impudent heathen and dangerous amoralist, whereas to later generations he became a teacher of reverence and humanity. And so we see that he has many faces, each of which is Janus-like, with a reverse side that is no less clear and evident.[103]

11

THE OLD MAN OF THE MOUNTAINS

Hesse's Continuing Journey Inward

1945: The *Rigi Diary;* Debates about National Pride with Ricarda Huch and Luise Rinser

In August 1945 Hesse ascended the Rigi. He had visited the Rigi-Kulm (the mountain's highest peak) once before, decades ago, but had felt "out of place there and repelled by the tourist industry." At that time he had been working on *Hermann Lauscher,* and had taken a rowboat out onto Lake Lucerne on his own. He preferred seeing the Rigi from below, and called it "the most boring of all mountains."

But now he ventured up the mountain once more, to Rigi-Kaltbad, to stay in a grand hotel there. His perspective on the place changed in old age—and the wide panoramic vista this high vantage point gave him would also clarify his view of the Germany that lay conquered, liberated, and in ruins far to the north. The text he wrote on this occasion begins, like so many of Hesse's, as a personal travel report. Reminiscences are combined with small, precisely observed events, plus information on what reading matter he has brought with him—to produce an atmospheric piece of prose writing in which Hesse found himself increasingly addressing a single theme: German nationalism. The end result is a stock-taking of the misery that Germany inflicted not only upon itself but also upon many other peoples: "Now that it has become pointless and convenient to hate the Germans, now that we can leave all that to the people who remained behind and the stupid, we may gradually begin to realize the losses that Germany and the world have suffered, the loss of homeland, of beauty, of memories, and of the wellsprings of imagination, and in among this almost unbearable impoverishment, we may set about searching with a new urgency for those wellsprings that are still flowing, and from which we are still allowed to drink: namely, the German writers from the good times."[1]

Hesse was looking both backward as well as forward in this text—composed in the open air of the Swiss Alps, which afforded quite different prospects than the smoking ruins of the landscape in Germany. Perhaps his viewpoint came across as somewhat detached, but it was certainly clear-sighted for all that. However, in offering his opinions on nationalism, his aim was reconciliation, for when writing Hesse had in mind that stratum of the German intelligentsia who were neither Nazis nor members of the resistance: "The history of this echelon of German society has not yet been written, and its existence is scarcely known about abroad." Who was he referring to here? Perhaps authors like Ricarda Huch or Erich Kästner, who were by no means suspected of having sympathized with the National Socialist regime, but who had nonetheless stayed in Germany throughout and had remained largely unmolested—and who within their narrow circle of acquaintances had tried to set an example of humanity.

Hesse was well aware that he lacked the experience of living under the surveillance of Nazi terror while maintaining a critical distance to the regime. Yet he also suspected that it must have been a difficult and unheroic struggle, day after day to try and wrestle some scope for displaying humanity from a regime whose stock-in-trade was brute force. Accordingly, it sounded very restrained, almost humble, when he now began to put into words the experience that had formed a major part of his perception both of himself and of the world since the First World War: "I have absolutely nothing to say to these friends of mine. How could a man who is sitting in a house that has not been destroyed, who always has something to eat every day, and who over the last ten years has certainly experienced plenty of aggravation and worry but has never been directly threatened or violated possibly have anything to say to these people who have gone though every conceivable suffering!" Yet he still felt himself able to formulate some "advice and encouragement," precisely because he had been observing Germany from beyond its borders for so long: "Though you are far superior to me in all other things, in one matter I do have longer experience than you: namely, in disengaging myself from nationalism. I didn't do this under Hitler or under the impact of Allied bombing, but back in the years 1914 to 1918." There then followed a proclamation that was to plunge the entire German nation into a kind of culture war—and in which Hesse would once again represent the voice of an outsider who for the most part was misunderstood:

> I should like to cry out to you, at the top of my voice: Don't let what little good has come your way from this destruction pass you by again! Back in 1918, all that was on offer in place of a monarchy with a bad constitution was a republic. And now, in the midst of your misery, you can have and experience something—a new element of evolution and humanity—that will put you at an advantage over the victors and the neutral nations: you have the opportunity to see through and liberate yourself from the insanity of all forms of nationalism, which at root you have already hated for so long.[2]

The text first appeared in September 1945, in the *Neue Schweizer Rundschau,* and from there went on to be rapidly disseminated in Germany. The reaction to this clear voice of reason, which only made one error—misjudging the emotional mood in Germany—was unexpectedly violent. For Hesse, it was a case of déjà-vu—the same willful misunderstanding as when he had written "O Friends, Not These Tones!" back in 1914. The war was over, and lost, but only a minority of Germans felt free—not many more, in fact, than those who had been liberated from the country's prisons and concentration camps. A whole people found itself at rock bottom and invoked the only thing it still thought it possessed: its national sense of dignity, its pride. Not, of course, the false pride that had been abused by the Nazis to foment hate propaganda, but the genuine, true, and laudable pride as exemplified by Goethe and Schiller! There was a collective national movement of all willing parties, a national project of renewal, and in the east of the country right up to the collapse of the German Democratic Republic even a "National Front" that transcended all individual differences among its members and proclaimed the cultural unity of all Germans.

Hesse recognized from the outset that this was primarily one great exercise in self-deception. Yet it is another question how vital such a movement was at a time when people yearned above all to look forward to the future.

When intellectuals speak of nationalism, one might reasonably imagine that it ought to be free of such mass-psychological calculations. Certainly, one cannot impute such ulterior motives to Ricarda Huch, who like Hesse had firm roots in German Romanticism. It was another matter that divided them: Hesse had long since made a clean break with the false conclusions that were drawn about the national consciousness that emerged from Romanticism (without rejecting it outright as a concept, however)—yet most Germans still lived in this continuity, and were only capable of seeing the two world wars as natural disasters, and as injustices that had been undeservedly perpetrated against them. This was the ultimate bone of contention in the fierce argument that now flared up.

The position of most Germans living in a state of postnationalism was now represented by Ricarda Huch, with the enthusiastic approval of—of all things—the *Tägliche Rundschau,* the daily newspaper in Berlin licensed by the city's Soviet military administration. In her response to Hermann Hesse, which appeared under the heading "Freedom from Nationalist Sentiment?" on April 12, 1946, she challenged him in the following terms: "Can it really be possible that a German, a German writer, should rebuke his own compatriots for their nationalist sentiment? While all the nations around us proudly proclaim their national consciousness, ought Germany to be divesting itself of its own?" This was the voice of an unsuspicious humanist, who was the author of unquestionably erudite works on German intellectual history—and who now refused to accept the contention that, in the year 1946, any form of national pride could only represent a form at worst of continuing National Socialism and at best of repression. In actual fact, Hesse had said nothing about national pride, nor had he called for shame or remorse—that healing catharsis through which a nation of perpetrators had to pass before it could ever feel pride again! Hesse focused unerringly on the act of rupture—both as a demolition of German tradition in a negative sense and as an opportunity for radical change in a positive sense—whereas the highly esteemed Ricarda Huch rather astonishingly took the view that the need for continuity should be self-evident. In favor of this standpoint, however, she did advance an argument that derived from her own long experience and that therefore could not

simply be dismissed out of hand: "It does always seem to have been difficult for the German people to combine a secure self-awareness with proper
respect for other nationalities. Instead, the German people forever alternated between self-loathing and self-aggrandizement."[3]

This was without a doubt a correct assessment of things. Nothing good
ever grows from feelings of inferiority, only the next violent and unpredictable display of excess. And yet what the aged Ricarda Huch intended
simply as an appeal to a just and pragmatic sense of proportion was reduced in public discourse merely to a defense of national pride against the
"traitor to the people" Hermann Hesse, and hence confirmed its diagnosis
of him as such. Accordingly, in the *Tägliche Rundschau* Heinrich Dietze
wrote an article of effusive gratitude to Huch for her contribution, couched
in the veiled, treacherous language of the so-called LTI (*Lingua Tertii Im-
perii,* or "Language of the Third Reich"), which the German philologist
Victor Klemperer was to trenchantly analyze in his 1947 book of the same
name. Dietze wrote:

> Week after week I had hoped that a German voice that is familiar, recog-
> nized, and loved might be raised in public opposition to counter Hesse's
> unpleasant incitement. . . . Hermann Hesse, who only knows the war and
> its effects from the perspective of peace and comfort, has insulted our Ger-
> many. That is shameful. How many Germans must have been instilled with
> strength, clarity, and self-confidence by your words. . . . You, most revered
> Frau Ricarda Huch, have put yourself forward like a protective mother of
> our Germany, and so for me you have now become the "Mother of the
> Germans."[4]

Once again Hesse was forced to confront the fact that the Germans apparently only loved those writers and thinkers who told them what they
wanted to hear—and he found himself sickened by such wrong-headed
pronouncements as that offered by Heinrich Dietze, who in writing what
he did set himself up as the spokesman for a new academic young generation in Germany who regarded Hesse as a bogeyman.

When he wrote his *Rigi Diary* pamphlet, Hesse did not remotely intend
it to be a polemic on the current state of Germany, and so he now tried to
explain his position in an open letter to Luise Rinser—yet as so often happened, his explanation only succeeded in further arousing the wrath of his
accusers. It still struck many Germans as an unacceptable impertinence to

have to read sentences such as the following about themselves: "Otherwise they only talked about what they had had to suffer, and complained bitterly about the injustice of their long imprisonment. But they never uttered a single word about the other side of the coin, namely about what they, as German soldiers, inflicted upon the world for many years."[5]

Luise Rinser's previous letters of approval to Hesse led him to believe that he had found an ally in her. Discovered by Peter Suhrkamp, Rinser had published her first work *The Glass Rings (Die gläsernen Ringe)* in 1941. By way of introduction, Hesse wrote to her: "So, you are the person who, like our faithful friend [Peter Suhrkamp], was under surveillance for a long time, spied upon, thrown in jail by the Gestapo and even sentenced to death!"[6] How shocked Hesse would have been if he had known that this was only half of an unpalatable truth and that—as in many biographies of twentieth-century figures subsequently discredited by history—victim and perpetrator coexisted in very close proximity in the person of Luise Rinser. For she too was complicit and had denounced many others to the Nazis before being denounced herself.

Yet there was also a response to Hesse that broadened the narrow German horizon of the debate: Jan H. Bruell, a Polish physician who had survived incarceration in a concentration camp and was now working in Heidelberg, wrote a piece in *Die neue Zeitung* on September 28, 1946, in which he stated: "Cruelty is not a special prerogative of the German people. In the camp, I met representatives of all European nations. Regardless of whether they were Germans or Russians, or French, Italians, or Poles, none of them were human enough, when they were given power over others, to wield that power in a humane way. And so, Herr Hesse, you have no reason to turn your back on the Germans. Who, then, is to lead the German people if even their own writers spurn them?"[7]

Bruell's proclamation is an impressive testimony to how fundamentally Hesse's intentions were misunderstood among the German public in the immediate postwar period. He had, after all, only said that he was warning against falling into the trap of nationalism again, which had already been responsible for so much misery, and yet he was being traduced as someone who had turned his back on the German people. One thing this Polish doctor's statement did accurately reflect was the question Hesse himself had posed in *The Glass Bead Game:* Is there a form of knowledge that is immune to the temptations of power?

And so this led Hesse to a conclusion that had been clear to him since writing "Zarathustra's Return" in 1919—the Germans first had to learn that they did not need any leader. No writers should lead the people, either—indeed, especially not writers—instead it was incumbent upon individuals to lead themselves.

However, as Heinrich Heine had also learned in his time, this was a resolution that Germans always found it hardest of all nations to make: to empower themselves to attain freedom.

Hesse on the Blacklist? The Dispute with Hans Habe

Winning wars generated a victor's mentality—and that was something that Hesse could not abide. Least of all could he bear to see people striking such attitudes in Switzerland, as he wrote to Felix Braun in London on October 10, 1945: "Here, people are zealously setting about 'cleansing' the country of Nazis and of Germans in general . . . after people kept their mouths shut for many years, perhaps even sympathized with Hitler's Germany, they are now sweeping the land of William Tell clean with a firm, foolish hand. Well, I suppose it was always, and still is, the same story in other countries."[8]

But worse was to come for Hesse, as something took place that not only he but also all those who knew him had not thought possible. He was placed on the blacklist of proscribed authors in the American zone of occupation in Germany. The trigger for this was an argument between Hesse and Hans Habe, the chief editor of all authorized newspapers within the American sector. Hesse had protested to Habe over a poem entitled "Toward Peace" *(Dem Frieden entgegen)* that he had written at Easter 1945 for the ceasefire celebration organized by Radio Basel, and which Habe had reprinted without his permission. The conclusion of the poem reads:

Yet still we hope. And in our breast
Resides a burning sense
Of the wonders of love.
Brothers! For us the gates now lie open
To the spirit
And to the return of love
And to all our lost paradises.

A fine enough ending, one might think. But Hesse appended two further lines: "Wish! Hope! Love! / And the Earth will be yours once more." These lines did not appear in the reprinted version, for whatever reason—though it is open to question whether the poem really suffered from their absence. But in any event, Hesse was furious. He accused Habe of "barbarism"—an unfortunate choice of words, as it turned out. In his response, Habe stated that "barbarism" had been something else entirely, something to which Hesse had turned a blind eye "in aristocratic seclusion in Ticino" whereas the likes of Thomas Mann, Stefan Zweig, and Franz Werfel had "screamed their condemnation of the Nazi regime over the airwaves." Habe concluded: "However, we do not believe Hesse will ever be entitled to speak in Germany again."[9]

Habe no doubt wanted to demonstrate his power; and without Hesse's indignant letter regarding the "barbarism" allegedly inflicted upon his poem, things would surely never have come to this pass. On receiving Habe's reply, Hesse realized that it would now be best to hold his peace: "I have no intention of bandying words with the man who was capable of writing this stupid and malicious letter. After all I'm not some conquered and occupied Teutonic slave and have no desire to justify myself to this officious little man."[10]

Hesse's son Martin saw things differently and believed that the affair needed airing in public; accordingly he wrote to various Swiss newspapers to inform them that his father had been blacklisted in the American zone. Shortly afterward *Der Bund* ran stories on what had happened, and quoted Habe's letter—much to Hesse's irritation. He wrote to the editor of the newspaper *Basler Nachrichten* in November 1945:

> I was very averse to the whole stupid business being brought to the attention of the press, and what's more through the indiscretion of my son, who I know meant well. For the letter, in which the press officer in question informed me that he counted me among those authors whose voices should no longer be heard in Germany, was curiously enough not the result of the customary American cluelessness in intellectual and European matters, but was written out of personal mean-spiritedness and spite. . . . Well, let my name appear on all the blacklists you like, I've grown accustomed to such things since the First World War and have always seen it as a badge of honor that I always seem to find those in power at any given moment against me. Long may it continue so.[11]

Hesse was particularly incensed when he discovered that Hans Habe's real name was Janos Békessy and that he was the son of Imre Békessy, a notorious press baron in Vienna who had been convicted (largely thanks to the investigative journalism of Karl Kraus) on charges of extortion and the exploitation of subordinates. Although the son actually had nothing to do with his father, Hesse was so frothing with indignation that he wrote Habe a furious letter in which he overreached himself in drawing the following false analogy: "It seems to me that your statements could well have come from a letter from Békessy Senior to Karl Kraus."[12] In the end Hesse thought better of it and did not send Habe the letter. Instead he wrote to Thomas Mann in Pacific Palisades to sound off about the idiotic and presumptuous son of the "biggest newspaper-proprietor crook and gutter-press journalist of his age."

In his reply, Thomas Mann could not refrain from issuing a mild rebuke to his friend:

> It is unfortunate that you furnished him with the catchword "barbarism," to which the whole of the American world—even, it would appear, its most recent manifestations—is extremely sensitized, and for which there are all kinds of other terms available nowadays. But now he's latched onto it and is milking it for all it's worth, comparing what happened to your poem to Belsen and Auschwitz, and accusing you of not unleashing any thunderbolts at Hitler. Quite how you were supposed to have done that, as a Swiss citizen living in neutral Switzerland, where I too was obliged to keep my mouth shut for five years, he doesn't explain. I could only let rip and make a clean breast of how I felt once I was in America—where you would never have felt at home.

The letter then went on to confirm to Hesse how his friend Thomas Mann—who at the time was busy in Stockholm working to ensure that Hesse was made the next Nobel Literature laureate—really saw his relationship to the National Socialist state (where, incidentally, the books of the entire Mann family had also been banned): "Every child in Europe knew full well that you had no time for that diabolical German filth and in a pantomimic way you provided ample evidence of where you stood."[13] One wonders whether Hesse chose to ignore the gentle irony of these lines. "Pantomimic" indeed! If that was the case, he would have done so because Thomas Mann—who now likewise found himself increasingly subjected to unfair attacks (not least because he refused to be summoned back to liberated Germany without more ado)—now showed himself more and more to be his most steadfast friend.

So, had Hesse's name really been placed on a blacklist? That would have entailed a ban being issued on the publication of his works, such as that imposed—for a while at least—on those of Ernst Jünger and Gottfried Benn. Or had he simply been confronted with an expression of opinion that he found unacceptably drastic by a fellow journalist for whom he had scant regard? If one reads the writer's correspondence with Peter Suhrkamp, one is tempted rather to assume the latter. In general, it is true to say that, after the liberation of Germany from fascism, Hesse appeared somewhat disgruntled. During this period, too much was not going to expectation for him—such as the business with reproduction rights for his texts. Poems of his were being reprinted everywhere, without anyone seeking his permission, let alone paying him any royalties. It is only understandable that this irritated him, but the depth of his anger suggests that he had little idea of the scale of the destruction in Germany (and throughout Europe) at this time. When Hesse wrote to Suhrkamp on February 9, 1946, to tell him: "I am sick to the back teeth with this state of affairs."[14]—it comes as a shock to the reader to realize that his wrath had been incurred by nothing more than a handful of pirate editions and his suspicions about the legality of an Italian edition of *Siddhartha*. Suhrkamp was unsure whether the Frasinelli publishing house in Turin had legally acquired the rights to the novel; after all, as he told Hesse, he had been absent from his desk for quite some time (during his spell in a concentration camp), and it may well have been the case that foreign editions of the book had been licensed during that time; he needed to check first with Kasack, who had run the business during his absence. And in any case, it wasn't worth getting upset, Suhrkamp took the liberty of writing to Hesse in Montagnola, since the Italians never paid their dues anyhow.

Suhrkamp also tried to defuse the situation concerning the blacklist on which Hesse assured him Hans Habe had placed him; his first move in this regard was to calmly establish the facts of the matter. Mail found its way to Switzerland from Germany at this time by some very roundabout routes; for the most part, Suhrkamp got traveling Allied servicemen of his acquaintance to carry his letters across the border. Accordingly, on January 31, 1946, he informed Hesse by one such courier letter:

There was a rumor going round here for a while that your books were on a "Black List" that the Americans had drawn up. This rumor originated from a broadcast on Swiss radio. Of course, I looked into the matter without delay. Quite apart from the fact that the Americans don't even keep "Black Lists" of this kind, no one has ever suggested banning your books. All I discovered when I investigated was this argument between you and the chief editor of the *Neue Zeitung* in Munich, one Captain Hans Habe. The potential for misunderstandings in these turbulent times is greater than it ever was.[15]

In 1969, when Siegfried Unseld published the correspondence between Hesse and Peter Suhrkamp (which unfortunately does not include their letters from 1945), he asked Erich Kästner, who had been working at the time for the *Neue Zeitung,* for clarification on this point. Kästner wrote back to tell him that the newspaper, which had only been founded in 1945, had never had an archive—something that seriously hampered the day-to-day business of editing the paper:

One day—it would have been around the end of 1945 or the beginning of 1946—when one of our colleagues turned up with some old newspaper cutting containing a poem by Hesse, we were so delighted we printed the poem straight away without checking that it was complete. It was not complete, as Hermann Hesse himself lost no time in informing us. As far as I can remember, this letter to the chief editor (then Hans Habe) was extremely indignant in tone. Hesse suspected malicious intent, and I know that, in his reply, Herr Habe tried to clarify the misunderstanding. It is perfectly possible that the tenor of his letter matched that of Hesse's in its irritability. It is also possible that the misunderstanding, which would have been simple to resolve, was never cleared up.[16]

A Stoical Reaction to Winning the Nobel Prize

The whole jamboree is taking place today in Stockholm, first the Nobel ceremony with a big gala, then a banquet, where some wise words by me will be read out.

—Hermann Hesse, letter to Gunter Böhmer, October 11, 1946

Gottfried Benn once offered some advice for a successful career as a writer: only start winning prizes late in life! As long as one is not awarded any prizes, at least none of those worth having and that one

truly covets, one can live in relative obscurity and untroubled by that
false kind of attention that goes hand in hand with jealousy and ill-will.
That spotlight then falls upon a major prizewinner like a stroke of fate.
Why does she / he, of all people, deserve this award? This is generally
the most innocuous of the questions that people ask—for the most part,
people insinuate things that they would never have lighted upon had
the prize not been given.

Hesse was almost seventy years old when he won first the Goethe Prize
of the City of Frankfurt and then the Nobel Prize for Literature. He tried
to sidestep the whole affair—in other words, to accept the prize but not to
go and receive it, as that seemed to him to be less of a snub than refusing
it point-blank. For his relationship to prize-giving committees of whatever origin was a tense one from the outset—he could never really take
external honors seriously. Yet here it was also about diplomacy, and
hence about politics, and Hesse's relationship with Germany was extremely tense and fraught with misunderstandings. Was the Goethe Prize
an opportunity, therefore, for a rapprochement with Germany?

This proved difficult, since the City of Frankfurt did not even inform
him about the award; he first learned about it—or to be more precise, his
son Martin learned about it—from the newspaper. Given that he had not
been officially informed of his success, he could scarcely express his gratitude publicly either.

Perhaps that also had something to do with the manner in which he
had previously received the envoy from the city's prize-giving committee.
He gave his son Bruno an account of proceedings in September 1946:

> Incidentally, the first person to learn about the Goethe Prize was our Martin,
> who surprised me one morning by coming to visit me in Bremgarten and
> giving me the news that someone had come to ask me on behalf of the City
> of Frankfurt whether I would accept the prize. Angrily, I replied "no" and
> Martin departed, but nonetheless some discussions did take place with that
> emissary that same afternoon. We quizzed him in detail about all the po-
> litical aspects, etc., and also took into consideration his assurance that, for
> the first time in the history of voting for the prize recipient, their decision
> had been unanimous.[17]

Even so, Hesse did not travel to Frankfurt am Main to receive the
prize; instead an acceptance speech was read out on his behalf. Naturally,

in this he could not resist making a grand declaration of his detached attitude to the awarding of prizes as such, even when—or perhaps particularly when—they were associated with the name of Goethe: "Prizes and honors are not quite what they might appear to be to us when we are young. From the point of view of the recipient, they are neither a pleasure nor a celebration, nor are they something that he has earned. They are a small constituent part of that complicated phenomenon that goes by the name of fame, which is largely made up of misunderstandings, and should be taken for what they are—namely, as attempts by the official world to assuage its embarrassment regarding unofficial achievements."[18]

Thus, Hesse's speech of thanks was utterly devoid of any flattery—according to him, it should at all costs "not give the impression of any kind of reconciliation with official Germany." After all, as a result of the position he took toward the catastrophe of nationalism, he had once more been deluged with hate mail from Germany that sounded exactly like the letters he had received in 1914. He also described his relationship to that Germany, in whose sudden spiritual revival (which it was eagerly proclaiming at every opportunity) he could not believe: "How prickly and complicated, how double-edged and difficult the relationship has been between this puzzling, great, and moody people and myself has been since the First World War."[19] Not that Hesse himself was without his moods. His refusal to collect in person either the Goethe Prize or the Nobel Prize the following year in Stockholm can be seen as just such an act of capriciousness. But it can also be construed as a natural consequence of his long journey from the outer to the inner life, and as a confirmation of what he saw as his role as an author—a role that, unlike for Thomas Mann, comprehended no personal sense of himself as an ambassador for his profession. But for all that it was hardly polite.

Hesse had always had a fear and loathing of public appearances and of having to give speeches. Every reading of his works in a small gathering resulted in a spiritual crisis that left him ultimately with only feelings of bitterness and regret; he concluded that he was fated to be misunderstood. Why, he reasoned, put himself through such stressful experiences? What did he owe anybody? The readers, perhaps, who expected something from him? Well, he would write for them, not speak to them. And so we can read in his essay "Acknowledgment and Moralizing Reflection" the real subtext behind his acceptance of the Goethe Prize; this reflects his attitude to the times far more accurately than any gracious gesture on the part of an author at an official prize-giving ceremony: "In my view the current state of humankind is the result of the actions of two mental disorders: the megalomania of technology and the megalomania of nationalism. They have given the modern world its appearance and self-assurance, they have given us two world wars and their consequences, and they will continue to give rise to further such events before they finally run their course. Organizing resistance to these two global illnesses is the most pressing task and vindication of the intellect in today's world."[20]

His Nobel Prize acceptance speech the following year, which was read out in Stockholm by the Swiss ambassador to Sweden, had the same basic tenor.

In October 1946 he wrote to Felix Braun about the Frankfurt Goethe Prize:

> But did you really take all that business with the prize seriously? I certainly didn't. Years ago, when the *Reflections* and *Steppenwolf* were published, and were by turns laughed at and vehemently rejected, I could have predicted to you that, when the economic cycle turned around and Germany suffered its next defeat, I would find myself showered with prizes and distinctions and new editions of my work—things that at such a moment have as little value as, say, the sum of money attached to this current prize, with which (assuming I don't just give it away) I couldn't even buy a loaf of bread and a glass of wine.[21]

Following the award of the Nobel Prize, public interest in Hesse grew in leaps and bounds once more. Thomas Mann had already proposed Hesse for the prize in 1930, but at that time the committee had seen Hesse as an "ethical anarchist" whereas now they saw in him a guardian of the German cultural legacy, albeit one with "attitude and style." Hesse as a "keeper of the flame"? He shunned such a role, preferring to remain at home, to hide from the press, and to celebrate among a close circle of friends. He wrote to Max Wassmer on this subject: "It's a shame that external fulfillments in life only ever come to you when they no longer give you any pleasure. At least Ninon is as happy as a child about it, and my friend Bodmer and his wife spent a really enjoyable evening with her drinking the best champagne; by contrast, for the first time in decades I have been a teetotaler for the past three weeks."[22]

Hesse struggled with all the hullabaloo and hype surrounding him, fleeing from Montagnola and taking refuge in a sanatorium. He noted grimly that the world had decided to "stone him to death" with letters and messages of congratulation—and that those who had sent them should not expect any gratitude from him. Hesse was not to be bribed with honors, and his reactions to the importunate overtures of an external world that tried to monopolize him grew no friendlier. In the spring of 1946, before the committee chose him as the laureate, he had offered the wholly jaded view that the Nobel Prize was "by and large awarded according to the considerations of trade policy."[23] What was he to think now that he was the chosen one? For whom was he—and the position for which he was being honored—important? Worse still: Had he already become so innocuous that he could safely be showered with prizes?

So, who was he writing for in general, and to whom could he turn in this confusing postwar Germany? Hesse clung tenaciously to one single hope: "That stratum of intellectuals I was referring to in the *Rigi Diary,* those people who really seriously opposed Hitler and who remained free of his corruption—though this is a vanishingly small group of people, I fear."[24] Yet they did exist, those isolated individuals, and for their sake it was worth exerting himself and continuing to work. They included his publisher Peter Suhrkamp. It was primarily for Suhrkamp's sake, in the first place, that he accepted the Goethe Prize and the Nobel Prize, which were ultimately more of a nuisance to him.

More Than a Publisher: Peter Suhrkamp

Reading the correspondence between Hermann Hesse and Peter Suhrkamp, which was compiled and edited by Siegfried Unseld and published in 1969, and yet which only begins in the autumn of 1945 after the fall of the Third Reich, one finds oneself irritated by Hesse's demeanor immediately after the end of the war. His entire attitude is one of constant complaint, reproachfulness to the point of unfair allegation, and thoroughgoing pessimism from November 1945 to 1950, when, following the final separation from Gottfried Bermann Fischer, the Suhrkamp publishing house was founded. At that point Hesse's tone changed; his mood was also lightened by the fact that the German mark was now finally permitted to be exchanged in Switzerland, meaning that Hesse could now (for the first time since 1933!) earn a sizable income from his book sales in Germany.

★   ★   ★

The nonexistence in Germany of his major work, *The Glass Bead Game,* which he had completed in 1943 but which thus far had only appeared in a small edition published by Fretz & Wasmuth in Switzerland, plunged Hesse into a deep depression. The old Steppenwolf with his adages about suicide still held sway over him. Yet by the summer of 1945 he seemed to have rallied somewhat and, almost in poetic high spirits once more, he set about writing his *Rigi Diary,* which contained a perfectly friendly and restrained warning to the Germans about the dangers of nationalism. Subsequently—just as had happened after the appearance of "O Friends, Not these Tones!" in 1914—he found himself deluged by a flood of invective and unpleasant insinuations, which in turn awakened in him a revulsion for all things German that he was unable to overcome to his dying day. He remained mistrustful and detached. His relationship with Suhrkamp was also colored by this animosity, though only at the outset.

To cut back to the past for a moment, it was Samuel Fischer himself who had brought Peter Suhrkamp on board at his publishing house—on January 1, 1933! Suhrkamp took over the editorship of the Fischer in-house magazine *Neue Rundschau.* In the fall of that year, Fischer appointed Suhrkamp to the board of S. Fischer Verlag. So who was this Peter Suhrkamp, a man who was already in his forties? He was a restless spirit, a person whom his friends and acquaintances described both as a charmer with a shrewd feel for negotiation and yet at the same time a stubborn individual to the point of pig-headedness who refused point-blank to listen to reason on certain topics. Furthermore, he was a go-getter who was drawn to danger. In his 1959 obituary "My Friend Peter," Hesse described Suhrkamp's difficult character in the following terms: "Throughout his life, these reserves of tenacity, of down-to-earthness, of organizational skill, and of patience were at variance with his individual temperament and character, which impelled him to spurn the inheritance of his father's farm, avoid returning to his home region, change his career several times and conquer the world, alone and independently, as a teacher, soldier, officer, dramaturge, editor, publisher, and writer."[25] Suhrkamp, who commanded a raiding party in the First World War and later became a keen athlete who regularly visited Berlin's Olympic Stadium to train (at javelin-throwing), worked at Fischer Verlag first as a reader and then as a publisher; he became known for generating lots of ideas for books that his authors might write for him (Hesse hated nothing more than these "suggestions"!). Suhrkamp was also very headstrong and had no compunction about changing titles, even of Hesse's texts (for which he was subjected to the writer's unbridled fury). On the one hand, he was as riven by inner conflict and as driven by obstinacy as Hesse, but on the other, they were dissimilar in two very significant aspects. For one thing, Suhrkamp loved Berlin, whereas Hesse loathed the place. And secondly Suhrkamp was a fan of the theater, and tried his hand at writing for the stage and worked for some years as a dramaturge at the regional theater in Darmstadt; Hesse despised the theater (except his own creation of the Magic Theater), just as he also had no appreciation whatever of cinema. After spells as a teacher in the Free School Community of Wickersdorf (he would bring his enthusiasm for education with him into the publishing world), as a magazine editor at the Ullstein title *Uhu* ("Owl"), and as a copywriter for the *Frankfurter Zeitung* and *Berliner Tageblatt* newspapers, he seemed finally to have found a safe haven at Fischer Verlag—but then 1933 drove him out once more into open waters. The old publisher Samuel Fischer was being tyrannized by regular house searches—it spoke to Suhrkamp's imperturbable nature that, on learning of this harassment, he would occasionally stay at Fischer's and repel the invaders.

Initially Hesse was less than enthused by Fischer's new colleague; Suhrkamp first approached him in his capacity as editor of the *Neue Rundschau,* and Hesse was astonished at what he saw as his high-handedness. For instance, Hesse wrote to Bermann Fischer on January 28, 1933, to complain about Suhrkamp:

> He wrote to tell me that he'd be happy to publish a short essay of mine, since it fitted in well with his program—I took this to mean that, in future, my work will need to have the episcopal imprimatur of the editorial board confirming that it chimes in with Suhrkamp's program before it is accepted. He also suggested an alternative title for my essay; he wanted it to be more punchy and allusive and programmatic. I wrote back to inform him that I thought about my titles just as deeply as I did about my text, and that in the future he was welcome to change anything I wrote as he saw fit, but that if

he did so he should add a footnote explaining that the author was not responsible for the title of the piece.

After Samuel Fischer's death in 1934, Suhrkamp and Fischer's son-in-law
Gottfried Bermann Fischer (a surgeon who had switched to publishing)
jointly managed the press to begin with. By 1936, however, the pressure
on the "Jewish publishing house" had grown so intense that its enforced
"Aryanization" could no longer be avoided. To ensure that the firm did
not fall into the hands of circles with close ties to the Nazi party, the Fischer
family and Suhrkamp—with the full support of the authors and employees—
decided that the running of the enterprise should immediately be taken
over by Peter Suhrkamp.

As a hero of the First World War, Suhrkamp had some acquaintances
among the Nazis who held him in high esteem and who were prepared to
lend him their ear—and, at crucial moments, no doubt also to shield him
from attack. Yet a lot of Suhrkamp's tangible achievements were also
down to his own tactical skill—for this reason, Max Frisch called him a
"partisan of the resistance." He negotiated the takeover of the publishing
house with the acting president of the Reich Chamber for Literature,
Heinz Wismann, whose son had been one of Suhrkamp's pupils in Wickersdorf (and had, it seems, fond memories of his former teacher). In 1937
Wismann himself was dismissed from his post on the grounds that he was
"interrelated to Jews."[26] Yet the outcome of the Fischer negotiations produced a settlement that was quite extraordinary for the time: the Fischer
family was granted 240,000 reichsmarks in compensation, together with
permission to transfer abroad author rights that were not wanted in Germany. Plus the stock of 780,000 books associated with those authors. Yet
the rights to Hesse's work were not released. Bermann Fischer, who had
meanwhile founded a new publishing venture in Vienna, was not allowed
to take Hesse with him. To get the money together for the purchase in
the first place and to manage the press as a limited partnership, Suhrkamp
needed to find associates who would provide the necessary capital: these
duly appeared in the form of Philip Reemtsma, Christoph Rathjen, and
Clemens Abs.

Bermann Fischer was perfectly content with the result of Suhrkamp's
negotiations—in the light of prevailing circumstances, as he informed
Hesse from Vienna on April 25, 1936: "S. has proved his worth beyond

all measure in the way he has handled my and my family's affairs. There are no words to describe the personal courage he has shown in fighting our corner for us. I have him to thank for the fact that our disengagement from Germany has been managed in a reasonably tolerable fashion. In the current climate, such loyalty and comradeship to the last, especially given the prevailing conditions in Germany, is so rare that its value cannot be overestimated."[27]

Hesse, however, was not at all happy about his rights remaining behind in Nazi Germany when Bermann Fischer founded his publishing house in exile. Wouldn't he be better off as one of his authors? Indeed, if his rights had been released, he would almost certainly have gone with Bermann Fischer without hesitation.

Accordingly, in 1936 he asked Suhrkamp how much he would ask for signing over his book rights to him should the necessity arise; Suhrkamp did not deign to reply. Of course, Hesse's financial worries in this whole affair were enormous. Without regular subvention from his Swiss patrons, he could not have survived—although Hesse's books sold a total of half a million copies in Nazi Germany during the twelve years of the Reich, it was only possible to transfer a tiny proportion of the royalties to Switzerland. As a result, Hesse received only some 20 percent of his royalties in Swiss francs.

The first meeting between the author and publisher, which took place in August 1936 in Bad Eilsen, during Hesse's final book-reading tour to Germany, was preceded by a great deal of tension. Both men were prepared for an unsatisfactory outcome, and Suhrkamp admitted in retrospect that he had been in a "rather fractious" mood beforehand. His train was delayed and he didn't arrive in Bad Eilsen until around ten o'clock in the evening. When he got to his hotel, he found a note waiting for him:

> In it, Hesse told me that he had waited up for me but had now gone to bed. He included his plans for the following day. He knew that I only had a day and a half at my disposal. According to his schedule, we could only see each other at midday the day after next, when we could talk for an hour before taking lunch together. The rest of his day was completely taken up with his treatments and periods of rest. The note gave no indication of either

annoyance or recalcitrance on his part. That night, I resolved to leave the following afternoon.[28]

As things transpired, the two of them did meet the following morning. Suhrkamp was sitting in the hotel drawing room, attending to his correspondence. He suddenly noticed someone pacing up and down outside the door. It was Hermann Hesse, he realized. But Suhrkamp pretended that he hadn't noticed. According to the timetable that the writer had provided him with, they were not due to meet yet. But Hesse was also stubborn—and inquisitive as well: "He seemed equally determined to besiege the doorway. Eventually, I stood up and announced myself. He offered me his hand in greeting; all the while, he kept his gaze fixed on my face. I can only describe the look he gave me as a sharp burst of light."[29]

The meeting was a success; the two men hit it off. This marked the beginning of a friendship that would not be without its tensions, hurtfulness, and some harsh words on Hesse's part—after all, two very strong personalities were colliding here—and yet it grew increasingly strong over the years, right up to Suhrkamp's death.

On April 13, 1944, Peter Suhrkamp was arrested and charged with high treason. He had fallen into a trap set for him by the Gestapo. The agent assigned to his case was a Dr. Paul Reckzeh. This young physician was sent by the Gestapo to Suhrkamp with a supposed letter of recommendation from Hermann Hesse. His mission, so the cover story went, was to secure the publisher's collaboration with subversive circles in Switzerland around the former Reich chancellor Joseph Wirth, who were making plans for a post–Adolf Hitler Germany.

Suhrkamp was too clever to let himself be drawn into this intrigue, but he did make one crucial mistake nonetheless, in failing to immediately report the *agent provocateur* to the police. Suhrkamp wasn't given to denouncing people; he simply dismissed the young man as a "fantasist" and drew a line under the affair. The authorities tried to make a noose for his neck from the mere fact that he knew about the story that the Gestapo had fed to him. Suhrkamp was now disabused of any illusions he may have had about people like Dr. Reckzeh; if he was any kind of "fantasist" at all, he was one who had been misled in a perverse way. A photograph of Reckzeh shows a young, good-looking man of not-unsympathetic appearance; one is tempted to ask what made him act in the way he did? Manfred Hausmann, who had first recommended Suhrkamp to Samuel Fischer, remarked: "This Dr. Reckzeh was one of those creatures with an unnatural desire to send other human beings to the torture chamber and the gallows. He was what is commonly known as a 'stool pigeon.' When the people in power at that time were unable to deal with a person by legal means, they deployed men like Reckzeh."[30]

Reckzeh was also the informant within the "Solf Circle," which he spied on for the Gestapo. He had inveigled his way into the tea salons held by Elisabeth von Thadden and collected incriminating material to use against the group. His evidence formed the basis of numerous death sentences and executions—Elisabeth von Thadden herself was put to death on September 8, 1944. After the war, Reckzeh was arrested by a special unit of the Soviet secret service (SMERSH). After being interned in a number of camps run by the NKVD (including Buchenwald), he was handed over to the newly founded German Democratic Republic for sentencing. In the "Waldheim" series of political trials, Reckzeh was sentenced to fifteen years in prison, but he was given an amnesty in 1952 in return for committing himself to work in the GDR health service. Instead, he moved to West Germany. There, however, relatives of his victims urged that he be put on trial—in response, he fled back to the GDR and claimed political asylum there. In the East he ultimately ended up as a senior physician in the hospital at Perleberg and as the head doctor at the polyclinic attached to the Heinrich Rau heavy engineering plant. A request from the Antifascism Committee of the GDR's Ministry for State Security that Reckzeh's license to practice medicine be rescinded was turned down, on the grounds that he had already paid his debt to society.

Peter Suhrkamp wrote about the odyssey he went through following his arrest: "Because the cellars in the Albrechtstrasse [the Gestapo headquarters in Berlin] had suffered bomb damage at the time, I was transferred to the Gestapo prison in the concentration camp at Ravensbrück in Mecklenburg. There I was interrogated until July 14. Ultimately I was sent to the remand prison Alt-Moabit 12A in Berlin to await trial before the People's Court."[31]

Thanks to an argument over respective areas of jurisdiction between various Nazi agencies, the commencement of Suhrkamp's trial was delayed—a chance occurrence that was to save his life. Hesse would later compare Suhrkamp's fate with that of Dostoyevsky, who was pardoned shortly before his execution. Yet Suhrkamp had not escaped unscathed; under torture in Gestapo custody he had suffered a compression of the spinal cord, which would later result in the repeated temporary paralysis of both his legs.

What happened next seems hard to imagine. On January 25, 1945, Suhrkamp was transferred to the Sachsenhausen concentration camp. There he came down with double pneumonia and pleurisy. He was as good as dead. But late in the evening of February 8, he was released quite unexpectedly. Suhrkamp explained: "The background to this was an argument between the [renowned Third Reich] sculptor Professor Arno Breker and the Gestapo leader Müller about me. Müller wanted me liquidated. Professor Breker threatened to indict him if he did this. Müller saw a way out of his dilemma by having me released from the camp in the condition I was in on a winter's night." Suhrkamp made his way to Potsdam to Hermann Kasack, who had been running the publishing house in his absence. Henry Goverts reported to Hesse on May 1, 1945, that Suhrkamp had appeared at Kasack's door at four in the morning, showed him his release papers, and sat down in his living room. All that he had suffered came pouring out of him in one long monologue of woe. "Then he collapsed, suffered forty bouts of fever and more pneumonia. The doctors did not think that they would ever be able to pull his extremely weakened body through, especially because he appeared to have lost all will to live."[32]

He spent the next two months in the municipal hospital in Potsdam in a serious condition. The pneumonia had left him with cardiac insufficiency and cardiac asthma. The hospital was hit no fewer than five times during Allied air raids, as Suhrkamp reported to Hesse in his first letter to him after the war, on November 13, 1945. By sheer good fortune, he survived.

When the hospital was evacuated on April 15, Suhrkamp refused to leave, and instead moved in with a family in Potsdam, his own apartment in Berlin having been destroyed by bombing.

Peter Suhrkamp received his license to operate as a publisher as early as October 17, 1945, from the British occupation authorities in Berlin. He was permanently disabled, suffered from recurrent bouts of pneumonia, and found it hard to stand up for any length of time: "But for me the worst thing was when I realized that, no matter how much I exerted myself, an inner stiffness and slowness meant that I was unable to achieve even half of what I could do before. My current condition thus resembles my former only inasmuch as I mostly find myself dogged by a guilty conscience."[33]

Trying to reopen a publishing house in the sea of ruins that was now Berlin was a labor of Sisyphus. The stocks of books had for the most part gone up in flames, there was no paper to be had, and the book trade had collapsed. Suhrkamp was prepared to hand the business back to the Fischer family—but after 1949, when the firm looked set to be operating at a profit once more, a dispute over conflict of competence broke out that would ultimately lead to a complete rift between Suhrkamp and Bermann Fischer. Meanwhile, Hesse responded on November 23, 1945, to the first signs of life from Suhrkamp ten days previously: "I wrote to Bermann to tell him that I would of course be happy to work with a newly constituted Fischer Publishers, but only if you were part of it, for in the interim you have been my sole German publisher. . . . Besides, I'm hardly writing anything new anymore, I'm utterly tired of writing in general, and I feel that I've done my bit."[34]

During the war, to enable Hesse to derive any income at all from his books, Suhrkamp had signed over to him the foreign rights to his works (these were transferred back to the Suhrkamp Verlag by Hesse only in the late 1950s). This situation now led to repeated misunderstandings, when Suhrkamp acted in cases where Hesse thought he had no business doing so, or conversely when he failed to act when it would have been appropriate. In general, Hesse's mood worsened from month to month: when would Suhrkamp finally publish *The Glass Bead Game* in Germany, along with his other titles that were no longer in print, Hesse wanted to know. Suhrkamp was having to contend with difficulties of which Hesse could have had no real understanding. He was indeed busy assembling paper stocks to print *The Glass Bead Game*. Finding a printing press that had not been destroyed was just one of the stumbling blocks in the way of resuming publishing operations. And time and again, Suhrkamp fell ill and struggled with all the last vestiges of energy left to him against the creeping onset of inactivity, as he told Hesse in a letter of January 30, 1946: "For the past few days I have been feeling feverish, and a cough that I have been unable to completely shake off since the spring of 1945 has taken on a more alarming form of late. So I am crouching in front of the only stove in the entire house. And from this position I am trying to keep the publishing business running on a shoestring."[35]

Hesse, meanwhile, was grappling with the problem of whether the Italian edition of his *Siddhartha* was legal or not. It irked him that Suhrkamp was unable to give him a straight answer on this matter. In a letter of February 9, 1946, for instance, he wrote: "Since the Italians will never pay anything, I'm inclined to let this matter drop. What displeases me far more is that a large number of German newspapers and some radio stations as well are constantly reproducing texts of mine without seeking my permission first. If things go on like this, I intend to respond to this ongoing theft with a declaration in which I will distance myself even more energetically from the political and literary Germany than even Thomas Mann has done. I am heartily sick of this state of affairs."[36]

Suhrkamp kept assuring Hesse that he had no way of controlling these kinds of reprints, since no international press monitoring service had yet been reestablished. But he was quick to send his author his royalty statement for the year 1945. Hesse was mired in a crisis at the time and saw "the value of my life's work frozen." And book production remained at a standstill; it sounded distinctly like a reproach when Hesse wrote to Suhrkamp on May 8, 1946, and pointed to the steady stream of letters that he was receiving: "People remember me and are minded to give me a hearing again, and they upbraid me for not getting a better publisher who could republish my books quickly, and yet it does not occur to anybody to draw moral or political lessons from my works and my life or to look for anything in them other than what is pretty and musical. So that's that!"[37]

The correspondence between the writer and his publisher was increasingly disrupted by the censorship imposed by the Allies on letters, and time and again Hesse's letters were sent back, such as one on August 20, 1946, with the comment that discussing commercial matters was prohibited.

Over the course of 1946 Hesse lapsed into an ever deeper form of Steppenwolf-like gloom. It almost seemed as if the award of the Goethe Prize and the Nobel Prize had exacerbated this crisis. He flung out accusations at all and sundry, including Suhrkamp, such as when the idea of a separate Calw edition of Hesse's work was mooted, something that Suhrkamp naturally could not endorse: "But now I have lost my entire life's work to Germany and to you, and can look forward to nothing by way of recompense from that quarter, and you are punishing me once again by keeping silent for months on end, I too will let things take their course. It's all the same to me now whether it comes to fruition or not."[38]

Hesse ended this letter with a self-pitying lament that must have appeared wholly inappropriate to someone who was genuinely as seriously ill as Peter Suhrkamp: "In any event: I send you warmest greetings from the hell of my nervous breakdown."[39]

Shortly afterward Hesse announced: "I have lost the war of nerves that the world has been waging against me."

Suhrkamp, who was overjoyed at the award of the Nobel Prize to Hesse, was no doubt rather casual in his responses to Hesse's jeremiads about the poor state of his health. This prompted an indignant outburst from the writer on January 15, 1947: "Unfortunately I cannot fulfill your wish by letting you know about the state of my health or the place where I have been recuperating, etc. You saw fit to joke about my 'illness,' so I can only respond with silence. I have no doubt that you have been through all kinds of purgatory over the years. But you can have no idea of the hell that I have been living in constantly for the past two years and more, my dear Suhrkamp." He went on to claim that the Nobel Prize had brought him no pleasure, but that it had only succeeded in "making my life four times more onerous than previously." In February he planned to move on from Marin to Baden for a rest cure, and then to return to Montagnola in March. However: "Things are so difficult there and my life there has become so utterly pointless and joyless that I am not looking forward to returning, despite the fact that I have found it really hard doing without my house and library and garden and so on for months."[40]

A subsequent communication in March 1947 made it clear that Hesse was in a deep crisis regarding his state of mind and his nervous disposition: "Now I have to go back to Ticino, though I would rather be heading to the cemetery."[41]

The dispute between Bermann Fischer and Peter Suhrkamp finally came to a head at the end of the 1940s. Suhrkamp had never been under any illusion that the Fischer family could resume their proprietorship of the publishing house if they so wished. Yet the relationship between the two men grew steadily worse. On Maundy Thursday 1947, Suhrkamp wrote to Hesse: "Any collaboration will always be extremely difficult. Gottfried is thinking in ever more commercial terms and along 'broad lines.'"[42]

The retransfer negotiations stalled when Suhrkamp realized that Bermann Fischer no longer wanted him on the firm's board, but was planning to offer him a consultancy role that could be terminated at any time. He refused to accept such a post. Hesse was alarmed at this, and got Ninon to send Suhrkamp a telegram on February 6, 1950, which read: "Think of Hermann Hesse, who is greatly concerned. Don't hand back the publishing house."[43]

Bermann Fischer obtained an injunction that barred Suhrkamp from setting foot inside the company's offices; a court case was pending, which was only averted by a last-minute settlement. One provision of this agreement was that Suhrkamp would leave the firm and establish his own company—and that it was left to the authors to decide whether they wanted to go with Bermann Fischer or with Suhrkamp. Thirty-three of the forty-eight writers opted for Peter Suhrkamp. Bertolt Brecht wrote: "Dear Suhrkamp, come what may of course I should like to be with a publishing house run by you."[44]

Hesse got Ninon to cast his vote for Suhrkamp by telephone. This was a major prerequisite for the new publishing enterprise; to have on its books a best-selling author like Hesse! Suhrkamp, however, was entirely lacking any capital. Hesse played an active role in this regard, too—his friends and patrons Georg Reinhart and H. C. Bodmer ensured a sound economic basis for the new venture. Suhrkamp Verlag was a success in its very first year of operation—and not just thanks to its ambitious list of publications. In the first two years, works published by the company included, among others, *Selected Essays* by T. S. Eliot, Max Frisch's *Diaries 1946–1949,* Theodor Adorno's *Minima Moralia,* Walter Benjamin's *A Berlin Childhood around 1900,* Brecht's *Essays Vols. 10 and 11,* and Hermann Hesse's *Late Prose.*

In economic terms, too, the company was faring by no means badly, although generating large profits had never been at the top of Suhrkamp's publishing agenda. In any event, in 1950 Suhrkamp paid Hesse royalties to the tune of 50,000 deutschmarks, all of which could be legally transferred to Switzerland.

The publisher and author had by this time begun to address one another with the familiar "Du" form, although Hesse remained one of Suhrkamp's most difficult authors, whose first inclination was to reject every innovation as a matter of principle. But Suhrkamp—and later Siegfried Unseld—knew what a valuable asset Hesse was to the publishing house and so made strenuous efforts to show forbearance, mollifying him by showing flexibility and yet gently shepherding him onto new pastures nonetheless.

When Peter Suhrkamp died in 1959, Hesse had, as he said, lost not only his "most loyal" but also his "most indispensable" friend. In his obituary "My friend Peter," he wrote:

> When Peter first made my acquaintance, I was the older, successful author whom he had read in his childhood, and later, at the decisive turning-point in his career after the war, when he was vacillating between giving up completely and making a tentative new start in life, I provided the firmest support for him. I, on the other hand, apart from revering him as a hugely talented publisher and writer, admired him even more for his suffering and heroism—he was a man who had had to endure and survive immeasurably more dreadful hardship and hostility than I or any of my other friends had ever experienced.
>
> My friend Peter was much loved, and he was immensely charming—and not only when he consciously meant to be so. Even in his darkest and most suicidal hours, when people perhaps railed against him or at least felt sorely tempted to do so, you could not help but love him.[45]

Long-Standing Friends? A Loyal Specter: Ludwig Finckh

One of Hesse's oldest friends was Ludwig Finckh: the first time they had set eyes on one another had been in 1897, at Heckenhauer's bookshop in Tübingen, and over sixty years later Finckh was to publish an (albeit very brief) appreciation of Hesse on the occasion of his eighty-fifth birthday. "Ugel" Finckh had been a loyal acolyte of Hesse's ever since the youthful, inspired times they spent together in the *petit cénacle*.

But was he in fact a friend, or rather a ghost from the past who like a dark doppelgänger from their time as neighbors on Lake Constance embodied a potential path for Hesse that he never went down: that of the Romanticizing regional writer? Someone who had taken the shortest route from being a Swabian-German patriot to a militant nationalist and a supporter of Hitler? Hesse clearly saw all the limitations of his old friend, yet still displayed a remarkably tolerant attitude toward him—notwithstanding the fact that such limitations had quickly turned to bigotry in the First World War, and that bigotry had in turn spawned a militant ideology that would have induced Hesse, had it been anyone else, to sever all contact for good.

Perhaps he gave Finckh credit for the fact that his espousal of National Socialism had been a form of naive credulity and that there had been no cynicism or calculation behind it. "Ugel" had simply been reeled in with cheap propaganda and a fomenting of old resentments, like millions of other Germans. Or maybe Hesse just recalled the days when he and his neighbor in Gaienhofen would go off walking or fishing together, in that period after Finckh's house had been rebuilt following the fire that had consumed it just before he was due to take occupancy, and Hesse was busy collecting books for his friend's library.

On January 25, 1918, Hesse noted a dream in which Ludwig Finckh appeared. In the dream Hesse had traveled to Germany to visit Finckh: "My relationship to him was very similar to how it was in reality: our attempts to pick up the threads again and to rekindle an atmosphere of bonhomie ran up against mutual nervousness and resistance." The problem was the kind of patriotism that Finckh displayed, and his enthusiasm for the war. There then comes a passage in this dream recollection that reads like an allusion to the fire in Finckh's house at Gaienhofen just before he planned to move in:

> I opened a window and a draft immediately started blowing between the window and the stove, which quickly dispelled the thick cigar smoke. At the same time, I put some more logs in the cast-iron stove, so that it would be warm when I got back. Suddenly I noticed that the draft had dispersed parts of the fire all over the room. It ran counter to all physical laws, but I immediately understood that this was what must have happened, so I shut the window and started gathering up from all round the room, namely from off the bed, glowing pieces of light charcoal or burning lumps of wood. The bedspread and bed linen had turned very black but showed remarkably little fire damage.[46]

In 1925 Hesse replied in the following terms to Finckh's complaints about the Weimar Republic: "I have also had cause to note the hypocrisy and unscrupulousness of the German government of which you complain; indeed, I lost my house in Gaienhofen as a result of it. But it is nothing new, the foundations were laid a long time ago, and it first reared its head during the war, when the emperor, the Foreign Ministry, the press, the war reports and dispatches from the front all started lying like mad to us day after day, and our warning voices from our sober vantage point abroad were either mocked or directly punished."[47]

Hugo Ball fiercely repudiated Finckh. In a letter to Hesse in 1931, Erhard Bruder complained that the chapter in Ball's Hesse monograph that dealt with his sojourn at Gaienhofen was "one long vilification of Ludwig Finckh." Hesse replied: "I know that Ball's judgment of Finckh is very harsh and that this must wound him—but at the time I did stop Ball from publishing the very harshest things he was going to say about Finckh."[48]

What Hesse then went on in this same letter to say about Ball and Finckh does not sound very indulgent toward the latter: "But in spite of all this, if you still don't understand Ball's attitude toward Finckh, let me remind you of the most salient point: Ball was the most unyielding critic of German warmongering and jingoism, and Finckh was a very active and vocal supporter of that kind of war-drunk mentality, which I also condemned and which has helped destroy German both intellectually and politically."[49]

Remarkably, despite this fierce attack, Hesse declared himself willing to "write a correction that will put Finckh in a more favorable light"[50] in a future edition of Ball's monograph. Wasn't that a clear case of him infringing upon the authorship rights of that work, which didn't belong to Hesse, just out of a long-standing friendship with Finckh?

In February 1932 Hesse reacted to Finckh's diatribes against the Weimar Republic and his praise of the National Socialist movement by referring to "that blockhead Hitler," whom he conceded might have an important role to play in German politics in due course. Although Hesse stood apart from the rough and tumble of politics, if faced with the choice, he saw himself on the opposing side and made no bones about telling Finckh as much: "Believe me, it would be simpler and better for me if I could sing and march along in support of some cause. If only Germany had a halfway decent and genuine form of communism, I would put myself at its disposal. But where is such a thing to be found? Whether it be about communism or Hitlerism or whatever, thinking and wishing is futile; it is sentimental and unproductive. A lot of things still need to die for the grass to grow once more. But it will grow again, for sure."[51] That was the starting point for *The Glass Bead Game*—this question of what had to decline in order for something new to arise, and what needed to be preserved, for the very same reason.

When Finckh placed himself in the service of the Nazis, he toed the official party line in ceasing to regard Hesse any longer as a writer who was important for Germany. Privately, though, he continued to send him letters with a friendly tone. Hesse was irritated, and reacted strongly, but still refused to burn his bridges with Finckh, as he wrote to tell him in 1944: "We two have taken opposing paths. . . . For you, my name no longer belongs to any canon of German literature that you are permitted to speak of. . . . You yourself concede that nobody can write anything under a regime of terror. But one cannot live or breathe in such circumstances either. I cannot go along with that, I do not think it possible that we can ever understand one another: I do not share your militant ideals."[52]

After the war, Finckh turned to Hesse, now a Nobel Prize laureate with an influential voice, to ask him to act as a character witness on his behalf at the denazification tribunal. Hesse's response was measured: he replied on March 6, 1947, sending his friend a letter that he said Finckh could present to the tribunal. But he expressly ruled out any personal involvement: "It is totally out of the question for me to appear personally in front of this or any other official body, whether it be German or convened by the occupying powers."[53]

In the letter he appended, he stated that Finckh was well aware of his, namely Hesse's, stance on the political views that Finckh had espoused since the First World War and that he had "always found his kind of patriotism abhorrent." And his judgment on Finckh was unequivocal. "You were and are a typical German Nationalist, and it is they who have visited Hitler and his whole diabolical regime upon us. The fact that you believed in Hitler himself and his party as a pure, patriotic and idealistic cause is sad and inexcusable, but it is a sin that you share with 90 percent of German intellectuals, and the German people and the world at large have had to pay dearly for this grand German sin." A harsh judgment that Finckh surely would have done better not to put before the tribunal. But then Hesse continued—and what he had to say was not a qualification or relativization but simply an attempt to place Finckh's individual case in its context: "But this guilt or sin or stupidity, or whatever you wish to call it, is one that you share with thousands of colleagues, who have had no punishment meted out to them. Even people like Gerhart Hauptmann have committed this sin, and in spite of that his work and his memory are still celebrated today."[54]

Hesse, then, had no desire to roundly condemn all those who had lived in Germany and believed in Hitler. According to him, a new start had to be possible for them too, as long as they were sincere and admitted their guilt. Finckh was not inclined to do that—nor did the atmosphere of the 1950s in West Germany require that he do so—quite the contrary, in fact.

Instead, as a supposed "sybarite"—as his enemies dubbed him—Hesse was the one who found himself under pressure to justify his position. Hadn't he lived a secure and comfortable life in Switzerland while Germans were either dying at the front or suffering countless nights of bombing at home in the cities, to say nothing of the privations of hunger and the harassment that ensued after the war? Meanwhile the German émigrés and their fair-weather fellow-travelers asked what Hesse's contribution had been to the struggle against Hitler.

Certainly, Hesse himself was well aware quite how lucky he had been. But ultimately who was to blame for the global catastrophe that was heralded by Hitler's seizure of power in 1933—him or people like Finckh who had rejoiced at the new regime?

Finckh, who officially had wanted nothing to do with Hesse during the twelve years of Nazi rule, now showed himself to be profoundly grateful. He dedicated his 1948 collection of poems *The Rose Garden* to him. Hesse felt somewhat hijacked, but was studiedly relaxed in his response:

> You ask me to extend the hand of friendship to you once more, old Ugel. Yes, I'll do that, indeed I have been doing it for quite some time. We shared some good times together back in the day. Our paths did not diverge when I moved to Bern, but only some years later, when you started singing war songs and chose as your masters the Emperor and the generals and later the Brownshirts. . . . I know that you personally did not torture any Jews or burn or proscribe any of my books and that, all things considered, you meant well, Ugel, but on the other hand you did follow blindly, and this barrier between us still remains and because of it I find your dedication to me unnecessary: it gives readers the false impression that we are bound

together not by our recollections of our splendid youth but instead are conjoined and of one mind in our thoughts and our innermost consciences. . . . Nice for you that you can forget so easily! But I take a different view.[55]

Hesse attempted to do something that not everyone was doing during this period: to admit the political mistakes of his fellow travelers and not to hush up the complicity of individuals in the crimes of the Nazi period, while still keeping faith with them as human beings. Generally speaking, however, this approach won him no new friends among either former Nazis or returning émigrés. Finckh was grateful to him, but Hesse again found it very suspect, this kind of overeagerness for reconciliation that appealed to the spirit of a shared youth, as he wrote to Erwin Moser, his former fellow pupil in Cannstatt, in February 1949: "Sometimes I'm really at a loss how to deal with good old Finckh. I always remained friendly with him on a personal level, and even helped him in his hour of greatest need, but he has never uttered so much as a single word of comment on the fact that he was a Nazi."[56]

Hesse knew the Germans; after all, he was one himself—albeit with the proviso that he was concurrently other things as well—Swiss, Alemannic, Swabian, and in spirit a citizen of the world. In a letter from Hesse in April 1952, Wilhelm Gundert learned about the absurdities of life in Germany—a phenomenon with a long tradition stretching right up to the present day. Hesse told Gundert that there had once been a street named after him in the city of Konstanz—but in 1916, when Hesse's name was suddenly no longer so opportune, it disappeared from the street sign and was replaced by that of Ludwig Finckh, of all people: "But then when Finckh, who had spent the past twelve years staunchly shouting 'Heil Hitler,' was out of favor, the good burghers of Konstanz quickly took down the Finckh sign and painted my name over it. This sort of thing could recur every couple of years."[57]

When Finckh finally published his autobiography *Heaven and Earth (Himmel und Erde)* in 1961, he made great play of his friendship with Hesse. This proved the last straw for Heiner Hesse, who demanded that his father explain to him why he had shown such excessive indulgence toward Finckh. A few weeks prior to this, on the occasion of Finckh's eighty-fifth birthday, Hesse had written a message of congratulation in the *Blätter des schwäbischen Albvereins* (Gazette of the Swabian Jura Society)—but had not omitted to mention there the differences between them. He also recalled the happy memory of Finckh coming to visit him in Montagnola in November 1957.

In a letter of July 1961 to his son Heiner, though, Hesse conceded that he was right:

> Up the First World War the book [Finckh's autobiography] is delightful and reveals something of the charm of the young Finckh, even though much of what he recalls is completely fabricated. But from 1914 on, it is the book of a conventional German nationalist and jingoistic patriot. And from 1933 on it is the book of a narrow-minded Nazi who spent 12 years yelling "Heil Hitler" and would still like to be doing so now. As far as he is concerned, there was no Himmler, no Eichmann, no Auschwitz or Stalingrad. It is ghastly and sad, and cannot be explained solely by Finckh's great stupidity. If I had known that he had never revised his views, realized the truth, and regretted his past, then I would never have received him.[58]

Daily Life in Old Age

Hesse had now become a grand old man. He could at this juncture have turned into a figurehead of German literature—yet that was a role he firmly rejected. He gave no radio interviews and (unlike Gottfried Benn or Thomas Mann) disliked being photographed or filmed. The only extant moving images of him are cine-camera footage taken by friends. And the sound recordings of Hesse, reading his "Thanks to Ticino" and "A Dream Gift," total just 27 minutes. It need hardly be added that he was not one for participating in panel discussions, either. And yet his decisive shunning of the real world, a position he had defended for so long, nevertheless began to crumble—due in no small measure to Ninon. Was that of benefit to his writing? Hardly—Ninon would have been all too happy to be his muse, but Hesse did not need a muse; indeed, he did not need any women at all in his life in order to write.

After all, he wrote the whole of *The Glass Bead Game* without including any principal female characters; he could only conceive of the spiritual realm as a confraternity of men. This society did not lead a life of celibacy, though; for all their espousal of asceticism, this did not include sexual abstinence, as Hesse expressly noted. The middle-class girls were

Hesse in 1957 with his youngest grandson, David

happy to enter into erotic relationships with prospective players of the Glass Bead Game, as that was an integral part of both parties' education, so to speak. The girls knew that and did not even want to get married. This was a bitter pill for Ninon to swallow, who wanted to be more to Hesse than just a perfect homemaker!

What's more, there were other authors whom she had got to know and who appreciated her intellect—Hans Carossa, for instance, whom she liked. Or Joachim Maass, who had included Ninon in *A Testament,* the last novel he wrote before emigrating, under the pseudonym of Xenia, a woman who played a significant part in the work of her beloved husband. Yet Ninon had no stake in Hesse's work. The reasons for this, however, lay in their divergent opinions of what art should be. For Hesse it was a form of defense against the encroachment of reality, whereas this form of Romantic esthetic was totally alien to Ninon, who was oriented toward reality and who had a real hunger for the world.

As a result, Hesse felt he had to defend his writing, his inner world, against Ninon, and that pained her deeply.

Ninon entered into an intense correspondence with Joachim Maass. Sadly, their letters no longer exist, as they were destroyed by his family. Hesse got to learn about this erotically charged friendship between

Heiner Hesse on November 6, 2002 (the last photo of him before his death)

soulmates when a letter intended for Ninon accidentally fell into his hands. He reacted with jealousy and wounded pride. Ninon confided to her diary at the time:

> October 7, 1949: Went to see H., feeling full of the joys of life. Rebuffed by his sour demeanor. With every day that passes, suicide seems increasingly the only solution. October 8, 1949: H. is enraged. Hasn't spoken a word to me. At 8 o'clock, before I was due to read to him, I asked him what "crime" I'd committed. Words exchanged. H. "excuses" himself. Separation or suicide? October 9, 1949: For the most part, it is hard to tell whether H. is sad or in a foul mood. . . . I want to throw myself under a car. How can one live like this? October 10, 1949: The loveliest letter from J. M. that he has ever written me. I am not alone anymore.[59]

Time and again, Ninon tried to find just one area of life in which she could express her creative urge. She edited a selection of Grimms' fairy tales for the Gutenberg Book Guild, but under the impact of the terrible war that had just ended, she decided she ought not to include some of the more grisly stories like "The Juniper Tree"—a curious attitude on her part

toward that "esthetic of terror" that had been present even in the mythology of ancient Greece and with which Ninon was very much at home.
Her judgments on art repeatedly irritated Hesse, as when she went to a
concert while on her travels and was outraged by what she regarded as the
dreadful kitsch of Gustav Mahler's "Lied von der Erde."

After the war Hesse received long-awaited visits from his elder sister, Adele,
and his younger sister, Marulla. He was especially delighted by Adele's visit,
as she had always been the only member of the family who had not taken
refuge in general philanthropy and who had fostered a special personal relationship with her brother—something that was otherwise lacking
among the Hesse family, in accordance with their Pietist principles. Adele
had married her cousin Hermann Gundert, a pastor. She died in 1949, and
Hesse wrote her obituary. At the time of Adele's death his sister Marulla
(who had remained single) was visiting Hesse, and she left to attend the
funeral in Korntal. Hesse gave her a bouquet of flowers to place beside the
grave, but never even entertained the idea of going to the funeral himself
(the same was true after Marulla's death in 1953). In his obituary "In
Memory of Adele," we read that she had been "a friendly guiding star, a
good spirit," who had the gift of "enchantment." A convivial soul, whose
"charisma" far outstripped that of her "rather solemn" siblings. Hesse's late
confession is surprising: "Adele always remained the most enduring love
of my life. There were stronger emotions, more passionate dalliances and
friendships, yet even those who are closest to me—my wife, my sons, and
my few intimate friends—do not have that bedrock of memories and our
childhood and homeland in common with me like she did."[60]

Daily life at Casa Rossa was strictly regulated. Hesse spent his time
writing, principally letters, sorting addresses, and arranging publication of
special editions—he kept a controlling eye on anything associated with
his name. He also continued painting, as well as working in the garden.
He could often be found crouching over a small bonfire, looking like an
old Red Indian waiting for death. Occasionally he would play *boccia* with
Ninon in the garden, where a special area had been laid out for the game.
Now and then he would even organize little tournaments involving family
members and domestic servants, to whom he issued special invitations.
Sometimes his sons would turn up with Hesse's grandchildren, and the
old man would play with them or they would go on walks together. Most

of all, though—and this was something he did have in common with Ninon—he enjoyed the company of cats, and there were always several in evidence at Casa Rossa.

The preparation of meals in the Hesse household for the excessively fussy cats proved to be a complicated business. And whenever Ninon went off traveling, she would leave behind long lists of special instructions relating to the individual animals.

There is a photograph showing the eighty-year-old Hermann Hesse crouching down on all fours on the verandah in pursuit of his tomcat Porphy. His face in this image is anything but that of the grand old man of letters—one can see the playful child still in the old man. The fact that such unposed images exist of him at all is thanks to the efforts of his son Martin. The third and youngest child of Hermann Hesse, Martin was born in 1911 and became a professional photographer. Shunned by his father as a child when he displayed behavioral problems following a bout of meningitis, Martin was actually the most artistically gifted of the three Hesse sons—though he also had the most unstable personality. Shortly before his death, Heiner Hesse pronounced his brother Martin's architectural photographs as truly significant works of art in their monochrome sparseness. Martin, who was always melancholic and sometimes depressive as well, was the only one of Hesse's sons who could not get over his father's death and ended up taking his own life in 1968.

Bruno, the eldest of the sons (born 1905), was raised by the painter Cuno Amiet, who was close to the group of German Expressionist artists known as "Die Brücke"; he recalled his childhood at the Amiets as a happy one. Bruno became a painter himself—however, he did not possess the unconditional artistic urge required to pursue a lifetime's career as a painter. The author Georg A. Weth, who visited him not long before his death in 1999, described him as a man at peace with himself. Bruno was living "wholly oblivious to the outside world"[61]—though he did feel that he had failed utterly as a painter and, like all three of Hesse's sons, remained dependent on his father's support throughout his life.

After a long childhood odyssey through various children's homes and boarding schools, Heiner Hesse, the middle son, who was born in 1909, rebelled repeatedly against his father. He learned the profession of store window-dresser and was for a spell a staunch communist. Heiner Hesse often came across to visitors as someone who was constantly bemoaning his fate. But also, rather impressively, as a self-sufficient hermit-like figure who had put all fear of life far behind him. On a visit in November 2002, a few months before his death, when he was suffering from emphysema and could barely walk and even found speaking very difficult, he nonetheless kindly set a great deal of time aside to meet the author of this biography and talk to him about his father. He was at pains to point out, repeatedly, that he had never hated him—and that chimed in totally with the peaceful accommodation he had reached in the interim not just with his father's work but also with his life. He was aware that such a body of work never comes without sacrifices.

In the final years of his life, Heiner Hesse lived on his own in a former mill building in the woods near Ronco sopra Ancona in Ticino, where he always kept the door unlocked. On the wall was a painting showing a turtle trying to mate with a steel helmet, and beneath it the legend "Fuck you." Heiner Hesse declared himself to be a pacifist with regard to the looming US-led invasion of Iraq. His face looked so "birdlike" that one could easily have imagined one was talking to Hermann Hesse himself. In an almost ascetic way, he lived very frugally where the material comforts of life were concerned, and he accepted his illness with a heroic stoicism. He left his body to medical science.

Returning to the business of daily life in Casa Rossa during the final decade of Hesse's life, Ninon's relationship with the domestic staff proved a constant source of problems. Self-possessed Swiss employees in the 1950s did not take kindly to the sort of imperious tone that might have been appropriate in Czernowitz half a century earlier. Many of them resigned soon after taking up their jobs—in Montagnola the Casa Rossa earned itself a reputation as a very uncomfortable place to work. Even house guests noticed how inappropriately severe Ninon was in her dealings with the staff. Maria Geroe-Tobler, a carpet-weaver friend of Ninon and Hermann Hesse, who stayed at Casa Rossa for a few weeks in 1948 following a stroke, was so incensed by Ninon's behavior that a furious argument erupted, with both women flinging insults at one another; Hesse was forced to strike Maria Geroe-Tobler's name from the list of family friends.[62]

Hesse's niece Trudel took a particularly harsh view of Ninon. Trudel was the daughter of Hesse's favorite sister, Adele, and came to Montagnola to help with the preparations for Hesse's eighty-fifth-birthday celebration. Decades later, she still had a vivid recollection of the expedition to purchase the wine that was to be offered to the brass-band players who were going to serenade the writer. To this end, she and Ninon had gone into Lugano together to buy five bottles. Trudel recalled: "We spent three hours wandering round the town trying to find the cheapest wine. . . . Ninon was a very punctilious woman, but also extremely miserly. For instance, one time when a housekeeper bought 100 grams too much meat, she was made to return it to the butcher's. Little wonder that most cooks didn't stay on the job under her for very long."[63]

Was Ninon truly stingy, though? Before her marriage to Hesse, when she was living in Vienna, she had a reputation for being very casual in everyday matters and generous with money. And after Hesse's death, when she was responsible for disbursing his estate, all his sons testified that they never had any money problems with her and that she had always been open-handed.

So was it Hesse who forced her to be so fussy and nitpicking in money matters? Certainly he could be both miserly and generous. Sometimes postal charges seemed too high to him and he refrained from sending a letter as a result. Conversely, after the war he supported his two sisters and their families in Germany with regular transfers of funds, and his three sons remained dependent upon his help. He even sometimes sent money to complete strangers whose begging letters touched a nerve with him.

It must, instead, have come down to a clash of two characters who were intent on showing each other that they were exemplary in household affairs, right down to arguing about minutiae.

Hesse suddenly saw his position in Casa Rossa as being like that of the old Goethe in his house on the Frauenplan in Weimar, shackled to a domestic routine. He accepted it, though it never really suited him—hence the charged atmosphere in the house, which they attempted to prevent from escalating into open feuding through written correspondence—the famous–notorious "house letters." By means of expressing themselves in writing, rather, they managed to inject a playful element into the serious business of daily life.

Thus, meals were prepared by the cook under Ninon's supervision and then brought to table by a parlor maid, who was then required to formally "serve" it to him in the manner of haut-bourgeois households of a bygone era. In Casa Camuzzi, Hesse had always drunk his wine out of water tumblers, whereas now he was served it in an appropriately grand crystal-cut glass on a silver platter.

Hesse appeared to have accepted this daily arrangement, which is to say that with Ninon's assistance he cultivated his malaise, which was more than the sum of his various ailments—rather, it was an expression of his sense of being totally at odds with the modern world.

By now they also owned an automobile. Ninon had passed her test and chauffeured Hesse around. Hesse, it seemed, had switched sides from that of the "automobile hunters" in *Steppenwolf* to that of the prey—and was thoroughly enjoying it. He could no longer walk very far, so instead they cruised around their locality in their Mercedes; a solution that was not only practical but also elegant.

The garden at the house, which for Hesse was a place where he could sit and meditate while staring into the flames of a bonfire, was for Ninon a place of sheer drudgery, which she dreaded. She wrote to her ex-husband, Fred Dolbin, to tell him about the harvesting of the vines that formed part of their property:

> This year the vines have to be cleared of excess foliage: the job of picking the grapes is a very laborious and unpleasant business. You find lots of rotten grapes between the good ones; ones that have shriveled or split or never ripened—your fingers get stickier and stickier and it reeks of mildew and mold. I said jokingly to H.: "I'd love it if some townie were to appear right now, one of those types who have read Hamsun's *Growth of the Soil* and who romanticize life on the land . . . just let him come and spend half an hour helping us with the grape harvest. I bet he couldn't wait to get back to the paved streets of his home city and start breathing in the healthy coal dust and petrol fumes again."[64]

Ninon thirsted after the world and gaining recognition in it. So it was all the more painful for her that over the years, despite studying Greece intensively, she never found a way of giving truly individual expression to her wealth of knowledge about Hera and the rest of the Greek pantheon. She felt as though she had failed.

"It's a shame that I've remained such a torso. Time and again I try writing, but it never really passes muster, either as a critical essay or as a piece of solid writing on art history or as literature. All it succeeds in doing is making me unhappy in my lot running the household."[65]

To the very end of her life, Ninon suffered from feelings of guilt over the suicide of her sister, Toka. She believed that she'd failed to spot the warning signs and had been deaf to her cry for help. On one level, she had been too harsh. For a long time she had not even been able to conceive of the possibility that someone could take their own life. But now she kept on talking about wanting to end her own life: "Death can't possibly hurt as much as life does!"[66]

Hesse, to whom she had sacrificed her own mission in life, completely failed to appreciate that sacrifice and instead almost completely overwhelmed her with his sensitivities and neuroses. Hence her almost constant state of irritability and her flirting with the idea of suicide. Where Hesse was concerned, suicide as a means of escape, one that he always kept open for himself was a way of cleansing the soul. By contrast the prospect of such a death, which was a permanent presence between them, threatened to crush her. Certainly they were two potential candidates for suicide, but even in this matter they were poles apart.

In March 1962 Peter Weiss came to visit Hermann Hesse again. Exactly twenty-five years had passed since he had first walked to Montagnola—it perhaps it might be more accurate to call it a pilgrimage, or an escape. Now he found himself standing outside the red house with the sign on the gate reading "No Visitors, Please," and he glanced into the garden and saw that it was just the same as it always had been: "a wilderness, full of dying foliage." And as if that one sign wasn't enough, his eyes now lighted upon a second, far wordier sign hanging in the window next to the front door—and the message it conveyed provided, so to speak, the reason for the neurotic, almost hysterical phobia of visitors by a man who was accustomed to justifying his actions in writing. The effect was embarrassing and at the same time comical—wouldn't it have been sufficient to simply disconnect the doorbell, to not answer the telephone and simply to consign all letters from unknown senders to the wastepaper bin without more ado, just as Gottfried Benn did, without the slightest qualms? But it went against the grain for Hesse to disappear like that without a word; he felt it was incumbent on him to give some justification for his action. And so it was that Peter Weiss, who had announced his visit and yet who now could not help but feel like an unwelcome interloper, found himself confronted with the following statement: "By the time a person has grown old and done his bit, he is entitled to acquaint himself with death in peace and quiet. He doesn't need people. He knows them well, and he's had enough of them. What he needs is peace. It's not very seemly to come calling on such a person and pester him with chit-chat. Better to just walk on past his house like it belongs to nobody."

On this visit, less than six months before Hesse's death, Weiss found him "wizened and haggard"; his suit had become too large for him, and yet he "was very youthful in the way he carried himself and walked."[67] His eyes were "inflamed and bloodshot" and his hands "gnarled" but his mind was sharp and clear. Ninon, he noted, "kept close watch over the old man" (Karl Kerényi spoke of her "religious devotion" to Hesse)—and hardly had Weiss's visit begun than she brought it to a close: "I'd not managed to say any of the things I wanted to before he was spirited away again into his wooden cubbyhole."[68] Weiss came to the sobering conclusion that his visit was just one "among thousands." Hesse would not allow himself to become some kind of visitor attraction, not even if they treated him with reverential awe, and he refused to play the role for others that he claimed for himself as the author of *The Glass Bead Game*. And he resented the fact that his readers lusted after the sensation of having him before them in person, when they ought to have been content with the written word.

In these late years Hesse remained the same pessimist he had shown himself to be previously. The only difference was that he withdrew increasingly from the world in the years that remained to him up to his death, and insisted upon living in ever greater seclusion. He was calm and composed, but was never reconciled to an age that he saw as being ruled over by Shiva, the Hindu god of destruction.

And so, as he surveyed the ruins of defeated Nazi Germany, Hesse was far from any euphoric feelings of liberation. He looked upon the Federal Republic of Germany and the German Democratic Republic with equal mistrust. Consequently, he did not grace either state with a visit; in fact, the last time he visited Germany was in 1936, for an ophthalmologist's appointment.

The extent of his embittered pessimism is revealed by a letter he wrote to Rolf Schott on October 2, 1945: "Supposedly, 'good' has now triumphed, but victory really belonged to the generals, the artillery, the atom bombs, and the engineers, and the rest of us are, as we always have been, 'not of that world,' and consequently often long to leave it behind completely."[69]

Hesse saw ideology as the archenemy of the spirit, that civilized mode of intercourse between human beings. As a result, he regarded West Germany in the 1950s as an unholy combination of old Nazi ideology with a new market-led euphoria, something that was complete anathema to him. And in East Germany, the ruling communists were completely in thrall to Stalin, whom Hesse identified as a criminal long before many of his writer colleagues did. Hesse wanted nothing to do with them, either.

Yet, unlike the Federal Republic, in the 1950s the GDR made strenuous efforts to woo Hesse, just as it did Heinrich and Thomas Mann, Bertolt Brecht, and Lion Feuchtwanger, Ernst Bloch and Hans Mayer. All of them had been émigrés and were prepared, at least initially, to give the "other Germany" the benefit of the doubt over the Federal Republic, which seemed intent on restoring the old order.

Hesse, though, was free of such hopeful illusions. In the first instance this was for the very simple reason that publishers in the GDR were stealing from him, publishing his novels in large print-runs and paying him either a pittance or nothing at all (hard currency was in short supply there after the war). To add insult to injury, his works were widely read in the GDR—and many readers longed for him to publish some new books. In March 1954 Hesse responded to a female reader of his from East Berlin, who had written to him expressing such a wish, in a manner that she would no doubt have found shockingly mundane: "Those works of mine that have been published so far in your country and have been dishonestly called 'licensed editions' have in fact been stolen. The books in question are *Camenzind* and *Beneath the Wheel;* about 80,000 copies of these two titles have been sold in the East, though we have not received a penny in return, nor did we give our permission for them to be printed in the first place. And yet now you think that I should ask these gentlemen to steal more books from me? That's really beyond the pale."[70] Yet when Walter Janka of Aufbau Verlag, the GDR publishing house that had been pirating

Hermann Hesse and his wife, Ninon

his works, was arrested in 1956 in the wake of the Wolfgang Harich affair and given a long prison sentence, Hesse was up in arms, incensed that such a capable, cultivated man should be locked up by the likes of the GDR leader Walter Ulbricht!

Hesse would not allow himself to be co-opted into anything, however noble a cause it might be. Since the summer of 1914, over and over again he had seen where such causes could lead once they became a political agenda—to chauvinism, the persecution of those who thought differently, and ultimately to political assassination and war. And so he brusquely rebuffed East Berlin's attempts to persuade him to attend the Congress of the Peoples for Peace in Vienna in December 1952. Anna Seghers, whose book *On the Way to the American Embassy* he had reviewed back in 1931, tried in person to win him round but without success. Hesse wrote to Ninon, who was on her travels in Athens at the time, to tell her: "The communists are preparing another 'Peace' offensive for this October, and this time I was personally ambushed, by a very venerable and charming lady who tugged at my heart strings but who believes in Stalin and his ideology like a devout Catholic believes in the sacraments, and who was completely deaf to any refutations of her position, even when they consisted of facts. Of course, she did not achieve her objective of getting me to sign on the dotted line."[71]

The surprising thing about this is not that Hesse refused to put his name to any joint appeal, but that he called Anna Seghers a "venerable lady": at the time she was only fifty-one years old (whereas he was seventy-five)! By couching it in these terms, he was presumably attempting to avoid Ninon becoming jealous. Many of the leading European avant-garde artists and thinkers of the day, including Matisse, Picasso, Vercors, and Sartre, had signed the Vienna Appeal. The long letter that she wrote Hesse after their meeting to try to win him round has survived. In it, she outlined the aims of the People's Peace Congress, at which "people of all nations, all colors, all parties (or none), all persuasions and professions will come together. They are united by just one thing: their wish to save the world from a Third World War. . . . Year after year, your books have made the lives of countless people happier, richer—in a word, better. If a writer is capable of doing this, then his thoughts, once expressed, have the capacity to improve the lives of everyone on Earth. You can defend peace."[72] This was a highly personal and moving letter from the former émigré writer. A note on the letter in Hesse's handwriting reads "No reply."

In 1955 Hesse received an invitation to join the Academy of Arts in East Berlin as a corresponding member. For Hesse, the very mention of academies—whether in the East or the West—brought back bad memories of the Prussian Academy. His brief membership in that institution had caused him a great deal of trouble. Accordingly, he declined politely but firmly:

> I am seventy-eight years old and I have managed thus far to avoid all such memberships. Just as I have not joined the PEN-Club or any West German academies, neither can I become a member of your academy.
>
> I would implore you to in no way see my response as a repudiation of your endeavors, but just as an adherence on my part to a principle to which I must remain true.[73]

This was a period of intense Cold War hysteria, which saw an invisible enemy at work behind everything and everyone. Even in Switzerland, Hesse was not spared this. Any hint of a political position that was not expressly anticommunist was enough to raise suspicion. In this period, a modern witch hunt could swiftly grow out of the slightest of causes. Hesse also experienced this when he wrote an open letter to the "warriors for peace" who staged an uprising against communist rule in East Berlin in March 1953—this was greeted with mistrust because he showed sympathy for the principal concern behind the revolt (fear of a nuclear world war) without throwing his weight behind those who had made this cause the basis of their political struggle. Hesse's contention was that the same malaise existed everywhere. Hesse saw his position as being vindicated by the reaction and noted: "But as if to demonstrate that the bourgeois–capitalist–hawkish front is just as powerful and violent as the communist one, the *Zürcher Zeitung* has refused to print my 'reply.'"

Hesse was a firm nonbeliever in public rallying cries and in putting his signature to appeals.

As a consequence, he never tired of repeating his position: "My works have all been written with no ulterior motive or bias. But if I search retrospectively in them for a common thread of meaning, then I can indeed find one: . . . a defense of (sometimes even a desperate plea on behalf of) the human personality, the individual. . . . The individual, unique human being with his past heritage and future potential, his talents and inclinations, is a tender, fragile entity that could certainly use an advocate."[74]

Having such an agenda made it hard for one's motives not to be misunderstood in that ideologically highly charged era, where one was forced to think in terms of friend and foe and where people adopted opposed and entrenched intellectual positions. The eye of suspicion fell on him, especially in Switzerland, as the blunt question was posed: Is Hermann Hesse a Communist? Thus ran the title of an article on July 11, 1955, in the *Schaffhausener Zeitung*. What had happened to occasion this? All he had done was respond to a request to send a few words in greeting to a Women's Congress in Lausanne entitled "Mothers against the Atom Bomb." It subsequently transpired that the Communist Party was behind this conference. Once again, the artificially fomented furor was whipped up to the point of hysteria, forcing an irritated Hesse to issue the following disclaimer: "I did not address my greetings to the 'Communist Congress in Lausanne.' Rather, some six months ago, I simply fulfilled a request from a Swiss Women's Organization to contribute a few words to a congress of mothers against nuclear war. I could not have known that this women's group was affiliated with the Communist Party."[75]

This was exactly the kind of thing that Hesse was fleeing from and trying to insulate himself against; he wanted nothing to do with the prevailing malevolent spirit of the age and believed that neither of the opposing ideological camps was better than the other. He preferred lighting bonfires in the garden and staring into the flames, or painting and being read to by Ninon, or any activity involving intellect and wit.

Enter Siegfried Unseld

In 1951 the twenty-seven-year-old Siegfried Unseld, who was later to become a leading German publisher and head of the Suhrkamp Verlag, found himself en route to Montagnola. The year before, Hesse had written to him: "Do come and visit me should you ever find yourself in Switzerland."

Unseld was carrying a copy of Hesse's *Wandering,* and made his way first, half walking and half hitch-hiking, to Lugano, then to Locarno, and finally to Montagnola. This was the first trip to the South for this young bookseller from Heidenheim, and he had felt his senses overwhelmed and his imagination fired right up until he arrived at his journey's end:

> There I stood, in front of the oak door of the house. Behind the barred window in the door a sign yellowed with age carried the warning words of Meng Hsiä [a fictional Chinese sage invented by Hesse]: "By the time a person has grown old and done his bit, he is entitled to acquaint himself with death in peace and quiet. He doesn't need people. He knows them well, and he's had enough of them. What he needs is peace. It's not very seemly to come calling on such a person and pester him with chit-chat. Better to just walk on past his house like it belongs to nobody."
>
> I felt that these words were neither a joke nor an intellectual game meant to test my literary knowledge.

So, Unseld forbore to ring the doorbell and turned to go, though he was loath to have made the long hitch-hike from the Rhineland for nothing. Shortly afterward, he learned that Hesse wasn't in Montagnola just then, but staying at Schloss Bremgarten, the home of his friend and patron Max Wassmer. Was there a sign there too reading "No Visitors, Please," he wondered?

The young bookseller decided to try his luck—and succeeded. Admittedly, he had an advantage over other visitors: he had written his doctoral dissertation on Herman Hesse. And yet with someone who had such a hostile attitude to all things academic as Hermann Hesse, that could have quickly proved to be a disadvantage.

Unseld immediately saw in Hesse that "Chinese hermit" to whom Josef Knecht makes a pilgrimage in *The Glass Bead Game:* "A frail man, dressed in biscuit-colored linen, with spectacles over blue eyes that had an observant look, stood up from a flower bed over which he had been bending and slowly approached the visitor. His manner was not unfriendly, but it had that somewhat awkward shyness common among recluses and people who live on their own." Unseld had bookmarked his copy of the novel with a picture of Hesse at the point where this passage appears.

Was this a magical act on Unseld's part, an attempt to conjure up that spirit that had the capacity to link the most disparate of things without thereby robbing them of their distinctiveness? He sat opposite Hesse and was fascinated by the living embodiment of the subject of his dissertation: "A face betraying a faun-like spirit, his senses, and his intellect seem here to have entered into an alliance that radiates a peculiar kind of sensibility."[76]

The young bookseller forgot what they spoke about at this first meeting, but what stayed with him was an impression of the magical atmosphere at Schloss Bremgarten, that place "where the travelers to the East celebrated their union." The only clear detail imprinted on his memory was Hesse's tone of voice, that "Swiss inflection," through which "a Swabian bass-note" resonated.

Hesse noted about this first encounter: "And on Sunday, while we were sitting over a cup of black coffee, a young stranger appeared. He had come down from Ulm and was called Unseld. He was very nice, and made a good impression on us."[77]

As it turned out, Unseld hadn't forgotten everything that he and Hesse talked about during their first meeting at Bremgarten. They chatted about what Unseld did. The fact that he was a bookseller prompted Hesse to recall his own experiences, not all of them positive. He also told Hesse that he wanted to start his own publishing house, with some friends near his age as his authors. In that case, Hesse suggested, why didn't he get in touch with his publisher Peter Suhrkamp, who was looking for a young man to take over the business? It sounded like a crazy idea, but it wasn't so crazy as to stop Unseld from applying to Peter Suhrkamp—not as his successor but for a position in the firm. And Suhrkamp liked the idea of the publishing company having this "young whippersnapper" on board specially to look after Hermann Hesse, who as an author wasn't always easy to manage. How to publicize the work of a writer like Hermann Hesse in a high-profile manner? That was the question that would preoccupy Siegfried Unseld for the next fifty years—the Unseld era at Suhrkamp, which could not have existed without Hermann Hesse, or for that matter without Peter Suhrkamp himself.

In 1955 Hesse was even instrumental in getting Unseld enrolled in a Harvard University course that was being taught by Henry Kissinger. Hesse the Nobel laureate wrote a letter saying that Unseld was a worthy candidate with high aspirations, and this did the trick. As to why his young friend should particularly want to travel overseas, Hesse could only shake his head in bewilderment. In his eyes the average American was a "blithe and easily satisfied half-human." Or as Unseld put it: "He disliked Americans just as much as they appeared to like him."[78]

On January 1, 1958, Peter Suhrkamp wrote to Hesse to tell him that he had indeed "nominated Siegfried Unseld to be my successor." Suhrkamp had been very concerned to find someone to take over the business. At the same time Unseld was also made a partner of the firm, a privilege hitherto reserved for the Reinharts and Suhrkamp himself. There was also another reason for this hasty and emphatic vote of confidence in their new sales-oriented colleague, who was breaking new ground in marketing strategies: "Otherwise Dr. Unseld would be poached from under my nose by Ullstein; they made him a very tempting offer."[79]

Siegfried Unseld would later report that Peter Suhrkamp, on the eve of his death on March 31, 1959, gave him the following advice—and it sounded so typical of the great eccentric as to prompt genuine concern over how any sort of continuity might be maintained in the company's publishing program after the major rupture occasioned by Suhrkamp's death: "Never try to run the company in the same way that I did. You couldn't do that, anyway. Remake the firm in the way that you think is right. And if you're fortunate, everything will work out fine."[80] Unseld was well aware that being lucky was one thing, but that having his own ideas and formulating them in such a way that would win over customers was quite another.

Hesse was Unseld's sworn enemy in all innovations that affected his books. He had remained stubbornly stuck in around 1900 as to what constituted a well-produced book. New combinations of texts? What for, that wasn't what he wanted! Unseld spent many long hours persuading him to agree to his work being reprinted in modern fonts rather than the old Gothic "black letter" type. Unseld also fought long and hard—but ultimately in vain—to try to win Hesse round to cheap paperback editions, which were attractive predominantly to younger readers. Hesse also found the typography designed by Willy Fleckhaus, which Unseld made into the trademark of the Suhrkamp Verlag, simply dreadful and forbade the first edition of the *Hesse Illustrated Biography* by Bernhard Zeller from appearing with such horrors on its cover. The fact that such a book was even commissioned in the first place only came about through Unseld showing him a similar work on Goethe produced by the Insel publishing house: *Goethe and His World*. That pleased Hesse: why not have something on "Hesse and His World" too, in that case?

And yet, for all Hesse's conservative attitude, there was also something innovative and new and stimulating about his way of thinking, as many of his peers would only come to realize in retrospect. For instance, Unseld's initial suggestion that he sell the rights to *The Glass Bead Game* as a licensed edition to a paperback publisher was met with a vehement objection from Hesse. That would entail the destruction of a work of lasting value, and a cut-price selling-off of his life's work that he would find completely unacceptable, Hesse told him. Consequently, the license was never granted. However, Hesse followed up his angry outburst by saying something that now set the publisher thinking: If there absolutely had to be a paperback edition, the author told him, then why not produce it yourself, in-house? This marked the genesis of the edition suhrkamp series of paperbacks, a highly successful publishing program that continues to the present day.

Music, Death, and Silence

For a long time now, Hesse had sensed that death was approaching. He welcomed it—maybe he would allow himself a decent amount of time to depart this life.

In the winter of 1961–1962 he had been struck down by a bout of flu from which he never fully recovered. He remained very weak, felt tired all the time, and also suffered from boils and muscle spasms. Henceforth, Hesse knew, anything pleasant and good would be a bonus. In his "Letter in May" he wrote: "I have by now—though I don't rule out the possibility of exceptions to this rule—grown weary of wanting to comprehend and interpret things and have instead reverted to that naive and childlike manner with which artists view the world and the world of dreams—as an apparition, an image, and a visual and sensory experience or even as a grotesque mental game."

As Ninon wrote to Siegfried Unseld after Hesse's death: "It was always so lovely to be there and experience how intensely H. saw everything—he was like a hawk."[81]

At the same time, though, he also listened in an intense way—not so much to Chopin, the Romantic favorite of his youth, but more to Bach and above all Mozart, over and over again. His own poems had been set to music, as well—he enjoyed the compositions of his friend Othmar Schoeck (a pupil of Max Reger) best—whereas the artistically momentous "Four Last Songs" that Richard Strauss composed shortly before his death (which included three pieces based on works by Hesse: "Spring," "September," and "When Falling Asleep") were something of a closed book to him—it is likely that he only heard them once anyway, on the radio. He would also have been prejudiced from the outset against Strauss, who during the Nazi period had been president of the Reich Music Chamber (until 1935). Hesse became increasingly intolerant of art putting itself at the service of political objectives.

Hesse's physician, Dr. Molo, had known for some time that Hesse had leukemia. The doctor didn't divulge this diagnosis to him; instead, there was just talk of a deficiency of red and white blood cells, which curiously did not alarm the lifelong hypochondriac. In the short term, repeated blood transfusions restored a little of his vitality.

Hesse's eighty-fifth birthday was looming, and he wrote grumpily to Siegfried Unseld: "This time the whole village has ambushed us: brass-band music outside the house in the evening, and the other day a visit from the mayor and the local council and the radio people, to record the handing-over of the document conferring honorary citizenship on me. The doctor gave me some injections to help me along."[82]

On July 2, 1962, Hesse celebrated his birthday among a small gathering of family and friends. A string quartet from Bern played Mozart, and at the invitation of Max Wassmer, everyone assembled at his house in the village of Faido near the St. Gotthard Pass. Hesse gave a speech of thanks and seemed in good spirits. The remainder of July was taken up with replying to hundreds of people who had sent their congratulations on his birthday—Hesse continued to be punctilious about such things. After his death, a small pile of letters that he had already written but not yet posted, plus a large pile of letters containing birthday greetings that he had not yet read, were found in his study. Alongside them was the list of addresses that Hesse kept so fastidiously, with occasional remarks about this or that sender.

Short walks in the company of Ninon were part of his daily routine—and every time they went through the wood and passed a particular false acacia tree, he would pull with all his might on a dead branch. Without fail, he would say to Ninon: "It's still holding!" This kind of tenacity displayed by something whose demise was long overdue delighted him. Some things that had long since decided to quit the scene simply kept clinging on.

Even on his very last day, August 8, Ninon recalled that "he was cheerful, relaxed, and full of the joys of life." It was a beautiful summer's day, not too hot. Again, they took a little stroll together and he tugged at the dry false acacia branch and again said: "It's still holding!" That evening, Ninon found a poem in her room that Hesse had been working on during his final days:

Creaking of a Bent Branch

A splintered, bent branch,
Hanging there for years on end,
Creaking its song drily in the wind,
Bereft of leaf and bark,
Bare, bleached and tired of living
Too long or taking too long to die.
Its song sounds harsh and dogged,
It sounds defiant and secretly scared
Just last one more summer
Just one more winter through.

For Hesse there were to be no more summers or winters—it was the final evening of his life. Ninon read to him, as always, while he lay on the sofa. Then she retired to bed. Hesse stayed up until eleven o'clock to listen to some music on the radio: Mozart's Piano Sonata No. 7 in C Major, K. 309.

The next morning, Ninon and the servants waited and waited for Hesse to rise. But there were no sounds of activity. Even Ninon did not dare to enter his room unbidden:

> I sat in the connecting vestibule between our two rooms and read—and listened—and then read some more. Eventually I tiptoed to the door and opened it; there was no sound from within. I didn't want to wake him. Only at about 9.45 A.M. did I approach him; he didn't move a muscle. After another 45 minutes the doctor appeared and pronounced him dead. He had had a stroke. He had passed away peacefully in his sleep, just the way he had always wanted to go. He was lying in his usual sleeping position, with his eyes shut, and he looked at peace and relaxed.[83]

Hermann Hesse died on the morning of August 9 sometime between seven and nine o'clock. He looked as though he was resting, but for a small trickle of blood from the corner of his mouth.

On hearing the news, Siegfried Unseld traveled down to Montagnola and reported: "That [Hesse's death] had been on Thursday morning. On Friday, a death mask was taken. On that day, by all accounts Hesse had looked like he was still alive, but when I first set eyes on him on Saturday, his skin was already ashen and pallid. His appearance was supernatural in a double sense; he lay there relaxed and peaceful like someone who has fully attained their goal." Hesse's body was placed in a zinc coffin, which was then promptly soldered shut. At Ninon's request, Unseld was in attendance with Hesse's sons and two of his grandsons. He remarked on this procedure: "This may have been the first and last time that technology found its way into this room."[84]

On August 11, Hermann Hesse was laid to rest in the cemetery at San Abbondio. Bernhard Zeller recalled the burial, which took place at four in the afternoon: "The number of those who had come to pay their last respects was not very great, and there were some spa guests dressed in summer clothes on the fringes of the group of mourners."[85]

Siegfried Unseld read out Hesse's poem "Farewell, Lady World!":

> In shreds the world's now lying,
> Though once we held her dear
> But now the thought of dying
> For us holds little fear.

She should not feel our rages
So wild and bright is she
The magic of the ages
Still colors all we see.

But gladly we'll be leaving
Her game. We'll say adieu
To all the joy and grieving
To all the loving too.

Lady World, Farewell now
Be young and lovely still
But of your heaven and hell now
We have had our fill.
[*Translation © David Henry Wilson (from "Hymn to Old Age," Pushkin Press, London, 2011)*]

Once again, then, anticipated farewells encompassing many renunciations were read out as a summation of Hesse's core belief in life at his graveside. In its rhythm and atmosphere, this poem was reminiscent of Goethe's "Prometheus"—the destructive power of the external world finds its limits in the Self, which it must leave to its internal world. Skepticism or faith? Maybe both simultaneously.

In his "Diary Jottings 1955" he had, in observing a butterfly, prefigured the peaceful nature of his own summer death. Right at the very end of his entries, he wrote of the butterfly: "And after a short while, without my being aware that I had let it go, it wafted away from me, up into the warm expanse of brightness."[86]

Yet even at the cemetery at San Abbondio, technological progress dogged Hesse like a dark shadow. Directly below his grave there now runs the route of the motorway from the St. Gotthard Tunnel to Milan.

A Life Shrouded in Mystery

Together with Ninon, the publisher Siegfried Unseld now entered Hermann Hesse's work room. Ninon did not think that they would find any manuscripts there that were unfamiliar to her. And yet: "We found file after file containing drafts and different versions of poems. Hesse had collected and organized all the newspaper reprints of his works in a truly ingenious way. The cuttings had all been numbered and arranged into individual stacks according to newspaper title, and the keys to all the numbers had been recorded in a notebook." Even after his death, Hesse continued to embody the contradictory personae of the anarchist and the pedant.

Despite suffering for years with a weak heart, Ninon now threw herself into the task of going through Hesse's unpublished works and letters and editing the first volume of his early correspondence: "Childhood and Youth pre-1900." She was beset by doubts over whether it was appropriate to Hesse's work to make so much private material public.

In 1963 she came to an important decision, which Hesse would never have made. In the face of objections from his sons, who wanted to keep their father's literary legacy in Switzerland, she donated it in its entirety to the German Literature Archive in Marbach. She even went so far as to threaten to "do herself a mischief" if any further pressure was brought to bear on her to change her mind. Ever since the exhibition held at the Schiller National Museum in Marbach to mark Hesse's eightieth birthday, Bernhard Zeller had maintained good contacts with the author. It was to him first and foremost that Ninon entrusted Hesse's unpublished writings.

Zeller recalled the day when the manuscripts were transferred to the archive: "After a year's work, when we finally had the lorry full of books, manuscripts, and letters all securely packed up in many bundles, and were just getting ready to set off, she asked us to open up the tailgate that we'd already closed and locked. I will never forget how, with some difficulty, she clambered up into the truck and without a word stood looking for one last time at all the material that was just about to be transported and that had been an integral part of her life for so long."[87]

In spite of her physical impairments, in the years remaining to her Ninon continued to pursue her studies of ancient Greece, especially on the figure of the goddess Hera. In April and May 1963 she took one last trip to Greece, her chosen spiritual home.

When, in the early morning of September 22, 1966, she suffered a heart attack, no local doctor was available to attend her; all of them claimed they were "busy elsewhere." Only her friend Elsy Bodmer was by her side, but she could do little more than hold her hand. By the time a female doctor from Lugano finally showed up, after several hours, Ninon was already dead. She too was buried in San Abbondio.

One poem of Hesse's that sums up his passage through life like no other is entitled "In the Fog":

> It's strange wandering in the fog!
> Each bush and stone stands isolated,
> No tree sees the next one,
> Every one is alone.
>
> My world was full of friends
> When my life was still filled with light,
> Now as the fog descends
> No one is visible anymore.
>
> Truly there is no wise man
> Who does not know the dark
> Which quietly and ineluctably
> Separates him from everything else.
>
> It's strange wandering in the fog!
> To live is to be alone.
> No man knows the next man,
> Everyone is alone.

Spelled backward, the German word for fog *(Nebel)* reads *Leben,* meaning "life." An uncertain wandering state is conveyed in this *Nebel-Leben,* this life in the fog, which remains shrouded in mystery despite the need for enlightenment. The darkness does not cease when we try to illuminate it—all it does is keep drawing further away.

One should learn to love this mystery of the creative individual who conceals himself within his contradictions rather than trying to fight against it. For unambiguous things are always deceptive, they are nothing but ideology, which misleads one into actions that are immeasurably more base than those informed by a living spirit.

Hermann Hesse's great vision was to create an indissoluble connection between people's spirits and their lives.

★　　★　　★

"In the Fog" reads like the poem of an old man, with the same outlook on life as "Creaking of a Bent Bough," written on the eve of his death. And yet it dates from 1905, when Hesse was only twenty-eight years old.

Hermann Hesse is among that handful of writers who seem old before their time, but then who do not seem to age. What comes across from reading this poem is a striking consistency both in his self-image as an author and in his relationship to the world as a person. It is not some piece of juvenilia that is left behind; it carries within it a sense of what is to come. And that in turn is the secret of all mysticism. The alpha and the omega, the beginning and the end, are one and the same.

Three years after Ninon's death, the Casa Rossa stood empty. There were still some signs of who had once lived here, but redevelopment of the site seemed on the cards. Perhaps Hesse should, after all, have let H. C. Bodmer gift him the property, as he had originally suggested, then his sons could have taken on the house and its garden.

Karl Kerényi, who had first visited Hesse there in 1936, returned to the house in 1969. All he could do was survey a largely derelict and forlorn place:

> The infamous sign "No Visitors, Please" (I can hear Hesse's imploring voice as I write) is still there, on the left-hand gatepost, which is the only piece of the wall left standing. The rest of the gate has gone, and beside it on the right-hand side lie felled tree-trunks, clearly dragged here from somewhere in the vicinity and waiting to be taken away. There's nothing to stop people from the neighborhood from parking their cars right in front of the derelict house.
>
> The house still appears from afar to the approaching visitor in the same striking shade of Pompeian Red it always had, but now it stands there with lowered blinds and with the entrances to the garden on the right and left open to all and sundry. It seems an impossible fancy that one or other of the two teasingly adjacent doors, Hesse's special personal door and the one reserved for the postman and other mere mortals, might suddenly open. It is still possible to steal a glance into the guest room on the ground floor, once a place of exquisite comfort occupied by the writer's friends, but all it now reveals is a dusty void. Arrangements have been made for the resident

tomcat. He lets himself in and out of the house through the cellar window and eats his food out of cans left open for him. A special provision in the will must have been made for him. At least that much remains of what was once a meticulously well-organized household![88]

And Bernhard Zeller reported: "Soon after, the Casa Hesse was put up for sale by Bodmer's heirs and purchased by an Italian. There is no access to it nowadays, and there's nothing left there to remind you of Hesse, even the color of the house has been changed. I was there not long ago for one last time, and tried to peer over the hedge into the garden, but even its surroundings are starting to change as a result of new buildings going up."[89]

Ultimately even the Casa Camuzzi suffered a similar fate. Heiner Hesse lobbied for its preservation—but to no avail, since nobody joined him in opposing a lucrative plan by its new owners to turn the palazzo into an apartment block. This destruction of sites of genuine literary history is sad, but perhaps also inadvertent in the sense of Hesse's work: the internal must become what the external once was. The sites thus live on—in myth.

Hesse was inordinately matter-of-fact about such matters. In his "Letter in May" of 1962, we read of a dream in which André Gide, who wanted to see him one last time, first appears and then promptly vanishes again: "And so he left me standing there, with no explanation or word of farewell."[90]

CHRONOLOGY

NOTES

ACKNOWLEDGMENTS

INDEX

CHRONOLOGY

1877   Hermann Hesse is born in Calw, the son of the Pietist missionary
        couple Johannes and Maria Hesse (*née* Gundert)
1881   The Hesse family moves to Basel
1886   The Hesses return to Calw
1890   Hesse attends the Latin School in Göppingen under Rector Bauer
1891   Hesse passes the state examination and becomes a seminarian in
        Maulbronn
1892   Hesse absconds from Maulbronn (after seven months); spends time
        with Pastor Christoph Blumhardt in Bad Boll; declares his intention to
        commit suicide; incarceration in the insane asylum at Stetten; becomes a
        pupil at the high school in Cannstatt (from November)
1893   Apprenticeship as a bookseller in Esslingen (for three days); time with
        his parents in Calw
1894   Trainee at Perrot's clockmaking workshop in Calw (for 14 months);
        Hesse considers emigrating to Brazil
1895   Apprenticeship as a bookseller in Tübingen (at Heckenhauer's
        bookshop)
1896   Hesse's first poems are published in *Das deutsche Dichterheim*
1898   Hesse's *Romantische Lieder* appear (published by the vanity publisher
        E. Pierson in Dresden)
1899   The prose volume *Eine Stunde hinter Mitternacht* is published by Eugen
        Diederichs; Hesse moves to Basel; sales assistant in Reich's bookshop
        (until January 1901)
1900   Begins contributing regular articles to the newspaper the *Allgemeine
        Schweizer Zeitung*
1901   First trip to Italy (from March to May); bookseller at the Wattenwyl
        antiquarian bookshop (until spring 1903); *Hermann Lauscher* is published
        by R. Reich

1902   Death of Hesse's mother, Marie

1903   Second Italian journey in the company of the Basel photographer Maria
       Bernoulli; invitation to become an author for the S. Fischer publishing
       house; *Peter Camenzind* appears as a preprint in the Fischer in-house
       magazine *Die neue Rundschau*

1904   *Peter Camenzind* becomes a best-seller; Hesse marries Maria Bernoulli
       and becomes a full-time writer; Hesse and Maria move into a house at
       Gaienhofen on Lake Constance

1905   Birth of Hesse's first son, Bruno

1906   Publication of *Unterm Rad* (written 1903–1904); Hesse co-founds
       the anti-Wilhelmine magazine *März* (remaining its co-publisher
       until 1912)

1909   Hesse's second son, Heiner, is born

1910   *Gertrud* is published by the Verlag Albert Langen in Munich

1911   Hesse's third son, Martin, is born; Hesse travels to "far India"

1912   Hesse moves permanently to Switzerland; takes up residence in the
       Welti house in Bern

1913   Publication of *Aus Indien*

1914   Outbreak of the First World War; volunteers for war service, rejected as
       unfit for active duty; publication of *Roßhalde*

1915   Assigned to war work at the German embassy in Bern; active in the
       prisoners of war welfare service (1919); publishes the newspaper
       Sonntagsbote für Kriegsgefangene (1916); instigates a book-donation
       service to POW camps; *Knulp* published

1916   Death of Hesse's father, Johannes; Maria Bernoulli shows the first signs
       of serious neurological disease; Hesse suffers a nervous breakdown and
       spends time at the Sonnmatt sanatorium near Lucerne; start of Hesse's
       friendship with the psychoanalyst J. B. Lang; undergoes first course of
       psychoanalysis

1917   Hesse publishes an antiwar article under the pseudonym Emil Sinclair;
       begins painting regularly

1919   *Zarathustras Wiederkehr* is published; Hesse becomes the co-publisher
       of the magazine *Vivos voco;* leaves his family and moves to Montag-
       nola in the Swiss Alpine canton of Ticino; takes up residence in
       Casa Camuzzi (where he lives until 1931); *Demian* is published
       (under the pseudonym Emil Sinclair); makes the acquaintance of
       Ruth Wenger

1920   The most prolific phase in Hesse's writing sees the appearance of
       Klingsors letzter Sommer and *Klein und Wagner;* publication of *Wanderung,*
       and *Blick ins Chaos* (essays on Dostoyevsky)

1921   Hesse writes the first part of the novel *Siddhartha;* suffers writer's
        block and severe depression; undergoes a course of psychoanalysis with
        C. G. Jung in Küsnacht near Zurich
1922   Hesse completes *Siddhartha*
1923   Divorce from Maria Bernoulli, who will thereafter spend many years in
        psychiatric institutions; takes the first of his rest cures at a spa in Baden
        near Zurich (a practice he maintains until 1952)
1924   Hesse readopts Swiss nationality; second marriage, to Ruth Wenger
1925   Publication of *Kurgast*
1926   Hesse is made a member of the Prussian Academy of Arts (which he
        leaves in 1931)
1927   Hesse divorces Ruth Wenger; publication of the *Nürnberger Reise* and
        Der Steppenwolf; the first biography of Hermann Hesse, by Hugo Ball,
        appears on the occasion of his fiftieth birthday; death of Hugo Ball;
        Ninon Dolbin moves into Casa Camuzzi (officially as Hesse's
        secretary)
1928   The *Krise* cycle of poems is published
1929   *Eine Bibliothek der Weltliteratur* appears in the Reclam Universal Library
        series
1930   Publication of *Narziß und Goldmund*
1931   Marriage to Ninon Dolbin and shared occupancy of the newly
        constructed Casa Rossa in Montagnola (built by the benefactor
        H. C. Bodmer for Hesse and placed at his sole disposal for his lifetime);
        Hesse begins work on *Das Glasperlenspiel*
1932   Publication of *Die Morgenlandfahrt*
1943   *Das Glasperlenspiel* is published by Fretz & Wasmuth in Zurich (Nazi
        authorities refuse Peter Suhrkamp the rights to publish the novel in
        Germany)
1946   Award to Hesse of the Goethe Prize of the City of Frankfurt am Main,
        and of the Nobel Prize for Literature; first German edition of *Das
        Glasperlenspiel*
1950   Hesse becomes a leading author of the new Suhrkamp Verlag
        publishing house
1959   Death of Peter Suhrkamp; Hesse's reader Siegfried Unseld becomes the
        new head of Suhrkamp and remains in this post until his death in 2002
1962   Hermann Hesse's eighty-fifth birthday; death of Hesse on August 9
        in Montagnola

NOTES

Abbreviations

GesBr = *Gesammelte Briefe* = *Collected Letters*
Hermann Hesse, *Gesammelte Briefe,* 4 vols., ed. Ursula Michels and Volker Michels (Frankfurt am Main, 1973–1986).

KuJ 1 = vol. 1, *Kindheit und Jugend (vor Neunzehnhundert)* = *Childhood and Youth before 1900*
Hermann Hesse, *Kindheit und Jugend vor Neunzehnhundert,* 2 vols., vol. 1: *1877–1895,* ed. Ninon Hesse (Frankfurt am Main, 1984) (1st ed., 1966).

KuJ 2 = vol. 2, *Kindheit und Jugend (vor Neunzehnhundert)* = *Childhood and Youth before 1900*
Hermann Hesse, *Kindheit und Jugend vor Neunzehnhundert,* 2 vols., vol. 2: *1895–1900,* ed. Ninon Hesse, continued and expanded by Gerhard Kirchhoff (Frankfurt am Main, 1985) (1st ed., 1978).

SW = *Sämtliche Werke* = *Complete Works*
Hermann Hesse, *Sämtliche Werke,* 20 vols. (plus *Registerband*), ed. Volker Michels (Frankfurt am Main, 2001–2007).

Introduction

1. *Briefwechsel, 1945–1959, von Hermann Hesse und Peter Suhrkamp,* ed. Siegfried Unseld (Frankfurt am Main, 1969), epilogue, 470.

2. Compare Georg A. Weth, *Hermann Hesse in der Schweiz* (Munich, 2004), 62ff.

3. Volker Michels, ed., *Hermann Hesse in Augenzeugenberichten* (Frankfurt am Main, 1991), 371.

4. Gottfried Benn, *Gesammelte Werke,* vol. 1, ed. Dieter Wellershoff (Stuttgart, 1989), 484.

5. Hermann Hesse, *Magie des Buches* (Frankfurt am Main, 1977), 33.

6. Michels, *Hermann Hesse,* 373.

7. Hermann Hesse, *Sämtliche Werke,* 20 vols. (plus *Registerband*), ed. Volker Michels (Frankfurt am Main, 2001–2007) (hereafter cited as *SW*), 15:802.

8. Ernst Robert Curtius, *Kritische Essays zur europäischen Literatur* (Frankfurt am Main, 1984), 214.

9. Erich Mühsam, *Tagebücher, 1910–1924,* ed. Chris Hirte (Munich, 1994), 15.

10. *SW* 15:598.

11. *SW* 15:816.

12. Volker Michels, *Über Hermann Hesse,* 2 vols. (Frankfurt am Main, 1977), 2:177ff.

13. Compare Karlheinz Deschner, *Kitsch, Konvention und Kunst* (Munich, 1957).

14. Der Spiegel, 40 / 1968.

15. *SW* 12:286.

16. Hermann Hesse, *Eine Bibliothek der Weltliteratur* (Leipzig, 1948), 50.

17. Ibid., 8.

18. Walter Rathenau, Theodor Heuss, Romain Rolland, et al., *Die vielen Gesichter Hermann Hesses: Ein Dichter im Urteil seiner Zeitgenossen* (Eggingen, 1996), 13.

19. *SW* 15:808.

1. A Child's Soul

1. Hermann Hesse, *Kindheit und Jugend vor Neunzehnhundert,* 2 vols., vol. 1: *1877–1895,* ed. Ninon Hesse (Frankfurt am Main, 1984) (hereafter cited as *KuJ* 1), 514 (1st ed., 1966).

2. Hugo Ball, *Hermann Hesse: Sein Leben und Werk* (Frankfurt am Main, 1977), 12 (1st ed., 1927).

3. *KuJ* 1:125.

4. Hermann Hesse, "Ein paar Erinnerungen an Ärzte," *SW* 12:524.

5. Hesse, "Kindheit des Zauberers," *SW* 9:176.

6. *SW* 12:72.

7. *SW* 12:17.

8. Ibid.

9. *SW* 9:176.

10. Hermann Hesse, "Der Bettler," *SW* 8:458.

11. *SW* 12:303.

12. *SW* 12:307.

13. *SW* 12:71.

14. Marie Hesse, *Ein Lebensbild in Briefen und Tagebüchern,* ed. Adele Gundert (Frankfurt am Main, 1977), 12.

15. Ibid., 14.
16. Ibid., 15.
17. Ibid., 12.
18. *SW* 12:18.
19. *SW* 12:19.
20. Marie Hesse, *Lebensbild,* 18.
21. Ibid., 21.
22. Ibid.
23. Ibid., 28.
24. Ibid., 49.
25. Ibid., 48.
26. Ibid., 60.
27. Ibid., 54.
28. *SW* 12:73.
29. Marie Hesse, *Lebensbild,* 160.
30. Ibid., 169.
31. Ibid.
32. Ibid., 167.
33. Hermann Hesse, *Hermann Lauscher* (Frankfurt am Main, 1996), 13.
34. Ibid., 16.
35. Hermann Hesse, *Calwer Tagebuch, SW* 11:196.
36. Ibid., 197.
37. *SW* 12:74.
38. *SW* 12:121.
39. *KuJ* 1:465.
40. *SW* 12:122.
41. *SW* 12:123.
42. *SW* 12:78.
43. *SW* 12:411.
44. *KuJ* 1:9.
45. *KuJ* 1:12.
46. *KuJ* 1:11.
47. *KuJ* 1:13.
48. Ibid.
49. Ibid.
50. *SW* 12:35.
51. *SW* 12:46.
52. *KuJ* 1:20.
53. *KuJ* 1:22.
54. *KuJ* 1:18.
55. *KuJ* 1:29.

56. *KuJ* 1:21.

57. *KuJ* 1:22.

58. *KuJ* 1:31.

59. *KuJ* 1:34.

60. *KuJ* 1:36.

61. Hermann Hesse, *Aus meiner Schülerzeit, SW* 12:87.

62. Ibid., 91.

63. Hermann Hesse, "Kinderseele," *SW* 8:191.

64. *KuJ* 1:84.

65. *KuJ* 1:61.

66. *KuJ* 1:62.

67. *KuJ* 1:66.

68. "Kinderseele," *SW* 8:191.

69. *KuJ* 1:160.

70. Ibid.

71. *KuJ* 1:162.

72. *SW* 12:415.

73. *KuJ* 1:103.

74. *KuJ* 1:104.

75. *KuJ* 1:106.

76. *KuJ* 1:109.

77. *KuJ* 1:110.

78. *KuJ* 1:130.

79. *KuJ* 1:132.

80. *KuJ* 1:169.

81. *KuJ* 1:170.

82. *KuJ* 1:182.

83. *KuJ* 1:180.

84. *KuJ* 1:187.

85. *KuJ* 1:201.

86. *KuJ* 1:189.

87. *KuJ* 1:190.

88. *KuJ* 1:204.

89. *KuJ* 1:205.

90. *KuJ* 1:208.

91. *KuJ* 1:210.

92. *KuJ* 1:213.

93. *KuJ* 1:215.

94. *KuJ* 1:220.

95. Ibid.

96. *KuJ* 1:222.

97. *KuJ* 1:223.
98. Ibid.
99. *KuJ* 1:230.
100. *KuJ* 1:236.
101. *KuJ* 1:238.
102. *KuJ* 1:234.
103. *KuJ* 1:241.
104. *KuJ* 1:242.
105. *KuJ* 1:241.
106. *KuJ* 1:243.
107. *KuJ* 1:246.
108. *KuJ* 1:247.
109. *KuJ* 1:248.
110. *KuJ* 1:252.
111. Ibid.
112. *KuJ* 1:256.
113. *KuJ* 1:258.
114. *KuJ* 1:263.
115. *KuJ* 1:261.
116. *KuJ* 1:267.

2. The Self-Proclaimed Writer

1. *KuJ* 1:268.
2. *SW* 12:23.
3. *SW* 12:8 ff.
4. *SW* 12:46.
5. *SW* 12:18.
6. *SW* 12:41.
7. *SW* 12:48.
8. *KuJ* 1:271.
9. *KuJ* 1:272.
10. Ibid.
11. *KuJ* 1:277.
12. *KuJ* 1:283.
13. *KuJ* 1:285.
14. *KuJ* 1:218.
15. Hermann Hesse, *Kindheit und Jugend vor Neunzehnhundert,* 2 vols., vol. 2: *1895–1900,* ed. Ninon Hesse, continued and expanded by Gerhard Kirchhoff (Frankfurt am Main, 1985) (hereafter cited as *KuJ 2*), 68 (1st ed.,1978).
16. *KuJ* 1:286.

17. *KuJ* 1:296.
18. *KuJ* 1:305.
19. *KuJ* 1:310.
20. *KuJ* 1:316.
21. *KuJ* 1:325.
22. *KuJ* 1:324.
23. *KuJ* 1:326.
24. *KuJ* 1:330.
25. *KuJ* 1:341.
26. *KuJ* 1:342.
27. *KuJ* 1:343.
28. *KuJ* 1:346.
29. Ibid.
30. *KuJ* 1:358.
31. Ibid.
32. *KuJ* 1:362.
33. *KuJ* 1:264.
34. *KuJ* 1:371.
35. *KuJ* 1:372.
36. *KuJ* 1:381.
37. *KuJ* 1:384.
38. *KuJ* 1:385.
39. *SW* 11:186.
40. *KuJ* 1:402.
41. *KuJ* 1:406.
42. *SW* 1:186.
43. *KuJ* 1:408.
44. *SW* 1:186.
45. *SW* 12:20.
46. *KuJ* 1:493.
47. *KuJ* 1:475.
48. *KuJ* 1:473.

3. Awakening of Individuality

1. *KuJ* 2:11.
2. *KuJ* 2:16.
3. *SW* 12:136.
4. Eike Middell, *Hermann Hesse* (Leipzig, 1990), 47.
5. *SW* 1:156.
6. *KuJ* 2:18.

7. *KuJ* 2:20.

8. *KuJ* 2:23.

9. Ibid.

10. *KuJ* 2:43.

11. *KuJ* 2:42.

12. *KuJ* 2:41.

13. *KuJ* 2:93.

14. *KuJ* 2:37.

15. Hermann Hesse, *Gesammelte Briefe,* 4 vols., ed. Ursula Michels and Volker Michels (Frankfurt am Main, 1973–1986) (hereafter cited as *GesBr*), 1:99.

16. *KuJ* 2:94.

17. *SW* 1:116.

18. *KuJ* 2:168.

19. *SW* 1:117.

20. *KuJ* 2:360.

21. *KuJ* 2:220.

22. *KuJ* 2:107.

23. *KuJ* 2:140.

24. *KuJ* 2:139.

25. *KuJ* 2:140.

26. Karl Heinz Götze, *Palmenwald* (Freudenstadt, 1995), 21.

27. *KuJ* 2:204.

28. *KuJ* 2:207.

29. *KuJ* 2:205.

30. The German verb *lauschen* means "to harken"; "Hermann Lauscher" was Hesse's poetic alter-ego in the collection of poems and prose pieces, *Hinterlassene Schriften und Gedichte von Hermann Lauscher,* Hesse published in 1900.—Trans.]

31. *KuJ* 2:226.

32. "Fever-Muse" is the title of a story in his 1898 collection *Eine Stunde hinter Mitternacht (An Hour Behind Midnight),* Hesse's second publication.—Trans.

33. *KuJ* 2:303.

34. *KuJ* 2:305.

35. *KuJ* 2:306.

36. *KuJ* 2:260.

37. *KuJ* 2:231.

38. *KuJ* 2:221.

39. Hermann Hesse, *Hermann Lauscher* (Frankfurt am Main, 1996), 46.

40. Marie Hesse, *David Livingstone* (Calw, 1900), 7.

41. Ibid., 9.

42. Ibid., 251.

43. *KuJ* 2:237.

44. *KuJ* 2:241.

45. Ibid.

46. *KuJ* 2:242.

47. *KuJ* 2:245.

48. *KuJ* 2:264.

49. *KuJ* 2:250.

50. *KuJ* 2:378.

51. *KuJ* 2:341.

52. *SW* 1:170.

53. *KuJ* 2:358.

54. *KuJ* 2:359.

55. *SW* 1:191.

56. Gabriele D'Annunzio, *Der Kamerad mit den wimpernlosen Augen* (Frankfurt am Main, 1996), 7.

57. *SW* 1:170.

58. Ibid.

59. Ibid.

60. Rainer Maria Rilke, *Von Kunstdingen* (Leipzig, 1981), 54.

4. At Home Crossing Borders

1. *SW* 12:17.

2. *SW* 12:117.

3. *KuJ* 2:390.

4. *KuJ* 2:412.

5. *SW* 12:137.

6. *KuJ* 2:394.

7. Böcklin died in Italy not long after, in 1901.—Trans.

8. *SW* 12:80.

9. *SW* 16:19.

10. *KuJ* 2:423.

11. *SW* 14:279.

12. *SW* 14:280.

13. *SW* 14:283.

14. *KuJ* 1:430.

15. Hugo Ball, *Hermann Hesse: Sein Leben und Werk* (Frankfurt am Main, 1977), 20.

16. *KuJ* 1:474.

17. *KuJ* 2:278.

18. Ibid.

19. Hermann Hesse, *Magie des Buches* (Frankfurt am Main, 1977), 10.

20. Friedrich Nietzsche, *Zarathustra* (Stuttgart, 1983), 97.

21. *SW* 14:394.

22. *KuJ* 2:422.

23. *KuJ* 2:423.

24. Ibid.

25. *KuJ* 2:619.

26. *KuJ* 2:524.

27. Ibid.

28. *KuJ* 2:525.

29. *SW* 1:485.

30. *SW* 1:441.

31. *SW* 1:483.

32. *KuJ* 2:419.

33. *KuJ* 2:432.

34. *GesBr* 1:34.

35. *KuJ* 2:205.

36. *GesBr* 1:47.

37. *SW* 12:499.

38. Ball, *Hermann Hesse,* 78.

39. *SW* 1:247.

40. *SW* 12:63.

41. Hermann Hesse, *Hermann Lauscher* (Frankfurt am Main, 1996), 72.

42. *KuJ* 2:53.

43. *KuJ* 2:115.

44. *KuJ* 2:54.

45. *KuJ* 2:117.

46. *KuJ* 2:103.

47. *SW* 1:490.

48. *SW* 1:367.

49. *SW* 11:198.

50. Hermann Hesse and Stefan Zweig, *Briefwechsel,* ed. Volker Michels (Frankfurt am Main, 2006), 18.

51. Joseph Roth, *Orte* (Leipzig, 1990), 5.

52. Stefan Zweig, *Die Monotonisierung der Welt,* ed. Volker Michels (Frankfurt am Main, 1988), 83.

53. *SW* 13:29.

54. *SW* 13:31.

55. *SW* 13:21.

56. *SW* 11:200.

57. *SW* 11:202.

58. *SW* 11:210.

59. *SW* 11:223.
60. *SW* 11:241.
61. *SW* 11:242.
62. *SW* 11:244.
63. Mark Twain, *Bummel durch Europa* (Berlin [DDR], 1963), 409.
64. *SW* 11:245.
65. *SW* 1:403.
66. *GesBr* 1:85.
67. *GesBr* 1:72.
68. *GesBr* 1:70.
69. *KuJ* 2:438.
70. *GesBr* 1:83.
71. *KuJ* 2:584.
72. Ralph Freedman, *Hermann Hesse* (Frankfurt am Main, 1999), 133.
73. *GesBr* 1:89.
74. *GesBr* 2:90.
75. Hermann Hesse, *Peter Camenzind* (Berlin, 1919), 51.
76. *GesBr* 1:93.
77. *SW* 11:188.
78. *SW* 13:12.
79. Ibid.

5. Portrait of the Successful Artist as a Young Man
Wandering beneath Clouds

1. *SW* 12:330.
2. Hermann Hesse, *Peter Camenzind* (Berlin, 1919) (hereafter cited as *PC*), 18.
3. *PC* 20.
4. *SW* 13:60.
5. *SW* 13:61.
6. *SW* 13:63.
7. *PC* 127.
8. *PC* 106.
9. *PC* 109.
10. Hugo Ball, *Hermann Hesse: Sein Leben und Werk* (Frankfurt am Main, 1977), 88.
11. Eike Middell, *Hermann Hesse* (Leipzig, 1990), 62.
12. *PC* 101.
13. *PC* 39.
14. *PC* 257.
15. *SW* 2:555.

16. *GesBr* 1:107.

17. *GesBr* 1:111.

18. *GesBr* 1:95.

19. Hermann Hesse and Stefan Zweig, *Briefwechsel,* ed. Volker Michels (Frankfurt am Main, 2006), 13.

20. Stefan Zweig, *Die Monotonisierung der Welt,* ed. Volker Michels (Frankfurt am Main, 1988), 218.

21. Ralph Freedman, *Hermann Hesse* (Frankfurt am Main, 1999), 144.

22. "E. Marlitt" was the pseudonym of the popular German novelist Eugenie John.—Trans.

23. Robert Musil, *Gesammelte Werke II,* ed. Adolf Frisé (Reinbek bei Hamburg, 1978), 1304.

24. *Die vielen Gesichter Hermann Hesses: Ein Dichter im Urteil seiner Zeitgenossen von damals bis heute* (Eggingen, 1996), 22.

25. *GesBr* 1:288.

26. *GesBr* 1:100.

27. *SW* 11:296.

28. *SW* 11:303.

29. *SW* 1:595.

30. *SW* 1:619.

31. *SW* 1:640.

32. *SW* 1:645.

33. Hesse and Zweig, *Briefwechsel,* 22.

34. Ibid., 21.

35. *SW* 13:22.

36. *SW* 12:50.

37. *GesBr* 1:136.

38. *GesBr* 1:126.

39. Ibid.

40. *SW* 12.

41. *GesBr* 1:123.

42. *GesBr* 1:125.

43. *GesBr* 1:124.

44. Ibid.

45. *SW* 13:57.

46. *SW* 12:140.

47. *SW* 12:99.

48. *GesBr* 1:137.

49. Hermann Hesse, *Beschreibung einer Landschaft,* ed. Siegfried Unseld (Frankfurt am Main, 1990), 166.

50. *SW* 12:142.

51. *SW* 11:308.

52. *SW* 11:312.

53. GB 1:149.

54. *SW* 12:445.

55. *SW* 12:447.

56. *SW* 12:343.

57. *SW* 12:342.

58. *SW* 2:137.

59. Hermann Hesse, *Unterm Rad* (Leipzig,1980), 28.

60. Ibid., 72.

61. Hermann Hesse and Stefan Zweig, *Briefwechsel,* ed. Volker Michels (Frankfurt am Main, 2006), 77.

62. Hesse, *Unterm Rad,* 83.

63. *GesBr* 1:139.

64. Hermann Hesse, *Unterm Rad: Erläuterungen und Dokumente* (Ditzingen, 1995), 78.

65. *SW* 13:412.

66. *SW* 13:81.

67. *SW* 13:82.

68. *SW* 13:83.

69. *SW* 13:84.

70. *SW* 1:576.

71. *SW* 1:577.

72. *SW* 1:578.

73. Ibid.

74. Hermann Hesse, *Knulp* (Berlin, 1915), 15.

75. Ibid., 73.

76. Ibid., 75.

77. Ibid., 137.

78. Ibid., 145.

79. *GesBr* 1:140.

80. Robert Landmann, *Ascona—Monte Verità* (Frauenfeld, 2009), 18.

81. Ibid., 118.

82. Ibid., 113.

83. Ibid., 56.

84. Ibid., 73.

85. *SW* 11:314.

86. *SW* 11:322.

87. *GesBr,* 152.

88. Hermann Hesse, *Gertrud* (Munich, 1910), 115.

89. Ibid., 243.

90. Ibid., 298.

91. *GesBr* 1:189.

92. *GesBr* 1:190.

93. Hermann Hesse and Josef Bernhard Lang, "Die dunkle und wilde Seite der Seele," in *Briefwechsel mit seinem Psychoanalytiker Josef Bernhard Lang, 1916–1944,* ed. Thomas Feitknecht (Frankfurt am Main, 2008), 71.

94. *SW* 11:331.

95. *SW* 13:211.

96. *SW* 13:275.

97. *SW* 13:263.

98. *SW* 14:173.

99. *SW* 13:264.

100. Ibid.

101. *SW* 13:353.

102. *SW* 13:354.

6. A New Beginning in Switzerland and the First World War

1. *SW* 12:145.

2. *GesBr* 1:206.

3. *GesBr* 1:209.

4. *GesBr* 1:210.

5. *SW* 12:146.

6. *SW* 12:95.

7. Albert Welti, *Gemälde und Radierungen. Gebundene Ausgabe mit einer Einführung von Hermann Hesse* (Berlin, 1917), 9.

8. Ibid., 8.

9. *SW* 12:95.

10. *GesBr* 1:224.

11. Hugo Ball, *Hermann Hesse: Sein Leben und Werk* (Frankfurt am Main, 1977), 110 (1st ed., 1927).

12. *SW* 12:148.

13. Conversation with the author on November 6, 2002, in Arcegno. Compare "Begegnung mit Heiner Hesse," in Gunnar Decker, *Der Zauber des Anfangs: Das Kleine Hesse-Lexikon* (Berlin, 2007).

14. *GesBr* 1:227.

15. *GesBr* 1:230.

16. Hermann Hesse and Stefan Zweig, *Briefwechsel,* ed. Volker Michels (Frankfurt am Main, 2006), 92.

17. Ibid.

18. Hermann Hesse, *Roßhalde* (Frankfurt am Main, 1980), 57.

19. *GesBr* 1:241.

20. *GesBr* 1:243.

21. *GesBr* 1:241.

22. *SW* 12:320.

23. *SW* 12:324.

24. *SW* 12:322.

25. *SW* 12:325.

26. Wilhelm Raabe and Karl-Maria Guth, *Die Chronik der Sperlingsgasse* (Berlin, 2016), 10.

27. *SW* 12:326.

28. Ball, *Hermann Hesse,* 110.

29. *GesBr* 1:246.

30. *GesBr* 1:244.

31. *Neue Rundschau,* November 1914, 1475.

32. *SW* 11:408.

33. *SW* 11:440.

34. *GesBr* 1:247.

35. *SW* 15:13.

36. *SW* 15:14.

37. Eike Middell, *Hermann Hesse* (Leipzig, 1990), 106.

38. *SW* 17:445.

39. Ibid.

40. *GesBr* 1:342.

41. *SW* 12:52.

42. *GesBr* 1:254.

43. *SW* 11:442.

44. *GesBr* 1:263.

45. Ibid.

46. *GesBr* 1:266.

47. *GesBr* 1:289.

48. Volker Michels, *Materialien zu Hermann Hesses Demian,* 2 vols. (Frankfurt am Main, 1997), 1:94.

49. Hermann Hesse, *Magie des Buches* (Frankfurt am Main, 1977), 99.

50. *GesBr* 1:270.

51. *GesBr* 1:527.

52. *GesBr* 1:271.

53. *SW* 11:584.

54. *SW* 11:587.

55. *Briefwechsel mit seinem Psychoanalytiker Josef Bernhard Lang, 1916–1944,* ed. Thomas Feitknecht (Frankfurt am Main, 2008), 92.

56. *SW* 12:55.

57. Hermann Hesse, *Ausgewählte Briefe,* expanded edn., ed. Hermann Hesse and Ninon Hesse (Frankfurt am Main, 1974), 456.

58. *Briefwechsel mit seinem Psychoanalytiker,* 54.

59. Hesse, *Ausgewählte Briefe,* 456.

60. *Briefwechsel mit seinem Psychoanalytiker,* 159.

61. Hermann Hesse, *Demian: Die Geschichte von Emil Sinclairs Jugend* (Leipzig, 1977), 73.

62. Ibid., 83.

63. Hermann Hesse, "Nachwort des Herausgebers," in *Blätter aus Prevorst* (Berlin, 1926), 189.

64. Ibid., 190.

65. *Briefwechsel mit seinem Psychoanalytiker,* 192.

66. Ibid., 194.

67. *SW* 12:58.

68. *SW* 12:60.

69. *SW* 12:63.

70. *SW* 11:521.

71. *SW* 20:352.

72. *SW* 18:89.

73. *SW* 15:451.

74. *Briefwechsel mit seinem Psychoanalytiker,* 27.

75. Ibid., 80.

76. Hesse, *Demian,* 5.

77. Ibid., 6.

78. *Briefwechsel mit seinem Psychoanalytiker,* 30.

79. Hesse, *Demian,* 34.

80. Ibid., 23.

81. *Briefwechsel mit seinem Psychoanalytiker,* 96.

82. Hesse, *Demian,* 24.

83. *SW* 14:353.

84. *SW* 14:356.

85. *Briefwechsel mit seinem Psychoanalytiker,* 69.

86. Hermann Hesse, *Eine Bibliothek der Weltliteratur* (Leipzig, 1948), 45.

87. Helmut Zander, *Rudolf Steiner Die Biografie* (Munich 2011), 16.

88. *Briefwechsel mit seinem Psychoanalytiker,* 168.

89. *GesBr* 2:70.

90. Hermann Hesse, Hugo Ball, and Emmy Ball-Hennings, *Briefwechsel, 1921–1927,* ed. Bärbel Reetz (Frankfurt am Main, 2003), 113.

91. *SW* 11:653.

92. Miriam Gebhardt, *Rudolf Steiner: Ein moderner Prophet* (Munich, 2010), 10.

93. Ibid., 13.

94. Volker Michels, *Hermann Hesse: Sein Leben in Bildern und Texten* (Frankfurt am Main, 1987), 307.

95. Hermann Hesse, *Zarathustras Wiederkehr,* ed. Volker Michels (Frankfurt am Main, 1993), 21.

96. Ibid., 32.

97. Ibid., 33.

98. *GesBr* 1:433.

99. Hesse, *Zarathustras Wiederkehr,* 7.

100. Fyodor M. Dostojewski, *Briefe,* ed. Ralf Schröder (Lepizig, 1981), 23.

101. Lászlo. F. Földényi, *Dostojewski liest Hegel in Sibirien und bricht in Tränen aus* (Berlin, 2008), 16.

102. Dostojewski, *Briefe,* 101.

103. N. F. Beltschikow, *Dostojewski im Prozeß der Petraschewzen* (Leipzig, 1977), 206.

104. Julius Meier-Graefe, *Dostojewski* (Frankfurt am Main, 1988), 364.

105. Dostojewski, *Briefe,* 281.

106. *GesBr* 1:423.

107. *GesBr* 1:424.

108. Ibid.

109. *GesBr* 1:430.

110. *GesBr* 1:469.

111. *SW* 18:84.

112. *SW* 18:117.

113. *SW* 18:119.

114. *GesBr* 1:392.

115. *SW* 18:137.

116. *SW* 18:135.

117. *SW* 15:92.

118. *SW* 15:111.

119. *SW* 15:116.

120. *SW* 15:292.

121. *SW* 15:193.

122. *SW* 15:295.

123. *SW* 8:163.

124. *SW* 8:172.

125. Ibid.

126. *SW* 11:553.

127. *GesBr* 1:387.

128. *GesBr* 1:390.

129. *GesBr* 1:386.

130. *SW* 8:182.

131. *SW* 8:191.

132. *SW* 8:192.

133. *SW* 8:193.

134. *SW* 8:196.

135. *SW* 8:173.

136. *SW* 8:177.

137. *SW* 12:148.

138. *SW* 12:149.

7. Escape to Ticino

1. Hugo Ball, *Hermann Hesse: Sein Leben und Werk* (Frankfurt am Main, 1977), 162 (1st ed., 1927).

2. Hermann Hesse, *Wanderung* (Frankfurt am Main, 1989), 9.

3. Ibid., 11.

4. Ibid., 10.

5. Ibid., 47.

6. Ibid., 49.

7. Ibid., 51.

8. Ibid., 67.

9. Ibid., 68.

10. Hermann Hesse, *Kurgast: Aufzeichnungen von einer Badener Kur* (Frankfurt am Main, 1997), 24.

11. *SW* 12:150.

12. Hermann Hesse, "Stunden am Schreibtisch," in *Hermann Hesse: Magie der Farben,* ed. Volker Michels (Frankfurt am Main, 1980), 69.

13. *SW* 11:456.

14. *SW* 11:461.

15. Hermann Hesse, *Die Märchen,* ed. Volker Michels (Frankfurt am Main, 2006), 184.

16. Ibid., 185.

17. Ibid., 222.

18. Ibid., 212.

19. *SW* 11:460.

20. Michels, *Hermann Hesse: Magie der Farben,* 77.

21. *SW* 11:461.

22. Michels, *Hermann Hesse: Magie der Farben,* 54.

23. Ninon Hesse, *Lieber, lieber Vogel: Briefe an Hermann Hesse,* ed. Gisela Kleine (Frankfurt am Main, 2000), 162.

24. *GesBr* 2:120.

25. *SW* 12:149.

26. *GesBr* 1:418.

27. Hesse, *Die Märchen,* 205.

28. *SW* 18:269.

29. *GesBr* 1:402.

30. *GesBr* 1:407.

31. *GesBr* 1:422.

32. *GesBr* 1:423.

33. *SW* 8:220.

34. *SW* 8:216.

35. *SW* 8:227.

36. *SW* 8:215.

37. *SW* 8:280.

38. *SW* 8:281.

39. *SW* 8:284.

40. Ibid.

41. Ibid.

42. Ball, *Hermann Hesse,* 20.

43. Novalis, *Heinrich von Ofterdingen* (Berlin, 1983), 13.

44. Ibid., 119.

45. Ibid., 116.

46. *SW* 12:59.

47. *SW* 8:285.

48. *SW* 8:286.

49. *SW* 12:61.

50. *SW* 8:290.

51. *GesBr* 1:408.

52. *SW* 8:165.

53. *SW* 8:169.

54. Ball, *Hermann Hesse,* 153.

55. *SW* 8:285.

56. *SW* 12:58.

57. Ibid.

58. Ball, *Hermann Hesse,* 153.

59. *SW* 8:293.

60. *SW* 8:332.

61. *SW* 8:293.

62. *SW* 8:317.

63. Ibid.

64. Hermann Hesse, Hugo Ball, and Emmy Ball-Hennings, *Briefwechsel, 1921–1927,* ed. Bärbel Reetz (Frankfurt am Main, 2003), 71.

65. Ibid., 74.

66. Ibid., 71.

67. *Briefwechsel mit seinem Psychoanalytiker Josef Bernhard Lang, 1916–1944,* ed. Thomas Feitknecht (Frankfurt am Main, 2008), 101.

68. *GesBr* 1:419.

69. *GesBr* 2:21.

70. *GesBr* 2:17.

71. *GesBr* 2:21.

72. Hermann Hesse, *Siddhartha* (Frankfurt am Main, 2000), 12.

73. Ibid., 17.

74. Ibid., 13.

75. Ibid., 20.

76. Ibid., 35.

77. Volker Michels, *Materialien zu Hermann Hesse. "Siddhartha,"* 2 vols. (Frankfurt am Main, 1976), 1:258.

78. "Brief an H. Gohlke, Febr. 1955," in *Materialien zu Hermann Hesse. "Siddhartha,"* 1:260.

79. *SW* 11:641.

80. Michels, *Materialien zu Hermann Hesse. "Siddhartha,"* 1:262.

81. Ibid., 39.

82. Ibid., 148.

83. Ibid.

84. Ibid., 162.

85. Ibid., 163.

86. Hesse, *Siddhartha,* 43.

87. Michels, *Materialien zu Hermann Hesse. "Siddhartha,"* 2:295.

88. *SW* 11:655.

89. *SW* 11:656.

90. Michels, *Materialien zu Hermann Hesse. "Siddhartha,"* 1:266.

91. Ibid., 1:267.

92. Hesse, *Siddhartha,* 45.

93. Ibid., 49.

94. Ibid., 64.

95. *SW* 11:629.

96. Ibid.

97. *SW* 11:628.

98. Hesse, *Siddhartha,* 83.

99. Ibid., 84.

100. Ibid., 47.

101. Ibid.

102. *SW* 11:630.

103. *SW* 11:638.

104. Hesse, *Siddhartha,* 116.

105. *GesBr* 2:50.

106. *GesBr* 2:44.

107. *GesBr* 2:26.

108. *GesBr* 2:52.

109. *GesBr* 2:57.

110. *SW* 15:266.

111. *SW* 15:267.

112. *GesBr* 1:429.

113. Hermann Hesse and Ruth Wenger, *Briefwechsel mit seiner zweiten Frau Ruth,* ed. Ursula and Volker Michels (Frankfurt am Main, 1969), 634.

114. Ibid., 32.

115. Ibid., 41.

116. Ibid., 604.

117. *Briefwechsel mit seinem Psychoanalytiker,* 178.

118. Hesse and Wenger, *Briefwechsel,* 600.

119. Ibid., 604.

120. *Briefwechsel mit seinem Psychoanalytiker,* 212.

121. Ibid., 224.

122. Hesse and Wenger, *Briefwechsel,* 308.

123. Ibid., 327.

124. Ibid., 331.

125. Ibid., 330.

126. Ibid., 329.

127. Ibid.

128. *GesBr* 2:80.

129. *GesBr* 2:82.

130. Hesse and Wenger, *Briefwechsel,* 620.

131. Ibid., 621.

132. Ibid.

133. *GesBr* 2:110.

134. Hesse and Wenger, *Briefwechsel,* 600.

135. Ibid.

136. Ibid., 611.

137. Ibid., 622.

138. Ibid., 623.

139. Ibid., 628.

140. *GesBr* 1:208.

141. Hesse, *Die Märchen,* 208.

142. Ibid., 209.

143. Ibid., 211.

144. *GesBr* 2:166.

145. Hermann Hesse, *Freude am Garten,* ed. Volker Michels (Frankfurt am Main, 1998), 10.

146. Ibid., 13.

147. Ibid., 61.

148. Ibid., 63.

149. Ibid., 65.

8. The Awakening of Steppenwolf

1. Hermann Hesse, *Ausgewählte Briefe,* expanded ed., ed. Hermann Hesse and Ninon Hesse (Frankfurt am Main, 1974), 118.

2. Hermann Hesse, Hugo Ball, and Emmy Ball-Hennings, *Briefwechsel, 1921–1927,* ed. Bärbel Reetz (Frankfurt am Main, 2003), 7.

3. Ibid., 6.

4. *SW* 11:458.

5. Hesse, Ball, and Hennings, *Briefwechsel,* 8.

6. Ibid., 27.

7. Ibid., 30.

8. Ibid., 36.

9. *SW* 11:455.

10. Hesse, Ball, and Hennings, *Briefwechsel,* 103.

11. Ibid., 78.

12. *SW* 11:648.

13. Hesse, Ball, and Hennings, *Briefwechsel,* 68.

14. *SW* 11:636.

15. Hesse, Ball, and Hennings, *Briefwechsel,* 76.

16. *GesBr* 2:116.

17. *SW* 11:632.

18. Ibid.

19. *SW* 11:634.

20. Hesse, Ball, and Hennings, *Briefwechsel,* 98.

21. Ibid., 105.

22. Ibid., 104.

23. Ibid., 105.

24. Hugo Ball, *Byzantinisches Christentum* (Göttingen, 2011), 243.

25. Gustav Landauer, *Skepsis und Mystik* (Cologne, 1923), 7.

26. *SW* 18:413.

27. *SW* 18:432.

28. *SW* 11:510.

29. Eike Middell, *Hermann Hesse* (Leipzig, 1990), 151.

30. *GesBr* 2:139.

31. *GesBr* 2:62.

32. Stefan Zweig, *Essays, 1925–1928* (Leipzig, 1985), 288.

33. Hermann Hesse, *Kurgast: Aufzeichnungen von einer Badener Kur* (Frankfurt am Main, 1997), 8.

34. Hesse, Ball, and Hennings, *Briefwechsel,* 172.

35. Ibid.

36. Ibid., 305.

37. Ibid., 332.

38. Hesse, *Kurgast,* 94.

39. Ibid., 53.

40. Ibid., 108.

41. Ibid., 93.

42. Hesse, Ball, and Hennings, *Briefwechsel,* 188.

43. Hermann Hesse, *Die Nürnberger Reise* (Frankfurt am Main, 1994), 20.

44. *GesBr* 2:125.

45. Hesse, *Nürnberger Reise,* 9.

46. Ibid., 15.

47. Ibid., 16.

48. *SW* 8:117.

49. *SW* 8:118.

50. *SW* 8:119.

51. Hesse, *Nürnberger Reise,* 17.

52. Ibid., 34.

53. Ibid., 39.

54. Ibid., 65.

55. Ibid., 61.

56. Ibid., 38.

57. Ibid., 102.

58. Ibid., 103.

59. Ibid., 102.

60. Ibid.

61. *GesBr* 2:227.

62. *SW* 11:661.

63. *SW* 11:663.

64. *SW* 11:231.

65. Volker Michels, *Materialien zu Hermann Hesse "Der Steppenwolf"* (Frankfurt am Main, 1972), 199.

66. Ibid., 200.

67. Ibid., 49.

68. *GesBr* 2:33.

69. *GesBr* 2:34.

70. Hermann Hesse, *Der Steppenwolf* (Berlin, 1986), 12.

71. Hugo Ball, *Hermann Hesse,* 20.

72. Hesse, *Steppenwolf,* 184 (afterword).

73. Ibid.

74. Ibid., 10.

75. Hesse, "Rückkehr aufs Land," in *Beschreibung einer Landschaft,* ed. Sieg-fried Unseld (Frankfurt am Main, 1990), 155.

76. Hesse, Ball, and Hennings, *Briefwechsel,* 409.

77. Ibid., 436.

78. Ibid., 409.

79. Fritz Böttger, *Hermann Hesse* (Berlin [DDR], 1982), 323.

80. Hermann Hesse and Thomas Mann, *Briefwechsel,* ed. Anni Carlsson and Volker Michels (Frankfurt am Main, 2007), 54.

81. *GesBr* 2:154.

82. Ibid.

83. Hesse, Ball, and Hennings, *Briefwechsel,* 438.

84. *GesBr* 2:156.

85. *GesBr* 2:158.

86. *GesBr* 2:174.

87. Ibid.

88. *GesBr* 2:155.

89. Hermann Hesse, "Brief an Alice Leuthold," in Michels, *Materialien zu Hermann Hesse. "Der Steppenwolf,"* 62.

90. *GesBr* 2:165.

91. *GesBr* 2:130.

92. *GesBr* 2:134.

93. Hesse, Ball, and Hennings, *Briefwechsel,* 96.

94. Hesse, *Steppenwolf,* 147.

95. Ibid.

96. Ibid., 148.

97. Ibid., 150.

98. *GesBr* 4:213.

99. Michels, *Materialien zu Hermann Hesse. "Der Steppenwolf,"* 161.

100. Hesse, *Steppenwolf,* 175.

101. Ibid., 176.

102. Ibid., 177.

103. *GesBr* 2:178.

104. *GesBr* 2:181.

105. Hesse, Ball, and Hennings, *Briefwechsel,* 499.

106. *GesBr* 2:187.

107. Hesse, Ball, and Hennings, *Briefwechsel,* 503.

108. *GesBr* 2:183.

109. Hesse, *Ausgewählte Briefe,* 118.

110. Hesse, Ball, and Hennings, *Briefwechsel,* 530.

111. Ibid., 529.

112. *GesBr* 2:187.

113. *GesBr* 2:188.

114. Michels, *Materialien zu Hermann Hesse. "Der Steppenwolf,"* 209.

115. Ibid., 347.

116. Hermann Hesse, *Eine Bibliothek der Weltliteratur* (Leipzig, 1948), 24.

117. Charles Baudelaire, *Die künstlichen Paradiese* (Zurich, 1988), 81.

118. Walter Rheiner, *Kokain* (Leipzig, 1985), 224.

119. Michels, *Materialien zu Hermann Hesse. "Der Steppenwolf,"* 210.

120. Ibid., 336.

121. Ibid., 400.

9. Traveling to the East

1. Quoted in Gisela Kleine, *Zwischen Welt und Zaubergarten: Ninon und Hermann Hesse, ein Leben im Dialog* (Frankfurt am Main, 1988), 35.

2. Quoted in ibid., 36.

3. Ninon Hesse, *Lieber, lieber Vogel: Briefe an Hermann Hesse,* ed. Gisela Kleine (Frankfurt am Main, 2000), 97.

4. Ibid., 49.

5. Ibid., 56.

6. Ibid., 95.

7. Ibid., 79.

8. Ibid., 83.

9. Ibid., 87.

10. Ibid.

11. Ibid.

12. Quoted in Kleine, *Zwischen Welt und Zaubergarten,* 533.

13. Ninon Hesse, *Lieber Vogel,* 102.

14. Quoted in Kleine, *Zwischen Welt und Zaubergarten,* 215.

15. Quoted in ibid., 253.

16. Ibid.

17. *GesBr* 2:190.

18. *GesBr* 2:191.

19. Ibid.

20. Quoted in Kleine, *Zwischen Welt und Zaubergarten,* 255.

21. *GesBr* 2:208.

22. Quoted in Kleine, *Zwischen Welt und Zaubergarten*, 260.

23. *SW* 12:151.

24. Kleine, *Zwischen Welt und Zaubergarten*, 261.

25. Ibid., 265.

26. Ibid., 268.

27. Ibid., 264.

28. Ibid., 256.

29. Ralph Freedman, *Hermann Hesse* (Frankfurt am Main, 1999), 417.

30. Hermann Hesse, *Magie des Buches* (Frankfurt am Main, 1977), 29.

31. Hermann Hesse, *Eine Bibliothek der Weltliteratur* (Leipzig, 1948), 3.

32. Hesse, *Magie des Buches*, 90.

33. Ibid., 91.

34. Ibid., 129.

35. Ibid., 77.

36. Ibid., 53.

37. Ibid., 54.

38. Ibid., 73.

39. Ibid., 41.

40. *GesBr* 2:236.

41. Hermann Hesse, *Ausgewählte Briefe,* expanded ed., ed. Hermann Hesse and Ninon Hesse (Frankfurt am Main, 1974), 49.

42. Hermann Hesse, *Narziß und Goldmund* (Berlin, 1982), 291.

43. Ibid., 279.

44. Ibid., 282.

45. Ninon Hesse, *Lieber Vogel,* 160.

46. *GesBr* 2:272.

47. *GesBr* 2: afterword.

48. Ibid.

49. Hermann Hesse and Thomas Mann, *Briefwechsel,* ed. Anni Carlsson and Volker Michels (Frankfurt am Main, 2007), 56.

50. Fritz Böttger, *Hermann Hesse* (Berlin [DDR], 1982), 368.

51. Hesse, *Narziß und Goldmund,* 221.

52. *GesBr* 2:275.

53. Robert Musil, *Gesammelte Werke II,* ed. Adolf Frisé (Reinbeck bei Hamburg, 1978), 1235.

54. Quoted in Inge Jens, *Dichter zwischen rechts und links* (Leipzig, 1994), 64.

55. Hesse, *Ausgewählte Briefe,* 17.

56. Quoted in Jens, *Dichter,* 113.

57. *GesBr* 2:263.

58. Ibid.

59. *GesBr* 2:272.

60. Hesse and Mann, *Briefwechsel,* 59.

61. Hesse, *Ausgewählte Briefe,* 27.

62. Hesse and Mann, *Briefwechsel,* 59.

63. Ibid.

64. Ibid., 62.

65. Ibid., 65.

66. Hermann Hesse, *Die Morgenlandfahrt* (Frankfurt am Main, 2001), 10.

67. *GesBr* 2:299.

68. Hesse, *Die Morgenlandfahrt,* 16.

69. Ibid., 24.

70. Ibid., 92.

71. *GesBr* 2:308.

72. Hesse, *Die Morgenlandfahrt,* 52.

73. *GesBr* 2:255.

74. Siegfried Unseld, *Hermann Hesse: Eine Werkgeschichte* (Frankfurt am Main, 1973), 170.

75. Hesse, *Magie des Buches,* 66.

76. Ibid., 67.

10. On the Nature of *The Glass Bead Game*

1. *GesBr* 1:384.

2. *GesBr* 1:403.

3. Hermann Hesse, *Ausgewählte Briefe,* expanded ed., ed. Hermann Hesse and Ninon Hesse (Frankfurt am Main, 1974), 112.

4. *GesBr* 2:214.

5. *SW* 15:350.

6. Ibid.

7. *SW* 15:351.

8. Ibid.

9. *GesBr* 2:377.

10. Hermann Hesse and Thomas Mann, *Briefwechsel,* ed. Anni Carlsson and Volker Michels (Frankfurt am Main, 2007), 67.

11. Ibid., 70.

12. *GesBr* 2:317.

13. *GesBr* 2:318.

14. *GesBr* 2:322.

15. Hesse and Mann, *Briefwechsel,* 74.

16. Ibid., 105.

17. Ibid., 78.

18. *GesBr* 2:380.

19. Hesse and Mann, *Briefwechsel,* 82.

20. *GesBr* 4:71.

21. Hesse and Mann, *Briefwechsel,* 81.

22. Ibid., 110.

23. *SW* 11:664.

24. Hesse and Mann, *Briefwechsel,* 87.

25. Quoted in Regina Bucher, ed., *"Im Dienste der gemeinsamen Sache":* *Hermann Hesse und der Suhrkamp Verlag* (Montagnola, 2005), 16.

26. Hesse and Mann, *Briefwechsel,* 105.

27. Ibid., 106.

28. Ibid., 127.

29. Ibid., 122.

30. *GesBr* 2:373.

31. *GesBr* 2:384.

32. *GesBr* 2:378.

33. Hesse and Mann, *Briefwechsel,* 101.

34. *GesBr* 2:383.

35. Hesse and Mann, *Briefwechsel,* 96.

36. Ibid.

37. *GesBr* 2:396.

38. Ninon Hesse, *Lieber, lieber Vogel. Briefe an Hermann Hesse,* ed. Gisela Kleine (Frankfurt am Main, 2000), 305.

39. Ibid., 304.

40. Ibid.

41. Hesse, *Ausgewählte Briefe,* 100.

42. Ibid.

43. Ibid., 101.

44. *GesBr* 2:445.

45. *GesBr* 2:444.

46. *GesBr* 2:450.

47. Ibid.

48. Quoted in Fritz Böttger, *Hermann Hesse* (Berlin [DDR], 1982), 399.

49. *GesBr* 2:487.

50. *GesBr* 3:10.

51. *GesBr* 3:13.

52. *GesBr* 3:17.

53. Hesse, *Ausgewählte Briefe,* 160.

54. Quoted in Böttger, *Hesse,* 400.

55. Hesse, *Ausgewählte Briefe,* 141.

56. Ibid., 140.

57. Ibid., 179.

58. Ibid., 180.

59. *GesBr* 2:486.

60. *GesBr* 2:484.

61. Hermann Hesse and Peter Weiss, *"Verehrter großer Zauberer": Brief-wechsel, 1937–1962,* ed. Beat Mazenauer und Volker Michels (Frankfurt am Main, 2009), 24.

62. Ibid., 31.

63. Michels, afterword in Hesse and Weiss, *Briefwechsel,* 222.

64. Hesse and Weiss, *Briefwechsel,* 36.

65. Ibid., 43.

66. Volker Michels, ed., *Hermann Hesse in Augenzeugenberichten* (Frankfurt am Main, 1991), 217.

67. Hesse and Weiss, *Briefwechsel,* 46.

68. Ibid., 132.

69. Ibid., 134.

70. Hermann Hesse, *Magie des Buches* (Frankfurt am Main, 1977), 15.

71. Ibid., 16.

72. Maurice Maeterlinck, *Das Leben der Bienen* (Jena, 1920), 6.

73. *SW* 5:11.

74. *SW* 5:12.

75. Gottfied Benn, *Gesammelte Werke I,* ed. Dieter Wellershoff (Stuttgart, 1989), 426.

76. *SW* 5:14.

77. *SW* 5:519.

78. *SW* 5:35.

79. *SW* 5:523.

80. *SW* 5:525.

81. *SW* 5:15.

82. *SW* 5:21.

83. Gustav Landauer, *Skepsis und Mystik* (Cologne, 1923), 10.

84. *SW* 5:393.

85. Quoted in Gisela Kleine, *Zwischen Welt und Zaubergarten: Ninon und Her-mann Hesse, ein Leben im Dialog* (Frankfurt am Main, 1988), 336.

86. Hermann Hesse and Karl Kerényi, *Briefwechsel aus der Nähe,* ed. Magda Kerényi (Munich, 1972), 28.

87. *SW* 20:350.

88. *GesBr* 3:207.

89. Compare Gunnar Decker, *Kriegerdämmerung: Polemischer Versuch zu einem Porträt Ernst Jüngers* (Essen, 1997), 15.

90. *GesBr* 4:76.

91. *SW* 20:352.

92. *SW* 20:351.

93. *SW* 20:353.

94. Hesse, *Ausgewählte Briefe,* 96.

95. Hermann Hesse, *Dank an Goethe* (Frankfurt am Main, 1999), 22.

96. Ibid., 26.

97. Ibid., 13.

98. Ibid., 122.

99. Ibid., 123.

100. Ibid.,124.

101. Ibid., 125.

102. Ibid., 28.

103. Ibid., 180.

11. The Old Man of the Mountains

1. *SW* 11:722.

2. *SW* 11:729.

3. *SW* 15:630.

4. *SW* 15:633.

5. *SW* 15:634.

6. *SW* 15:638.

7. *SW* 15:644.

8. *SW* 15:597.

9. *SW* 15:598.

10. Ibid.

11. *SW* 15:607.

12. *SW* 15:599.

13. *SW* 15:602.

14. Hermann Hesse and Peter Suhrkamp, *Briefwechsel, 1945–1959,* ed. Siegfried Unseld (Frankfurt am Main, 1969), 23.

15. Ibid., 21.

16. Ibid., 418.

17. *GesBr* 3:374.

18. *SW* 14:476.

19. *SW* 14:475.

20. *SW* 14:476.

21. *GesBr* 3:377.

22. *GesBr* 3:389.

23. *SW* 15:624.

24. *SW* 15:608.

25. *SW* 12:509.

26. Volker Michels, "Ohne Hermann Hesse gäbe es keinen Suhrkamp Verlag," in *"Im Dienste der gemeinsamen Sache"—Hermann Hesse und der Suhrkamp Verlag,* ed. Regina Bucher (Montagnola, 2005), 15.

27. Siegfried Unseld, nachwort in Hesse and Suhrkamp, *Briefe,* 468.

28. Ibid., 469.

29. Ibid.

30. Quoted in Siegfried Unseld, *Peter Suhrkamp: Eine Biographie* (Frankfurt am Main, 2004), 104.

31. Ibid.

32. Ibid., 108.

33. Ibid., 111.

34. Hesse and Suhrkamp, *Briefe,* 9.

35. Ibid., 15.

36. Ibid., 23.

37. Ibid., 33.

38. Ibid., 39.

39. Ibid., 43.

40. Ibid., 47.

41. Ibid., 50.

42. Ibid., 112.

43. Unseld, *Peter Suhrkamp,* 138.

44. Hesse and Suhrkamp, *Briefe,* 463.

45. *SW* 12:510.

46. *SW* 11:554.

47. *GesBr* 2:104.

48. *GesBr* 2:299.

49. *GesBr* 2:300.

50. *GesBr* 2:301.

51. *GesBr* 2:318.

52. *GesBr* 3:244.

53. *GesBr* 3:405.

54. *GesBr* 3:406.

55. *GesBr* 3:509.

56. *GesBr* 4:17.

57. *GesBr* 4:148.

58. *GesBr* 4:403.

59. Gisela Kleine, *Zwischen Welt und Zaubergarten: Ninon und Hermann Hesse, ein Leben im Dialog* (Frankfurt am Main, 1988), 355.

60. *SW* 12:463.

61. Georg A. Weth, *Hermann Hesse in der Schweiz* (Munich, 2004), 54.

62. See Hermann Hesse and Hans Purrmann, *Briefe, 1945–1962,* ed. Felix Billeter und Eva Zimmermann (Berlin, 2011), 56.

63. Weth, *Hesse in der Schweiz,* 46.

64. Kleine, *Zwischen Welt und Zaubergarten,* 357.

65. Ibid., 358.

66. Quoted in Kleine, *Zwischen Welt und Zaubergarten,* 256.

67. Hermann Hesse and Peter Weiss, *"Verehrter großer Zauberer": Briefwechsel, 1937–1962,* ed. Beat Mazenauer und Volker Michels (Frankfurt am Main, 2009), 232.

68. Ibid.

69. *SW* 15:596.

70. *SW* 15:771.

71. *SW* 15:765.

72. *SW* 15:767.

73. *SW* 15:779.

74. *SW* 15:772.

75. *SW* 15:783.

76. Volker Michels, ed., *Hermann Hesse in Augenzeugenberichten* (Frankfurt am Main, 1991), 354.

77. Ibid., 358.

78. Ibid., 361.

79. Hesse and Suhrkamp, *Briefe,* 383.

80. Michels, *Hermann Hesse in Augenzeugenberichten,* 363.

81. Ibid., 479.

82. Ibid., 369.

83. Kleine, *Zwischen Welt und Zaubergarten,* 483.

84. Michels, *Hermann Hesse in Augenzeugenberichten,* 483.

85. Ibid., 449.

86. *SW* 11:741.

87. Michels, *Hermann Hesse in Augenzeugenberichten,* 450.

88. Hermann Hesse and Karl Kerényi, *Briefwechsel aus der Nähe,* ed. Magda Kerényi (Munich, 1972), 106.

89. Michels, *Hermann Hesse in Augenzeugenberichten,* 450.

90. *SW* 12:697.

ACKNOWLEDGMENTS

It is incumbent upon me to thank a number of people who either facilitated my writing of this book or stood loyally by me during its genesis. My two earliest—and in the interim sadly deceased—interlocutors were Hermann Hesse's son Heiner, who despite being gravely ill received me warmly at his mill-house in Ronco, and whose testimony about his father left a deep and lasting impression on me; and secondly Ezard Haussmann, the son of Hesse's second wife, Ruth Wenger, from her second marriage, who furnished me with important insights into her memoirs.

I am profoundly grateful to Carl Hanser Verlag and its managing director, Michael Krüger, for the trust he invested in me—when I had only just embarked on the project—in agreeing to publish my book. I would also like to thank my editor, Dr. Tobias Heyl, for his constantly stimulating collaboration, and his colleague Martha Bunk for the patient care she showed in clarifying countless details. My thanks are also due to my agent, Thomas Karlauf, for his thoughtful suggestions during the writing process.

I would especially like to thank Ursula and Volker Michels, who despite their own ongoing labors on the critical edition of Hesse's works took the time to read my manuscript and who—in addition to much friendly encouragement—provided invaluable help in resolving several outstanding questions. I recall with great fondness my visit to them at the Hesse Editions Archive in Offenbach.

Lastly, I must express my heartfelt gratitude to my wife, Kerstin, whose diligent reading of the manuscript and reflections on it greatly enhanced the end product, and to my father, Professor Heinz Decker, who gave me the benefit of his customary warmhearted support and precise scientist's viewpoint throughout my work on the book.

INDEX

Abraxas, in *Demian,* 328, 330, 331, 332–333, 338

Abs, Clemens, 682

Abu Telfan (Raabe), 304

"Acknowledgment and Moralizing Reflection" (Hesse), 677–678

Adorno, Theodor, 174, 690

"Age of the Feuilleton" (Hesse), 209, 643–654

"Alemannic Avowal" (Hesse), 28–29, 157–158, 295

Alemannic region, Hesse and, 156–157

Allen, Woody, 96, 496

Allgemeine Schweizer Zeitung (newspaper), 162–163, 201

"Alone" (M. Hesse), 38–39

Am Erlenlob (Gaienhofen), 237

Amiet, Cuno, 373, 374, 390, 701

"Among the Crags" (Hesse), 276

Anachronistic figures, Hesse and, 97

Andere Seite, Die (Kubin), 138

Andreae, Volkmar, 536

Andreas-Salomé, Lou, 567

Anthroposophy, 347–351

Anti-Semitism: Hesse and, 283–284; increase in German, 616

Apollonian and Dionysian principles (Nietzsche), 297, 414, 576

Apprenticeships: in Esslingen, 103–108; in Tübingen, 114–120, 137

Arndt, Johann, 651–652

Arnold, Gottfried, 181, 413, 593, 652

Arosa, Hesse and Ninon's visit to, 555–557

Arp, Hans, 480

Art: of the absurd, 509; communism and, 424, 607; *Narcissus and Goldmund* and, 580, 584; primitive pleasure of creation and, 409; purpose of, 353–354; religion of, 155; Ruth Wenger and, 460

"Art for art's sake," Hesse on, 164

"Art Is a Weapon," 424

Artist: Hesse and sacrifice role as, 486–487; as neurotic, 491–500; psychoanalysis applied to, 345–347, 434–435

"Artist and Psychoanalysis, The" (Hesse), 345–346

"Art of Idleness, The" (Hesse), 644

Art of idleness, Hesse and, 211

Asceticism: Ball and, 484, 486, 574; Hesse and, 275, 276–277, 486–487, 618

Ascona—Monte Verità (Landmann), 272–273

Assassination, Hesse's fantasies about, 58–59

Assimilation, Hesse and problem of, 284

Astrology: Englert and, 91, 334, 336; Hesse and, 91, 333, 334, 338; Jünger and, 656

Atheism (Dostoyevsky), 360–361

Atheistic mysticism, Hesse and, 483

Atman, 426, 428

"At the Eye Clinic" (Hesse), 189–190

At the Wall of Time (Jünger), 655, 657

Augsburger Abend-Zeitung (newspaper), 370

Ausländer, Jakob, 543–544

Author readings, Hesse and, 504–505, 509–510, 526

Autobiographical accounts, in Hesse's writings, 3–4

"Autobiography" (M. Gundert), 25

Autodidact, Hesse as, 573

Autoeroticism, in *Demian,* 331

Automobiles: big-game hunt for in *Steppenwolf,* 509, 529–534; critique of modern culture and, 529, 530

"Autumn Nights" (Hesse), 238

Baader, Franz, 334

Baal (Brecht), 211

Bach, Johann Sebastien, 610, 715

Bachofen, Johann Jakob, 332, 607

"Back to nature," Monte Verità and, 273–274

Bad Boll sanatorium, Hesse at, 16, 73–77, 100, 125, 127

Ball, Hugo, 569; on anthroposophy, 349–350; asceticism and, 484, 486, 574; background of, 479, 480–481; bond with Hennings, 477–478; on Casa Camuzzi, 411–412; death of, 534–537, 574; on *Demian,* 327, 328; as eyewitness to Hesse's crisis, 517; on Finckh, 206; on Hesse and beginnings of human soul, 177; on Hesse and Romanticism, 165, 516; on Hesse and spirit and the senses, 492; on Hesse at outbreak of

World War I, 306; Hesse on misgivings about marrying Ruth Wenger and, 458; Hesse's advice on Ball's monograph on Hesse, 518; on Hesse's affinity for van Gogh, 395; Hesse's description of participating in nightlife in Zurich and, 526–527; Hesse's elegy to, 536; on Hesse's move to Welti house, 296; on Hesse's Romanticism, 405; as inspiration for *Steppenwolf,* 514; interest in exorcism and, 338; on *Klingsor's Last Summer* (Hesse), 418–419; on Maria Bernoulli, 234; on Marie Hesse, 46; monograph on Hesse, 518, 519; move back to Ticino, 488; move to Munich, 487–488; on *Peter Camenzind,* 210–211; photo of, 478; on *Psychologia Balnearia,* 500; relationship with Hesse, 473–479, 481–490; repudiation of Finckh, 693; on role of grandfather in Pietism, 18; Roman Catholicism and, 430, 480, 482, 483–485; on Romanticism, 414; on the Steppenwolf, 541; on *Wandering,* 378, 381. *See also* Hennings, Emmy

Balzac, Honoré de, 577–578

Bang, Herman, 470

Barbizon School, 274

Barns, John, 37–38

Barth, Christian Gottlob, 26

Barth, Max, 636

Barth, Paul Basilius, 453–454

Basel: Hermann's return to after Stetten stay, 94, 95–96, 98–99; Hesse as child in, 45–51; Hesse at Reich's bookshop in, 158–162; Hesse at Wattenwyl antiquarian bookshop in, 198; Hesse ready to leave, 173

Basel Mission, 125

Basler Anzeiger (newspaper), 196–197

Basler Nachrichten (newspaper), 672

Baths of Lucca (Heine), 189

"Battle of the Machines" (Hesse), 529–530

Baudelaire, Charles, 539

Beauty, connection between wickedness and, 48–49

Beauvoir, Simone de, 562

Becher, Johannes R., 601, 645

Beethoven, Ludwig van, 117

Békessy, Imre, 673

Békessy, Janos, 673

Bellamy, Edward, 96–98, 640

Beneath the Wheel (Hesse), 90, 264; child-soul and, 230, 247–260; counterculture and, 10; criticism of, 258–259; education and, 36, 65, 247–249; existence of intellectual in mechanized world and, 250–251; friendship in, 255–257; Hans Hesse and, 251–253; individuation and, 249–250; philistinism and, 250–251, 253–255; process of acquiring self-knowledge and, 258; wayfarer and, 259–260; Zweig on, 219

Bengel, Johann Albrecht, 651

Benjamin, Walter, 690

Benn, Gottfried, 657; blacklisting of, 674; father of, 74, 129; hallucinatory style and, 538; on Hesse, 8, 10, 525; on Knulp, 266; Nazis and, 614, 615; "The New Literary Season," 645; on Nietzsche, 3; on purpose of art, 353; "Satzbau," 570; situation underlying *Siddhartha,* 423; on winning prizes, 675

Berlin: Dolbin and, 547–548; Hesse's distaste for, 185, 263, 555, 589

Bermann Fischer, Gottfried, 615, 627, 634, 679, 681–683; photo of, 556; rift with Peter Suhrkamp, 687, 689–690

Bern: Hesse living in, 157, 268; move to Welti house in, 293–297

Bernhard, Georg, 627–628

Bernoulli, Maria (Mia), 49; adulterous relationship of, 321–322; burden of son Martin's illness and, 301–302; as burden to Hesse, 277–278; divorce from Hesse, 333, 454–455, 456; following Hesse to Ticino, 420; Hesse's assessment of, 301; Hesse's dream of her death, 400–401; Hesse's engagement to, 230–231; marriage to Hesse, 169–170, 234–235, 236–238; mental health of, 83, 322, 420; as mother figure, 437; move to Bern and, 294–295; photo of, 249; psychoanalysis and, 321; trip to Italy with Hesse, 222–224

Bie, Oskar, 288

Bierbaum, Otto Julius, 209

Biographical monographs, Hesse's, 4–5

Biographical Notes (J. Hesse), 28

Biography of the soul, *The Glass Bead Game* and, 638

Bird, Hesse's caricature of himself as, 1, 28

Bisexuality, Hesse's, 475–476

Black Forest, 43, 44, 45

Blei, Franz, 479

Bloch, Ernst, 261, 625, 707

Blue Flower, The (Jacobsen), 162

Blue flower motif, 147, 164, 166, 180, 186, 406

Blumhardt, Christoph, 73, 74–77, 255

Blumhardt, Johann Christoph, 16, 31, 74, 75, 337–338

Boarding school, Hermann Hesse at, 50

Boccaccio, Hesse's monograph on, 4–5, 224–227

Böcklin, Arnold, 116, 161, 295

Bodmer, Elsy, 719

Bodmer, H. C., 488, 560, 561, 690, 721

Böhme, Jakob, 215, 255, 662

Böhmer, Gunter, 390, 617, 618, 620, 628, 635

Bonhoeffer, Dietrich, 649

Bonniers Litterära Magasin, Hesse's work as reviewer on, 623–631

Book reviews, Hesse's, 162–163, 399, 571, 572, 708; for *Bonniers Litterära Magasin,* 623–631

Books, Hesse's relationship with, 566–574

Bosch, Hieronymus, 514

Bote für deutsche Literatur, Der (journal), 154

Böttger, Fritz, 583

Bourgeois culture: Hesse and attempt to save, 643–644, 645–647; *Journey to the East* and demise of, 595–598

"Boyhood" (Hesse), 43

Braun, Felix, 671, 678

Brazil, Hesse and, 114, 183

Brecht, Bertolt, 211, 339, 424, 628, 636, 690, 707

Breker, Arno, 686

Brentano, Clemens, 334

Bright Night (Hennings), 488

Bronnen, Arnolt, 88–89, 256, 339

Brotherhood, Hesse and, 229

Brothers Karamazov, The (Dostoyevsky), 361, 428

"Brothers Karamazov or the Decline of Europe, The" (Hesse), 366–367

Brown, Charles, 487

Bruckner, Ferdinand, 255

Bruder, Erhard, 693

Bruell, Jan H., 670

Brümmer, Franz, 235

"Bruno Book" (Hesse), 242–243

Buber, Martin, 317

"Bücher-Ausklopfen" (Hesse), 318

Buddenbrooks (Mann), 249–250

Buddha, *Siddhartha* and, 429, 440

Buddhism: Hesse and, 288, 445; at Monte Verità, 277

Bund, Der (newspaper), 672

Bunsen, Olga, 36

Burckhardt, Jacob, 161, 183, 190

Busse, Carl, 196, 198, 199, 211

Butterflies, Hesse and, 289–292

Byzantine Christianity (Ball), 485, 487, 488–489, 490, 519, 534–535, 569

Cabaret Voltaire, 480–481

Calderón, Pedro, 3

Call of Roland, The (Johst), 339

Calw: adult stays in, 81–82, 108–109, 230–232; childhood in, 51–56; as symbol in Hesse's writing, 42–45

"Calw Diary" (Hesse), 43, 52–53

Calw Publishing Union, 22, 26, 31, 105, 318

Cannstatt, Hermann at high school in, 99–108

"Canticle of Brother Sun and Sister Moon," 214

Carona, excursion to, 409, 410

Carossa, Hans, 698

Casa Camuzzi (Montagnola): Ball on, 411–412; fate of, 722; Hesse at, 377, 385–386, 394–397, 545, 558; photo of, 396

Casanova, Hesse as spa guest and, 494

"Casanova: A Study in Self-Portraiture" (Zweig), 494

Casanova's Conversion (Zweig), 494

Casa Rossa (Montagnola): after Ninon's death, 721–722; Hesse and Ninon at, 1, 559–565, 616–617, 700–701; Ninon's management of household at, 562–564, 616–617, 702–704; photo of, 560; regulation of Hesse's daily life at, 700–701; view from, 663

Catcher in the Rye (Salinger), 541

Cats, Hesse's, 701

Century of the Child, The (Key), 252

Ceylon, Hesse's journey to, 287–288

Chairos, 440

Chamberlain, Houston Stewart, 284

Change theme, 70

Chaos, Dostoyevsky and gazing into, 353, 355, 407, 422

Chaplin, Charlie, 268, 392–393

Chastity, Pietist neurosis about, 138

Cherubinic Wanderer, The (Silesius), 652

"Cherubinic wanderer," Knulp and, 270–271

Chesterton, G. K., 228

Chicherin, Georgi, 425

Childhood, Hesse's, 15–17; Hesse characterized as difficult child, 40–41; Hesse delving far back into, 388–390; as idyll and abyss, 51; as imaginary realm for Hesse, 41–42; "Journal to Nuremberg" and Hesse's, 501–502; "Kinderseele" and, 374–377; purpose of writing and, 90–93; recollections of after mother's death, 247

Childhood and Youth Before 1900 (N. Hesse), 20

"Childhood of the Magician, The" (Hesse), 23, 30, 50–51, 90–91, 388, 389–390, 636

Children, treatment of in German Second Empire, 50–51

Child-soul, 11, 90; in *Beneath the Wheel*, 230, 247–260; discovery of, 166; "Kinderseele" and, 374–377; in *Peter Camenzind* (Hesse), 214; as theme in Hesse's writing, 43, 324

"Child's Soul (Hesse), A," 58–59, 61

Chopin, Frédéric, 173–176; Funeral March movement, 175–176; "Grande Valse," 174–175; Hesse's poem on, 132, 135; as role model for Hesse, 116, 122

Chronik der Sperlingsgasse, Die (Raabe), 304, 305

Chronos, 440

Church, *Journey to the East* and history of the, 593–594

Cicerone, The (Burkhardt), 190

Cioran, Emil, 439

Civilization, Hesse's concerns for in time of war, 309

Clairvoyance, Hesse and, 333–334

Clocks, Hermann and, 109–112, 654–657

Cloud metaphor: for Elisabeth La Roche, 168–169, 170; *Peter Camenzind* and, 206–207

Collected Works (Hesse), 3, 13, 213, 221

Color: Hesse and use of, 388, 393–394; memory and, 262–263

Communism: art and, 424, 607; Hesse and, 601–602, 603, 604–606, 709–711

Communist Party, writers and, 424

Comrade without Eyelashes, The (d'Annunzio), 153–154

Concentration camp, Suhrkamp in, 686

"Confessing Church," 649

"Confession of a Poet" (Hesse), 602

Confessions of an English Opium Eater (De Quincey), 539

Conrad, Joseph, 147

Contemporary age, *Wandering* as picture of, 379–380

"Conversation with a Stove" (Hesse), 396–397

Cosmic humor, Goethe and, 182–183

Counterculture: Hesse as figurehead of in early twentieth century, 220; Hesse's popularity with American, 6–7, 10–11, 220, 537–542

Courths-Mahler, Hedwig, 8

"Creaking of a Bent Branch" (Hesse), 600, 716, 721

Creative ecstasy, in *Steppenwolf*, 540

Crisis: Hesse as author of, 11–12, 130; *Rosshalde* and, 297–298; *Siddhartha* and, 423, 426, 429–430, 435, 437, 485; *Steppenwolf* and, 420, 511, 514, 516–517, 532; *Wandering* and, 379

"Crisis—A Diary Fragment" (Hesse), 532–533

"Crisis" poems (Hesse), 523, 529–530, 599

Criticism of Knulp, 269–270

Curtius, Ernst Robert, 7

Dadaist movement, Ball and Hennings and, 480–481

Damaschke, Adolf, 316

D'Annunzio, Gabriele, 122, 153–154

David Livingstone (M. Hesse), 40

"Dealing with Books" (Hesse), 5

Death: Hesse and allure of, 101–102; Hesse approaching, 714–718; Narcissus and Goldmund and, 579, 580, 581, 582

Death in Venice (Mann), 256

Death mask, Hesse's, 717

Decameron (Boccaccio), 226–227

"Declaration of Aryan Heritage," 630, 631

Decline of the West, The (Spengler), 286, 363–364

Decline of the West, Vivos voco as forum for discussing, 424

Delaune, Étienne, 548

Demian (Hesse), 326–333; Abraxas and, 328, 330, 331, 332–333, 338; as bridge to Klingsor's Last Summer, 365; childhood and, 90; dream interpretation and, 166; fire motif in, 163; first description of Max Demian in, 344; Hesse as modernism's myth-maker in, 342; identity of Demian, 328–329; Magic Theater and, 343–344; reviews of, 339; significance of for Hesse, 332; spiritual concerns and, 320; symbiosis of art and psychoanalysis in, 346; Zweig on, 219

Demons (Dostoyevsky), 360

Depression: Hesse's, 3, 141–142, 211, 418, 498, 515, 564, 680; Maria Bernoulli's, 302; Ninon and, 564

De Quincey, Thomas, 539

Deschner, Karlheinz, 10

Deutsches Dichterheim (journal), 44, 132, 135, 599

Diary 1900 (Hesse), 177–178

"Diary Jottings 1955" (Hesse), 718

"Diary of Psychoanalysis" (Hesse), 373

"Diary of the Journey to Indonesia" (Hesse), 286

Diederichs, Eugen, 139, 148, 149, 151–152, 162, 163, 198

Dietze, Heinrich, 669

Discipline, Hesse learning, 110

Divorces: from Mia, 333, 454–455, 456; from Ruth Wenger, 525

Dix, Otto, 530

Döblin, Alfred, 442

Doctor Faustus (Mann), 301, 541, 639, 644

"Doctor Knölge's Demise" (Hesse), 277

Dolbin, Fred, 548, 551–552, 553, 559, 561, 563, 704

Dolbin, Ninon (née Ausländer), 284, 468, 510, 543–553; association between love and death in Hesse, 581; blocking publication of Ruth Wenger's correspondence with Hesse, 450; blossoming of Hesse's relationship with, 524–525, 534; correspondence with Hesse, 543–544, 545–550, 553; daily walks with Hesse, 716; death of, 718–719; editing Hesse's unpublished works, 717–718; first marriage, 548, 551–552, 553, 561; on Hesse family history, 20; on Hesse's intensity, 715; Hesse's reluctance to marry, 551–553; as Hesse's secretary, 555–556, 558, 561; Hesse's treatment of, 565–566; horoscope, 551;

Jewish family of, 544–545; knowledge of Hesse's works, 557–558; living arrangements with Hesse, 554–555; Maass and, 698–699; management of Casa Rossa household and, 562–564, 616–617, 702–704; marriage to Hesse, 558–567, 620–622, 698–699; as moderator of outside world for Hesse, 566–567; Nazism and Hesse's marriage to, 612; need for outlets for creative urges, 699–700, 704–705; photos of, 549, 556, 708; trying to tame Hesse, 553–558; visit to Arosa with Hesse, 555–557; vote for Suhrkamp and, 690; watch over Hesse in old age, 706

Dolbin, Toka, 705

Doppelgänger motif, 13, 65, 219, 499; in *Hermann Lauscher,* 177; in *Klein and Wagner,* 398; Nietzsche and Hesse's, 297; in *Steppenwolf,* 511

Dostoyevsky, Fyodor: Europe and, 360–362; Hesse and, 353, 355, 362–367; *Klein and Wagner* and, 400; mock execution of, 356, 686; in Siberia, 356–357; Slavophilia and, 358–359, 360, 361; view of history, 358

Dostoyevsky, Mikhail, 356, 358

The Double (Dostoyevsky), 398

"Dream Diary of Psychoanalysis" (Hesse), 321, 387, 392, 476, 481

"Dream Gift, A" (Hesse), 697

Dream of a Ridiculous Man (Dostoyevsky), 400

Dreams, analysis with Lang and, 325–326

Drehdichum, 179

Dr. Jekyll and Mr. Hyde (Stevenson), 398

Drug use, *Steppenwolf* and, 538–540

Drunkenness, Hesse and, 523–524

Dubois, Julie, 24–26

Dystopia, in utopia, 97–98

"Early Spring" (Hesse), 268

East Germany, Hesse and, 10, 707–709

Ecce Homo (Nietzsche), 83

Eckermann, John Peter, 320

Education: *Beneath the Wheel* and, 247–249; in Göppingen for schooling, 55–58; Hesse as autodidact, 112–113, 115–116, 120–125, 180–183; Hesse at monastery, 64–73; Hesse's high school education, 99–108; Hesse's preoccupation with ideal, 12, 567–568; link with play in *The Glass Bead Game,* 650–651

Eichendorff, Joseph von, 100, 165, 191, 206, 263, 660

"Ein Dichter Sein" (Hesse), 132

Eisner, Kurt, 365

Eliot, T. S., 690

Elites: in *The Glass Bead Game,* 436, 640, 646–647, 648, 649; in *Journey to the East,* 593, 595, 597

Émigrés from Nazi Germany: attacks on Hesse, 627–628; continued criticism of Hesse after war, 695; Hesse on, 645

Emmerich, Katharina, 334

Employment: at Heckenhauer's bookshop, 115–116, 117, 119–120, 137, 149; at Reich's bookshop, 149, 158–162; at Wattenwyl antiquarian bookshop, 198, 230

Encyclopedia of German Poets and Prose Writers (Brümmer), Hesse entry, 235

"End, The" (Hesse), 268, 528–529

End state, Hesse and discovery of, 91–92

Englert, Joseph, 419, 487; astrology and, 91, 334, 336, 474; Ball and, 535; Hesse's letters to, 602, 620; *Journey to the East* and, 594, 596; Steiner and, 348

Eros, 101–102; *Narcissus and Goldmund* and, 575, 580

Erotic fantasies, Hesse's, 150

Eroticism: in *Demian,* 331, 332; Elisabeth
     La Roche as symbol of, 169; of
     friendship, 575–576; Hesse's own, 512;
     Hesse's relationship with Ruth Wenger
     and, 451–453; in Hesse's writing, 137;
     in *Klingsor's Last Summer,* 408–410; of
     music in *Gertrud,* 277–285; in *Steppen-
     wolf,* 511–512, 522–523, 533; of travel
     for Hesse, 501
Esotericism, Hesse and, 333–338, 345,
     348–349, 350
Estheticism, Hesse and, 153
Esthetic Theory (Adorno), 174
Euphoria, Hesse and, 141
Europe: Dostoyevsky and, 360–362;
     Hesse and vision of, 611
Europe (magazine), 660
"Evening with the Author, An" (Hesse),
     504–505
Evola, Julius, 340
Exorcism: Ball and, 483, 514; Hesse's
     parents and, 338
Expressionism, Hesse and, 13
Extramarital affairs, Hesse's, 550, 551
Extremisms, Magic Theater and,
     531–532

Faber, Otto Erich, 142, 143
Fairy-tale logic: as esthetic defense against
     the world, 170–171; in Hesse's writing,
     91–92
"Fairy Tale of a Wicker Chair" (Hesse),
     387–388
Fairy tales: Hesse and, 4, 324–325, 337;
     Klingsor's Last Summer and, 416
Faith, "Trees" as Hesse's profession of,
     384–385
Fame, Hesse on, 302–306
"Farewell, Lady World!" (Hesse), 717–718
Faustian man, 658, 661
Feuchtwanger, Lion, 707

Feuerbach, Ludwig, 29
"Few Reminiscences about Doctors, A"
     (Hesse), 22
Finckh, Ludwig, 608; as German
     nationalist, 447; on Hesse in Gaien-
     hofen, 235; Hesse's relationship with,
     691–697; Julie Hellmann and, 150, 167;
     as neighbor in Gaienhofen, 241, 243;
     Peter Camenzind and, 206; *petit cénacle*
     and, 140–141, 142–143, 691; photo of,
     143; review of *Romantic Songs,* 137
Fire: Hesse's fascination with, 2–3, 59–64,
     375–376, 656; at Maulbronn monastery,
     61–64; as medium of life in Hesse's
     writing, 216; in "New Romanticism,"
     163–164; water *vs.,* 59. *See also*
     Pyromaniac tendencies, Hesse's
Firework, Hesse's injury from, 63–64
"First Dada Evening," 480
Fischer, Samuel, 211; death of, 615, 682;
     Demian and, 326; Hesse on, 204–205;
     Hesse's clash with, 288; Hesse's contract
     with, 278–279; Hesse's instruction to
     regarding unpublished manuscripts,
     404; on *Peter Camenzind,* 217; *Steppen-
     wolf* and, 521; Suhrkamp and, 680, 681.
     See also S. Fischer Verlag
Flake, Otto, 326
Flametti or the Dandyism of the Poor (Ball),
     480
Flatt, Jeremias, 23
Fleckhaus, Willy, 714
"Flight Out of Time" (Ball), 479, 483
Florence, Hesse in, 190–191, 223
Flute Dream (Hesse), 340–341
Four Books of True Christianity, The
     (Arndt), 651–652
"Fourth Life of Josef Knecht, The"
     (Hesse), 619
Franciscan ideal, Hesse and, 213–214, 215
Frank, Leonhard, 308

Franz von Assisi und die Anfänge der Kunst der Renaissance in Italien (Thode), 229

Freedman, Ralph, 415, 444, 565

"Freedom from National Sentiment?" (Huch), 668–669

Fretz & Wasmuth (publisher), 654, 680

Freud, Sigmund, 331, 415, 547

Friends: circle of, in Tübingen, 120–122, 140–144, 149–150

Friendship: in *Beneath the Wheel,* 255–257; in *Narcissus and Goldmund,* 575–576, 581

Frisch, Max, 682, 690

Fromm, Erich, 353

"From My School Days" (Hesse), 57

From the Life of a Good-for-Nothing (Eichendorff), 191

Fühmann, Franz, 640

Fulda, Ludwig, 585

Funeral March: Memorial Sheet for a Young Comrade (Hesse), 175–176

Gaienhofen: Hesse as family man in, 235–243; sale of house in, 515

Games in the Family Circle (J. Hesse), 31

Garden of Eden, 468, 470

Garden of Paradise (Arndt), 652

Gardens, Hesse and, 466–472, 564, 700, 704

Gassner, Philipp, 372

Gauguin, Paul, 274

"Gazing into chaos," 353, 355, 407, 422

Gazing into Chaos (Hesse), 363

The Genius of War and the German War (Scheler), 312

Genoa, Hesse in, 190, 223

George, Henry, 316

George, Stefan, 154, 177

Gerbersau, fictional name for Calw, 43

"Gerbersau" stories (Hesse), 65, 247

German character/spirit, Hesse on, 355, 503, 607–616

"German Letter on Literature" (Hesse), 624–625

German Literature Archive, Hesse's papers at, 719

German nationalism, Hesse and, 157, 369–372, 421, 665–671

German nationalists, antipathy for Hesse, 369–371, 381, 447–448, 613–614, 625–626

Germany: devaluation of Hesse's property in, 514–515; Hesse on blacklist in American zone of occupation, 671–675; Hesse's ambivalent relationship with, 9, 311–313, 413–414; Hesse's and two Germanies, 706–708; Hesse's distancing from, 448–449; reaction to "Zarathustra's Return" in, 352. *See also* Nazi Germany; Weimar Republic

Geroe-Tobler, Maria, 702

Gertrud (Hesse), 169, 277–285; criticism of, 280–281, 283; as self-portrait, 279

Gide, André, 9, 617, 722

The Glass Bead Game (Hesse): attempt to publish in Germany, 649, 653–654, 680; chapters published in *Bonniers Litterära Magasin,* 624; clocks and rules of game in, 111; criticism of journalistic age in, 571; critique of "Age of the Feuilleton" in, 643–654; early steps toward, 163–167; elite and, 436, 640, 646–647, 648, 649; European Nirvana and, 429; goal of, 639; Hesse on what Glass Bead Game actually was, 642–643; Hesse's debt to Goethe and, 658–661; Hesse's knowledge of significance of, 563; *Homo ludens* in, 650–651; imagining future in, 8–9; inward path of, 652–653; *Journey to the East* and, 592, 596–597; Jünger and, 657; knowledge in, 642, 646–647, 670; lead-up to, 637–643; *Looking Backward*

The Glass Bead Game (Hesse) (*continued*)
and, 96–98; Maeterlinck and, 641–642;
Magic Theater and, 638; monastic
principle and, 569; music and, 651;
mysticism and, 490; as Platonic dream,
619; quasi-cosmological perspective
and, 609; recapitulation of Hesse's life
in, 24; science fiction setting for, 640;
spirituality in, 648–649, 650; supraindividual perspective in, 516; theme of
terminal decline in, 647–648; writing,
618–619, 622
The Glass Rings (Rinser), 670
Glauser, Richard, 481
Gnosticism: *Demian* and, 330; Hesse and,
350; Lang and, 324
Gnostic motif of two kingdoms, 511
"Goat-Song Rising" (Strauss), 353
God: Dostoyevsky and question of, 360;
immanence in every living thing, 384
The Goddesses (H. Mann), 233
Goebbels, Joseph, 627, 630
Goethe, Johann Wolfgang von, 639;
Demian and, 329; Hesse and, 658–664;
Hesse reading, 107; Hesse's admiration
for, 111, 112, 116, 121, 122–123,
181–183; inner harmony and, 3; Steiner
and, 347–348; on xenophobia, 320
"Goethe and Bettina" (Hesse), 661–662
"Goethe and Nationalism," 663–664
Goethe Prize awarded to Hesse, 1, 676,
677–678, 689
Golden Pot, The (Hoffmann), 407, 596
Goldschmidt, Hermann Levin, 635
Goldziher, Ignaz, 284
Good Soldier Švejk, The (Hašek), 269
Göppigen, Hesse in, 56–58
Gottfried, Gustav, 129
Goya, Francisco, 138
"Grande Valse" (Hesse), 135, 174–175
Gräser, Gusto, 328

Grass, Günter, 10
"Gratitude to Goethe" (Hesse), 660
"Great Mother" myth, 332
Grosz, Georg, 530
Groves, Anton Norris, 24
Grüne Heinrich, Der (Keller), 205
Gruppe 47, 9
Guerrilla fighter, in *Steppenwolf,* 530–531
Guessing Games (J. Hesse), 31
Guest at the Spa, A (Hesse), 123, 385, 491,
497–500; Palmenwald spa hotel and,
125–131; *Psychologia Balnearia* and, 461;
Steppenwolf and, 519–520
Gunddrum, Maria, 222–223
Gundert, Christine Louise (Ensslin), 23
Gundert, David, 73, 76
Gundert, Emma, 55
Gundert, Fritz, 633
Gundert, Henrietta, 52
Gundert, Hermann (grandfather), 16, 18,
22–26, 700; death of, 105; on Eugenie
Kolb, 79; on Herman Hesse's schooling,
57; on Hermann and fire, 60; on
Hermann's nervous disposition, 64–65;
on Hermann's return to Calw after stay
at Stetten, 81–82; on Hermann's time at
Maulbronn, 66, 67; on Johannes's
nervous breakdown, 55; library of,
112–113; Marie Hesse and, 33;
relationship with Herman Hesse, 48,
49–50; return of Hesse family to Calw
and, 51–52
Gundert, Julie (Dubois), 24–26, 32, 45, 52
Gundert, Marie, 25, 26
Gundert, Wilhelm, 432, 696
Gundert family, Pietism and, 16

Haas, Willy, 7
Habe, Hans, 8, 671–675
Haeckel, Ernst, 307
Haines, Fred, 541, 542

Hammelehle, Carlo, 140, 141, 142, 143

Hamsun, Kurt, 303

Handke, Peter, 9

Handwritten manuscripts, Hesse's skill at producing, 184

Hartmann, Otto, 296, 574–575

Hašek, Jaroslav, 269

Hate campaigns against Hesse by German nationalists, 369, 447–448, 613–614, 625–626

"Hate Mail" (Hesse), 370–371

Hauptmann, Gerhart, 116, 307, 629, 695

Hausmann, Manfred, 685

Haussmann, Conrad, 283, 294, 310

Haussmann, Erich, 450

Health and sickness, Hesse's relationship with, 101, 241, 403–404, 407–408, 461

Heart defect, Hermann diagnosed with, 101

Heart of Darkness (Conrad), 147

Heathens and Us, The (J. Hesse), 31, 198

Heaven and Earth (Finckh), 696

Heckenhauer's Antiquarian Bookshop, 115–120, 137, 149

Hees, Walter, 613

Hegel, G. W. F., 357–358, 430, 643

Heimann, Moritz, 204

Heine, Heinrich, 101, 106, 107, 108, 112–113, 165, 671

Heinrich von Ofterdingen (Novalis), 166, 331, 406, 407

Hellmann, Julie, 142, 150, 167, 169, 179

Hennings, Annemarie, 480, 488, 537

Hennings, Emmy, 431, 432, 458, 528; background of, 479–481; bond with Ball, 477–478; death of Ball and, 535, 536, 537; Hesse and, 473–479, 565; on *Klingsor's Last Summer*, 418–419; move back to Ticino, 488; move to Munich, 487–488; Ninon and, 560; photo of, 478. *See also* Ball, Hugo

Hennings, Joseph-Paul, 480

Heraclitus, 429, 440

Herman Hesse in Eyewitness Accounts, 450

"Hermann Hesse and the American Subculture" (Haines), 542

Hermann Hesse Prize, 637

"Hermann Hesse's Journey" (Zweig), 219

Hermann Lauscher (Hesse), 41–42, 176–180; doppelgänger motif in, 65; Fischer publishing house and, 204; Hesse's relationships with women and, 168–169; Julie Hellmann and, 150; *petit cénacle* and, 141, 142–143; success of, 169

Hermes, as archetype of writers, 117

"Herr Claassen" (Hesse), 47–48, 63

Hesse, Adele (sister), 40, 41, 55, 60; correspondence with, 301, 302, 425, 460, 492–493, 601, 609, 633; on Hermann at high school, 104–105; Hermann's obituary of, 700; photos of, 53, 112

Hesse, Agathe, 20

Hesse, Bruno (son), 2, 302, 373, 491, 597, 701; birth of, 238; "Bruno Book," 242–243; father's Nobel Prize and, 676; photos of, 242, 370

Hesse, Carl Hermann (grandfather), 16, 19–22, 30

Hesse, David, 698

Hesse, Hans (brother), 65, 160, 198, 496–497; *Beneath the Wheel* and, 251–253; photos of, 53, 112; suicide of, 632–633

Hesse, Heiner (son), 28, 298, 322, 420, 491, 653, 722; birth of, 241; on brother Martin, 701; communism and, 601, 603, 605, 612, 702; Finckh and, 696–697; photos of, 242, 699; relationship with father, 701–702

Hesse, Hermann: on answering question why he wrote, 12; caricature of Hesse as gardener, 465; daily life in old age, 697–711; death of, 716–717; eighty-fifth birthday, 715–716; photo of 1889, 53; photo of 1898, 134; photo of around time writing *The Glass Bead Game*, 590; photo of as naked rock-climber in 1910, 172; photo of at age four, 48; photo of at Arosa, 556, 557; photo of before outbreak of World War I, 308; photo of from 1895, 115; photo of from 1899, 112; photo of from walk in Ticino region, 389; photo of Hesse on walk near Carona, 409; photo of in 1925, 502; photo of on verandah of Am Erlenlob at Gaienhofen, 237; photo of while mountaineering, 370; photo of with Ball and Hennings, 478; photo of with glass of wine in 1910, 233; photo of with grandson David, 698; photo of with *petit cénacle*, 143; photo of with wife Ninon, 708; photo with Ruth Wenger ca. 1920, 454; portrait of, 374; sketch of by Gunter Böhmer, 618

Hesse, Jenny (grandmother), 20

Hesse, Johannes (father), 18, 20, 25, 28–32, 39–40; in Basel, 45–46; biography of Hermann Gundert, 26; death of, 321, 323–324, 325; Hermann at Stetten and, 77–79, 81–85, 86–87, 93–94; Hermann missing from Maulbronn and, 71, 72; Hermann's relationship with, 31–32, 48–50, 125, 485–486; instructions to son, 103, 104, 118; letter to Hermann stating end of son's studies, 88; living in father-in law's home, 54–55; marriage to Marie, 39–40; nervous breakdown of, 55; photos of, 18, 53, 112, 322; response to *An Hour Behind Midnight,* 152

Hesse, Klara, 2

Hesse, Marie (mother), 18, 32–40; in Basel, 46; biography of Livingstone and, 144–147; childhood of, 33–37; criticism of son's poetry, 137–139; death of, 198–199; on disappointment with son Hermann, 64; frustrations with son Hermann, 48–50; Hermann asking forgiveness from, 98–99; Hermann at Stetten and, 80–81, 82–83; Hermann missing from Maulbronn and, 69; on Hermann returning to Basel, 94; illnesses of, 109, 197–198; letters to son about family matters, 198; living with father in Calw, 54; marriage to Johann Hesse, 39–40; photos of, 38, 53, 112; Pietism and, 47–48; poems of, 38–39; relationship with Hermann, 32–33, 40, 124–125, 131–135, 633; on removing Hermann from Maulbronn, 73; response to *An Hour Behind Midnight,* 152–153; response to Hermann's running away from Bad Boll, 76; return to Calw and, 52; taking Hermann to Maulbronn, 66; visit to Hermann in Cannstatt, 100, 101

Hesse, Martin (son), 2, 49, 491, 560; birth of, 241, 286, 298; communism and, 603; defense of father in press, 672; father's Nobel Prize and, 676; Hermann Hesse's dislike of, 298; illness of, 298, 301–302; mother's strangulation of, 322; photo of, 299; photos of father, 701

Hesse, Marulla (sister), 41, 124, 163, 229, 624, 700; photos of, 53, 112

Hesse, Sibylle, 2

Hesse family, photos of, 53, 112

Hesse Illustrated Biography (Zeller), 714

Hesse, Renaissance of in 1960s, 6–7, 10–11

Heuss, Theodor, 281, 311

Heydt, Eduard von der, 272

Heym, Georg, Hesse on, 13

Himmel und Erde (Finckh), 141

Himmler, Heinrich, 613

Hippies, Hesse and, 6–7, 10–11, 537–542

History, Dostoyevsky's view of, 358

History and Description of Mystical Theology (Arnold), 652

History of the City of Basel (Wackernagel), 163

Hitler, Adolf, 513–514; Finckh's support for, 691, 692, 693; Hesse on, 608–609

Hodler, Ferdinand, 309

Hoffmann, E. T. A., 142, 163, 177, 356, 407, 508, 596, 640

Hoffmann, Ida, 273

Hofmannsthal, Hugo von, 177, 443

Hölderin, Friedrich, 97, 326, 643

Homesickness, as theme of Hesse's later writing, 239

Homoerotic tendency, in Hesse, 475–476

Homo ludens, 650–651

Homosexuality, in Hesse's writing, 256

Horoscopes: for Hesse, 91, 334; for Ninon, 551

Hotel Kraft (Basel), Hesse at, 459–461

Hour Behind Midnight, An (Hesse), 151–155, 164, 177, 198, 408; parents' response to, 152–153; reviews of, 154–155

"Hours at My Writing Desk" (Hesse), 386

"Hours in the Garden" (Hesse), 59

"House letters," between Ninon and Hesse, 553–554, 557, 621, 703

House of Life, The (Rossetti), 162

How I Found Livingstone (Stanley), 144

Huch, Ricarda, 629, 666, 668–669

Huelsenbeck, Richard, 480

Human, All Too Human (Nietzsche), 5

Human contact, Hesse as contact-phobic, 140, 491

Humm, Rudolf Jakob, 623

Humor in "Journey to Nuremberg," 506

Hunnius, Monika, 21

Huppenbacher, David, 128

Huxley, Aldous, 532

Hyperion (Hölderin), 97

Hypnosis, Johannes Hesse on, 67–68

Identity, in *Demian,* 329–330

Ideology, Hesse on, 707

Idiot, The (Dostoyevsky), 364–365, 510, 515

"If the War Lasts for Another Five Years" (Hesse), 371–373

"If the War Lasts for Another Two Years" (Hesse), 371–372

Ilg, Paul, 200, 204

Imitation of Christ, The (Thomas à Kempis), 652

Impartial History of the Church and of Heresy, An (Arnold), 181, 413, 593, 652

Incest motif, in *Steppenwolf,* 533

India: Hermann Gundert and, 22, 24, 26; Hesse's journey to, 286–289, 292; Hesse's picture of, 423–424; Hesse's relationship to, 443–445; Marie Hesse and, 33–34, 37

"Indian Butterflies" (Hesse), 289, 291

Indian myth, *Siddhartha* and, 421

Indien, Aus (Hesse), 287, 289

Individuality, Hermann learning to conceal self from world to preserve, 87

Individuation in *Beneath the Wheel,* 249–250

Indonesia, Hesse's journey to, 287

"In Memory of Adele" (Hesse), 700

"In Memory of S. Fischer" (Hesse), 204–205

Inner harmony, Hesse and, 3

Inner life, Hesse's path inward, 353–355

Inner voice, Hesse and listening to, 380–381

Inner world, Hesse writing about, 337

"In Remembrance of Hans" (Hesse), 251–252

"In Remembrance of Knulp" (Hesse), 268

Insanity, Hermann and diagnosis of primary, 93

Intellectual: existence of in increasingly mechanized world, 250–251; soul biography of modern, 519; transforming into sensory, 386–387

International Women's League for Freedom and Peace, 445

"In the Fog" (Hesse), 720–721

"In the Garden" (Hesse), 469

In the Mine (Fühmann), 640

"In the Mist" (Hesse), 600

"In the Old Sun" (Hesse), 264–265

"In the Penal Colony" (Kafka), 275

Inwardness, shift to in Hesse's writing, 327–328

"Iris" (Hesse), 300

Isenberg, Carlo, 595, 612–613

Isenberg, Charles, 39, 94

Isenberg, Karl, 39, 64, 72, 104, 105, 106, 109, 258–259, 612; as musician, 94–95; nervous breakdown, 197–198

Isenberg, Marie, 613

Isenberg, Theodor, 39, 76, 77, 94–95, 105–106, 160

Island motif, 138, 153

Isle of the Dead (Böcklin), 116, 161

Italian Journey (Goethe), 189

Italy: Hesse's first journey to, 184–196; second trip to, 221–224

Jacobsen, Jens Peter, 122, 123–124, 162, 166

Janka, Walter, 707–708

Jazz, as rhythm of modern life, 520–521

Jazz Singer, The (film), 520

Jews: anti-Semitism, 283–284, 616; Narcissus and Goldmund and, 579

Joachim of Fiore, 648–649

Johnson, Uwe, 10

Johst, Hanns, 339, 615

Jolson, Al, 520

Joseph and His Brothers (Mann), 619–620

Journal de Genève, 309

Journalism, Hesse and, 209, 571–572

"Journey to Nuremberg" (Hesse), 501–510

Journey to the East (Hesse), 436, 516, 591–598; demise of bourgeois world and, 595–598; The Glass Bead Game and, 592, 596–597; history of the Church and, 593–594; monastic principle and, 569

Joyce, James, 522

Judas tree, 385–386, 396

Jung, Carl, 324, 331, 337, 345, 389, 434–435, 482

Jünger, Ernst, 221, 314, 338, 638, 655–657, 674

Jungk, Robert, 8, 635

Kafka, Franz, 12, 275, 541, 625

Kaiser, Joachim, 9

"Kandy Diary Entry" (Hesse), 288

Kant, Immanuel, 29

Kapff, Ernst, 114

Kappeler, Berthli, 444–445

Kasack, Hermann, 686

Kassner, Rudolf, 162

Kästner, Erich, 629, 666, 675

Keller, Gottfried, 205, 208, 254, 303, 318, 589

Kerényi, Karl, 655, 706, 721–722

Kerner, Justinus, 333

Kerr, Alfred, 7

Key, Ellen, 252

"Kinderseele" (Hesse), 245, 374–377, 404

Kisch, Egon Erwin, 645

Kissinger, Henry, 713

Kläber, Kurt, 611–612

Klabund, 417–418

Klein and Wagner (Hesse), 330, 362, 404; suicide in, 398–402

Kleine, Gisela, 565

Klingsor's Last Summer (Hesse), 363, 398, 399, 402–420; astrologer in, 417–418; Ball's interpretation of, 414; bridge from *Demian* to, 365; Casa Camuzzi and, 411–412; as centerpiece of Hesse's work, 415–416, 417; eroticism in, 408–410; fantasies in, 412–413; letter writing in, 20; Li Tae Pe figure in, 417–418; "The Painter" and, 410–411; psychoanalysis and, 415; Romanticism and, 405, 411; Ruth Wenger and, 449; spiritual source of, 405–406; Van Gogh and, 414, 415; Zweig on, 219

Knapp, Albert, 37

Knowledge, *The Glass Bead Game* and, 642, 646–647, 670

The Knowledgeable Playmate (book), 63

Knulp (Hesse), 264–265; "Tales about Quorm" and, 265–272. *See also* "Journey to Nuremberg" (Hesse)

Kokain (Rheiner), 539–540

Kolb, Annette, 467, 627, 628

Kolb, Eugenie, 77, 79–80

Kolbenheyer, E. G., 586, 588, 615

Kölner Tageblatt (newspaper), 311

"Konigskind" (Hesse), 138

Korntal Brethren, 31, 36–37

Korrodi, Eduard, 327

Kraus, Karl, 548, 673

Kreidler, Horst Dieter, 532

Kubin, Alfred, 138, 275, 390, 594, 635

"Kunst des Müßiggangs: Ein Kapitel künstlerischer Hygiene, Die" (Hesse), 232

"Lake Constance Memoir" (Hesse), 237–238

Landauer, Gustav, 489–490, 573

Landmann, Robert, 272–273

Land Reform (Damaschke), 316

Lang, Josef Bernhard (J. B.): Ball's funeral and, 535; in *Demian,* 332; esotericism and, 335–336; etching of, 323; hedonism and, 528; Hesse exchanging roles with, 340–347; Hesse's decision to leave family and, 300–301; Hesse's diary about treatment with, 387; Hesse's discussions of sex life with, 364, 451; Hesse's divorce from Mia and, 333; Hesse's early therapy with, 324–326; horoscope for Ninon and, 551; on identity of Demian, 328–329; Jung and, 434; letter to Hesse, 284; Ruth Wenger and, 453; Steiner and, 348, 349

Lang, Wilhelm, 73

Langbehn, Julius, 352

Langen, Albert, 205, 279

Lao-Tse (J. Hesse), 31

La Roche, Elisabeth, 167–173, 198, 206, 280

Late Prose (Hesse), 690

"Late Summer Flowers" (Hesse), 393

Lauscher, Hermann (Hesse pseudonym), 162, 163; Hesse on posthumous writings of, 179–180

League of Proletarian Revolutionary Writers, 424

Leary, Timothy, 10, 538, 539, 542

Leavetaking (Weiss), 636–637

Dem Leben eines Taugenichts, Aus (Eichendorff), 165

Lechler, Paul, 128–130

Legends, Hesse and, 4, 424, 4250–4426
Leipzig Museum of the Book Trade, 200
Leonhardt, Rudolf Walter, 8
"Letter in May" (Hesse), 714–715, 722
Letters, Hesse's: to Andreae, 536; to Ball,
    458, 495–496, 524, 529; to Carlo
    Isenberg, 595; to Elisabeth La Roche,
    170–171; to Englert, 602, 620; with
    father, 88, 103, 104, 118, 152, 217; to
    Finckh, 447, 515, 608; to grandfather
    Gundert, 48; to Hartmann, 296; to
    Haussmann, 283–284, 294, 310; with
    Helen Voigt, 135–137, 147–149; to
    Heuss, 281; to Kappeler, 444–445; to
    Karl Isenberg, 258–259; to Kolb, 467;
    to Kreidler, 532; with Lang, 331,
    340–341, 343, 347, 400–401, 420, 453,
    455; to Leuthold, 423–424; to Lisa
    Wenger, 482; with Mann, 9–10, 614,
    615–616, 617, 618, 619–620, 626–627,
    629–630, 673; to Moillet, 410; to Molt,
    493; to Morgenthaler, 552; with
    mother, 98–99, 138–139, 152–153, 198;
    with Ninon Dolbin, 543–544,
    545–550, 553, 556; to parents, 66–69,
    74–75, 85–86, 93–94, 95, 104, 106–107,
    120–121, 126, 133, 134, 159–160, 161,
    173–174, 184–185, 314; to Paul Ilg,
    200–201; to Prussian Writer's
    Academy, 587; to Reinhart, 402, 425,
    448–449, 474, 498, 513; to Rinser,
    655–656; to Rolland, 319, 445, 446; to
    Ruth Wenger, 450–452; to Schädelin,
    463, 535; to Schlenker, 391; to
    Schrempf, 583–584; to Seelig,
    362–363, 431; to Seidel, 394; to sister
    Adele, 301, 302, 425, 460, 492–493,
    601, 609, 633; to son Bruno, 597; to
    son Heiner, 605, 653, 697; to son
    Martin, 654; to Stefan Zweig, 217–219,
    230, 234, 235; with Suhrkamp, 340,

675, 679; to Unseld, 715; to Wenger,
    364; to Wolff, 313; to Zweig, 298, 445,
    525–526
"Letters to Elisabeth" (Hesse), 185
"Letter to a Communist" (Hesse), 604
"Letter to a German Scholar" (Hesse),
    631–632
"Letter to a Wounded Soldier" (Hesse),
    315–316
Letterwriting: Hesse and Gundert
    families and, 20; Hesse's devotion to, 3,
    5, 416
Leukemia, Hesse's diagnosis of, 715
Leuthold, Alice, 423, 520
Leuthold, Fritz, 520, 605
Leybold, Hans, 479
"Library of World Literature, A" (Hesse),
    12, 318, 567–569, 631
Liebermann, Max, 307, 585
Lieder vom Leben (Hesse), 131–132
"Lied von der Erde" (Mahler), 700
Life, Journey to the East and the meaning
    of, 592–593
Life Is a Dream (Calderón), 3
Life of Jesus, The (Strauss), 23
Life of Saint Francis of Assisi (Sabatier), 229
Life of the Bee, The (Maeterlinck), 641
Life Story Briefly Told (Hesse): on alien-
    ation from Germans, 413; on begin-
    nings of art, 409; on being a writer,
    92–93; on childhood, 51; closing image
    of, 179; as conjectural biography, 90,
    91; effects of war and, 313–314; on life
    as outsider in Bern, 323; on magic, 337;
    on own sense of reality, 336; Steppen-
    wolf as reprise of, 513; on success of
    Camenzind, 233
LIT (Language of the Third Reich), 669
Li Tae Pe figure in Klingsor's Last Summer,
    417–418
"Little Songs" (Hesse), 79

Livingstone, David, 144–147

Loerke, Oskar, 326, 585–586

Loneliness: Hesse and lyricism of, 153; of Hesse in Tübingen, 120–121

Looking Backward (Bellamy), 96–98, 640

Lord Chandos Letter, The (Hofmannsthal), 443

"Lost Penknife, The" (Hesse), 470–472

Love: of Dolbin for Hesse, 549–550; Hesse and nature of, 172–173, 215–216, 278, 279–280; Hesse's for Eugenie Kolb, 77, 79–80; Hesse's phobia toward, 581–582; in *Peter Camenzind,* 214, 215–216; in *Siddhartha,* 437

Love's Heart (correspondence between Hesse and Wenger), 450

LSD, *Steppenwolf* and, 10, 538–539

Ludendorff, Erich von, 614

Ludendorff's Fortnightly (magazine), 614

Lukács, Georg, 601

"Lulu" (Hesse), 179, 180

Lustless love: in *Peter Camenzind,* 215; Saint Francis and, 229

Lyric poetry, Hesse on future of, 598

Maass, Joachim, 698–699

Maeterlinck, Maurice, 122, 153, 154, 162, 177, 641–642

Magic, as theme for Hesse, 336, 337

Magic Flute, The (Mozart), 394, 492, 520–521

"Magician, The" (Hesse), 90, 91, 92

Magic Mountain, The (Mann), 128, 607

"Magic of the Book, The" (Hesse), 569–572

Magic Theater, 529–534; art of the absurd and, 509; *Demian* and, 343–344; dreams and, 3; *The Glass Bead Game* and, 638; Leary's understanding of, 538; split personality in, 257–258; supraindividual perspective and, 516; transfor-mation into magic landscape of the soul, 583; women and, 410

Magnetism, Hesse and, 333–334

Magnus, Albertus, 647

Mahler, Gustav, 700

Maimonides, Moses, 625

Malte Laurids Brigge (Rilke), 154–155, 210

Manifesto of 93, 307, 309

Mann, Heinrich, 233, 308, 318, 586, 588–589, 707

Mann, Katia, 559, 561, 563

Mann, Klaus, 628

Mann, Thomas, 318, 573; *Buddenbrooks,* 249–250; correspondence with Hesse, 9–10, 614, 615–616, 617, 618, 619–620, 626–627, 629–630, 673; diaries of, 5; *Doctor Faustus,* 301, 541, 639, 644; East Germany and, 707; German character and, 503, 607–616; *The Glass Bead Game* and, 639–640; on Hans Habe, 673; on Hesse as antithesis of Greater Germany, 157; Hesse meeting, 233; Hesse's Nobel Prize and, 678; homosexuality and, 256; *The Magic Mountain,* 128, 607; move to Switzerland and then United States, 611–612; on *Narcissus and Goldmund,* 582–583; Nazi regime and, 609–610, 611; preoccupation with national identity, 625; Prussian Writer's Academy and, 586–587, 588–590; "secret of identity" and, 575; on *Steppenwolf,* 521–522; "Thoughts in Wartime," 307; *Tonio Kröger,* 171, 219, 250; war and, 312

Man of God, A (J. Hesse), 31

"Man with Many Books, The" (Hesse), 376–377

Markwalder, Franz Xaver, 495–496

Markwalder, Josef, 495

Marriage, *Rosshalde* and problem of the married artist, 297–302. *See also* Bernoulli, Maria (Mia); Dolbin, Ninon (Ausländer); Wenger, Ruth

Marti, Fritz, 445

März (magazine), 276, 279, 446

Matisse, Henri, 709

Matriarchy, Hesse and concept of, 607

Maulbronn: engraving of monastery seminary at, 86; fire at monastery in, 61–64; fountain in the cloisters at, 68; Hesse and monastery at, 58, 64–73; Hesse missing from, 69–72

Mauthner, Fritz, 483, 489, 573

May, Karl, 209

Mayer, Hans, 541, 707

Mayer, S., 108

Maync, Harry, 306

Mechanics, Hesse and, 109–112

"Media in vita" (Hesse), 442–443

Meier-Graefe, Julius, 361, 387–388, 404

Mein Kampf (Hitler), 513

Melancholy, Hesse and, 177

"Memories of Hans" (Hesse), 633

Memory: colors and, 262–263; "Schoolmate Martin" and, 243–246; visit with Raabe and, 305

Mental institution at Stetten, Hermann Hesse at, 76, 77–87, 93–94

Merkur (journal), 7

Mescaline, 539

Metamorphosis, Hesse's, 13–14

Metzner, Ralph, 538

Michelangelo's Nose (Ball), 479

Middell, Eike, 312, 442, 492

Milan, Hesse's disappointment in, 187, 189, 190

Military service, Hesse and, 160, 195, 306, 317

Miller, Henry, 9, 424

Mind, connection of sickness with, 493

Mines at Falun, The (Hoffmann), 640

Modern Times (film), 268, 392–393

Moilliet, Louis, 390, 399, 410

Molt, Emil, 349, 493, 509

Monastic principle, books and, 569–570

Money: Hesse's attitude toward, 703; income from book sales in Germany after World War II, 679, 683; issues for Hesse during Nazi regime, 615, 624; issues for Hesse during World War I, 373–374; Reinhart patronage and, 396, 481–482

Monograph, Hesse on form of, 5

"Monotonization of the World, The" (Zweig), 232

Mont, Emil, 487

Montagnola: daily life for Hesse during Nazi regime, 616–623; Hesse living in, 354, 377, 385; Hesse's move to, 296. *See also* Casa Camuzzi (Montagnola); Casa Rossa (Montagnola)

Monte Verità, 272–277

"Mood Pictures from Northern Italy" (Hesse), 187, 194–196

Moral insanity, 249; Hermann diagnosed with, 104, 108

Moravian Brethren, 173–174

Morgenthaler, Ernst, 390, 552

Mörike, Eduard, 75, 304–305

Moser, Erwin, 696

Mozart, Wolfgang Amadeus: Hesse's love of, 117, 175, 610, 715, 716; *The Magic Flute,* 394, 492, 520–521; in Magic Theater, 532, 533, 573

Muehlon, Johann Wilhelm, 366, 399

Mühsam, Erich, 7, 275

Müller, Georg, 205

Müller, Heiner, 65, 247

Münchhausen (Kästner), 629

Munich soviet republic, invitation for Hesse to join, 365–366

"Muse of sleeplessness," 173

Music: eroticism of, 277–285; *The Glass Bead Game* and, 651; Hesse's enjoyment of, 173–176, 715; Maria Bernoulli and, 231, 278; *Steppenwolf* and, 520–521

Musik des Einsamen (Hesse), 311

Musicology, Glass Bead Game and, 644

Musil, Robert, 7–8, 220–221, 256, 584–585

"My Friend Peter" (Hesse), 680

"My Horoscope" (Hesse), 91

"My Love and Marriage with Hermann Hesse" (Wenger), 450, 461–463

"My Mother" (Hesse), 32, 40

Mystical forms of expression, *The Glass Bead Game* and, 489–490

Mysticism: atheistic, 483; *Demian* and, 328; Hesse's pantheistic, 127, 130, 271–272, 721; words and, 567

Mysticism, Artists, and Life (Kassner), 162

Mystic union *(unio mystica)*, *Narcissus and Goldmund* and, 577, 584

Myth, Hesse and, 619–620

Mythical dimension of *Steppenwolf*, 537–542

Myth of the Twentieth Century, The (Rosenberg), 339, 619

Nag, Kalidas, 445

Narcissus and Goldmund (Hesse), 510, 557, 574–584; backdrop to tale, 577–579; reviews of, 582–583

National identity, Hesse and, 156, 625

Nationalism: Hesse and German, 157, 369–372, 421, 665–671; Hesse's rejection of, 28–29, 428

Nationalists, German, antipathy for Hesse, 157, 369–371, 381, 447–448, 613–614, 625–626

Nature: Goethe's conception of, 181–182; Hesse's conception of, 181–182, 283;

Hesse's love of, 130; Saint Francis's conception of, 227, 228; as writer, 570

Nazi Germany: Finckh's support for Nazi regime, 691, 692, 693–695; German nationalism after fall of, 667–670; Hesse accused to being figurehead of Third Reich, 627–628; Hesse and refugees from, 617, 620, 645; Hesse's attitude toward, 158, 602–603, 606, 608–609, 610–611, 612–616, 620; Hesse's Kingdom of the Spirit in opposition to, 648–649, 650; Hesse's position of neutrality and, 627, 629–633; polemic against Hesse and, 625–627; position of writers in, 625–626, 627–628, 629–631; Suhrkamp and, 682–683, 684–685

Neue Deutsche Rundschau (magazine), 204; "In Remembrance of Knulp" in, 268; *Peter Camenzind* in, 219; Suhrkamp and, 681–682; travel reports in, 288–289

Neue Literatur, Die (magazine), 625, 626

Neue Rundschau, Die (magazine), 431, 490, 649

Neue Schweizer Rundschau (magazine), 667

Neue Tage-Buch, Das (magazine), 627

Neue Zeitung, Die (magazine), 670, 675

Neue Zürcher Zeitung (newspaper), 198, 309, 327, 399

Neurosis of the intellectual and spiritual individual, 492–500

Neuroticism, Hesse's, 123

Neutrality, Hesse's position of during Third Reich, 627, 629–633

"New Literary Season, The" (Benn), 645

"New Romanticism" (Hesse), 163–165

News from Heathen Lands (magazine), 23

Newton, Isaac, 182

"New world," Hesse's fascination with, 96–97

Niekisch, Ernst, 96

Niels Lyhne (Jacobsen), 123–124, 166, 176

Nietzsche, Friedrich, 3, 5; affirmation of
the danger and, 265; Andreas-Salomé
and, 567; dichotomy of the Dionysian
and Apollonian and, 297; Dostoyevsky
and, 360; *Hermann Lauscher* and, 177;
Hesse and portrait of, 116; Hesse
reading, 183; Hesse reading Goethe
through filter of, 662; Hesse's admiration for, 161, 381–382, 493; Hesse's trip
to Italy and, 186; motto for *Psychologia
Balnearia* from, 498; music and, 284; as
role model for Hesse, 116, 122,
351–355; as Romantic, 166; *Thus Spoke
Zarathustra,* 166, 173, 342

Nightlife, Hesse enjoying, 521, 526–528

Nihilism, *Steppenwolf* and, 515

"1920–1921 Diary" (Hesse), 437–438

Nirvana: as goal, 428, 429–430; path to,
439

Nobel Prize for Literature, awarded to
Hesse, 1, 6, 611, 675–679, 689–690

Notes from the Underground (Dostoyevsky),
400, 494

Notturni (Hesse), 184

Novalis, 296; "blue flower," 147; *Heinrich
von Ofterdigen,* 166, 331, 406, 407;
Hesse's admiration for, 163–164, 165,
642, 660; Hesse's review of collected
works, 162; *Journey to the East* and, 596;
"stranger" figure, 138

"November Night, The" (Hesse), 177, 178

November Revolution of 1918, 623

Nudity, Hesse and, 172, 491

Nuremburg Laws, 612

Obituaries: Hesse's, 8; of sister Adele, 700

Objects, Hesse and life hidden within,
117–118

Obstinacy, Hesse's, 265

Oedenkoven, Henri, 273

Oetinger, Friedrich Christoph, 651

"Old Music" (Hesse), 285

"Old Painter in His Studio, An" (Hesse),
390–391

"O My Friends, No More of These
Tones!" (Hesse), 309–310, 625, 667,
680

"On Butterflies" (Hesse), 290

"On Moving to a New House" (Hesse),
241, 296–297

On the Marble Cliffs (Jünger), 638

"On the Nature and Origin of the Glass
Bead Game" (Hesse), 647

*On the Psychology and Pathology of So-Called
Occult Phenomena* (Jung), 337

On the Way to the American Embassy
(Seghers), 708

"On Traveling" (Hesse), 188–189

On Visiting Wilhelm Raabe (Hesse),
302–306

Orphanages, Pietist, 21

Other Side, The (Kubin), 275, 594

Outsider: Dostoyevsky and, 365; Hesse's
sense of self as, 167–168; *Peter Camenzind* and, 205–206; *Steppenwolf* and,
514–529, 530–531

Pacifism, Hesse on, 368–369

Padua, Hesse in, 192–193

"Page from My Diary, A" (Hesse), 314

Pages from Prevorst (Hesse), 333–334, 335,
612

"Painter, The" (Hesse), 410–411

"Painter Paints a Factory in the Valley,
The" (Hesse), 393

Painting: Dolbin's interest in, 548; exhibit
of Hesse's watercolors, 394; Hesse and,
379, 386–387, 403, 423, 700; *Rosshalde*
and, 297–302

Palmenwald spa hotel, 125–131, 159,
161

Pantheism: Goethe and, 181; Hesse and, 107, 126, 127, 466–467; "On Butter-flies" and, 290; trees as evangelists of, 383–386

Pantheistic mysticism, Hesse's, 127, 130, 271–272, 721

Paperback books, Hesse's dislike of, 541–542, 714

Paquet, Alfons, 121, 221

Parents: feelings of betrayal by, 83–86; Hesse's relationship with, 133–135, 137; independence from, 122–123, 141, 302. *See also* Hesse, Johannes (father); Hesse, Marie (mother)

Pariser Zeitung (magazine), 627

Parsifal (Wagner), 411

Patience, Hesse's recognition of need for, 441–442

Patricide motif, 88–89

Paul, Jean, 90, 303, 660

Peace Prize awarded to Hesse, 1

"Pedagogical Province" (Goethe), 658

Perrot, Heinrich, Jr., 109, 111, 655

Peter Camenzind (Hesse), 53; brotherly love and, 214; change of direction in life and, 208; creating homeland in, 210–211; distortions of modern outlook on life in, 205–206; Dolbin letter and, 546–547; doppelgänger motif in, 65; Elisabeth La Roche and, 168, 169; "Journey to Nuremberg" and, 507–508; Keller and, 205; love of wine and, 212–213, 260; neuroticism of an age and, 209–210; portrayal of mother's death in, 199–200; publication and success of, 219–220, 232–234, 281; style in, 212

Petit cénacle, 140–144, 149–150

Petraschevsky, Nikolai, 356

Pfisterer (Pastor), 64, 95–96, 99

Phenomenology of Spirit (Hegel), 643

Philistine, world of in *Beneath the Wheel,* 250–251, 253–255

Pia desideria (Spener), 27

Picaresque novel, *Peter Camenzind* as, 212

Picasso, Pablo, 709

Pietism: Carl Hermann, Hesse, and, 21; dualistic image of world in, 26–28; as evangelical revivalist movement and way of life, 26–28; Hermann Hesse and, 16, 17, 46–48, 89, 90, 92, 104; Hermann's parents continued proselyti-zation of him, 100, 105–107, 125; Hesse family and, 16; Hesse's reading of Pietist writers and biographies of Pietists, 618, 651–652; history of the spirit within a story of decline and, 593; Johannes Hesse and, 89; Marie Hesse and, 33, 39, 47–48, 124; Palmenwald spa hotel and, 125–126, 128–129; personal role models in, 18–19; reverence for Word of God in, 27–28; view of childhood, 34

"Piktor's Metamorphoses" (Hesse), 463–466

Pilgrimage, *Siddhartha* and, 421–422

Pisa, Hesse and, 190

Planck, Max, 307

Plato, 9, 643

Plauderabende (Hesse), 122, 124–125

Poems (Hesse), 217

"Poet, The" (Hesse), 171–172

Poetry: butterflies as symbol for, 289; Hesse and others' opinions of, 598–599; Hesse on, as mirrors of the soul, 600; Hesse's abandonment of, 595; Hesse's love of, 4; Hesse's radical realization of, 164; of Marie Hesse, 38–39; Ninon Dolbin's love for, 546; Prussian Writer's Academy and, 586; in *Steppenwolf,* 522

Poetry, Hesse's, 44; "Battle of the
  Machines," 529–530; "Creaking of a
  Bent Branch," 600, 716, 721; "Crisis"
  poems, 523, 529–530, 599; "The End,"
  528–529; "Farewell, Lady World!,"
  717–718; "Grande Valse," 174–175;
  Heinrich von Ofterdigen, 406, 407; "In the
  Fog," 720–721; "In the Mist," 600;
  "Media in vita," 442–443; *Musik des
  Einsamen,* 311; *Notturni,* 184; "An Old
  Painter in His Studio," 390–391; "The
  Painter Paints a Factory in the Valley,"
  393; "Pruned Oak," 466; "Ravenna,"
  191–192, 600; "Refusal," 605–606;
  Romantische Lieder (Romantic Songs),
  137–140, 198, 599; set to music, 715;
  "Steps," 600; "Toward Peace," 671–672;
  "Transience," 383–384; "Wave," 195
Poetry and Truth (Goethe), 181, 593
Polgar, Alfred, 625
Politics, Hesse and, 286, 320, 601–606,
  622–623
Politics of conscience, Hesse's, 320
Poor Folk (Dostoyevsky), 359
"Portrait" (Hesse), 265, 266–267
Poverty: Hesse's Franciscan sympathy for,
  568; poeticized, 265–266
Principle of contrasting pairs, in *Demian,*
  329
Prisoners of war, Hesse's work for,
  315–320, 354–355
Progress and Poverty (George), 316
"Pruned Oak" (Hesse), 466
Prussian Writer's Academy, Hesse and,
  584–591
Psychoanalysis: applied to artists,
  345–347, 434–435; "Dream Diary of
  Psychoanalysis," 321, 387, 392, 476,
  481; Hesse's own, 321–326; with Jung,
  482; *Klingsor's Last Summer* and, 415;
  Magic Theater and, 540

·*Psychologia Balnearia or Glosses of a Spa
  Guest in Baden* (Hesse), 127–128, 461,
  491–500. See also *Guest at the Spa, A*
  (Hesse)
Psychological realm of darkness, as theme
  in Hesse's writing, 147
Psychopath, justification of, 498–499
Ptolomäer (Gottfried), 538
Puberty, Hesse examining own, 343, 344
Publishing House of the Central Book
  Depository for German Prisoners of
  War, 318
Purrmann, Hans, 390
Pyromaniac tendencies, Hesse's, 2–3,
  59–64, 375–376, 656

Raabe, Wilhelm, 205, 302–306
Radardenker (Gottfried), 538
Radiations (Jünger), 656–657
Raft Journey (Hesse), 45
Raftsmen of Calw, 44–45
Rathenau, Walther, 425
Rathjen, Christoph, 682
"Ravenna" (Hesse), 191–192, 600
Ravenna, Hesse in, 191–192
Reading, Hesse and, 12–13, 314, 567–574
"Reading in Bed" (Hesse), 570–571
Reality, Hesse's sense of, 331, 336–337
Reckzeh, Paul, 684–685
Red Zora and Her Gang (Kläber), 611
Reemtsma, Philip, 682
Refugees from Nazi Germany, Hesse and,
  617, 620, 622, 634
"Refusal" (Hesse), 605–606
Reich's bookshop, Hesse employed at,
  158–162, 184
Reineke Fuchs (Goethe), 181
Reinhart, Georg: as Hesse's benefactor,
  396, 481; letters to, 402, 425, 448–449,
  474, 498, 513; Suhrkamp Verlag and,
  690

Religion, Hesse on, 292

"Religious Conversion" (Ball), Hesse on, 484–485

Religious faith, monograph on Saint Francis and, 227–228

Reports from India (Hesse), 287, 289, 423

Republic (Plato), 9, 643

Rest-cures, Hesse's, 127–128, 129–130, 494–496, 537. See also *Guest at the Spa, A* (Hesse)

Revolt against the Modern World (Evola), 340

Revolution (magazine), 479

Rheiner, Walter, 539–540

Rigi Diary (Hesse), 157, 368, 665–671, 679, 680

Rilke, Rainer Maria: estheticism and, 170; *An Hour Behind Midnight* and, 154–155; Jacobsen and, 123; journalism and, 209, 571; *Malte Laurids Brigge,* 210; on marriage, 458, 562; memorial address on, 584–585; narcissism and, 475–476; in Paris, 185

Rinser, Luise, 655, 669–670

River Nagold, 43, 44–45

Robber Barons at the Gates of Munich, The (Valentin), 509

Robbers, The (Schiller), 88, 361

"Robert Aghion" (Hesse), 291–292

Rolland, Romain, 269; Hesse's "Gratitude to Goethe" and, 660; response to war, 309, 311, 628; *Siddhartha* and, 431, 433, 445, 446

Roman Catholicism: Ball and, 430, 480, 482, 483–485; Hesse and, 483

"Romantic: A Conversation" (Hesse), 166

Romanticism: in Basel, 161; Dostoyevsky and, 356; Hesse and, 113, 137, 163–167, 516; Hesse's rejection of dark, 607; *Klingsor's Last Summer* and, 405, 411;

national consciousness and, 668; nocturnal world and, 343

"Romanticism and New Romanticism" (Hesse), 164–165, 641, 642

Romantic Songs (Hesse), 137–140, 198, 599

Röntgen, Wilhelm, 307

Rooks, Conrad, 541

Rose Garden, The (Finckh), 695

Rosenberg, Alfred, 339, 619

Rosenhof, Die (Wenger), 449

Rossetti, Dante Gabriel, 162

Rosshalde (Hesse), 48, 219, 265, 268, 278, 297–302

Roth, Joseph, 187–188

Rousseau, Jean-Jacques, 130

Rowohlt, Ernest, 479

R. Reich publishing house, 163

"Rückkehr aufs Land" (Hesse), 518

Rümelin, Theodor, 111–112, 165

Rumi, Jalal ad-Din Muhammad, 581

Rupp, Elisabeth, 452

Rupp, Oskar, 140, 141, 142; photo of, 143

Rural and village life, attractions of at turn of the century, 263–264

Russian Orthodox Church, Dostoyevsky and, 360

Sabatier, Paul, 213–214, 229

Sacred, in *A Guest at the Spa,* 500

Sahl, Hans, 503

Saint Francis of Assisi: Hesse's admiration for, 213–214, 272; Hesse's monograph on, 4–5, 225–230, 427, 483

Salinger, J. D., 541

Sanatoria: Hesse at Bad Boll, 16, 73–77, 100, 125, 127; Hesse at Stetten, 76, 77–87, 93–94; Hesse fleeing from hype surrounding Nobel Prize award at, 679; rest-cures, 127–128, 129–130, 494–496, 537

Sanda, Dominique, 542

Sartre, Jean-Paul, 562, 709

"Satzbau" (Benn), 570

Schädelin, Walter, 463, 535

Schäfer, Wilhelm, 586, 587, 588

Schaffhausener Zeitung (newspaper), 710

Schall, Blessing, 104

Scheffel, Josef Victor von, 508

Scheler, Max, 312

Schiller, Friedrich, 58, 88; Dostoyevsky
and, 361; Hesse and, 112, 182–183, 356;
Hesse's parents and, 175; Marie Hesse
and, 37

Schlegel, Friedrich, 163

Schlenker, Alfred, 298, 391

Schoeck, Othmar, 279, 328–329, 476,
610, 715

Scholz, Wilhelm von, 154

Schöne Literatur, Die (magazine), 433

"Schoolmate Martin" (Hesse), 243–246

Schopenhauer, Arthur, 161, 391, 426, 573

Schott, Rolf, 707

Schrempf, Christoph, 583

Schubert, Franz, 414–415

Schumann, Robert, 117

Schwäbische Merkur, Der (newspaper), 114

Schwarzschild, Leopold, 627

Schweinigel (Hesse), 159, 201

"Search for lost time," Hesse's, 11

Seelig, Carl, 362, 431

Seghers, Anna, 708

Seidel, Ina, 394

Self, encounter with unfamiliar in Hesse's
writing, 289

Self-discipline, Hesse and, 213

Self-knowledge, *Beneath the Wheel* and
acquisition of, 258

Self-realization, Hermann and drama of, 94

Self-reflection, *Rosshalde* as document of,
298

Sensuality: Hesse's discovery of, 449; in
Siddhartha, 436–437

Sexuality, Hesse and, 215–216, 491

S. Fischer Verlag: Hesse's introduction to,
204–205; publishing contract with, 217;
Suhrkamp and, 680, 681

Sickness, connection with mind, 493

Sickness of youth motif, 255–256, 259

Siddhartha (Hesse), 166, 420–446; as
attempt to synthesize Eastern and
Western thinking, 429–433, 440; Ball
and Hennings and, 474; conflict
between urge to live and longing for
death in, 485; crisis Hesse had while
writing, 437–438; criticism of,
432–433; dual nature of humanity and,
442–443; Hesse's relationship to India
and, 443–445; impulsion to write,
429–430; legality of Italian edition,
674, 688, 689; the night in judgment of
the day and, 202–203; overcoming the
Self for the sake of the Self and,
428–429; patience and, 441–442; as
pilgrimage to self, 426–428; presented
as Indian legend, 424, 425–426; process
of writing, 422–423, 424, 425,
431–432, 437–439; question of "being"
in, 435–436; Rolland and, 445;
sacrificing role as artist and, 486–487;
screen adaptation of, 541, 542;
sensuality in, 436–437; Vasudeva and,
433, 439–440

Sieburg, Friedrich, 637

Silberne Saiten (Zweig), 217

Silesius, Angelus, 127, 270, 489, 652

Simplicissimus (magazine), 309

Sinclair, Emil (Hesse pseudonym), 179,
326–327, 331

Sinclair, Isaac von, 326

Skepticism and Mysticism (Landauer),
489–490

Slavophilia, Dostoyevsky and, 358–359,
360, 361

Sleep, Hesse and, 201–203

Sleeper (film), 96

Sleeplessness, Hesse and, 201–203

"Sleepless Nights" (Hesse), 201, 203

Sleep of Reason Produces Monsters, The (Goya), 138

Smoke (Turgenev), 77, 84

Smoking, Hesse on, 351

Society of the Tower (Goethe), 111

Socrates, 328

"Solf Circle," 685

Sonnewald (Herr), 119, 509

Sound recordings of Hesse, 697

Spartacist League, 353

Speeches of Buddha, The (Hesse's review of), 431

Spener, Philipp Jakob, 27

Spengler, Oswald, 286, 363–364, 644, 648

Spiegel, Der (magazine), 7

Spirit, *Narcissus and Goldmund* and concept of, 580

"Spirit of Romanticism, The" (Hesse), 166

Spiritual connection, travel and, 189

Spiritual dimension, Hesse's defense of, 10

Spirituality, war and, 312

Spitzweg, Carl, 219

Spring Breezes among the Nations (J. Hesse), 31

Sramanas, 427–428

Stanley, Henry Morton, 144

Steiner, Rudolf, 347–351

Steppenwolf (Hesse), 27; American counterculture and, 6–7, 10–11, 220, 537–542; apotheosis of the outsider and, 514–529; as a chronicle of self-knowledge on verge of self-destruction, 515–516; criticism of, 523; criticism of city life and, 520; *Demian*

motifs and, 343–344; Goethe and, 659–660; *A Guest at the Spa* and, 519–520; "Journal to Nuremberg" and, 503, 504; LSD visions and, 10, 538–539; Mann on, 521–522; misunderstood mythical dimension of, 537–542; music and, 520–521; 1942 afterword, 516; prologue to, 510–514; romanticism and, 166, 516; screen adaptation of, 541, 542; supraindividual perspective in, 516–517. *See also* Magic Theater

Steppenwolf (rock group), 6

Steppenwolf and Everyman (Mayer), 541

"Steps" (Hesse), 13–14, 600

Stevenson, Robert Louis, 398

Stifter, Adalbert, 205

Stilpe (Bierbaum), 209

Storm, Theodor, 303, 318

"Storyteller, The" (Hesse), 168

Stowe, Harriet Beecher, 146

"Stranger" figure, Hesse and, 138

Strasser, Gregor, 96

Strauss, Botho, 353

Strauss, David Friedrich, 23

Strauss, Emil, 588

Strauss, Richard, 715

Stunde hinter Mitternacht, Eine (Hesse), 138

Sturzenegger, Hans, 287

Subconscious, Hesse and, 355

Subconscious regions of human history, 342

Success, Hesse and success as writer, 281–284

"Suffering and Greatness of Richard Wagner, The" (Mann), 610

Suhrkamp, Peter, 340; attempt to publish *The Glass Bead Game*, 653–654; in concentration camp, 686; death of, 691; Hesse as blacklisted writer and,

Suhrkamp (*continued*)
674–675; Hesse's relationship with,
679–691; on meeting Hesse for first
time, 1, 2; Nazis and, 682–683,
684–686; own publishing house, 679,
690; publishing after the war, 686–691;
publishing in Nazi Germany and, 627,
629; rift with Bermann Fischer, 687,
689–690; Rinser and, 670; on Unseld
as successor, 713
Suhrkamp Verlag, 679, 690; Unseld and,
711, 712–713
Suicide: of Hans Hesse, 251, 253,
632–633; of Hermann Lauscher,
178–179; Hesse contemplating/threat-
ening, 76, 100, 517–518; Hesse's suicide
attempt, 420; of Marie Isenberg, 613; of
Martin Hesse, 701; Ninon's thoughts
of, 564, 705
Suicide motif: in "Kinderseele," 376; in
Klein and Wagner, 398–402; in "The
Man with Many Books," 376–377
"Summer Evening in Ticino" (Hesse),
260–261
Sunday Courier for German Prisoners of War
(magazine), 317, 318, 354–355
Supraindividual perspective, in Hesse's
writing, 516–517
Swabia, Hesse and, 114, 506–507
Swiss-German relations during Third
Reich, Hesse and, 631–632
Switzerland: Hesse in, during Nazi
regime, 612–613, 616–623; Hesse's
battle with bureaucracy concerning his
residence, 371–372; Hesse's position as
émigré in, 318–319; publication ban on
German émigrés to, 611–612; Swiss
citizenship for Hesse, 455, 456

"Tagebuch eines Entgleisten" (Hesse), 511
Tägliche Rundschau (newspaper), 668, 669

"Tales about Quorm" (Hesse), 265–272
Technology, Hermann's view of, 110–111
Testament, A (Maass), 698
Thadden, Elisabeth von, 685
Thanatos, 101–102, 580
"Thanks to Ticino" (Hesse), 697
Theater: Goethe and, 182; Hesse's
suspicion of, 637–638, 681. *See also*
Magic Theater
Theosophy, 348
Thiess, Frank, 638
Thode, Henry, 229
Thomas à Kempis, 652
"Thou Shalt Not Kill" (Hesse), 448
Thus Spoke Zarathustra (Nietzsche), 166,
173, 342
Ticino, Hesse's move to, 260–261, 377.
See also Casa Camuzzi (Montagnola);
Casa Rossa (Montagnola); Montagnola
Tieck, Ludwig, 163, 178
Time: Hesse and clockwork mechanism
of, 654–657; in *Siddhartha,* 440
To Have or To Be? (Fromm), 353
Tolstoy, Leo, 273
Tonio Kröger (Mann), 171, 219, 250
"To the Pacifists" (Hesse), 368–369
"To the poet Hermann Hesse" (hate
poem), 369
Tourism industry, Hesse's aversion to,
187–188
"Toward Peace" (Hesse), 671–672
Trakl, Georg, 177
Tramp Abroad, A (Twain), 194
Transformation, as theme for Hesse, 336
"Transience" (Hesse), 383–384
Translations of Hesse's writings, 5–6
"Traveling or Being Traveled" (Zweig),
188
Treaty of Rapallo, 425
Trees: as evangelists of pantheism,
383–386; "Pruned Oak" poem, 466

Tristan (Mann), 171

"Tristan" phase, Hesse's, 101–102

Tristan und Isolde (Wagner), 412

Troeltsch, Ernst, 27

Trog, Hans, 162

Trumpeter of Säckingen, The (Scheffel), 508

Tübingen, apprenticeship with bookseller in, 114–120, 137

Tucholsky, Kurt, 13, 297, 506, 599

Turgenev, Ivan, 77, 84, 101, 360

Twain, Mark, 194

Twentieth century, sense of unease at start of, 263–264

Tzara, Tristan, 480

Ulbricht, Walter, 708

Ulysses (Joyce), 522

"Umbrian principle," 328

Uncle Tom's Cabin (Stowe), 146

Unconscious, Hesse's exploration of, 290, 334, 342

Unio mystica, 350

United States, Hesse's popularity in, 6–7, 10–11, 220, 537–542

University Library of Vienna, 598

"Unpublished Prose Works" (Hesse), 619

Unseld, Siegfried, 715; buying back American rights, 6; death of Hesse and, 717–718; on Hesse's Nuremberg travel report, 503–504; mollifying Hesse, 691; paperback editions of Hesse's writing, 542; on personal testimonies in Hesse's writings, 3; publication of correspondence between Hesse and Suhrkamp, 675, 679; unpublished works and, 718; visit to elderly Hesse, 711–714

Utopia, dystopia in, 97–98

Valentin, Karl, 509

Vampirism, "Piktor's Metamorphosis" and, 464–465

van Gogh, Vincent, 274; Hesse's affinity for, 388, 395; Hesse's monograph on, 404; *Klingsor's Last Summer* and, 414, 415

Venice, Hesse in, 191, 193–195, 223–224

Venner, Johannes Vincent, 274–275

Vercors, 709

Verlaine, Paul, 217

Versailles Peace Treaty, 447

Vesper, Will, polemic against Hesse, 625–626

Vienna Appeal, 709

Villa by the Sea (Böcklin), 116

Violence, Hesse's hatred of, 604

Virginity complex, Hesse and, 214–215

Vision, Hesse and, 189–190

Vita activa, 436, 468, 650

Vita contemplativa, 436, 468, 650

Vita experimentalis, 484

Vivos voco (magazine), 327, 339, 398, 399, 424, 446–449. See also *Werkland* (magazine)

Voice of conscience, Demian and, 328

Voigt, Helene, 135–137, 139; photo of, 136

Voigt-Diederichs, Helene, 147–149, 151, 169, 175, 180

von Salomon, Ernst, 425

von Sydow, Max, 542

von Trier, Lars, 477

Wache, Die (magazine), 204

Wackenroder, Wilhelm, 508

Wackernagel, Rudolf, 163, 173

Wagner, Richard, 284, 400, 411–412, 607, 610

Waldo, Peter, 227

Wallenstein (Schiller), 58

Walser, Martin, 10, 637

Walser, Robert, 318

Wanderer figure, 45, 70, 127, 130, 270, 382

"Wanderer's Night Song (I)" (Goethe), 662–663

Wandering (Hesse), 378–383, 502; Hesse as illustrator of, 386–387; "Trees," 383–386; Unseld and, 711

Wandervogel movement, 211, 220

War: criticism of Hesse's stance on World War I, 367–374; Hesse on effects of, 313–315

War jingoism, Hesse and, 307–310

Wassmer, Max, 678, 711, 715

Water: fire *vs.*, 59; as medium of death in Hesse's writing, 216; symbolism of in Hesse's writing, 44–45, 116

Wattenwyl antiquarian bookshop, 198, 230

"Wave" (Hesse), 195

Wayfarer figure: Boccaccio and Saint Francis as, 226, 230; in Hesse's writing, 259–260; as symbol of Hesse's life as writer, 156–157; in "Tales about Quorm," 267–268, 270–271; in *Wandering,* 379–383

Weber, Carl Maria von, 117

Wedekind, Frank, 479

Weimar Republic: Finckh's complaints about, 692–693; Hesse and, 425, 590–591

Weiss, Peter, 10; Hesse's recommendation of, 12–13; Hesse's relationship with, 617, 628, 634–637; visit to elderly Hesse, 705–706

Weissen Blätter, Die, 319

Welt, Die (newspaper), 12

Welti, Albert, 293, 294, 295, 390

Welti, Helene, 281

Welti house, Hesse's move to, 293–297

Weltwoche (magazine), 637

Wenger, Lisa, 410, 449, 452; Hesse's relationship with, 431, 454–455, 456, 457, 482, 524

Wenger, Ruth, 364, 410, 449–463; art and, 450, 460; Ball's monograph on Hesse and, 519; as daughter figure, 437; divorce from Hesse, 525; fairy tale for, 463–466; Hesse on marriage to, 467; Hesse's dissatisfaction with, 460–461; Hesse's misgivings about marrying, 455–458; Hesse's repressed eroticism and, 451–453; illness of, 460, 461; living apart from Hesse during marriage, 458, 459, 524; male admirers, 453–454; photos of, 454, 462; recollection of marriage to Hesse, 450, 461–463; visit to Hesse at sanatorium, 497

Wenger, Theo, 364, 455, 456, 459, 488

Werkland (magazine), 490

West-Eastern Divan (Goethe), 660

West Germany, Hesse's opinion of, 707

Westhoff, Clara, 458, 562

Weth, Georg A., 701

"What I Love" (Hesse), 124–125

White House, The (Bang), 470

"Who Is the Author of *Demian?*" (Korrodi), 327

Wickedness, connection between beauty and, 48–49

Wiegand, Heinrich, 523, 588, 595, 603, 617, 620

"Wiese, Auf der" (Klabund), 417–418

Wilde, Oscar, 397

Wilhelm Meister's Apprenticeship (Goethe), 111, 121, 181, 639, 649

Wine, Hesse's love of, 212–213, 260–263

"Wine Studies" (Hesse), 261–263

"Winterreise" (Schubert), 415

Wirth, Joseph, 684

Wolf, Friedrich, 424, 645

Wolff, Kurt, 313

"Wolken" (Hesse), 207

Woltereck, Richard, 315, 317, 399, 447, 448

Women, Hesse's writing and, 168–169, 410, 697–698. *See also* Eroticism

Woolf, Virginia, 4

Word, Pietism, Hesse, and reverence for the, 27–28

World War I: attacks on Hesse's patriotism and, 310–313, 316–317, 367–374; *Demian* as voice of generation who lost their innocence in, 327, 338–339; Hesse and outbreak of, 306–315; Hesse's work for prisoners of war, 315–320, 354–355; mission statement of Cabaret Voltaire and, 480; money worries for Hesse during, 373–374

World War II, criticism of Hesse's stance on, 368. *See also* Nazi Germany

Writer, Hermann Hesse proclaims self to be, 89–93

Writer's Diary, A (Dostoyevsky), 358–359

Writers on Hesse, 7–9

Writing: Hesse engaging with the world through, 1–2; Hesse on, 572–573; as substitute for life, 582

Writings and Poems from the Estate of Hermann Lauscher (Hesse), 179

Wunderdoktorin, Die (Wenger), 449

"Zarathustra's Return" (Hesse), 351–355, 671

Zasulich, Vera, 360

Zeitmauer, An der (Jünger), 338

Zeit, Die (newspaper), 8

Zeller, Bernhard, 714, 717, 719, 722

Zeller, Gustav, 328

Zetkin, Clara, 96

Zola, Émile, 214

Zurich, Hesse in, 419; Hesse enjoying nightlife in, 520–521, 526–529; as Hesse's winter home, 397; Ninon and, 543, 550, 554, 556, 558–559; psychoanalysis in, 387, 435

Zweig, Stefan: on attacks on Hesse, 368; on *Beneath the Wheel,* 257; on Casanova, 494; friendship with Hesse, 217–219, 230; on Hesse's affinity for van Gogh, 395; on Hesse's physical appearance, 319–320; Hesse's views on *Siddhartha* and, 445; on Knulp, 269, 298; "The Monotonization of the World," 232; "monotonized world" and, 567; snapshot of Hesse's mood in Zurich finishing *Steppenwolf,* 525–526; stance against war, 308; on technological change, 529; trip to Italy and, 185, 187–188; visit to Hesse at Gaienhofen, 239